5/12 24x L¹²/₁₁   24/2016   08/17 24x L¹²/₁₁ C.1

796.32   Green, Jerry .
G   The Detroit pistons : capturing a
         remarkable era / Jerry Green. -- Chicago :
         Bonus Books ; Detroit, Mich : Detroit News,
         c1991.

             301 p. : ill.

             ISBN 0-929387-57-0: 24.95

OP
NSC
13 x L³/00   7164

K⁶/02
             1. Detroit Pistons (Basketball team).   I.
         Title.

The Detroit Pistons

The Detroit Pistons

Capturing a Remarkable Era

Jerry Green

Co-published by Bonus Books, Inc., Chicago
and the Detroit News

95 94 93 92 91   5 4 3 2 1

Library of Congress Catalog Card Number: 91-75668

International Standard Book Number: 0-929387-57-0

Bonus Books, Inc.
160 East Illinois Street
Chicago, Illinois 60611

The Detroit News
665 Lafayette Blvd.
Detroit, Michigan 48231

Printed in the United States of America

*All Photographs courtesy of the Detroit News. Photographers include Kirt
Dozier, William Anderson, Michael S. Green, Barbara McClennan, Drayton
Holcomb, and the Detroit News staff.*

To The Past Masters . . .
Doc Greene . . . Red Smith . . . Jimmy Cannon . . . Shelby Strother

Contents

Preface

Back before pro basketball became America's state-of-the-art sport, making a nation vibrate with a confrontation between Michael and Magic, long before the television announcers came up with exotic terms such as pick-and-roll, there were—the Rollers. That was short for the Providence Steam Rollers. And they played in what is now the National Basketball Association, a.k.a. the NBA, at a time when . . . well, shoot, before most of our homes were equipped with television sets.

This is all the truth, believe it or not. The Providence Steam Rollers played their games in a dingy ice hockey rink, with the basketball floor set down on planks atop the ice.

And if you had a student ID card and a quarter, you were permitted to sit in a corner of the semi-lit arena and watch the Rollers play their games.

They became a favorite team. And although they survived for three seasons and then vanished from the face of the earth, never to return, after the 1948–49 campaign, they have remained a favorite through the decades.

They were not a spectacular team. They were not even a good team. But there was some passion in the audience when they made a run at victory in the fourth quarter, before fading away to one more defeat. They did something to stir you. In the second of their three seasons, the Rollers did something to establish their immortality.

They won six games—in the 48-game schedule. Their storyline remains etched in the *NBA Guide* for posterity: Fewest victories in season, Providence Steam Rollers, 6, 1947–48.

Bless 'em! They provided an excellent starting point for what I would do later on, cover the Detroit Pistons.

I was no longer required to cough up two bits to see a pro game. I got in free in my role as a writer and columnist for the *Detroit News*. But then, most of the others in audience also were invited in to watch the Pistons for free. The Pistons, to my mind, were the Providence Steam Rollers incarnate. In moments of fantasy, I can even imagine that the Rollers might have become NBA champions some forty years or so after they were founded—had they been allowed to stay around.

The Pistons were. And did.

And by the time they did, ticket prices had gone up a bit, so that if you had to pay for a seat courtside where I sat for free, it would cost you $150. For one game. And there was never an empty seat in this glittering, flashy building called The Palace of Auburn Hills.

There is only token value to a quarter now in pro basketball. Dennis Rodman, when he is so inclined, has a trick in which he can place a quarter in his ear.

Pro basketball is the only sport that I have been privileged to watch develop from birth through a weak infancy, a laughable childhood, an unpromising adolescence, an unprosperous young adulthood to an awesomely successful middle age.

This is a book of many memories—of reflections of conversations and winter nights in arenas . . . of articles that have yellowed, written by both myself and many other sports journalists, whose work is packaged under the label of research.

It is a book about a basketball franchise that seemed destined for perpetual failure and survived and won.

I call it an anecdotal history.

To give you an idea, I'll offer up right here, now, my favorite anecdote of all the years of the Detroit Pistons. It happened during the 1964–65 season, when the Pistons were forced to struggle for any victory. They were playing the New York Knickerbockers. And in the final minute of the game, with the Pistons scrambling to maintain a two-point lead, Tom Gola of the Knicks batted a loose ball backwards as he plunged out of bounds into the scorer's table, not quite at midcourt. The loose ball bounced once near the foul circle and went untouched up, up onto the rim of the basket fifty feet from midcourt. It teetered and went in, as though it had been homed in by radar.

"It bounced over my head," Terry Dischinger of the Pistons told me that night. "I chased it. I don't know if I could have caught it, but I couldn't believe it when it went in."

The fluke basket, scored when a player was trying to save a loose ball, pushed the game into overtime. Of course, the Pistons lost it in OT.

It was that way then.

John Salley told me a story during the 1991 NBA playoffs, when the Pistons played the Chicago Bulls, coached by Phil Jackson. Jackson had played for the Knicks; Salley grew up in Brooklyn.

"My mother and aunt used to clean houses of richer whites," Salley said one day in conversation. "My aunt cleaned Phil Jackson's house."

Pro basketball is a game with powerful sociological undertones.

When Michael Jordan and Earvin "Magic" Johnson, at last, played against each other in the NBA finals in 1991, America cooed and fawned and NBC, which purchased the TV privileges, gushed.

ESPN likened Michael-Magic to Hercules-Zeus. The same jock cable network brought on Billy Crystal, the exceedingly humorous Hollywood personality, to disclose his impressions. Crystal said: "Michael is Picasso; Magic is Stokowski or Bernstein."

This pro basketball game has moved along a bit since the days of the Providence Steam Rollers and 25-cents admissions.

A few acknowledgments: This book could not have been written without the research material gleaned from the articles by Bill Halls, who covered the Pistons and the NBA with such expertise for so many years for the *Detroit News*. Thanks to Terry Foster, the *News'* beat man on the Pistons during the Back-to-Back championship seasons for use of his material. Thanks to Kirthmon Dozier, whose excellent photographic work is included in this book. And thanks also to Matt Dobek, public relations director of the Pistons, who always provided a place to sit along with his counsel. And thanks to the multitude of other writers, broadcasters and such who are mentioned in the text. And thanks, before he examines every word, to Bill Laimbeer.

Jerry Green
Grosse Pointe Woods, Michigan
September 1991

First Quarter

I—The Rose Garden

LATE NIGHT—or so it is made to be in America's television make-believe, and Isiah Thomas is standing, grinning, gripping Arsenio Hall's water bottle on a show that began with Sam Kinison peeing into a glass tumbler. That, too, was make believe.

We see the squeeze-it water bottle vanishing as Arsenio pokes around for it.

"Where's my water?" says Arsenio, marvelously chic in his shredded blue jeans. He dances around. "I do my monologue. I work up a sweat. I need my water."

America's insomniacs watch, enrapt, as the camera's eye slides along the studio floor—to Isiah in the corner. There, in focus, is the water bottle, deftly lifted, in Isiah's fast hand, just as he had lifted the last can of MINUTE MAID from Patrick Ewing and Dominique Wilkins in the original of the commercial of which we have just viewed the parody.

"I got thirsty just watching you, Arsenio," says Isiah. "This ain't no Patrick Ewing-Dominique Wilkins gig," says Arsenio. "That commercial's very popular."

Isiah hands Arsenio his water bottle. They sit down.

"Congratulations," says Arsenio. "I got to say that. It's hard to get out."

Isiah Thomas beams. He is dressed in a khaki jumpsuit and the great grin that is part of his every-day wardrobe.

Arsenio switches to a voice full of gravel. Deep. Condescending.

"Con-grat-uuuuu-lations," he says again. "OK twice." Arsenio raises two fingers to show the audience. "Twice."

It is late June 1990, and it is all part of the championship ritual. Earlier in the month, the Detroit Pistons, that team named for a part in an automobile engine, won their second National Basketball Association championship. Back-to-Back. They bounced the Portland Trail Blazers in five games in the NBA final series—and set off the chain of events that have become normal in the afterglow of championship-winning.

1

The champagne squirting in the locker room in Portland, sloshed champions flat on the tiles of the shower room, hugging their ladies. Camp followers clogging the room. Print reporters, on deadline, being nudged, and then nudged again by television cameras, responding with elbows to the guts of the cameramen.

Dancing in the streets back home. In Detroit. A city bent on having a party. The rioting. The deaths. The World War-sized headlines the day after.

The plane ride home. The continued cheering. The parade through the downtown streets, un-visited by the champion athletes themselves since the parade the year before. The multitudes lin-ing the streets in celebration of a team that they have never been able to afford to see play in the flesh.

And then the summons to Washington, the White House.

The ritual. The afterglow.

And part of it, the talk show appearances. From Hollywood. The humorous Arsenio Hall, syndicated . . . Arsenio, diehard supporter of the Los Angeles Lakers . . . those erstwhile champions whose dynasty had been ended a year earlier by the Detroit Pistons.

Isiah is the first guest this late night across America, sort of a warm-up act for Kirk Doug-las and the pig-visaged comedian Sam Kinison. Before Isiah, the audience has been teased into watching by a scene from the men's room, the top of the show, as they say in the biz. Arsenio standing outside the stall. Sam emerging, black bandanna wrapped around his skull, the jar containing a yellow fluid in his hand, a doctor analyzing the stuff.

"You're clean," Doc proclaims.

"I told ya so," Sam says to Arsenio. Then Sam reaches back and secretively hands a bill, five, ten bucks, to a kid.

"Thanks kid," says Sam as Arsenio marches away. End of introduction.

The band explodes into the theme of "The Arsenio Hall Show."

The ritual.

Now, after the monologue and the water-bottle routine, we have Arsenio and Isiah chatting.

"Does it put a lot of pressure on you," says Arsenio, "because now everybody is talking three-peat?"

"No," says Isiah, "it's much easier now. You know. We want to see if we can three-peat also. I think the rest of the country wants to see if we can do it, and everybody wants to see if we can do it. So it gives us much more incentive [the grin stays on] to work much harder to try to get there to see if you can do it yourself."

Arsenio says, "And then you went to see the president." It is known as a segue in the studio, something like Isiah driving toward the hoop, then passing off while suspended in the air.

"Yeah," says Isiah, his eyes now mirthful along with the smile. "It was hot that day. We won the championship. We flew back to Detroit. It was real hot going into Washington. And Washington is very humid. So we *was* standing in the Rose Garden. Myself. Joe Dumars. Bill Laimbeer . . . I was going to present President Bush with a Pistons jersey. So I'm standing there with the jersey, and you know, we got on our suits—we don't normally dress like that—we got on ties and everything—looking like we were ready to go to church on Easter—so I'm stand-ing there with the jersey and we start sweatin' —and I take the jersey and wipe my face with it. Laimbeer, he takes the jersey, and he wipes his face with it—and you know, Joe, real quiet, he snuck over there—he grabs the jersey and wipes his face . . .

"And then I gave it to President Bush.

"But I didn't mean it that way. It just hap-pened."

II—The Bad Boy

The black Bruise Brothers hat is perched atop Bill Laimbeer's head, pulled down across his brow. And across his neck and chest, his bruises flame in red anger.

"That's my job, to do the dirty work," Laim-beer says. "It's my job to bang some bodies around. I had to do the dirty work."

This is late on a Sunday afternoon in the Memorial Coliseum in Portland. It is June 1990. For years and years, Sunday afternoons in June for Bill Laimbeer had meant a game of golf and perhaps a peek at the TV set to see what was going on in the basketball game. The Lakers and Celtics would be engaged in the NBA finals,

Larry Bird vs. Earvin Johnson; Pat Riley, his hair slicked plaster-style on his head, vs. Sam Jones. Or it would be the 76ers, from Philly, with Julius Erving, Dr. J, performing through the air with dazzling skills.

Before then, for earlier generations of Pistons, it might have been the New York Knickerbockers —Willis Reed, Walt Frazier, Dave DeBusschere; the St. Louis Hawks, with Bob Pettit. And even, through the years, such clubs as the Portland Trail Blazers, the Milwaukee Bucks, the Seattle Supersonics, the Washington Capitols, and the Golden State Warriors in the finals, becoming champions.

But never the Pistons, the comedy franchise of the pro basketball league. Never for more than thirty years of tears and laughter; giggles and heartbreak. Never until 1988—and then more agony, more heartbreak in the seventh game of the finals.

Now on this Sunday in 1990, in Portland, the Pistons are playing in the NBA finals for the third consecutive year. Not the Celtics. Not even the Lakers.

And Laimbeer is doing the dirty work. Banging. Bumping. Shoving. Mashing. Intimidating. Laimbeer's head and chest press into the bulky bodies of the enemy. The villain on the foreign floor, raising the wrath of his opponents, the hostility of their fans.

On this Sunday, America watches a gory display of vintage Pistons basketball. Detroit muscles away the edge in the NBA finals. It had been an even series, a victory apiece, and the Trail Blazers had Games 3, 4 and 5 at home. On this Sunday, the Pistons pound the Trail Blazers 121–106. In the process they break what the nation's press has referred to as the Portland curse. The Pistons have not won a single ballgame in Portland since 1974—sixteen years in the past. Twenty failures in succession in Portland, for the Pistons; the carry-over from long before Isiah and Laimbeer and Joe Dumars, Dennis Rodman, Mark Aguirre, Vinnie Johnson, John Salley. The carry-over from sixteen departed, mostly sacked, coaches before Chuck Daly.

"Laimbeer chests up people," Portland's Jerome Kersey complains in defeat, "and pulls up his arms, and he throws you off-balance, and they don't call it. One time I went to the hole,

and he stuck out his leg and knocked me down. The referee was standing there and didn't call anything. That's not basketball.

On the floor, during the battle, Kersey has shouted to Laimbeer: "You do it again and it's going to be me and you."

Laimbeer looks back at him. There is a trace of a smirk on his face. A trace of mischief in his eyes. A trace of choir boy on the face, too.

"That's textbook basketball," he says later, after victory, the black hat on his head.

"He was fantastic, unbelievable, he clogged up that lane, three men," says Chuck Daly, the coach in the custom-tailored suit.

The welts on Laimbeer's neck, and on his jaw, are red badges of honor.

On the floor, during the battle, the Blazers' Buck Williams delivers a forearm karate chop across Laimbeer's throat and face. Laimbeer flops to the floor and stays down.

"It's not important," he says later when the finals were no longer even. "I never hit back.

"I got hit five times on the head. Some by accident. Some on purpose."

"You know they're going through all the antics," says Buck Williams, in the locker room down the passageway. "Everybody knows their mindset and that Laimbeer is going to flop."

Laimbeer laughs. He is a known actor when bopped, collapsing to the floor, writhing. Theatrics, part of his dirty work.

"This is hostile here," he says. "You can feel the hostility. When our team feels this way, we play our best ball. And we felt threatened by this team.

"When we feel threatened, we raise it up a level. Our work ethic rises. We were all a little mad.

"We had it easy so long."

On the floor, late in this battle, Laimbeer fouls out. The Pistons are far ahead. The Portland crowd cheers his departure. Near the bench, Laimbeer delivers a mock bow, the actor in him emerging. The Portland fans respond with deep boos.

"I came off and heard 12,666 cheering," Laimbeer says. "So I thought they were cheering for me."

Two nights later, the Pistons win again in Portland, 112–109, but it is scary. And two nights after that they win again, 92–90, on

Vinnie Johnson's pop shot with seven-tenths of a second displayed on the game clock. Scarier still. The Pistons finish it in Portland, champions again, back-to-back!

In Detroit, people dance in the streets. In Portland, in the Mayfair Ballroom of the Benson Hotel, Bill Laimbeer wears the black Bruise Brothers hat at the team party, until somehow, it is destroyed when somebody fills it with champagne.

To the team it is more enjoyable the second time.

"Last year was too easy," says Laimbeer.

Sure. The first time the Pistons swept the Lakers in the finals. The Lakers without Magic Johnson.

Bill Laimbeer is tolerated, perhaps even loved, as the foremost of the Pistons' Bad Boys in Detroit. Elsewhere, particularly in Boston, he is unpopular to the point of hatred. It was Robert Parish of the Celtics who punched Laimbeer in the chops in 1988 playoffs. It was Larry Bird, who threw a basketball at Laimbeer the next game, aiming at the sometimes angelic face.

"Villain?" Laimbeer says. "Despised is the word."

He is dining in the Ponchartrain Wine Cellars in downtown Detroit with his wife, Chris—something of a feast/interview.

The interviewer offers: "But you've sort of mellowed, haven't you?"

"I've gotten harder," says Laimbeer.

There are those who claim Laimbeer is part theatre performer. That he's not the ogre he pretends to be when arousing the ire of opponents and hex-poking witches and assorted other unfriendly fans around the NBA.

"He's a far more clever, far more compassionate and distinctively, a much nicer guy than he will let the world know," says Dick Versace, then coach of the Indiana Pacers and formerly an assistant to Chuck Daly in Detroit.

"I've always admired him, his work ethic. He's maxed out as much as anybody in the NBA. I told him, 'Billy, you never fooled me. I've seen through this facade all the time.'

"He said, 'Well, never tell anybody.' "

The face—this boyish, puckish, moonbeam face—looks at you and grins. Then the game begins. The eyes become slitted, narrow, afire, emitting rays of intensity, the message of a single purpose. The intimidation expert; the in-your-face practitioner of his team's dirty work. The villain.

"I think I sometimes play to that reputation," Laimbeer says. "Sometimes I'm having fun. I'll play to the crowd on the road. Oh yeah, I can really egg 'em on at times. That's when I feel like doing that, though.

"I do it just by antics, facial expressions."

He admits, prodded, that *villain* is the apt description.

"We're in the entertainment business," Laimbeer says, "so it's probably the appropriate word. It's the way Americans grow up. You cheer the good guy and boo the bad guy. Cowboys and Indians.

"But sometimes it goes beyond that, which is why I used the word despised. Some people cross the line between when it's a game and, you know, being personal."

Chris Laimbeer adds: "People have come up to me and said, 'You're so nice. How can you be married to such an asshole?' I'm like, 'Have you ever met my husband?'

" 'No.'

" 'Have you ever talked to him?'

" 'No.'

"Then you don't know what you're talking about, do you?

" 'No, but I read this and heard this . . .'

"So you don't pay any attention to it."

Laimbeer tells reporters he regards as semi-friendly: "I don't want anybody knowing any more about me than they have to. I don't want them to get to know the real me."

There are problems when you are 6-foot-11 and your mug is plastered post-office style in basketball arenas across America. Celebrity can be a pain. Laimbeer doesn't like it.

"Well, there are varying degrees of LIKE," Laimbeer says. "Obviously, a lot of perks come with your *quote* celebrity status. Monetary. Advantages I wouldn't have if I wasn't a basketball player.

"But as far as celebrity status, I don't need it. I could give or take it."

Ego gratification?

"I've never had that problem, have I?" says Laimbeer. "I never asked to be in the spotlight. I have a job to do. I go about my job and go home. A lot of people have a turnoff about competitive people. I always use the example of

Pete Rose. He played to win every time. But there's a lot of people who dislike him because of his style of play. They thought he was too competitive. It scares off a lot of people.

"I'm perceived in two different ways. I'm perceived by the fans who've read the morning newspapers, the local columnists who've called me all kinds of names, from thug, to the 'Prince of Darkness,' as the Milwaukee paper headlined.

"'Ax murderer,' Johnny Most called me. There you have a guy who was listened to all over New England calling me all kinds of names . . . He knew nothing about me as an individual. He was just making stuff up because of my style of play. But, you know, people believe what they read in the newspaper or they might hear on the radio from somebody they think is an authority on whatever, like Johnny Most might be.

"There's nothing I can do about that. So!"

In the season of their first championship, 1988–89, the Detroit Pistons enhanced their image as 'The Bad Boys.' Laimbeer crunched. Rick Mahorn punched. *Rolling Stone* magazine, ordinarily devoted to other forms of the entertainment industry, featured The Bad Boys. The Bad Boys reigned. The marketing parasites hit a bonanza. T-shirts. Peaked caps. Everything black. Laimbeer and Mahorn became poster children leering menacingly in The Bad Boys poster. Laimbeer received nearly $100,000 in royalties for posing.

What was not known by those who hooted and hexed him in the arenas around the NBA is that Laimbeer donated most of the money to charity.

"I don't believe in making money off an image like that," says Laimbeer.

If it is possible to gauge the degrees of hatred, Bill Laimbeer is despised most in Boston. Bird disdains him. Parish detests him. It took the Pistons so many years of anguish before they could climb over the Celtics in the playoffs, there are terrible lingering animosities. In both directions.

Still, it is the fans, in the ancient Boston Garden, who carry the most hatred for Laimbeer, this man who had made himself into a villain on purpose. A courtside witch, descended perhaps from those who were burned at the stake in Salem, crosses her fingers and hexes Laim-beer. The hooters, in less-dignified style, vilify him from the balconies.

The Celtics, the enemy players themselves, refuse to badmouth him.

"I don't have anything with Bill or against him," says Kevin McHale. "Hell, he's probably a good guy. I don't know him as a person. You play against a guy, you don't know him. I don't know how many kids he has. I don't know where he lives. I don't know anything about him."

"Boston sucks," says Laimbeer.

Amusing!

Laimbeer's father, also Bill, attended Harvard as a graduate business student. "I'm the only player in the NBA whose father makes more money than he does," Laimbeer would say long after he attained his reputation as a star, or villainous, professional basketball player. Laimbeer grew up in wealthy circumstances in Palos Verdes Estates, California. But he was born while his father was at Harvard.

Bill Laimbeer was born in Boston.

III—Oh, Isiah

Isiah is seated in the dining room of a suburban Detroit country club, talking heart-to-heart, one-on-one.

"They pay by the inch in this league," he says. "Very few players took a team from the bottom to the top.

"Magic. Bird. Kareem. Wilt. Russell.

"I built the arena for this team."

He lists the names of the gods of the NBA. This is back in 1988, not long after the Pistons finally destroyed the curse of the Celtics and reached the NBA finals for the first time. Not long before their back-to-back championships. The Pistons had lost these first finals in seven games to the Lakers. They'd had the advantage, ahead three victories to two, and then went out to the Fabulous Forum in L.A., and it slipped away. By one point, 103–102, in the sixth game, and by three, 108–105, in the seventh game.

Isiah Thomas destroyed his ankle, playing with heroism, in the sixth game. And in the interim between Games 6 and 7, the doctors said Thomas was too severely injured to play again.

Isiah pushes the ball hard up court. (*K. Dozier*)

The papers echoed the doctors. The TV stations echoed the papers. Nobody believed Isiah Thomas could play Game 7 on an ankle, torn and swollen and terribly painful, except a few who knew him so well they understood his intensity and desire. Those few—and Isiah Thomas himself.

He played, damaged, and was heroic again, and his team lost and the throbbing pain became worse in defeat.

And then he had to go home and fight for a new contract.

Now he is in this country club, participating in Bill Laimbeer's charity golf event to help the people in his city. The negotiations are nasty.

"It's getting to be embarrassing," Isiah says. "Kelly Tripucka got more money—$900,000 when I was making $400,000. Then Adrian Dantley was making more."

Isiah is 6 feet 1, and he mentions this business about payment by the inch in the NBA. Magic Johnson, Larry Bird, Kareem Abdul-Jabbar, Wilt Chamberlain, and Bill Russell are towering men. Thomas' point is clear.

Seven years earlier, he had jumped to the pros after playing for Bob Knight's NCAA champions at Indiana. The Pistons were the dregs of the NBA. Ridiculed through 16–66 and 21–61 seasons, back-to-back. Thomas was the catalyst in the gradual, then the stunning climb of the Pistons. He had played in the seventh game of the NBA finals, with the throbbing pain, risking his body and his career before Jack Nicholson and that devout Forum clientele.

Devotion had developed in Detroit, too, during those first years of Isiah. The Pistons had become a whopping financial success playing in the jerry-rigged football stadium, the Pontiac Silverdome. Their attendance became the highest in the league. One night, when they played the Celtics, they had drawn 61,983 fans. Detroit had fallen in love with the Pistons, after so many years of apathy. And in the fall, the Pistons would be moving to their own new arena, The Palace of Auburn Hills—regal, plush, state of the art. The house Isiah Thomas says he built.

And now, as Isiah sits at the country club, his discontent spilling out him, there are rumors the Pistons are trying to trade him to the Utah Jazz. It is part of the bargaining leverage the club is using.

So Isiah, despairing, hurt, says: "I feel I've been cheated."

There is anger behind the sweetest smile in sports.

It works out, of course. The negotiations drag through the summer and into the fall of 1988. Then settlement, near midnight, the night before the opening of training camp. Isiah going to Utah is so much jazz.

The contract is for sixteen million bucks, to cover eight seasons.

Isiah Thomas is happy, smiling sweetly again. The next contract, at this time of rampaging escalation in the NBA, puts Isiah on the list behind Michael Jordan, behind Patrick Ewing, behind Magic.

"It took some very creative minds to get this done," Isiah says. With his smile.

They play in noise and party in noise. M.C. Hammer hammers out in "U Can't Beat Us" during the breaks of the games at Palace. Hammer Time! It hurts the ears.

And it hurts the ears again on this late spring night in 1990 as the party in Portland swings past midnight and into the morning. Joe Dumars is at the door of the ballroom. He nods and tries to smile to writers in the bittersweetness of the moment. Joe Dumars, Sr., died on Sunday, the day Joe, Jr., played Game 3 of the finals. Now, business done, he will go home to Louisiana for the funeral. He says thanks for the condolences and thanks for the congratulations. He is a silent, beautiful hero in the cacophony of victory.

Chuck Daly has stripped off his double-breasted suit. He is in a sweater, grinning, and is telling how he won his championships back-to-back and, now he must solve his inner battle. The visions of trying to Three-peat, that cockeyed word invented by Pat Riley, are tremendously seductive. NBC wants him for his intelligence, his looks, his wizardry. The offers to hit TV, become basketball's John Madden/Bill Walsh, are terribly appealing. The Pistons want him to stay as coach, with a new deal. It is a decision that must be mulled, and wrestled with, and Daly cannot escape the curious who grill him with questions he cannot answer.

Near the dance floor, Bill Laimbeer pours champagne and surveys the view in the room. He still wears the black Fedora. It has not yet been used as a container for the champagne. Laimbeer squeezes everything, all of it, the entire scene, the total picture, into four words.

"This is Isiah's team," he says. "This team has his personality. The determination, the desire and the heart revolve around him."

It is impossible, if you were a white youth in America, to imagine what it is like to grow up on the streets of the black ghetto. Bill Laimbeer, the rich man's son, could not know. Most of the journalists could not guess.

Isiah Thomas grew up on the West Side of Chicago. He grew up raised by a strong mother in a house with eight brothers and sisters; some got into trouble. Isiah was the youngest. The mother, Mary, was powerful and tough. She kept Isiah out of too much trouble.

These were cruel, mean streets. Rats and garbage, drugs and muggings, violence and broken homes—and the schoolyards, what Hollywood once called The Asphalt Jungle. Basketball, with sharp, digging elbows and digging clenched fists, halfcourt games through the afternoons and into the nighttimes, almost pitch black, the court illuminated by dim, pale, yellow lights.

Chicago Stadium was nearby. Isiah Thomas fantasized playing there, some day, for the Bulls. That was his mind game on these days of boyhood, his knees scraped and bloodied from rides on the concrete, his ribs bruised from the pummeling under the basket. Isiah Thomas emerged powerful and tough.

A rare chemistry fuels the Pistons. Perhaps the sociologists should ponder this mix the Pistons have—the rich white suburban giant, with the competitive fires and the comedians' stagger and the glowering visage, and the poor black urban playground player, with the awesome drive and the mighty motivation and the engaging smile.

Beware of that smile. It does not always transmit the message received.

There are times when there is anger behind that smile. The anger reappears. A fist, a fight, a grab, a choke.

He is the millionaire now, with the basketball court in his home in the exclusive, affluent suburb of Bloomfield Hills. But something of the street, the violent jungles of the West Side of Chicago, sticks to him. Sticks to his moods, to his personality, to his performances, to his public persona.

Controversy traps Isiah Thomas. He can never escape.

In 1987, the Pistons were within a flicker of defeating the curse of the Celtics at last. Command of the series switched in Boston, in the fifth game, when the Pistons were so certain of victory they pranced up the floor. Dennis Rodman's arms were raised in triumph. The Pistons needed only to flick the remaining split seconds off the clock. They needed only to inbound the ball without some silly mistake. Isiah passed the ball in without caution. Bird snatched it, passed to Dennis Johnson, and there was barely time for a layup. Boston won Game 5. Boston won the series in seven games and returned to the finals to face the Lakers.

Same stuff.

Except the finals were obscured by the mouthings of the Pistons. Rodman, in defeat, after the Game 7, told the press that Larry Bird did not deserve to be most valuable player in the NBA, that he would be just another guy with a basketball player's salary if he were black, not white. The press rushed over to Isiah for a comment about what Rodman had said. Isiah, in defeat, agreed.

The fires of racism upstaged the playoffs. Isiah had to go to Los Angeles to explain himself, to apologize.

In the following season, the Pistons traded Adrian Dantley to the Dallas Mavericks in midstream. Isiah and Adrian did not create good chemistry. The player the Pistons received in the deal was Mark Aguirre. Aguirre grew up on the West Side streets of Chicago with Isiah Thomas. There was considerable speculation that Thomas went to Bill Davidson, the Pistons' owner, and engineered the trade.

Adrian Dantley's mother certainly believed that.

"He's a con man; whatever his royal highness wants he gets," said Virginia Dantley to the media in the days after Adrian was traded away.

Thomas smiled and said it wasn't true. Read his smile.

Isiah gets what he wants.

Usually.

The day after the Pistons achieved their back-to-back mission, their second championship, the athletes boarded Roundball One, their own aircraft. They were flying home, across two-thirds of the nation, from Portland to Detroit. It was a time of euphoria. Of celebration.

America believed at last.

Isiah Thomas had been voted the most valuable player of the NBA playoffs. He had been on the edge, all his years in Detroit, the years of cajoling and prodding the Pistons from the dregs to twin championships. And now, now at last, he had qualified without dissent for the elite of the game. He was in the class with Magic, his kissing friend, and with Bird, the man he once accused of lacking the necessities. He was in the class with Michael Jordan, who did not possess enough of a cast around him to win a championship. He belonged to history—with Dr. J and Kareem and, going back, Bill Russell, Wilt Chamberlain, Bob Cousy and Bob Pettit, superstar heroes from other ages.

Isiah had reached the pinnacle—measured in achievements, not in inches.

And then a gambling probe caved in around him.

Roundball One was over America with the Pistons aboard, aimed toward Detroit for the heroes' welcome. In the large house in Bloomfield Hills on this June Friday afternoon, Isiah's wife, Lynn, flipped on the television. She switched to WJBK-TV, Channel 2 in Detroit. Vince Wade, an investigative reporter for the station, appeared in the screen. Wade reported that Isiah Thomas, embraced by a city, was linked with an FBI investigation of a sports-betting ring. Wade said millions of dollars were involved. The reporter stated that the Feds were concerned with checks written by Isiah Thomas and cashed by Emmet Denha, who operated supermarkets in Detroit. Denha was a friend of Isiah's and a onetime neighbor. He was the godfather to Joshua Thomas, the young son of Isiah and Lynn. WJBK said Denha was being investigated in connection with a nationwide gambling probe. The station also said Mark Aguirre had contacted a Ned Timmons, a former FBI agent, and said that Isiah had a gambling problem. The allegations reported by the station included information that Aguirre purportedly had informed Timmons that Isiah had been involved in high-stakes dice games. The reports said that Isiah himself was not under investigation.

But . . . but he had been smeared by the hints of scandal.

Isiah walked through the door of his home shortly after the news broadcast. Lynn was seated in front of the TV set. She was crying.

A day later, all the triumphs, all the heroism, the back-to-back championships, Isiah Thomas, were tarnished. The statement that Isiah personally was not being investigated by the FBI was smothered by the fog of the report. The other TV stations, the radio stations, the newspapers, the wire services picked up the story. Isiah was innocent, they reported, not guilty.

Except, Isiah Thomas was the most prominent citizen of Detroit on this day, this weekend—and he was judged guilty by association.

"I'm really mad," Isiah Thomas told interviewers that weekend, "because none of this has anything to do with fact. I didn't deserve this. I'm sure this will blow over. At least my part in it."

And a few days later the government publicly exonerated Thomas. Stephen Markman, the U.S. attorney for the Eastern District of Michigan, announced that the federal investigation was not targeting Thomas.

This same day Detroit clogged the walkways of Woodward Avenue to cheer the Pistons in parade. Championship parades back-to-back in center city Detroit. Downtown, near the streets where eight persons were killed in celebration the night they won their second championship, a few nights earlier.

"I promise I'll never let the city of Detroit down," Thomas told the people.

Then the Pistons dashed back to suburbia, to Auburn Hills to the delirium of The Palace, and another praise-the-Pistons celebration with shooting lights and grinning athletes and hugs and cheers.

Isiah Thomas stood up and spoke again.

"When you have a problem," he said to these suburbanites, middle-class hero-worshippers, "think of me. Say to yourself, 'If Isiah can handle what happened to him, I can handle any problem.'"

The crowd shook the rooftop with its cheers.

How could this man be accused of any wrong-doing?

But he was marked, soaked by suspicion. And he was angry. And the anger carried over, within him, through the summer of 1990.

In the autumn, a few days before the opening of another training camp, Isiah Thomas, captain of the Pistons, was practicing informally with some teammates at Oakland University. Outside, after practice, he was approached for an interview by Virg Jacques, a sports reporter for WJBK. Thomas refused to be interviewed. Jacques persisted. There were some angry words. Jacques persisted further. Thomas became angrier. Jacques claims Thomas slammed him against a car, grabbed him around the neck and tried to choke him.

More roaring headlines.

Jacques threatened to sue. His own television station interviewed him.

It does not take much to create a mountainous issue in Detroit when the media and athletes are involved.

On the day training camp opened in Windsor, Ontario, Isiah Thomas apologized to Jacques. The apology was accepted.

Another story faded with the winds of autumn.

A few days before the 1990–91 season opened, Isiah Thomas spoke out about himself, what drives him, in an interview with Corky Meinecke, of the *Detroit Free Press*.

"In my neighborhood, you had to fight every time you moved to another block," Isiah said. "That's just how it was. After you had a couple of fights, then nobody messed with you. But if you didn't fight, they would rob you every day.

"See, most people don't really want to fight. They just want to bully and woof and take your money. They don't want to go through the confrontation of tussling and wrestling with you. If they know they'll have to tussle and wrestle with you, then they'll probably want to be friends.

". . . I don't know if I feel angry, if I feel hurt, if I feel cheated. I feel like somebody flipped my life upside down for five months and then said, 'Oh well, it was a mistake. Forget about it.'

"Well, I can't forget about it. You have no idea what this has done to my family.

". . . I'm not going to conform and live in a cave. I'm not going to live like that. I'm human, and it's unfair to expect me to live by a different set of rules. I'm not perfect. I can't live by those rules. I can't."

IV—Daddy Rich

Chuck Daly is dressed in his black velour Sergio Tacchini warmup suit at the epicenter of the basketball court. He dips into a pocket and withdraws a comb. He proceeds to treat his pompadour as all around him limber up with an assortment of jumpers and slams.

The crowd in the grandstands overflows, about 2,500 in the St. Denis Centre on the campus of the University of Windsor, across the

Detroit River. The Pistons start their championship defense by going to Canada for training camp. And this is the Canadian holiday of Thanksgiving. It is the first Monday in October. These Canadians are dressed up in Pistons' t-shirts. They wear Pistons' caps.

Once upon a time, in Detroit, pro basketball used to battle ice hockey for the wintertime attention of the sporting fans. The Red Wings were entrenched. The Pistons were carpetbaggers, moved from Fort Wayne in Indiana. It was not much of a battle. Detroit did not adapt to pro basketball, to the Pistons. The Pistons were vagabonds in Detroit. They moved from arena to arena. They were orphans. Nobody cared, no matter how the Pistons tried to lure in some honest, genuine customers who were willing to pay for tickets.

Now 2,500 people pack a university gymnasium to watch a team practice layups and shoot at each other in a scrimmage.

Once upon a time the Pistons were incapable of drawing 2,500 fans, half them on freebies, to their regular season games at Cobo Arena. Or the University of Detroit's Memorial Building. Or the Olympia Stadium, their first home in Detroit, where they were tenants of the Red Wings and were given the leftover dates after the hockey schedule was prepared.

Daly finishes combing his hair. He peeks at the gold watch on his wrist beneath the sleeve of his warmup jacket.

"Let's go," he says.

Then he retires to an elevated seat at the corner of the court.

Once upon a time, the coach of the Detroit Pistons, whomever he happened to be at the time, worked the job solo. He conducted the practices. He coached the team in the games. He handled a lot of the travel arrangements. He was available, constantly, for interviews, because publicity was invaluable to a team that was No. 4 in a four pro team market.

Now the coach, Chuck Daly, has an entourage. He has two assistant coaches, Brendan Suhr and Brendan Malone. They can direct practice. Daly sits watching this practice on his perch and with him sit, Jack McCloskey, the general manager; Will Robinson and Stan Novak, the scouts; two public relations guys; George Blaha and Dick Harter, the team's broadcasters.

Once upon a time, the Pistons fired and hired their coaches in the middle of seasons, at the end of seasons, for peculiar reasons, for good reasons, for no apparent reason, with predictable regularity, at the whim of the owner. Coaching the Pistons put a man in constant jeopardy.

Now Chuck Daly is a coach maker. He trains coaches for other NBA teams. Dick Versace went from Daly's staff to become head coach of the Indiana Pacers. Ron Rothstein coached for Daly and became head coach of the Miami Heat.

11

Harter, the new broadcast analyst, was Daly's assistant and went into the perilous head coaching position with the Charlotte Hornets, remaining as long as possible.

Chuck Daly—who has coached at the high school, college, and pro levels . . . whose first head coaching job in the NBA with the Cleveland Cavaliers had lasted forty-one games (he was 9–32) before he was fired—stood against a locker room wall in full glory.

"Firings," he said "that's part of the business. I've been doing this thirty years. I feel like I'm a solid career coach.

"Look at me. Look at my face. You don't look like me. Look at me. I'm going to be fifty-seven. You don't see any lines. You don't see any gray hair.

"I've spent my whole life without working. This is a culmination. It's a helluva long way from Cleveland.

"I told my guys we were going to win it here."

Chuck Daly had to scramble through life until he was past fifty. He came out of Kane, Pennsylvania, and graduated from Bloomsburg University, not your perennial basketball powerhouse. Chuck became a coach, honing the leadership and strategic skills, which would some day be instrumental in winning back-to-back NBA championships, first at Punxsutawney High School. He was a biology teacher; coaches doubled up. In Punxsutawney, Daly might have been the town's second foremost resident. Number one was the groundhog, that critter that tradition says emerges from a Punxsutawney hole in the ground each February 2 to see if it can see its shadow.

Daly left Punxsutawney while the groundhog stayed. Chuck continued on in coaching. He was an assistant at Duke. He was head coach at Boston College. Eventually, he became head coach at Pennsylvania, and his team became a winning factor in the tough, sometimes cruel Philadelphia college competition. Penn won four Ivy League championships in Daly's six years. He hit the NBA as assistant to Billy Cunningham on the 76ers. After four seasons of that, he figured he was ready for anything. So he took the job as head coach of the Cleveland Cavaliers in 1980. He got three years, guaranteed, for half a million bucks.

The Cavs were owned by a man named Ted Steptien, who had his own ideas about running a sports franchise. He told the coach how to coach. Some of the owner's other ideas were bizarre. Daly kept the job for those forty-one games of the 1981–82 season. Or by his reckoning, he kept it for ninety-three days.

"Ninety-three days in a Holiday Inn," he recalls.

Daly returned to Philly, his roots, and became a television basketball analyst. Somewhere along the way he was invited to shake and wiggle on a hot rock-and-roll MTV video; he became the only mature basketball coach to appear on MTV.

In spring 1983, the Pistons fired another basketball coach for another lame reason. Scotty Robertson went, joining the procession of fifteen other coaches who had gotten the Detroit ziggy in the first twenty-six years after the Pistons had been carpetbagged out of Fort Wayne. The Pistons had Isiah Thomas for two seasons with Robertson as head coach. The club was too slow in making progress, still below .500.

So Robertson went after the 1982–83 season. Chuck Daly was hired, after Jack McCloskey toyed with the idea of making Jack McKinney, who had been successful with the Lakers, the Detroit head coach. Supposedly, McKinney was the first choice.

Chuck Daly was fifty-three years old.

The Coach Maker. Chuck Daly and Dick Versace (right) listen to strategy from Ron Rothstein. Both Versace and Rothstein went on to become head coaches in the NBA.

"At this point in my coaching life, the authoritarian figure has gone," Daly told Bill Halls of the *Detroit News* during his first season with the Pistons. "I like to be part of the group. I give them a lot of freedom. But with freedom comes responsibility."

Daly appointed third-season pro Isiah Thomas his team captain at age twenty-three. He gave additional responsibility and support to a mean-faced but nondescript center who had been a benchwarmer on his team during those terrible forty-one games in Cleveland—a charming thespian named Bill Laimbeer.

From a column in the *Detroit News* by Jerry Green, June 12, 1985, after the Pistons' rebuffed Daly's attempts to accept the offer from the Philadelphia 76ers:

Chuck Daly has bunches of style. It is the theory here that any man who accepts employment as a basketball coach is daft. He has to be. Coaches are not driven loony by the heat of the game. They are loony before they ever go to work.

The case example of this is Dick Vitale. Dick Vitale was around the bend long before he was dragged from courtside screaming and foaming at a Pistons' game. It all erupted at the untimely toot of a whistle. That was it.

Chuck Daly is not such a severe case. He has rational moments. He is a tap dancer on the edge of the court, but he does it with a precise tempo, then sits down. He sits and folds his arms and glowers at the referee, or the player, who has flipped his mood.

Daly dresses up for the performance, which is part of his style. The NBA record book collects all sorts of data, but it is not clear on this matter. Daly must lead the league in haberdashery.

Frankly, he makes a better sight on the bench than say, Pat Riley, of the new champions from Malibu Beach. Greased down hair, slicked back, is quite gauche nowadays. Nobody shows up at the Pistons' games riding in limousines, but, beyond that, Daly outstyles Riley.

This is Detroit, after all. Parking a limousine outside Joe Louis Arena would result in parts scattered all over town with the skeleton found the next day in a lot along Gratiot.

It was Daly's idea during the playoffs to show up in something finer than one of his browns or blues or pearl grays.

"I think I'll wear a tuxedo," Daly said before a game with the Celtics.

Too bad, he chickened out.

And too bad now, Daly might as well be coaching next season in gray fatigues with broad stripes running through the cloth.

The guy is a captive now, a prisoner.

He is a guy with style, with class, kept shackled by a classless organization that traditionally has lacked style.

It was immoral to tease him around when he had the chance to coach the 76ers. It was obscene to tantalize him with the opportunity to make more money in another, more secure job—then yank it all back.

Either do it, or don't, as they say, but don't putter.

For sure, the Pistons warranted compensation. They had so magnanimously given Daly a one-year contract extension for next season. But after virtually agreeing on two second-round draft choices as the price, it was unfair to renege. The demand for a first-round draft choice was outrageous.

The Pistons have themselves a mess, again.

They don't want to pay Daly enough to keep him; they refuse to rush to sign him beyond one year. But they don't want to let him go so he could double, perhaps treble, his $110,000 for 1985–86.

Thus, they have themselves a disgruntled coach. They have a confused ballclub. They have a coach dangling, angry, unsettled and wondering.

Asked how a coach can handle such a situation, Daly responded with style.

"It's what they call living on the edge," Daly said. "That's one of the reasons you go into it. You like the excitement of winning and losing. The ecstasy of it.

"You like living on the edge—and that's part of it."

Chuck Daly did not terribly want to leave Detroit, his adopted city, for Philadelphia, where he has roots.

"I don't know that I wanted to be somewhere else," he said. "I like this city, this club, the fans here. It was a professional decision in terms of contract and money—professional in quotes."

It was not totally that. Daly is stifled in Detroit.

"We haven't had any help in the two years I've been here," he said. "Now the East is murder. Patrick Ewing is going to be in New York, three of the top nine players are going to come into our division. Atlanta, Indianapolis and Cleveland."

The Pistons owe Daly something. They owe him a promise beyond one more year, at a salary comparable to the other well-dressed coaches in the NBA.

Sadly, the Pistons' organization lacks deep commitment—and it keeps showing.

Chuck Daly, who didn't hit it rich until he was past fifty, arrived in Detroit with terrific smarts. It was as though he had popped out of a hole in the ground in Punxsutawney, spied his own shadow and decided he had to move. He developed quickly into the master of leverage. Skilled in his approach. Sharp in his timing.

Jack McCloskey had provided the inner necessities of a team that was on the verge of winning. Isiah, Laimbeer, Kelly Tripucka, and Vinnie Johnson were on the ballclub. Still the Pistons had not been able to win, to reach the level of .500. So Scotty Robertson was fired, amid criticism for McCloskey for dumping a man who seemed to be making some progress. The Pistons had endured six consecutive losing seasons when Daly arrived in 1983. The club had gone through Herbie Brown, Bob Kauffman, the illustrious Dick Vitale, Richie Adubato and Robertson in their coaching turmoil of those half-dozen seasons.

In popped Chuck Daly and the Pistons, with the inherited players, immediately turned about and finished with a 49–33 record in 1983–84. They were 16 games over break-even. They reached the playoffs for the first time since 1977. A year later Daly coached them to a 46–36 record. And again they reached the playoffs. Both times in the playoffs the Pistons were eliminated early, first by the New York Knickerbockers in a pitched battle, and the second year, natch, by the Celtics. But it was so far so good for Daly in a town that has an inbred playoffs mentality rooted from the years when ice hockey was the premier wintertime sporting passion.

It was then that Daly tried to check out of town. He himself was rooted in Philly. Billy Cunningham, who had brought Daly into the NBA as an assistant, gave up coaching the 76ers.

Chuck Daly, his coaching mettle proven in Detroit, was the obvious candidate. The 76ers wanted him. They were willing to pay a fee to the Pistons for Daly. But the Pistons were going to play a close shuffle for this man whose career did not start to blossom until late-career. Daly had a year to go on his contract in Detroit. The Pistons had picked up the final-year option on Daly's contract three months earlier. They gave him a raise to $110,000. They were enthused about Daly and his accomplishments.

Chuck checked his options—a young, developing team in Detroit vs. winning tradition and home in Philly, plus more money—and opted to abandon the Pistons. Julius Erving might have become less marvelous than he was at his prime time, but the 76ers wanted to jump Daly's income to something close to triple.

The Pistons put a price on Daly. The price, according, to all published reports in Detroit and Philly in June 1985, was two second-round draft choices. The 76ers were jumping at the bargain.

The negotiations dragged through two weeks. Pat Williams, the 76ers' general manager, kept Jack McCloskey glued to long distance. They talked just before midnight on a June Sunday night.

McCloskey told Williams the fee for Daly was a first-round draft choice. Take it or leave it. "Non-negotiable," said McCloskey, the tough bargaining man.

"Too high a price," Williams told Bill Halls of the *Detroit News*.

And McCloskey told Halls: "They weren't willing to give up a first-round choice. So that ends it. I'm happy it's over."

Chuck Daly accepted the setback without public complaint. He has a way of covering his feelings.

"I don't know if you'd call it a disappointment," he said. "I lived there twelve years, and obviously, I was interested. But I like it here, too."

The Pistons denied they had switched the price for Daly late in the negotiations. Oscar Feldman, the club's legal counsel and number two in the ownership hierarchy, said the price had never been two second-round choices. "It was always a No. 1," Feldman said.

But other sources felt the Pistons had reneged

and trapped Daly to a lower-paying contract with a team he'd prefer to leave.

Asked about some sort of hanky-panky regarding the Pistons' supposed switch in price for his coaching body, Daly responded: "It was a little bit of a surprise."

Then he said: "There's nothing I can do about it. I don't know if any team has ever given up a first-round pick for a coach in this league. If it were to happen now, it would create a precedent. It's a pretty steep price. But that's the way it goes. I'm under contract here. It goes with the territory."

Daly had learned something about the art of leverage and negotiating. He would not forget

The following autumn, as the training camp for the 1985–86 season opened, Chuck Daly started applying his new knowledge. The Pistons had held him captive for the final year of his original contract. Now they wanted to make certain of retaining him for the future. Daly suggested an extension. He knew he was hot. He knew he was becoming loved in Detroit. He knew that the base had been put in for a championship team a few seasons away. Daly went to McCloskey and suggested an extension.

"Every guy in town was asking me what was going to happen next year," Daly said. "I felt it was best to work something out."

McCloskey felt Daly was hot, but not that hot. He asked Daly to name his price.

"At least the average salary," Daly said. This was in midsummer, about a month after Daly had been dangled at Philly and then yanked back.

The figures were in the ballpark of $200,000 to $225,000 for the two years following the existing contract. Daly and McCloskey shook hands on the deal, according to reports by Dave Dye in the *Detroit News*.

"He said it was exactly what he wanted but he was going to talk it over with his financial adviser anyway," McCloskey was quoted as saying. "Then he came back a few weeks later and said he had changed his mind. I agreed to what he asked. I thought we had an agreement. I think he needs to make up his mind what he wants."

Daly's financial advisers were based in Philly. Back with his roots. He consulted them, Art Kania and Albert Linder by name. They told him to tell the Pistons no deal.

"We decided it wasn't really what I wanted to do right at this point," Daly said in the *News*. "It was neither the money nor the time that I was really looking for. I agreed to it because I'd like to stay here. I love it here and I really like this team. They're young and enthusiastic and fun to coach."

The Pistons went into training camp at Windsor for the 1985–86 season with their coach a quasi-lame duck. Daly and McCloskey were far apart on all terms. Money. Daly was said to want about a quarter million. More than that, he wanted a contract for four more years, or at least three. He was fifty-five. He had thoughts. He had ambitions.

"I'll probably coach only three more years," Daly said. "This most likely will be the last coaching contract of my career. It's a very volatile job. The nerves can get to you.

"After coaching, I'd like to stay in the game, maybe as a general manager, director of player personnel. Something like that."

Other clubs, it was reported, secretly approached Daly to learn if he would be staying in Detroit. Daly had a certain wedge. But it was neutralized by the NBA's tampering laws.

Daly and McCloskey haggled and negotiated through much of the season. For the first time since they had evacuated Fort Wayne three decades earlier, the Pistons were playing through a third-successive season with a winning record.

But before that season ended—the Pistons gave Daly an ultimatum. He was told he had five days to accept the last offer, or forget it. Take it or else. Final offer. That's the bottom.

Or the pits!

The Pistons were on the road in California when Daly was given his quick choice of acceptance or departure. It was late March. The playoffs would be starting in a few weeks. The final package for two years, according to the *News,* would be worth $445,000, including incentives based on team's season records.

Daly capitulated to McCloskey's squeeze in less than five days. It was a roll of a dice cup for Daly; he could accept the Pistons' proposal or starting dickering with whatever team or teams had approached him with sly promises that could not be written down on pieces of paper. Daly was being rewarded with a contract above the median wage for NBA coaches, a package sweetened by a few more grand to $455,000 for the two seasons of 1986–87 and 1987–88. He had a team on the rise in a league in which the dominant clubs, the Lakers and Celtics, were starting to fray so slightly with age. The chances of Chuck Daly becoming very rich in a few years seemed excellent. Signing before the Pistons yanked their offer off the table was the wisest decision Chuck Daly could make.

Asked why he went for what might have been a bluff by McCloskey, why he blinked, Daly said, simply: "I think it had a lot to do with the guys on this team. I like it here. You could pick up and go somewhere else . . . It would be sort of like starting over again, having to learn the personnel and how to deal with new media there. To be honest, I never really had strong feelings about leaving Detroit. I felt all along I'd be back."

Daly fast forwarded from the deal in 1986, through two seasons, and he was worth every penny. The Pistons were not quite as good as the Celtics, not quite as good as the Lakers, Daly kept saying, his constant theme. But the Pistons were getting there. Then they suffered the terrible jolt in the 1987 playoffs when they might have beaten the Celtics.

After such a disaster, in such a depression, Chuck Daly's Pistons might have self-destructed in the following season, 1987–88. They did not. Daly kept them directed, kept them motivated. They had become superior to the Celtics. They had reached, at least, a level with the Lakers. For the first time, since they played in Detroit, they reached that point never before imagined by those who suffered the agonies of a comic, pratfalling, joke of a franchise. They whipped the Celtics in the 1988 Eastern Division finals. And the night they did, suddenly, the multitudes rolled out of the grandstands and onto the court at the Silverdome and fast danced. A jubilant mob of the suddenly faithful, vaguely familiar people who wanted only to rub themselves in the sweat of the Pistons.

"Well, critic of many years, what do think now?" one of these creatures bellowed at me, down from the hills, during this frantic ritual that night. "See."

"I see," I said. "And it took only thirty-one years."

Chuck Daly captured it all in that heavy room. His eyes glistened. His team was headed toward L.A., and the NBA finals. And he, Chuck Daly, with his professional roots dug deep at Punxsutawney, was a coach without a contract.

They had been haggling for months over contract length in a new deal. McCloskey was offering two years. Daly, now fifty-seven, wanted four more years. He believed, again, that this could be his last contract. Money, too, was an issue. Daly had received $275,000 in the second and last season of his expiring contract. Rick Pitino, in his first year as stopover coach of the Knicks in his personal coaching tour, was making 350 grand. So was Mike Fratello from the Atlanta Hawks. Daly did have a legitimate gripe. He had a team capable of winning a championship, which Pitino and Fratello didn't have. He was the coach who managed to get Thomas, Dantley, and Laimbeer to perform on the same team. The coach who sublimated their considerable egos for the good of the team, as Bill Halls wrote in the *News* during the contract dispute.

Daly told McCloskey no when the Pistons offered two years at $300,000. That's not what Pitino or Fratello made, and this was Chuck Daly, who'd helped to build a ballclub that captured the largest audience in the NBA.

This was Daly again "living on the edge" in a period of personal insecurity. He wanted to stay in coaching. The ambition to be a general manager had slipped away. Chuck had a team that could win a championship, and he wanted to stay in coaching. In Detroit.

Past negotiation struggles had made Daly slick and cool in the springtime of 1988. The Pistons went off to L.A. to play the Lakers in the finals. And Chuck Daly played a fine tune. He gathered sympathy in the papers. He plain snookered some journalists; poor Chuck, he was coaching the Pistons vs. the Lakers and he didn't even have a contract; the guy deserves more, he deserves security of a new contract; such shabby treatment.

Tisk, tisk. Poor Chuck played on this sympathy with a full symphony orchestra, even though a few reporters in the know were aware that the Pistons were willing to continue the negotiations, but that Chuck himself, voluntarily, had broken off any negotiations for the remainder of the playoffs.

But tisk, tisk, the fiddlers continued on, with the same song, that poor Chuck was mistreated because his heartless Pistons bosses were not paying him a penny while he sweated through the climactic playoffs.

At Daly's tempo, the negotiations would resume when they would no longer conflict with the playoff efforts. They began again after the Pistons' gutty downfall in the seven close games of the 1988 finals, with Isiah bussing Magic, with Jack Nicholson glowering at courtside.

A column from the *Detroit News*, by Jerry Green, June 29, 1988:

Chuck Daly came into the room with his shirt collar open and a chain around his throat and glowed, typically, about the Pistons' draft.

Daly? The Pistons? Their supposed former coach? Slaving loyally for the Pistons, although he technically no longer is employed by the team?

". . . I anticipate I'll be back," Daly said after speaking his pleasantries about the draft choices. "I like to use the word anticipate."

There was much ado during the playoffs that the Pistons had left Daly dangling when his contract expired.

But Tuesday, Daly confirmed that negotiations had been suspended at his request to allow him to concentrate on coaching. And he said that his old contract had been extended during the business with Boston and L.A.

"Yes," Daly said when asked if he had gotten paid after the old contract expired.

He had been portrayed as a lame-duck coach, with no income.

But Tuesday he said the Pistons had not treated him shabbily in these contract talks. There should have been no onus placed on the Pistons' management.

Daly's reasoning for not wanting to talk contract during the NBA semifinals and finals was smart and simple to understand.

"We got into Boston and L.A., I didn't want to have anything negative going on," Daly explained. "It was best to concentrate on what we were doing. There was no reason to get into contract talks when we were in the two most important series.

"In Boston, L.A., my phone never stopped ringing. When I put it down, it rang again, and when I was on the phone, there was always a message when I was finished. I wanted to focus on what I was doing."

Daly is not the vagabond, nor the misinformer Larry Brown is. Be happy for that. The deal that ripped Brown out of Kansas for the San Antonio Spurs cannot be matched for Daly. Brown will get $700,000 annually for five years. But that deal has to aid Daly's cause.

"Larry Brown's a unique situation," Daly said. "I don't have the marquee name he has."

A couple of days later it was over.

Daly and McCloskey agreed on a three-year contract. McCloskey sealed it on the transatlantic telephone, from the Netherlands, while on a scouting mission.

The deal would be worth $1.35 million. The newspaper beat writers started calling Daly by the nickname Daddy Rich. The name stuck.

"The contract puts me with the top people in the league," Daly said, coming off a day on the golf course. "No question I wanted to stay here. I've grown up with this team.

"I'd really like to win the title. And I think we're close."

He admitted he had proper leverage in these dealings. The 76ers again had wooed him, this time to be general manager, the position once at the top of his aspirations. And the Miami Heat, brand new as the NBA was giving itself more stretch marks of expansion, wanted Chuck. An expansion team, after the Pistons in the NBA finals, might have made Chuck wretch.

So he'd worked himself into a sweetheart of a contract. And this contract had an escape clause in it. If Chuck Daly, after two seasons, felt like doing something else he would be free to go. If he wanted to retire and count the daisies, he could. If he became fed up at hearing the constant bleat of whistles, he could depart. If the concept of pancake makeup and envy of Dick Vitale made broadcasting appealing to him, he could junk the contract and take a hike. He would be sixty then. No obligation to stick around. The contract gave Daly thirty days after the Pistons' last game in 1990 to decide if he would elect to serve the final season of his three-year contract.

The gossip started in December 1989, around

Christmas time. He was getting bored, and NBC was conducting a manhunt for a well-dressed, good-looking, bright coach who knew an X from and O and could speak well enough in the English language. NBC had outbid CBS for rights to the NBA telecasts, spending multi-millions. Daly fitted the profile for the man NBC wanted to be a talking head and force information between ears of America's dribble-pounded pro basketball fanatics.

All these stories made sense, when you figured out each X and each O and summed it all up. Daly could diagram plays in chalk on one of those TV gizmos.

"I have not talked to NBC nor has NBC talked to me," Daly said as the 1989–90 season dragged along.

Another time, Daly coyly dropped hot words onto the speculation: "I will continue to evaluate the situation because it's obvious I can't do this forever. At my age, I'm going to have to give up basketball at some point, whether it's this year, next year or the following year."

The gossip raged on through February, March, and into April, toward the end of the regular season, as they clinched the division coasting and advanced into the playoffs.

Out of New York, people who claimed to know, folks in the NBA and in television, stated that NBC had offered Daly a four-year contract worth between $2 million and $3 million. WTBS, the cable TV station owned by Ted Turner, was willing to go as high as $800,000 for Daly to sit courtside and deliver commentary and analysis.

Chuck Daly had worked a lifetime. He had suffered on the bench. He had pained. He had sweated. He had flown hundreds of red-eyes after pressurized games, landing at dawn in new towns, unsure sometimes where he was, and conducted practices in the late morning and played games at night, and then rushed back to the airport again. He had replayed games in his mind at four in the morning. He was the oldest coach in the league, soon to turn sixty—and now he possessed all the leverage a man in his business could ever wish to have in his command.

Other clubs competed for him and his knowledge and experience. The Charlotte Hornets and the Los Angeles Clippers, it was said, wanted

him to become their general manager. Chuck Daly—instant turnabout, instant success.

A friend of Chuck's told Terry Foster, the beat writer for the *Detroit News* in early April 1990: "There is no doubt in my mind that he will go. If NBC offers the job, he is gone. He could play golf in the winter all the time. That's what he really wants to do."

Daly, playing his role, told Foster: "I haven't done anything else in my life. Sure it's tough. There's the practice, travel, crisis management. But when summer comes, as tired as I am, when a plane goes overhead, I think maybe I should be on that plane."

It was as close to a hint that Chuck Daly had ever dropped about his future, about his plans, about his deepest thoughts.

The day after Game 3 of the 1990 NBA finals, Pat Riley resigned as coach of the Lakers. He had beaten Daly two years earlier the first time the Pistons qualified for the finals. But Pat, with Magic Johnson essentially running the Lakers in an ex-officio capacity, was looking for a cushion so he could fall on it.

Happily for him, NBC was as hot for Riley as it was for Daly. The new NBA network coveted both coaches. It was not a secret that Riley would switch to television in some sort of expert commentary role after he chucked the Lakers.

In Portland, engaged in the Finals, Daly spoke to the media gathered from across America, from Italy, from Spain, from Canada, about Riley and his resignation.

"It's obviously been in the works," Daly said. "Obviously he did a great job because you guys voted him coach of the year. He is a very smart and marketable guy and he will be a success in whatever job he takes, whether it be coaching, television, or marketing. He's an extremely gifted guy."

The sarcasm oozed. NBC's Terry O'Neill, the executive producer, had met secretly with Daly while the Pistons played the New York Knicks in the second round of the playoffs. O'Neill obviously regarded Chuck Daly as very smart, marketable and that he would be a success in whatever job he worked, be it coaching or television.

It was written than NBC would outbid the Pistons for Daly. And it was written that NBC would outbid cable's TNT.

"Anything can happen," Daly said, his head shampooed with champagne. This was the night in Portland, moments after the Pistons had won their second championship. It was CBS' NBA finale, and the cameras grabbed graphic scenes of grown athletes returning to the sandbox. Pat O'Brien, who'd boasted in *USA Today* that he used to be a newsman and therefore could ask penetrating questions, had asked Daly about his future. The stories that Daly would move to television, NBC, were rampant.

"Anything can happen." Reporter O'Brien neglected to follow up, pushing Daly for something better than three inconsequential words.

Two hours later, Chuck Daly, changed to a sweater from his coaching double-breasted suit, breathed heavily at the champions' ballroom bash.

"Tough, tough," said Daly, his face aglow. "It's great. I don't know what I'm going to do. It's tough, tough."

But the message was there, written in his unlined face and his unspectacled eyes. Right in the ballroom of the Benson Hotel, as Bill Laimbeer wore the black Fedora and Joe Dumars smiled despite the personal hurt inside, Daly was telling you, NBC be damned.

He would be back to coach.

The crowd packed the Palace on the late afternoon of June 18, after the parade honoring the back-to-back champions in downtown Detroit.

Detroit is a hard town for coaches and managers. Sparky Anderson got booed changing pitchers for the Tigers. Once upon a time, Harry Gilmer, was bombarded with snowballs as his Lions finished another disastrous season in the NFL. They serenaded Gilmer: "Goodbye Harry, Goodbye Harry, we hate to see you go."

"At least the snowballs didn't have rocks in them," the imperiled Gilmer said as he retreated from town.

Chuck Daly, too, was greeted with chanting from the passionate fans. "One more year. One more year," they yelled. Daly heard it all, and it had to overload his ego.

He looked up and spotted a sign strung out from the balcony.

"Chuck Daly, don't leave. Go for 3."

"This is a very hard decision to make," Daly said. "I will make that decision once we get things out of the way."

It was auction time in Detroit.

Though he already had a contract to coach the Pistons in 1990–91, that contract had the escape clause. McCloskey was forced to bid against O'Neill of NBC and against Ted Turner. There were other players in the bidding. Now, the Denver Nuggets joined the clubs offering Daly a general manager's job.

Daly had the thirty days to flee, to take it on the lam.

Carl Peterson, the Denver club president, realized the hopelessness of his club's offer to lure Daly into exile in the Rocky Mountains.

"He's the master of leverage," Peterson told reporters in Colorado. Daly bristled at the description. "I don't know why he would say that," Chuck said in Detroit.

In late June, Daly was pacing in the hallway at the Pistons' inner sanctum in the Palace. He was fixed in meditation. McCloskey came out of his office. They started talking, in private.

"I'd really miss coaching," Daly told McCloskey.

"I would like to look down the road a little bit," Daly told Terry Foster when it was reported in early July that the Pistons were willing to throw away the existing contract and offer him a sweeter, longer deal. Eight hundred thousand bucks a year, which with Daly's Detroit endorsements, might bring him a million dollars a year, for as long as he wished to fly airplanes in the middle of the night and coach Isiah and Laimbeer and Dennis Rodman and Joe D.

"I'm struggling with the decision," Daly said

"I think Chuck could be our coach as long as he wanted to be," McCloskey said as the speculation switched one way and then the other.

"First of all he's got to tell me whether he wants to stay. It's his decision."

But the pressure was McCloskey's.

Once he had given the sign-or-else ultimatum to Daly.

Championships back-to-back, and now it was Daly, in essence, giving McCloskey an ultimatum: shove the existing contract into the shredder and write out a new one, richer and longer. Mighty was Chuck's leverage.

Matt Dobek, the Pistons' public relations man, ushered us into the swank room in the Palace of Auburn Hills. It was late in the midsummer afternoon. July 10, 1990. Ten days before Chuck Daly's sixtieth birthday. A podium was set up in the front of the room with microphones stationed on the tabletop. TV cameras stood on their stilts behind rows of chairs for the reporters. The crowd for the press conference was about the same size as the crowd for an actual ballgame thirty years before.

Chuck Daly and Jack McCloskey filed into the room.

"Chuck has signed a new contract," McCloskey said. "No terms are announced. But I want to check the new *Forbes* list."

"I couldn't see October coming and me not going back to training camp," Daly said.

He was a victor in this eternal battle of bargaining with his own employer, this victory that men can rarely feel. He was in a jocular frame of mind—twice a champion, desired everywhere at age sixty, no wrinkles on his face, little gray in his pompadour hair, slim, fit, happy, secure.

"I didn't want to quit until we got it perfect," Daly said at that summit moment in his life. "We lost a game in the finals.

"I didn't want to leave until I have one of those games where we allow no second shots. In order to do that, you have to continue coaching."

He turned serious. He turned to his roots. There were moments of melancholy at this press conference.

"I talked to Al Davis," he said. "I talked to John Madden. I talked to Billy Cunningham. I talked to Dick Motta."

To people in sports who had walked away, they to return to other jobs. To some in football, Davis and Madden, men who had helped build and toiled for the Pistons' alter-egos in the NFL, the roguish, infamous Raiders from Oakland and Los Angeles.

"Winning a championship, it's an incredible feeling," Daly said. "I want to go back and try again. I understand the difficulty of winning three in a row. We have a chance.

"The lure of winning three in a row—I would always look back and say I didn't try to get that third championship, and it would always bother me.

"Easily, this was the most difficult decision I ever had to make in my life. How many times are you offered the opportunity to go on network television?"

A week earlier, Terry O'Neill, the NBC player in this taffy pull, suggested that the network fly Daly to London. There, during a break in the coverage of tennis from Wimbledon, Daly would announce his retirement from active coaching to join NBC and its basketball talking team. Television does things that way: it manages the news and then covers that news as events.

NBC was waving $800,000 at Daly for two years to experience the joys of television. Daly said no to the trip to Wimbledon, he said he still had to make his mind up.

"I was concerned," said McCloskey when asked if he actually ever thought Daly would be leaving the Pistons, "until we had that little walk in the hallway a few weeks ago."

The Pistons' deal was $675,000 to $700,000, for at least one additional year, through 1991–92. He had become the NBA's second best paid coach, second only to Larry Brown, the man with all that marquee value down by the riverside in San Antonio.

Daddy Rich turned nostalgic.

"I did this for $3,600 a year," Daly said. "Coaching is in your blood."

He was guaranteed two more years, at least, by the Pistons, but again, he had the escape clause written in.

Just in case he wanted to use his mastery of leverage one more time.

"The only time I have a problem with Jack is at contract time," said Daly.

Chuck Daly walked into another press conference in February 1991, as the Pistons were staggering in their effort for the Three-peat. Isiah was out with a severely injured wrist, and the Pistons were playing .500 basketball without him. But now, at this press conference, Chuck Daly was about to be recognized as one of the most respected and best-known coaches of basketball in America.

There were speeches. The United States Olympic people, in their quest for victory, had decided to make NBA plutocrats eligible for the once-sacrosanct amateur Olympic Games. Those dastardly Soviets had whipped the American college kids at the Seoul Olympics in 1988. So now we'd see how they'd like a taste of Earvin Johnson,

Michael Jordan, Charles Barkley, Patrick Ewing, and Larry Bird. They'd kick some Soviet ass.

Chuck Daly was introduced as the head coach of the USA team for the 1992 Olympics. From Punxsutawney to Barcelona.

"I'm very happy to represent all the coaches around the country who, like me, are lifers," Daly told the press at the conference. "This has been a way of life for me."

Daddy Rich was going for Gold.

V—Joe

An article in the *Detroit News*, June 13, 1990:

PORTLAND, Ore.—It was the second quarter, and Joe Dumars had the basketball behind the key. John Salley was maneuvering in the lane.

It was then that Salley heard Joe Dumars yell: "Salley, I'm moving to the basket. Move."

"OK, Joe," Salley said, recalling the brief exchange. Salley got out of the way. Dumars scored.

On this night, Joe Dumars played the game he had played since boyhood with a heavy heart. And a courageous heart. His father had died in Louisiana on Sunday, and Dumars stayed in Portland to play with the Pistons on Tuesday against the Trail Blazers in Game 4 of the NBA Finals.

"It was funny," Salley said after the Pistons had won, 112–109. "Those guys didn't want to touch him. And when he wanted me out of the way, I got out of the way. He didn't say, 'John.' He said, 'Salley.'"

Joe Dumars played 43 of the 48 minutes on this night two days after his personal tragedy. He scored 26 points. He ran the club in the second quarter after Isiah Thomas had collected three personal fouls and was confined to the bench.

The Pistons were 10 points behind when this quarter started. They were five points ahead when it ended.

The second half was wild and theatrical and controversial. But without Joe Dumars' presence in the second quarter, the end of the game might have been nothing.

A year ago Joe Dumars III had given his championship ring to his ailing father, Joe Dumars Jr. after the Pistons won their championship. It was a matter of love and respect.

And Dumars now stayed with his team in the crisis of the Finals because his family in Louisiana believed it was what his father would have wanted.

His teammates realized this. His coach realized it.

"Joe is a very strong human being," Salley said. "Joe has the biggest heart I've ever seen. He realized playing this game was something his father wanted him to do."

"He's special," said Coach Chuck Daly. "His father dies. He knows it's coming. But even so, it's very difficult for Joe.

"He's a man's man. So was his father, from what I understand. It takes a lot of courage."

"Joe is a very strong-minded guy," said Vinnie Johnson. "He really showed his character with his father passing away, yet he knew we had a game to win."

Mark Aguirre lost his mother while he was involved in the playoffs while playing for the Dallas Mavericks. Only Aguirre could know Dumars' true feelings.

"This [the game itself] is a relief for him," Aguirre said. "He gets to take his mind of things for a while. Right now, I'm sure he's thinking something else. I'm sure he wishes he had his dad to talk to."

Dumars, a quiet, dignified man always, did not wish to talk to the media. He was permitted to dress in an isolated area and was escorted from the Memorial Coliseum by team Dr. Ben Paolucci and other Pistons' officials.

Joe Dumars is standing at the door in the darkened Mayfair Ballroom two nights later. The Pistons are champions again, back-to-back, and Joe Dumars is to get another ring. The music blares inside. Bill Laimbeer pours champagne for sports writers. Chuck Daly nibbles at the hors d'oeuvres and keeps repeating how tough it was and now how tough it would be to decide his future.

It is a deliriously happy time for the back-to-back champions.

Except for Joe Dumars, quietest of the champions. His joy is muted. There is no smile. Just nods and thank yous for condolences, not congratulations.

Death was figure in this second championship.

The Pistons are a team of heart, blood and, passion. And if there is to be a favorite on this team, it must be Joe Dumars.

The nation regards Laimbeer, the pratfalling actor, as a thuggish villain. America knows Isiah's enormous fortitude and drive to win and commanding ability to control a game in the tightness of the clutch. But America wonders if his smile is not a touch too sweet, a might too cynical. Dennis Rodman, The Worm, with his arms flailing, is respected for his defensive skills, but the nation's fans of basketball think he is, perhaps, too flamboyant, a hot dog. Vinnie Johnson is known for his shooting abilities that enable him to take over games with microwave heat, but there are times, too, when he endures slumps of frozen inaccuracy. John Salley is a humorous giant, blessed with a comic's disposition and a flair that lures the ladies. James Edwards plays with a rare strength and a special experience, and he is viewed as a man with a glowering visage that makes him more feared than he might be.

Joe Dumars is the true basketball player of the group. There is no flair to him, no hot dog, no cynicism, no villainy, no glowering expressions. There is only a purity of the game.

To reach the finals the Pistons must go through the Bulls. They must, somehow, defend against and beat Michael Jordan. They must take this magnificent athlete and neutralize his mighty motivation, his acrobatics. The Pistons eliminated the Bulls in 1988 and made the finals. They eliminated the Bulls in 1989 and won the finals. They eliminated the Bulls in 1990 and won the finals. Joe Dumars is Chuck Daly's man on Michael Jordan.

Sports Illustrated used the Dumars vs. Jordan scenario for its cover photo in the NBA preview issue before the 1989–90 season. The picture mocked Michael Jordan. A clever artist had made Michael to seem like a cardboard cutout with his tongue hanging as a flag of surrender. Dumars was depicted with a hand on Jordan's head with a nothing-to-it gesture. It was terribly unfair to Michael Jordan.

But Joe Dumars had become famous.

Chuck Daly speaks of some occult defensive scheme known as The Jordan Rules. The press has picked up on the tricky phraseology, and Daly is pictured as some sort of genius mastermind because the Pistons were able to dominate the Bulls with Michael Jordan.

Daly's genius, simply, is shown in his assignment of Joe Dumars to guard against Michael Jordan.

"Look, this is my job," Dumars told the late Shelby Strother of the *Detroit News* before one of his mano-a-mano series against Jordan. "That's the perceptive I keep. I'm going to workhard, hard as I can, no matter whom it is we're playing. Because it's my job to work hard."

The style and skills Joe Dumars III brought to the Detroit Pistons had their roots in the backyard of a home in Natchitoches, Louisiana. There was a rim and a backboard there, as there are in millions of other homes across America. But this one was different. It wasn't store bought, it didn't bear the stamp of NBA marketing approval.

The basket Joe Dumars, future MVP of the Pistons' first world championship team, shot at was hand crafted by his father. Joe Dumars, Jr., built that basketball apparatus with manual work. He took a door, an old one, and sawed it in half. That could be used as a backboard. Then he took an old bicycle wheel rim and hooked it to the half-door with a hammer and nails. That could be used as a hoop. Then he hooked the backboard and rim to a post and settled the post into the ground in the backyard at Natchitoches.

Joe Dumars, the son, spent hours and weeks and months and years shooting baskets at the old door and converted bicycle wheel rim. He got so he could hit and then hit again. He was the seventh child in the family of seven children of Joe, Jr., and Ophelia Dumars.

Young Joe went on to college at McNeese State. He would make the All-Southland Conference team all four years he was in college. He would lead the league in scoring three of those years. The McNeese State media guide listed the favorite pro athletes of the school's players. Joe Dumars' favorite player was a young guard with the Detroit Pistons—Isiah Thomas.

Despite his heroics at McNeese, Joe Dumars received scant publicity attention from the media. He was unknown. Down there in Louisiana, Joe Dumars, with the outside shot learned shooting at a sawed-in-half door and a bicycle rim, was discovered by a canny scout from Detroit named Will Robinson. Robinson was an old coach, a coach of champions in Detroit high schools and the first black to become head coach at a major college, Illinois State. He later returned to Detroit and went to work for the Pistons, touring the south, discovering talent.

Thus, Will Robinson discovered Joe Dumars. He recommended Dumars to the Pistons. And in 1985, the Pistons drafted Joe Dumars with their pick on the first round of the NBA draft. He was selected eighteenth overall. The selection surprised the growing legion of followers of basketball in Detroit. Most of them, no matter how devout they were in their attention to basketball, had not heard of Joe Dumars.

That year, 1985, Joe Dumars, the father who had built his sons a basketball backboard and rim for the backyard, contracted diabetes. Soon he was bed ridden.

In his rookie season, Joe Dumars, the son, became an integral piece in the team being put together by Jack McCloskey. He was in the backcourt, the foil and mate to his favorite pro player, Isiah Thomas. The father caught his son's games, those he could, on television.

Joe Dumars was a four-year veteran, well-known across America by the 1988–89 NBA season. In June, when the Pistons played in the NBA finals for the second time and when they won the first of their championships, Dumars was selected as the MVP. His team had beaten the Celtics and the Bucks and the Bulls and Michael Jordan, and then the Lakers in four. Dumars averaged 27 points per game as the Pistons swept the injury-strapped Lakers in the finals.

Joe Dumars, the father, watched the games on television back in Natchitoches. The diabetes and heart trouble had cost him both legs. Most of the time he was in bed, his back propped against pillows.

The night Joe Dumars led the Pistons to their championship, he spoke on television as the traditional champagne scene was carried live onto the screen in the bedroom in Natchitoches. The young man said he would never wear the diamond championship ring he had worked so hard to earn.

"The ring goes to my father," said Joe Dumars, the son.

"He'll wear it a lot more than I would."

That season, Joe Dumars, the son, telephoned Joe Dumars, the father, after every game the Pistons played.

"There were a lot of days I'd like to be sitting on the edge of the bathtub or in the backyard talking to pop," Joe Dumars told Charlie Vincent of the *Free Press* after the season.

Dumars told Vincent: "He always told us, 'As hard as I had it growing up, as hard as your mother had it growing up, we made it. You kids have got it great today, so don't sit here complaining about what you don't have and the reason this didn't work out. Just get it done and don't say anything about it.'

"That has been instilled into me all my life. 'Don't complain. Just get it done.' Those are the best things my parents gave me—teaching me about hard work and learning to accept things as they are."

"People think I should be jumping up and down, saying, 'I'm so proud of Joe,'" Joe Dumars, the father, told Vincent. "And I am! He has gone as far as he can from a little town like this and is still the same person."

On the Sunday afternoon in June 1990, in Portland, Joe Dumars III, shooting with magnificent accuracy, scored 33 points as the Pistons beat the Trail Blazers, 121–106, in Game 3 of the NBA finals. Two hours, or so, earlier Joe Dumars, the father, died at age sixty-five of congestive heart failure in a hospital in Alexandria, Louisiana. Joe Dumars, the son, had not been told of his father's death. When the game ended with victory, Dumars was taken to the operations office of the Portland Memorial Coliseum. Joe's wife, Debbie, was on the telephone from Detroit. She passed the crushing news on.

Only Chuck Daly, Jack McCloskey, Isiah Thomas, and Matt Dobek, the Pistons' public relations chieftain, knew of the death of Joe Dumars' father before the game.

"I was carrying around a heavy load," Thomas said in the press interview room at the Coliseum, his team back in command of the finals.

"I knew something was going to shatter his world in a couple of hours. It was hard to look at him at times.

"He made one shot running down the lane today, and it went in. After that, we looked at each other and smiled, and I said to myself, 'your father put that one in. You sure didn't have anything to do with it.'"

That night Ophelia Dumars spoke to her son on the telephone. It was decided that Joe would remain in Portland to play with his team, in the style his father had taught him, in Games 4 and 5. The funeral would not be until the following Saturday in Natchitoches. Dumars would go to Natchitoches for the funeral, then fly to Detroit for Game 6 on Sunday.

Joe Dumars scored 26 in Game 4, when the Pistons won by three on Tuesday, and 8 in Game 5, when they won by two on Thursday, in Portland. There would be no Game 6 on Sunday. The Pistons had won championships, back-to-back.

VI—Worm

The functionaries bring Dennis Rodman to the podium set up for a press conference in The Palace of Auburn Hills. He stands there, his face serene, the back of his head displaying the name Alexis, his daughter, carved into his hair. He listens to a speech. This is a trophy presentation in May 1990, early in the playoffs in the Pistons' drive to their second championship.

Rodman is introduced as the NBA's Defensive Player of the Year, by vote of the sports writers. He looks over the collection of ink-stained wretches in the audience. Rodman's mind goes back one year, when his heart was broken because the sports writers then did not vote him the award.

He finished third then, behind Mark Eaton, who lumbers along the court at 7-4 for the Utah Jazz, and Akeem Olajuwon, 7-0 tall and center for the Houston Rockets. Rodman is 6-8, skinny, with prominent stick-out ears, and a flashy style that is loved in Detroit for its natural ebullience and regarded in the other towns of the NBA as very hot dog. With customary candor, Rodman said he was robbed then. He vowed to win the

Rodman's defense results in an easy bucket on the other end. (*K. Dozier*)

award the next season, or else . . . or else. he said, he'd retire from basketball.

"It's unfair to a guy who works harder," Rodman said in his disappointment the year before in his trophy loss to Eaton.

"If you stand in the middle and that's all you can do is block shots, that's not defense."

The memory of all this hurt returns to Rodman now as he stands at the podium. He starts to speak of his thrill, of his gratitude . . .

"I take great pride in stopping great players," he says. "What makes me different is I am willing to do the dirty work."

He looks over the audience.

"I thought . . ." he says. And he is crying. Tears drip down his gaunt face. His eyes pour out with his emotions. The TV cameras whir on, capturing his unashamed passions for the 6 o'clock news.

"I wanted this award so bad."

That is all Rodman can say. Jack McCloskey puts his arm around Rodman. He leads Rodman to the Pistons' locker room.

The ceremony is finished.

The Garden in Boston is a relic, in the manner that Stonehenge is and the ruins from ancient Greece. It is a place the historians relish, where they can assemble and scrutinize the leftovers from the time of the classics. They gawk at the basketball floor, sectioned into wooden squares, the parquet floor, the most famed court in all the world.

The Garden is perched atop a building that houses the old North Station down below. Trains emerge from the Boston underground and rattle by on elevated tracks, disgorging the most fanatical of pro basketball fans who recall the days of the classic Bob Cousy and the classic Easy Ed Macauley and the most classic Bill Russell. It was in this old and revered building that the Celtics, put together by Red Auerbach, won eight successive NBA championships. From 1959 to 1966.

Back-to-back-to-back-to-back-to-back-to-back-to-back-to-back! Then after missing one year, they won two more.

The dressing quarters assigned to visiting foes in the Boston Garden are cramped and very hot during playoff time in the spring. It is to this tight locker room that the Pistons retreat in aching defeat on May 30, 1987, the first time they have reached the Eastern Conference finals.

They are a team in ascent. In swift order, they eliminated Washington in a three-game sweep and Atlanta with four victories in five games. They have qualified to play the Celtics.

The Celtics—with Larry Bird, Robert Parish, Kevin McHale—are the reigning world champions. Proud and dignified, steeped in tradition. The Pistons have won 52 games during the 1986–87 season. They are upstarts, a team lacking heritage. But they are a team emerging, with true talent. And quickly, in Boston, they lose the first two games of the best-of-seven Eastern finals series.

The Celtics think sweep. But, back in Detroit, the Pistons win two. They square the series. Game 5, the Boston Garden, is itself a classic. The Pistons, this team without tradition, minus any proud heritage, have lost 17 games in succession on the parquet floor of the Celtics.

Now the Pistons, gripped by some sort of sense of destiny, take a lead by a single point with seconds seconds to play. Isiah shoots the basket, a jumpsshot from maybe 18 feet. Now the Celtics bring the ball in the other direction. They do not panic. They feed the ball to Bird, who has scored 36 points. This time he starts to drive the baseline. He brakes, goes up for the jumper and the ball is stuffed back, blocked, by Dennis Rodman, leaping. The ball ricochets off the leg of Boston's Jerry Sichting and bounces out of bounds. Five seconds left and the Pistons are ahead by one point and have possession of the ball.

As the ball goes out of bounds, the Pistons go delirious. Dennis Rodman, his arms flailing, races up the court in utter jubilation. In his joy, he has vacated the area where the Pistons must pass in the ball. The Boston Garden hex, or whatever brand of witchcraft it is, is dead, over; the Pistons need only to compete the routine pass in from the side, in Boston's end of the court.

The Pistons ignore the idea of taking a time-out. Rodman and teammates are at the wrong end of the court, in celebration. Isiah takes the ball from the referee at the sideline, gets set to inbound the ball. Laimbeer cuts toward the baseline, prepared to catch the pass. Strictly routine. But this is the Boston Garden and these are the Celtics and they have Larry Bird. Bird slices down the lane toward Laimbeer. Isiah's pass in is soft. It fails to reach Laimbeer. Bird cuts in front, intercepts the pass and relays the ball to Dennis Johnson driving underneath. Johnson lays in the basket. The score is 108–107, Boston, as the buzzer goes. Again.

The Pistons return home, brokenhearted, to face elimination. With grit, character, mettle, they beat the Celtics a third time to tie the series once again. The reward is Game 7 in Boston Garden.

And the series has been marked by fighting—Laimbeer is at his most combative. Bird throws the ball at him. Parish punches him. Now in Game 7, all the anger and all the hostility are compacted into one afternoon—the champs playing for their very survival against the upstarts, playing to advance to the NBA finals, which their Detroit franchise has never reached.

It is a bloody, gory, tough game. Adrian Dantley is conked, when he bangs heads with Vinnie Johnson late in the third quarter. Dantley is knocked to the parquet floor, out cold. He is carted off, taken to the hospital. Still the Pistons are mighty in this game, playing with their hearts, their emotions. The fourth quarter grips America on Saturday afternoon TV. Late in the fourth quarter, it is 99–99. Tied. The Celtics miss four successive shots. Each time they grab the offensive rebound away from the Pistons. Finally, Danny Ainge gets the ball and shoots from distance, for three points.

The Pistons still fight mightily. With twenty-five seconds left, Isiah Thomas takes the long shot, from three-point range, trying to tie the score again. The shot arches, hits the back of the rim, and bounces off. The Celtics grab the rebound. At the end, the Celtics win. They move on to the NBA finals for the fourth consecutive season, vs. the Lakers. The Pistons lose. By three—117–114. This time Larry Bird has scored 37 points.

And the Pistons must trudge into the tiny, tight locker room to face the hordes of media people.

It is here, in this madcap scene, that Dennis Rodman, Worm as he is called, an NBA rookie, the Piston who had run up the floor with his arms flying in celebration with seconds left in Game 5, faces his interrogators and speaks.

"Larry Bird is overrated in a lot of areas," Rodman says to the reporters. "I don't think he's the greatest player. He's way overrated."

The reporters glance around. Here is a guy, a rookie in the league, from a tiny college out west, a guy off the bench, from a team of upstarts, spieling away for their benefit, criticizing the NBA's MVP, one of the premiere athletes in the country. They sense story. But the story has hardly started. Rodman is unstoppable.

"Why does he get so much publicity?" Rodman says to the reporters. "Because he's white. You never hear about a black player being the greatest."

And now, suddenly, the story is no longer just an athlete in oratory after a crushing defeat in a basketball game. It is a story of race and bitterness and sociological anger. It is a story that goes from a sidebar at a ballgame to story that evokes flaming headlines and enormous repercussions.

The reporters, armed with Rodman's dialogue, squeeze toward Isiah Thomas in the tight dressing room. They repeat Rodman's words and ask Isiah for his opinion about Larry Bird, how would Bird rank in the league's hierarchy if he happened to have been born black.

"If Bird was black, he'd be just another good guy," Isiah says to the reporters.

And so the story, with its raging headlines, with its tones of racism, breaks in Sunday newspapers all across America.

The 1987 NBA finals are about to begin, Celtics vs. Lakers again. But the NBA finals are secondary. All hell has broken loose—the words of Rodman and the supportive words of Thomas rattle through the consciousness of pro basketball and all of American sport.

Rodman, realizing the impact, says he is sorry in a short public apology. He should have known better.

Isiah is represented as speaking his words about Bird in a vain, futile attempt to diffuse the criticism he knew would smack into the gaunt face of the rookie Rodman. Thomas calls Bird to explain; he has been misquoted; his facial expressions have shown that he was only kidding. Bird doesn't even bother to listen to Isiah's pleas.

Thomas is summoned to L.A., where the NBA propaganda people out of New York arrange a press conference. The NBA places Thomas and Bird together at a table to answer the questions of the hundreds of reporters covering the upstaged NBA finals.

Dennis Rodman, Worm, meanwhile has dashed off to Bokchito, a town of 600 or so citizens, in rural Oklahoma. It is there that he takes his retreat, where he has lived when he was playing basketball in college, where the people who are closest to him can embrace him and soothe him and hug him. Where a family has taken him in.

A white family.

Each of the Pistons has his individual story. Dennis Rodman's is the strangest, the most remarkable. He was born in Dallas, and when he was three the family broke up. Phil Rodman left his family—the mother, Shirley, two daughters, Debra and Kim—and tiny Dennis. It was a women's family. Dennis would tell *Sports Illustrated* years later that even as a small boy he always had to look out for himself.

Even Mother Nature played him an odd trick. His sisters grew tall and sturdy. Debra would grow to 6-feet-3 and play basketball so brilliantly she would become an All-America at Louisiana Tech when it won a national championship. Kim would grow to 6-feet-1½, and like Debra, become an All-America, at Stephen F. Austin.

Dennis, the remaining male, meanwhile, seemed destined to live life as a runt. He went to South Oak Cliff High School, where he couldn't make the football team because of his size. He was too small. "He was devastated by that," Shirley Rodman told *SI* when it profiled her son. "He went to pieces, stayed in his room for days." His friends taunted him, she said, for always trailing around with his sisters.

Next Dennis tried to make the basketball team at South Oak Cliff. It was his senior year. He sat on the bench for half a season, and that was no fun. He realized he didn't have the stuff. "I couldn't even make a layup right," he would tell *SI* years later. He was 5-feet-9, towered over by his sisters, victim of nature's cruel joke.

Dennis Rodman was eighteen, graduated from high school, short, confused, presumably angry, without even one varsity letter-jacket among his property. He found work at the sprawling Dallas-Fort Worth Airport, cleaning up. He was hired as a janitor.

He was at work late one night, performing his chores—"mopping, sweeping, cleaning up." It was at a time when there were few travelers making the long rush through the corridors. The shops were shut, iron gates drawn across their doorways. Dennis paused in front of a jewelry shop. Hmmmm. Curiosity drove him to try to shove his broom handle through the gate and toward a display case containing watches. A bit of nimble jiggling and Rodman discovered he could scoop out the watches on the end of his broom stick. He left with fifty or so, and he gave most of them to his friends.

But the cops caught him. He spent much of a day in jail and convinced friends that his generosity was misplaced. Would they please return the gift watches? The charges of stealing were dropped.

At nineteen, when most young adult males have reached their full height, 5-foot-9-inch Dennis Rodman started to sprout. He grew eleven inches in the next two years. At twenty-one, Dennis Rodman stood 6-feet-8. He was now working as a car cleaner for an Oldsmobile dealer. His hourly salary was $3.50.

He tried the basketball court again. Suddenly, he knew how to make a layup. Like magic. The awkwardness had vanished as he grew taller. "Once I started growing," Rodman told *SI*, "I picked up the game like that."

He took his late-blooming talents to Cooke County College, a junior college in Texas, and was awarded a scholarship. He was gone after fourteen games. The academics troubled him.

"It got to me," *SI* quoted him as saying. "I said, 'I ain't going to make it no how. What do I want to do this for?'"

He went back home to Dallas. He hung out on the streets. Shirley, his mother, gave him some money to help look for a job. He didn't bother. He continued to hang out on the streets, doing nothing, eyeing the passing cop cars, loafing.

He spent hours playing pinball machines, twisting as the metal ball bounced off the bumpers, contorting his now long and skinny body, pumping the machine with a series of grinds. "Hey, Worm." The nickname stuck as Dennis Rodman roamed the streets.

"I would have ended up in jail for sure . . . Finally, [my mother] told me she was sick and tired of me sitting around the house bumming, so she threw me out."

Rodman vanished, became, virtually, a missing person. He moved from place to place, living with friends. He was unaware that a basketball coach, Jack Hedden, from Southeastern Oklahoma State, was trying to trace him down, offer him a second chance to play college basketball. Hedden finally located Rodman and made the offer to play at the small-college, NAIA, school in Durant. Rodman was twenty-two, a drifter.

"I figured I had to try again to get off those streets," Rodman said.

He entered school.

Some fifteen miles from Durant, in the out-back Oklahoma town of Bokchito, a thirteen-year-old boy named Bryne Rich was struggling to regain his life. The *Dallas Morning News* reported these details, which were reprinted by *SI*:

A year earlier, in the late summer, Bryne Rich had gone into the woods with three friends behind his family's 600-acre farm. They were just boys, and they had taken a shotgun with them. They planned to shoot at horse apples on the trees. The accident occurred with stunning impact. Bryne had opened his shotgun to reload. He put a new shell into the shotgun. He snapped close the shotgun.

As he did, Brad Robinson, Bryne's best friend, walked toward him. Somehow the firing pin had stuck. When the shotgun snapped shut, contact was made, and it fired. The shot hit Brad. Brad Robinson died three days later.

Bryne Rich could barely exist with his regrets.

His mother Pat picked up the story for *SI*:

"At one point he came to us and said, 'Maybe if you'd adopt me a little brother I could teach him to play basketball.' He was missing Brad something awful that night. I told Bryne that if God intended for him to have a little brother, maybe he'd send him one. Then we said a prayer together. Three weeks later, God sent us Worm. I never dreamed our little brother would be black. I think God must have a sense of humor."

As therapy for Bryne, the Riches sent him to attend a basketball camp at Southeastern Oklahoma. He was shooting baskets one day, in his solitude, when a guy with a quarter fitted into each of his prominent ears, walked onto the court. He said his name was Dennis Rodman. He said he'd rebound Bryne's shots.

That night Bryne went home and asked his mother if he could invite his rebounding friend, Worm, over for dinner. Pat Rich said, sure. Then Bryne said he'd forgotten to tell her something.

"Worm is black."

"Black?" said Mrs. Rich.

Guess who is coming to dinner?

"I almost swallowed my tongue when I heard," Pat Rich told *SI*. "I assumed he was a white boy. If everything had been normal, I'd have questioned it a lot more. But I tolerated it

because it was good for Bryne. We thought, what harm could it do to let him have a friend for dinner? We didn't know he was going to become part of our family. It's hard to believe a family like ours could love a black boy like Worm."

The night after Dennis Rodman had come for dinner, Bryne asked his parents if his friend could stay over for the night. The Riches wrestled with their consciences and could not come up with a clever way of saying no. That night, for the first time since the shooting accident, Bryne Rich slept the night through in his own room. Rodman slept on the floor of the room.

"Worm brought Bryne out of the depression he was in," Pat Rich said. "But at the same time, I think Bryne helped save Worm."

The bond between Bryne Rich and Dennis Rodman, the little brother, became thicker. Eventually, they became so attached that Rodman was treated as a member of the family. He sort of moved into the house on the farm.

"All of a sudden I'm driving a tractor and messing with cows," Rodman told *SI*. "But I never went back to Dallas, I never did. I figured if I was going to make it, if I was going to steer that street crap out of my life, I couldn't go back there."

There were times Rodman sought to move back to his dorm on campus. "But every time they begged me to come back," he said. "I knew they just wanted me there for Bryne's sake. But in time they accepted me as part of their family."

At a time of life when other young athletes were becoming stars in the NBA, Rodman started to excel playing for a small college in Oklahoma. He became stronger, better. One night he scored 51 points, against Bethany Nazarene. He was selected three times as an NAIA All America. He led the small-college group twice in rebounding. He flapped his arms, he thrust his fist, his emotions poured from him as he played the game they'd said he'd never be able to play.

And he was hellish on defense.

He would sit there at times watching the NBA on television and fantasizing.

"I'd see Bird on TV and say, 'I could guard that guy,'" he said. "I wasn't afraid of anybody."

And the NBA found him down there in the Oklahoma boonies. Marty Blake, the NBA man who scours the world for undiscovered talent, found him. He recommended him. And Jack McCloskey made Dennis Rodman, age twenty-five at the time, the kid with the prominent ears, the Pistons' second-round draft choice in the spring of 1986. He was the twenty-seventh player off the board.

Rodman was so excited the day he signed his contract with the Pistons his breath grabbed him and he hyperventilated.

But he made the club.

A year later, Dennis Rodman had played against Larry Bird in the NBA playoffs, and he wasn't that impressed. One Saturday afternoon in the ancient Boston Garden, the Pistons lost the seventh game of a brutal playoff series to the Celtics. Dennis Rodman stood in the visitors locker room, in defeat, his emotions stretched, and stated to a mob of reporters that Larry Bird was overrated, nobody would think he was so good if he were a white guy.

Dennis Rodman, Worm, scooted off to take refuge and read the all the hate mail he received, in the one place he could feel he was safe—with his white family in Bokchito, Oklahoma.

One Sunday afternoon in February 1991, in Madison Square Garden, on display on NBC-TV for the nation, the Pistons crumble before the Knicks by twenty-eight points. Isiah is out for months, indefinitely, his right arm in a huge cast after a delicate operation by the surgeons. No alibi for Dennis Rodman. It is a shameful performance by a club aiming for a championship.

In the second half of this game, Daly benches The Worm.

He goes into the locker room, and again in this scene, after damaging defeat, he is approached by the reporters.

He is mad as hell again. He yells, he shrieks. He accuses his teammates of dogging it. He accuses his coaches of losing their intensity. The words are treasonous.

"I just told the coaches if you're going to bench me, give me a valid reason why," Rodman says to the reporters. "They sat me down to rest me. I didn't like it because they pay me to play, not to sit."

He says he told his mates: "We're all men." Cutting words.

"They may not like my opinion, but they're still going to have to listen to it," Rodman tells the reporters. "We needed to play hard like the Pistons have done the last three years.

"I didn't like what was going on. I had to reach out to certain players. I don't care if they hate me. Just go out and play hard."

Next night, back in Auburn Hills, the disgraced Pistons play the Seattle Supersonics.

Again the Pistons are lifeless, lacking drive, motivation. They are dead ass, and they fall eleven points behind the Sonics. Isiah has shown up for the first time since his surgery. He has spoken to his falling team, rendering the captain's pep talk. He is sitting on the bench in civvies, his right arm immobile.

In the third quarter, the Pistons' struggle goes on. There is a loose ball beneath their basket. Three of the Sonics go to grab the ball and into the melee Dennis Rodman dives alone, without help. He wrestles the ball from the three Sonics and is fouled. Isiah is off the bench, flipping his left arm in triumph, cheerleading, and the crowd wakes up.

And so do the Pistons.

Now Dumars is hitting and Rodman is battling. Worm, between free throws, backs off from the line and waves his arm to the sullen crowd. Wake up, he is saying.

The Pistons win the game two seconds before the buzzer, 85–83, on Dumars' twisting drive through three of the Sonics to a victorious layup.

"Anything to get us over the hump," says Rodman in another statement in another locker room. "Anything to light a fire."

"I know one thing," says Chuck Daly, "after the game Sunday, he was not very happy, and he let everybody in the room know, including the coaches. And I respect that. But he's a determined guy."

That night, Dennis Rodman has played the entire 48 minutes, without a rest, without a letup.

Chuck Daly says of Worm, one day in 1991: "He's the best there is. He's a joy to coach. In all my years in high school, college, and the pros, he's the only player who goes all out every game. He never gets involved in the agenda. The head stuff."

Second Quarter

I—Vignettes from the Edge

Wilt Chamberlain, known as Wilt The Stilt because he stands 7 feet 1 inch, comes down the escalator of the Book Cadillac Hotel in downtown Detroit. He steps out onto Washington Boulevard to look for the bus. It is an autumn afternoon in the early 1960s. Chamberlain is the premier drawing card of the National Basketball Association. He is the one recognizable athlete in this struggling league. He is in Detroit because the Pistons, still new in the city, have arranged an exhibition game with his team, the Philadelphia Warriors.

"The team bus is right there," the functionary tells Chamberlain.

He is dubious, but climbs the steps and folds his huge body and legs into a seat. The other basketball players, from both his team, the Warriors, and the opposition, the Pistons, get aboard the same bus.

The door closes—and the bus chugs off, out of the city, and down the highway to Toledo, Ohio. Exhibition games mean money, and the Pistons smell a rich box office with Chamberlain playing, and they have gone on the lam with the game, taking it to another town to lure an appreciative crowd.

The game and the arrangements are the Pistons' responsibility, and they have arranged to rent the bus to take both teams to Toledo.

The bus is a Little Yellow School Bus.

Wilt Chamberlain, 7-feet-1, is crammed into a sweaty seating space, usually occupied by kids being transported to high school or junior high. His legs are twisted and his knees are crushed against the back of the seat ahead of him.

Thus, professional basketball has arrived in Detroit. Sheer symbolism. The Pistons are vagabonds in their own hometown.

It is a huge secret. The Pistons have discovered a way to get ink in town. They have traded away George Yardley. But they refuse to name the player they will receive in exchange, or even identify the team to which they are sending Yardley. The papers publish with large headlines: Pistons Trade Yardley for Mr. X.

And the Pistons refuse even to hint about the identity of the phantom Mr. X.

It is February 1959, and the Pistons have no box office name, other than George Yardley. He has been imported with the team when Fred Zollner moves from Fort Wayne to Detroit to start the 1957–58 season, based at the Olympia out on Grand River. That first season, Yardley breaks George Mikan's scoring record for pro basketball. Yardley scores 2,001 points.

Time magazine discovers pro basketball and writes about Yardley and his phenomenal scoring: "When he puts on his basketball uniform he looks like an absent-minded scientist who left home without his trousers." *Time*'s cute phraseology is accurate. Yardley is a graduate of Stanford's think tank, he has a degree in aeronautical engineering. He is balding, lean, knock-kneed, 6-6 and his nickname is the Bird. Bird shot. He is a marvelous shooter.

And he is Fred Zollner's favorite. Z had signed him personally, when the Pistons played in Fort Wayne.

George Yardley broke George Mikan's league scoring record with 2,001 points in the first year of the Detroit Pistons existence.

But then Yardley and Zollner have a flap. It is about money, basically, although Yardley has a handsome salary as the most productive scorer in pro basketball, said to be $25,000. Yardley himself says years later he is a physical wreck that second season in Detroit. He wheezes and complains. He has been the first player to reach the 2,000-point milestone and he feels pressure because of greater expectations. The Pistons management says he is a hypochondriac, nothing more. In a magazine article, Yardley says the NBA is a bush league. Yardley is benched, demoted from the starting unit. He accuses Zollner of meddling with Coach Red Rocha, ordering the club's best player be banished to the bench.

To top it, Yardley breaks his hand.

He says, publicly in an interview with Pete Waldmeir in the *Detroit News*, in early February that he wants to be traded.

"It would be foolish to go back to Detroit when I'm not wanted."

Nick Kerbawy, the general manager Zollner hired away from the champion Detroit Lions, says he would talk to three clubs about trading for Yardley.

Yardley knocks Zollner in print.

"Frankly, I haven't talked to him in a month," Yardley tells Waldmeir. "It has been bothering me. I know I wasn't playing much before I got hurt. I sensed something was wrong, but I didn't want to complain. Evidently, Zollner is the one who wants to swing the trade."

Zollner denies it, says there never has been any animosity.

The trade deadline is in a week. The rancor and the speculation go on for the entire week.

Kerbawy spends full work days on the telephone trying to arrange a trade. He says: "We figure one or two top players are all we need to have a good club. This trade will give us one of those players."

Mr. X.

The deal is made, days before the deadline. But there is no name announced, no other team identified, because Yardley's hand is broken. Five days go by.

Who is this Mr. X, this phantom player who can do for the Detroit Pistons what George Yardley could not do—make them a good club?

He remains a secret.

And then, at last, the mystery ends. The headline reads: Pistons Get Conlin in Mr. X Swap.

The Pistons have just traded George Yardley, the top scorer in the history of pro basketball, for Ed Conlin, a low-scoring, nondescript benchwarmer for the Syracuse Nationals.

But Fred Zollner is quite happy. He has rid himself of George Yardley.

And he has established a method for the Pistons' way of making trades. It would be more than two decades before the Pistons could escape from this pattern: George Yardley for Ed Conlin, even up.

* * * * * * * *

"C'mon," says Don Wattrick, general manager of the Pistons, to the tall, dark-haired hometown hero, "we're going out to dinner."

"Where you going?" says the hero, smiling, twenty-four, a product of Detroit's large Belgian community.

"How about Pinkey's," says Wattrick.

"Good," says the hero. "I thought you'd want to go to one of those fancy places downtown."

Wattrick invites two writers to join them at Pinkey's.

"Meet the new coach," says Wattrick when we get there.

Dave DeBusschere sits down with us. He orders a beer. He always orders a beer. He could lead the NBA in beer drinking.

Pinkey's—it's still there—stands at the corner of Grand Boulevard and East Jefferson, near the Belle Isle Bridge. The location for this little get-to-know-you soiree is symbolic. It is East Side Detroit. Dave DeBusschere has grown up on the East Side. His father ran a saloon down East Jefferson, near the Chrysler plant, at Lycastle. The neon, in the window, advertised simply: BAR.

The Pistons are in a turmoil. Again. They are playing their eighth season in Detroit. In this time span, they have employed five coaches. There have been four general managers. Wattrick is the fourth, freshly commissioned on the side of the battlefield—or the court. He has qualified, eminently, for the position by doing the play-by-play broadcasts of the Pistons' games on radio.

Fred Zollner, flying in from his plant that manufactured pistons in Fort Wayne, Indiana, handpicks Wattrick for the job. Wattrick turns around and fires Charley Wolf as coach. Then Wattrick handpicks DeBusschere to coach the team.

The year is 1964, November, just after the season has started with 9 losses in 11 games. The ballclub is near mutiny. The players gather in bars and curse their coach.

"I never saw a coach who was hated so much," DeBusschere says.

Before the season, Wolf has traded three players he considers leaders of the anarchy in his locker room. Don Ohl has openly criticized Wolf to me in an interview in the airport bar before a roadtrip.

"Charley deals with personalities rather than the abilities of his players," Ohl says. "He told me he didn't like me, but that shouldn't interfere with basketball."

These comments, printed in the *Detroit News*, break open the strife between players and coach. Wolf has to get rid of his dissident player even though Ohl is a deadeye who could rally a club with his outside shot. Ohl is traded along with Bailey Howell, Bob Ferry, Wali Jones, and Les Hunter to the Baltimore Bullets. Wolf gets three players in exchange—Terry Dischinger, Rod Thorn, and Don Kojis.

Charley Wolf gets himself mugged in the eight-player deal.

"I'm glad I'll be able to play under a coach who played in the NBA," says Bailey Howell, in his drawl. Howell, once in the Pistons' early days in Detroit, had been considered the savior of the franchise when he was drafted out of Mississippi State. That belief is too optimistic, but Howell becomes the Pistons' top scorer for four years and floor leader, playing with a dignified style. Beyond that he is never controversial, never trouble for a coach, always religious and honorable. But he leaves, not with a blast, but with a mild rebuke for his coach, who has complex theories but has never had the practical experience of playing in the NBA.

"Valuable players are never troublemakers," Howell says over the phone from his home in Mississippi the night Wolf had traded him away.

Bob Ferry is considerably more outspoken.

"I wouldn't play any more for that man," says Ferry. "I have no regrets in leaving."

Ferry, later on, would become general manager of the Washington Bullets, before becoming a television voice for NBC.

Gene Shue—the courtside announcer would shriek "Two for Shue" to the handpicked group of spectators in his day—is retired. But he joins the chorus of Charley Wolf's favorite critics.

"It's the biggest steal since the Boston Brink's robbery," says Shue. He had been a Detroit original with the Pistons, coming with the franchise in 1957 when it moved from Fort Wayne. Zollner, piqued, had dumped Shue earlier. Shue adds: "The Bullets really raided Detroit, and if there's any club in the league you can do that to, it's Detroit.

"They have the worst management in the league. I know. I played for them. Over the years, they've gotten rid of their stars cheap."

With such venomous words escaping into the public domain, Zollner makes Wattrick, the broadcaster, his general manager. And Wattrick, scanning the Pistons' roster, goes to DeBusschere and asks him to become player/coach.

"I'm not going to be a tyrant," DeBusschere says that night at Pinkey's.

The cadre of pro basketball fans in Detroit glances at the choice with disbelief. DeBusschere is local. He has played for a state championship team at Detroit Austin High. He'd stayed in town to play at the University of Detroit, leading his team into postseason tournaments.

The problem with DeBusschere is his age. He has just turned twenty-four and is just two years out of college. He is the youngest man ever to coach in the NBA. At the time he becomes the Pistons' coach, he is the youngest coach, or manager, of any team in any major-league sport. Research reveals that only Roger Peckinpaugh, who managed the New York Highlanders at age twenty-three in 1914, had been younger. Lou Boudreau was also twenty-four when he became the boy manager of the Cleveland Indians in 1942, but he was an older twenty-four than DeBusschere.

So the Pistons have this tender, young coach who could not devote his total efforts to basketball. Out of U. of D., he has also signed a baseball contract with the Chicago White Sox with high potential as a major-league pitcher.

With that background, DeBusschere says at Pinkey's: "Somebody makes a mistake, so somebody makes a mistake. I thought everybody on the team had been playing scared. They were afraid to shoot and miss. They had one eye on the bench."

Don Wattrick, the new GM, beams at his new coach that night, proud of his decision.

What Wattrick doesn't say to his guests that November night in 1964 is learned later.

While mulling over his decision to make DeBusschere his coach he has gone into the office of Earl Lloyd. Lloyd then is a scout for the Pistons, a longtime employee, a man wise in pro basketball technique and the ways of the league. He has finished his playing career with the Pistons. Fourteen years before Chuck Cooper followed by Earl Lloyd and Sweetwater Clifton had been the first black players signed by NBA teams. On October 30, 1950, Earl Lloyd, on the floor with nine white guys, playing for the Washington Capitols, breaks the NBA's color line, the first black to play in an NBA game.

Wattrick now goes to Lloyd and solicits his thoughts about the coaching change and a successor to Wolf.

"You'd be the answer to all my problems," are the words Earl Lloyd hears that day in 1964, "if you weren't black."

* * * * * * * * * * *

It is a season or two later, the mid-1960s, a chilly night in January. An usher comes up to George Maskin, the man running the business at the press table in Cobo Arena. Maskin is the Pistons' press agent, tubthumper, drumbeater—all those boiled under the euphemism of public relations director. The usher hands Maskin a slip of paper. Some numbers are written in pencil on the paper: 1,365. The numbers are based on the number of people who are in the arena to watch the Pistons this night. Some have even paid cash money for their tickets; among them those who have paid a half dollar for promotional tickets.

"Tonight's attendance: 5,158," says Maskin to the couple of writers who have drawn the assignments to cover the game.

One night I lean over to peek at the numbers. The general manager comes charging toward the press table to shoo me away. He doesn't want me to print the actual attendance total.

Maskin tells me years later, when the Pistons have become champions and tickets cannot be purchased by ordinary fans: "The usher had the true figures. They were so ridiculous I'd add to it."

One night, Maskin says, the attendance was so low at Cobo, he asks a guy, "What year are we in?"

The guy says: "1967."

"Tonight's attendance," Maskin announces, "one, nine, six, seven."

* * * * * * * * * * *

The gunman walks into the party store on Detroit's East Side. The man's head is covered with a pulled over stocking to mask his face.

"Empty your register," orders the man, pointing the pistol at the shopkeeper.

"C'mon, Reggie, cut it out," says the proprietor.

"I ain't Reggie, and I ain't foolin' around," says the gunman through the stocking.

Reggie Harding lived his entire, short life on Detroit's East Side. He was 7-feet tall and he could be smooth on the basketball floor. He first got his name in the papers when he played basketball for Eastern High in the inner city. Mostly, he got his name in the papers for his arrests. He got nailed for auto theft and on a morals rap. He beat the morals charge. He was arrested for felonious assault, but he beat that charge. The bouncer of a Detroit saloon had accused Reggie of drawing a gun. The judge threw the case out of court when Reggie testified that it was a cigarette lighter that looked like a gun.

With Reggie, Eastern High had won three City League championships. Reggie didn't go on to college. But the Pistons decided he was tall enough and smooth enough to match up with a Bill Russell and with a Wilt Chamberlain and play center in the NBA. This is acute desperation, but the Pistons were seeking to build a clientele in Detroit. It was the summer before the 1963–64 season, and the Pistons, in the six years they'd played in Detroit, never had a winning season.

So they signed Reggie Harding, 7-feet tall, with a growing police record tailing him. Maurice Podoloff, the league commissioner, rejected the contract. But Reggie beat that rap, too. He was cleared to join the Pistons. One night, with the Celtics in Detroit, he outplayed Bill Russell.

But more often, he missed planes, showed up late for games, and kept getting himself into trouble and getting fined.

Funny, when he came into the Pistons' locker room, he'd flip his wallet into bottom his cubicle. He didn't bother to padlock it, as his teammates did.

"Anybody who stole that would get disappointed," Reggie told the writers. "So why lock it?"

He was actually a congenial guy, with a small, cynical sort of smile.

He lasted two seasons with the Pistons. One night he drove through a stop sign. It took six cops to apprehend him. He paid a fine in lieu of going to jail. Six months later, he was arrested for assaulting a cop. He said he knocked off the cop's cap by accident. He was acquitted. But the Pistons and then the league suspended him. He lost his family, his home, and the Thunderbird he once owned. He didn't even have a driver's license. He'd been too successful as a collector of traffic tickets.

The next fall, 1966, he was back in training camp, seeking a job. He got room and board and was in dire need of the $10 per diem for meals. Dave DeBusschere, the young coach, predicted the Pistons could finish second.

"Second place?" said Ray Scott, one of the bulwarks of the ballclub. "We got to change that, eh Reggie? Where we goin', Big Cat?

"To the top, man," Harding said. "Right to the top. They talk about black power and white power. Well, I believe in green power. Money, man, money."

He didn't make the ballclub. A year later, the Pistons traded Harding to the Bulls for a third-round draft choice and cash. It was one of the Pistons' better trades. When he left the team, vanishing, the Bulls fined him, suspended him —and at last released him.

Harding returned to the streets of Detroit's East Side. In 1968, the Detroit police shot him in both legs when they were investigating an armed robbery. He was arrested again several times for

Reggie Harding's run-ins with the law were legendary in Detroit.

He was on the street on the night of September 1, 1972, when a stranger walked up to him and started an argument. The man slapped Harding, according to police reports. Harding slapped the man back. The man left and returned with a handgun. He called Harding's name and then fired two shots. Two bullets went through Harding's skull.

He died the next day, his name in the papers one last time.

* * * * * * * * * *

There is a press conference. The Pistons call it. The media show up, ink-stained wretches from the papers, TV crews with one reporter, one cameraman to lug the huge picture-taking machine and tethered to him a guy with a microphone called a sound man. Major league stuff.

Which is why, shortly before the press conference, some individual in the Pistons' front office takes one look at Herbie Brown and says:

"Put on a suit for the press conference."

"I don't have a suit," says Herbie.

"Better go buy one," suggests the boss. "Better get a shirt you can put a necktie on, too."

So Herbie Brown, the thirty-nine-year-old world traveler, goes out and buys a suit, a shirt, and a tie so he can look spiffy when he is introduced to the media critics in Detroit. Herbie, of course, believes he looks spiffy in blue jeans, a fluorescent open-neck sports shirt, a vest, and cowboy boots to complement his shoulder-brushing locks.

Then the Pistons introduce Herbie Brown as the Pistons' new assistant coach and chief helper to Coach Ray Scott. At the same time, they announce that Ed Coil is being replaced as general manager by Oscar Feldman. Coil, capable and true, is a holdover from Fred Zollner's regime. It is June 1975, and a year before Zollner has sold the Pistons at long last to a consortium headed by millionaire industrialist Bill Davidson. Feldman, the number 2 stockholder and a lawyer, has been the team's general counsel.

The Pistons have had considerable success with Ray Scott as coach. He took over early in the 1972–73 season for Earl Lloyd, who had been given his chance after years of faithful service.

burglary, given a 2½-year jail sentence. He admitted in court he had a $100-a-day drug habit. As a police prisoner in Detroit Receiving Hospital, Harding ran from his room and escaped, outlegging the chasing cop assigned to guard him. The cops arrested him again a few days later. They found him walking down a street on the East Side. He told the judge he bolted from custody because he was sick and wanted to go to his own doctor for medication.

In court, Harding told the judge: "I would like another chance."

The judge gave it to him . . . if he would seek treatment for drug addiction in a federal narcotics program. Harding accepted the condition and returned to the street.

Sometime soon thereafter, the tall gunman walked into the party store on the East Side intending to hold up the owner. He'd disguised his face with a stocking. "I ain't Reggie," said the seven-foot gunman and walked back out into the street.

Scott has some players. Dave Bing is a veteran star, a slender guard who slices through the defenders to score and score. Bob Lanier, with his size 20 feet—sometimes exaggerated to size 22 in erroneous reports by fact-stretching reporters. Lanier, a massive pillar in the post, quickly becomes the best young center in the league.

In 1973–74, the Pistons go 52-and-30, and Detroit, at last, accepts pro basketball. The town can take a winner. Scott is voted NBA Coach of the Year.

The Pistons qualify for the playoffs for the first time in six years. There is genuine excitement in the city, if not hysteria. The Pistons play the Bulls. It is a hellishly tough series. The Pistons win the first game in Chicago with Detroit watching on TV. Now there is hysteria in the city. The series goes seven games—and the Pistons lose the seventh game by two points, with a chance to tie, when Bing's pass-in is intercepted in the final seconds.

But the Pistons have become a basketball team that is close to championship caliber. Championship dreaming, anyway. But, of course, they fade in the next season. Bing is hurt. He holds out. He squabbles with Scott. The club falls to 40–42. They get blown out of the playoffs in three games by the Seattle Supersonics.

Two months later, Herbie Brown shows up as Scott's assistant.

"In terms of big time credentials, I don't have them," he says at the press conference. "I think I can coach. All I need is a break."

His credentials are something like this: He has coached the Tel Aviv Sabras in an international league; he has been head coach at C.W. Post on Long Island; he has coached at Stony Brook College on the same island; he has coached teams in Puerto Rico and Pakistan.

But he has rich bloodlines and is ready to take on the NBA. His brother is a well-known pro/college coach named Larry Brown. Traveling from job to job must be a family trait.

Two months later the Pistons dump Bing in another one of their trades, just before the start of the 1975 training camp. The Pistons send Bing plus a first-round draft choice to the Washington Bullets for a scooting guard, Kevin Porter. Bing must go because Davidson is miffed about his holdout. And Scott and Bing are no longer in synch.

Herbie Brown's first coaching is in the exhibition season. The Pistons are playing a game against the Kentucky Colonels in Cincinnati. Brown is off the bench shrieking at the players. He is off the bench waving his arms. He is off the bench hollering at the referee. Scott just sits there. He is calm. It's a bloody exhibition game against a team from the American Basketball Association.

"Who the hell is that guy?" I say to Scott in the locker room after the game. "He acts like he's trying to steal your job."

"Nah, he isn't," says Scott.

Without Bing, the Pistons collapse at the start of the 1975–76 season. They are 17–25 in January.

Scott is conducting practice one evening when his bosses march onto the court and submit the coach to a lynching before his players. They fire him, without the common decency to take him into an office and administer the "Ziggy"—that distinctive Detroit word for firing the coach. The reason is that cliche copout that is offered whenever an owner fires a coach—"Lack of communications."

The new coach is Herbie Brown, who learned the basketball game on the gutters of New York. He has his break.

I express my regrets to Scott. "I should have listened to you," he says.

Herbie Brown is named coach through the remainder of the season. In essence, he has a twelve-week contract—and about as much security as scoutmaster of a Boy Scout troop. Or head coach of the Detroit Pistons!

I write: "There is a legion of discarded Pistons coaches. One has a radio show. Another sells basketball sneakers. Another hopes to return to the college classroom. Another is commissioner of another failing league. One sells booze, and another sells real estate."

In nineteen seasons in Detroit, the Pistons have gone from Charley Eckman to Red Rocha to Dick McGuire to Charley Wolf to Dave De-Busschere to Donnis Butcher to Paul Seymour to Butch van Breda Kolff to Terry Dischinger to Earl Lloyd to Ray Scott to Herbie Brown. A full dozen around the maypole.

"They said they would talk about next year after the season," Herbie Brown says. "I'd like to be here in training camp.

Herbie Brown, at the bench, does the fast-shoe shuffle along the floor. He is up, he is down, he is back up, he is yelling. Coaches wear suits on the bench, not blue jeans. The prize of Herbie's closet seems to be a leisure suit, pea green.

He is trying to work his own ideas with this ravaged team. His style differs from Scott. One night, during a time out at Cobo Arena, Herbie is diagramming a play to Lanier, Chris Ford, and the others. There are some season ticket holders and some are devout fans and the most devout is Leon the Barber. His seat is in the front row, behind the Pistons' bench. Herbie is scribbling out the play onto a memo pad. And Leon the Barber is in the aisle, yelling into the Pistons' huddle: "Two, two, two."

The fans, the devout ones, become privy to the play nomenclature by the simple method of eavesdropping the coach and his signal calling. "Two. Two." Herbie looks at Leon and issues his final instructions.

"They yell these numbers out and don't realize we haven't had these plays for three weeks," Herbie Brown says later.

Leon the Barber has been trying to call Ray Scott's plays, plays that Herbie Brown had junked for his own ideas.

The morning mail arrives in the newspaper office soon after Herbie takes over. There is a stack of public relations stuff for the waste can. But there is straight truth from the Pistons' offering. The press release begins: "Woe is us."

It is the first time I have been tempted to quote from a PR handout.

Funny, Herbie Brown gets by with beginner's luck, because it could not be some new coaching mystique. The Pistons finish the season and Herbie's personal record is two games below .500. The club makes the 1976 playoffs.

But Herbie has already started to lose his players. He has had a nasty spat with Bob Lanier. He has had them with John Mengelt and Eric Money, and the brooding Kevin Porter. There are shouting matches, at halftime, in the locker room. There are shouting matches, at the bench, in full hearing of the customers—and the guys jotting notes and taking numbers in the press row.

"Why should I get mad when Bob Lanier says in New York the thing he can't stand about Herb Brown is that I'm a yeller and a screamer,"

Brown tells me one night after a playoff game. "Basketball is a course in family living. You can't expect in forty games for the guys to understand me and for me to understand them.

In that game, Brown benches Lanier for 13½ minutes during the first half. Bob has picked up three fouls. The Pistons dissipate a 12-point lead. Once during the lengthy bench confinement Lanier's eyes meet mine. We erupt into mutual laughter.

"Why did you laugh?" Lanier asks me later.

"Because I thought you were getting ticked off by being kept on the bench so long," I say.

"I was laughing," Lanier tells me, "because I knew exactly what you were thinking, that you thought I was on the bench too long."

"You know," I tell Lanier, "the man was right."

"He was," says Bob.

That night, despite the shrieking and darting and shuffle, Brown coaches a devilish game. Lanier fires the Pistons back in the third quarter. He finishes with 35 points. The Pistons beat the Milwaukee Bucks, 126–123. They actually win a playoff series, two of three from Milwaukee.

But the Warriors blow the Pistons out in six games of a best-of-seven series.

"I hope whoever the coach is they let him stay three-four years to get the team together," says Lanier. "It's better than change, have it take three years, then change and take another three years.

"I'll be forty years old."

The new owners are encouraged. Herbie gets something longer than a twelve-week contract. A one-year contract. Herbie Brown, given a reprieve, goes into a temper tantrum. He figures the Pistons owners lack gratitude, that he has earned a three-year contract. Management suggests take it or leave it, after all Herbie should be counting his blessings that he ever got an NBA assistant's job.

It is January of 1977 when the mutiny starts. Lanier argues with Herbie Brown after a game with the Kansas City Kings. Chris Ford, so knowledgeable about the game of basketball, gets into a spat with Brown. But mostly it is the inscrutable Kevin Porter, who goes to war with his coach.

Porter, the man the Pistons have gotten for the popular superstar Dave Bing, is a slick, playmaking guard. Porter is a player of moods and shifting angers. He pouts and makes accusations against his coach. Brown fines Porter a grand. The fans remember this is the player the Pistons gave up Bing to get, and they boo Porter on his home court. Porter speaks out publicly against Brown. He claims the coach is against him, is benching him unfairly, is calling him names.

One day there is a scrimmage in practice. Porter, who is 5-11, winds up on a switch guarding a guy eight inches taller. Brown is prancing along the court. He yells at the taller player with the ball in a fit of class:

"You got a midget on you, put it up, you got a midget on you."

"Midget?" snarls Porter, justifiably irked.

The feud is on the verge of becoming physical. Lanier becomes the peacemaker. Through it all, the Pistons are playing well, in second place, though Lanier says the club should have won twelve to fourteen more games. It is a club with some talent. But there are strange strategies.

One night Brown sets up a right-handed play for Lanier.

"I'm left-handed," Lanier says to the coach.

It is openly speculated that Herbie Brown is about to be canned by the Pistons, today, tomorrow, the next day.

Rather, Oscar Feldman works to create a truce between Porter and Herbie Brown as the season heads into February. He invites the two of them to his house for Sunday brunch, lox and bagels. They talk. Feldman mediates.

"I've been caught up in a lot of bickering and stuff and I'm tired of it," Porter says. "I've been wrong at times and I can't accept being booed by the home fans."

Feldman announces peace in our time at a press conference. He also announces that Herbie Brown has been given a contract for at least another season as coach of the Pistons.

"This is probably the first time in a year I've been really happy," Brown says at the press conference.

"Perhaps I was remiss in not bringing them together sooner," Feldman tells the press. "With the help of my wife's cooking, they were able to sit down and discuss their differences."

Lox and bagels diplomacy has worked wonders. Herbie preens.

"I've had coaches come up to me and say I deserve the Congressional Medal of Honor," Herbie tells me. "I've gotten a lot of strength out of this year. How many did we win before I was here? All the players here are those I wanted to be here.

"I got four guards who are bitching. I got Chris Ford, who has been bitching since he got to the Pistons. I can deal with that. How long has it been since Bob Lanier played this well? Nobody says how well I get along with Marvin Barnes."

The Pistons finish the 1976–77 season with a 44–38 record. But they are belted out of the playoffs by the Warriors in three games. Herbie Brown reveals he tried to trade Kevin Porter three times during the season and was vetoed by Bill Davidson and Oscar Feldman.

It is written that Kevin Porter must be traded over the summer if Herbie Brown is to return as coach in 1977–78 and be successful. Just before the season, the Pistons purge themselves of Kevin Porter. They send Porter, who had cost the heroic Dave Bing, plus Howard Porter to the New Jersey Nets for one Al Skinner plus two second-round draft choices. The Pistons get rooked again. Herbie Brown is free at last. But the trade is too late to rescue him.

He is fired twenty-five games into the new season, his team slumping. He is replaced by the

Kevin Porter was a participant in Oscar Feldman's attempt at lox and bagel diplomacy.

38

new GM, Bob Kauffman, who has never coached before in the NBA.

Lox and bagels diplomacy has been a failure, after all. Kauffman coaches less than one season, elects to remain as general manager, and starts his manhunt for the next coach.

* * * * * * * * * *

The brand new coach comes out with a trumpet fanfare as an artificial waterfall roars behind him and the outline of the Detroit skyline is etched in lights on the messageboard and a roll of drums blends with the trumpets and smoke funnels upward through the air and a cannon that—that is supposed to explode backfires.

The TV cameras whir and the tape recorders spin until they run out of tape and the newspapermen flex their fingers as they catch writer's cramp. The brand new coach speaks for twenty-six minutes, nonstop, a monologue.

Dick Vitale is the brand new coach of the Detroit Pistons. The man selected as savior of pro basketball in Detroit. The man all the columnists in Detroit have advocated for the coaching job if the Pistons ever expect to sell tickets and succeed. Dick Vitale, the fourteenth coach of the Pistons in the franchise's twenty-two years in Detroit.

"I vow, I pledge that if a player on this team plays without excitement, without enthusiasm, and without feeling for two hours, I'll get fired first," Vitale swears. "Because I'll stand by my principles. That player will be on the bench or he'll be gone."

Our fingers ache, but his mouth feels great. He continues to bleat. Vitale talks of his boyhood in New Jersey. "A boy, a ball, and a dream," he says. He takes us back to East Rutherford High School, in Jersey, and to Rutgers. We're all aware that he came to Detroit, unknown, unheralded, for less than $10,000 a year, and created excitement, and victories, in the University of Detroit program. We know how he burned himself out and had to give up coaching with a chronic stomach ailment and internal bleeding.

And now here he is preaching a program of ReVITALEization of the Pistons. The Pistons finally have listened to the media do-gooders

Dick Vitale conducts a session of his daily road show.

and hired Vitale for three seasons at $100,000 per.

He squeezes life from a microphone on this day in the Silverdome, where the Pistons have moved their base of operations from downtown Detroit. It is the first of May 1978, and management is going to the drastic to try to place fannies into the seats in the new building built for football. The consortium of owners needs a huckster. If this doesn't work, they hint darkly they'll be forced to peddle the franchise down the river, convinced that pro basketball can never sell in Detroit.

Vitale has plans. He has had plans for months, throughout the media-backed campaign. Seven weeks before he is anointed coach, while the Pistons struggle to finish their season under Bob Kauffman, he tells me:

"I know what I'm goin' to do that first game in the Silverdome. I'm gonna get myself kicked

39

out. Ejected. The first game. The crowd'll go wild. Absolutely mad. Dick Vitale kicked out of his first game in the pros. Dick Vitale gets the boot."

It seems a plausible plan for Dick Vitale.

Kauffman stands by as the GM on this day of martial music and aborted cannon blasts. "We wanted a big boom, but something went wrong," Kauffman says. He hears Vitale, in his rantings, vow allegiance to Kauffman as the general manager, the boss.

The new era of pro basketball has begun in Detroit: PISTONS PARADISE! Vitale's words.

Two months later, Kauffman is the first casualty of this new era of ReVITALEization. Outmaneuvered in the inevitable power struggle, Kauffman resigns as GM. Vitale now is employed in a dual capacity, coach and, in essence, his own GM.

It becomes a road show. Vitale hits the podium, daily. He displays the finesse of a carnival barker, which essentially is what he is.

His first 113 days in the job, he hits 125 banquets, a line for the record book agate type the NBA buries itself in.

He is at a speaker's dais in September. His first training camp has not yet started. Suddenly, there is a barrage of T-shirts thrown from the dais. "ReVITALEized Pistons," across the shirts. This is the light fire. The heavy stuff follows. Vitale propels autographed basketballs into the luncheon crowd.

"What other coach in town throws out t-shirts, basketballs?" he yells at me. "Better not break the chandelier! Last place I was at I broke the chandelier.

"Talk about rich people. I was at a place they could afford to buy them. I throw them out and they're fighting for them like they're in heat."

Then he tells me what it means to be coach of the Pistons, in the lineage with Red Rocha and Charley Wolf and Herbie Brown.

"What it means to be the Pistons' coach? The other night it gave me the opportunity to meet the *man* I have the greatest, greatest admiration for because he's tested time. And any time, whether you're a great athlete, a great journalist, a great lawyer, a great doctor, a great broadcaster, in any walk of life, you can deal with time, you can survive for X number of years,

baby, that is a superstar. Well, I met Francis Albert Sinatra."

Dickie comes up for air.

"And I tried to meet him five years ago and I went back and said Dick Vitale. The guy said, screw you big fella, get out of here, we're not going to let you backstage. So all of a sudden I go now. Dick Vitale. Yeah, come on in, baby. And I go backstage, there's Francis Albert Sinatra. I can't believe it."

Dickie comes up for air.

"And after I got done, I said, 'Sinatra, you run around with Lasorda, you run around with Garagiola, they say they're the biggest dagos you know. Baby, get ready now. If you don't give me a chance to meet you, Francis,' and I told him this, 'if you didn't give me the chance to meet you and come backstage, when we come to Los Angeles and we win the world championship in the future and you want to get into my locker room, I say the hell with you and don't let you in.' And he began to laugh and I gave him a ReVITALEized t-shirt with the name Frank Sinatra on it, and I tell you something, I wish somebody would revitalize me."

Dickie comes up for air.

The next day, with camp approaching, Vitale swings his first trade for the Pistons. He says: "One word epitomizes the Pistons and it's *dissension*."

To clear up his serious problem, Vitale offloads the player he considers his top troublemaker. He dumps Eric Money to the Nets, even up in exchange, for, for Kevin Porter. Somewhere, off in limbo, Herbie Brown must be clutching his stomach in uproarious laughter.

It is October, and the 1978–79 season starts in *Pistons' Paradise*. The ReVITALEized Pistons lose their opener, Vitale's debut, to the Nets, 107–105. They lose their second game in Atlanta. By the third game, Vitale has been rushed to the hospital with something the matter in his stomach. The doctors diagnose it as only a tummyache.

Vitale is well enough to swing another trade. He wants Earl Tatum, playing for the Celtics. In exchange, Vitale swaps Chris Ford, who has been a reliable floor leader through years of dissension, anarchy, and disaster. Plus, Vitale gives up a second-round draft pick.

A few nights later Vitale is at the Pistons' bench again in the Silverdome.

He is up at the screech of a whistle, yelling at the offending referee. Now Vitale is ripping off his jacket, ready to go after the offending ref, ready, it is written in the *News*, for a fistfight. He is booted out with his quota of technical fouls, disqualified in the euphemistic parlance of the NBA. He keeps screaming. Curses, yells obscenities, bleeps, and his voice carries all over the jerry-rigged basketball corner in the huge Silverdome. A mammoth rent-a-cop, hired to protect the coaches and players from intruders, at last grabs Vitale to lead him from the court. Vitale keeps shrieking, his arms flailing, a man no longer trying to huckster tickets. The guard wrestles Vitale, picks him, and carries the coach of the Pistons up the runway to the locker room.

A column from the *Detroit News* one month later, November 16, 1978:

AT THE CIRCUS, there is also the one with the weepy eyes and the saddest of grease-painted faces.

"What coach ever was ejected, suspended, hospitalized and lost five in a row in the matter of a week?" said Dick Vitale, the ringmaster. "His first week on the job? I started on Friday the 13th. From now on I'm not doing anything on Friday the 13th.

"I lost those five in a row and you know what I was thinking? I was thinking 0 and 82, 0 and 82 really.

"It was all fear of failure. I've changed all my attitudes.

"I was so uptight, worrying about fear of doing the job."

Do you know fear? It is a dreadful emotion. It can tear a man's guts. But it is an emotion that is understandable in Dick Vitale, a man of bravado. Maybe the admitted fear explains his actions in his first weeks as coach of the Pistons.

OK, he shrugged off advice that he chuck his new job following a maniac display when he had to be dragged to the locker room. Maybe he needed some sympathy. Now he has survived the first month of the job.

Will he survive the season?

"If I can only get through this year," said Vitale, dodging one way for he would dodge another later.

"We have three No. 1 draft choices next year. I have general managers calling me from all over the league. They say they'll trade you a veteran for one of the No. 1's. Why do it? What's the difference if we win 25 or 30 games? The Pistons have always done that, traded away their draft choices. That's why they've had one No. 1 draft choice in four years."

. . . A month after getting ejected, dragged off the floor, suspended, hospitalized and losing his first five games, Dick Vitale guarantees:

"One thing I know. I can coach in this league. The whole key to coaching in this league is no bitching, no dissension, getting along with the players . . . and ultimately having enough talent so you can survive."

Herbie Brown couldn't have said it any better.

The Pistons make it to exactly 30 victories in Vitale's rookie pro season—30 and 52. It is an eight-game dropoff from what the Brown/Kauffman combo had *accomplished* the previous season. They fail to make the 1979 playoffs. Bob Lanier's knee bothers him. Lanier's moods are bothering him, too. Though he, too, campaigned for Vitale as coach the year before, he has feuded with his coach, and partner in business. Lanier sees a club still in decline. He hears that his coach has called him a malingerer, behind his back. And there is Kevin Porter. Vitale says he is a greedy player who is asking too much money for one who doesn't play defense.

Vitale says such things as though he is a conspirator sharing secrets. Then he denies it all when his criticisms work their way to the media.

It is not Pistons Paradise at all. It is the same *Pistons Purgatory*.

With the end of the season, Vitale makes plans to rebuild his club. Vitale trades Tatum, the player he received for Ford, to the Cleveland Cavaliers to pay for one Jim Brewer.

The 1979 draft is in June. The Pistons are fifth in the rotation. Earvin Johnson is first off the board, taken by the Lakers from Michigan State's national champions. Vitale drools. But Dick has his own secret scheme. He swings a deal with Milwaukee to advance a spot in the draft rotation, up from fifth spot to fourth. Vitale throws in $50,000 to certify the transaction and guarantee the drafting of the man he wants.

The Pistons conduct their draft via conference phone from the Main Event Restaurant at the Silverdome. The public is invited to cheer the picks in the Theatre of Vitale. They had everything under the big top but the cotton candy.

"We're on, we're on," yells the strident voice of the court jester over the amplifier. "The Pistons take Special K, Greg Kelser."

Kelser has been Magic's teammate at Michigan State. A smart enough pick. Sort of.

After that, the Bucks pick, in what had been the Pistons' original spot, and select Sidney Moncrief, from Arkansas.

Vitale pops out for the crowd, not with Kelser, who is at draft headquarters in New York, but with a box of Special K, munching the cereal flakes from his hand.

Out of Milwaukee giggles are heard from the Bucks. The Pistons have made them a gift of the fifty grand for swapping places in the draft. They say they had planned to draft Sidney Moncrief all along, that they intended to pass on Special K, Greg Kelser, anyway.

Soon after the draft Kevin Porter jumps the Pistons to sign as a free agent with the Bullets. The Pistons are awarded two first-round draft choices in exchange, Washington's number 1 in 1980 and the No. 1 in 1982. The Pistons have a neat stockpile of No. 1's, if used wisely.

Vitale buries himself in the trademart. Just before he opens training camp before the 1979–80 season, he swings another deal with Red Auerbach in Boston. Dick wants Bob McAdoo, who has been a brilliant scorer for years in the league. One season McAdoo averaged 34.5 points per game. He has played for the Buffalo Braves and the Knickerbockers before the Celtics. He comes with a reputation. Trouble for coaches. A terrible attitude. That's why so many teams have traded him.

McAdoo's reputation does not deter Vitale.

The deal is complex. The Celtics have signed M.L. Carr, a tough, hustling player, as a free agent from the Pistons. The two clubs, Auerbach and Vitale, dicker and dicker. The result: the Pistons agree to give the Celtics two first-round draft choices in 1980, their own and the one received for Porter from Washington, plus the rights to Carr for Bob McAdoo. Auerbach shakes hands on it and lights up his cigar.

The Pistons struggle at the start of the 1979–80 schedule. A dozen games into the season, the club calls a press conference. The date is November 8, 1979. The Pistons' record is 4–8 for the 12 games. The Pistons announce that the era of ReVITALEization has ended. Dick Vitale is fired as the coach of the Pistons. His assistant, Richie Adubato, is appointed coach for the rest of the season, the fifteenth coach in twenty-four years.

In a league in which the basic rule is *twenty-four seconds to shoot*, it has taken the Pistons twenty-four years to shoot and all they've shot have been coaches.

From a column in the *Detroit News*, November 9, 1979:

The mouth would always be working in overtime, running off in overdrive. Dick Vitale did it to himself. He talked himself out of his job of a lifetime with the Pistons.

It wasn't his endless harangues or his nonstop soliloquies. The Pistons ownership could abide them. That was the Dick Vitale they hired, the one who stimulated interest in a sport few folks cared about in this town. That was the Dick Vitale, who helped up fannies in the seats. That was the Dick Vitale, the showman, the Dick Vitale, who compensated for his drawbacks as a coach with a special flamboyance.

What killed Dick Vitale was his incurable habit of talking behind the backs of his players, of his bosses, of people who befriended him. The statements made in a stage whisper into a receptive ear. They are called leaks. They are made off the record. Don't quote me, but look what I'm up against, says the leaker in a conspiratorial tone.

That was the kind of sweet talk that got Vitale into deep trouble.

He spoke confidentially a year ago about Bob Lanier, his center, business partner and friend. The suggestion was that Lanier was goofing off, dogging it. I saw Lanier sizzle about the remarks made behind his back.

Vitale said such things about Kevin Porter.

And last week he said them about the men who own the Pistons after they unceremoniously dumped John Shumate and his huge salary. The implication was that Vitale considered his employers a bunch of cheapskates. Bill Davidson and Ozzie Feldman were portrayed as men more interested in saving bucks than winning basketball games.

I believe all those quiet, whispered, confidential remarks of complaint were the self-sabotage which cost Vitale his job.

. . . Looking it all over, I can't say whether Vitale failed as a pro basketball coach. He never had a proper chance. One season and a dozen games were not enough.

But he did do the job the Pistons owners hired him to do a year ago. He provoked people into an awareness that there is a pro basketball team in town . . . He was hired to be an entertainer, not a basketball coach. He was a ringmaster, an animal tamer, boffo.

. . . I worried what would happen when the novelty wore off . . . Dick Vitale had no new gimmicks. The guy dressed in the shaggy chicken suit couldn't save him. Only Lanier and the guys on the court could. And they couldn't.

. . . "We have made errors in judgment in the past," said Feldman, who was the management observer at Vitale's execution yesterday. "Just as coaches have made errors and players make errors. The best franchises in this league have made errors.

"We hope to learn by our errors."

A month later, in December 1979, the Pistons hire a veteran basketball vagabond to be their new general manager—a man unknown in Detroit, named Jack McCloskey.

The Pistons play out the 1979–80 season with Richie Adubato as coach. They finish with a 16–56 record. Bob McAdoo manages to rouse himself to play in 58 of the 82 games. He would be waived during the following season.

In June of 1980, the Celtics utilize the two first-round draft choices Vitale had traded them. They use one to draft Kevin McHale, out of Minnesota. They use the other in a trade to obtain Robert Parish from the Golden State Warriors.

Years later, in reflection, after he has succeeded hugely as a television voice and the Celtics have won three NBA champions, Vitale tells me:

"Red Auerbach ought to give me a championship ring."

It is a night for nostalgia in April 1982. The rookie, Isiah Thomas, sits on the bench in the Silverdome. It is a quarter-century since the Pistons have evacuated Fort Wayne to play in Detroit. In these twenty-five years they have played home games at Olympia Stadium, at the University of Detroit Memorial Building, at Grosse Pointe High School, at Cobo Arena, at the Silverdome, and at Joe Louis Arena. They have remained a vagabond franchise in their adopted hometown.

Through these twenty-five years, they have some outstanding players, superstars they might be called, even if they have never finished a season in first place or been anywhere except a distance from the NBA finals. And on this night in 1982, the Pistons are honoring the six best players to play pro basketball for Detroit in the twenty-five years.

The names of the six are read over the public address system, as Isiah watches, and thinks some day that he might be added to the list:

George Yardley
Gene Shue
Bailey Howell
Dave Debusschere
Dave Bing
Bob Lanier

They are names that ought to be cherished in Detroit.

And the six of them, they have something in common that discloses so much about the Pistons' first twenty-five years in Detroit.

Each of the six had been traded away by the Pistons. In each of the six trades, from 1959 to 1980, the Pistons were rooked.

February 7, 1959—The Pistons trade George Yardley, first NBA shooter to reach the 2,000-point milestone in a season, to the Syracuse Nationals for Ed Conlin. Yardley goes because he has irked Fred Zollner, the owner. Conlin stays two seasons in Detroit, mostly as a bench-warmer, and is sent apacking to the St. Louis Hawks.

August 28, 1962—The Pistons trade Gene Shue to the New York Knickerbockers for Darral Imhoff and cash. Shue, club leader, playmaker and accurate outside shooter, goes because he has irked Zollner. Imhoff plays two seasons in Detroit, averages 3.9 points per game, and is sold to the Los Angeles Lakers.

June 16, 1964—The Pistons trade Bailey Howell with Don Ohl, Bob Ferry, Les Hunter, and Wali Jones to the Baltimore Bullets for Terry Dischinger, Rod Thorn, and Don Kojis. Howell, the team's top scorer for four seasons and work-ethic leader, goes because he does not fit into Coach Charley Wolf's style. He would later start for the Celtics in two NBA championship seasons. Dischinger plays six fine seasons in Detroit and is traded to the Portland Trail Blazers.

Thorn plays a season and a fraction and is traded to St. Louis. Kojis plays two seasons and is left unprotected in an expansion draft to stock the new Chicago Bulls.

December 19, 1968—The Pistons trade Dave DeBusschere to the Knicks for Walter Bellamy and Butch Komives. DeBusschere, the club's former coach and top player for seven years, goes for no reason at all. He would later be an integral player for the Knicks when they win the

Two of the best of the Pistons—Bob Lanier (16) and Dave Bing (21)—were both traded from the Pistons. Number 24 of the New York Knicks is future U.S. Senator Bill Bradley.

NBA championship and then become commissioner of the American Basketball Association before it is annexed by the NBA. Bellamy plays two years in Detroit and is traded to the Atlanta Hawks. Komives plays four seasons and is traded to the Buffalo Braves for a second-round draft pick.

August 28, 1975—The Pistons trade Dave Bing plus a first-round draft choice to the Washington Bullets for Kevin Porter. Bing, one-time NBA scoring champion, one-time Rookie of the Year, the best player in the club's history and a Naismith Hall-of-Famer-to-be, goes because management is irked with his contract demands. Porter plays four seasons in Detroit, in two terms, is traded once to the New Jersey Nets, is reacquired in a trade for Eric Money, and then signs with the Bullets as a free agent.

February 4, 1980—The Pistons trade Bob Lanier to the Milwaukee Bucks for Kent Benson and a first-round draft choice. Lanier, the Pistons' leading scorer for eight seasons, goes at his personal request to move to another team. Benson plays decently for six seasons in Detroit and is traded to the Utah Jazz. The Pistons used the draft pick for Larry Drew, who never plays for them and is traded to the Kansas City Kings for two second-round draft choices.

II—The Roots

He would sit in a box—three rows, five seats in each row—and watch the Pistons play their basketball games. He would sit there all alone, nobody with him, surrounded by fourteen unoccupied seats just behind the aisle, in some sort of solitary confinement, and he would suffer. When the game was finished, usually, in defeat, Fred Zollner would enter a limousine to be chauffeured to the airport and fly back home to Fort Wayne, Indiana, in his own plane, The Flying Z. It was there that he lived then, it was there that the factory he owned manufactured pistons for the engines of automobiles and tractors.

And it was there that Fred Zollner, in the war-stricken and prosperous 1940s, founded his basketball team. The team he named the Fort Wayne Zollner Pistons.

Fred Zollner, The Z, who had a vision and sat alone, 1957.

He was a kind man, a gentle man, a quiet man, but an eccentric rich man. Myron Cope, the Pittsburgh wordsmith, once wrote about him:

"Fred Zollner is short and stocky, a dapper man sporting peak lapels, a silk shirt, a constant tan and an unruly coiffure that suggest he is about to mount a podium and conduct Beethoven's Ninth.

"He is the sort who would not harm a fly; rather than swat one, he would catch cold holding the door open until the fly got ready to leave."

Zollner was known, simply, as The Z. And without The Z as its benefactor, the National Basketball Association would not be the prospering, crazed, media-hyped enterprise it is in the 1990s. Without his charity, the NBA could well have died an ugly death in the 1950s.

The league, then, would be gerrymandered every season, franchises joining, franchises folding, franchises on the lam going to new towns. There were clubowners who needed stakes to remain in business. And Zollner would give them loans so their teams could keep on playing and keep the league active.

"Through all adversity, he stuck to the ship," Eddie Gottleib, who owned the Philadelphia Warriors when the NBA was new, said in a 1975 interview. "He never thought of quitting. Fred was very devoted to basketball and devoted to the league. He did everything he could to help this league grow and prosper."

Zollner established his basketball team at his plant just before Pearl Harbor in 1941. The Zollner Pistons competed in an industrial league, the National Basketball league.

It was shortly after V-J Day—victory over Japan in the war in 1945—that America started to break out in a sporting renaissance. A new fangled gadget called television with tiny, snowy, flickering black-and-white images was just reaching the marketplace. The nation was in a heady, adventurous mood. Dreamers, men ready to gamble away their bank accountants, entrepreneurs, were jumping into the romantic arena of professional sports. Not just in basketball, but in football also. The Z was one of the adventurers. He believed America would embrace pro basketball. The federation of teams called the National Basketball League, with his Zollner Pistons, was minor league. Mostly, the NBL, consisted of small town clubs owned by industrialists wishful of publicizing their products. Zollner envisioned something more glorious.

There was another group of adventurers—men involved in the operations of arenas in larger cities. Collected by Maurice Podoloff, a visionary sports/businessman out of New Haven, Connecticut, and Ned Irish, from New York's Madison Square Garden, they organized a flashy, new league. They gave it a catchy name—the Basketball Association of America. The BAA. In a somewhat elastic exaggeration, the BAA advertised itself as a major league.

This new league started business with the 1946–47 season and eleven franchises. Among the teams were the Knicks in New York, the Celtics in Boston, the Warriors in Philly—and such other clubs as the Pittsburgh Ironmen, the Toronto Huskies, the Cleveland Rebels, the Detroit Falcons, and my wonderful, all-time favorite Providence Steam Rollers.

By the second season, four clubs had folded and failed—Toronto, Cleveland, Pittsburgh . . . and the Detroit Falcons.

It was in 1948 that Fred Zollner's grand dreams turned into reality, for a price. He jumped leagues and took the Zollner Pistons into the rival BAA for its third season. Zollner paid a $25,000 fee to join the BAA. The Chicago American Gears from the NBL joined the BAA along with Zollner, moving to Minneapolis, where they adopted the nickname of Lakers.

With such stalwarts as Leo (Crystal) Klier and Dick Triptow, the Zollner Pistons went 22–38 the first season, finishing fifth in the BAA's Western Division. The Minneapolis Lakers, with George Mikan, won the BAA Finals, rushing to the championship over such rivals as the Chicago Stags, Rochester Royals, and Washington Capitols.

After the season, the two enemy leagues merged into one entity. The new league would be named the National Basketball Association. It, essentially, was a continuance of the BAA. But this 1949–50 season, the first under the banner of NBA, the league was formed in the shape of a camel.

There were seventeen teams in the league. Among them were the Waterloo Hawks, who played somewhere in Iowa, and the Sheboygan Redskins from Wisconsin, and the Anderson Duffy Packers from Indiana. Along with the Tri-Cities Blackhawks, who played along the banks of the Mississippi and represented Davenport in Iowa and Rock Island and Moline in Illinois. The Syracuse Nationals, Denver Nuggets and Indianapolis Olympians, replacing the BAA's Indianapolis Jets, also joined the NBA. The Zollner Pistons went 40–28 against the competition, finished tied for third in the Central Division, and made the playoffs. They beat Rochester in the first round, then lost to the Minneapolis Lakers in the division finals.

Its first four seasons as the BAA and then the NBA, America's major pro basketball league was an exclusively white society. Every player was white. At the 1950 draft, Walter Brown drafted Chuck Cooper out of Duquesne on the second round for the Boston Celtics.

Jackie Robinson had been the great pioneer to break baseball's color line three years earlier.

"Walter," one of the other NBA clubowners

was quoted as saying by the *New York Times* when the Celtics drafted Cooper, "don't you know, he's a colored boy."

Brown glowered at the admonishing fellow owner and said sharply: "I don't give a damn . . . Boston takes Charles Cooper of Duquesne."

On the ninth round, the Washington Capitols drafted Earl Lloyd, out of Virginia Union. At the same time, the New York Knicks signed Nat "Sweetwater" Clifton, who had been playing for the Harlem Globetrotters.

Earl Lloyd would become the first black man to play in an NBA game.

The 1950–51 season started with the NBA boiled to eleven clubs. Anderson, Sheboygan, Waterloo, Denver, the Chicago Stags and St. Louis Bombers all had vanished from the map of the NBA. At midseason, the Washington Capitols gave it up, too, disbanding with their players dispersed to other clubs.

But the Zollner Pistons persevered. There was little else to do for entertainment in Fort Wayne —and Indiana was rich in basketball heritage.

The Z went after players, Larry Foust and Frank Brian, who had been college stars. In 1953, he personally persuaded George Yardley, trained to be an engineer, to play pro basketball in Fort Wayne.

Zollner also sharpened his ziggy. Carl Bennett, the first coach when the Zollner Pistons entered the BAA in 1948, survived six games. The club had lost all six. Zollner hired Paul Armstrong for the remainder of the season. Murray Mendenhall became coach and lasted two seasons. Paul Birch actually coached the Fort Wayne club for three seasons.

It was Mendenhall, long forgotten, who on the night of November 22, 1950, made an unwitting contribution to the future fortune of the NBA. The night before his Zollner Pistons had been clobbered by George Mikan and the Minneapolis Lakers at the Coliseum in Fort Wayne. Mikan, 6 feet 9, with an arching hookshot was unstoppable. He was the premier player in the sport.

After he beat the Zollner Pistons, the two teams boarded a train for Minneapolis and a rematch. Mendenhall spent his time figuring out a strategy to neutralize Mikan. He came up with an idea. Hold the ball, slow the tempo. It was hardly a unique concept, but it had not been tried in pro basketball, which was a sport needy for action and scoring. On November 22, the Zollner Pistons passed the ball back and forth, back and forth, from John Oldham to Fred Schaus to John Hargis to Jack Kerris to Larry Foust. Occasionally, to break the monotony, one of them would cut in and shoot a layup.

Then the Lakers would grab the ball and feed it to Mikan for a basket.

Then the Zollner Pistons would hold onto the ball again, back and forth, ostensibly working for a good shot.

Mendenhall's plan worked. The Zollner Pistons won the game, forty-eight minutes of non-stop boredom, by an effective, if not overwhelming score of 19–18. Foust scored the winning bucket with three seconds left.

Mikan lead all scorers with 15 of the Lakers' 18 points. Johnny Oldham led the victorious Zollner Pistons. He scored 5 points—on one basket and three free throws. In all, Fort Wayne scored only four baskets.

It was not what the NBA considered hot box office. Minneapolis fans lined up to demand their money back. Others had passed the time of the game reading newspapers and playing cards.

Somebody in the league had to have a better idea than 19–18 ballgames as entertainment. It was Danny Biasone, boss of the Syracuse Nationals club, who figured out the solution. Why not have a time limit on how long a team can hold the ball before it must shoot? Like a 24-second clock?

The 24-second clock was the miracle discovery that might have saved pro basketball from death before the sport climbed out of its crib.

Before the 1953–54 season, Zollner signed a tall, dark Ivy League rookie out of Columbia named Jack Molinas. Molinas was the top candidate for NBA Rookie of the Year in January 1954, when, suddenly, he was suspended indefinitely by Maurice Podoloff, now league president. Something had been fishy about some of the Zollner Pistons' games. Paul Birch, the coach, said he became suspicious "about things Molinas was doing at games." Like, in one game, Birch recalled, according to accounts in aging clippings of the *Detroit News*, Molinas took only one shot. In another he took only two shots. New York papers, with pipelines to gamblers, printed that bookmakers had taken Fort Wayne games off the boards—stopped taking bets on them. There had been unexpected fluctuations of pregame point spreads.

The league's suspension cited Molinas for betting on games and for feeding information by telephone to a New York bookmaker about the team. He was quoted as saying he bet only on his own team to win. Molinas was quoted by police investigators as saying: "At no time was there a payoff to throw any game, nor was there any mention of one. The only reimbursement I received was for my phone calls and about $400 in winnings, including phone bills."

Podoloff said of the scandal: "I don't think this will have any effect on pro basketball. It was simply an isolated case."

Two months later a Bronx County Grand Jury in New York announced that it had not found any evidence that Molinas had been involved in a criminal activity.

It was a time before the NBA athletes had a Players Association and agents and lawyers. Podoloff, the president, ran the league with dictatorial powers. Molinas would not be reinstated.

"We are not concerned with whether Molinas committed a crime," Podoloff said after the Grand Jury findings. "To us, betting means that he broke faith with us. It was a flagrant violation of a written contract."

Jack Molinas was outlawed for life by the NBA. But he would be heard from later.

Paul Birch was finished as coach of the Zollner Pistons at the end of the 1953–54 season. It was a time when athletes played their games with gratitude, happy to draw $9,000 for a season if they were exceptional. The age of the prima donna player was in the future, but in Fort Wayne the players bitched about Birch's intensity and that his harangues destroyed their confidence. Zollner decided in midseason that he would need to make a coaching change. The club had become a contender by then. And the Z found the next coach in a strange place— tooting a whistle on the basketball floor.

Charley Eckman was 5-feet-5, cigar smoking, obscene, crusty and semi-lovable. He refereed NBA and college games and did some baseball scouting, some work as a radio man, when he could harness his language. Zollner thought Eckman would be a perfect NBA coach and talked him into joining the Zollner Pistons.

And if Charley wasn't quite perfect, he was quite good. His first season, 1954–55, the Zollner Pistons went 43–29 with Yardley, Foust, Fred Scolari, and newcomer Mel Hutchins. The club finished in first place, in the West, for the first time in its history. In the playoffs, Fort Wayne knocked off the three-time reigning NBA champion Minneapolis Lakers, 3 games to 1, in the Western Division finals.

The Zollner Pistons moved on to the 1955 NBA finals versus the Syracuse Nationals. Zollner switched his home games out of Fort Wayne to a neutral court in Indianapolis. It was a heated, intense final series that went all of seven games and to the final buzzer of Game 7. Syracuse won the championship in the final game on its own court, by one point, 92–91. The Zollner Pistons' other three losses, all at Syracuse, were by four, three, and five points. They had held a 3–2 advantage in games before losing Games 6 and 7.

It would be thirty-four years before the franchise would be so near to winning its first NBA Championship.

Still, Charley Eckman coached the Zollner Pistons back into the NBA finals in 1956. Again the club finished first, but the season record was a lackluster 37–35. They defeated the vagabond St. Louis Hawks—the erstwhile Tri-Cities Blackhawks and Milwaukee Hawks—in their first playoff round to reach the NBA finals against the Philadelphia Warriors. Philly blew the Zollner Pistons out in five games.

It was becoming a league of moveable franchises. And by the 1956–57 season, Zollner started considering transferring his club out of Fort Wayne, where it had been intensely popular with the locals, to a larger market. The Detroit auto companies were Zollner's major customers for the pistons manufactured in his plant. Detroit was a logical spot to move the basketball team—a town with a large, sports-oriented population and a rich sporting heritage. The Lions and Red Wings were winning championships. It was the fifties, after all. The Tigers struggled, but were one of the most valuable franchises in major league baseball.

Detroit was ripe for another pro basketball team—or so Zollner reasoned.

So as the Zollner Pistons played the 1956–57 out of Fort Wayne, Zollner maneuvered in the background, negotiating to move the club out of town.

For the third successive season, the Zollner Pistons contended. They finished first again, sharing the spot in a three-way tie with St. Louis and Minneapolis, with 34–38 records. They were already lame ducks in Fort Wayne by playoff time. The Lakers blew the Zollner Pistons out of the playoffs in the first round, in a year in which the Boston Celtics won their first NBA Championship.

On February 14, 1957, Fred Zollner signed the deal to switch his beloved basketball team's base to red-brick Olympia Stadium, near downtown Detroit.

On that day, the Detroit Pistons were born, kicking, squalling infants to be greeted by rejection and apathy in their adopted city.

III—Detroit, The Early Years

Excerpts from an article in the *Detroit News*, June 12, 1990

If the man who owned the ballclub had listened to the pleadings of his coach, they would have been the *Cincinnati* Pistons! It could have been Cincinnati that became hysterical in the Junes of 1989 and 1990 with the pandemonium of the Pistons' championships.

If . . .

"I wanted to go to Cincinnati," Charley Eckman said. "We'd have gotten Oscar Robertson as the territorial draft choice. I'd have been coaching another 10 years."

"When I got to Detroit nobody cared about basketball," said Eckman, reminiscing at age 68 during the 1990 NBA Finals from his home in Glen Burnie, Maryland.

"We had no place to practice. We were the last kid on the block. They had the Tigers, Lions and Red Wings. The first time I saw our home floor was the night we played our opening game on it."

Meanwhile, the Rochester Royals, also seeking to move to a major-league town, grabbed the Cincin-

nati territory. They drafted Oscar Robertson in the territorial, which at the time awarded a local team the first right to the best college player in its home region.

Once he left coaching, Eckman returned to his original craft—refereeing basketball games . . . "After I got fired Eckman said, "I reffed in the ACC and Ivy League."

It was as a referee that Eckman encountered Jack McCloskey, destined to become the champion Pistons' general manager, and Chuck Daly, who one day would work the job that Charley used to have.

"Jack was a gem at Penn," Eckman said years later. "He knew what it was all about. Jack was a holler coach. But I was a holler ref.

"I knew Daly when he was an assistant at Duke. He worked for a guy named Vic Bubas. Daly was more laid back then. He's gotten more vociferous."

One thing about Charley Eckman, bantam, tough, carousing, cigar chomping: He has not toned down his language over the years. Profane words poured from his mouth; anecdotes were related in a machine-gun staccato . . .

For example, he was not much of a fan of Dick Vitale, who happened to be one of the 16 men following in Eckman's lineage as head coach of the Detroit Pistons.

"Vitale knows it all," Eckman said, in a yell. "What's he know? He couldn't teach a dog to bark. He says, 'I'm gonna coach the pros.' You don't coach pros. You manage pros.

"They know how to dribble."

Eckman did not really cotton to the NBA coaching methods and complexities of the '90s.

"Plays," he said. "X's and O's, pick and roll—you can shove it.

"I had one play. An out-of-bounds play. Plays, the only time they work is on a board. Such a phony thing. What's the guy on defense going to do? Let you run it?"

Among Coach Charley Eckman's original Detroit Pistons were George Yardley, Walter Dukes, Gene Shue and Sweetwater Clifton. It was the year Yardley broke the NBA's 2,000-point barrier and led the league in scoring.

"We still had the two-hand set," said Eckman. "He was a great shooter.

"He always thought he was sick. I used to give him water so he'd throw up. He looked like death until he got on the floor. He'd fall asleep as soon as he got on a plane or a train.

"I'd cover him up with a blanket. He was my bread-and-butter man.

Charley was reminded that he had Walter Dukes. Dukes claimed to have gone to law school and had become a lawyer.

"He posed as one," said Eckman. "Ten years later I found out he didn't have a degree. He was 7-1. Who's going to argue?

"Shue got on the court and ran our offense.

"Sweetwater Clifton had six wives, so that took care of him."

Charley Eckman maintained that he is one of a kind in the history of the NBA.

"I'm the only guy to coach and referee in the NBA," Eckman said. "I'm the only guy who refereed the NBA championships and coached a team in the NBA championships."

The moveable Detroit Pistons played their first game in their new hometown on October 24, 1957, before a sold out house of 10,965 of the more curious at the Olympia on Grand River. They lost.

The Pistons opened as the feature portion of an NBA doubleheader, a marketing device of the era. A team would sell a home game for $4,000 or so to another town, because it was more than they could pull in their own arena. So the New York Knicks and the St. Louis Hawks, the reigning NBA champions, provided the entertainment in the first act of this basketball theatre. Then the Pistons made their debut after long, long introductions, against the Boston Celtics. With Bill Russell intimidating them beneath the basket and Bob Cousy treating the customers to his sleight-of-hand basketball, the Celtics knocked off the Pistons, 109–94.

The night was marked in history.

It was a warm night. Water, formed by condensation, dripped down from the rafters of the Olympia, onto the customers and onto the court.

The doubleheader started at 7:30, soon after dinner, and lasted until after midnight, 12:16 on the following calendar day.

Charley Eckman (left), the coach who came with the Pistons from Fort Wayne, with Bill Veeck.

"We gave the fans a show," Zollner said sometime around 12:20 on the twenty-fifth. "Those 11,000 will go out and tell 22,000 more what they saw. I think you'll see the day when we have to turn people away."

Regarding the length of the evening, The Z said: "We'll have to do some streamlining."

Zollner had hired Fred DeLano, a publicity man from the University of Detroit, as his general manager when the club moved from Fort Wayne. Just before the opening night ceremonies started, an Olympia usher urgently summoned DeLano into action. There was a gate-crasher, a guy trying to get in without a ticket. DeLano rushed to the ticket gates to quell the disturbance. There he saw the gate-crasher was Maurice Podoloff, the NBA president. Podoloff had forgotten his ticket.

It was about 12:30 when Charley Eckman summed up the Detroit Pistons' opening night performance.

"Our boys were scared stiff about running against Boston," Charley told the writers.

His statement would be turned into a prophecy for the franchise. Eckman's words would ring for the next thirty years, before they could be destroyed.

Eckman had come charging into Detroit with

another prophecy about the selling of pro basketball in the new town.

"It's going to go boom or bust," he said. "We're either going to go like wildfire or we're going to die."

The second declaration was somewhat less accurate.

Another slice of heritage was established that month of October 1957. In the third quarter of an exhibition game against the Hawks in Louisville, Bob Houbregs of the Pistons and St. Louis' Easy Ed Macauley went up under the basket in quest of a stray basketball. Elbows and nastiness were exchanged in the skirmish. Suddenly, fists were clenched, angry words exchanged, faces smashed.

Walter Dukes, the entire gangling seven feet of him, rushed to Houbregs' assistance. Jack McMahon jumped in to help Macauley. Then all hell broke loose. Players dashed onto the court and started fighting. Press accounts described it as a free-for-all. The Bad Boys legacy had been started for the Pistons, though no one back then had the imagination to coin such a phrase.

With the new sport in Detroit came the new philosophies of Charley Eckman. Zollner could not have had a better guy around to work on the selling of pro basketball. Charley was an enchanting quotesmith. His words got into the papers.

"What can you teach All Americas?" he said. "How to comb their hair."

They kept discussing his coaching style and one day Eckman was asked his favorite play.

Charley twirled his cigar and said:

"South Pacific."

Charley liked to flash back to his days as a whistletooter, before Zollner hired him to coach. There was a night in Moline, in an antiquated armory back when the NBA was still geographically misshapen.

"I was almost killed there one night," Charley told the writers. "I was refereeing and the Tri-Cities Blackhawks were playing the Philly Warriors and getting walloped. This was the worst town in the league to work in.

"At halftime, they trotted out some girls with canisters and people pitched money to the floor for the Heart Fund. We held up the game while they picked it all up, then went back to the massacre.

"There were about two minutes to go and during a timeout, my partner and I stopped for a breather. 'What a night this has been,' the other ref says, and with that he reaches into his pocket for his handkerchief.

"I didn't have to tell you what happened. As he pulled out the handkerchief all his change fell on the floor. Being a ref was bad enough, but that mob was convinced we stole the Heart Fund money, too."

Charley became a bon vivant in Detroit, a compadre of the legendary Doc Greene, who was noted for his nocturnal adventures before appearing in the office to write his memorable daily sports column in the *News*.

The Pistons had fastened themselves quickly into third place, with a losing record. Worse, the Pistons had troubles winning on their supposed homecourt. They lost seven of their first ten games at Olympia.

One night in early December, Doc and Charley were in some watering hole in town.

"That's not a home court," Charley told Doc. "The best you can call it is a neutral court. We don't get to practice on it. We're the only club in the league in that situation. They just put the floor down and take it up for games. We can't use it the rest of the time because of the Red Wings."

The club was going so poorly Charley couldn't sleep. Doc wrote that Eckman would pace his

Early style Pistons basketball.

apartment, captured by worry. Why even try to fall asleep?

"I guess I'll stay up and catch the bus to the airport," Charley told Doc Greene. "The team leaves for Philadelphia at seven o'clock. I wish I could get numb to losing, but I can't."

Charley Eckman became the first of the Detroit Pistons' coaches to catch the ziggy. After three first-place finishes in Fort Wayne, a near miss in the NBA finals, Charley Eckman was fired after twenty-five games in Detroit.

The Pistons were 9–16 when Charley went, actually forced to resign from his $12,500-a-year job. More convincing to Zollner than the stinking record was the Pistons' attendance in Detroit. They had lured more customers to their games in Fort Wayne. It was a vital matter. In the NBA then, the home team retained all the gate receipts. The road team received zero. Zollner was losing money fast.

He was not a quiet spectator in those days. He was a meddling owner. He debated Eckman's strategy. He told Eckman to dump Sweetwater Clifton, who had played for the Harlem Globetrotters. Eckman refused to release Sweetwater. Owner and coach argued. Zollner fretted for a month, considering a coaching change. Then he told Eckman to resign.

"Resignation is a nice way to put it," Eckman told Pete Waldmeir, then the Pistons' beat writer for the *News*.

Zollner's new coach stood fourteen inches taller than Charley Eckman. He was Red Rocha, true name Ephraim, a Hawaiian by birth, and a Mainlander by choice. At 6-feet-9, he had played at Oregon State and then nine seasons in the NBA. His last NBA stop was in Fort Wayne, in the Pistons' final season there. His coach was Charley Eckman.

"I bought him from Syracuse last year for $600 when he was on his way out," Eckman said of his successor.

Rocha retired and returned to Syracuse after his brief time in Fort Wayne. He was working there as a sheet metal salesman when Zollner bugled him back into basketball as the man designated to wow Detroit and show the town the merits of pro basketball.

"I know Red will teach the right moves and plays to some of our younger players and he'll be able to adjust the patterns of play to fit game situations as they arise," Zollner told Waldmeir.

"Also, he's not an extrovert and he has no bad habits.

Rocha was thirty-four years old—and he had never coached a game of basketball in his life.

Of course, he had some fresh ideas.

"I know when I played at Fort Wayne under Eckman last year, his style of basketball made me inclined to be a little lazy," Rocha said.

Zollner gave Rocha a rather odd contract, for less than ten months. It extended through the 1957–58 season until the following October 1. It would expire in the midst of the 1958 training camp, a few weeks before the start of the regular season.

In January 1958, Zollner flew to Detroit from Fort Wayne to attend another NBA doubleheader at Olympia. He watched his team defeat the Syracuse Nationals, 109–107, the Pistons' fourth victory in five games since Rocha became coach. That, of course, pleased Zollner and convinced him that he had made the correct decision in changing coaches.

But even so, it was a distressing night for The Z. The Pistons drew 2,818 customers to the

Nat "Sweetwater" Clifton (left) looks to the hoop during a game in 1957. George Yardley is the other Piston pictured.

doubleheader. Afterwards Zollner announced a long-range plan for the Detroit Pistons.

He said: "We are prepared to risk as much money in Detroit over a six-year period as we lost in fifteen years of operation in Fort Wayne. And it may surprise a lot of people, but although we had the largest per capita attendance in the league in Fort Wayne, we showed a profit only one year.

"We've completed our first phase in Detroit. We've let people know we are here and we've done it pretty well. Now we intend to move into a second phase and try to get more people interested in the game."

What interest Detroit fans showed was stirred by George Yardley's bid to reach 2,000 points and break George Mikan's NBA scoring record. Yardley started gunning. He scored 51 points against the Celtics in January. Then 52 against the Nationals in February. In March, he scored 49 points against the Lakers, Mikan's old team, to break the league record.

The last game of the schedule was against Syracuse. Paul Seymour, the Nats' coach, vowed that Yardley would not get to 2,000 points. In the first quarter, Al Bianchi tried to defend against Yardley and couldn't. George scored 14 points in the first quarter. He reached 1,999 points. Seymour put three defenders on Yardley. Yardley couldn't get the ball in the fourth quarter. Then "Balding George," as the press called him, took off with the Pistons on a fast break late in the game. He crashed his barrier/goal with his last basket of the season to finish with a grand total of 2,001 points.

The record would survive just one year. Bob Pettit broke it the following season by scoring 2,105 points for the St. Louis Hawks. And then Wilt Chamberlain came into the league as a rookie one year later.

Under Rocha, the Pistons did treat the Detroit faithful to some playoffs histrionics that first NBA season. They managed to finish second in the West despite a 33–39 record. And they whipped the Cincinnati Royals in the first round of the playoffs before losing the Western finals, 4 games to 1, to the Hawks, who were bound for the NBA championship.

The 33–39 season tally was something of a signal for what pro basketball would be in Detroit. The Detroit Pistons would not have a winning record over a season until 1970–71. The string of futility went thirteen seasons—and would become the NBA record for franchises with the most consecutive losing seasons.

The NBA record book is chock full of numbers. The league tends to keep records for everything. This one acquired by the Pistons exists still into the 1990s.

In May, after the first season in Detroit, Zollner dealt another change. In another of the forced resignations, Fred DeLano resigned as general manager. Zollner wanted more glitz, more oomph. Pro basketball was failing to sell in Detroit and . . . skulls had to crash when it didn't. The great minds on the Detroit newspapers had trouble discovering the captivating appeal of the game Zollner was trying to peddle.

Doc Greene wrote: ". . . He expected it and thought it was his due. This was sort of a fundamental mistake. Nobody owed him anything . . . DeLano got his season off the ground with more publicity than all basketball is probably worth . . . It's his silly game that's to blame. It has become a ridiculous idiocy of back-and-forth and back-and-forth spectacle. These herons that participate trade baskets until the last few minutes and then decide the contest. Detroit has turned it down before.

"As a charter member of the Hockey Haters' Association of America, it is my unpleasant duty to inform them that perhaps we are hating the wrong sport. Two or three nights of professional basketball could make a hockey fan of you . . .

"By this time you may have decided that there is a prejudice here against professional basketball and this is true. They wanted to eliminate the center jump and all that and speed up the game.

"They eliminated the spectators, too, and how do you trade to get them back. As stated, the subject is dull, but the dismissal of Fred DeLano and Charley Eckman isn't going to change things . . ."

The burning words sent Zollner out to hire the sharpest sports promoter in town to make pro basketball work. He snatched W. Nick Kerbawy away from the Lions and made him general manager with a free ticket.

"Lion Boss Quits For Million-Dollar Job," was a front page headline in the *News* in June 1958.

"It's for life and it's fabulous," Kerbawy said.

Zollner smothered Kerbawy with a hug at the press conference.

"I'm lucky to be able to hire a talent like this," said The Z. Then Zollner added: "My worries are over."

For certain. Nick Kerbawy possessed some sort of magic touch. The Lions had become the trend-setter team of pro football, which was just beginning to shuffle from its roots with its discovery by television. Over the previous six years, the Lions had won three NFL championships. Zollner was envious. Every team owner in America was.

The Lions were a team that featured Bobby Layne, and his nocturnal activities often placed his name in the news sections of the newspapers. His on-the-field heroics made him invulnerable to newspaper criticism, police captivity, and judge's rulings. Layne owned the town. And Nick Kerbawy worked this charisma and popularity to sell pro football in Detroit.

But what Kerbawy, as general manager/entrepreneur, sold most were victories and championships.

The Lions had the talent. The basketball team didn't.

It was going to be a hard sell for Nick. He retained Red Rocha beyond the ten-month contract for the Pistons' second season in Detroit. He came up with some gimmicks aimed at drawing crowds. He made one deal, purchasing Earl Lloyd from Syracuse. But the 1958–59 season was a rerun of 1957–58. The team struggled and the attendance was sparse at the Olympia.

And occasionally, there was Walter Dukes. The Pistons had acquired Dukes from Minneapolis for Larry Foust the year before. But when Rocha opened training camp in the fall of 1958, Walter Dukes was an absentee. A week passed. Dukes still had not shown up in camp. It was then that Nick Kerbawy, with his roots in the press agent's business, notified the Bureau of Missing Persons. One seven-foot basketball player had vanished.

Two days later, Nick Kerbawy got a phone call from some place back East.

"Mr. Kerbawy, I read in the papers that you were looking for me."

"Who's this?" said Kerbawy.

"Walter Dukes."

"Do you realize the team has been training for more than a week already?" said Nick.

There was silence—and then Kerbawy heard the voice over the phone: "Man! Where has the summer gone?"

Dukes arrived at last as the Pistons went off to display their wares in outstate Michigan, in hopes of piquing some interest. The Pistons took off for Lansing, to play the first exhibition, and were scheduled in Flint the next night.

They got to Lansing and Kerbawy wondered where the in hell Walter Dukes was. At halftime, Kerbawy was notified that he had a phone call.

"Mr. Kerbawy?"

Walter Dukes, with a 50–50 shot of getting it right, had gone to Flint.

When the season started and the Pistons had a game at Minneapolis, Dukes was AWOL again. Kerbawy finally traced him to the Garfield Hotel in Detroit.

"Would you like to speak to Mr. Dukes?" the hotel operator asked Kerbawy. "He's right here."

"That's why I'm calling," said Nick.

"I'm sorry," said the operator, "he just went out the door."

Kerbawy told Doc Greene: "Funny thing about Dukes is he's not a dummy. He took eight hours this summer at New York College of Law. He'll get a law degree in September. One year he went to France and studied law at the Sorbonne. I asked him afterwards:

"'That's in French. How do you do in French?'"

"He said, 'well enough to get along,' and he went out and shot a basket."

Part of the reason the Pistons struggled so futilely in the 1958–59 season was George Yardley. He complained of various illnesses—asthma, a shortage of blood sugar. He felt weak. He had said in a magazine story that the NBA was a bush league. His outspokenness irked The Z. Zollner openly started accusing Yardley of dogging it. Then in a game on the parquet floor in the Boston Garden, Yardley broke his hand. Zollner had Yardley come to his box. In their conversation, Zollner supposedly told Yardley that he never wanted to see him again, that George was finished with the Pistons. It was January 1959, and the flap between Zollner and Yardley continued through the next several weeks.

Stories appeared in the daily newspaper stories about the Yardley for Mr. X trade. The deal was announced, and the Pistons got themselves stuck with Ed Conlin. The club's first superstar was gone, off to Syracuse, for hardly anything in return—very much because of a stubborn, meddling owner.

A week or so after the trade, Yardley got his revenge. The Nats played the Pistons. Yardley scored 33 points in a victory over the team that sent him away.

In an interview with the Associated Press out of New York in March 1959, Yardley said he was sick of the Pistons. He spoke with sharp anger at Zollner.

"I was ready to quit the game before the Pistons traded me to Syracuse," he said, offering the interviewer a list of his illnesses. "Naturally, I wasn't scoring or rebounding too well. When I began feeling better, they started using me less and less. I heard that this was under orders from Zollner to Red Rocha.

"After I broke my hand, I was called into the office . . . I was told that Zollner did not want me to sit on the bench or go into the team's dressing room. He never talks much to the players. In fact, I hadn't talked to him more than a few times in my six years with the club.

"I was fed up . . . "

Yardley went on, speaking words of poison against his former employer.

"I think I played harder in that game against the Pistons than I ever did before. Zollner was sitting right there in the front row. I played 27 minutes and got 33 points. I got a lot of satisfaction out of it."

The Pistons finished the season in the doldrums. The second season had been worse than the first. Even with a 28–44 record and a third-place finish 21 games from first, the Pistons qualified for the playoffs. The Minneapolis Lakers eliminated them 2 victories to 1.

Kerbawy operated via power lunches, late nights, and smooth sell. He was a newspaperman's friend, an old PR specialist self-made into a club general manager. In the same era, a guy named Pete Rozelle had traveled the same tour in pro football. As with Rozelle, Nick understood the star system. He knew he had to have a drawing card for pro basketball ever to have a chance in Detroit.

Also, Nick knew how to deal. He'd done it in pro football. Now, he worked a deal at the 1959 NBA draft, to slice off an edge.

Bailey Howell was the premier, available player coming out of the college in 1959. Wilt Chamberlain, too, was coming out of college, eligible for the NBA draft, but previously consigned. The territorial draft was in effect; in essence, a

Gene Shue goes in for a layup on Pistons original homecourt, The Olympia. Note the hockey boards in the background; the court was placed over the Red Wings ice.

club owned first approval on all players in its home territory. That gave the Pistons first-round draft rights to any player it might ever want from the University of Detroit or Michigan.

Wilt Chamberlain was coming out of Kansas and it was conceded that at 7-1, he would be the player to alter the shape of pro basketball. Kansas did not happen to be in the territory of any NBA franchise. But it so happened that Chamberlain grew up—to his giant's height— in Philadelphia and went to Overbrook High School there. Eddie Gottlieb, powerful proprietor of the Philadelphia Warriors, tried to stake his claim to Wilt, even as a high school player. Chamberlain opted for college and not at one of Philly's basketball daffy schools.

But . . . not having specialized in grade school geography—or perhaps in a fit of sympathy for a fellow owner with the influential might of un-elected, unofficial league commissioner—the NBA governors allowed Gottlieb's Warriors to exercise the territorial draft to claim Chamberlain. Apparently, Lawrence, Kansas, served as a suburb of Philadelphia.

Not bad at maneuvering himself, Kerbawy forged a deal with the Cincinnati Royals, who had the first two picks in the first round of the regular draft. The Pistons sent Phil Jordon to the Royals for Archie Dees plus a second-round draft choice—plus a gentleman's agreement to cooperate. Thus it was, the Royals passed on the coveted Howell for the less desirable Bob Boozer. Kerbawy drafted Howell for the Pistons.

Writing for the *Associated Press*, I proclaimed Howell, a high-scoring, 6-foot-7 forward from Mississippi, to be the *savior* for the Pistons and for pro basketball in Detroit.

Zollner took credit for the trade that made the draft choice possible.

"I've had Howell's picture in front of me for three months," The Z told the press. "I wanted him very much."

In the fall of 1959, Walter Dukes became involved in a contract hassle with Kerbawy. He was in camp—until the day the Pistons were scheduled to fly off for a game in Minneapolis. Just before the team was to leave for the airport, Dukes walked into the Pistons' offices and plunked his plane ticket on Kerbawy's desk.

"I'm not going," said Dukes. And he left for New York and home.

The season started without him. Dukes held out through the first five games before coming to an agreement in November. He planned to drive to Detroit to rejoin the team on a Sunday. On Saturday night in New York, a thief broke into his parked car. The loot, according to Dukes' statement to the New York cops, included seven suits, eight trench coats, four pairs of shoes plus accoutrements, packed in luggage.

Imagine the crook's reaction when he went to try on Walter's suit.

Bailey Howell was a distinguished southern gentleman who blended in as a rookie in the chosen group of Detroit sports stars. He wore a close-cropped haircut, displayed a frequent smile, and played with a steady flow and much gusto. To the Pistons, he became what Al Kaline was to the Tigers, Gordie Howe was to the Red Wings, and Joe Schmidt was to the Lions. They all played in Detroit at the same time, as America turned into the sixties. And as Detroit teams started pratfalling into the tank.

It was beyond the ability of one man to be the savior of pro basketball in the city at that time, three decades ago. Bailey, as hard and as well as he played at the very beginning, could not even be savior to Red Rocha.

The Pistons got off in the 1959–60 season, their third in Detroit, with a 13–21 record. Three nights after Christmas, Nick Kerbawy summoned the local press. We were invited to a high-up suite in the Book Cadillac Hotel, where the Pistons had set up their offices at street level. Kerbawy always operated with a flamboyant touch; thus, the suite with its deep easy chairs and atmosphere of comfort.

There he announced that Red Rocha was gone as the Pistons' coach, another ziggy. Dick McGuire, the veteran guard who had played mostly with the Knicks and then with the Pistons, was appointed the new head coach. McGuire had been an All America at St. John's in New York, quite a famous player. Much more famous than his brother Al, who would win an NCAA championship as coach of Marquette before hitting the highway into television. And Dick was much quieter than Al, too.

Dick McGuire would smile sometimes, and nod, and he could coach some basketball. But he was an awful interview. This was unfortunate for a team still seeking any way to sell tickets and influence fans.

Zollner spoke for the Pistons that night. He had flown in from Fort Wayne for the Christmas week beheading of Rocha.

Doc Greene quoted Zollner, saying The Z spoke as if he were delivering a speech to the Cub Scouts: "They've got to win or else. He knew where he stood and said so last season after he'd lost nine straight . . . Detroit has refused basketball before and I think it was because they want a winner. I think Dick'll get 'em playing together. I think he'll inspire 'em to go out and play the game."

Doc described the press conference scene in these words: "As the background music of violins and marimbas swelled against the potted palms in the hotel, the audience wiped off a tear . . . Even your little boy knows that what the Pistons need is not coaches as much as ball players. So where do you get ball players? Well, occasionally you might find one strolling down Michigan Avenue, but that's doubtful and is generally regarded as an undependable source . . ."

Kerbawy, going next at the press conference, said it was a business decision, even then in the last week of the fifties, an ancient cliche. "We have to do something for the public's sake and we've done it," said Nick.

These were the years when Detroit became afflicted with the playoff mentality. Those fans that supported the Pistons—and other Detroit teams—became immune to losing seasons, provided there could be some playoff competition in the postseason. I've seen impromptu celebrations of people dancing, cheering, raising triumphant fists after Detroit teams backed into the playoffs with records that loosely could be considered mediocre.

This time the Pistons finished 30–45, which was sufficient for second place in the West—a bare sixteen games behind the first-place St. Louis Hawks.

Ice hockey had invented the system in which almost every team in the sport made it to the playoffs—and the Red Wings were in their own

The 1960 version of the Detroit Pistons play tight man-to-man defense against the St. Louis Hawks.

playoffs. So, the Pistons had to tote themselves out to the University of Detroit for their playoff games. The Minneapolis Lakers bumped the Pistons out of the playoffs in two games.

The Z was becoming fed up with GM-forever Nick Kerbawy.

As the 1960–61 NBA season moved along with results unchanged from the previous three seasons, the Lions' rich mob of owners was engaged in a bitter—nasty—internal struggle for control. It was a battle for proxy votes. Zollner heard that the former general manager of the Lions— his own GM of the Pistons—had become secretly involved in the intramural conflict for the football team.

At the time, the Pistons still were playing the odd game in their former hometown of Fort Wayne, out of courtesy to natives down there. They had a game in Fort Wayne on January 12, 1961.

It was during that game that a letter was hand-delivered to Nick Kerbawy by Otto Adams, one of Zollner's aides and an official of the Pistons.

In the text of the letter, Kerbawy was told: "It is common knowledge that you are active in the present situation of the Detroit Lions.

"Therefore, effective as of this date, you are granted a leave of absence with full compensation to . . . July, 1, 1961. This leave of absence from your duties with the Detroit Pistons is being made so that you can devote full time to other activities."

"Nick is involved in a conflict of interests," Zollner told the *News*. "He has been working part-time at full-time pay. At this point of the season the team needs attentive management."

One friend of Kerbawy's was quoted as saying: "So Kerbawy's out in the open now. What's he going to do with a leave of absence? Get a haircut?"

In March, Zollner fired Kerbawy. In effect, the million-dollar contract Kerbawy had called fabulous and for life, agreed to in 1958 and actually to run for twenty years, was being broken.

Nick had called it an ironclad contract, and he did more than get a haircut. He went out for a lawyer.

It was recalled about this time that Walter Dukes had become a lawyer. But then Kerbawy, in reflecting on Dukes and his reactions to timetables and schedules, said: "I'll name you one person he'll never represent. Me!"

Kerbawy got himself a high-profile Detroit lawyer. They sued Zollner for $5.5 million charging libel, slander, and conspiracy.

The Pistons finally received all the newspaper attention Zollner had been begging for—but not on the court of his choosing.

Kerbawy versus Zollner raged in the papers and the courtrooms for four years. The trial itself went on in Federal Court for seven weeks, at times filling the papers with tabloid stuff. Then with the judge acting as referee, the two rivals agreed to a legal jumpball. Kerbawy won the tip—but for only $255,000.

Meanwhile, the games went on with continued apathy. Attendance had climbed some; according to the Pistons' bookkeeping figures, the average had risen to more than 5,000, promising, but still not nearly enough to make the club a money earner. What the Pistons never added in announcing their figures was that the 5,000 plus included everybody entering Olympia on freebie tickets, two-for-one ducat deals, certain captives, and everybody aboard the Grand River bus when it passed by during game hours.

The Pistons improved their record to 34-45 in the 1960–61 season. This time it was a third-place finish, but McGuire's Pistons made their annual trek to the playoffs. The Pistons again had to make do with a playoff site. Their first-round opponents were the Lakers, who had abandoned Minneapolis to move to Los Angeles. The NBA was now coast-to-coast, transcontinental.

One Saturday during the NBA playoffs, even the University of Detroit's Memorial Building had a prior event scheduled. The Pistons had to scrounge around for a place to play a nationally televised NBA playoff game. They moved it to a high school gym in Grosse Pointe. Carpetbaggers in their own town, the Pistons still beat the Lakers in their two so-called home games. But they lost the three games in Los Angeles and were toppled from the playoffs.

IV—The Sixties

The Pistons moved into Cobo Arena for the 1961–62 season. They would no longer be pushed out, the homeless. Cobo Arena stood on the riverfront in downtown Detroit; a new building attached to a huge convention center. Walk outside toward the Detroit River, and there was a spectacular international view—across the band of water, with the huge Great Lakes iron ore carriers passing by slowly—to Canada, the city of Windsor, Ontario.

It was a brand new atmosphere for the Pistons, starting their fifth season in Detroit.

Fran Smith, who had written sports for the *Detroit Times* and had been the Pistons' PR man, took over the operations with Kerbawy sacked. Another sports writer turned honest, George Maskin, had left the failing *Times* to do the Pistons' public relations. As such as they were.

Gene Shue was the Pistons' popgun from the outside. He would take the ball up court, feed it off to Howell or circle behind a screen set up by Dukes and his pointed elbows, and pop from the corner. Sometimes, Gene would pass off to Ray Scott, the first-round draft choice, who could connect from distance with an odd, flat trajectory shot. No arc at all.

Shue's style had a sweetness. And at the time, the Pistons figured noise could be translated into success in the NBA. So it was, the public address announcer's voice bounced and rattled around the empty seats of Cobo every time Shue hit one of his jumpshots. "TWO FOR SHUE!" Hardly a mutter from the crowd added to this orchestrated cacophony. Shue had a touch of class and might have preferred to play his game in silence.

But most nights, there was barely a crowd in Cobo to watch him and Howell. Strangely, now that they had their own arena after the tenant years at Olympia, the Pistons were less attractive to the populace. Average attendance that had been announced at 5,300 the final year at Olympia, in a blighted neighborhood, dwindled by 500 per night the first year at Cobo. And it would dwindle even more until the Pistons averaged 3,300 by the middle 1960s.

And this was after George Maskin had rigged the figures to something more than the count of real fannies in the seats. This was after all the free tickets that were given away at the cashiers' counters of all the fast-fry chicken joints in town. This was after all the promotional gimmicks designed to attract the curious to a basketball game, as an afterthought.

The Pistons came up with Turkey Pop Gun Night. Naturally, it was Thanksgiving time, and the Pistons gave away turkeys to lucky ticketholders. But everybody at the gates was given a paper turkey pop gun. The idea was, on cue at courtside, for everyone to snap his, or her, wrist and the accordian-packed paper in the musket-shaped cardboard pop gun would whip out and go bang. Or pop. There were so few people there, the sound was sort of poof.

All this—plus an improved basketball team, and still the attendance dropped. Dick McGuire, somehow, cajoled 37 victories out of the Pistons, most in their five seasons in Detroit, against 43 defeats. Gee, it was promising. It wasn't much further to .500. The Pistons finished third in the West and then blasted the Cincinnati Royals in four games in the playoffs. But the Lakers got them again, in the Western Division finals, 4 victories to 2.

Still, there were snatches of hope for 1962-63.

And it seemed more promising, when the Pistons exercised their territorial draft option to select Dave DeBusschere. Leader of a state high school championship team at Detroit Austin, leader of NIT and NCAA postseason tournament teams at University of Detroit, DeBusschere was deemed the Pistons' player of destiny.

He was Detroit through and through—except when he rejected the Tigers' offer to sign a baseball contract. The Tigers refused to allow DeBusschere to play two pro sports. And DeBusschere—The Buffalo, to his friends all over Detroit—wanted to be a basketball player more than a baseball player. So he signed with the White Sox and the Pistons.

The Pistons had DeBusschere, his popularity, and his drawing power. But they no longer had Gene Shue and his popularity and deadeye and floor leadership. Shue wound up on the bad side of Fred Zollner. The Pistons traded Shue to the Knicks for Darral Imhoff, a towering, non-scoring center, and a wheelbarrow of cash.

So it was that the Pistons darted off to a seven-game losing streak to start the 1962-63 schedule. The players blamed it on Zollner's trading of Shue.

"The big thing is, I think, we miss having a superstar," Bailey Howell told the *News'* Pete Waldmeir. "We aren't playing together as a team.

"The trade, that's Mr. Zollner's business. But . . . we have to find Shue's 20 points somewhere else in the lineup, and it's tough."

Howell had something to say about the Detroit fans: "They don't know a great deal about basketball, because they haven't grown up with it. It isn't their fault. They don't know what to look for. It's not simple, like a forward pass."

Smash.

The Pistons weren't unique in their inability to attract a crowd. The entire NBA was suffering. The league had lost its national TV contract, after eight seasons of at least some television exposure.

"The games were low-rated on TV any way," said Howell.

The Pistons qualified for the playoffs, for the sixth successive season, despite their sixth successive losing record. This time it was 34-46—and Dickie McGuire was getting jittery. He had said barely anything worth saying and had coached for nearly four seasons. It was a depressing situation. The Pistons were blitzed out of the playoffs in the first round in four games by the St. Louis Hawks.

After the season, McGuire decided he wanted to go back home to New York. He contacted Zollner and told him he was committing a self-ziggy.

Zollner was without a coach. But he had been impressed with that young coach who had been just canned by the Cincy Royals, Charley Wolf.

Charley Wolf, signed as head coach number four of the Detroit Pistons for the 1963–64 season, was full of theories and ideas. He discussed techniques and concepts. His players, behind his back, shook their heads in confusion. They said they had no idea what Wolf was talking about.

Wolf had what seemed to be a decent team, perhaps a team that could succeed in the eternal push toward the .500 level. He had Howell and DeBusschere and Ray Scott plus Bob Ferry, who had been acquired a couple of years earlier from St. Louis in trade for Ed Conlin, the erstwhile Mr. X. Don Ohl had been around for a couple of seasons, after a deal with Philadelphia. In the draft the Pistons were happy with their top choice—Eddie Miles, the "Man with the Golden Arm" out of Seattle University.

There was also a seventh-round draft choice who wasn't quite yet eligible to play—Reggie Harding, the former Detroit schoolboy star with the somewhat imperfect past.

Walter Dukes was gone after six seasons of being here and there. Wolf did not want Dukes on his club. Walter was not asked to training camp. The Pistons tried to trade him. They tried to sell him. No other NBA club was interested. The Pistons put him on waivers.

The day Dukes' name went out on the waiver wire, Fran Smith, the club's staff director, received a telephone call in the Pistons' offices at the Book-Cadillac. The caller inquired about Walter Dukes.

"Well," the caller told Smith, "I'm calling from the parking lot at Metropolitan Airport. Does Mr. Dukes own an automobile?"

"Yes," said Smith.

"Have you seen him lately?" asked the caller.

"No."

"When you see him, please tell him we're keeping his car for him," said the parking lot man.

"Thanks for your interest," Smith said.

"That's OK," said the man from the airport. "We were a bit worried. The car has been here for thirty-six days."

"If you find him," said the affable Fran Smith, remembering Dukes' other missing-persons capers, "tell him we're not looking for him."

George Maskin, the Pistons' PR guy and general factotum, tried to pump up interest in the ballclub. George had been the beat man for the *Detroit Times* the Pistons' first year in Detroit. He remembered his own experience covering the team.

"They'd played five, six, eight decent games when I wrote another story in the *Times*," Maskin recalled. "I went into the office. Edgar Hayes, the sports editor, came over to me and said, 'Don't you ever write another story glad-handing the Pistons.' I'd written if the Pistons continue to play like this they'll attract interest. Edgar thought I was cheerleading."

The situation back in the 1960s was that the Pistons were low team in town, and the media treated them with disdain. The *News* and *Free Press* sent their writers on the road with the Tigers and Lions and much of the time with the Red Wings. But writers never traveled with the Pistons.

George Maskin, in the team's employ as the PR guy, reported the road games for the two papers. He'd sit down after a game, bang out a quick game story for the *Free Press*, then turn around and bang out a second story with quotes for the *News*. He'd file to both papers via Western Union.

The practice might seem fishy, except for one thing. George Maskin was totally objective in writing facts and details about his own ballclub. The Pistons lost in Boston, and Maskin, the old reporter, told it just like it happened, complete with odors.

He had some other duties. For example, he served as traveling secretary, too. He arranged for the team busses to meet the Pistons when the Flying Z landed at the airport. He arranged the busses when the Pistons had to roll down to Toledo, too. Sometimes for both teams. Sometimes getting Wilt Chamberlain squeezed between two seats designed for school kids on a yellow school bus.

"I rented the bus," George Maskin would reveal three decades later after the Pistons had won championships back-to-back in the NBA. "I was flabbergasted when the bus showed up. It was supposed to be a larger bus. The company sent the school bus."

Maskin also took care of the details of switching the schedule so that some of Detroit's home games could be played elsewhere, one method of Zollner recouping some of his financial losses. In return the Pistons were rewarded with the odd NBA doubleheaders, another method of bolstering attendance at Cobo.

"Zollner swapped games to New York, Boston, and Philadelphia for doubleheaders," Maskin said in 1990. "Originally, they were swapped. Then later he sold games to New York for about $4,000 or $4,500 per game. Now fifteen or twenty front row seats bring in more than that."

Attendance was so poor in the time from 1960 on, the NBA tried to talk Zollner into moving the franchise to another town.

"There was that desire by people in the NBA who wanted him to move the Pistons," Maskin said. "Zollner was loyal to Detroit. He refused to move."

Maskin recalled some of those roadtrips on snowy winter nights, flying back to Detroit from New York or Baltimore.

"The club had a DC-3 for the trips, the Flying Z. It was a fancy plane. The players and coaches all sat up front. Zollner sat in the back with his mistress."

Then, Maskin recalled, there was a night in the NBA when only one referee showed up. Maskin moonlighted as a referee and umpire at college and school games around Detroit and Michigan. On this night, he was the Pistons' PR guy; he wrote the newspaper stories; and at the request of Maurice Podoloff, the league president, he worked as an NBA referee.

"The league sent me an unsigned check," said Maskin.

It was by the middle of the 1963–64 season that the Pistons started griping openly about Charley Wolf. Don Ohl broke open the situation in his airport interview with me in which he complained Wolf personally disliked him. Howell wondered, privately at first, about Wolf's credentials to coach the game. Bob Ferry, also speaking private thoughts, doubted that Wolf could handle players.

The Pistons were in total disarray by the end of the season. They failed to reach the playoffs for the first time in their six seasons in Detroit. The record was 23–57. For the first time, the club finished in last place—frustrated, and united in their anger toward the coach.

Wolf, a lone wolf, was angry and frustrated in his own right. He started plotting changes for the following season, to assemble his own kind of ballclub. Even though Bailey Howell and Don Ohl had been good enough to play in the NBA All-Star Game, they were dead in Detroit.

In the spring of 1964, Charley Wolf attended the Olympic Trials, where America's best collegians—best pro prospects—would be on display. The Olympics, four years earlier, had turned out an astonishing collection of superb pros. Oscar Robertson, Jerry Lucas, and Terry Dischinger were on that team. Oscar went from winning a Gold Medal in Rome to scoring better than 30 points per game in then NBA in Cincinnati.

Now Wolf went off to the 1964 Olympic trials in full resolve to examine the crop and then, on draft day, tap a giant center, the position at which the Pistons had a major gap. It was a league dominated by Russell and Chamberlain. Foremost on the Pistons' list was Lucious Jack-

Don Ohl, the outside deadeye, feuded with Charley Wolf and was finally included in an 8-player deal with Baltimore.

son, out of Pan American in Texas. Wolf had spent much of his first season drooling about Jackson as a pro prospect in conversations with reporters. And when he wasn't praising Jackson, Wolf was talking about a little-known player out of Grambling named Willis Reed.

Either center might have lifted the Pistons out of their doldrums, certainly lifted them some in the standings.

And with their last-place finish, the Pistons were near the top in the draft rotation, once the teams desiring territorial picks had made their choices.

Wolf was at the Olympic Trials when he spotted a quick leaping forward with a pretty good shot. The player was Joe Caldwell, out of Arizona State, and Wolf pictured an amazing NBA career for this young player.

So it was on draft day, the Pistons ignored the center they needed and selected Joe Caldwell higher than any scout on any other club had him tabbed. Luke Jackson was picked off by the Philadelphia 76ers, their first acquisition with that franchise name. The 76ers were the transferred Syracuse Nationals, who jumped into the basketball hotbed vacated when the Warriors moved cross-country from Philly to San Francisco.

Charley Wolf had one more shot at a center as the second round of the draft started. But alas, one team had finished weaker than the Pistons in 1963–64, the New York Knicks. And picking at the start of the second round, in the spot one ahead of the Pistons, the Knicks, with what must have been a sense of historic clairvoyance, selected Willis Reed. Slugged, Wolf had to settle for Les Hunter out of Loyola-Chicago as the Pistons' replacement pick.

The misadventure at the draft would have impact on the future of Charley Wolf.

Wolf made his expected trades between seasons. First, he sold Darral Imhoff to the Los Angeles Lakers—the player the Pistons had received two years earlier in exchange for Gene Shue.

Then on June 16, 1964, Wolf made the eight-player trade with the Baltimore Bullets that shredded the very heart of the Pistons and their franchise. The biggest steal since the Brink's robbery!

The Pistons surrendered Howell, Ohl, and

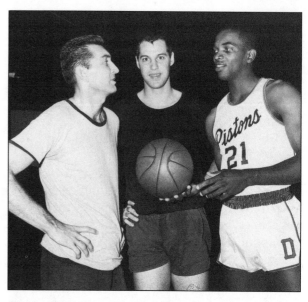

Charley Wolf (left), Terry Dischinger (center), and Joe Caldwell. Wolf drafted Caldwell ahead of Willis Reed and Luke Jackson, two big men who could have solved the Pistons problems at the center spot.

Ferry plus new draftees Hunter and Wali Jones, their second and third-round choices. The Pistons got themselves an outstanding player in Dischinger, a plugger of a guard in Rod Thorn, and a whirling dervish in Don Kojis.

It was so lopsided a deal that, in phone interviews that night, Howell, Ohl, and Ferry laughed at Wolf. But he was rid of them, and that's what he wanted.

"I don't intend to get into a name-calling contest with them," Wolf said. "As soon as last season ended, I started thinking of how we can help ourselves for next year.

"I'm real happy with this trade."

The new-look Pistons opened the season by losing nine of their first eleven games. There was some talent on the club—Dischinger, Dave De-Busschere and Ray Scott up front, Eddie Miles and Thorn at guard. Caldwell made the club, but was inconsistent. The Pistons' most terrifying weakness was at center—where Luke Jackson or Willis Reed might have played. Charley Wolf had to use Reggie Harding at center, mano-a-mano against Wilt and Russell That is, when Reggie managed to show up for the plane to road games or bothered to get downtown at least five minutes before tipoff at Cobo Arena.

The Z sensed a problem with his ballclub. He figured Wattrick, sitting courtside blabbing into a microphone, was close enough to the problem to understand it. So Wattrick became GM, the job Nick Kerbawy once was supposed to handle for life, and the job Fran Smith had been doing without the title or power.

Kissing the mike goodbye, Wattrick charged into his new job with authority. He put the guillotine to Wolf after eleven games. He had always admired Dave DeBusschere. So the Pistons had themselves a twenty-four-year-old coach with Detroit roots, two seasons of pro basketball experience, and ambitions to become a major-league pitcher on the side. He also had the requisite white skin.

DeBusschere got the Pistons hustling. He brought about harmony on the ballclub. He kept fining Harding. At the end of the 1964–65 season, the Pistons had actually improved a shade. They escaped last place with a 31–49 record, good for fourth, as the transplanted San Francisco Warriors astonishingly managed only 17 victories with Wilt Chamberlain traded back to Philadelphia and the 76ers halfway through the season. The Pistons failed to qualify for the playoffs for the second straight spring.

Plus, Detroit was becoming more apathetic. Despite, the presence of Coach DeBusschere, the Pistons' home attendance dwindled to an average of less than 3,400.

It could get worse. It did.

Terry Dischinger, the Pistons' leading scorer, went onto active duty as a second lieutenant in the Army. He had been an ROTC student at Purdue. And now, his number came up in the summer of 1965, as America was just starting to become serious in a military way in a country named Vietnam. Most Detroit basketball fans would have had a devil of a time pinpointing it on a map.

Reggie Harding, due to his adventures with the Detroit cops, had been suspended by the league.

Bill Buntin, the number-one draft choice taken as the final territorial pick from Michigan, had showed up lugging excessive avoirdupois—270 pounds worth. Also, Tom Van Arsdale, the second-round draft choice from Indiana, had been so shook up over being split from his twin brother Dick, drafted by the Knicks, he quit the Pistons' camp. In the process, Tom blasted Detroit. Two days later, Tom returned to the Pistons.

And there had been tragedy—Don Wattrick, the general manager, died two weeks before the season, after suffering a heart attack.

All of this happened before the start of the 1965–66 season.

There had been a single light glowing ahead. Cazzie Russell would be in his senior season at Michigan out at Ann Arbor.

But, of course, the Pistons being the Pistons, there was a matter of timing.

The NBA, the previous spring, abolished the territorial pick that allowed teams to capitalize on the drawing power and playing abilities of home-grown collegiate talent. The territorial, by vote of the NBA's board of governors three years earlier, went out *after* the 1965 draft. Thus, the New York Knicks still were able to claim Bill Bradley, whose arched-eyebrow, pointed elbows, and marvelous skills had made him a glamourous sports figure—and future national leader—at Princeton, for delivery following completion of his studies at Oxford as a Rhodes Scholar. The Lakers took Gail Goodrich from UCLA. And the Pistons took Buntin. But that was the end of it, the NBA governors had decreed.

"Only three teams used their territorial rights," Zollner told Pete Waldmeir after the 1965 draft session. "The other teams didn't have anybody worth picking in their areas. When we voted the territorial out three years ago, we didn't have anybody either.

"It's ironic, now, that we are pretty much alone."

Zollner planned to appeal, beg the NBA governors, to extend the territorial draft for one more year. The Z wanted Cazzie; Cazzie wanted the Pistons. The Pistons had been the NBA's weakest franchise in quality and in allure among the townsfolk for nearly a decade. Now, here, forty-five miles from downtown Detroit, the best, most dazzling, most famous college player in America during the 1965–66 season, was about to turn eligible for the NBA draft. In all the prior years, the Pistons could have staked their territorial claim, and Cazzie Russell would have been theirs.

Player/Coach Dave DeBusschere (third from left) reacts to the action on the floor during a Pistons game. Players seated with him are Jackie Moreland (left) and Donnis Butcher (center), who would eventually succeed DeBusschere as coach in 1967.

Fred Zollner wore his usual beaten, weathered look when he went before his fellow governors to beg for a waiver and extension of the territorial draft for one more year.

He told the other owners that a strong Detroit franchise would benefit all of them. He cajoled them. He didn't have to stir up their memories that there were times Zollner had loaned, or given, money to some owners who were out of cash and needed a handout so they could continue to operate their franchises. He didn't have to remind them that the Philadelphia Warriors were deeded territorial rights to Wilt Chamberlain—OUT OF KANSAS. He didn't have to remind them that the Cincinnati Royals were awarded Jerry Lucas as a territorial even though Ohio State was outside the club's territory.

All of this, and the other owners told Fred Zollner to go to hell.

"I tried to get a player assigned on the basis of strength, on the basis that Detroit is a good franchise, and it would make a better all-around league situation," Zollner told me that night in 1965, after the owners' meeting. "We failed there.

"Then I proposed that each club would get the chance to make one territorial selection over the next four years with each club holding the option to choose the year it wants. We failed there.

"The third suggestion was to restore the territorial rights. We failed there, too.

"But there is no failure like failing to try."

Only the Boston Celtics, winners of seven

consecutive NBA franchises, and the Philly 76ers, backed Zollner. He lost by a vote of 6–3.

Among those listening to Zollner's pleas were Ben Kerner, owner of the St. Louis Hawks, and Lou Mohs, agent for owner Bob Short of the Los Angeles Lakers. When Kerner's franchise was withering in Milwaukee, Zollner aided his efforts to move to St. Louis. When the Lakers were drawing zilch in Minneapolis, Zollner actively campaigned for Short in his bid to move to L.A.

Both clubs voted against the Zollner in his plaintive pleas to guarantee the Pistons the rights to Cazzie Russell.

"I thought we had a concession of some kind coming after the other clubs had received so much in the past," The Z said, seething inside.

The Pistons would still have a shot at Cazzie. All they'd have to do was finish last, again, something they could certainly manage. But then they'd have to win a coin flip with the last-place club in the other division. Heads or tails.

DeBusschere talked about making the playoffs. It was boyish dreaming. The club got off to the traditional poor start in 1965–66. It was making desperation trades by Christmas. Rod Thorn, one of the three players acquired in Charley Wolf's months-in-the-making trade with Baltimore the previous year, was sent to the St. Louis Hawks for two guys on Christmas Eve. The two guys were Charles Vaughn and John Tresvant. DeBusschere needed bodies.

Then three days after Christmas the Pistons' dumped Joe Caldwell, Wolf's pet draft choice when he bypassed two dominating centers. Caldwell also was traded to the Hawks. For an obscure player named John Barnhill.

There was a night in January, when the Pistons were hosts to an NBA doubleheader. Cazzie Russell wanted to drive in from Ann Arbor for the game. My assignment with the *News* was covering both Michigan basketball and the Pistons. So I arranged for Cazzie to get a ticket. He arrived between games. The attendance was about 4,000, one of the better crowds.

Cazzie walked into Cobo Arena and down an aisle near the basketball court. By the time he reached his seat in the stands, he was in the middle of a mob. More people spent more time gazing at Russell in street clothes than they did at the ten players in uniform on the floor.

After the game I took Cazzie over to the loge seats, where Fred Zollner watched games in solitude, surrounded by fourteen unoccupied seats. Zollner's eyes sparkled as he met Michigan's triple All-America for the first time. This was the potential superstar Zollner had dreamed about for his team in the nine years since he moved the Pistons from Fort Wayne.

Heads or tails!

In March, the Pistons finished last again, at 22-58, the worst record at the time in the franchise's history. And the worst record in the NBA. They had assured themselves of a spot in the coin flip, with the Knicks, bottom in the East.

And in late April, the Celtics beat the Lakers 4 games to 3 in the NBA finals. The Celtics were pro basketball's champions for the eighth straight season—a dynasty never matched in professional team sports.

Two weeks later, on May 11, 1966, the Knicks and Pistons went at each other in the coin flip for pickings in the NBA draft. The Cazzie Russell Lottery.

Cazzie Russell sat in his Ann Arbor digs on the morning of the coin flip/draft with a single visitor—me. Russell said he had an offer with the Harlem Globetrotters, which would interest him if the Pistons didn't win the flip.

At draft headquarters in New York, Walter Kennedy, the NBA commissioner, held a $20 goldpiece. He nodded at Dave DeBusschere, telling him to make the call with the coin flipping end over end in the air.

"Tails," called DeBusschere.

The goldpiece landed on the carpet.

Of course, the Pistons didn't win it. The coin landed heads.

Cazzie's phone rang and it was the Knicks calling from draft headquarters. Eddie Donovan, the Knicks' general manager, and their coach, Dick McGuire, who had left the Pistons years before to go home to NYC, were on the phone. "Congratulations, Cazzie, you're with the Knicks."

Russell's face sank.

"I kind of feel sorry for Detroit," Russell said that morning. "They lost their best scorer, Dischinger, to the Army. They lost Mr. Wattrick, who passed away. They finished in last place. They lost the flip of the coin."

Disappointed, the Pistons had to take the second fiddle. Ed Coil, appointed the Pistons' new general manager after years of loyal service to Zollner at the plant in Fort Wayne, made the selection with DeBusschere. They picked the player from Syracuse—the player named Dave Bing.

The Pistons cursed their luck.

"Nobody in Detroit including the Pistons wanted Dave Bing," Ed Coil, the onetime, gentle general manager, would say to a banquet audience twenty-five years later, in the winter of 1991. "We flipped a coin. We wanted Cazzie.

"That night Earl Lloyd said, 'Don't worry, we just got the best player in the country.'"

The banquet that night was "A Salute to Dave Bing."

The luck the Pistons had cursed, heads or tails, brought them the best player in franchise history; the NBA's Rookie of the Year in 1966-67; an NBA scoring champion; a player who would eventually be elected to the Basketball Hall of Fame.

But back then, in May 1966, even Dave Bing was aware he was unwanted in Detroit.

"I thought about that," Bing told the *News* a few hours after he was drafted. "It's worried me whether I'll be accepted in Detroit."

BINGO!

Dave Bing showed up in Detroit out of college with a wife and two daughters and all their worldly possessions packed into a trailer.

"He got a $500 bonus," Ed Coil would recall so many years later, at the salute in 1991.

In the years since he had arrived in the summer of 1966, family in tow, Dave Bing had played a Hall of Fame NBA career, had been exiled in trade, returned to live in Detroit, totally transplanted; and had established a million-dollar industry called Bing Steel that helped diminish the city's unemployment. There was talk about him becoming the city's next mayor.

Dave Bing grew up in Washington, the American city with the White House, the Capitol and the Washington Monument, and the most huge pockets of gnawing poverty. Basketball is rooted in this ghetto so near our most loved historic shrines. And the ghetto has always been a fertile growing-ground for some of the most precious NBA stars. Elgin Baylor emerged from Washington before Dave Bing. Adrian Dantley would be developed a dozen years later, after Bing.

Bing came out of Springarn High School and went off to Syracuse to play basketball in the early 1960s. And maybe college sports were nearer to purity then. And he came with a work ethic instilled by his father, who was a bricklayer.

"I wasn't a typical jock," Bing once told the *News'* Bill Halls. "I didn't get all that cash. When I got married I had to move out of the dormitory and into married housing. The scholarship didn't pay for that.

"I had to work all summer on construction. We got $4.50 an hour and I worked twelve hours a day. But during the season, I had to work. I cleaned the nursery. I scrubbed floors and emptied trash."

So there was very little dickering when Coil offered Bing, the second player taken in the NBA draft, the $500 bonus and a $15,000 contract.

A quarter-century later, Bing would tell the Detroit audience at his salute: "I had some

DeBusschere shreds the Lakers defense for a layup in a 1965 game as Donnis Butcher (16) watches.

misgivings about coming here because of our media. The first question was, 'what's it like not to be wanted?'"

BINGO!

It would take some time, but Dave Bing would become cherished and then loved in Detroit.

DeBusschere had given up his baseball aspirations to serve one master—his player/coach job with the Pistons. He opened the training camp in September 1966 with the usual hopes. He had been a coach for two years and was not quite twenty-six. He had become comfortable playing the game and making the decisions while active on the court. But the system had not been productive, not yet. And at this camp, DeBusschere had to be wondering if the burden of coaching might be detracting from his skills as a player. There was still a rawness to his play.

Zollner had remained steadfast in support of DeBusschere. He liked DeBusschere's intelligence and his intensity.

"To get along in life, you have to have a head like a grapefruit," The Z had told Pete Waldmeir. The Z put his hands over his ears in demonstration, then flicked two fingers at the right side of his unkempt head.

"You have to be able to pluck a piece out like this and have the rest stay together," Zollner explained. "Then you put that piece back." He smacked the imaginary segment of brain/grapefruit back into his skull. "And grab another piece from somewhere else.

"DeBusschere has a head like that. He can coach and he can play. They are separate things and he does each individually . . . he can do anything he wants right now. He can quit coaching anytime and just play or do both. He says he wants to continue to coach and I think he wants to do the best job possible and I'm for him."

But for sure, the grapefruit was feeling squeezed as this training camp continued on.

Dave Bing was a revelation at his rookie training camp. Unwanted but accepted, Bing displayed a dazzling amount of ball-handling and shotmaking skills. DeBusschere was so impressed he likened Bing to Bob Cousy, who had been so masterful with the basketball in his hands for the Celtics.

"He does things out there that make him too good for us," coach/player DeBusschere said one day, when his veterans could not keep up with the rookie. "We're not ready for his passes."

Bing became an immediate force in the NBA. Slender and 6-3, his game was to slice through the towering forests in the lane with acrobatic moves and then twist underneath to score. He was so much faster and so much slicker than the bigger men. And he could shoot from the outside. He could pass off with accuracy. And he was the playmaker, working well within the framework of the team, especially in the backcourt with Eddie Miles. Bing, from the outset of his rookie season, was the Pistons' leader in scoring and in assists.

The Pistons had become a better team . . . because of Dave Bing, the rookie. Soon Detroit did not miss Cazzie Russell too much. The city adopted Dave Bing.

Attendance did not rocket, but it did jump. Bing had an early marquee value. A club that once had difficulty drawing crowds of 4,000 with free tickets and promotions and pick-your-numbers estimates was now hitting 7,000 and sometimes 8,000 for selected games.

And the people were making basketball-arena noise, with the blaring music speakers behind them, every time Bing would slip through the massed giants to twist underneath and score.

"BINGO," shrieked the PA announcer, as if somebody in the building might have missed who put in the bucket.

The Pistons were winning more, but even Dave Bing could not hoist them to .500. So it was in January 1967, in an effort to bolster the scoring, the Pistons ventured back into the trade market.

The trade fit the club's historical pattern. This time they dealt Ray Scott, a onetime first-round draft choice, to the Baltimore Bullets in a three-pronged swap with the Lakers. The player sent to the Pistons was Rudy LaRusso from the Lakers.

LaRusso had gone to Dartmouth and with an Ivy-League mindset decided that he didn't want to play in Detroit for the Pistons. He refused to report.

Again, there were daily trade stories, as there had been when George Yardley was dealt away, about a phantom athlete.

LaRusso could not be persuaded to play for the Pistons. He said he'd rather retire. Eventually, the Pistons and the league surrendered to

Eddie Miles, nicknamed the Man with the Golden Arm because of his shooting ability, led the Pistons in scoring (19.6 ppg) in 1966.

his wishes. The Pistons were awarded in compensation the Lakers' No. 1 draft choice for 1967, in lieu of the flesh-and-blood LaRusso.

Meanwhile the Pistons were stuck with a manpower shortage.

It was in March 1967, that the decision was enacted to strip Dave DeBusschere of his coaching toga. GM Ed Coil took DeBusschere and Donnis Butcher, an assistant coach and former reserve guard with perhaps only an orange for a head, to a tavern. The place, appropriately enough, was located on Detroit's West Side, the opposite end of town from DeBusschere's origins where Wattrick once had introduced him as coach to a couple of writers. There, in the West Side saloon, the change was discussed among the three men, with the suggestion that DeBusschere, concentrating only on his playing game, could help the Pistons into playoffs.

At the time, the Pistons were a half-game behind the Chicago Bulls in a struggle for fourth place and the last available playoff position. Eight games remained in the season. The Pistons were 28–45 under DeBusschere, a faster pace than the previous season.

DeBusschere accepted the proposals.

"We talked about it for two weeks," Coil said. "Dave was willing to give up the coaching job to concentrate his full attention to playing forward . . . He agreed that it would be best. That was it."

Whether DeBusschere was fired or merely agreed to what was tantamount to a demotion became a moot point.

"Frankly, I know if I had pressed the issue, I could still have the job," he said. "But it's better this way."

Despite the smooth play of Dave Bing, it had become an increasingly stormy season. Club sources told Pete Waldmeir that DeBusschere had been having disciplinary problems with some of his players who he felt were not playing at capacity. Beyond that, there was the fiasco of the Scott deal. And beyond that Ron Reed, a tough, popular, young board-crashing athlete, had left the Pistons to try out as a major-league pitcher (he made it) with the Philadelphia Phillies. Reed complained that DeBusschere didn't play him enough.

Coil absolved DeBusschere of fault and took the blame himself. He guaranteed that DeBusschere would continue to receive his double-jobs salary of $100,000 through the following season. And he said despite the trade overtures from the Knicks, who were willing to send the Pistons Cazzie Russell in exchange, DeBusschere would not be dealt away.

"This is Dave's town," Coil said. "As long as he wants to stay here, we'll have a place for him. We're not looking for any trades."

At last, the Pistons had admitted that making DeBusschere coach while he was still so young had been an unwise choice; that it had been made out of hero worship rather than practical sports sense.

Dave DeBusschere would become a stronger, better pro basketball player, ultimately a superior player, without the conflict of having to coach a team of older players and play with the same guys, too.

And he had the guarantee that the Pistons would always cherish him and have a place for him.

The Pistons were ending their tenth season in Detroit. Donnis Butcher, just twenty-nine himself, was their sixth coach since the franchise had moved from Fort Wayne.

In the final eight games of the 1966–67 season, in the supposed playoffs drive under Butcher, the Pistons had a 2–6 record. They finished fifth and last again at 30–51 and missed the playoffs for the fourth consecutive season.

But there was one honor after the season. Dave Bing was selected the NBA Rookie of the Year. He averaged 20 points a game—and because of Bing, the Pistons' average attendance climbed to 6,459, an improvement of 2,400 per game.

Going into the 1967–68 season, the NBA performed another geographic mix and shake. The Seattle Supersonics joined the jumble in expansion and the Buffalo Braves moved their franchise to San Diego, where they would fancy themselves as the Rockets. And when Wilt Chamberlain, perhaps recalling his ride in a little yellow school bus, loaned his name to an article for *Sports Illustrated* that was entitled "My Life in a Bush League," he was applauded for his candor and accuracy.

As part of the switches, the NBA hoisted the Pistons from the West and relocated them in the Eastern Division, with New York, Boston, Baltimore, Philly, and Cincy.

There was a matter for the history books, too.

Bill Russell had become the Celtics' coach, with Red Auerbach yielding that portion of his authority.

This was the late 1960s, an era of rage and madness and change in America. Because of a war in Vietnam, anger impacted on the college campuses from Columbia to Berkeley. Dissent spread across the American South, where, until recently, it had been impossible for certain citizens of this nation to ride in the front half of busses. Desegregation was an issue, along with this war, and along with student unrest and the burning of flags and draft cards. These matters were the news, in the forefront of the newspapers, sections ahead of game results and what was reported in the toy departments of journalism, the sports pages.

And now what was a sports story also merited reportage out front, on the first page of the papers. Bill Russell had become the first black head coach in the NBA. It was an honor that Earl Lloyd had deserved in Detroit three years earlier and had been deprived of unjustly because of the hue of his skin. But nobody knew about that snub of Earl Lloyd. Only Earl Lloyd did. It went unwritten, unreported.

Now Russell was a coach in of the NBA, in Boston. And beyond basketball, he was the first black man to coach, or manage, a team in any professional sports major league. It would take major-league baseball a while to catch up—and the National Football League another generation.

Properly planted in the East, the Pistons went off to Donnis Butcher's first training camp in the fall of 1967 with serious notions about hitting their modest goal of a .500 season for the first time in Detroit.

There was genuine hope. Terry Dischinger had returned from his tour as an Army officer. Dave Bing was no longer a rookie. And Dave DeBusschere was free to play basketball, stripped of coaching responsibilities. Beyond that, the Pistons went into the season with the player considered to be the prime catch from the draft. They had the first pick off the board. Their choice was Jimmy Walker, a guard, who had been college basketball's glamour player of the year at Providence College. In taking Walker, the Pistons bypassed lesser-known Earl Monroe. Monroe was taken by Baltimore. The Pistons also had a second draft choice in the first round, as compensation in the aborted deal in which Ray Scott

Jimmy Walker, the No. 1 pick in the 1967 draft, never quite realized his potential in the NBA.

went and Rudy LaRusso declined to show up. They took Sonny Dove, from St. John's in New York.

Although Butcher was in the first training camp of his first coaching job, he had considerable basketball savvy. He had been trained in rural Kentucky, the mountain town of Paintsville, where basketball ranks just after religion and family. It was a rugged drive to the hoop hanging near the barn door. Butcher and his brothers, when they weren't shooting buckets and exchanging elbows, went off to hunt for squirrel dinner and possum for breakfast.

"Every kid in Paintsville played basketball twelve months a year," Butcher said.

Donnis' brother Paul was his coach, both at Paintsville High School and then at Pikeville College. Butcher had not been a star player in the pros. He had been a smart player, for the Knicks and Pistons.

Fred Zollner felt Butcher needed an assistant coach and hired Paul Seymour. It was a dangerous mesh. Seymour had worked in the league for years as a player and as a head coach at Syracuse, St. Louis, and Baltimore. It could be a pain of pressure for a young, rookie coach to have to look at his practice court or his bench during games and see an older, more experienced, once successful ex-head coach there. Paul Seymour appeared very much like a coach-in-waiting, though he claimed he was too occupied by his business interests and never wanted the responsibilities of being a head coach again.

Still, Seymour confessed to reporters: "I don't want to sound off, but what's the sense of ducking the issue? To be honest with you, I suppose I'm more or less the Pistons' ace in the hole."

It was a nice sense of security for a young, new head coach, conducting his first training camp. Typically Pistons. And having to coach another ex-coach—DeBusschere—magnified Butcher's jittery situation.

DeBusschere accepted his defrocked status with grace and dignity. He could tolerate playing for the man who took his coaching job. Actually, no longer being burdened with the responsibilities of coaching the club and playing, too, was a tremendous relief.

"I guess you can say I failed," DeBusschere told Pete Waldmeir about of his coaching tenure.

"You can look at the records. They weren't good. There are a lot of things that didn't show in the records, but that'd be making excuses if I talked about them.

"I had nearly three years and it didn't work out. Look, they asked me to take this job when I was twenty-four years old. They came to me. I figured it might come to this some day. Now it's here, and I feel a little relieved, frankly. It wasn't do-as-I-say. It was do-as-I-do, and there were times when I made mistakes . . .

"I want to play in Detroit for a long, long time. As long as they want me here and we can get along. I wouldn't object to being traded, but I feel that I've helped get something started here that has a firm base and can grow. Detroit is my home. I want to be part of it."

Then DeBusschere added: "I recommended Donnis for the job. He's a fine guy and I can play for him. Let's face it, I'd have to play for someone someplace."

The Pistons, for the first time in five years, were viable contenders to reach the playoffs. The objective of a .500, break-even, season seemed remote. But there was some excitement attached to the ballclub. Attendance continued to climb, and, usually the crowds were above 7,000, occasionally touching 8,000 or 9,000.

Dave Bing became a drawing card in Detroit and in the cities around the league, too. He was scoring more points on more nights than other power names in the league—guys such as Elgin Baylor, Chamberlain, Earl Monroe, Oscar Robertson, and Jerry West.

DeBusschere provided strength in rebounding and scoring. Dischinger blended back into the lineup. Eddie Miles was a cog in the backcourt with his shooting. Tom Van Arsdale and the rookie Walker gave the Pistons a rare luxury, for them, some depth on the bench.

The other top rookie, Sonny Dove, was a dud.

The basic weakness remained in the middle. It was a time in pro basketball when center was the primary position. Teams had to have giant, dominant centers to win championships, to make the NBA finals. Other teams could make the playoffs, but they could not be serious about the championship.

So the Pistons, with Joe Strawder playing center, were shooting to get into the playoffs after five years of misses—the old playoffs men-

tality, again. Strawder was banged around, man-handled, just no match for Chamberlain and Bill Russell.

In January 1968, the Pistons made another trade to bolster the scoring and the rebounding. In a multiplayer deal, a very strange deal, they got themselves Happy Hairston from the Cincinnati Royals. They had to sacrifice Van Arsdale off their bench as part of the deal.

But the trade was a rarity for Detroit. Finally, they had made a trade that was beneficial to the club. Hairston had immediate impact. And the deal had a secondary effect—the strange part of it. Relocated in the East, the Pistons' battle for the final qualifying spot in the playoffs was with the very club with which they traded. The Royals missed Hairston in the stretch, the Pistons had him.

In the end, the Pistons won ten of their last thirteen games in March. Butcher had gotten the Pistons into the playoffs, in fourth place, by the margin of a one game. The club they beat out by that one game was—the Cincinnati Royals.

The goal for a .500 season was not reached; but Butcher's 40–42 was the Pistons' best showing for the eleven years in Detroit.

For the first time since George Yardley broke the 2,000-point barrier, the Pistons had a league scoring champion. Dave Bing scored 2,142 points, an average of 27.1 per game. He was abetted by Miles and Hairston, who each averaged better than 18 points a game; and by DeBusschere, whose scoring average was a fraction off the 18-point average.

The Pistons had become a power on offense.

Then, they went into the playoffs. For the first time they played the Celtics in the postseason, and that would provide a foreshadowing of history. With the series squared a victory each, the Pistons won the third playoff game on the parquet floor at Boston Garden, 109–98. The Pistons had the advantage in the series over these dynastic rivals, who until they had been dethroned the previous year by the Philly 76ers, had won eight NBA championships in succession.

And for the very first time, the Pistons had become a hot ticket in Detroit. The papers were gripped in the middle of a nine-month strike. But it didn't matter to the Pistons; they didn't need press help any more.

So it was, they went out to play the Celtics in

Jerry West (44) and Wilt Chamberlain (13) of the Lakers out muscle Eddie Miles (14) and Jim Fox (23) during a 1968 matchup.

Game 4 of their Eastern Division semifinals playoff series at Cobo Arena backed by a shrieking mob of more than 11,000. The date was March 27, 1968. These were the playoffs and these were the Celtics—Bill Russell vs. Joe Strawder.

Boston, with Russell and Sam Jones and John Havlicek and a familiar veteran named Bailey Howell, blew the Pistons out, 135–110. On the Pistons' court.

The Celtics continued rolling to win the series in six games, going onward to their ninth championship in ten years.

The Pistons had done their best and were still far, far away from being any true match for champions.

And whatever monstrous magic the Celtics would have over the Pistons in the playoffs, through the decades, it was begun in 1968, on a March night at Cobo.

The NBA again was a floating crap game, for the 1969–69 season. Two more expansion franchises, the Milwaukee Bucks and Phoenix Suns. And those carpetbagging Hawks—relics from Tri-Cities and Milwaukee—had now abandoned St. Louis, where they'd won a lone NBA championship—to set up a shop in Atlanta.

The Pistons remained firmly fixed with their Eastern Division brethren. With aims again to make the playoffs and break the monotony of below .500 seasons.

In the fall of 1968, when Donnis Butcher opened training camp in Marysville on the Michigan thumb, nobody much noticed. Detroit was going daft about baseball. The Tigers were about to win the American League pennant. Much more newsworthy, their Dennis McLain was about to become the first major-league pitcher to win 30 games since Dizzy Dean in 1934.

The Pistons trained for a new season, starting off with that ancient sporting boost known as momentum, in isolation. There was little space in the Detroit papers, printing again, for pro basketball.

But the Pistons were pretty much unchanged from the previous spring, when they had produced some excitement in town.

"It's the same old story," said Butcher. "We've got a great backcourt with Miles, Bing, and Walker. And a strong front court with DeBusschere, Dischinger, Hairston, and Dove. We don't have an adequate big man."

The persistent problem.

Joe Strawder was gone, unclaimed in an expansion draft, and a no-show for training camp. It didn't matter. The Pistons had finally drafted a center, they presumed. Otto Moore, the first-round draft choice, was quite promising. Otto was 6 feet 11 out of Pan American.

Before the season, there was a Meet-the-Pistons banquet in Detroit. Donnis Butcher introduced the players and then he introduced his assistant, Paul Seymour. "My next successor," said Butcher. The audience laughed at Butcher's gallows humor.

The season did not have an auspicious start to it. The Pistons lost their first three games and then six of their next seven.

Before they'd played those ten games, some television journalists were reporting that some of the Pistons players had turned mutinous against Butcher. The report said that the players were complaining about harsh tactics by Butcher, a traditional gripe. The story said further that Butcher was in jeopardy of losing his job as head coach to Seymour, his assistant in the wings.

The Pistons insisted it was a phony story. Bing, DeBusschere, and Miles met with Butcher and emerged to report that everything was hunky-dory. All harmony.

"The players' committee was really embarrassed by the story," Butcher told the press. "But what the hell, I didn't care. I know things can't last forever.

"I think we got a fine ballclub. We've been building this team from within for several years, and it's beginning to pay off now. One thing we've found is a good, tough center in our rookie, Otto Moore . . .

"He may not be another Bill Russell, but he's going to be good enough for us."

Zollner also waxed with enthusiasm. "Our problems at center are solved," The Z told Pete Waldmeir. "Now all we need is one more forward and we'll be all set."

Then the Z gave Donnis Butcher a vote of con fidence: "I'm not going to fire the coach because two or three guys are griping. Some of them make $40,000 a year and they should work for it."

Donnis Butcher, age thirty, got the ziggy from Fred Zollner twenty-two games into the 1968–69 season. It was December 2, the holidays just gathering momentum, that ancient word. The record was 10–12, and certainly through the years such a record less than two months into a season had not been regarded as any great criminal cause for firing action.

Paul Seymour, age forty-one, had been in the wings—the ace in the hole, in his own words—for more than a year, as Butcher's older, more experienced assistant. Seymour had his real estate and liquor store businesses in Syracuse and actually was commuting from there to his basketball employment with the Pistons. Now Zollner had to talk Seymour into accepting the head-coaching promotion. Seymour agreed to coach the club for the rest of the season, at least.

He popped back into Detroit prepared to dress for his new role. He was laden down with two suitcases and three hanging suit bags.

"What guy in his right mind would leave a liquor business with the holidays coming up?" Seymour said. "I've got to be nuts. Why did I take the job? It's simple. Once a jock, always a jock."

After the introspection of Butcher, the press welcomed Seymour. He always had been gabby, extroverted. He was prone to deliver the audacious. The brushcut was still a popular hairstyle, and Seymour wore one, close cropped.

He had grown up in Toledo, down the pike from Detroit, a place where the townsfolk rooted for Detroit teams even though they played across the dreaded border in enemy Michigan.

"I saw my first baseball game and my first burlesque show in Detroit," Seymour said. He was regaling the press. "Both on the same day, too. I was eleven or twelve and the Toledo Boys Club had won the softball championship and we came up here to see the Tigers. The guy who managed the team was a little kooky and let us go to the burlesque show after the game."

It had been inevitable that Paul Seymour would coach the Pistons, regardless of what innocent might get the ziggy in the neck. It mattered only when Zollner would get the urge. The Z and Seymour had been friends for years, back to their years with the Fort Wayne Zollner Pistons and Syracuse Nationals. Seymour became the Pistons' seventh coach in their twelve seasons in Detroit.

Ed Coil, the GM, told the players of the switch at a mid-afternoon practice session.

"I don't know whether this was his fault or their fault," Coil said, referring back to the reports about a players mutiny against Butcher, a story previously considered untrue.

"This team needs an awakening," Butcher told the *News'* Bill Halls. "Nearly half the players are not giving 100 percent. Maybe they will for Paul."

"The players were noncommittal when they heard about it," said a player among them, Dave DeBusschere. "I guess when things are going bad, the thing to do is change coaches, especially in basketball."

Paul Seymour had been head coach of the

Pistons for fifteen days when they made another trade. This one was with the New York Knicks. A one-for-two swap. The Pistons got the two, Walt Bellamy and Howard "Butch" Komives.

The player they sent to New York was Dave DeBusschere, grown to manhood on Detroit's East Side, catalyst to a Michigan high school championship team at Detroit Austin, All America at University of Detroit, former coach of the Detroit Pistons, NBA All-Star, and beer drinker *celebre*.

The exile of Dave DeBusschere to New York shocked the city of Detroit. It shocked those who cared about this gradually growing sport of pro basketball. It shocked those who could not give a hoot about basketball.

DeBusschere went to join the Knicks, leaving a lot of friends in town. Bellamy, a towering, brooding center, and Komives, a flashy guard, joined the Pistons. They were strangers.

Bellamy, 6 feet 11, was known around the league, though. He'd played with a bunch of teams. He was a licensed mortician during the offseason.

"He should be an undertaker," the joke went around the NBA. "He's buried enough basketball franchises."

The flak hit the fan in Detroit. Seymour caught it. He was the culprit who had traded away a local hero . . . Dave Debusschere, who had said: "I want to play in Detroit for a long, long time."

There was a sharp drop in attendance at Cobo Arena.

Seymour countered sharply: "I expected a lot of reaction when I traded DeBusschere. But all I got where three letters."

Then the new coach explained his methods, his philosophy, his style—all of it effective because he had been a winning coach elsewhere:

"I'm a grinder. I've got no time to fool around with people who don't want to play basketball. If somebody has a problem and he wants to sulk about it, he might as well sulk on the bench. You do the job and I'm yours. Don't do the job, and I get somebody who does."

Seymour did not mention any player by name in this post-trade scenario. He did not have to; it was clear that he meant DeBusschere was the sulking player.

"Bellamy's a big-league ballplayer, all right," Seymour said. "DeBusschere had seven years and Detroit never won anything. So why all the fuss? You don't win with him, try something else. Another thing, Dave was starting to have trouble with some of the other players. Nothing serious, but I had a feeling they weren't giving him the ball when they could.

"I had no time for that stuff, either."

"Hell, I did DeBusschere a favor trading him. He'll make out in New York just fine."

Done with his critique on DeBusschere, Seymour turned to Dave Bing, now in his third season as a force athlete in the NBA.

". . . We need to get Dave Bing straightened around," Seymour said as the struggle continued in the 1968–69 season. "You know there were times when they told Bing just to take the ball, run down the floor, and shoot it. How the hell are you going to win that way? What do you tell the other four guys?

"I tell Bing to quit messing around, turning your back to the basket and making all those funny moves going to the hoop. I tell him to keep his face to the basket and concentrate on taking his best shot."

"The Pistons are in bad shape," ousted Donnis Butcher would tell Pete Waldmeir later in an interview. "Seymour traded away DeBusschere as soon as he got my job because he didn't want Dave around as a threat to his own popularity.

"DeBusschere is tight with Zollner. And as long as he was in Detroit, Seymour couldn't feel safe."

The former coach also unburdened himself on some other matters: That DeBusschere never would have been traded had he, Butcher, been retained as coach. The very day Butcher was fired as coach, he said, he'd agreed to a trade with the Knicks and their general manager, Red Holtzman. Butcher's projected trade had the Pistons getting Bellamy, all right—straight up for Jimmy Walker, still a reserve guard and still a disappointment.

"Holtzman and I shook on the trade and I was to get it approved the next day," Butcher said. "But I was relieved of my job on the plane trip back to Detroit that night and the deal was off."

Then Butcher complained that he had been stifled on other deals when he was coach. One would have brought Lenny Wilkens, then with the Atlanta Hawks, to the Pistons for Eddie Miles.

"I had arranged to trade Miles for Wilkens," Butcher said, "But Zollner said we'd have to pay Wilkens too much money, so he said, no."

The Pistons were in such bad shape they dropped back to sixth place in what was now an expansion-engorged division of seven clubs. They believed they had the strong, intimidating center they'd wanted for years in Bellamy, but that was short of Russell and Wilt, too. So close to touching what for them had been the magic .500 level the year before, the Pistons finished the 1968–69 season with a 32–50 record. No playoffs for them.

The club had reeled after the firing of Donnis Butcher and the exile of Dave DeBusschere. After Butcher got the ziggy with his club at 10–12, they went 22–38 under the auspices of grinding Paul Seymour. It seemed that they had quite a few sulking ballplayers. "We have to sit down and face cold facts," Seymour said when the season ended. "We may be two years away from a winner."

And as he spoke those words in March 1969, with the NBA playoffs going on in other towns, there was doubt that Seymour would be back to coach in Detroit. Zollner had to cajole him into taking the job 3½ months earlier, when Butcher was dumped. Now The Z tried again, but Seymour was reluctant.

By mid-April, as the 1969 NBA finals started, the Pistons had not made any announcement about their coaching situation. Seymour, when contacted, was coy in stating: "Mr. Zollner doesn't want to talk about it at this point. There are a lot of things to be decided."

And when Bill Halls of the *News* contacted Zollner at his retirement home in Golden Beach, Florida, The Z said: "I can honestly say Paul hasn't said yes and he hasn't said no. I would never release him and he would never quit unless he left me in a very good position."

Then Zollner said he had five offers to buy the Pistons and had rejected them all.

"They were what I call explorers," Zollner said. "Five of them. They shouldn't even be listened to. I'm not going to listen to any more of these explorers."

A day or two later, the 1969 NBA finals started between the Celtics and the Lakers in L.A.

The Lakers had gotten themselves Wilt Chamberlain in a deal with the 76ers and were instantly transformed into a championship quality club. They were coached by a fiery, humorous, beer-chugging, independent, tempestuous soul named Butch van Breda Kolff, a.k.a. VBK. Butch had coached Bill Bradley and Princeton to national prominence before he got tired of working in the Ivy League. He was a Princeton man himself, but he was a migrant, too, in the habit of so many basketball coaches. Before Princeton, he'd coached at Lafayette and Hofstra. After Princeton, he jumped to the pros, to coach the Lakers in the league in which he had once been a player for the Knicks.

Chamberlain was a bundle for a coach. By midseason, VBK was looking for a cushioned landing field.

"I can't take this any more," he said privately.

One day VBK told an interviewer: "If the basketball court were made of grass, Wilt would wear out a three-foot-square area."

Fred Schaus, one of the long-ago Fort Wayne Zollner Pistons and then GM of the Lakers, played diplomat. The season went on to its end and through the playoffs with VBK and Chamberlain in a state of truce.

VBK's Lakers, on their homecourt, bumped off the reigning champion Celtics in the first two games of the finals. The Celts won the next two in Boston, then the Lakers took another edge, 3 games to 2 in the series, in L.A. Back in Boston, the Celtics forced the series into the seventh game with another victory in the Garden.

All the while, there was speculation that Butch van Breda Kolff, entwined in a hectic NBA finals series, was so fed up with coaching the Lakers that he would be jumping ship after the season.

They played the seventh game in L.A. on May 5, 1969. With five minutes left, the Celtics led the Lakers by seven points. Then Chamberlain wrenched his knee. VBK had to take him to the bench. With Chamberlain sitting on the bench, the Lakers cut into the Celtics' lead. Chamberlain kept asking van Breda Kolff to put him back into the game. VBK ignored Wilt. He kept ignoring Wilt.

In the end, the Celtics edged VBK's Lakers, 108–106, in the only game in the finals won by the visitors. It was the Celtics' tenth NBA championship in eleven years.

One day later, a source told Bill Halls that Seymour had already quit as coach of the Pistons—and that another coach, unidentified, had been hired to coach the team.

The Pistons denied the story.

One day after that, the NBA conducted its draft in New York. Fred Zollner said no decision had been made on the Pistons' coaching job, but that Paul Seymour would remain if needed. Oddly, there was an interloper sitting at the Pistons' table during the draft. Butch van Breda Kolff, coach of the just defeated Lakers.

He had nothing to declare.

Two weeks after the seventh game of the NBA finals, Butch van Breda Kolff resigned as coach of the Lakers at a meeting with the owner, Jack Kent Cooke. VBK, afflicted with an insatiable wanderlust along with a terrible temper, had a year to go on his contract, but wanted out so much Cooke said goodbye.

Willem Hendrik "Butch" van Breda Kolff, age forty-seven, beer and basketball lover, habitue of steam baths and former Marine and Ivy Leaguer at Princeton, became the Detroit Pistons' eighth head coach in thirteen seasons on May 21, 1969. Fred Zollner, it seemed, had put on his pith helmet and gone off to do some exploring of his own. Butch had agreed to a two-year contract, which presumably would thwart his wanderlust for at least the duration, though a signed deal didn't prevent him from escaping from L.A. There was a large press conference to introduce the new coach to his new town.

Van Breda Kolff told the story about how he'd met his wife, Florence. Butch called her Sarge. They'd both been in the Marine Corps. Butch had joined up the first time he flunked out of Princeton. One night he went out on the town, had some beer, and bought himself a new pair of shoes. He was swinging the shoes around his head as he returned to the Marine base at Cherry Point, North Carolina. Butch was stopped by the Shore Patrol and asked to show his liberty card. The SP guy told Butch to hurry up.

"I hit him over the head with the shoes and the next thing I knew I was in trouble."

Florence—Sarge—was in a mess of trouble, too. She was a radio operator and was apprehended for unauthorized use of a transmitter when she did some extracurricular chattering.

Butch met his future wife in the brig.

And now, after his coaching wanderlust had taken him on the not-so-grand tour to Lafayette, Hofstra, Princeton and L.A., Butch was in Detroit, feeling free at last.

VBK was free of Wilt the Stilt and into the pot of basketball turmoil in Detroit. He had Walt Bellamy instead of Wilt. He had a brooding Jimmy Walker instead of Jerry West. And he had Dave Bing and Terry Dischinger, who could play the game.

Only the Milwaukee Bucks had finished below the Pistons during the 1968–69 season. So it was that the Bucks had themselves first pick in the NBA draft. Their selection was a 7-foot-1⅜-inch center who had just led UCLA to three NCAA championships. His name was Lew Alcindor, but he would change in the pros to Kareem Abdul-Jabbar.

Going high in the order of this same draft, the Pistons claimed Terry Driscoll, a forward out of Boston College.

Beyond the first man picked, it was not an especially fertile draft crop. And then Driscoll signed with a team in Italy.

Butch van Breda Kolff started off his regime in the fall of 1969 with the identical objective that had eluded his seven predecessors. To be the first Detroit coach lucky enough, or astute enough, or possessed with enough magical powers, to coax his team to the .500 level and above it. He yearned to cross that infinitely tiny barrier between a losing season and a winning season.

VBK had the experience, the background, the history of success to be a winning coach. A championship coach.

He was also the champion referee-baiter of all the coaches in basketball. His first year with the Lakers, he was issued thirty technical fouls. He drove his players.

One night at the Lakers' bench, *Sports Illustrated* caught VBK in full tirade: "Do you want to win this game? Do you listen when I say before the game that each man has to check his man? This looks like high school . . . What the hell do you want me to do? Do I have to look like an idiot? You guys been playing seven, eight, nine years in the league . . . I got freshmen in college know more than this . . ."

Guys like Jerry West and Elgin Baylor stood there in silence, nodding at their coach.

Butch arrived back in pro ball, boasting that he'd been an outcast in the Ivy League.

"I was more like a townie," he told *SI*. "I chewed tobacco and wore crazy hats, anything to be different, and my friends were cops and bartenders . . . I didn't make it on the society scene. I also did a very un-Princeton thing—I flunked out. Not once, but twice. That at least ties the track record. All I cared about was sports, competition."

Butch arrived, saying: "Bulling your way in for a layup doesn't impress anybody. People want to see movement, the nice passes underneath, stuff like that. And these pro players are capable of doing all of it, too. They have a rhythm, almost a poetry, some of them. When the pro game is played right, it makes the college game look downright dull."

Butch arrived with an opinion about his fellow NBA coaches, as quoted again in *SI*: "Too many of these guys don't seem to be having any fun. They sit there on the bench and look like they're slowly dying. They've all got pretty good personalities, but they're a little odd in their own ways, too. Look at all the concentration that's involved, the intensity, and it lasts for ten, eleven months, counting practice and all . . . one of the toughest things about it is the sheer length. We used to play 25 games in college, but now it's 82 games in the pros plus exhibitions plus playoffs and you've got to be up for every one of them. I'm wringing wet after every game. I don't care if we win by fifty, I'm still a wreck, and I'm off to the nearest saloon as soon as I can get there. I can't imagine a coach not having a few beers after a game. To me, that would be the weirdest thing off all."

Weird was a word his fellows around the NBA attached to Butch. Said an NBA guy about the newest Detroit coach: "He's an absolute hedonist. He loves steam baths and beer. When the typical NBA coach gets to a new town, he looks for the nearest bar. Butch looks for the nearest steam room. Then he looks for the nearest bar. He thinks nothing of taking two or three steam baths a day."

Butch arrived in Detroit with a victory. The Pistons opened the 1969–70 season at Cobo against the Celtics—without Bill Russell, who had retired as a player and a coach. The game introducing the new Detroit coach against the reigning world champions drew all of 4,892 of the definitely most curious. The Pistons won, 98–97, with Jimmy Walker hitting two free throws seven seconds before the end.

What VBK had to say in the postmortem after his first game in town, a coaching victor against the champs, in a dramatic finish, was this: "These are the worst fans I've ever seen. You get three points behind and you've done everything wrong. Some of these fans don't deserve a winner, but we won despite them. I give Butcher and Seymour all the credit in the world. DeBusschere was lucky. At least he was on the court."

It was explained that the Detroit faithful had been frustrated by a dozen years of losing basketball.

"I don't care," said VBK. "We're not trying to go out there and lose."

Welcome to town!

Butch then went out to find a steam bath and have some beer.

Butch van Breda Kolff made his first trade two weeks into the 1969–70 season. By Pistons' standards, it was neither a giant deal nor the traditional giveaway. The Pistons obtained Erwin Mueller from the Seattle Supersonics. Mueller saw the basketball through bottle-thick spectacles. He was not a star, but he had personality. He cost the Pistons a second-round draft choice and may have been worth it. Not for his basketball, but . . . Mueller was sure-handed and gifted as a beer drinker.

Van Breda Kolff's first deal might not have done much to strengthen the Pistons' bench, but he got himself a companion for his postgame beer sojourns.

VBK had never been the occupant of last place before. Now, after steaming the fans on opening night, he could see the reasons for their frustrations. The Pistons quickly buried themselves into last place in the NBA East.

In January 1970, the coach issued the VBK Doctrine—not too different than what Paul Seymour, Donnis Butcher, and Dave DeBusschere had once declared.

"We've got the nucleus of a good young team," VBK told the *News*. "We just need a little bit of help, either through a trade or the draft this spring, and then next year we could really be something."

It was suggested he'd spent too much time in the steam.

As Seymour had before him, van Breda Kolff delivered a criticism of Dave Bing in a public forum.

"Dave's big trouble is trying to win it all by himself," Butch told Bill Halls. "He feels he's got to score the key basket. The team has got to learn that in the normal movement of the game whoever is open takes the shot."

And there were more serious concerns about Bing. The new American Basketball Association had established itself as a business competitor of the NBA. Teams in both leagues were losing money. But that didn't prevent them from spending it to sign players. Washington had one of the ABA clubs and was Dave Bing's boyhood hometown. Word was he'd signed a $500,000 contract with the Washington ABA club for future delivery.

Meanwhile, VBK took care of the others in his personal doghouse. He made three trades in a whirlwind forty-eight-hour period. Gone were Walt Bellamy, Happy Hairston, and Eddie Miles. Young Otto Moore would have to handle center by himself. Jimmy Walker had already replaced Miles as Bing's partner in the backcourt. Erwin Mueller could play some forward in Hairston's spot.

In this trio of trades, the Pistons basically enriched themselves with additional draft choices. The players obtained were basic cannon fodder for the bench.

As VBK announced the trades, a writer yelled at him: "The press was holding out for another coaching change."

Van Breda Kolff grinned. "Yeah, it was me or Bellamy, and we flipped a coin." He grinned even more. "I lost," he said.

As the NBA season went along, it was noted clearly in Detroit that there was a new power in the division. The New York Knicks had climbed into command in the NBA East. The Knicks really did need twenty-four years to shoot.

A charter club in the old BAA in 1946, the Knicks had never won a championship. Now fortified through the draft and some sharp trades, the Knicks were genuine contenders. Among the athletes who turned them into winners were Bill Bradley, Walt Frazier and Dick Barnett plus Cazzie Russell, Willis Reed, and that tough forward acquired only the previous season, Dave DeBusschere.

The last-place Pistons publicly admitted that they regretted the exile of Dave DeBusschere the day Walt Bellamy was dispatched to the Atlanta Hawks for somebody named John Arthurs.

"Looking back on it," said Ed Coil, the general manager, "I don't think we would have ever made that trade if we had known Paul Seymour was not going to coach this year."

The Pistons finished their thirteenth season in Detroit with their thirteenth consecutive losing record. Van Breda Kolff was heated and angry. He had been within two points of winning the NBA championship with the Lakers the year before. He had coached a perennial Ivy League championship team when Bill Bradley played at Princeton. An Ivy League team making it to the Final Four of the NCAAs was a near miracle. Bradley and VBK made it. Now Butch was saddled with a Detroit team that finished in last place with a 31–51 record.

VBK could only note wistfully how one player had hoisted the previous season's last-place club, the Milwaukee Bucks, to double their total of victories and into second place. That one player with such an impact in the NBA was the rookie, Kareem Abdul-Jabbar.

The Pistons had never had such a treasure, a dominant center who could hook the ball into the basket, who could clog up the middle, who could rebound—who could intimidate.

Finishing last, the Pistons again had to flip a coin for the privilege of going first in the draft. They tossed with the San Diego Rockets. This time the Pistons made the correct call of the spinning coin. They won their choice of any senior playing in all the colleges in America. One such center was available. His name was Bob Lanier, and he played for St. Bonaventure. A week earlier, in the NCAA tournament, he had torn up his right knee. On draft day, he was in a hospital bed in Buffalo, New York, his future uncertain as a pro basketball player because of the severity of his injuries.

For thirteen years, the Pistons had been, pretty much, the comedians of pro basketball—the team that couldn't win; the team that made nonsensical trades; the team that made foolish draft choices.

Now because of Lanier's injury, the Pistons considered drafting Pistol Pete Maravich from Louisiana State, a pure shooter with a winning style. VBK mulled it over in a fit of indecision. Then he suggested what the hell, the Pistons could never win without a center, let's plunge and gamble.

They selected Bob Lanier, 6 feet 11 and 260 pounds, as their first draft choice, as the top player off the board in 1970, while he was flat on his back in a hospital bed, his encased leg held aloft in traction by a rope and a pulley.

The 1970 NBA finals were hellacious and heroic. For the first time, they went transcontinental—New York to Los Angeles, the Knicks and the Lakers. In the end, the Knicks beat the Lakers in seven games. They won very much because of the play of Willis Reed, lost years before by the Pistons at the NBA draft, and very much because of the rugged play of Dave De-Busschere, traded into exile from Detroit to New York.

V—The Seventies

Ed Coil, the bookkeeper cum GM, flew over to Buffalo to visit Bob Lanier in the hospital and to discuss a contract.

"We're 99 and 44/100ths percent sure we'll sign Lanier," Coil said on draft day, March 23, 1970.

It was just a matter of agreeing on the proper figures for a bonus and salary.

Lanier had already been signed to turn pro in the NBA, while he was still playing for St. Bonaventure in upstate New York. It was known as a John Doe contract, no team identified in the proper entry and the money amount blank for future settlement.

Pro basketball was enmeshed in its own war, much in the manner of pro football during the early sixties, before the merger of the National and American Football Leagues. Athletes agreed to play in one league or the other, while still in college. It wasn't kosher, but there always has been an elastic quality to pro contracts.

So, while still with the Bonnies, before his surgery, Lanier was ticketed to play in the NBA. The new, rival American Basketball Association was working the same trick with other college kids as player payments streaked off into the wild blue yonder.

"It was a five-year deal," Coil would say years later. "We paid him $1.2 million and that was a lot of money in those days. His leg was in a full cast.

"We didn't even know if he could play."

Lanier reported to Pistons' training camp at Ypsilanti, Michigan, with a limp and a prayer. The knee was healing, and the Pistons had to keep him off the court for much of the camp period. Then Bob was permitted to scrimmage with his teammates.

In one of the early scrimmages, he tripped over a teammate and tumbled to the floor, his 6-11 frame falling in sections. There was a frightening hush as a series of pops exploded from Lanier's knee.

Lanier arose and he was fine. The pops were the adhesions breaking inside the knee, a medical necessity before a surgical knee can become fully operative again.

"Bob broke them all in one day," said VBK. "The doctor said he'll be better off in the long run. So that fall turned out to blessing in disguise."

And you could count the blessings the Pistons had on one middle finger.

The NBA went through another spate of geographic gyrations. The league was growing, lots faster than dictated by business practicality. Three more expansion clubs were added to make a total of seventeen member franchises in the NBA, as it continued its expensive battle with the ABA.

The new NBA clubs were the Buffalo Braves, Cleveland Cavaliers, and Portland Trail Blazers. What it meant was a league with too many incompetent ballclubs.

To avoid clogging, the NBA split from its two divisions, like amoeba, into four divisions. They were given the names Atlantic, Central, Midwest, and Pacific. The Pistons were spotted in the Midwest with the Milwaukee Bucks, Chicago Bulls, and the Suns from that Midwestern mecca, Phoenix.

Bob Lanier's pro basketball debut occurred on the night of October 14, 1970, in the Pistons' opener at Seattle. The box score of the game showed that Lanier took 18 shots, several of them left-handed jumpers from outside, and connected on 10 of them and finished the game with 22 points. The Pistons beat the Supersonics, 123–117, and then continued down the coast and beat the Warriors on their court in San Francisco and the Suns on their court in Phoenix. "Bob Lanier, you know, the critics have started already," said van Breda Kolff. "They say he can't use his right hand, he can't rebound, he can't do this, he can't do that. All I know is, he's played about 23 minutes a game for three games and averaged 20 points, made some passes and got us a few rebounds. There aren't too many players in the league that can do that."

Lanier, quickly, became competitive against the top centers in the NBA—Willis Reed, of the champion Knicks, among them.

"I thought we were pretty evenly matched," Lanier said. "Of course Reed has more experience and can get away with a lot more than I can. But I catch on pretty fast."

The hottest controversy about Lanier dealt with the size of his basketball shoes. There were only a few companies that provided basketball shoes for the players. Bob wore Converse. Size 20, he said. Converse disputed that, announcing publicly: "They're size 22 and have to be specially made."

The riddle regarding Lanier's actual basketball shoe size would continue for many years.

By then, Ruth Coil, Ed Coil's wife, had commandeered one of Lanier's sneakers to use as a conversation piece in a floral display. She figured the basketball shoe was an ideal place for a potted plant.

By then, the innovative minds that created the series of Lite Beer commercials had hired Bob and his arch rival Dave Cowens, from the Celtics, to act in one of the beer-selling spoofs that ended with a mockery of the NBA's largest foot.

By then, Lanier's basketball shoe size had been the topic of countless bar bets—size 22D vs. size 20.

Jerry Dziedzic had won fifty bucks in one bet by producing one of Lanier's mammoth sneakers with the numbers etched inside.

It was the spring of 1991 when Dziedzic, an expert voice, settled the matter with a definitive ruling.

"Lanier wore size 20, not 22," spoke Dziedzic. "I ought to know."

Dziedzic has been the Pistons' equipment man since . . .

"I started when DeBusschere was a boy coach," Dziedzic said in the spring of 1991. He is the Pistons' oldest employee in time of service, privy to a lot of secrets, with memories of many quaint moments in all the suffering years and now owner of two shiny championship rings, one on each hand.

"I handled a lot of jocks," he said. "I took care of the equipment of all of them. Bob wore a 20 basketball shoe and an 18½ street shoe. He didn't wear a 22. I ought to know."

Bob Lanier was moody and powerful. He was a rookie, but he refused to take any guff in the professional league. He banged elbows and bodies in the middle. He played with anger. At last, the Pistons had the essential ingredient. Dave Bing's skills could be meshed into a team concept. The Pistons won the kind of ballgames they had lost for thirteen years. And, they could stop faking the attendance counts in order to make them appear respectable in the wire-service box scores.

Still, these were the Pistons and they could not rid themselves of the bizarre and the ugly.

The ugliness in what had been the Pistons' longtime dream season started in February 1971. The Pistons lost four games by three points or fewer in a span of two weeks. Bing took an elbow in the cheekbone and suffered a depressed fracture, underwent an operation, and kept on playing. One night, as March began, the Pistons had a twenty-point lead against the expansion Cleveland Cavaliers and blew it away. They lost —to the team with the poorest record in the league.

The locker room was mutinous. A schism had developed between Coach VBK and his players.

"It's more like the Grand Canyon," one of the disgruntled players told the *News'* Bill Halls, who had asked about the seriousness of the split between the paid players and their coach. The player begged to remain anonymous, lest his mouthiness cause him to have his butt placed in a sling.

Willing to be quoted and identified, Dave Bing, now the team captain said: "We haven't had time to sit down and talk about it. Most of us will be here next year and the most important thing is to keep the same kind of rapport we now have between the players on this team."

Bing was openly critical of VBK's substitutions of four bench players as the Pistons were taking their pratfall against the Cavs. Bing was one of the players yanked to the bench.

"I didn't want to come out then," he said.

"But second-guessing is the easiest thing in the world.

". . . Every coach is different. If it isn't him, it'll be someone else. But this team has got to stick together. This year is shot."

Strange, but true. The Pistons came down the stretch with the best team in their fourteen seasons in Detroit, with the best record since they were near champions in Fort Wayne in pro basketball's early years. And the frustrating irony was that the year was shot anyway.

Van Breda Kolff did not respond to the critique of his players, as he once had to Wilt Chamberlain with the Lakers. But he was truly ticked off at them.

"I was unhappy," he said, "the players were unhappy. You can't go around with sweetness and light when you're losing. I got naggy and some of the players reacted. It's a normal chain of events. But I don't think any permanent damage was done. Time heals a lot of things."

He had never been a peaceful coach. One night, as the club sagged, VBK got into a flap with a fan. He drew two technical fouls, resulting in automatic ejection. He led the league in Ts, with forty-one. And he was kicked out of seven games during the season.

His contract was finished.

"I want to come back," he told Halls when the season ended.

There was some doubt that Zollner wanted him back.

At last, at last, the Pistons reached the .500 barrier, crossed it, finished their season with a winning record. For the first time in Detroit. They rode in at 45-37. The 45 victories were more than the games won by all but six other NBA clubs.

And the utter bitter irony was that the Pistons didn't qualify for the playoffs, even with their spiffy record. They were victims of the NBA's rejumbled geography. With the league gerrymandered into four divisions, spotted in the Midwest, the Pistons' 45 victories placed them fourth—AND LAST—in the division. Milwau-kee, Chicago, and Phoenix all won more games. The Pistons were out—even though Atlanta with nine fewer victories and San Francisco with four fewer made the playoffs out of other divisions.

Indeed, the Pistons would have finished first with their 45 victories, if they had been spotted in the Central Division. As it was the Baltimore Bullets won the division, with 42 victories.

No wonder the Pistons turned cranky late in the season, when they lost 20 of their last 30 games.

"If we'd finished strong like we started out," VBK said in postmortem, "I would say this was a successful season. But we didn't. We never won a game big, even when we were winning. Teams we beat by three or four points would beat other teams by twenty or thirty points. It would appear we weren't as strong as we should have been . . .

"In any other division we wouldn't have been out of it. But we were in the toughest division, and when we lost the other teams in our division won.

"One thing I liked is Bob Lanier. Bob played his best basketball the last two weeks of the season."

As the playoffs began, with the Pistons on the outside, Lanier was selected as the NBA's Rookie of the Year.

A couple of days after the season ended, Dave Bing signed a new three-year contract to stay with the Pistons. He had been signed to a contract by the Washington club of the ABA, effective for the 1971-72 season. But the contract turned to junk when the Washington team moved to Virginia, as the ABA did some geographic jumbling itself.

The new contract with the Pistons put Bing in the class with Oscar Robertson, Jerry West, and Wilt Chamberlain—for $450,000 per season, estimated.

How long does it take to create a championship team? The Bucks won the NBA finals their third season in the league, after being started from scratch. That was the impact of the young Kareem Abdul-Jabbar, playing with an aged and still highly skilled Oscar Robertson in the backcourt. The Bucks won 66 games during the season, then crushed the Warriors and Lakers in the playoffs, then swept the Bullets in the finals.

A few weeks after the Bucks won their championship, the Pistons signed Butch van Breda Kolff to another two-year contract. VBK earned a raise to $45,000, estimated—about one-tenth of Dave Bing's salary, if the estimates were accurate. The press conference was chock full of joke-making.

"I'll bet he doesn't even know he signed for two years," said Ed Coil.

"Hell," said VBK, who never had much appreciation for the written word. "You can quit if you want to and they can always fire you.

The Pistons were encouraged going into camp for the 1971-72 season. They had a winning record to defend. There was progress. Bob Lanier was NBA mature beyond his one year of experience, and his knee had held up for the long duration of the 82-game pro season. Dave Bing was hitting his prime, bunched with Jerry West as the best two guards in basketball. Plus, the club had some stability in the coaching position, after some many years of flux and fire.

Not all was perfect as the season opened.

The Pistons were being jobbed again by the league. They had traded Otto Moore, an erstwhile No. 1 draftee, to the Phoenix Suns. They were supposed to receive Mel Counts in return. But Otto signed a contract with the ABA's Virginia Squires. He then signed an NBA contract with Phoenix. Possessor of two valid contracts, Otto opted to join the Suns. Phoenix, to certify its contract with Moore, took the case to court.

The NBA season began with Moore playing for Phoenix. And because the situation was not resolved, Phoenix also held onto Counts. He, too, was playing for the Suns, Moore's teammate.

Zollner, of course, protested to the NBA board. And of course, The Z's fellow owners told him to go to hell. Phoenix kept playing both players, while the Pistons were held up short. Zollner had shot himself in the big toe again. He refused to go to court to get an injunction against the Suns playing both players.

Worse than losing a backup center for nothing, the Pistons lost Dave Bing at the very start of the season. Bing had been poked in the right eye by Happy Hairston, his old teammate, in an exhibition game with the Lakers. David was held out of the last three exhibitions, then played in the season opener. He was sharp, with 24 points, as the Pistons jumped on the Knicks to win in the Garden. He had hit a basket that appeared to him as a fuzzy loop.

"I can't shoot from too far out," Bing said. "I'm very concerned about it."

Bing already had vision problems. His left eye was weak and off the court, he wore eyeglasses. Now the doctors discovered that the poke in the eye had detached his retina. He underwent surgery three days after the new season started. The prognosis was he'd be lost to the Pistons for two months, at least.

Butch Komives replaced Bing as a starter at guard in tandem with Jimmy Walker. Curtis Rowe, off John Wooden's invincibles at UCLA, had meshed onto the ballclub as the No. 1 draft choice. The Pistons got off to a decent start. They won six of the first ten games.

On the morning of November 1, 1971, the cream of Detroit sports journalism was with the Lions in Milwaukee for a Monday Night Football game against the Green Bay Packers. They stood around in a hotel lobby as Howard Cosell baited Joe Schmidt, the Lions' coach.

"Joe Schmidt, he couldn't motivate a frog," said Cosell.

It was about that time that the newspaper offices started sending rockets to their columnists.

All hell had broken loose back in Detroit while the writers were in Milwaukee with the Lions. Doug Barkley had quit as coach of the Detroit Red Wings, stumbling through the National Hockey League.

Moments later, the Pistons made an announcement: Butch van Breda Kolff had resigned as their coach. Ten games into his brand new two-year contract. He had been absolutely correct—he could quit if he wanted to. And he wanted to, very much.

VBK told Bill Halls: "There are two things about my job I'm not enjoying, and whether I'm doing it well is circumspect. I don't know if that's the right word, but it's getting to the point where I'm uptight. Life is too short to prostitute yourself. If that's the case, I'll do something else."

The two things that were bothering him, VBK said, were the players' attitude—so selfish that individuals regarded themselves as more important than the team—and crabby, criticizing fans.

"He told me he was quitting last Thursday, but I asked him to wait until the two weekend games were over," said GM Ed Coil. "Then when we won the two games, I thought he'd change his mind . . .

"Mr. Zollner was shocked. He didn't know what to say.

"Bill said there was so much pressure, he wanted to get out . . . It almost sounded as if Barkley and van Breda Kolff were together."

"I don't know why he'd do it," said Terry Dischinger, the club's elder statesman.

The Pistons were practicing at the University of Detroit when VBK resigned at the club offices downtown. Coil phoned Dischinger to tell him to relay the information to the players—that their coach had abandoned them.

Coil's first thought was to make Dave Bing the coach while he was recovering from eye surgery. When Bing was ready to play again, he'd be player/coach. It was an idea that hadn't worked before with DeBusschere. Then Coil changed his mind. Instead, he appointed Dischinger the player/coach for the time being, while the club went off on another manhunt for a permanent —ha!—bench head coach.

No matter what coach the Pistons managed to find, Butch van Breda Kolff figured the guy would have an awful time. The day after he quit, VBK disclosed the basic reason for his decision to quit. He had talked to a friend a few nights earlier when the Pistons had been beaten by the Bullets by thirty points. The guy told Butch: "They didn't play for you."

The players had become too much to handle. "The philosophy of the game," said VBK. "It's changed." The fans, too, had become a bother. They'd become too hot, even though the Pistons' attendance was decreasing again. Butch complained how he almost dove into the stands to fight with the critics.

He talked about going off to the Jersey shore, walking his dog in solitude.

"I won't coach again," he vowed. "I'd like to be a liaison between the league and the players. Attend all the owners' meetings, the referees' meetings, the players' meetings. Just be there and straighten things out."

But he had not been able to straighten things out with the Pistons. Maybe they could never be straightened out. Maybe.

The search for the next coach of the Pistons took Ed Coil to the point where, seven years earlier, Don Wattrick had ducked. There was a man steeped in NBA experience, a man loaded with NBA expertise, available right in Detroit.

Earl Lloyd was still in town, no longer a token employee in the Pistons' front office, but in the corporate business world of the city. He worked for Chrysler. Coil hired Earl and gave him a week to settle his business matters.

Meanwhile, Terry Dischinger coached the Pistons for two games, against Boston and Milwaukee. The Pistons lost both games. Terry Dischinger entered the Pistons' record book, etched for eternity in the expansive list of coaches, stuck with a career record of 0–2.

Earl Lloyd had served the Pistons with dignity and honor as a player, as an assistant coach, as a scout and as a TV commentator, in a series of regimes, before he was, at last, summoned to solve their manifold problems.

"I'm not a black coach," he said, simply, "I'm a coach who is black . . .

"A lot of people tell you you'd be a great coach. But you don't know until you do it. It's always gnawing at you."

He was forty-three years old, when he returned to pro basketball. He had the usual two-year contract to serve as the Pistons' tenth coach —Dischinger included for his two games. "This is a strange business, you know," he told Halls. "When you sign to coach any professional sport, you're signing your termination papers . . ."

The first black man to play in the NBA, he became the fourth black man to serve as coach. Bill Russell, Al Attles of the renamed Golden State Warriors, and Lenny Wilkens of Seattle were ahead of Lloyd.

"I think all this talk about black athletes being hard to handle is blown out of proportion," Lloyd said. "I don't see black as an issue. This is a professional organization. It's predicated on winning and losing.

"Ed and I didn't talk black and white, green or polka dot. Black and white never entered the conversation with Ed Coil.

"I'll take it a step further. If I thought he was hiring me because I was black, I wouldn't take the job."

Earl Lloyd addressed this issue of handling highly paid ballplayers, the issue that van Breda

Three NBA coaches (from left to right): Bill Russell, Earl Lloyd, and Ray Scott. Russell was the first black NBA coach; Lloyd was the first black player in the NBA; and Scott succeeded Lloyd as coach of the Pistons.

Kolff said drove him to dog-walker duties on the beaches of New Jersey.

"You don't handle people," Lloyd told Pete Waldmeir. "You handle animals. I want to deal with players. If I can do that, I'll have no problems."

Earl Lloyd's belated debut as coach of the Pistons occurred in Cobo Arena on November 10, 1971. He juggled the lineup, returned Dischinger and Butch Komives, who both had been benched by VBK, to the starting lineup.

All the new coach's moves worked. Jimmy Walker had a career night with 31 points. Bob Lanier was immense with 23 points. The Pistons raced up the court and back down it, gunning, shooting, passing. They drubbed the Portland Trail Blazers, 139–122.

And afterwards, Earl Lloyd could barely talk in his postmortem: "I lost my voice the first night . . . You sit on the bench with an eighteen-point lead and seven minutes to go and you still worry."

That was the start.

The Pistons were a team that had a winning record for the first time the previous year. It was a young team, but it was trying to win games without its best player. Without Dave Bing, the Pistons were doomed. The Pistons still had not received the payment due for Otto Moore and Bob Lanier was becoming bedraggled from overwork, and thus, the club was further doomed. So, Earl Lloyd was doomed.

A month after Lloyd took over the Pistons were in a tailspin.

Lloyd raised hell in a closed-door meeting. He lost his temper.

"They've got to have some pride," Lloyd said. "Everybody's got pride."

But not on this ballclub. It was December and the Pistons were quitting so soon in the season.

Earl Lloyd's problems intensified before New Year's. The Pistons were losing, last and dead. The mutiny that had confronted van Breda Kolff the previous season now returned in a form of insidious dissension.

Bing had come back after Christmas, sooner than expected. That put Butch Komives back on the bench.

Then, Lloyd juggled his roster, getting rid of some bench fodder, questing for a winning mix. Three reserve ballplayers were dropped—Steve Mix, Harvey Marlatt and Bob Quick.

One night, in late January 1972, when the

Dave Bing scores 2 of his 15,235 points he accumulated as a Piston on a typical drive. Erwin Mueller is the other Piston shown.

Pistons beat Baltimore for one of the rare victories, Lloyd kept Komives hooked to the bench. It so happened that Komives had a consecutive game streak of 264 games, and on this night it was broken. Fiesty and outspoken, Komives accused Lloyd of racism.

"It should be evident to everyone who's been around," Komives, fuming, told Halls when the game ended. "I'd say he's trying to phase the white players out. I was very pissed off because he broke the streak. But I wasn't surprised. Just look what's happened."

Of the three players released by Lloyd in his brief time as coach, two happened to be Caucasians. Mix and Marlatt.

Komives' gripe ignited an ugly situation in the Pistons' locker room. This was a time of sociological impact in the NBA, once lily white. In the early 1970s, more and more blacks were playing on more and more NBA teams, because they were the more skilled guys.

The Pistons had three white players left, after Lloyd's roster shuffling, and eight blacks. On the night of the dispute, Bing and Jimmy Walker started at guard.

"I used two guards almost 48 minutes each," Lloyd explained when Komives' complaint was relayed to him. Rookie Bunny Wilson, black, went into the game twice, when Lloyd wanted a player to commit deliberate fouls as a strategy measure.

Erwin Mueller and Terry Dischinger were the two white guys on the Pistons, with Komives. Mueller was out hurt on the night in question. Dischinger played much of the game and when asked if he agreed with Komives' opinion that Lloyd was phasing out white players, he responded, tartly: "I'm still playing, so he must not be. Everyone has his own opinion, and if he feels that way, he feels that way."

Mueller said, more tartly: "It's unfortunate his streak ended." The sarcasm oozed.

Said Bing, the team captain: "When Earl was playing him all the time and when van Breda Kolff was playing him, I guess you didn't hear that from him then."

The Pistons' mud hit the fan all over the country. A team that had trouble getting its box scores in the papers in other towns now had all its bitterness and anger heralded in headlines. And on the network news.

"I guess we made big time this time," said Lloyd. "Even NBC's 'Monitor' called me. The phone started ringing at 7:30 in the morning. Radio, newspaper guys. Even some from New York. And people asking me what's going on and telling me not to let it bother me.

"Of course, most of the dudes calling to cheer me up were black guys.

Bing called a team meeting to rattle around the situation. Afterwards, Komives apologized to Lloyd and his teammates. Lloyd took the apology and said: "I want to kill it right here. If you fine or suspend a guy, you give him a sounding board. The more you stir the garbage, the more it stinks."

Then Earl said: "If I wanted to get rid of Howard Komives, I wouldn't have to phase him out. I'd just cut him."

Earl added: "When I played, the whole quota in the league was three blacks. Nobody said nothing."

During these difficult days, Fred Zollner's seats were empty on game nights at Cobo. The Z was now seventy-one and he lived in semi-retirement and semi-seclusion at his beach digs near Miami. He had attended one game during the entire 1971–72 season, and just a couple the season before.

The word was now out that Zollner was encouraging explorers to make offers for his basketball team. There was a price tag on the Pistons. Fred was asking $5 million for the franchise he had started from scratch and brought into the major pro basketball league, the BAA, for a stipend of $25,000.

The 1971–72 season ended at last for the Pistons. It ended the same way it had ended the year before, with the Pistons stuck in last place in the Midwest Division, out of the playoffs. Except this time there were no What-Ifs . . . no rationalization copouts about how mighty the Pistons could have been if their geographical situation had them in another division. After their first season with a winning record in Detroit, the Pistons were back in form. They wound up 26-and-56 and only three other clubs had lousier records. And a huge chunk of fans turned away from the team, again; attendance was off by 2,300 per game to an average of 4,600.

The L.A. Lakers, with Wilt and Jerry West

and Elgin Baylor and a slick-haired mustachioed young player named Pat Riley, won the NBA championship. They beat the Knicks and De-Busschere in the finals, 4 games to 1.

There was a brief wire-service piece in the papers early in the offseason of 1972. The Phoenix Suns had hired a new coach for the next season. He was New Jersey dogwalker named Butch van Breda Kolff.

"I just missed everything about basketball," VBK was quoted as saying. "The game. The competition. The people. I like to win, and you have to fight for your team."

The Pistons were busy in the trademart between seasons. Terry Dischinger, who had completed dentistry school, was dealt away in a three-way trade. Dischinger had issued an ultimatum—"Trade me or else." Or else, I'll retire and drill molars.

The final remnant of Charley Wolf's bizarre regime nearly a decade earlier, Dr. Dischinger went to the Portland Trail Blazers, a struggling young club. The Pistons received Fred Foster in this trade, from the Philly 76ers, who received a draft choice from Portland as their payment.

A day after this trade, the Pistons dealt Jimmy Walker, first player taken in the 1967 NBA draft, to the geographically transplanted Houston Rockets, formerly based in San Diego, for Stu Lantz. Walker had been a sometime starter in Detroit, a sometime behavior problem for the coach, and a sometime companion of Detroit's sweetest young things. But he was never the catalyst the Pistons had hoped.

And late in training camp, the Pistons traded Coach Lloyd's critic, Howard "Butch" Komives, to the depressed Buffalo Braves for a second-round draft choice.

The Z did not peddle his basketball franchise before the 1972–73 season, as had been expected. It was still being offered to selected explorers. There were certain qualifications for the bidders.

"One of the requisites Fred has is that he sell the team to a local group or local individuals," Ed Coil said. "But the price has got to be right, I'm sure. If it's not, I'm just as sure Fred Zollner won't sell. Like he said, he doesn't need the money.

"Fred definitely wants the team to be kept in Detroit."

The new season began with a rotted sense of deja vu. It became a struggle for Earl Lloyd, and after seven games, he got the ziggy as had so many of the Pistons' coaches before him. The Pistons were 2–5 when Lloyd got it.

The new coach was Ray Scott, elevated from assistant coach under Lloyd. The change was orchestrated by Zollner, long distance from Florida. The Z telephoned Ed Coil in Detroit. Coil took a plane to Portland, where he personally defrocked Lloyd and gave Scott his battlefield commission.

"Zollner . . . felt we haven't been playing like we should and that a change was needed," Coil told reporters by phone back in Detroit. "So he made it."

Coil then said he had advised a change in coaches during the past season. The Z had vetoed that.

"He wanted Lloyd to finish out the year."

So in essence, Lloyd had spent the summer as a lame-duck coach. Only he didn't know it.

"Ever since training camp, we seemed to be going backward," Coil said. "The team has been regressing. We have the talent to play better."

It was the same refrain.

Ray Scott became the Pistons eleventh coach.

Scott had come out of Philly as a schoolboy, played two years of college ball at Portland University—and then turned pro with Allentown in the Eastern League. If pro is the accurate word. His pay was thirty-five bucks a game. In the summertime, he played in the Borscht Circuit in the Catskills. It was in the mountains of New York state that Red Auerbach spotted Scott. Red was going to draft Scott for the Celtics. But the Pistons, somehow, heard about it and figured Red always knew what he was doing. So they drafted Scott as a first-rounder in 1961, before the Celtics had a turn. He played most of six seasons in Detroit, averaging 16.0 points per game.

When last seen in prominence with the Pistons, Scott was the forward with the flat trajectory shot who'd wiggled into the doghouse of then-coach Dave DeBusschere. Ray was the Pistons' donation in the slapstick trade with Baltimore for Rudy LaRusso, who refused to play in Detroit. Sonny Dove, the player whom the Pistons finally received in the shape of a trade choice, was a total waste. He had spent two terrible seasons in Detroit before he was sent apacking.

"I'm shocked," Scott told the Detroit press via phone from Portland when queried about his promotion to head coach. The Detroit papers still did not ante up to send their own writers on the road with the Pistons. "There is nothing that Earl has done I can improve on—except win some games."

That, simply, is why Earl Lloyd was not coach of the Pistons anymore. His club hadn't won games. The coach is always vulnerable, when the team loses, even though the players lack the necessities to win games.

Earl Lloyd accepted his scapegoat's role with characteristic grace and class.

"It's the nature of the beast," he told the Detroit press, again via a phone connection from Oregon. "If you're a man you handle it. Basketball has been good to me. I never rapped it coming in and I'm not going to rap it going out . . .

"The guys tried, they hustled. I think Ray needs some help."

Scott, a coach at age thirty-four, showed an immediate knack for his new assignment. As Lloyd had a year earlier, Scott won his first game as coach. He got Bob Lanier inspired, for one thing. Lanier scored 33 points, cleared 15 rebounds and blocked 5 shots. Such heroics make winners out of coaches. The Pistons beat the Trail Blazers 119–111.

Afterwards, Scott showed also he had a penchant for making the quotes that writers like. Asked about replacing Earl Lloyd, his friend and the man who had hired him, Scott said: "It's kind of like your mother-in-law driving over a cliff in your new Cadillac. Bittersweet."

Bittersweet would become a word for Ray Scott to remember.

Earl Lloyd was not alone among NBA coaches to leave his job early in the 1972–73 season. Butch van Breda Kolff had done some meditating about coaching, the attitude of athletes, walking his dog and the whistle-tooting of referees, and chucked his job at Phoenix. His tenure with the Suns lasted a grand total of seven games, just like Earl.

Two days after Ray Scott became coach of the Pistons he negotiated his first trade. The Pistons needed a forward fast and acquired Don Adams from the Atlanta Hawks. The price was a second-round draft choice.

Excerpts from a column, *Detroit News*, November 8, 1972:

There are certain words good for a laugh any time.

If a harassed comedian wants to break up his audience, all he has to do is say "Hoboken." They roar. Or Burbank. Or Hamtramck . . .

Now here's one that'll really make you laugh: "The Detroit Pistons . . . " That's funny. Brings tears to my eyes, my side is knotted up, I can't stop laughing.

The Pistons have been a civic joke for so long the people who know Detroit has a National Basketball Association team immediately guffaw.

Just don't laugh too heartily around Ray Scott.

Scott used to play for the Pistons. The other day they took a contract out on him for execution by appointing him head coach . . . It was an offer Scott couldn't refuse. Except that the club hasn't gotten around yet to telling him the duration of his contract or how much money he's earning.

Oh well, that's standard for a club which has a bookkeeper for a general manager and an owner who never sees it play. The bookkeeper, Ed Coil, wishes he could go back to his ledgers and numbers. The owner, Fred Zollner, has this fetish about canning coaches according to schedule.

Scott was innocently minding his own business as Earl Lloyd's assistant coach a week ago Saturday night when Coil caught up with the Pistons in Portland, Ore. . . .

It seems the players resented Lloyd's chewing them out for atrocious play. They did not like it last year when he criticized them publicly for carousing on the road. They did not like his sarcasm when he said they were so indolent nobody on the club got a floor burn all season.

Since several of the Pistons are locked in with ironclad salaries of $100,000 or more, it was time to fire the coach. Punctual.

Despite the mess piled upon mess, Scott talks of the positive approach.

"Why is there always the connotation THE Pistons?" Scott wondered. "When you refer to them around here it's almost like you're referring to failure. There has to be something positive.

"Every time they are referred to in a derogatory manner. These are human beings, too. Must you always pay for the sins of the past?

"We have 12 guys trying to win and for everybody to refer to them as 'THOSE Pistons' . . . it's unfair to my players. The past haunts them."

. . . "I took the job at the insistence of Earl and Ed Coil," said Scott. "In fact, Earl said, 'You better take it.' There was reluctance pouring out of my ears. I wasn't expecting it. It hit me flat . . . and there was a guy I love losing his job."

Ray Scott . . . is trying valiantly to stem an avalanche of negativism and turn it to something positive. Some day somebody will make the Pistons winners. Ray Scott has all the credentials to do it. No joke.

The Pistons added another player soon after Scott's elevation. John Mengelt came over from the Kansas City-Omaha Kings—another geography lesson courtesy of the NBA—for the draft choice obtained when Komives was traded to the Buffalo Braves. "Crash" Mengelt added fire to the Pistons. He was one player who definitely suffered floor burn.

Fired up, the Pistons now sported a lineup of Curtis Rowe, Don Adams, Lanier, Bing and Chris Ford, a young rookie who had something to learn. This was hardly the nucleus of a contending ballclub. But Scott forced some cohesiveness upon it. And it had a bit of bench depth.

Lanier made it unnecessary for Bing to slip and slide and twist through the towering defenders as much as before. Bob became the top scorer and Bing controled the team on the floor.

"In spots we're immature," Scott said early in his regime. "We make some dumb mistakes. But so does everybody. I don't think it's fair to criticize those mistakes. I say that because most of the mistakes we're making occur when the guys are trying to do the right thing."

Scott was continuing his combat role against negativism.

Yet, he knew there was only one safe, sure method.

The Pistons were not yet blended into winners.

But Scott had managed to give some impetus. The Pistons won 20 of their last 31 games, ending the 1972–73 season with a 5-game winning streak.

They had generated some added interest. Insufficient to add to Zollner's vaults of cash. But sufficient to supply promise for the following season, with that ancient bleat of *next year*. The cry of all losers; the cry of the Pistons.

Not winners, the Pistons had become the symbol of that copout word—*representative*. They completed Scott's first season with a 40–42 record, back, almost, to that *cherished* .500 plateau. Scott himself, after taking over for Lloyd seven games into the season, compiled a 38–37 mark. But as he, and all coaches in the Pistons' legacy have so carefully pointed out, basketball is a team, not an individual, game.

So it was, the Pistons finished third in their Midwest Division, behind Jabbar's Milwaukee club and the Chicago Bulls. But they beat out the Kansas City-Omaha vagabonds (ex-Rochester and Cincinnati Royals), who had been repositioned in the division while Phoenix was moved to Pacific Division.

Scott spoke of the motivation the Pistons had when they finished with the winning streak.

"Here they were at the end of a long season, out of the playoffs, and they all sat around the locker room telling each other they wished the season went on a little longer. They were really succeeding those last couple of months. And they didn't want it to end."

And thinking again what might have been, the New York Knicks, led mightily by the drive of Dave DeBusschere and the guts of Willis Reed, won the NBA championship for the second time in four years.

The Pistons entered the 1973–74 season with this summary:

One season of sixteen with a record that touched .500 or above—in other words, fifteen losing seasons in sixteen tries. One appearance in the postseason playoffs, in a town afflicted with the playoff mentality, in the previous ten seasons.

With a history of flux—whim-spurred coaching firings and hirings; whim-spurred sacrifices of GMs; whim-spurred trades that could only damage; as a moveable franchise that had played home games in four different arenas in the same town; as a franchise on the block, being offered in auction to the highest bidder; as a franchise operated, meanwhile, by a septuagenarian absentee owner.

And Ray Scott's avowed goal was to rid the Pistons of the aura of negativism that surrounded and trapped them.

Another goal! Scott believed he had enough talent on this team to make it into the playoffs, an honor they'd been deprived of even in their single winning season.

"They know this is the elite," Scott said in an interview with Al Stark, a writer for the *News'* Sunday Magazine. "Only eight teams out of seventeen make the playoffs, and if you get past the first round you are only one of four teams left. That's the elite, and they know that, and they want to be part of that."

And the Pistons started off the 1973–74 season as if they had suddenly peddled their souls in exchange for one year as a member of the NBA elite.

Scott was only thirty-five; two years earlier he had been a player himself. Now he sat on the bench and coached with a rare understanding, with a rare wisdom. He had grown a goatee and he could have fit the Hollywood stereotype for a professor. He had to remain separate from his players, although some of them were in their thirties, too, nearly in his age group.

"I'm the cheese," he told me one day.

"The cheese?" I said, incredulous. "How's that?"

"The cheese stands alone," said Ray Scott. So wise, he had resorted to a nursery rhyme to make his mature point.

Whatever method that had failed in prior regimes, Scott learned the knack of handling Lanier and Bing.

The Pistons were winning and appealing to Detroit as they never had before. Don Adams meshed in with Bing and Lanier. Scott had a nickname for Adams—Smart. As in, "Smart, you break for the basket when David reaches the key." Bing teamed in the backcourt with Chris Ford or Stu Lantz or Mengelt, when the Pistons needed a guy to crash into the end court grandstands.

And there were nights at Cobo, now, when those seats had paying bodies sitting in them.

"I can tell you the secret of this team and its success in one word—sacrifice," Scott said one day. "Take Lanier. He could average 30 points a game. He could lead the league in scoring. You ask Bob to be a complete offensive and defensive player, to get the ball now and then to someone else who's open, so the other guy can get a few points, too, and keep his head on right. Sure, Bob can get the ball in the basket. But this way, the other guy, who the team needs, too, feels part of everything.

"Then take Bing. Do you realize that David's lifetime average is 23 points a game? Lifetime! So you go to David and tell him that maybe he won't be scoring as many points because he's going to become a defensive guard and a passing guard.

"You start with your exceptional people when you're trying to get things going in your new direction. If they agree and give it what they have, you might have something.

"If they don't agree, you have chaos . . . "

One day, as the Pistons proved they could play with the Celtics and the Lakers, the Knicks and the Bucks, and the Bulls—with the NBA's acknowledged elite, I wrote a simple column in the *News*. In a fit of boosterism, I suggested in print that Ray Scott, of the eternally rundown Detroit Pistons, deserved to be selected as NBA Coach of the Year.

Ray Scott, we know, read the papers.

How was that for being positive?

Excerpts from a column by the author in the *Detroit News*, December 20, 1973:

Bob Lanier is just like any 6-foot-11 guy who wears size 20 (22?—23?) canoes on his feet, is earning $1.5 million, is black and lives next door.

I say that with gratitude to Wilt Chamberlain, for I have just plagiarized the blurb from his autobiography. But it applies to Bob Lanier . . . he gets lost in the milling crowd, he roams unnoticed in a city which lionizes its hero athletes.

At least, he gets scanty recognition in this town, which is still rather cynical toward professional basketball . . . He's the largest, highest-paid, most-ignored superstar we have in Detroit.

Through his veneer of put-on and jiving, there is some bitterness in Lanier because of this void.

"I started here on a bad foot," he said last night after the Detroit Pistons bumped the Chicago Bulls, 89-87. "I had the bad leg. They thought I'm the super mechanicalman; I'm super human.

"What I mean is people just tend to look at big dudes. People got empathy for little dudes . . . "

Ray Scott (left), the brooding, wise coach, led the Pistons to their first 50-win season (52–30) with the help of Bob Lanier.

So the man is 6-11 and yet he lacks the stature in the city he represents and it grinds him?

"No," Lanier said. "You never get recognition if you don't win. If we win on a consistent level, I'll get recognition."

This is the pat answer . . . and then Lanier dropped a pungent inner feeling.

"If I played in New York, I'd own the town," Lanier said.

It is true. Basketball is a New York sport. The Broadway wise guys, squashing their cigars in their teeth, clog Madison Square Garden when the Knickerbockers play. They comprehend the sophisticated choreography of the game. They are wise to the point spreads and the Garden is, in truth, a gambling hall.

Dave DeBusschere went from Detroit, his hometown, to become a revered celebrity in New York. Walt Frazier is worshipped as a high priest of basketball. Willis Reed is a civic monument on Manhattan.

Bob Lanier has been a better, more valuable basketball player to his team than any of them this year. But this gigantic man who could own New York endures anonymity in Detroit.

Ray Scott, the mystic who coaches the Pistons, oozes optimism about his team—and he has a vision about Bob Lanier.

"He could own this town," said Scott, whose mission is to sell professional basketball to the people of Detroit. "He is the first good big man to come here and he's going to make this town go crazy. He'll own Detroit."

Fred Zollner still had his basketball franchise for sale at a fair market price. In January 1974, The Z was offered $5 million to sell the Pistons to a mixed bag of New Yorkers—diamond and garment merchants and Wall Street lawyers. Five mill was higher than the going price for NBA franchises in 1974.

Zollner wanted it guaranteed that any new owners would keep the Pistons in Detroit. The offer from the New Yorkers did not fly.

But the club, increasing in value, remained for sale.

There were nights of madcap nonsense at Pistons' games in Cobo. Some of the swells from ritzy Bloomfield Hills and Birmingham in the northern suburbs and aristocratic Grosse Pointe to the east showed up in three-piece gray-flannel suits. Going to dinner and having a few pops and then taking in the Pistons' game had become chic in Detroit.

To entertain a larger, more adoring, more suburban clientele, the Pistons picked up some new marketing techniques.

They opened up a postgame watering spot in Cobo and treated their favored customers in the F.O.B. Room. F.O.B. stood for Friends of Basketball, very catchy in an autumobile city, although the F might better have stood for Freeloaders.

Lots of teams had mascots. The Pistons presented a mascot. They dressed a guy in a huge cylindrical encasement that resembled a piston in an auto engine. They called him the Magic Cylinder and had him prance along the court during time outs.

The Magic Cylinder was Jerry Dziedzic, the long-serving equipment guy. Jerry never quite lived down the embarrassment of the experience.

"Yes, it was humiliating," Dziedzic would recall in 1991. "Let's face it, they were trying to generate some interest.

"Out of all the time I spent in that thing, there

was one time that made it worthwhile. It weighed twenty-five pounds. And I couldn't see out of it. I'm on the floor and we're playing the Bulls and they have a bull mascot on the floor at the same time. I feel a bang. And then the bull's hooves are over my face and he's laughing. So I knocked him over and put my foot on his stomach and raised my fist. The crowd went crazy. It was the biggest cheer all night.

"As I said, it weighed twenty-five pounds and I had to take it off to take care of the equipment.

"We had the Magic Cylinder only one season. Then it was retired, into the Mascot Hall of Fame."

Then, there was the attraction of Gus the Vendor, who started his belated dancing career during the giddiness of the 1973–74 season. He was a roly-poly guy with a huge gut and nimble legs, a round red face, and usually the beginnings of a scraggly beard, dressed in a candy-striped blue uniform. He actually worked as a vendor, peddling drinks, programs, whatever, in the upper reaches of the balcony, which for the first time actually had basketball fans sitting there.

"Gus would be hanging over the balcony in Section C," Dziedzic said.

He generally began his act during a time out in the third quarter. The music would start, amplified to a deafening volume, as it always has been in NBA arenas. Gus would start with a wild twist, to the music, as all the spectators below, as all the players on both teams below, would look up and watch his crazy gyrations at the railing of the balcony. Up. Down. Sideways. Until he almost fell over the side and then pulled himself back.

The house went nuts.

The Pistons had discovered, so suddenly, the magic for winning—and in their seventeenth season in Detroit, pro basketball had become fun.

The ghosts from the Pistons' past rattled around in the minds of the newspaper columnists in this rare season. Rod Thorn. Shellie McMillon. Walter Dukes. Larry Staverman. Darral Imhoff. Wayne Hightower. Joe Strawder. Some names vaguely remembered, others that forced up a laugh. They were names of transients, athletes who passed through town and performed. They were the relics of the tragicomical past.

"An era has ended for the Pistons and a new one has begun," I wrote, puffing up my pomposity, in the *News* one afternoon in February 1974. The bandwagon was rolling. Why not jump aboard?

"We knew when the season started we were good," Dave Bing said, "but we didn't know how good. We lost some close games then. We're a better team now than we were when the season started.

"I think we're just as good as any team in the entire NBA!"

The bandwagon was rolling hell bent for leather.

"It is not a case of emotional braggadocio by a frustrated athlete who has excelled for years on a dinky basketball team," I shrieked in print. "It happens to be truth. The slapstick pantomime has been transformed into fine theatrical art."

The words pour now from a yellowish newspaper clipping. Unluckily, you do not write for a newspaper in invisible ink.

But Ray Scott loved the new positive press. And Dave Bing flowed with his true confessions.

He had turned thirty. He was the Pistons' elder statesman. He had been a genuine star on a team clobbered with ridicule and now awash with praise. He had endured the agony of defeat, the agony of injury. And now he spoke with humble candor:

"You're embarrassed when you're down. I don't care how good you are as an individual. It's a team sport. You're part of the team. If you get 30 points and your team loses, you're still a loser.

"The fans . . . have been great and I think we played the way they supported us. I'm glad to be around here when we started winning. A lot of faces come and go. Now we've passed respectability.

"I've seen the team built from the bottom. The team and the front office.

"We've got a very intelligent team. On the road we go out together. There's a closeness."

I likened Dave Bing, in print, to another Detroit sports star who had been deprived throughout his career. Al Kaline was finishing up his years with the Tigers. Kaline would collect his 3,000th big league hit and later go into the Baseball Hall of Fame in Cooperstown just as

Dave Bing would, one day, go into the Basketball Hall of Fame in Springfield, Massachusetts. Kaline, so late in his career, had reached the World Series in 1968. There had been stardom and laurels and personal applause. But there had been no ultimate victory, until one year it finally happened—and now the comparison was being made between Kaline and Bing.

"I can't say I'm excited," Bing said. "I had a lot of patience waiting for this to happen. I'm happy for myself. There's a selfish motive."

The Pistons finished the regular season over .500 for the second time since Fred Zollner had moved them to Detroit from Fort Wayne. That was the longtime goal, to finish over .500, and this season the Pistons finished 22 games above their old standard. They were 52 and 30, and now there was another standard of measurement for them, a much more difficult objective.

"I think we've got as good a chance as any to win it all," said Bing.

Despite their glittering record, the Pistons still won fewer games than the Bucks and Bulls from their own division. Detroit was one of elite eight teams included in the playoffs, as the NBA went to a wildcard system. Only three clubs in the entire league won more games than the Pistons. It was the first time in six years they reached the playoffs.

Their opponents in the first round would be Chicago. The Pistons and the Bulls pretty much hated each other. The rival coaches, Ray Scott and Dick Motta, were more than rival coaches. There was an ingrained dislike between the men. Scott, dignified, brooding, vs. the preening, smaller, cockier Motta, who himself had built a strong basketball team with patience and knowledge.

The matchups seemed quite balanced. But the Bulls would have the home-court advantage in the best-of-seven conference semifinal series with four games in the creaky, cobwebbed Stadium situated on the West Side of Chicago.

It was a hard, tough area, as everybody living in the neighborhood well knew. One twelve-year-old had more passionate loyalties than most, in favor of his home team. Already he was developing his skills and an imagination that fancied himself, some day, playing in such an NBA series for the beloved Bulls—maybe against the despised Pistons. It was pretty much all the boy,

Isiah Lord Thomas III, could think about in the springtime of 1974.

It was a time when the Tigers were in the doldrums, the Red Wings were suffering from ineptitude and apathy and the Lions were perennial failures. Detroit needed to embrace a winner. And the Pistons, the once upon a time number four guys in town, supplied that love object. The Pistons drew 300,000 fans at Cobo over a season for the first time.

The Pistons went into the Chicago Stadium on March 30, 1974, cast as heavy underdogs in their first playoff game in six years—the first of Bob Lanier's career. It was a brutal defensive game that provided entertainment for America—and in the end, Lanier and Bing won the game, on the road, 97–88. The Pistons had captured the home-court advantage, which was supposed to be something special.

The teams traveled the 250 miles for the second game in Detroit. There had never before been quite a night such of this in Cobo Arena. The place was packed. The Magic Cylinder did his routine and then rushed back to the locker room to make sure all the water bottles were full. Gus wondered where he might find footspace for his dance. The Arena was festooned with slogans on banners and pennants.

One banner that somebody hung over the side of the balcony said, simply: "Muck Fotta."

"That's not very nice," said Scott.

The game began and the defense wasn't quite as tight as it had been in Game 1. The Pistons had some problems before their enrapt home crowd on their own court. They struggled. Scott called a time out.

We meditated in the press row, waiting for time in, for the game to resume. I was sort of dozing when I looked up, toward a passageway in a corner of the grandstands. In my reverie, I was not quite thinking of this, but I had always realized that America was a nation of fads. Such fashionable crazes as the hoola hoop and the leisure suit and the miniskirt had captivated the people. The fad in the nation, at the time of this playoff game, consisted of stripping off one's garments down to the bare skin and then dashing, before a shocked mob of fellow citizens, in an arena, on a city street, in a ballpark. It was called streaking—a unisex sort of event.

Well, during this time out, as Ray Scott lectured the Pistons, a streaker—a male streaker, by the look of things—dashed through the runway and out into the grandstands, a huge grin. On his face.

The cops tackled him.

But the streaker upstaged the Pistons on this April night. The Bulls won, 108–103, to knot the series. Home court had meant piddle, so far.

But now it did. Back in Chicago, the Pistons were edged 84–83, in Game 3. In Detroit again, the Pistons won, 107–87. The series was tied at two games apiece. Back in Chicago, the Bulls won for the third time, 98–94, in a game in which the Pistons once had been down behind 25 points. If the Pistons were not quite as elite as the Bulls, they did prove their mettle.

"For a team to be down 25 points and come back the way we did has to show you something," said Don Adams, Smart, as Scott called him. "It would have been easy for us to cop out now."

Game 6 was back in Detroit. The Pistons were at the edge, one game from elimination, after all they'd endured, after all the hope and promise.

Before the game, the NBA held a ceremony on the court. Ray Scott was handed a trophy, as the duly selected NBA Coach of the Year.

Excepts from a column by Jerry Green in the *Detroit News*, April 12, 1974:

The Trophy is a rather garish and grotesque hunk of metalwork, really . . . two tiers, four columns at the corners and a half dozen or so figurines holding basketballs.

It was richly deserved by the recipient, though—for his intellect, his handling of athletes and his patience and subtlety in disposing of foolhardy questions.

Ray Scott raised aloft his bric-a-brac—it resembles a miniature of a Roman monument. The multitudes emitted a thunderous roar of approval. Then to hush the din, Ray Scott hugged his trophy and deposited it purposefully at my station at the courtside table.

Right on . . .

"I thought you deserved it," said Ray Scott, using his deepest sarcasm, "you and Frank Saunders from the Michigan Chronicle. You and Frank said early in the year I should be Coach of the Year."

Ray Scott has his trophy as the National Basketball Association Coach of the Year back today. You see, if anybody could have doubted his qualifications for the prestigious award, Scott quashed those minority dissidents last night.

There was a masterpiece of a coaching job performed at Cobo Arena, where the Pistons were enmeshed in all those frightening cliches . . . backs to the wall, no tomorrow, doomsday, fighting to stay alive, and such rot.

Scott coaches, when it is necessary, by a lottery shuttle. He takes out Stu Lantz and shuttles in Chris Ford. He yanks Curtis Rowe and shuttles in George Trapp. And vice versa.

Last night in the must (ah) 92–88 playoff victory over the Chicago Bulls, Scott wound up the game by using offensive and defensive platoons. As the clubs pattycaked through the last hectic 45 seconds there were four strategy time outs.

When the Pistons had possession of the basketball, Scott used his three guard offense. The plan was to ballhandle and expend time. Then when the Bulls got the ball back Scott yanked Lantz and put in Trapp to create a three-forward defense.

It was all very brainy and very successful. And this was one reason why Scott was coach of the year.

So, by winning Game 6 in front of their home fans, 11,134, the Pistons set up the most critical game in the sixteen years they'd played in Detroit. They were square again with the Bulls and Motta. Game 7 would be decisive. One game, the winner goes into the next series, the loser is out, done for the season, TV spectators, with extra time to figure plans for next year. Always that next-year cliche.

"Las Vegas had made Chicago a 5-to-1 favorite when this thing began," Scott said. "I think Chicago thought it would win the championship this year.

"Some people in Chicago thought this could be a piece of cake . . . and they're choking on it."

Game 7 was scheduled for Saturday afternoon in Chicago Stadium. CBS-TV set it up as its NBA Game of the Day. The neighborhood kids taunted the Pistons as the bus pulled up in the asphalt parking lot outside the players/press entrance.

It was April 13, 1974, and inside the grimy Stadium, it was hot and choking humid.

Ray Scott sat at courtside before the game for a taped interview. Then the CBS producer informed him of the exact second the game would start. Scott nodded. He had his team in a situation it had never been in ever before, and he understood that TV established many of the rules.

What TV could not control was the amount of drama.

This was the Bulls' homecourt, and they were the stronger team. They were playing without their best guard, Jerry Sloan, who was hurt, causing Motta to moan.

But even so, the Bulls soared. They were in command, early. They were turning the game into a rout. Clifford Ray, their center, was neutralizing Bob Lanier. The Bulls were ahead by 14 points in the second quarter. They were ahead by 19 in the third quarter. The Stadium jumped with its sardined 13,000 fans. But who knows? Across America, TV sets had to be clicking. Either to off, or to the baseball game on the other channel.

Game 7, with the Bulls in front 64–45, had been devoid of drama.

It was then that Dave Bing started working the ball inside to Lanier and to Trapp. Lanier went in quickly; Trapp hit a jumper. Lantz drove through the key.

And one more time, at the edge and confronted with all those other cliches, the Pistons rallied. They sliced away all 19 points of the Bulls' lead. With 2:04 to play, Lanier sank two free throws. The score was tied 92–92.

Chet Walker put the Bulls back in front with a basket. Bing missed a shot. Norm Van Lier made two free throws for the Bulls, and their lead was back to 96–92. With twenty-eight seconds left, Bing scored, and the Pistons cut it to 96–94.

Now the Bulls had the ball again. They ran the entire twenty-four seconds off the clock without shooting.

And the Pistons received the ball, out of bounds near midcourt, with three seconds left, and time to tie the score and take this series into overtime in the seventh game.

Scott called time out. At the bench, the CBS cameras, now catching every ounce of drama, focused in on the bearded coach. He set up the play: Bing to inbound the ball, get it worked to Lanier, for the vital shot.

Motta, at the Chicago bench, sent his second center, Dennis Awtrey, into the game to provide twin towers with Ray on defense.

Excerpts from a story in the *Detroit News*:

David Bing stood at the inbounds line with the basketball in his hands and three seconds left to influence history.

The Pistons were down by two on the enemy court in Chicago. It was Game 7 in a playoff series punctuated by unexpected heroics and surprise endings. Now it was all reduced to three seconds in Game 7, winner to advance, loser to be eliminated. The Pistons had this final chance for the last shot, tie the score, force the game into overtime, beat the Bulls.

So many details flashed across your mind as you looked across the court at Chicago Stadium and watched the dignified Bing with the ball in his fingers.

He had joined the Pistons in 1966 . . . and in his eight seasons, he had been in the NBA playoffs just once before . . . And the ne'er-do-well Detroit club had not won a playoff series in 16 years, since 1958, the first season in Detroit . . .

And now there were the three seconds left, an entire season dwindled to one play. Bing readied to inbound the ball. Then he lobbed his pass. Awtrey, standing in front of him, flapping long arms, leaped and flicked the ball. Norm Van Lier, the Bulls' quick guard, grabbed it. He dribbled away the last seconds with it. The Pistons had lost, 96–94.

Ray Scott met the press in the bowels of the Stadium, in a dim corridor. Inside, behind a closed green door, in the locker room, grown men sobbed because they had been a single basket from magnificence. Scott sucked in a deep breath and delivered his eulogy in soft, somber voice.

"I told them I'm proud of the year we had," Scott said in the corridor, "proud of the things they've done in the eighteen months I've been coach. I told them not to forget about the things we've done because next year we can be better. And I'm proud of them,"

Dick Motta, a pipsqueak of a man and coach of the Bulls, pushed through the assemblage.

"Ray, I'd like to talk to your team," said

Motta. He slammed the green door behind him and held it shut.

When Motta finished, Scott allowed the writers into the tomb of a locker room. David Bing, in his depression, reconstructed Motta's speech to a defeated enemy.

"Good luck. You didn't play dirty. The best team was knocked out of the playoffs."

Motta's speech did not dry the tears. This had been a bitter, angry, physical series that went seven brutal games. A deflected pass and one basket were the difference.

"Much as I dislike Motta, it was a helluva thing to come over here," said brainy Don Adams.

It was written that the Pistons departed with honor. And again, the Pistons had to look ahead to next year.

Motta was right about the better team losing the Detroit-Chicago series. The Bucks blew the Bulls out in a four-game sweep in the next series. Then the Celtics, rebuilt, beat Jabbar and the Bucks, 4 victories to 3, in the NBA finals of 1974.

Before the next season started, in midsummer, Fred Zollner peddled the Pistons. The Z was seventy-three. He had seen the sport he imported to Detroit grab a hold on the city. The selling price was $8.125 million, a fair return on his original franchise fee of $25,000.

Now Zollner told Bill Halls: "If I was twenty years younger, I wouldn't have sold the team."

The franchise had been for sale for several years. And when Fred sold it, it was to an eleven-member group of Detroit industrialists, professional men, and sportsmen led by Bill Davidson, multimillionaire head of Guardian Industries. Included in the group were Oscar Feldman, Herb Tyner, Ted Ewald, Warren Colville—all prominent in Detroit, all basketball lovers.

Funny, after looking hither and yon Zollner sold the club to Davidson.

"Bill Davidson is a neighbor of mine in Golden Beach," The Z said, "and I think he'll take care of the franchise in the same manner that I took care of it.

"This is like searching all over the world for a bride and ending up marrying the girl next door."

Something like it, anyway.

Zollner had been a force in the league for twenty-eight years, one of the pioneers. The men whom he had favored so many times with his generosity, with his support, who in turn rejected his attempt to draft Cazzie Russell, to obtain equity in disputed trades, now were overwhelming with their praise.

"He was the last of his breed," said Walter Kennedy, the league commissioner. "Without Fred there wouldn't have been an NBA. He gave his money and a sense of stability to the league."

Then the NBA governors unanimously approved the sale to Davidson and confederates and presented Zollner with an award for meritorious service.

There were two financial matters settled under the new management. Before the 1974–75 season began, the owners refused to renegotiate David Bing's contract and they refused to renegotiate Don Adam's contract; but they agreed to renegotiate Ray Scott's.

Scott was given a three-year contract, in the range of $70,000 to $80,000 a year plus additional powers beyond the authority of coach. He was made director of player personnel, in essence assuming the talent-procurement responsibilities of the general manager.

Actually, Scott's new deal was the last vestige of Zollner's ownership. Zollner had promised to rewrite Scott's existing contract when Ray won the Coach of the Year trophy the previous spring. Scott's new contract was written into the sale agreement by The Z.

Bing and Adams, meanwhile, held out to get their contracts rewritten. Bing had a contract for two more years, but he believed he deserved a better arrangement because of his status on the team and the team's elevated status in the league. Adams felt his contributions during 1973–74 merited a better deal.

As the two dissidents skipped training camp, Scott tried to prepare his team for the 1974–75 season. He figured it would be a season in which the Pistons could make a serious run at first place in the Midwest Division and do some winning in the playoffs and, perhaps, reach the NBA finals.

Things were happening around the rest of the NBA. In Portland, the Trail Blazers, still expansion fresh and struggling, fired their coach of two seasons. Apparently, he didn't have the right stuff. Or the right players. So the fired coach, a man named Jack McCloskey, moved onward. It was McCloskey's misfortune that the Trail Blazers did not sign the right player until he became a goner. The very same month McCloskey was booted out the Trail Blazers signed Bill Walton to play center for them.

Meanwhile, Kareem Abdul-Jabbar was becoming disillusioned with the joys of Milwaukee. He was figuring out ways to escape.

And in its continued scheme to take the pleasures of pro basketball to all the towns and hamlets of America, the NBA situated an expansion team in the city of New Orleans. The man appointed to coach the brand new New Orleans Jazz was Scotty Robertson.

Dave Bing's holdout ploy was doomed when he started it; his contract was firm and valid. He and Adams rejoined the team. Dave was not happy. Davidson was upset. He was a business wizard, in the glass and photography businesses. He was a tough negotiator. But he was new at dealing with the brooding moods of athletes and the quirks of sports business. Davidson soured on Dave Bing.

And Ray Scott, the Cheese standing alone, soured on Dave Bing and Don Adams.

It was not starting well for the Pistons in 1974–75.

Despite the contractual unpleasantries, Bing spent the season etching his name into the league's record book. In November, he passed Dave DeBusschere and Jerry Lucas on the scoring lists, with his 14,054th point. He was in the NBA's Top Twenty All-Time Scorers. The next target was Bill Russell. Bing passed Russell in January, then he passed Richie Guerin to move into the eighteenth spot, all time. In March, against the Knicks, he reached the 15,000-point milestone.

But these were individual heroics.

Ray Scott's team was struggling. The Cheese, indeed, was alone. There was considerable sulking among the players.

The successes of the previous season became a bewildering memory. The Pistons were back to being a team that aspired to hit .500. They had severe problems winning on the road. Oh, they did manage to win a road game in Portland early in 1974–75. The club would win its next game there, in the glass arena in Portland, sixteen years later, in a Sunday playoff game in the NBA finals of 1990.

But in one stretch in early 1975, the Pistons lost fourteen straight games on the road.

In mid-February, with the season vanishing, with a five-game losing streak and ten losses in eleven games, Scott made his decision to shake up the club. He had the authority of director of player personnel, and he cut Don Adams from the roster. Adams was furious at being dropped.

The players were shaken and all but one remained glumly silent. Dave Bing was the captain, the elder statesman of the team. So Bing, speaking for all, stated that Adams had been made the scapegoat for the team's misfortunes. Bing said it for public consumption. And when he read the new negativism in the papers, Ray Scott was ticked off.

"They're a bunch of party boys," added Ed Coil, the GM.

The surprise cashiering of Adams did not correct the Pistons' troubles. They continued to lose, always on the road, it seemed. Then they went into New Orleans in mid-March and beat the Jazz, the sadsack new team in the league.

By then, of course, the first-year Jazz had verified their credentials as an NBA franchise. They did what all NBA clubs historically do when the players cannot shoot, and dribble basketballs off the tops of their sneakers. They fired the coach, Scotty Robertson. Scotty got the New Orleans version of the ziggy after the fifteenth game in the franchise's history. Elgin Baylor handled the Jazz for one game, also a loss, as coach pro tem. Then the Jazz, 1–16, introduced their permanent, sort of, coach.

Butch van Breda Kolff said it was great to be back coaching a team in the NBA. "The fans are great," said Butch of the people who went to watch basketball in New Orleans.

His comments about Bourbon Street were, unfortunately, not preserved for history.

The Pistons, in a season-long decline with new ownership and locker room friction and sagging morale, missed making it to .500. They wound up 40-and-42, 12 games below the achievement of the previous season. It was an embarrassment in a season in which they had the best attendance (averaging nearly 7,500 a game) since the move to Detroit.

But there are those ironies in this sport. In an effort to honor mediocrity, the NBA had expanded the group of playoff qualifiers from eight to ten clubs for 1975. Losing record and all, finishing third in their division, the Pistons made the playoffs. Milwaukee had collapsed from first to last and finished below Detroit.

The Pistons drew the Seattle Supersonics in a best-of-three first round series. In a five-day span, the Pistons flew to Seattle and lost, flew back to Detroit and won, then flew back to Seattle to lose again.

They were out of it, so quickly; no bitter, angry, physical, brutal series this year; no nearness to magnificence. No honor.

The season would end with the Golden State Warriors—a BAA original in Philadelphia thirty seasons earlier and the league's first champions in 1946, that had later played out of San Francisco and eventually ensconced in Oakland —winning the NBA finals in a four-game sweep over the Washington Bullets, who in fifteen years had been the Chicago Packers, the Chicago Zephyrs, the Baltimore Bullets, and the Capital Bullets.

In this league, the Pistons were not the only franchise on the lam.

After the season ended, Bill Davidson said, openly, he did not want Dave Bing on his ballclub any longer. He said the Pistons would trade Bing before the 1975–76 season. Davidson was not the kind of man who changes his mind over a matter of sentiment.

The trade rumors persisted all summer.

It happened the final week of August, 1975, the twenty-eighth, with the summer heat shimmering in a city already sickened by the Tigers' twenty-game losing streak. The Pistons dumped Dave Bing. They traded him to the Washington Bullets, a team that had been to the NBA finals the previous spring. They got Kevin Porter, six years younger than Bing, in exchange. But Davidson and Scott were so eager to get rid of Bing they sweetened their part of the exchange by including the Pistons' No. 1 draft choice for 1977 in the deal.

And rather ironically, they had to beg Bing for his approval of the trade. A clause written in the contract the Pistons' ownership had chosen not to renegotiate gave Bing the power to veto any trade involving him.

Excerpts from a column by Jerry Green in the *Detroit News*, August 28, 1975:

David Bing played with a gusto that made basketball an appealing sport in Detroit.

He was an immense player and the games for the first time were fun because he played with sweet skills. The assisting passes were the sweetest . . . Bing dribbling downcourt, thump, thump, on the hardwood . . . and like lightning, the open man was catching the ball underneath and the layup became so simple . . .

There was no sweet talk from Bing in Washington last night when we conversed on the telephone. The bitterness and angers of last season persisted . . . joined with the new joy of belonging to a contending club.

"I'm feasting," said the departed Bing, whose reward was a new contract from the Washington Bullets. "Like just after the big hunt, you make the kill and you have the feast."

He spoke hotly of the new owners of the Pistons, the syndicate which paid $8 million for the privilege of making silly decisions.

"They did me a helluva favor," Bing said. "They've done the city of Detroit and my former teammates a helluva disservice."

There were two issues of dispute: Bing's abortive efforts to renegotiate his lucrative contract last year and the midwinter firing of Don Adams. Those caused the severing of Bing's friendship with Ray Scott, the Socratic coach who had welded a contending club.

"I don't give a damn about management," Bing said last night.

"I'm a strong man and I've got backbone and I'm not kissing anybody's tail to make money.

"They don't want people to be men. They don't want people to have dignity.

"Ray? Maybe he does what management tells him. But then he doesn't have backbone.

"Two years ago we had the best team in the club's history, and now three starters are gone. I'm gone. Don Adams is gone. And Stu Lantz. And it's a good thing for Curtis Rowe that he's on the last year of his contract because he wants to leave."

The Pistons historically have made atrocious trades because of vindictiveness or stumbling stupidity. They pathetically banished George Yardley, Gene

Shue, Bailey Howell, Don Ohl, Joe Caldwell, Ray Scott himself, Dave DeBusschere and Jimmy Walker. Never in these exchanges did they receive proper value.

Now Bing has been exiled to Washington in anger. The Pistons' other trades of caliber players were more feeble. For Bing, the Pistons received Kevin Porter. He is a pugnacious little guy who is a marksman and he is six years younger than Bing. He may never be as sweetly stylish, but he is a worthwhile addition.

To compensate for the age disparity, the Pistons also awarded the Bullets a No. 1 draft choice for 1977 delivery. The Pistons are so wasteful.

"They're paying a helluva price to get rid of me," Bing said. "They must think I'm a troublemaker or a helluva bad ballplayer."

The other evening two men sat up through the night and talked. Bob Lanier and Dave Bing.

"Bob came over to my house and tried to talk me out of leaving," said Bing, whose contract contained a trade-veto clause.

Now Lanier remains alone in the lineage of stars the Pistons have owned—Yardley and Shue and Howell and DeBusschere and Bing.

"Tell Bob to be careful," said Dave Bing, who played here with gusto."

The day after Dave Bing was sent into exile, the Pistons held a press conference to welcome Kevin Porter. Porter, 5 feet 11, out of St. Francis of Loretto, Pennsylvania, had led the NBA in assists the previous season.

"He's an excellent fast-break player," Scott said. "He's a winner.

"We always want to trade a lead guard for a lead guard."

Porter was a sack of movements, energetic, electric, to the edge of being jittery. Hypertense, it seemed. Angry, perhaps.

"Coach Scott has a lot of trust in me and I'm going to give it all I got," Porter told the Detroit writers. "Pressure, I think that's what basketball's all about. We want to get out and run, and that's my game. "I think I'm the best penetrater and passer in the game."

There were some people in Detroit who thought that was the description for David Bing.

The Pistons opened the 1975–76 season in late October. Herbie Brown, outfitted in his new wardrobe, had waltzed and jitterbugged through training camp and the preseason games. Herbie was showing up as the foil to Ray Scott, supposedly the head coach.

To Scott's dignity, Brown provided shrieking. To Scott's mystic cynicism, Brown offered a lack of subtlety. To Scott's controlled poise, Brown displayed a horrid temper and uncontrolled emotion. To Scott's pro basketball savvy and experience, Brown presented a travelogue.

There was no doubt, in my mind, that Herbie Brown was gunning for Ray Scott's job from the day he arrived in Detroit in a bum's duds.

One night as the Pistons barnstormed through exhibition season, Scott stood in the locker room, in a sullen mood.

"Well, it's different," I said to him.

"What do you mean?" Scott said.

"The Cheese no longer stands alone," I said. "You've got an assistant coach now."

Scott reflected for about five seconds, a response spinning through his mind.

"I was an assistant coach once," he said, the words carefully measured. "The Cheese always stands alone."

He disregarded any idea that he might be in jeopardy.

But the notion persisted here that the Pistons must be immediately successful with the start of the season or that Scott would no longer toil as the franchise's coach. It was a valid notion in Detroit. This was the method, repeatedly, in professional sport in the city. Most certainly with the Pistons.

Such an abuse to Scott would be a tragedy, it was written. Ray was the most successful coach in the franchise's history. Indeed, he alone, among the eleven coaches of this organization since it relocated in Detroit, had managed his athletes sufficiently well to have a winning record. But the sport/business was ruthless and its rationale was based on current events. So the eloquent Scott was logically declared, as the 1975–76 season opened, vulnerable for the ziggy. There was an aura of insecurity around the man, or so it seemed.

"We brainstorm, brainstorm," Scott said

"Feelings of security or insecurity come from winning or losing on the floor. I feel very good about myself. I feel very good about my situation. We are building toward a secure situation.

"If you think that builds an insecure situation, you're crazy."

The moot point was whether the Pistons, under Scott, could win with the frequency to satisfy the hungers of the business-mogul ownership headed by Bill Davidson. Scott was the lone policymaker, a year later, to survive from the regime of Fred Zollner. Ed Coil had left, gone back to Fort Wayne and the corporation, while his wife grew roses in Bob Lanier's boot. Oscar Feldman, lawyer by profession and high in the syndicated ownership hierarchy, took the title of GM. Other changes were made in the publicity department and in the office staff. Even the old trainer had been sacked.

"I think we have departments that are necessary," Scott said. He was stamping his approval on the manifold office changes. "It's not a stopgap thing. It's not run by people who are striving to get to a higher plateau.

"It becomes a very pressured situation, trying to win games because we have a revamped organization. Everything is discussed among us from the standpoint: Will it be successful or will it be unsuccessful? You sit down, and it's discussed among all departments.

"That's the way we do it—we brainstorm.

"Davidson is going to make this team damn successful."

Around the league, there was a new commissioner and proof that it was not impossible to escape from Milwaukee.

Lawrence O'Brien replaced Walter Kennedy as commissioner. O'Brien, before he went into the business of governing tall, angular, overrich guys who jump and sweat, had been adviser to Presidents Kennedy and Johnson. He once had been boss of the Democratic National Committee, when Democrats actually could be voted into the White House. Now he made sure the 24-second clocks worked on time and that the referees weren't too abused.

The other major shift featured Kareem Abdul-Jabbar, the league's prize player. Kareem begged to be traded out of Milwaukee, where he had won one championship, to either the Lakers or Knicks. He preferred New York, because that's where he grew up to be 7 feet 1⅜ inches in height. The Bucks traded him to the Lakers.

He was out of the Pistons' division.

And in the beginning, the Pistons responded by moving into first place in the Midwest. They could handle opponents. On opening night against the Lakers, Bob Lanier handled Jabbar. Bob scored 41 points.

Excerpts from a column in the *Detroit News* by the author, December 3, 1975:

Bob Lanier curled his 6 feet 11 inches into a courtside seat that costs ordinary citizens $7 and will cost eight bucks after New Year's.

The practice sessions were over, lights had been cut and Lanier was observing some stragglers finish their schoolyard frolic of one-on-one.

Lanier, when the mood strikes, can be Othello, the brooding Moor, and he has been suffering from an aching knee. There are times of joy for him, too, when he is healthy. Then he is glib and puckish.

This should have been one of those pleasant times because the Pistons have begun to dominate their division. They are a first-place team in a town which needs one.

On this night in Cobo Arena he was part Othello, part a giant Puck—not the sarcastic joker of other times, but not totally morose, either.

There are been hard feelings on the Pistons. A year ago this team was torn by the infidelity of certain people.

Now the old camaraderie has been restored.

Lanier was a confidant of the exiled David Bing, the cause of much of the trouble. Lanier himself was said to be an accuser of Coach Ray Scott, whose fragile psyche had been bruised by the skirmishing.

"Ain't no doubt there's harmony here again," Lanier said as the basketball thumped in the game on the floor.

Lanier had been an outspoken critic when the Pistons tried to trade Bing in punishment for his indiscretions. But now Lanier is a diplomat. He does not fault his friend, Bing, for last year's tumult, yet you sense that he believes it. And he praises the contributions of Kevin Porter, whom the Pistons got from Washington for Bing.

"We bolstered ourselves at the position—guard—that we were weakest at," Lanier said in what sounded like the start of a shot. But he pirouetted.

"I'm not saying David was the weak link. Kevvy gives you that generalship as David did. But he finds the open man as good as anybody in the league."

Scott, dressed like a Russian professor, came into the darkened arena. He stood, imperiously, wearing a fur-collared coat, and he carried a briefcase stuffed with papers about basketball theory and philosophy.

There was banter between the coach and star player. There had been some friction last year.

"You yourself were his critic last year," said the person sitting with Lanier.

"No," he said and he did not seem angry. "People say a lot of things about people when they're successful. Envy takes over. Then when you start losing a negative atmosphere takes over.

"Everybody gets off in a corner and if you can't degrade a player, you degrade a coach. It's a bitch for a coach with contract disputes among his players, the problems we had here last year. I wouldn't want to change places.

"I don't agree on everything with Ray. But he gives you a chance to speak. He might say bleep you, but at least he's given you the chance to speak before saying bleep you.

"He did have to win. I think he's gained back the confidence of the players. He is relating.

"Everybody believes in Ray Scott again. That's because he's done what he had to do, get people prepared mentally and ready to play."

Scott, who began this season in insecurity, has been vindicated. There is harmony. Bob Lanier says so. And there is some help in the coaching for Herb Brown, the new assistant. Lanier says Brown has strengthened the Pistons in fundamentals.

Tonight Lanier has another duel with the forbiding Kareem Abdul-Jabbar of the Los Angeles Lakers. Their meeting spurred Lanier to a 41-point output last time.

"I'm not average," Lanier said, "and he's more not average than I am."

The new owners raised ticket prices at New Year's 1976—and the Pistons went through another spell of the staggers. Afflicted by injuries, their offense damaged with Kevin Porter among the casualties, the Pistons skidded through a period in which they lost 19 of 25 games. Porter

Coach Herbie Brown, dressed for success, calls one of his plays.

had wrecked a knee and was gone for the reason. Before the month was over, the new management delivered its first coaching ziggy.

Ray Scott got his the last week of January. In the middle of practice. With his executioners marching onto the court, stripping him of his silver whistle, and marching him off the court. They did it all to him, except offer him a blindfold and last cigarette.

In the end, The Cheese still stood alone.

But Herbie Brown was the new Cheese.

And Ray Scott admitted his neglect in not listening to the warnings that he was in jeopardy, that he was vulnerable right between the shoulder blades. Scott had, it was written, contributed more than any human to the ultimate popularity of pro basketball in Detroit.

The excuse offered by Oscar Feldman was that there had been a communications breakdown between Scott and the players. The new owners had not been successful in business and the professions without smarts. They were quick studies. They'd learned the proper cliche for canning an unwanted coach in a little bit more than one year.

The Pistons were 17-and-25 when Herbie Brown took over as the club's twelfth coach in twenty seasons. He changed everything; the plays, the numbering system, the atmosphere, the attitudes. Scott had been stoic and intellectual. Brown was wild and flamboyant.

His wildness and flamboyance soon scratched the nerves of his players.

The ranting and raving of the new coach started to pound at the mood-ridden Lanier. Bob, simply, could not figure out Herbie Brown.

It became a joke.

The Pistons had so much talent, with Lanier and Curtis Rowe and Eric Money and Chris Ford, they qualified for the playoffs despite the idiosyncrasies of their new coach and the absence of Porter. The record was not distinguished —36–46 for the season. But it was enough for second place in a division won by Milwaukee with a 38–44 record, two games better than the Pistons.

Detroit did manage to eliminate the Bucks in three games in the first round of the playoffs, as Lanier winked at the press row while Brown ranted. But then the reigning champion Golden State Warriors dumped the Pistons out in six games of a best-of-seven.

It was enough for the new owners to bring Herbie back for another season, ignoring his squawks that he had earned a longer contract.

The season finished with another championship for the Celtics, now coached by Tom Heinsohn and captained by John Havlicek. Red Auerbach had rebuilt the Celtics pretty much from scratch around another marvelous center, Dave Cowens. The Celts beat the upstart Phoenix Suns, formed twenty plus years after the Pistons, in the NBA finals in six games.

Pro basketball's geography underwent another revision during the bicentennial summer of 1976. The American Basketball Association—the league that shot red, white and blue basketballs —had fought the NBA for nine years. They pirated each others players, battled each other for rookies, and forced salaries to rise and explode.

The ABA had gotten itself some prominent athletes. Julius Erving, Moses Malone, David Thompson, Artis Gilmore, Marvin Barnes. But the league was so shaky, the NBA seemed sophisticated in comparison. The final ABA season, the league attempted to add a team called the Baltimore Claws. The Claws had no money to support them. The ABA's young commissioner ruled that the Claws could not operate and unilaterily folded the franchise by decree before

it ever pumped up a basketball. That commissioner's name was Dave DeBusschere.

The NBA decided to annex four clubs from the ABA for a franchise indemnity of $3.2 million apiece. The four additions were the Denver Nuggets, San Antonio Spurs, Indiana Pacers, and New York Nets. The fee left the Nets so strapped they had to peddle their best player, Julius Erving, to the 76ers in order to operate in their first year in the NBA.

The remaining ABA players, not on the four teams merged into the NBA, were tossed into a pool for a dispersal draft, actually a money-raiser. The Pistons had the fourth pick in the go-around. They were torn between two players who had belonged to the ABA's Spirits of St. Louis.

Examining the roster, and the statistics, they saw Moses Malone, a powerful, young giant, with a physique and work ethic ideal for the NBA. Then, of course, the Pistons drafted Marvin Barnes, 6 feet 9 and occasionally inclined to use his huge talent. The price tag was only a half million bucks.

The Pistons' owners might have been the new guys on the block—but that did not mean the old suicidal traditions would change. It seemed, when Marvin "Bad News" Barnes came to Detroit, that the franchise would remain slapstick forever.

Marvin Barnes, out of Providence College and U.S. District Court, was overjoyed that the Pistons had so much faith in him that they spurned Moses Malone.

"I'm going to get my game together early, two months early, and I'm going to be ready," Bad News (Call Me News) Barnes told the *Detroit News'* reporter, Vartan Kupelian, when reached on the phone dispersal draft day in early August of 1976.

Reaching him by phone was never too much of a problem. Barnes had thirteen telephones in his apartment in St. Louis.

"I'm very pleased," he said into one of them. "We're going to have a contender in Detroit. Lanier and Kevin Porter are superstars.

"I hope I can hold my own . . . and the record shows I'm a player. I can see the championship banner hanging in that building now . . . what do they call it? Cobo? I want to play."

And Ozzie Feldman was just as delighted with the prospect of Marvin Barnes playing for the Pistons, with visions of championship banners waving, and bugles tooting.

"We talked to coaches and players and they're unanimous in their opinion that when Barnes comes to play, he's a superstar," Feldman said, thrilled to be forking over the 500 grand. "He was our first choice, the best man available, and we aren't concerned with other things." The Pistons assembled in training camp on September 24 to get their game together for the 1976–77 season. Herbie Brown had the bugle. He counted the players who had reported, and oops, somebody was missing.

Marvin Barnes!

He had, it was assumed, gone off to buy some bunting to display in, what was the place? Cobo! At the NBA finals.

For sure, he had not arrived at training camp. But he was expected. Wasn't he?

Next day, it was reported that Barnes had missed two practice sessions and by actual count, three airplanes. It was one of the few times Barnes was not reachable by phone.

A check with his agent disclosed that News wanted to renegotiate his contract.

The Pistons suspended him.

Kevin Porter was back, recovered from his knee problems and eager. For the first time in five years, the Pistons had a first-round draft choice with special promise, Leon Douglas out of Alabama. And the Pistons had purchased another player from the dead ABA's dead Spirits, M.L. Carr, who brought with him a reputation for hustle and intensity.

Herbie Brown had a prophecy for the season: "This team will be made up of twelve good human beings as well as twelve outstanding basketball players. I think Kevin's play is back to where it was at the beginning of last season. I can't wait to get started."

Marvin Barnes showed up a week into training camp.

"My off-the-court activity draws attention," News said. "I'm just a fun-loving guy. I had a Rolls Royce in St. Louis, but they weren't ready for that, and I got rid of it this summer. I just stand up for what I believe in. I'm not a yes-man.

"I'm here to play ball and give 101 percent. I'm a forward, strictly a forward, and one of the best in the game.

"Herb Brown put himself on the line for me when he took me in the draft. I'm not the stablest person in the world, but I'm not going to make him sorry."

Once, when he played college ball for Providence, Marvin Barnes was arrested for striking a teammate with a tire iron in response to catching an elbow in the mouth in practice. The teammate suffered a broken jaw. The judge gave Marvin three-years probation.

Now in Detroit, during training camp, he injured his right ankle. He insisted on a walking cast. It was put on his ankle. He missed a practice. He was fined and suspended again.

Next, the Pistons scheduled a doctor's examination of the ankle in Ann Arbor. Marvin neglected to show up. He was located in St. Louis, visiting his personal physician.

A couple of weeks later—the season had started now—Marvin returned to St. Louis, a trip unauthorized by the Pistons, to have the cast removed.

The trouble was, mostly, that Marvin set off the alarm at security at Detroit's Metropolitan Airport. He had, it seems, a .38 caliber revolver and five loose bullets for it, in his luggage.

When that incident hit the papers, the judge in Rhode Island charged Barnes with violation of probation.

Meanwhile, Ozzie Feldman was quoted in the *New York Times*: "I've rejected dozens of offers for Barnes. We have no intention of getting rid of him. We're still convinced he'll help our club."

Feldman planned a little get-together with Barnes, just to talk things over.

With the season going along, Herbie Brown was appearing more and more like the genius the Pistons had been seeking for all these years. Upstairs Gus was doing his dance in the balcony, twisting and turning and wiggling. Down at the bench, Herbie was twisting and turning and wiggling himself. The Pistons were off to a phenomenal start. They won eight of their first nine games.

Kevin Porter was a virtuoso on the floor, slithering through the opponents at speed and firing the basketball off to Lanier or M.L. Carr or Howard Porter for baskets. In Cobo, on a

November Saturday before a shrieking crowd, the Pistons dished it out to the reigning champions, the Celtics. Kevin Porter contributed 20 assists, a club record.

Barnes was ready to play, at last, just around Thanksgiving when the Philly 76ers, with Dr. J, went into Detroit.

The *News* headlined that Barnes was getting his third try with the Pistons, after the talk with Feldman.

"I didn't go in there begging for no third try," Barnes said. "I don't have to play for them . . . .

"I've been pegged as a rebel, but I'm not a rebel. I just happen to be a black man trying to get on . . . .

"They're not doing me no favors letting me play. I'm a talent. I'm a superstar.

"I didn't go in there saying I'm gonna be a good kid from now on."

Herbie Brown's genius started to tarnish around New Years's, 1977. The club was doing fine. But Brown's antics started to wear on the athletes. He got into it with Chris Ford and Lanier. There was a spat in Kansas City.

Kevin Porter was fast and clever with a basketball in his hands. But he was twitchy and tempestuous. Brown's shouts and insults quickly started to eat at Kevin.

When Brown yelled in a practice session that a tall guy had a midget on him, that's when all hell broke lose. Kevin wouldn't take it anymore.

Oscar Feldman had to try to serve the peacemaker's role, once again. He went to the lox-and-bagels diplomacy—that unique strategy for curing anything that ills a pro basketball team. Almost as good as chicken soup.

Certainly, the chicken soup treatment must have clicked with Marvin Barnes. While all this flurry went on around him, Marvin was playing, happy, showing up usually, frequently on time.

In January, the judge in Rhode Island ordered him to spend a year in prison for probation violation, stemming from the time he got caught packing the revolver at the airport. But lawyers being lawyers, a deal was struck so that Marvin wouldn't have to start spending any time in stir until after the end of the basketball season. Barnes' jail date was scheduled for May 16.

". . . I want to say," said News, "I'm grateful for everything everybody has done for me. Oscar. Herb Brown. The team. The people.

"You know, when I went into a game the first time, the fans gave me a standing ovation. I appreciate that. I really do."

Detroit fans, for some reason, have supported the anti-social, the anti-citizen. They yelled mightily for Denny McLain the night he returned to the Tigers from his gambling suspension in 1970. They cheered hockey hooligans as if they were heroes.

Now they turned their love toward Marvin "Bad News" Barnes, the man with the jail sentence in his future.

The cries of "News, News" would chant out from the Cobo balconies. Then Herbie Brown would to go to Barnes on the bench. The joint would erupt.

One night in February, Barnes scored eight points in two minutes as Pistons rallied to beat the Portland Trail Blazers by seven points. Portland, with Bill Walton, had become a new power club in the NBA. And the Pistons had handled them.

"I get turned on when the crowd cheers for me," said Barnes. "They like it when I get a streak going. Anything might happen when I get the ball."

Fifteen years later, the recollections of Marvin Barnes remained etched in Jerry Dziedzic's memory.

"Call me News," Dziedzic said in 1991. "Him and his telephones. He had twenty-six telephones in a three-room apartment so he wouldn't have to reach any further than arm's length."

Lox-and-bagels diplomacy did not have the punch of chicken soup, after all. The troubles between Brown and Kevin Porter simmered and popped in March. And then Herbie got hit with a truly serious problem.

Catching a ball and drawing it toward him with his left hand, Bob Lanier moved his right hand over the ball to protect it. A defender reached out and swatted at the ball.

The swat hit Lanier's right hand. And bam, a bone in Lanier's right hand cracked and was broken. He was out, with the Pistons shooting toward the playoffs, in their own quaint style.

Late in the month, Marvin Barnes went AWOL again. The Pistons had lost three in a row. They were struggling to make the playoffs. And Marvin was a no-show for practice.

"He's played some good games for us, but he hasn't been consistent all year," said Brown, with typical tact. "In the past, when Lanier was healthy, we could play over Marvin's problems. Now Marvin has a great opportunity to prove his mettle as a player. I haven't given up on him."

But . . . Barnes said in an interview with the *Free Press* that he wouldn't play in the playoffs. He wanted to get to jail in Rhode Island before the May 16 date and start serving his time.

"You know, that's like waiting to die," he said. "I might as well die now . . .

"I'm not obligated to play in the playoffs for them. My contract doesn't say I have to play in the playoffs."

Barnes told Bill Halls of the *News*: "It's gotten to the point where I count the days. Thirty-five, thirty-four, like that. I've got to serve time. It's affecting my game, mentally and physically. It's on my mind; it's a heavy weight, a burden to know what's waiting at the end of the season, especially when I don't think I deserve to go to jail . . .

"It's unfair to knock me and say I'm dogging it—because I've played with broken bones and punched eyes. I never complained when I was playing less than thirty seconds on national TV . . .

"I didn't abandon my team. I'd never do that. I wasn't missing. I called the Pistons' office to say I had business and would miss practice. Do I have to report every move I make? Is someone on the Pistons my father?

". . . This has not been a beautiful season."

The Pistons made it to the playoffs, turmoil and all. Their 44–38 record allowed them to share second place with the Bulls in the Midwest Division, behind the ex-ABA Denver Nuggets.

Barnes opted to play in the playoffs. For as long as the Pistons lasted. The Golden State Warriors eliminated them in three games, two victories to one.

The playoffs went nearly two months, into June, for the first time. The Portland Trail Blazers, with Walton playing with his kerchief knotted around his head, won their first championship, beating the 76ers in six games in the NBA finals.

Just before the finals started, Marvin Barnes entered the Adult Correctional Institute in Cranston, Rhode Island, to serve his time in stir.

Indeed, it had not been a beautiful season.

Bob Kauffman became the Pistons' general manager during the summer of 1977. He replaced Oscar Feldman. Kauffman was in his thirties, but he was a basketball man. That was a switch on the way to run a sports franchise. Feldman was a lawyer. The man Ozzie replaced, Ed Coil, was an accountant. Attorneys and bean counters had become essential in the realm of sports as athletes went into contract meetings shoulder-to-shoulder with agents, and then sought to renegotiate what they had agreed to the year before, or got themselves caught with strange powder in their nostrils.

The NBA, as did major league baseball and pro football, had become a cruel world.

So there had to be lawyers and CPAs, but every once in a while, it was important to have a basketball man judge a basketball player on the basis of talent.

So the Pistons hired Kauffman as their GM to work with Herbie Brown, who was surviving as a jumping-bean coach while squabbling with the hired athletes and while existing on the diet of lox and bagels. It was thought that maybe Kauffman could smooth things over a slice in the diplomacy matter.

Even so, Herbie kept suggesting that the Pistons trade Kevin Porter—for the sake of the coach's sanity, at least.

Meanwhile, the Pistons were informed that Marvin Barnes would be paroled from the can in Rhode Island in time to start the 1977–78 season in their uniform. He would be sprung after serving less than five months of his one-year sentence, justice prevailing once again. And even more justly, Marvin would be freed just in time to miss Herbie Brown's training camp. He didn't even have to go AWOL this time.

Said Kauffman, hired to be tactful and diplomatic as well as for his knowledge that tall is good in basketball players: "We are terribly disappointed but we do, however, appreciate the consideration the parole board has given us in granting the October 14 release date."

Herbie Brown, whose survival swung on the possibility of a miracle happening, said: "He went in with the right attitude and fulfilled his obligation. I'm very, very pleased. Marvin called me recently and asked if it would be all right to use my name and address as a place for him to

Julius Erving helps out on D against Lanier. Erving, Caldwell Jones (11), and George McGinnis (30) all played in the ABA.

stay. They have to have a place to stay and he'll be with me until he can work something out with the parole board."

From Rhode Island came word that the parole board checked the NBA schedule in going over the request to release Barnes early.

And there also was some words for the Pistons from Marvin via a Rhode Island newspaper: "My season with them was probably my worst as a professional player and a person. I want to prove to them my worth. They're gonna get their reward this season. I'm gonna pay off. I'm gonna help them win a championship."

Curtis Rowe, in whom the Pistons had once invested a first-round draft choice, was not as expressive as Marvin. He insisted on being traded and boycotted training camp to emphasize his attitude. Kauffman arranged one of the

Pistons' patented three-club deals. The Pistons wound up with homebred Ralph Simpson, a veteran forward, from the Denver Nuggets. They shipped the disenchanted Rowe to the Celtics, who relayed Paul Silas to the Nuggets.

At least the Pistons had an athlete willing to do some playing.

While the Pistons were in training camp, Bob Lanier signed a four-year extension to his contract—a $2 million deal for Bob. It put him in a the same salary range as Pete Maravich, Julius Erving, and Kareem Abdul-Jabbar—the NBA's rich and mighty. Lanier refused to confess to the actual details of the contract.

"If I told you, then my wife would know and she'd spend more money," Lanier told the *News'* Tom Gage.

For once, Lanier was happy.

Barnes showed up for the opening of the season. So did Kevin Porter, in midseason pique. Herbie had tried to trade him, without connecting. Now Brown flatly benched Porter, granting him about sixteen minutes of usage per game. Kevin had a front row seat on the pines with Barnes and Howard Porter.

It was obvious that Herbie had himself a full doghouse.

Brown was starting young Eric Money at guard with Chris Ford, with M.L. Carr busting his buns up front along with a choice of the night plus Lanier.

Eight games into the season, the Pistons made their move.

They traded Kevin Porter and Howard Porter to the geographically relocated New Jersey Nets, formerly co-occupants of New York City with the Knicks. From the Nets the Pistons got a player named Al Skinner, sort of a 1970s Ed Conlin, and two second-round draft choices.

The trade in early November did not exactly send Roman candles shooting around Cobo. The Pistons continued in their downward spin. They were losing games in bunches. The losing streak hit four after Herbie had been freed of Kevin Porter.

Then Marvin Barnes vanished again. The Pistons had lost a game to the Lakers in L.A. After the game, there was another one of those shouting matches, which seemed to be Herbie Brown's forte. This one involved Kauffman, too,

obviously siding with the coach, two-on-one against Barnes. It soon turned into two-on-none. Kauffman told Marvin to go back to Detroit to get treatment on a paining foot while the Pistons continued up the coast to Golden State and Portland. Marvin didn't bother to return to Detroit to take care of his foot. Instead he remained in Los Angeles and hit a club to test his ailing foot—on the dance floor.

Asked about what had happened, Herbie Brown said: "Speak to Kauffman."

Asked about what had happened, Kauffman said: "When you have a family squabble, you don't tell your neighbors about it."

When the rest of the team returned to Detroit, Barnes was absent from a practice session, supposedly because he had to meet with his parole officer.

"Marvin is a very nice man," Kauffman said, believing he was letting Bill Halls in on some secret, "but he lacks responsibility."

The next day the Pistons made their second trade in two weeks. Somehow, Kauffman found a taker for Marvin (Bad News) Barnes. It was just around Thanksgiving, a few days left in November, plenty left in the season. The new club, which believed absolutely it knew how to appease Marvin Barnes and get him to show up, was the Buffalo Braves.

Bob Kauffman did know basketball. He rooked the Buffalo team by getting John Shumate, a decent forward, and Gus Gerard, decent bench fodder, plus a first-round draft choice—all for Marvin Barnes.

"I think it's a good trade for both teams," Kauffman said. He was a quick learner in the GM business. He did not gag while stifling his giggles.

"He always gave 100 percent on the floor," Kauffman said. "But we couldn't reach an understanding as far as team rules and regulations went.

"I'm not saying everything was peaches and cream. But this wasn't totally because of L.A. When it comes to the point where we can make a good deal, I'll make it. Maybe Marvin needs a change of scenery."

Marvin Barnes, who had several changes of scenery including a good look at the inside of prison walls, shuffled off to Buffalo.

Herbie Brown's doghouse was now empty. Kevin Porter was gone. Marvin Barnes was gone.

A few weeks later, so was Herbie.

The Pistons had tumbled to 9-and-24. Herbie got the ziggy in the traditional way the Pistons deliver it. With the season going on, the club floundering.

Somebody already working for the club in another job is wonderfully handy to replace the coach. Dick McGuire and Dave DeBusschere were promoted from the players' ranks. Donnis Butcher, Paul Seymour, Earl Lloyd, Ray Scott, and Herbie Brown himself were all promoted from assistant coach when their bosses got fired.

Now the Pistons tried a new approach out of the same, tired program. Bob Kauffman, the general manager, became the Pistons' thirteenth head coach.

Kauffman was admittedly a fill-in for the remaining fifty-eight games of the season. He had never coached before. It didn't matter. The club needed some sort of change in direction, and he'd give it a try while the management searched for a less temporary coach for the following season.

There was one footnote out of Buffalo as the Pistons played along aimlessly for the remainder of the 1977–78 season. The Braves suspended their new acquisition, Call Me News Marvin Barnes, two weeks after the trade from Detroit. Marvin, it seemed, wanted to renegotiate his contract.

He showed up to join the Braves a couple of weeks later. The Braves were soon riddled with dissension. They traded Marvin on to the Boston Celtics, where Red Auerbach had been running the franchise forever. Red thought he could tame Marvin. He failed this one. When Barnes walked out on the Celtics, Auerbach waived him.

In February, Ralph Simpson was shipped out again. Right back to the Denver Nuggets. It seemed like rent-a-player. The Pistons had Simpson for thirty-two games. End of lease.

But Kauffman was displaying skills, despite his tender experience, as GM. This time he got another first-round draft choice from Denver, which was gambling on a championship, plus a benchwarming body, Jim Price.

The Pistons had squandered away their first-round draft choices for 1977 and 1978. Now

When Kevin Porter was traded during the 1977–78 season, the burden fell on Eric Money (left), M.L. Carr (right), and Chris Ford to man the backcourt.

Kauffman, looking at the long-term, had squirreled away three first-round picks at the 1979 draft. He got them from the Barnes deal, the second Simpson trade, plus the Pistons still had their own choice for a year hence.

The club only had to use them with intelligence, and the Pistons could become a power club early in the decade of the 1980s.

But before then, there were other matters for the 1970s.

Dick Vitale's campaign to coach the Pistons started very shortly after Herbie Brown's demise.

Bill Davidson, learning quickly that winning basketball championships was not the same as making millions manufacturing glass, planned a break in all theories and traditions of the Pistons' past. It did not matter to him, at this juncture, if his next coach had never been involved in pro ball. It did not matter if the next guy stood on his head, did the bugaloo dance at center court, if he talked with his hands while shrieking at the top of his limitless lungs. It did not matter if the next coach knew nothing more than that a basketball must have air pumped into it and that the basket was a rim ten feet above floor level.

Somehow, Dick Vitale fit that profile.

With Dick Vitale, you got only what you saw —and what you heard. He had gone to Detroit from New Jersey, where he'd started at East Rutherford High School and never shut up telling about it. Nobody ever had heard of him when he arrived to become coach at the University of Detroit. But he must have sold the good fathers at U of D a great pitch, because he was hired to take over a program that better qualified coaches wanted to coach.

Basketball was dead at U of D. It had some history, with Dave DeBusschere and Spencer Hayward. But Vitale didn't bother selling the history very much to revitalize—to steal a word —the program. He gathered his team and sent them out to blaring music, jumping through a hoop in a darkened arena into floodlights for their introductions. He scrounged the ghetto neighborhoods of Detroit and talked street kids into playing ball at his university. He sold and peddled and hawked. He made a million speeches to booster groups and sports clubs in his grating machine-gun voice. He developed a schtick.

It worked. People showed up for his basketball games. He brought good players into school —Terry Tyler, John Long. Detroit got some national recognition. Vitale got some national publicity. The team got into some tournaments. He became athletic director on top of his basketball coaching job.

Then one day Vitale's stomach popped. He became the victim of his own intensity, his own pressure. His aim in life, then, was to emulate Al McGuire, the coach at Marquette. When his stomach backfired, Vitale called a press conference. He cried openly. In an emotional address, he sobbingly said coaching was over for him; that he'd have to concentrate on being athletic director.

But soon he was plotting to get back into coaching. Vitale wanted to coach the Pistons, and he said so to guys around town, like sports columnists and such riffraff.

The guy who was unknown when he reached Detroit was now one of the most recognizable people in town—for both his bald head and his stentorian voice.

As all this was going on, the Pistons finished their season in comparative silence. Kauffman did an acceptable job, going 29-29 in his part season. But the overall 38-44 record, placing the Pistons fourth in the Midwest, was not enough to make the playoffs.

So it was that both papers pumped in their sports columns for Dick Vitale. I figured that he was perfect for the job. Not so much as a coach, but because Davidson/Feldman and syndicate were moving the Pistons out of Cobo—and out of downtown Detroit after twenty-one years of chaos and general apathy. They were headed to the suburbs and the new Silverdome in Pontiac. The jerry-built basketball court in a corner of the vast football arena would have double the capacity of Cobo.

There were people who knew basketball who doubted if Vitale could coach much. But as Charley Eckman had said two decades earlier, you didn't have to coach these big lunks.

What Vitale could do best was stir up interest; put fannies in the seats; make whatever fans there were overlook the inadequacies of the team. The Pistons needed a brand new image. Providing that was Dick Vitale's strength; who knew, maybe he could coach a bit too and produce a winner.

Maybe Davidson was convinced by what he read, but I doubt it. More likely he swallowed the same bait, same hook and same line and sinker that Vitale doled out to the rest of us all over town. Davidson hired Vitale as the Pistons' coach No. 14.

Vitale made his first pro coaching appearance for us in front of the waterfall and the imaged Detroit skyline, with the martial music bursting our ears and with the cannon failing to go off, just as the NBA playoffs elsewhere were turning serious.

A month later, the Washington Bullets, with long-ago Piston Bob Ferry as GM and old pal

Happy days in Piston Paradise—Dick Vitale with owner Bill Davidson (left) and GM Bob Kauffman (right).

Dick Motta as coach, won the NBA championship. They dumped the Seattle Supersonics in seven games in the NBA finals.

After the season, the NBA, looking at a map undoubtedly published as a cover of the *New Yorker*, relocated the Pistons in the Central Division. They were grouped with such oasis spots as San Antonio, Houston, Atlanta, New Orleans and always scenic Cleveland. Using typical logic, the NBA left Detroit's natural rivals, Chicago and Milwaukee, in the Midwest Division.

But what the heck, Dick Vitale was coming into the NBA to set matters straight.

Other than his fifty dozen speaking engagements, the 1978 draft was Vitale's first act as coach of the Pistons. He immediately displayed his well-rounded qualifications to serve as a coach in the NBA. His two highest picks were Terry Tyler and John Long, on the twin second-round selections. Previous curiosities had traded away Dickie's first-round pick for that year when the Pistons acquired Archie Clark from Seattle in 1975–76.

Of course, it was only coincidental that Tyler and Long were the same Tyler and Long, who had played for Vitale at the University of Detroit. Bob Kauffman, the holdover GM and ex-part-time coach, was starting to become mystified. Although, it all was a family affair and quite secret.

Back went Vitale on the midsummer straw speech circuit, peddling his theories of ReVI-TALEization. He was cocksure he could coach in the pros and kept spouting his theories about his Pistons Paradise, somewhere out over the horizon.

And then, it was after Bob Kauffman had enough and surrendered as general manager that Vitale used his authority to make trades.

His first trade was the classic reacquisition of Kevin Porter from the New Jersey Nets for the ticked off Eric Money.

And it was doubtful that Vitale, boasting of his Italian heritage, had ever developed much of a taste for lox and bagels.

Dick traded again, quickly, frequently.

He had never been able to do this before in his life, swap athletes, trade players from his own team to obtain players from another team. Vitale was running amok in a candy store, where they sell bubble gum cards.

Give me your Rickey Green and I promise I'll give you something later. So the Pistons got Green from the Golden State Warriors for a draft choice.

Give me your Otis Howard and I'll give you something later, I promise. So the Pistons got Howard from the Milwaukee Bucks for a promised future draft choice.

Give me your Earl Tatum and I'll give you my Chris Ford and I promise I'll give you something else later when I get back to the candy story. So Chris Ford, a team co-captain, still young, bright enough about the game to be considered coaching material some day, was shipped to Boston. "Let's see how long Tatum lasts," said Ford, snappishly, about Vitale's fickle brain. In Detroit, Tatum was joining his fourth NBA club in less than three seasons.

And so it was, Vitale had this odd assemblage of athletes early in his rookie pro season—along with his vow and pledge that this would be a team of enthusiasm, a team of excitement.

Of course, it was a misfit team—playing basketball in a strangely configured basketball arena in the corner of a football field. And, of course, Vitale's stomach popped on him again in the first days of the first season. Then soon all of him popped and he had to be carted, dragged, lifted away from the court to the locker room by a security guard.

Pistons Paradise meant 0-and-5 at the start and Vitale's fantasies that he could coach in the NBA were being transformed into his ghoulish nightmares about going 0-and-82.

But no team can be that lousy. Still, this was a situation running full throttle out of control.

The ballclub was struggling on the floor, lucky when it could win one of three games. Lanier's left knee was killing him. He had had one operation over the summer. The doctors removed three large bone chips. But early in the season, he had to go back to the hospital for a second operation. This time the surgeons plucked out two more bone chips.

The club that had seemed so near championship contention five years earlier had disintegrated.

That could not be blamed on Vitale. The Pistons had been allowed to fragment before Davidson hired Vitale as a cure all measure.

But it kept getting worse. And worse.

And Vitale, no matter how loud he ranted about his players, his owners, his situation, could not be judged an innocent.

The first public outbreak of trouble occurred at the 1979 NBA All-Star Game in February. The game was in the Silverdome, showcasing all of what Vitale would classify as all the NBA's Rolls Royce performers, all on the same court. After the game, Bob Lanier, definitely Rolls Royce but charged with malingering, exploded with angry statements. Bob felt he had been dishonored and he responded with rage. He spoke standing in the

Chris Ford, a co-captain at the time, was traded by Dick Vitale to the Celtics for Earl Tatum, who lasted less than a year as a Piston.

Terry Tyler (41) was Dick Vitale's first draft pick. Both Tyler and John Long (second pick) played under Vitale at the University of Detroit.

locker room, towering above his listener, as the other All-Star players in the NBA strode nonchalantly toward the showers. It was a delicate, yet stormy scene.

Excerpts from a column by Jerry Green in the *Detroit News*, February 5, 1979:

The passions poured through this giant named Bob Lanier.

They stood and cheered, 31,745 people, and Lanier blew them a kiss and waved his thanks. Choked up, goose pimples, trembled, held-back tears—the words are Bob's own to express how he felt.

And the emotions swayed, a counterpoint at the very moment, to the deep, deep anger which comes from the hurt of gossip. Brooding Bob Lanier could not keep this pain inside himself.

He is terribly angered by an accuser who says he is coddling himself, dogging it for the Pistons. The accuser could be Dick Vitale, the man Lanier openly campaigned for when the Pistons scurried for a coach. There is a growing rift between player and coach—though Lanier refuses to identify who has angered him and Vitale denies mouthing any criticism.

Still, club sources do say Lanier believes privately that Vitale was the one who accused him of malingering in statements to the Pistons' executives.

"Something has extremely disappointed me," Lanier said when yesterday's National Basketball Association All-Star Game had ended. "I'm hurt. Hurt professionally.

"I've heard some rumblings. People that are close to me and it hurts. If you got something to say, say it to me. Say it to my face. Don't say it behind my back. Don't stab me in the back. You can fool people, fool them. They fooled me once.

"People think I'm allergic to work. I've played countless times when my knee was bothering me. People don't appreciate it. The doctors know how bad it is.

"I get blasted when it's sore. Other people think it's not sore, or don't have the sensitivity."

The anger overwhelmed the feeling of gratitude Lanier had for the people who had stood and cheered him before the game . . . and who cheered him throughout. His mood was bittersweet. When I caught him alone in the first minutes after the game, he was seething in a back room. He threatened at that time to refuse to play any more games for the Pistons.

"The doctor drained my knee so I could play in this game," Lanier said. "We're not going anywhere anyway. I'm taking off, man. I'm not playing."

Dr. Ben Paloucci, the team physician, and Dr. Gerald O'Connor, the Ann Arbor specialist who looks after Lanier's knee, came to the door.

"It's a question of value," Lanier told them. "Whether I value myself . . . or my team.

"I'm worried about my future."

. . . He continued to fluctuate and later said he does want to play for the Pistons tomorrow night in their game at Houston . . . But he did say he values himself and his personal future more than the team right now.

As Lanier's emotions swayed, Vitale was at the other end of the Silverdome at an NBA affair. I hit Vitale cold with a question about Lanier's performance of late.

"Bob has shown more courage than any athlete I've ever seen," Vitale said.

Only then did I say to Vitale that Bob was angry over alleged remarks.

"He came back in December after his knee surgery and played in 3½ weeks," Vitale said. "A lot of guys would have said, 'We're not going anywhere,' and would have taken off to protect their future.

"Bob has been playing, without question, at his maximum. We have an agreement. He plays at his own pace.

"If there's been any friction. I'm not aware of it. It's just sensationalism. Bob is the pride and guts of what we are, and he's a tireless worker."

The words are fine and dandy. But the Pistons have another of their player vs. management tempests here.

The dangerous part is that Lanier does believe Vitale has griped about him, whether or not it happened . . .

Supposedly Lanier's disenchantment with Vitale, also his close friend and business partner, began a while ago. Bob's statements tend to support this.

"It's a whole combination of events that are frustrating," Lanier said. "I've played sick, some times damn near dead. I don't like that weight thrown on me."

Same old Pistons.

The day the column appeared in the *News*, Vitale and Lanier met. Both claimed they had hashed out any problem.

"I'm assured he's not the guy who said that," Lanier said about Vitale and the purported accusations.

"What Bob's said was uncalled-for for," Vitale said. "He should have come to me first. But we're two guys in the limelight. Everyone wants to get close to you, wants a piece of you . . . I was very, very hurt by this. But the matter is closed. Dead. Dick Vitale and Bob Lanier never had a rift. We've argued about basketball, but that's part of the job."

In the same denial piece, basketball writer Bill Halls reported that one source close to the situation told him: "This is a very serious problem. It's not over yet."

It wasn't.

Vitale's first season droned to its conclusion. Lanier played when he could on his paining knees. He jammed a toe on his left foot and that injury cost him more time. He missed twenty-nine games over the season, but even so, he led the Pistons in scoring for the eighth successive season.

As the season ended in April, Vitale sent Earl Tatum to the Cleveland Cavaliers as payment for Jim Brewer, who had been acquired in February for future considerations. Chris Ford's statement about Vitale's fickleness—"Let's see how long Tatum lasts."—was bull's-eye accurate. Tatum was on the go to his fifth NBA club. Red Auerbach, who could recognize a fish across any court, had duped Vitale.

Of all of Vitale's preening statements, of all his vows and pledges, the only one that smacked of any credibility was his offhand remark, made the first month of the season: "If I could only get through this year."

He accomplished that—but it was a year of futility, hardly what any cockeyed optimist could call Pistons Paradise. The club finished the 1978–79 season with a 30-and-52 record, the worst since van Breda Kolff and Dischinger and Lloyd had coached in combo seven years before. The Pistons tied Cleveland for fourth in the Midwest Division. They weren't close to making the playoffs.

The lone improvement was in attendance. Their final year at Cobo the Pistons had averaged 5,448 customers per game. They jumped that by 4,000 out in Pontiac at the Silverdome, where the average for 1978–79 was 9,510.

Now Dick Vitale could prepare for the 1979 draft. He had those three No. 1 draft choices and plenty of ideas. Bob McAdoo, who had moved to Boston late in the season, caught his fancy.

But Vitale also had two guys who had qualified for free agency and urgently wanted to escape—M.L. Carr and Kevin Porter.

Bob Lanier gave another interview when the season ended.

He told Bill Halls: "This has been one of the most mentally painful seasons of my career. Mostly, it was because of the injuries. Right now I just want to get away from it all for awhile.

"The papers keep trading me, but that's nothing new. For the last four years I've been traded in the papers, and I'm still here.

"I got a letter the other day from a woman. She was a soothsayer, a seer. She said she had a dream about me and kept seeing the letters S.F. I guess that means San Francisco.

"But I can't see that happening. Detroit is my team."

Greg Kelser battles on the boards during his rookie season.

Dick Vitale's draft circus took place under the big top of the Silverdome, in the Main Event Restaurant. It was not a vintage year in 1979 for fresh NBA talent. Earvin Johnson had announced he was coming out two years early from Michigan State. But Magic was committed to the Los Angeles Lakers, who had been owed a future draft choice in a trade and so luckily wound up with the first pick off the board.

The rest of the group that year was hardly worth all the noise Vitale was making. Dickie had those three picks in the first round and invited the town to watch him draft. A few people did, not enough to be called a crowd. Then, Vitale raised his arms toward the roof as he announced that the Pistons had moved up a notch in the rotation, figuring he'd be accepted as a genius. But the rest of the league laughed.

Carelessly wasting fifty grand of the owners' money, Vitale had gotten the Pistons ahead of Milwaukee and claimed Special K, the man he wanted. Greg Kelser was a fine enough prospect, and he had been Magic's teammate at Michigan State, the team that had won the national championship. But the Bucks, happily accepting the donation of $50,000 from Vitale, had intended to skip over Kelser from the start.

There was a clown at this draft circus.

Next, as the first-round continued, Vitale grabbed off Roy Hamilton, from UCLA. Hamilton would last one meager-production season in the NBA before realizing he was better suited for employment in the television industry.

Vitale, with his third shot on the first round, went for Phil Hubbard, a center, out of Michigan.

The territorial draft had been killed off in Fred Zollner's face fifteen years earlier. Vitale managed to beat the system. In two years of drafting, four of his top five draft choices came out of local territory.

The matter that Vitale declared closed, dead, returned hauntingly during the summer. Bill Halls wrote that Vitale and Lanier had buried the hatchet. Thus, it was confirmed at last that there had been a feud between the two men.

"There was a period of noncommunication last season," said Lanier. "That's the worst thing that can happen. The key to any organization is communication. When you don't have communication, people begin to assume things. That always causes problems.

"Dick and I had a long talk recently. We aired our feelings. I think we understand each other. I think we're on our way to something big again. I'm extremely optimistic. For the first time in three years, I'm not facing a major injury and I feel I can fulfill the things I want to fulfill within myself."

A couple of weeks later, Kevin Porter left for the second time. He signed with the Washington Bullets as a free agent. The Pistons accepted two No. 1 draft picks, those for 1980 and 1982, in compensation. Thus, Dick Vitale had another lode of first-round draft picks to play around with.

As the summer moved along toward training camp, there was the matter of the Boston Celtics striking a deal to sign M.L. Carr as a free agent. The completion of the deal was hung up on the compensation factor. Carr wanted to go to Boston. Red Auerbach wanted him there. And Dick Vitale hemmed and hawed about it, as time passed by.

Actually, he was scheming up a proposal that would have, for sure, stamped him as a genius this time. Vitale had his good eye on Bob McAdoo. McAdoo had been the NBA's scoring champion three successive years when he played for the Buffalo Braves.

He was an immeasurable talent. When he cared to be, he was brilliant. He just didn't always care to be. Buffalo finally shipped him off to the Knicks. He was a mighty star, for a while, on Broadway. Then Auerbach figured McAdoo could revive the Celtics. Red traded three—by count, one, two, three—first-round draft choices to New York for McAdoo, and threw in a player.

Auerbach wasn't always a genius, himself. McAdoo played twenty games for the Celtics and did not rescue a club that was in last place and destined to remain in last. When Vitale mentioned McAdoo, Auerbach drooled.

On September 6, 1979, the trade was made. Vitale got McAdoo for the Pistons. Auerbach got Carr for the Celtics plus the Pistons' own No. 1 draft choice in 1980 plus the draft choice they'd received from Washington in the first round in 1980. Three-for-one!

Red had to gag on his cigar smoke. He had duped the same fish a second time.

Those two No. 1 draft choices Dick Vitale surrendered to get McAdoo would result in the ruination of one franchise through the early and middle 1980s. It would result in a championship dynasty for another franchise.

Eight, nine, ten years later, as the Pistons struggled to overcome whatever the mastery it was that the Boston Celtics held over them, they would see Kevin McHale and Robert Parish damaging them on the floor.

But Auerbach never did send Vitale a championship ring after converting the choices the Pistons had given away to him into McHale and Parish.

Still, Vitale had to make another deal, while in training camp. Jim Brewer, who had cost the Pistons Earl Tatum, who had cost Chris Ford, was sent to the Portland Trail Blazers for a draft pick. Brewer had been with the Pistons for all of twenty-five games.

Back when pro basketball was in its infancy, the Providence Steam Rollers won only six games in a forty-eight-game season. On a number of nights, when it was too tough to study, I sat there watching the beloved Rollers try to play this game that a band of arena owners and other entrepreneurs were trying to sell in America's cities. I paid my two bits by displaying my Brown University ID card and sat in the end seats of the dark, dim arena with the court spread over an ice surface in Rhode Island Auditorium. Maybe a thousand other spectators were there with me.

But the Rollers were fun to watch. They would give the St. Louis Bombers or the Philly Warriors with Joe Fulks a battle before collapsing into defeat sometime in the fourth quarter. They offered classic comedy.

Never again would pro basketball, the NBA, have a team as futile as the 1947–48 Providence Steam Rollers, with their six victories spread over an entire season.

But the Detroit Pistons possessed all the ingredients, plus Dick Vitale, that had been endearing about the Rollers of thirty-one years before.

Sadly, we did not have Dick Vitale to kick around much longer. The 1979–80 season started in much the same shape as the previous one had ended. The Pistons were not a match for their opponents in the NBA. They were, as the Providence Steam Rollers had been once upon a time, futile on the floor.

Porter was gone, Carr was gone. Bob McAdoo was in Detroit, but not truly happy about it. Kelser was playing some. Hubbard was playing less. Hamilton was playing less than the other two. Bob Lanier was sulking again, an enormous jewel on display in the back alley of some bazaar.

We the press were bugled back to the Silverdome on a sickly looking afternoon in November of 1979. A dozen games of the new season

had been contested. It was obvious, to the entire town, the entire league, that the Pistons were a franchise in disarray.

Bill Davidson's helicopter was parked in the parking lot, just outside the entrance to the club's offices. None of us could miss sighting it as we walked into the Dome.

Inside, Davidson was rendering the ziggy to Dick Vitale. No waterfall or images of the city's skyline or martial music accompanied this mercy killing. There was no cannon there to go poof and backfire.

Pistons Paradise had gone poof, instead. The short, unhappy era of ReVITALEization was ended. A miserable flop.

Vitale, bedraggled, looking defeated, admitted the ziggy was what he deserved—"I didn't get the job done." Making a confession was to his credit. He had, simply, self-destructed. Now he would no longer have to duck our brickbats. Dickie would head off in another direction, maybe into television, the medium that had welcomed Al McGuire, the old coach Vitale had envied and wanted to emulate. Perhaps Vitale had the essentials for TV.

But this was not time to think about that. The Pistons had another new coach, Richie Adubato. The fifteenth in the Pistons' twenty-three years in Detroit. Of course, Adubato had been Vitale's assistant. That Pistons tradition had to be carried on. Adubato had arrived in Detroit better dressed than Herbie Brown had a few years earlier, but he was just as obscure. He had been a coach somewhere in New Jersey. He was a quiet, self-effacing man. Vitale selected Adubato and brought him in—a foil to Vitale's emotional, arm-swinging, noisemaking extroverted persona.

Loudmouth boobs always seem to want quiet guys around them.

What Richie Adubato inherited from his coaching benefactor was a situation so broken it would take patience and a performer of miracles to repair at any time in the next decade. The Pistons were a franchise barren of draft choices, bereft of hope.

The 1980s were almost upon us.

But before the new decade began, Davidson and his syndicate made another move. They brought in another new general manager. There was no fanfare. Jack McCloskey wasn't the type.

He was a grizzled basketball man who had

kicked around—and had been kicked around—in the sport for thirty years or more. He was beyond age fifty at the time of his appointment, December 11, 1979. He did not arrive with an impressive resume. There was a bunch of Ivy League to him.

Davidson found McCloskey working the bench as an assistant coach for the Indiana Pacers.

"This is a positive step in the building of our franchise to NBA championship level," Davidson said.

There were some giggles when Davidson made this latest of changes in the operation of the Detroit Pistons. It was the old reflex reaction. We had seen it all so often before—a PR flack, a radio broadcaster, a newspaper guy, a bookkeeper becoming the general manager, with the usual optimistic outlook. If you didn't laugh, there was only one thing else for you to do.

Cry!

A week after Jack McCloskey became general manager he was hit with his first controversy. Bob Lanier demanded to be traded. Detroit might have been his team, but he was fed up with waiting for it to become competitive, again.

Bob spilled his gripes to a Philadelphia radio station, after the Pistons had been whipped by the 76ers and Dr. J in the Silverdome.

"Ten years is too long to wait," Lanier said into the mike. "I'm too old to wait."

Bob was thirty-one, with the creaky knees, and a huge anger whetted by a huge sense of deja vu.

That night, the Silverdome audience—just 9,000—had booed the 9-and-24 hometown team.

Lanier said he was mentally distressed by the Pistons' perpetual state of inertia.

"It'll be two or three years before these kids come around," Lanier said. "I'm down a lot. I had no oomph at all.

Next day, McCloskey said, sure, he'd trade Lanier—if the Pistons could get something of value in exchange.

Indeed, McCloskey was relishing the idea of a major trade in his new role.

"If we got a trade offer that would benefit the Pistons, and I don't mean immediately but in the long run, then we would certainly make that move," McCloskey told Bill Halls.

Reporter Halls had learned that the Pistons put out a memo on the league's twix wire, connecting all the clubs, that they were willing to conduct a garage sale. "If you have any interest in anyone, anyone on our roster, please contact us immediately," was the message out of Detroit that rattled into every other NBA inner sanctum. In Milwaukee, Wayne Embry, the Buck's vice president, made a phone call to Detroit.

That day, Lanier came out of a meeting with McCloskey to say: "I really don't see any hope. We don't have the kind of unit that is going to be productive and we've got to trade to get other players. I think the best thing to do is trade me."

The day after, the Pistons lost their fifth straight game to the Atlanta Hawks. But the news that day was Lanier and a pending trade. McCloskey spent hours on the telephone with his counterpart in Milwaukee.

The Bucks had resurfaced as a team with first-place aspirations years after they had been forced by Kareem Abdul-Jabbar to trade him to the Lakers. They imagined they could challenge seriously in the playoffs—if they had a center who could dominate guys in the post. Bob Lanier was perfect for that role—in size and in ability and in motivation.

McCloskey's price for Lanier was Kent Benson, the Milwaukee center, and Quinn Buckner, a guard who could operate the offense.

The Bucks told McCloskey to take a hike.

McCloskey switched his talks to another club, unidentified.

"The teams we're talking to feel he might be the one player who could mean a championship," McCloskey told the *News*.

Christmas was coming—and the other clubs thought McCloskey was too eager and wanted too much.

Lanier's frustrations spilled over again.

"The same old things," he said after the loss to Atlanta, at home." . . . Nothing ever gets accomplished. I wasn't inspired tonight. This was a normal performance for me. There's no sense of drama that the last points might be my last as a Piston. For that you have fond memories and nostalgia. Those things aren't there. The last three years have been too tough.

"I don't want to go crazy. I just want to go."

In the locker room, Richie Adubato, the laid-back coach, was vilifying the athletes, just as

Herbie Brown and Dick Vitale had with louder shouts.

Adubato had been appointed coach only until the end of the 1979–80 season, one of those so-called interim coaches. Naturally, he envisioned himself able to bring some sort of competitive desire to the Pistons. Then after a month in the job, McCloskey was brought in as his boss.

He had to impress a new guy with new concepts with the players he inherited from Vitale. No peach of a situation for any coach.

So when Adubato told the Pistons most of them weren't hustling, some of them started to sulk. Among the sulkers was Bob McAdoo, Vitale's precious acquisition from Boston.

Towering Bob McAdoo wasn't going to take any grief from little Richie Adubato.

"I don't appreciate hearing things like that," McAdoo said. "If there are some trades coming it wouldn't surprise me. Nothing surprises me anymore. Not in this game. Something's got to be done."

McAdoo had joined Lanier in volunteering to be traded.

The Pistons teetered—not on whether Bob Lanier would be traded out of Detroit, but how soon and to what team, and for what assortment of talent—as the world entered the 1980s.

Meanwhile, the Pistons pulled themselves down and down toward the dregs in the NBA. Lanier was hurt again, with a fractured pinkie of his left hand, his shooting hand. He would be incapacitated for eighteen games. His injury stalled McCloskey's trade talks with the Bucks, who were now offering Benson and perhaps two No. 1 draft choices.

Getting a No. 1 for the 1980 draft was foremost for McCloskey. Vitale had left the Pistons stripped naked, without a single draft choice in the first three rounds. McCloskey made his first trade in January, mainly to get some choices for the draft. James McElroy, who had been signed as a free agent, was traded to Atlanta for Ron Lee plus a second-rounder and third-rounder in the draft.

As the first month of the 1980s passed, the Pistons were the worst team in the league, without dispute. They were inferior to the Utah Jazz, who had fled New Orleans and apathy to Salt Lake City as the NBA had another geographical

Terry Tyler jumps out to contest Larry Bird's fallaway jumper. Tyler led the Pistons in blocked shots for five straight seasons.

upheaval. They were inferior to the San Diego Clippers, who had been the Buffalo Braves and imagined some sort of southern California tonic would make them better.

Changing towns failed . . . but that was ancient news to historians who followed the meanderings of NBA franchises.

In their twenty-third year in Detroit after leaving Fort Wayne, the Pistons were being compared, but not fondly, to the long-gone Providence Steam Rollers.

Bob Lanier got his wish with less than two months left in his tenth season in the NBA. He was permitted to escape Pistons Purgatory, for the promised land of Milwaukee. The town that Kareem Abdul-Jabbar couldn't get out of fast enough.

McCloskey shipped Bob to the Bucks for Kent Benson plus a 1980 first-round draft choice. The Pistons were being rooked again in the trade. Lanier was going, in the same pattern as George

Yardley once had and, after him, Gene Shue and Bailey Howell and Dave DeBusschere and Dave Bing.

But this time the deal was made because Bob had to get out. McCloskey's deal could be considered nothing more than a humanitarian act.

"I wanted it," Lanier said, bittersweetly. "But I felt sad about it when it happened. Milwaukee has some real talent. They don't care who scores and they move the ball.

"Hopefully, we can go to the far reaches of the earth together."

So Bob Lanier went off with his size 20s to join a new club in Milwaukee. The Bucks were five games behind the Kansas City Kings in the Midwest Division the day the trade was made.

And McCloskey had the first-round draft choice he coveted.

His next goal was to trade Bob McAdoo, offering the former scoring champ to any team that might be interested.

"But nobody's pursued it or pushed it," Mc-Closkey told the *News*.

Excerpts from a column about Lanier by Jerry Green in the *Detroit News*, February 19, 1980:

. . . Bob didn't laugh much during the decade he spent playing basketball in Detroit.

He was a brooding, bearded giant. He would have made the ideal Othello. So often there was the expression of pain on the Moorish face.

He was forced to chew on a lot of guff in this community. They said he dogged it, imagined a lot of his injuries. They accused him of being a clubhouse lawyer, eruptive. They say he was an unsettling influence on the team, particularly the youngsters. They said he never smiled. But the most painful stab of all, they said he could not win.

At last, as it got crazier and crazier, Bob Lanier begged the Pistons to trade him. So the Pistons obliged him a couple of weeks ago. They gave him away to the Milwaukee Bucks. They sent him packaged in gift paper and bows.

The evidence of this trade is overwhelming right now.

The Bucks have won six of seven games with Bob Lanier playing center for them.

The Pistons have lost 10 games in a row in the longest losing streak of their inglorious history.

Of course, it could be debated that the Pistons would also have lost 10 straight if they still had Lanier. But we'll never know.

The proof is recorded. Lanier can win. He can contribute to a team with other talented players. He can be a champion.

It is all in the CHEMISTRY. The word is Lanier's.

He was on the telephone and he was saying:

". . . Here everybody plays a role. The chemistry is here. I don't think the chemistry was there in Detroit.

". . . Remember when we were 52–30 with Ray Scott? It took a couple of years. Then five, six or seven of those guys were gone. We had some good players. Chris Ford. Don Adams. They weren't big names, but they played well.

"When you break the nucleus of your team with that kind of chemistry, that's what happens. But sometimes chemistry is more important than names."

. . . Being with a team with the genuine winning chemistry has got to be the happiest part of Bob Lanier's career at last.

"I wouldn't say it's the happiest part," said Lanier, the words spoken slowly and with deep thought. "There's one thing that makes me sad. I wanted it to happen in Detroit.

"If I'm happy in Milwaukee, there's no telling how happy I would have been if it had happened when I was in Detroit."

The Pistons finished the season with sixteen victories. They lost fifty-eight games. They were hit by another drop in attendance. They'd failed to rival my precious Providence Steam Rollers, after all. But nonetheless, the season had been a marvelous nostalgia trip— and I didn't even have to pay a quarter every time I wanted to get into the building.

Detroit's interest centered on pulling for the Milwaukee Bucks and Bob Lanier in the play-offs. Lanier had boosted the Bucks to a first-place finish in the Midwest in the last week of the regular season. The Bucks had won twenty of their last twenty-six games with Lanier playing center for them.

Sam Goldaper wrote about Lanier in the *New York Times*: ". . . he finally shed his image as a loser."

116

But Detroit's rooters were to be disappointed again from afar. Lanier and his new teammates were knocked of the playoffs by the Seattle Supersonics in seven games in their first playoff series.

The NBA finals that spring of 1980 would be remembered eternally as an epic because of Magic Johnson, the rookie. Magic lifted his team, the Los Angeles Lakers, to another NBA championship by beating the Philadelphia 76ers in six games. It was a moment for history.

And back in Detroit, the team that Magic Johnson had rooted for as a schoolboy in Lansing, Michigan, performed its ritual act. The Pistons gave their coach, Richie Adubato, the expected ziggy.

Jack McCloskey, the general manager, started scrounging for another head coach. His goal was quite simple. He wanted to construct a team from the dregs of a sixteen-victory season to a club that some day, some spring in the 1980s, might be good enough to play against Magic Johnson in a finals series for the NBA championship.

In twenty-three NBA seasons, the Detroit Pistons had reached over the .500 standard three times.

McCloskey's notions seemed very much like a ridiculous dream.

THIRD QUARTER

I—Trader Jack

Jack McCloskey is standing in a hard rainfall on a lush green of the Forest Lake Golf Course outside Detroit. In nine years, he has created a basketball team worthy of respect. The slapstick element of his team, throughout its history, has been eliminated in the years he worked for the Pistons as its general manager. The team that had struggled to win sixteen games of an eighty-two-game season the year he arrived in midstream and twenty-one the following year is now on the threshold of a championship.

The team and its players—the players he acquired—have become worthy of a city's love. The team that once gave away free tickets and hired a school bus to transport elongated athletes has become the most captivating franchise in the NBA. It has crumbled the curse of the Boston Celtics and has played almost square with the Los Angeles Lakers, with Magic Johnson and Kareem Abdul-Jabbar.

The cruelty of a one-point and then a three-point defeat with the championship within grasp has diminished some. The soothing relief of international travel has tempered McCloskey's moods.

The rain falls. He is in a storytelling mood mixed in with his game of golf. It is that way with all of them, Bill Laimbeer, Isiah Thomas, Jack. They seem to sense a destiny, that their championships will come to them.

Laimbeer is the day's host in July of 1988. Without much fanfare, he's killing the national image as the villain they love to hate in Philly and Boston and Atlanta and L.A. This is the day on which Laimbeer stages his Muscular Dystrophy Celebrity Golf Classic.

Fund-raising golf events such as this one are very popular in Detroit. They enable the athletes to return something to the town in which they earn their bread. And they provide the odd anecdote that can humanize the men who work in the games that entertain us.

So it is that McCloskey is gripping his putter in the rain on the cropped grass. He is covered with a slicker when a scribe rolls up to visit. It is a month after the Pistons have reached the NBA finals for the first time. A few weeks after the loss to the Lakers. In the weeks separating Game 7 in L.A., which the Pistons' lost by three despite the courageous efforts of a crippled Thomas, and this golf tournament, McCloskey has journeyed to Europe in the search for more talent.

He has been watching tall Dutch basketball players in Holland. A stop on his itinerary was Rotterdam. Jack's daughter is an artist. So he put in a call at Rotterdam's art museum.

"I went to see the Van Goghs and the Toulouse-Latrecs," McCloskey says. "I wanted to tell my daughter I touched a Toulouse-Latrec. So I touched it."

He starts laughing there in the rain.

"Alarms rang," he says. "Guards came rushing up with their guns drawn."

McCloskey has an honest mug, it seems. He tells his audience how the guards bought his story about wanting to tell his daughter he touched the famous artist's painting. They shoved their pistols back into the holsters and let him go, to return to America. To return to America, so he can keep swindling fellow general managers in the NBA.

Jack McCloskey thrives on competition. The fires had not receded at age sixty-five, with his back-to-back champions. They were as hot as they were at age nineteen, when he was a young Naval officer in warfare, the skipper of an LST fighting the Japanese in the Pacific.

"I liked the service," he told the *News'* Bill Halls. "Did I like the war? No! But, damn it, it was exciting. You become very mature, very fast, under those circumstances."

The intensity had not diminished from what it was when he was twenty-three, a high school coach so aggrieved over a whistletooter's call that he pursued the referee into the shower and applied a choke hold. It did not matter that McCloskey was in his courtside dress while the offending referee had stripped off his zebra garb and was outfitted in full and proper splendor for the shower, in his birthday garments.

Fortunately, for the ref, he was rescued from McCloskey's grasp.

"I've been accused of being too competitive," McCloskey said in a 1986 interview with the *News'* Dave Dye. "Some people tell me I want to win too much."

He believes it is impossible to want to win too much; that wanting to win is natural behavior. And so it is.

Otherwise, Jack McCloskey would have landed in the coal mines, gagging on the black dust.

McCloskey's origins—just as Chuck Daly's — were in small-town, Middle-America Pennsylvania. Jack came out of Mahoney City in a fiesty mood.

His grandfather was a miner and so was his father, Eddie. The grandfather once was trapped down the shaft for thirty-six hours before he was rescued. Eddie McCloskey took Jack down in the mine one day. Jack was a lad then.

"I'm taking you here one time and I want it to be your last time," the father cautioned the son. "I want you to have a better life than me."

Eddie McCloskey, the dad, would die of black-lung disease contracted in the coal mines in 1974.

Jack McCloskey joined the Navy at seventeen, fought in World War II and after V-J Day, he enrolled at the University of Pennsylvania. He was a three-sport athlete at that Ivy League establishment in Philly.

After school, he signed as a pitcher in the Philadelphia Athletics chain. But he tore up his shoulder in the minors. He played pro basketball —in the Eastern League, where the athletes played with clenched fists and needed heavy knees and sharp elbows to survive. Jack survived for eight seasons. His NBA playing career consisted of one game, for the Philadelphia Warriors, when he was summoned as an injury replacement in 1952–53. He recalls making something like nine shots and scoring six points.

He has a very sharp memory. The *NBA Guide* confirms his stats—adding that his entire NBA playing career totaled sixteen minutes.

But his boyhood ambition was to go into coaching. And as Daly did, McCloskey started in grass-roots territory. He got a job coaching the high school team at Collingswood, New Jersey. One night in a game at Atlantic City, the referee made a call McCloskey didn't care for. That was when he chased the official into the shower intent on strangulation.

"I wanted him bad," McCloskey said.

Three years later, at twenty-six years of age, he was an assistant basketball coach at Penn. He became Penn's head coach another three years later. He took his temper with him. One night after a game at Princeton, Jack jammed his fist through a blackboard. Jack got a bill in the mail back in Philly demanding $25 to pay for the broken blackboard. At Princeton, the blackboards were made from thin junk.

He moved on, to where the basketball quality supposedly was a tad better—the ACC. McCloskey became coach at Wake Forest. One night during the ACC tournament McCloskey was displeased by an official's call. Again. He went to the scorer's table and stuffed his foot through it. Then he tried to yank his foot free and he couldn't. It was trapped. In the ACC, they used sturdier materials.

"It got stuck," McCloskey said. "The referee didn't even give me a technical foul. He said I looked too funny and I was embarrassed enough."

At Wake Forest, one of McCloskey's assistants was a basketball person named Billy Packer, who would learn to talk about the games on television in lower decibels than Dick Vitale, or John Madden.

The pros were Jack's next stop.

The Portland Trail Blazers hired him in 1972, in their third season of existence. He had an awful team consisting of culls and dregs. The Blazers managed 48 victories in the next two seasons, with 116 losses. Jack got the Portland ziggy in May of 1974. A few days later, the Trail Blazers latched on to Bill Walton as their foundation. In another three years, Walton would win the NBA championship for Portland.

By then McCloskey was working on his first rebuilding project—his own life.

Getting booted in Portland devastated McCloskey, the intense, tense competitor.

"It was the low point of my life," McCloskey told Dave Dye in the *News*. "I didn't want to ever see another basketball game. I spent a year running back and forth to islands. It got my mind off basketball. I had an empty feeling. I felt I'd done a good job there. We'd made progress with the team. I couldn't understand it."

He tinkered with an idea to build a resort in the West Indies. The plan plummeted.

He spent two years in flux. He took a sabbatical from basketball, reflecting always on the horror of what had happened to him because he could not turn an expansion team with inferior material into a miracle winner.

"But it could never defeat me," he said.

Finally, he returned to the sport that he had vowed to forsake. He accepted a job as an assistant coach on the Lakers, working with Jerry West. He did that for three years. Then he took an assistant's post with the Indiana Pacers.

That was his job at the beginning of the 1979-80 season when Bill Davidson went on a search for a man to repair the mess wreaked by Dick Vitale in Detroit.

The Pacers, when McCloskey was first approached, refused to allow him to escape.

"There was no question it was something I wanted to do, but I didn't think it was going to happen," McCloskey told reporters later on. "The first time we talked, it wasn't going to happen. The second time we talked, we eventually worked it out. Then the owner said he wasn't going to let me go. But Bob Leonard (then the Pacers' coach) worked it out, and that's how we got up here."

Davidson hired McCloskey on December 11, 1979. The date would be remembered significantly in the history of the Pistons' basketball franchise, a team that had been a cruel joke most of the years it had conducted business in Detroit. McCloskey was fifty-four years old.

Davidson first considered McCloskey for the coaching job, being handled temporarily by Richie Adubato. Then the decision was made to allow McCloskey to mend and build the tottering franchise from the front office, in the role of general manager. Left open was the possibility that McCloskey could become the team's coach at the beginning of the next season, 1980-81.

"I looked at it as an expansion team when I first got here," McCloskey told Dave Dye in the 1986 interview. "There was so little here, that's what we had to do. I remember my wife and I sitting in a section at midcourt, and we'd be by ourselves almost. Heck, if I didn't have to be there, I wouldn't have gone either. But I also remember the first time we got into the playoffs [in 1984]. What a feeling it was to think back to how bad we were and see that big crowd standing for your team.

"We didn't want to go for a quick fix. We decided to go through the draft, make wise decisions in trades, and step by step, build this team up."

When Bill Davidson introduced Jack McCloskey to Detroit a month after Dick Vitale was cashiered, the greeting was spontaneous silence. Jack was known to only the hardcore Detroit pro basketball fan—and that was with memories of his dismal seasons in Portland.

The Pistons' heritage was change the coach, change the general manager, failure, apathy, and fire the coach, fire the general manager, and change again.

"I have the authority to make decisions, but I'm not going to make any quick, rash, implausible ones," McCloskey said. The traditional speech of the just-hired general manager.

The town's cynics didn't even bother taking cynical shots at the hiring of McCloskey. We'd seen it before. The town had abandoned the team. McCloskey was viewed as another guy starting with his head inside the noose.

What could he do that Nick Kerbawy and Ed Coil and Paul Seymour and Charley Wolf and Charley Eckman and Butch van Breda Kolff and Dick Vitale had failed to do?

And right away, when Bob Lanier begged in the public prints to be permitted to flee from the Pistons, the situation seemed as spoiled as it had ever been.

On February 4, 1980, when McCloskey traded Lanier to Milwaukee for Kent Benson and a 1980 first-round draft choice, it was noted that the Pistons had been rooked again in the trade market. The deal fit perfectly into the Pistons' image—the star sent into exile for a minimal return. McCloskey had been forced to make the trade, because of Lanier's demands, but the new general manager could not be forgiven. Same, same, same.

Step, step, step. Step by step.

The date, December 11, 1979, has been circled now, forever.

It was not the same. On that date, it all started to change, and years later we would realize this. Gradually, Jack McCloskey built the Pistons until they improved and improved some more. He drafted and he traded—and the Pistons were no longer dumb at the draft, they were no longer getting rooked in trades. And they got better and better until they became the best basketball team

in the world. And it was Jack McCloskey's doing. It took a decade to do. But he was the creator, the catalyst.

McCloskey had promised not to make quick, rash, implausible decisions the day he was hired in Detroit. It was years later that he admitted his attempt to make his first trade had flopped. It was too rash, too implausible.

It was a telephonic offer, in late 1979, to Bill Sharman, then the general manager of the Lakers. Bob Lanier was still with the Pistons—and McCloskey offered the Lakers their choice of any four players off the Detroit roster for a rookie guard. The rookie guard happened to be Earvin Johnson, fresh out of Michigan State.

As McCloskey recounted just before the 1988-89 season in a conversation in the *News* with writer Corky Meinecke, Sharman said: "Jack, I don't think we can do that."

McCloskey contacted Sharman again the next day. Jack offered the Lakers their choice of any six of the Pistons' players—supposedly, Lanier, Bob McAdoo, Greg Kelser, Terry Tyler, John Long and Phil Hubbard—for the one Magic Johnson.

As McCloskey recalled, Sharman said: "Let me get back to you."

Sharman rejected McCloskey's offer for the second time the following day.

McCloskey is competitive. He does not give up. He tried a third time.

"Bill, are you sitting down?" McCloskey said. Sharman assured him he was seated.

Then McCloskey proposed: "You can have every player on our roster for Johnson."

Sharman told McCloskey: "Jack, I better talk to Jerry Buss about that."

Buss, a swashbuckler, was the owner of the Lakers.

Sharman conferred his boss. Then the Lakers rejected McCloskey for the third time.

"They were thinking about it," McCloskey told Meinecke in the 1988 interview, "but their decision was right. It would have been great. We'd have taken Magic, some CBA players and anybody else we could have picked up. And that would have been the start."

Instead, the start occurred eighteen months later—in the spring of 1981, at the draft.

By then, the Pistons had finished the 16-

and-66 season, the remnants of 1979–80 that began with Dick Vitale and ended with Richie Adubato. They had endured the 1980–81 season with a 21-and-61 record under the first coach McCloskey hired, Scotty Robertson, who had once coached the New Orleans Jazz—for fifteen games before he was fired.

The 21-and-61 record positioned the Pistons second in the 1981 draft rotation. The Dallas Mavericks, created in another expansion the year before, had won fifteen games in their first season. So the Mavs had the priority pick, first off the board.

McCloskey was guaranteed that he'd get the second best player. He assumed that player would be Mark Aguirre, a forward out of De-Paul, an athlete with outstanding ability and an occasionally balky attitude. Dallas had a clear shot at drafting the best player with their first pick.

That best player had decided to enter the draft early, after playing for Bob Knight at Indiana and leading his team to the NCAA championship. That player was named Isiah Thomas.

The situation was such that McCloskey had already negotiated with Aguirre's agent and agreed on a contract.

Then Isiah Thomas let it be known that he preferred not to play in Dallas. The Mavericks

made a curious decision. Thomas didn't have much of a choice if the Mavericks drafted him. But they said the devil with Isiah Thomas, if that's the way he felt about things.

Dallas drafted Mark Aguirre first off the board.

McCloskey and the Pistons had been struck by enormous good fortune. Jack staked the Pistons' claim to Isiah Thomas, second in the draft.

"Even though a lot of people said you don't take a small guard that early, I really felt Isiah's spectacular play would be a shot in the arm for the franchise," McCloskey would recall years later.

That was the start—as soon as the Pistons convinced Thomas playing in Detroit was every bit as good as playing for his hometown Chicago Bulls.

But McCloskey was not finished that draft day in 1981. He had a second pick in the first round. It was the only positive leftover from Dick Vitale's regime. Kelly Tripucka, out of Notre Dame, remained untaken as the draft went through eleven picks. Tripucka's availability was unexpected, a surprise. McCloskey drafted Tripucka as the twelfth man off the board.

McCloskey wheeled through several trades his first two years with the Pistons. Other than the exile of Lanier, that had been forced on him, none of the trades was notable. Step by step, McCloskey worked to improve the ballclub.

He had drafted Larry Drew as a first-rounder at his first draft in 1980 and traded him away for two second-round draft choices after one season.

He had picked up Paul Mokeski from the Houston Rockets and Edgar Jones from the New Jersey Nets in draft choice deals. They were not earthshakers. The players were bodies for the bench and part-time play. There was nothing in McCloskey's deals to show that he had any special knack as a trademaker.

Then on November 21, 1981, as rookies Isiah Thomas and Kelly Tripucka were providing a new excitement for the Pistons and their fans, Jack McCloskey negotiated another trade. This trade, too, seemed routine—another shuffling of ballplayers.

McCloskey sent Greg Kelser to the Seattle Supersonics in a one-for-one trade. The player the Pistons received had played two unspectacu-

The number one and two picks in the 1981 draft—Mark Aguirre and Isiah Thomas.

lar seasons for Seattle. The player was Vinnie Johnson.

It was Jack's first trading coup. Vinnie Johnson would fit ideally into the Pistons' step-by-step program, as the gun off the bench when a scoring gun was vitally needed. And ten seasons later, it would be Vinnie Johnson's basket with 00.7 on the clock that would win the Pistons' second NBA championship in Game 5 of the 1990 NBA finals at Portland.

But back then, it was another small step for Jack McCloskey.

He negotiated another trade during that 1981–82 season, as the Pistons struggled toward that ancient franchise objective, the .500 mark. This one McCloskey made at the trade deadline, on the night of February 16, 1982.

McCloskey had realized the Pistons' old-time need—a tall, strong, tough center. The Cleveland Cavaliers had such a player on the trade block.

Earlier on that night, the Pistons had beaten Houston in the Silverdome. The game had drawn 5,370 customers. After the game McCloskey went upstairs to the Main Event Restaurant at the far end of the Silverdome, stayed a few moments and then went to his office. Being deadline day, he had been on the telephone for hours trying to make the trade for the Cleveland player. He talked to Ted Stepien and repeated the two names, plus the first-round draft choice, he was willing to include as Detroit's part of the deal. Then trying to complete the trade, he flipped in an additional draft choice, a second-round pick. Stepien told McCloskey he'd consider it and maybe get back to him before the deadline.

McCloskey drove home. It was nearly midnight, the witching hour, the trade deadline. The phone rang at 11:51, nine minutes to go. Stepien grabbed the deal—and turned the tough center over to Detroit in what amounted to a four-for-two trade.

The center the Pistons received from Cleveland was Bill Laimbeer. The Pistons also got Kenny Carr in this deal for Paul Mokeski, Phil Hubbard, the No. 1 draft choice in 1982 and the No. 2.

"Everyone thought the player we were interested in was Carr, and we were interested only in Laimbeer," McCloskey would say years later.

In Detroit, Bill Laimbeer would go on to

deliver some hard, grinding bumps, perform some histrionics and gather for himself some sort of reputation.

"It looked like the deal wasn't going to go through," McCloskey said, reenacting the trade for Laimbeer in 1988 for writer Corky Meinecke. "I think I closed the deal by adding that second-round pick, but one of the major factors was that Mokeski is Polish, and I brought that to Stepien's attention.

"I'm telling you, that helped."

Nothing like a little ethnic nudge to get a deal done.

Kenny Carr, who came across Lake Erie with Laimbeer, did not dally long in Detroit. Carr squawked, created some problems—and after twenty-eight games McCloskey dumped him in his next trade. Jack dealt with his old team, the Trail Blazers, and took their first-round draft choice in exchange for Carr.

So it was the Pistons had two No. 1s at the 1982 draft. McCloskey knew the advantages of hoarding the first-round picks. This time he used them to select Cliff Levingston and Ricky Pierce. If they didn't mesh in, McCloskey could always use them as trade fodder.

Jack was always tinkering. He was never reluctant to correct a goof. If a draft choice didn't quite fit in, the guy was used in the next trade. If a guy he got in a trade turned out to be a stiff, that guy was packed into the next trade.

He used this philosophy with his coach, too. The progress was step by step, no quick fix under Scotty Robertson. And this time Scotty got three seasons, not fifteen games. And then Scotty got the ziggy after the Pistons, even with Isiah and Laimbeer and Vinnie and Tripucka, did not reach .500 in any of those three years.

It was then that Jack McCloskey tapped Chuck Daly, his first choice three years earlier, to become coach of the Pistons. Funny, Daly wasn't the first choice this time. Jack McKinney, the coach of the Indiana Pacers, had the first crack and turned the job down.

McCloskey had some luck for the second time. The first was being able to get Isiah Thomas when he expected to get Mark Aguirre. Now he got Chuck Daly when he sought Jack McKinney.

Jack McCloskey had held a bunch of jobs in his life, after his father told him never to return to the mines. A Navy lieutenant in a war, a pitcher with a bum arm, a coach in high school, college and the pros, fired when it wasn't his fault and shunted aside into a period of depression, then serving in obscurity as an assistant pro coach, and then, when past fifty, hired to create something decent out of the most comical franchise in pro sports.

He was nearing age sixty when that the dice started to roll for him.

Levingston didn't mesh in, and after two seasons with the Pistons, he figured in McCloskey's next major deal. Jack was smeared with egg on this one—and with characteristic smarts, or good fortune, turned it around to the Pistons' advantage.

The date was June 18, 1984, at the end of Chuck Daly's first season, and the franchise's first season at .500 or above in seven years. McCloskey sent Levingston and Antoine Carr, the first draft choice of 1983 and never signed by the Pistons, plus two second-round picks to the Atlanta Hawks for Dan Roundfield.

Roundfield was a veteran and McCloskey/Daly figured he would be ideal for this improving ballclub. The aim was to advance into the company of the Celtics and the Lakers. And Roundfield had the experience and the expertise to boost a young ballclub—or so it seemed.

The trade bombed.

Roundfield was injured and didn't seem to give a damn. There are vivid memories of him sitting in uniform on the bench for the first half and then going to the locker room and changing to his civilian clothes and coming out to watch the remainder of the game. The excuse was that he was hurting.

"I was sure he was the answer," McCloskey told writer Dave Dye. "We took a chance to get to that echelon. Obviously, it didn't work. I'd take that trade back."

McCloskey did the best he could. He stuffed Roundfield into his next trade.

He made that one on June 17, 1985. And he received two players for Roundfield. One was named Mike Gibson, who lasted thirty-two games with the Pistons. The other was Rick Mahorn!

McCloskey thought he'd made another stinker of a trade.

Mahorn showed up twenty pounds over-weight. He, too, played like he didn't give a damn. Daly hardly used Mahorn. Mahorn went into McCloskey's office to gripe.

"If I were the coach, you wouldn't be getting any playing time at all," McCloskey said in a seething voice.

A couple of years later, he told Corky Meinecke: "We were taking a chance with Rick because he had slipped in the previous two years. People didn't like his work habits and he was getting the reputation of a thug."

The deal turned out to be slick and vital.

Rick Mahorn would become the original Bad Boy of the Pistons, playing ugly-rough on the floor, muscling the enemy, flashing a sinister smile, all in league with Bill Laimbeer.

Years later, he would leave the Pistons, with one championship ring . . . leaving in heart-break, when Jack McCloskey was forced to put a name in the 1989 expansion draft. And the name that went in, with Jack's deepest regrets, was Rick Mahorn's.

McCloskey had rooked Seattle, Cleveland and Washington in trades, Portland, too, for a draft choice. Attendance was no more a problem for the Pistons, when they played at the Silverdome and on occasion downtown at the Joe Louis Arena. The Pistons were averaging more than 16,000 a game—and had become the NBA's top draw, the league's attendance leader.

The club had discovered Joe Dumars as a prize in the draft. It had become a contending team, stepping up toward the echelon of the Celtics and Lakers. But still the curse of the Celtics choked the Pistons in the playoffs. And in 1986, the Pistons were not even able to survive through a best-of-five first-round playoff series with the Atlanta Hawks.

The Pistons were still steps away.

McCloskey's best smarts—or luck—occurred in the summer of 1986.

On draft day in June, McCloskey chose John Salley, not quite 7 feet tall, out of Georgia Tech on the eleventh pick of the first round. Next time around, McCloskey went for an unknown athlete with an unusual past and very strong yet very delicate emotions—Dennis Rodman, from Southeast Oklahoma State.

The draft is always a game of Pin the Tail on

the Donkey, spin the picker around until he's dizzy and then point him to the target. Jack hit it twice in the 1986 draft. And the Pistons took two more giant steps toward a championship.

Jack went off, played tennis, a game in which he is so competitive and so adept that he became the Michigan Over 55 Men's Singles champion. Before his basketball team ever won a championship. But his summertime thoughts did not stray from the NBA trade market.

Joe Dumars was another jewel in Jack McCloskey's drafting crown.

The Pistons still were short a scorer, a forward who could get inside, post up when necessary, work toward the basket.

McCloskey got him on August 21, 1986.

The player was Adrian Dantley, who had kicked around the NBA for ten seasons. He had been with the old Buffalo Braves, the Indiana Pacers, the Lakers, and the Utah Jazz. He had been traded four times. A player who moves around that much must be regarded with suspicion. Could he be a team player? Could he and Isiah Thomas share the one basketball that is the league maximum for use at one time in any game? Dantley had averaged more than 30 points a game in a couple of seasons. Twice he had been the NBA's scoring champion.

Plus, Adrian Dantley was thirty, not the sort of addition likely for a youthful team on the upgrade.

McCloskey had been trying for two years to acquire Dantley in a trade. The Jazz kept refusing. McCloskey kept asking. Then Dantley got into a contract flap with Frank Layden, the general manager/coach at Utah. Adrian had a habit of doing that, irritating management. He and Layden got into a spicy feud and the Jazz let the Pistons have him—for a considerable price.

"That had a lot to do with their attitude," McCloskey told Bill Halls. "So we were able to swing the deal."

McCloskey had known Adrian Dantley from their years with the Lakers. He understood the risks and made the deal. It was expensive for the Pistons. To get Dantley from the Jazz, McCloskey was required to surrender Kelly Tripucka and Kent Benson, who had been with the Pistons since the day he was traded for Bob Lanier. The Jazz gave the Pistons two second-round draft choices in the package with Dantley.

"If you're a coach and you try to change Adrian Dantley, which Chuck hasn't done here, you're going to run into problems," McCloskey told Corky Meinecke. "He's a bit of a loner and he's quiet. But when he does have something to say about basketball, you better listen."

Once again the Pistons had rooked the other team in a trade.

Flushed with that success, McCloskey made another trade the following day. He obtained Sidney Green to bulk up the Pistons' bench. The price was Earl Cureton, who had played well enough for the Pistons, and one of the second-round draft choices obtained in the package with Dantley the day before.

Jack's next trade was not that great. But it was necessary. Seeking a big man to spell Lanier, McCloskey made the deal with the Los Angeles Clippers for 6-foot-11 Kurt Nimphius at midseason of 1986-87. It was a costly deal. The Pistons gave up their first-round choice for 1987 plus one of their many seconds.

It was worse than not that great. It was a lousy deal, but McCloskey never claimed perfection. Nimphius played the half season in Detroit and left as a free agent.

The Pistons had not stepped as far as the NBA finals by the summer of 1987. But Jack McCloskey's skills as general manager were envied around the league.

He had dickered with his coach during the times Chuck Daly was faced with temptations of other jobs, with higher pay.

Now McCloskey himself was hit with temptation. The New York Knickerbockers, fallen into the dungeons of the NBA, offered McCloskey a carte blanche deal to reconstruct their club as general manager. The money, as reported out of New York, was to be $2 million.

"I'm interested in it," McCloskey told the Detroit reporters. "You have to have an interest. It would be a new project, an interesting new project."

He was sixty-one at the time—an interesting age to interview for a new job loaded with enormous challenges.

McCloskey had dickered in tough negotiations with Isiah Thomas and Chuck Daly, both of them armed with agents who had the angles figured. He had battled and squabbled with free agent players, all represented by pushy agents. He had handled the agents. Now, negotiating with the Knicks, McCloskey employed his own agent. It was a rare occasion in pro sports—a GM with an agent.

When the story broke, McCloskey had already been interviewed by the covetous Knicks. He was leaning toward accepting the New York job, and abandoning the Pistons. His agent told the *News* the deal was almost all completed. Then the day after the story broke, McCloskey made up his mind, with the aid of his wife, Leslie.

He rejected the Knicks and their reported $2 million to stay in Detroit at around half the dough.

"When it came time to pull the trigger, to say, 'Yes, we're going to New York,' it couldn't be done," McCloskey told Dave Dye.

His wife had more influence on him than his agent. Leslie McCloskey had found a home in West Bloomfield, Michigan, and did not want to leave it.

And Jack McCloskey had a challenge in Detroit that had not yet been won, an assignment that still had to be finished.

The competitor stayed put to compete some more.

Ten days after turning down the Knicks' offer, McCloskey was back in the risk-making dealing business. He surrendered another of the precious first-round draft choices for towering height. McCloskey traded for William Bedford 7 feet 1, from the Phoenix Suns.

The trade left Pistons bare of precious first-draft choices for two years. And the risk was that Bedford had a background of problems in Phoenix—including drugs and a lax work ethic. But Bedford had awesome potential.

McCloskey felt the Pistons were so close now he had to gamble. The club had been on the brink of the 1987 NBA finals, just succumbing as the curse of the Celtics got them one more time in the riotous, and horrible, seven-game series with Boston. The series with the errant pass from Isiah and the racial recriminations following Dennis Rodman's statements with regard to Larry Bird's skin color.

Bedford's drug problems would continue in Detroit to the point that his own teammates once ostracized him. He played one season, then missed the entire 1988-89 season on a drug-related suspension. He spent most of the season in drug rehab and was there when the Pistons won their first NBA championship.

But McCloskey steadfastly supported Bedford when he returned to the Pistons, despite the disapproval of some of the athletes.

"I guess I'm the eternal optimist," McCloskey said. "I think he's eventually going to do it, whether it's here or somewhere else. William has a chance."

McCloskey's optimism—his faith—was wise. William Bedford was a starter when the Pistons opened defense of their back-to-back championships in the 1991 playoffs.

As the 1987–88 season started, McCloskey turned active again in the trademart. He was now patching up on a team close to its eternal goals. Sidney Green, picked up from the Bulls the year before, was dispatched to the Knicks. The Pistons got Ron Moore and a second-round draft choice in exchange.

Just after the season began, McCloskey took a risk on the jovial/brooding Darryl Dawkins, who had been around the league for ages. Among his considerable accomplishments, Dawkins had shattered a backboard into a million fragments while making a slam dunk one night with Philly. He had been the strength on some fine teams there. But now he had become a problem player in Utah. McCloskey gave the Jazz a second-round draft choice and a bucket of dough for Dawkins. It was another risk to fill a need. And it didn't work. Dawkins was there sometimes, sometimes he was an absentee. The Detroit segment of his career lasted sixteen games.

If the gamble with Dawkins had worked, McCloskey might not have not made his next trade. But the Pistons needed a guy 7 feet or so to play up front as a power forward, get into thickest part of the battle as a post-up center, spell Laimbeer, and sometimes team with him in a twin-towers concept. McCloskey found his man to fill that role, in another of his special trades.

On February 24, 1988—again close to the trade deadline—McCloskey traded to get James Edwards from the Phoenix Suns. McCloskey paid for Edwards with Ron Moore, obtained earlier in the season from New York, plus a second-round choice in the draft three years in the future. The goal was to win now, in 1988 and the future be damned, the philosophy that George Allen had made famous, and occasionally successful, in pro football.

Edwards was 7 feet 1, with a glowering visage and a wealth of experience. He was called Buddha. He was thirty-two when he was moved to the Pistons. He had kicked around the NBA from 1978, much in the style of Adrian Dantley. Indeed, Edwards once had been included in a multiplayer trade in which Dantley moved on the other side. Edwards had been a paid performer

The Microwave, Vinnie Johnson, makes a pass to the wing against Charlotte.

for the L.A. Lakers, the Indiana Pacers and the Cleveland Cavaliers before going to Phoenix enroute to Detroit.

Again, Jack McCloskey rooked the other guys in a trade. James Edwards, a career journeyman, would become a starter in Detroit. And his team would make the NBA finals that very same year, and then win NBA championships back-to-back in 1989 and 1990.

The Pistons were one step away, after the 1988 finals, after McCloskey's trade to get James Edwards. Perhaps, the next step need not have been made. The Pistons had killed the curse of the Celtics. They had stuck their own curse on the Chicago Bulls. They had proven they were five points, or so, from matching the Lakers. They were aimed toward a record of sixty or more victories; they had become feared as the Bad Boys, plainly, and they were winning more games than any other club in the league.

The trade deadline was nearing again when Trader Jack struck. The papers were full of rumors about an impending trade for days. The rumors became truth. McCloskey dealt with the Dallas Mavericks, and the player he got was Mark Aguirre. This was the very player McCloskey had expected to draft back in 1982, when the Pistons were a dogmeat team, when Dallas, for some odd reason, left Isiah Thomas available by picking Aguirre first off the board.

Isiah and Aguirre had been boyhood chums in Chicago, out on the West Side where Michael Jordan now played for the Bulls in the seedy Stadium. Now, it was commonly gossiped in Detroit, that Isiah had campaigned for the Pistons to get Aguirre in a trade. Aguirre had become a dissident in Dallas. He sulked and strained. The fans booed him.

McCloskey made the deal. He sent Adrian Dantley to the Mavericks, packed with the Pistons' No. 1 draft choice for 1991. It was a heartbreak for Adrian. He had meshed in Detroit, performed the exact role for which Mc-

James Edwards, a career journeyman acquired by Jack McCloskey in 1988, was one of the final pieces to the championship puzzle.

Closkey had obtained him almost three seasons earlier. Now, at the edge of a championship for the first time in his career, he was being exiled to Dallas. It was the fifth time he'd been traded. This one was a rotten break and Dantley first refused to report. His mother, in Washington, complained publicly about the treatment of her son, stating that Isiah Thomas had engineered the trade to get his friend to Detroit.

And in Detroit, there were doubters who wondered if Mark Aguirre could alter his habits as a basketball individualist to fit into the Pistons' concept of team unity.

It all worked.

McCloskey had collected Vinnie Johnson, Bill Laimbeer, Rick Mahorn, Adrian Dantley, James Edwards and finally Mark Aguirre—all of them roustabout athletes, most of them with some sort of problem, all of them guys who had never won on other clubs. And he took his acquisitions and placed them on a team with extra-special draft selections—Isiah Thomas, Joe Dumars, John Salley, Dennis Rodman.

And they all contributed, in some way, to the molding of a championship franchise—a team that once had been a tragicomedy in a town that had shunned pro basketball.

"When I take a risk," McCloskey told Vartan Kupelian of the *News*, opening the secret of his philosophy for rooking the other guy, "I don't mean take a risk to the point where you're really going to hurt your team. It's got to be a very calculated risk situation. For instance, with James Edwards, I went down to Phoenix before we made the trade, saw him play two or three times, talked to a number of people and felt very comfortable about bringing James here. He's worked out well for us."

II—The Microwave

On a basketball court far away from home, Vinnie Johnson returned to the game of his youth, his sporting roots.

"I was built with confidence," V.J. said on the Sunday afternoon in Portland after his shooting touch returned and the Pistons had taken control of the 1990 NBA finals.

"I grew up on the playgrounds of New York. I was playing one-on-one all my life.

"This was what I learned in Brooklyn."

The game they play on the asphalt jungles, the playgrounds, is brutal and mean. They play it with hands in your face, the dribble, the sidestep, the maneuver, then the shot.

Always the shot.

Johnson was a pure shooter. And for the Pistons, as they and the Trail Blazers split the first two games of the NBA finals, he had been misfiring. His stats were two points in each of the games. Vinnie was in a slump.

He had been below double figures in all of the past six games, all physical playoff games with the Bulls and then the Blazers. The Microwave had shorted out.

"The first two games, I was 1-for-10," Vinnie said on this June Sunday in 1990, after his shot came back the way it used to on the Brooklyn playgrounds. "Some guys do that in a half. If you don't get the shot, you don't shoot.

"Now I don't have to read that I'm in a slump. My friends were calling me, 'Vinnie, what's wrong?'"

In Game 3, Vinnie came off the bench to score 21 points, double figures twice over. That's been his role, the sixth man, coming off the bench and firing, since he joined the Pistons in 1981. He scored 15 of his points in the second quarter, as the Pistons took command. As Chuck Daly put Vinnie into the game, Isiah Thomas ran over and said: "Make him wait till he gets warmed up before he takes a shot."

Daly responded: "Zeke, I've coached him seven years. I know when he hits his first shot, he's hot."

Vinnie got the ball moments after the second quarter started. He dribbled along the baseline, stopped short, bent his legs and unloosed the jump shot. It was dead-solid perfect through the iron and net. One shot and he'd matched his field-goal production for the first two games of the finals. It was just like on the school yard in Brooklyn.

"Chuck doesn't have to say, 'take the first shot,'" Johnson said. "I'm going to take it. I have to attack. That's my game. Sometimes it takes four shots, even if I miss.

"I'm a scorer, not a shooter.

"The first shot goes in and my eyes light up. Give it to me again. I'm ready."

Johnson felt the pressure of playing in Portland. The Pistons had lost twenty games in succession there before their 121–106 victory this Sunday afternoon.

"I never lost confidence," Johnson said. "Only a couple of times in my career have I lost confidence.

"Coming here, they were supposed to win on their home court. That's a lot of pressure.

"I wasn't ticked off with the media people. I felt totally confident with my shot."

But then the Pistons are a team on which the players lift each other, try to bolster the other guy's spirits. At the practice session on Saturday, with the finals square at one victory and the Pistons having forfeited their home court advantage, Bill Laimbeer took Johnson aside.

"He had a mental thing," Laimbeer said. "I told him we were all behind him, even if he shot 1-for-500. He's a shooter."

"Bill definitely gave me a big lift," Vinnie Johnson said. "He said, 'you're two men.' Then he said after we lost the second game, he almost called me at 3 o'clock in the morning."

Consider that Johnson, a.k.a. The Microwave got his wakeup call.

And four nights later, the ball would go from Isiah Thomas to Vinnie Johnson with the clock flickering through its countdown, each tenth of a second flashing away, down toward the end—to all zeroes. Vinnie would have it with four seconds showing in the deadlocked game. He would dribble, bend his knees, and unloose the ball with his right hand with one second left. The ball would travel seventeen feet in a McDonald's arch, above the head of Jerome Kersey, and slash, untouched, through iron and the cord netting, and go splat on the floor in Portland. The dwindling clock would read 00.7—a fraction of the final second of the long season from early November to the middle of June. Double O Seven, the number identified with James Bond, the fictional terminator.

But there was no fiction here. Only melodrama.

"Vinnie, vidi, vici!" read the headline in the *Detroit News*

Vinnie Johnson's shot terminated the Trailer Blazers, 92–90, and won the NBA championship for the Pistons. Back-to-Back!

It was vintage Microwave. A shot straight off the streets in Brooklyn.

"Isiah gave me the ball, he was double teamed," Vinnie said as the Pistons guzzled what champagne they didn't bathe themselves in. "I looked at the clock. There were four seconds and I knew it was tied. I wanted to take more seconds off the clock, and then I gave Kersey a head fake and let it go—and we're champions.

"No, no, I never hit a shot like that in my life before, and it's history, baby."

Vintage Pistons.

They were behind in the fourth quarter. They were behind Portland by seven points with two minutes and two seconds on the blinking red light bulbs that formed the digital game clock. In those last 122 seconds, the Pistons scored nine points, the last two on Vinnie's shot over Kersey's head. The Trail Blazers scored zero.

The Pistons overcame adversity, a large deficit, the hostile crowd and the Trail Blazers in that fourth quarter. Vinnie Johnson, on this night, totalled 16 points for the game.

He scored 15 of those 16 in the dozen minutes of the final period, when he turned on his instant heat. Coming off the bench.

Vintage Microwave!

There was a night against the Celtics, in the playoffs, in 1985, when the Pistons were enduring their growing pains. The Pistons were playing in Joe Louis Arena, downtown Detroit, home but away, again removed from their regular court in the Silverdome. The Dome's roof had collapsed. On this night, in May, during the playoffs, the Pistons trailed the Celtics all through the game. They were behind in the fourth quarter. Then they started feeding Vinnie Johnson. Vinnie pumped in 22 points in the quarter alone. The Pistons won, 102–99, a fine victory for this young team still four years distant from its first NBA championship. For the game, Vinnie had 34 points.

After the game in the locker room of the reigning champion Celtics, Danny Ainge muttered to a reporter:

"If that guy in Chicago, William Perry is The Refrigerator, Vinnie Johnson is The Microwave. He really heated up in a hurry."

In the other locker room, the CBS-TV producer chased after Vinnie Johnson. Vinnie was needed for the postgame interview on the national TV show.

"Oh, let Isiah do it," said Vinnie Johnson.

". . . That's my role, to make things happen," The Microwave told Skip Myslenski of the *Chicago Tribune* as the Pistons were winning a seven-game crunch war with the Bulls in the 1990 playoffs. That doesn't necessarily mean scoring. It means doing something in every aspect of the game. It's my job to provide the spark.

". . . I attack. I go in a game and attack. I'm very confident I can score on anybody.

". . . When I'm on a probe, I'll probe anyone . . . When it happens, I categorize it as being in a zone. You feel you can make every shot, bank it from any distance, put as much arc on it as you like. You feel you have the touch, and before you release the ball, you feel it's going to fall in.

"You're on top of the world. You know everyone's focusing on you. They're anticipating your next jump shot and so are you. It's just an incredible feeling. You know, everything you do, it's going to fall in. Your shot hits the rim, rolls around and falls in. You know it's your night, and when it comes, you appreciate it.

"You treasure the moment."

". . . I'm from Brooklyn," Vinnie Johnson told writers another time. "I was built with confidence. I grew up playing in neighborhoods where people wouldn't even drive their cars. I fear nothing."

He is not pretentious, he is not tall for this game—6 feet 2 and stocky. He moves in bursts with the ball, hunched over it as he dribbles, then uncoiling to make his shots. He started balding during his seasons in Detroit. He was well into his thirties before his team started winning championships; he was thirty-four when the 1990–91 training camp started and he was fighting again for a new contract—and winning.

But as it is with all of them, he can go back to his origins and spin an intriguing story.

As a boy, Vinnie would pedal his bicycle from game to game, from playground to playground, hopping off to shoot buckets, one on one, pushing through that bloody-nose lane beneath the basket.

"We went around and played all the best competition in the city," V.J. told the *News'* Dave Dye in a 1985 profile. "There would be guys running through the park, carrying guns every day. We just kept playing our games, and they were all battles.

"There was no such thing as an uncontested

layup. You'd get tossed to the cement. You had to learn how to take the shot and get fouled because you'd never get away with calling fouls all the time on the playground. They'd never let you. You just had to learn how to take your hits.

"And you learned to somehow get the shot, because if you passed it, you might not see it again. It taught you to score even if you weren't open . . .

"That's carried over."

The first bike Vinnie rode to take him from game to game was created out of nuts and bolts and chunks of metal, on a workbench.

"At first I had a homemade bike, then a better one, then a 10-speed," Vinnie told the late Shelby Strother of the *News*. "We'd ride into some pretty bad neighborhoods to play ball. I didn't worry, though. I had my chain and my lock and I'd hoist my bike about six feet up the fence and chain it there so I could keep an eye on it while I played.

"You do what you gotta do."

His mother was a seamstress and part-time maid. His father worked in an air conditioning plant as a foreman. Vinnie grew up rooting for the hometown team, the Knicks. It was during the early 1970s, when the Knicks won championships.

"I used to listen to the Knicks games on the radio with my father," Vinnie told Strother. "Clyde Frazier, DeBusschere, Willis Reed, Dick Barnett. The Knicks' heyday. I loved those nights. Then when I was big enough to play with the older fellows, I headed across the street, ready to be the next Walt Frazier.

"I never had any problems. Couple of times we got chased out of some white neighborhoods after we beat them in a game. But we were laughing all the way to the train station. It wasn't nothing real scary."

And there were the basketball shoes.

"I remember when I got my first pair of Chuck Taylor Converse All-Stars," Vinnie said to Strother. "Your first pair of Chucks is always a big deal. Man, I remember for a long time I'd wash those shoes every night, use a toothbrush to get any smudges off. I took care of them same as you might take care of your car."

From the tough part of Brooklyn, and the gym of Franklin Roosevelt High, Vinnie made it to Waco, Texas, with his basketball skills. He spent two years at McClennon Junior College and then two more years at Baylor. The Seattle Supersonics picked him off in the first round of the 1979 draft. Vinnie was an NBA rookie the same season Earvin Johnson and Larry Bird were rookies.

When the trade was made—Vinnie Johnson and cash for Gregory Kelser—the Pistons had just finished their two most disastrous seasons. The Pistons had just started their 1981–82 schedule, with a new regime, with a new approach. An NBA championship was a remote fantasy.

Vinnie Johnson would be the first of those assembled by Jack McCloskey on the team that most of a decade later would become the most intimidating and feared in the NBA.

Those early days were hell.

Scotty Robertson, the Detroit coach of the moment, and Johnson bickered with each other. Robertson complained that Johnson was overweight and wanted to trade him away.

But Vinnie Johnson, the one-on-one man, played the same way then as he did during the championship seasons.

One night the Pistons played the Golden State Warriors and actually won. Vinnie always claimed he was not a one-dimensional ballplayer. On this night, he scored 23 points. But also had 9 rebounds, 8 assists, 2 steals, and using all of his 6 feet 2 inches, he blocked 2 shots. The man he guarded was the renowned World B. Free.

"I was getting beat on every drive," Free told the media following the game. "It took me right out of my game."

One of Chuck Daly's tricks, successful at Portland in the 1990 playoffs, was a three-guard offense—Vinnie, Isiah, Joe Dumars—as a stunning triumvirate on the court. It was the precisioned slickness of Isiah with his snap passes and marvelous court sense, and the schooled control of Joe, mixed with the Brooklyn playground individualism of Vinnie.

When the Microwave heated up and started his gunning—pop, pop, pop, swish—his teammates became awed. They knew to feed him the ball and let Vinnie shoot it.

"I sit back and become a fan just like the rest," Joe Dumars told the *News*. "He's unreal. He unconscious. You start wondering what he could possibly do next."

"He's an offense by himself," Thomas added. "When he gets going like that, we just give him the ball and start watching like everybody else in the place. It's demoralizing for the other team. There's nothing they can do."

And said Chuck Daly, who knew to sit back and let Vinnie shoot and shoot, with the coaching caution coming out: "It's fascinating for everybody in the building. He's unstoppable. But it can act as a double-edged sword for us, too. Everybody stands around and admires Vinnie. It's tough not to respond that way. It sort of takes everybody out of the offense. But when he's hot you still got to ride him . . . "

As against Boston in 1985, when Danny Ainge discovered The Microwave. As in game after game, year after year, in the Silverdome, in Joe Louis Arena, in the Palace, when he came off the bench as the sixth man and fired up. As in Game 5, in the last quarter of the 1990 NBA finals at Portland. As he cut loose with 00.7 on the clock, just as if he were taking a shot on the playground back in Brooklyn.

Of all his trades—from Bob Lanier to Adrian Dantley for Mark Aguirre—Jack McCloskey harked back to the deal he made on November 21, 1981, as the one in which the Pistons rooked the other guy the best.

"Dollar for dollar, that was our best deal," McCloskey once told the *News'* Bill Halls. "We gave them Gregory Kelser, and I think they threw in $100,000."

Getting Vinnie Johnson, and his street basketball skills, was the first major step toward the back-to-back championships.

But in sports, the time eventually expires for all heroes. In late summer 1991, it expired for Vinnie, senior man on the Pistons, when they were champions. It was a sad day—the Pistons put Vinnie Johnson, who had scored once with a playground basket with 00.7 on the clock, on waivers so they could release him.

III—Spider

The season of their first NBA championship the Pistons move into the strange territory beyond the *Sports Illustrated.*

They are discovered by *Rolling Stone*, which ordinarily devotes itself to subjects of a different style of rap. Laimbeer and Rick Mahorn are featured as the masters of mayhem—the Bad Boys of Detroit. *Esquire* discovers Laimbeer and his unique ability to stir stuff and perform his on-stage theatrics in a lovely piece by Mike Lupica, the New York sports guru. Later on, *Gentlemen's Quarterly*, going for glitz as always, grabs Isiah for its cover as a fashionplate when he wasn't adorned in his basketball skivvies.

The Pistons have traveled a notch, maybe two, above being a curious franchise in the insular domain of sports. They have gone beyond the late-night humor/talk shows and Arsenio. They have burrowed into the exclusivity of the prime time network television sitcom society. One night in the 1990–91 wintertime, Kevin McHale, the Celtics' Frankenstein look-alike, does a cameo on "Cheers," which is high-level popular entertainment TV. The show is set in Boston, so McHale's appearance is seminatural. Sam, or somebody, shows McHale an X-ray picture.

"A male gorilla."

McHale scrutinizes the picture.

"It could be Laimbeer," says McHale, his key line for laughter.

And America does laugh.

The Pistons, that erstwhile funny little basketball team from some place out in the Midwest, has arrived among the rich and famous.

And then there is John Salley, the Spider, from the streets of Brooklyn, trained at Georgia Tech and various night spots and ladies locations. John Salley makes it all the way to *Vogue*. There is Salley all dressed up in high fashion, carrying an umbrella and wearing no socks, in 'Takin' Parties,' going to the premiere of Spike Lee's *Mo' Better Blues*. He is grinning, as usual, seven feet above the rest of the crowd.

Vogue never gives space to Chuck Daly and his double-breasted courtside wardrobe. Wrong list.

Wrong list, too, for John Salley, when it is Chuck Daly's list.

Daly does not often speak critically of his players. They have freedom of expression; he does not attempt to squelch their personalities.

Bill Laimbeer has shouted violently at the coach in mid-game at bench and received no consequence more serious from Daly: "That's Billy."

Thomas and Daly have not always been in synch.

But John Salley mystifies Daly, to the point of

outspoken criticism. Spider Salley's basic function is stuffing and stuffing back—the slam on offense and on defense, the rejection, as they mutter in the new lexicon invented by ESPN. The rap is Salley does not always play to capabilities, unless it is playoff time.

There is the aftermath of a loss to the Indiana Pacers, a.k.a. the Indiana Patsies to the Pistons, in February 1991, when everything was a struggle with Isiah injured. Daly drops some meaningful words on Salley via an interview with Frank Beckmann of Detroit's WJR.

"He gets seen on TV, either locally or nationally, every night," says Daly. "But papers around the country are writing about the maddening, frustrating John Salley, the inconsistent John Salley.

"He's a little more frustrating than other players on the team. We tell him how we plan to play something and he goes out and does it the way he wants. He's very frustrating."

One night later, on the road in hostile Milwaukee, John Salley goes out and slam dunks, he rejects shots, he scores. The Pistons, slumping, victimized twice in two games on their own court in Auburn Hills, where they seldom lose, bash the Bucks. John Salley is the hero of the victory.

"I love him, but he's frustrating," says Daly to Corky Meinecke. "All of his offense is happenstance. He'll take a hook shot, he'll take somebody off the dribble, and he'll make jumpshots. But none of it is consistent.

"Very frustrating.

"Maybe it's because . . . there's so much trade talk about him."

It is true that trade rumors have pursued Salley through two seasons—the Nets, the Clippers, the Mavericks, the Hawks. Such gossip tends to make a man with two championship rings and some strong commitments somewhat jittery.

And it rages again as the trade deadline approaches in February of the 1990–91 season, with Isiah out injured for months, Joe Dumars hobbled by bum toe, and the Pistons' desperate for a guard.

The Pistons now play what the late Pete Axthelm once described as the city game far away from the city. They used to play in the city, in downtown Detroit when they could find a spot that would take them in. But years ago they abandoned the city first for the Silverdome in Pontiac, and then their own Palace of Auburn Hills. It's a thirty-five-mile haul from downtown to see a basketball game. Since the team plays in suburbia, the Pistons players took up residence in the suburbs. All except Spider Salley.

John Salley has bought a mansion inside the very city limits of Detroit. The house happens to have sixty-two rooms complete with an elevator, a chapel with eight rows of pews, stained-glass windows, a dozen fireplaces, seven porches, a wine cellar, and the adornment of eight heads of angels carved into the walls. Lots of marble. Salley's digs once happened to be owned by the Archdiocese of Detroit and was lived in, most recently, by John Cardinal Dearden. But it is within the city limits, because John Salley expresses a unique desire to live where the people live. Besides, at half a million bucks, it was a real estate steal.

"It's good to have a big place in case I feel trapped by basketball or by fans," Salley explains to reporters.

Salley has a powerful social consciousness, among his varied attributes. He goes to schools and conducts clinics. He is aware. His life's ambition, after basketball, is to become a stand-up comedian.

At the Pistons' games in The Palace, the picture scoreboard displays a crashing, farcical scene for the amusement of the customers during an early first-quarter time out. At that juncture, Salley is still in his warmup togs, not yet in the game. So he gathers with the other Pistons during this time out respite as Chuck Daly expounds on some priceless strategy and delivers some motivational rhetoric. But Salley's attention is seldom on his coach in these moments.

Rather, you can see his eyes turn and lift toward the scoreboard to the comedy scene being shown to the crowd. Daly is ignored. Then when the climax of the slice of comedy is shown, usually with a character taking a pratfall of sorts, Salley grins and tries to suppress outright giggles. Often he fails and guffaws, in plain view of those sitting at the press table.

A portrait of Salley from the *Detroit News* shortly after the Pistons' second championship —the interview was conducted on the morning of the day Nelson Mandela, the African National Congress' freed leader, visited Detroit:

It is party time. The man about town is on the polished floor, slow dancing.

John Salley likes that description—man about town. His face lights up.

Anyway, he is slow dancing, cheek-to-cheek with a lady, when somebody tries to cut in.

"You know," Salley says, the flight of the Pistons' second championship never ending, "the funniest thing happened. I was at Joey's. That's a club down on East Jefferson, and I'm on the dance floor. The last dance. A slow record. Luther Vandross . . . one of my favorite artists . . . period . . . in the world . . . and I'm dancing with this real pretty girl. And this girl came up . . . I'm slow dancing now . . . came and tapped me and moved her, the girl, I was dancing with . . . and said, 'I'm about to leave and need your autograph.'

"This is on the dance floor. Now, I mean I'm in the middle of the dance floor, not like on the side. So I act like I didn't hear her. I grabbed the girl back. She came around the other side.

"I'm in the middle of my spin move. I'm a good slow dancer, and I could spin and move at the same time. She said, 'No, no. I have to go, and I need your autograph now.'

"It's been hectic at times."

Hectic it is in the nightly life of the 7-foot man about town, member of the city's Back-to-Back NBA champions.

"So did she get the autograph?" he is asked.

"Yeah," said Salley. "I didn't want her to stand there the whole time and mess up the rest of Luther's song. 'See ya. Have a good life.'"

Salley's days are equally as hectic. Basketball clinics at Detroit's high schools. Lecturing at Isiah Thomas' basketball camp at Oakland County Community College. Autograph sessions. His radio gig at WLLZ-FM. His endorsements for Chrysler, pushing his Osaga sneakers. A trip back to his roots in Brooklyn, and a clinic and some parties there. A whirlwind visit to the Bahamas with his Pistons teammates. Busy.

He is aware of the community, all spectrums. He is the rare Detroit pro athlete who actually lives within the boundaries of the city, in his famed 62-room digs in Palmer Woods.

"Some people relax on a boat," Salley says. "Some people go on a vacation. I spend most of my summer talking to kids. Black. White. Green. Purple. Rich. Poor. There's no such thing as in between any more.

"I do a lot of things that are socially active. Dealing in African-Americanism.

"I'll give you an example. I wear an ANC hat, and I explain what it means. My biggest experience is seeing Mandela. Getting as close as possible."

". . . Hopefully, getting a handshake. That'll make my whole season. My whole year."

"Think he'll know who you are?" he is asked.

"No, I don't care," Salley says. "I know who he is. That's all that's important. If he doesn't know, he'll know when I finish . . . breaking his hand with a hard handshake. 'Who was that 7-foot black man kissing on me?'"

That night Mandela is presented with a Pistons jacket and a Pistons cap. Towering behind Mandela on the TV cameras is Salley. Later, it is Salley assisting Rosa Parks up the stairs at Tiger Stadium, where she and Mandela would speak.

"You asked me about being a man about town," Salley says. "I don't mind being called that. When I go out to nightclubs, people ask me what I'm doing there. I let people see I'm human, you know.

"A lot of times . . . since we won . . . a lot of women have been tapping out when they see us. You know, breathing hard, hyperventilating. Things like that."

"They do that?" he is asked.

"Yeah," Salley says. "When I go to Perry Drugs and they don't believe I'm in a Perry Drugs."

Salley likes to do both voices of a conversation.

"'What are you doing in a Perry Drug store?'" he says, speaking in the high voice who spots his towering head from the next aisle over. "Buying deodorant and toothpaste," he says, in the other voice, his own. "So I don't scare you the rest of the day.

"Some people don't expect us to be human. I try to let them see it. Like I told a bunch of kids, I'm tangible. I'm human. I like to eat ice cream. Cookies. And laugh and giggle and go to the movies."

Man about town.

"I'll give you an example," he says. "We had a party at Clubland. Invited the whole city. You should have come, man. It was a blast. No one got hurt. No one was upset. Put on this video show with lasers and steam. I did it right this time.

"I got to get a bigger place. Maybe next year, Cobo Hall. That means we're gonna win next year."

They tell Salley he has 40 seconds before he goes on to speak to the 200 or so children at Isiah's camp.

"I'll give you an example. Any camp my teammates have, I show up for free . . . "

"And not for free?" he is asked.

"Some autograph sessions," he says. "Sometimes, when I'm in the suburbs, I don't do them for free. However, the inner city . . . usually, it's for free. A lot of people are coming up to me asking to do fundraisers at my house. A lot of times I've got to say no to them."

On a typical summer day, Salley can be seen delivering a clinic to children on the floor of a Detroit high school. He can be seen at lunch at a posh restaurant along the Detroit riverfront. He can be seen at a second clinic in a public high school. He can be seen dining in the suburbs at another posh restaurant. Then he can be seen, slow dancing, in some club in the city.

The man about town . . . he is asked about his favorite restaurant.

"I've got a couple of great restaurants," Salley says. "Let's go over them . . . so I don't get killed by any one person. I got Ginopolis. I got New Parthenon. The Rattlesnake is my newest. There's a place in West Bloomfield, if I'm ever in that neighborhood, which is not often, called Confetti's. My cook used to be the cook at the Golden Mushroom."

Thomas shows up to summon Salley out to the campers on the court.

"Hey, nice shorts," Salley says.

Isiah is dressed in blue jean cutoffs, with frayed edges, and a shirt proclaiming Isiah Thomas' Basketball Camp.

Outside, Salley grips a microphone. He has been trained to do this. He is an aspiring comedian, devoting spare time to writing comedy. He is the butt of jokes by Arsenio Hall on television. If Salley were not blocking shots for the Pistons, he would be doing comedy even now.

His message to the children is true life, tinged with humor.

"Hey, what's up," Salley says. "I play with this little guy, that's his name on your shirt. When I first came here, I had big dreams, you know, like Sean Higgins has."

The kids laugh. The night before, Higgins, who came out of Michigan early for the NBA draft, was the very last player taken in the draft. Salley had the line prepared.

"I had this really big ego. Big ego. I went to Isiah Thomas. 'I want you to find me a condo or an apartment . . . a condo with a jacuzzi for me and my lady. I want a Rolls-Royce.' I wanted him to find it. Isiah stayed there . . . nodded his head . . . smiled . . . yeah . . . he took this. (Salley is holding a basketball.) Hit me right in the head with it. My head got about as skinny as it is now."

Laughter.

"I had to say thank you for it," Salley continues, coming to the moral of his story. "Because if he didn't do it that way, I'd probably be . . . like Sean Higgins.

"He started helping me . . . because I was pretty beat up by Rick Mahorn. They were treating me real bad. I had coaches who didn't like me. Teammates.

"Then I became a Piston. Sacrifice is the biggest thing

. . . a healthy ego.

"You can't have a big ego, and it takes determination to win. It takes determination to do anything. Not cheating. But it takes hitting . . . and you're not known as a hitter . . . you hit somebody.

"Like Isiah."

Salley goes on for a half hour, gripping the mike, his words transmitted by hand signals for the hearing impaired. He holds the basketball. He delivers some parables. He shows the children how to pass the ball. He talks about the perils of drugs. He delivers some more jokes.

"I told Isiah something," Salley says, "good things happen to good people. Like, Isiah was shooting bad . . . well, Isiah wasn't shooting so good . . . "

"I was shooting bad," Thomas says. "For Isiah, I was shooting bad . . . "

"I told him, 'Zeke, good things happen to good people.'

"See what happened? He got an MVP trophy. He got a Cherokee truck. He got extra money.

"Do you think he gave me any of that?"

Salley has one final message for the campers.

"I'm going to do my neighborhood," Salley says of his trip back to his roots in Brooklyn. "Doing a dinner. Same neighborhood, same guys gonna be there who told me I couldn't play . . . had no potential . . . I shouldn't even think about picking up a basketball. Maybe I should be a truck driver."

"A 7-foot truck driver!

"These same guys gonna be at my park. I believe in positive thinking. I believe that good things happen to good people.

"As long as I was a good kid, good person, stayed away from negative people, bad associations, formed some useful habits.

"That's my speech to you."

He is in a hurry now. Got to rush to his next engagement, speaking to Boy Scouts at The Palace before he goes home to get ready to go to Nelson Mandela's rally.

He stops for a moment to discuss his touch for comedy.

"My mother is very extroverted, can find jest in everything," he says. "As far as the comedy thing, I understand how important it is to make fun of reality . . . to jest around, because if you would take everything serious all the time, you wouldn't have much of a life . . . you only live once, but if you do it right, once is enough."

He is asked about Arsenio Hall, who trashed him during the NBA playoffs.

"Arsenio used to be a comedian," Salley says. "I mean that was his full-time job. Now, he's a TV personality. Arsenio understands he has to be a talk-show host, as well as be funny and an entertainer.

"As far as the things he said about me, to say a joke you have to be able to take a joke, and don't get mad about it. He hasn't done anything to damage my popularity. All he's done is add to it."

The man about town . . . he is asked about his moments of repose in the house, the Palmer Woods mansion that was the home of the late John Cardinal Dearden.

"I spend an hour a day just sitting somewhere, looking up," he says. "I got this seat on the roof of my house, and I hear people drive by and say, 'this is John Salley's house.'

"'Yo . . . John . . . you there?' I can hear that all the time. And I got a chapel in my house. It used to be a chapel. Real quiet. You can't hear the telephone.

"I can sit in my house and not be bothered."

He is going to be late to speak to the Boy Scouts. He is now talking about Brooklyn, the Brownsville section, and he drops a Jewish expression into the conversation.

". . . if doesn't bother you, don't worry about it," Salley says. "Brownsville was all Jewish . . . My uncle's was the first black family there. I'm good friends with Mark Breland and Mike Tyson. Now I told my teammates I'm good friends with Mark Breland and Mike Tyson. They say, 'Sall, every time somebody comes from Brooklyn, you say you know them . . .' The year we lost the championship . . . my second year in the league . . . Adrian Dantley gets injured, Rick Mahorn gets suspended for fighting, and we go to New York to play on Christmas Day . . . and Mike Tyson saw us on television, and came down, and sat behind our bench."

The second voice becomes a whisper.

"Mike Tyson behind our bench. We wind up winning the game. He comes into the locker room. He sits right next to me, and we're sitting there talking . . . All these guys were sitting there petrified. He says, 'Think Isiah can get me a pair of sneakers.?'"

Salley now raises his voice.

"I said, 'Zeke, Mike wants your sneakers, Zeke.' (Whisper again) Anything you want, you get."

Now he must go. He says:

"I got a red, black and green button on my hat. I got ANC on my hat . . . and people ask me what ANC means, which either means they live in a capsule . . . or their television doesn't work.

"I went to a party the other night . . . and this white lady asks, 'Do you know Mandela?' I said, 'Yes.' She said, 'You know he's a communist?'"

"I said, 'So's Gorbachev. You never say anything about him coming to this country.'"

One afternoon during the summer 1990, John Salley is strolling through a shopping mall in Detroit.

"I saw one sixteen-year-old kid in a mall walking with a portable phone and a beeper and

136

wondered if he was doing the right thing or was into drugs," Salley tells an interviewer for the NBA's *Hoop* magazine. "We sat and talked for a half an hour. He gave me his phone number and said if I could show him an alternate to drugs, he'd try it.

"You have to struggle to get to the top, not take the easy road dealing in poison."

Another publication discovers John Salley, the man about town. *Metro Times*, a Detroit tabloid circulated for the Yuppy group, publishes its Best of Detroit Reader Poll. Salley is voted the towns Most Sexist Sports Figure. The text accompanying this announcement of his selection states: ". . . His charisma and semi-slick propensity for self-promotion may well make him a very visible national celebrity. Perhaps he will mature with fame and shuck off the sexist airs that make him appear as yet another adolescent millionaire with attitude and hormone difficulties, for otherwise the Spider may find himself trapped in the web with fun boys like Wade Boggs and Steve Garvey . . ."

Sporting fame in Detroit means heads placed in bull's-eye targets. A few pages beyond Salley's selection as Most Sexist Sports Figure, *Metro Times* publishes its lengthy list of classified personals . . . hawking sex by the agate line.

IV—Mark

Chuck Daly is off the bench, catapulted. His foot is stomping on the glistening floor; his double-breasted suitcoat is opened, flapping as he swirls, and his arms rotate in frantic flourishes.

This mad display of anger is provoked by a small moment on the floor. A moment of neglect. Duane Ferrell has slipped uncontested, unchallenged, in a dash through the lane in the blood-colored uniform of the Atlanta Hawks. Meanwhile, Mark Aguirre has been fastened beneath the basket, flat-footed, a spectator, when the idea was for him to be playing defense.

Chuck yells his lungs out at Aguirre. Chuck throws out the hook. Aguirre is out of the game. He is now to be fastened to the bench, to stew in his mistake.

These are the playoffs of 1991, and the reigning champions are in deep stuff. They have already lost the first game of the first-round of the playoffs on their home court in the Palace. They are in jeopardy. The Pistons manage to win this game, still endangered in the series, but Mark Aguirre plays only seconds more. There are stories that Aguirre refuses when Daly tells him to go back into the game. In the last minute, Daly sends him back in and Aguirre goes. Daly puts Aguirre back in for garbage time, that period of scramble and shoot in a lopsided game, when the rinky-dinks clog the floor until time runs out. The coach has punished the player—shown him up, embarrassed him.

After the game, Aguirre storms to the locker room. All his teammates are happy, at least satisfied, that they have rebounded from their loss in the first game. Aguirre dresses fast and sets some sort of NBA record for getting out of the locker room before the press can find him.

Club officials berate him.

Next morning, Aguirre shows up for practice with his left arm encased in a cast. Sometime during the night, he explains, he felt a twinge and took himself to the hospital.

He is hit upon by the reporters. Old criticisms of Aguirre's old habits are unearthed, retold. His desire and his commitment are questioned.

Unrecalled in this time of controversy in the playoffs is that the Pistons have won back-to-back NBA championships with Mark Aguirre performing in the role assigned to him. Unmentioned is the likelihood that without Mark Aguirre, the Pistons would not have won either of their championships.

Mark Aguirre is the confusing, enigmatic personality on this basketball team.

Mark Aguirre came to the Pistons with the reputation:

He was accused of pouting, when he sat on the bench.

He was accused of tossing too many temper tantrums.

He was accused of being a whiner, unwilling to sacrifice his individual aspirations for the welfare of the team.

He was charged with making himself unpopular with the home fans. They booed. He was accused of responding with an obscene gesture.

He was charged with developing phantom injuries, fakes, making them up.

He was charged with delivering ultimatums to

management; ultimately demanding to be traded.

All the accusations were made in the eight seasons Aguirre played for the Dallas Mavericks. Still, he was, without dispute, the best player in the brief and unspectacular history of the Dallas NBA franchise.

The Mavericks were forced to trade him.

The Pistons were not forced to take him.

Yet Jack McCloskey did, a week before the NBA trading deadline at the end of the 1988–89 season. Surrendering Adrian Dantley, who had squeezed into the Pistons' concept of total team, plus a first-round draft choice in 1991 when the club would be aging and so needy for fresh talent, McCloskey negotiated the riskiest trade of his life.

There is championship proof of McCloskey's good judgment and his faith in the untamed Mark Aguirre.

He was another playgrounds player. His playgrounds were on the streets of Chicago, where he was a companion of Isiah Thomas. Isiah went off to play in college with Bob Knight at Indiana and was the cog of a national championship team. Mark stayed in Chicago and went off to play in college for the pixieish legend Ray Meyer at DePaul, where George Mikan had played two generations earlier for the same coach.

During those years in the late 1970s and early 1980s, Aguirre was considered, by consensus of organizations that honor such athletes, as the most outstanding college player in America.

Aguirre was 6 feet 6 with a mighty torso, strong thighs, and he could caress a basketball with huge hands.

"He has hands as big as toilet seats," said Meyer one day to the Chicago media. Ray had a way with words.

Meyer's reputation soared along with Aguirre's —and DePaul was regarded by the pollsters as a team talented enough to become the No. 1 team in the nation. Until the tournaments. Then something went poof, and DePaul was beaten. In 1979, DePaul reached the Final Four. But so did Magic Johnson and Michigan State and Larry Bird and Indiana State. Bird and Indiana State beat Aguirre and DePaul. Then Magic beat Bird for the college championship, and their rivalry would endure for a decade in the pros.

The following year, when DePaul was upset in the NCAAs before reaching the Final Four, Aguirre was so disconsolate he fled the building as the game ended. He just ran out, off the court, up the aisleway and out the doors and into the parking lot, in his basketball uniform with the DePaul written across the chest.

The press had a fine time describing Aguirre's escape and probing his psyche.

It was then that Aguirre decided to turn pro. He came out early, entering the NBA draft as a junior in 1981, the same year Isiah declared himself available. The Dallas club, one year after expansion, had its choice of the two young athletes from Chicago. The Mavs went first. Isiah was regarded as the superior prospect. The Pistons, drafting second, were resigned to being left with Aguirre. McCloskey was all set to draft him.

And then the Mavericks drafted Aguirre and left Isiah Thomas for the Pistons.

The Pistons were given the foundation for their championship seasons years later. And with great irony, they would win them only after Mark Aguirre and Isiah Thomas were reunited to play on the same team.

Mark Aguirre and Isiah Thomas would become millionaires because they could play basketball with greater skills than normal mortals. It is part of the dream of youth to be able to do that. It is a dream nurtured in the playgrounds and on the streets of urban America. To be blessed with such a high degree of talent, it leads to escape from the blight of the ghettos, to the opportunity to gain a college education while playing games that arouse student bodies and college professors and cause coaches to bite on towels or dance as though boiling water had been poured into their pants. To be so blessed, it leads to the huge contracts and the endorsements —and the free basketball shoes that other kids and youths from the same neighborhoods where our heroes grew up sometimes rob and kill to obtain.

Little Mark and Little Isiah were the fortunate ones.

But as boys with the traditional dreams, they managed to crash the arena where now as visitors, as men, they try to halt the heroics of Michael Jordan. They would sneak into the Chicago Stadium, where the Bulls played their NBA games.

Aguirre explained to the *News'* Terry Foster how they managed to get inside their cruddy Stadium, without getting caught. It was a simple ruse, Aguirre said: A truck would roll up to the loading dock hours before gametime to deliver the hot dogs, soft drinks and beer, and the two lads would dart inside. Then, they'd vanish, pose as vendors or other Stadium workers who were lugging the beer to the stands. Then they'd hide behind the concession counters, slipping away when those stands were being serviced. They'd come out and stand with the standees during the games.

"I did it all the time," Aguirre told Foster. "I must have seen 100 games that way. Not many people knew about it because we kept it a secret."

The visiting teams that were most alluring to little Mark and little Isiah were the Lakers and the Celtics; and of course, the 76ers with Julius Erving. Mark did not mention the Pistons as one of his favorite draws.

The coach of the Bulls in those days was Dick Motta, the Napoleonic, poison-mouthed critic of enemy teams and his own athletes.

By the time Mark Aguirre decided it was time to leave DePaul and turn professional, Motta had moved on. To the Dallas Mavericks. It was coincidence, and Aguirre's misfortune, that brought him and Motta together on a struggling, one-star team trying to succeed in NBA expansion.

Aguirre became the Mavericks' top gun. They didn't have any other. They had no leader, few athletes with viable talent. So the game style boiled down to a simple bottom line—Aguirre had to shoot and shoot, for it was the only way the Mavs might have a chance to win. One year he averaged 29.5 points for the season. He'd just pop and pop. He'd have led the NBA in scoring that season, except that another guy with a similar reputation topped 30 points per game—Adrian Dantley, of the Utah Jazz. Aguirre's gunning led the Mavericks to a winning record and the playoffs in their fourth season. It might have been too early for the Dallas basketball fans. They hadn't suffered long enough, as the Detroit fans had.

The people turned on Aguirre. The Dallas media turned on him. The coach turned on him.

He was booed when he didn't hit. The media made mention of his frequent injuries, suggest-ing that not all the injuries were real, that Mark might be a hypochondriac. The media made further mention of his disinterest in playing defense . . . of his occasional displays of temper . . . of his occasional moments of sulking.

The coach—he was hardest of all.

One day Dick Motta called Mark Aguirre "a coward."

It was a tough charge, one that hardly qualified Motta as a motivational sort of coach who understands how to treat the high-strung and extremely well-paid and quite talented human athletes.

In 1984, Motta accused Aguirre of not hustling. Motta suspended Aguirre—and he called the player "a quitter."

"Put the whip to a thoroughbred and he responds," said Motta to the Dallas press. "Put the whip to a jackass and he balks."

Motta, too, had an eloquent way with words.

"The great ones are temperamental," he told a Dallas newspaperman back in 1986. "Little things set them off. A lot of times you don't know what it is."

"He tarnished my career from day one, and frankly, I'll probably never get over it," Aguirre said when he still played in Dallas.

Another time he said of his coach: "I have no feelings for Dick. He has no feelings for me."

Still, Aguirre could hit the basket. Still, there were moments when his temperament was evident to all viewers—the press, and his own teammates, some of whom regarded him as a selfish player because he continued to gun at the basket rather than pass them the ball.

His reputation carried around the league, gossipy stories were told and retold and embellished at every stop. He was a 25-point per game shooter and he made the NBA All-Star Game three times in his Dallas years.

One year, 1985, he didn't make the All-Star Game when he believed he should have. He stormed and fretted and fumed. He took his anger out in a regular-season game. He scored 49 points playing against Dr. J, his boyhood role model.

He could turn the lights on—or out.

On February 15, 1989, the day the of the trade, Adrian Dantley cried. He had become attached to the Pistons. He was being shoved into exile.

Mark Aguirre felt only joy. He had begged to be traded and now he had been liberated.

Next, he would be initiated—brought into the Pistons' method of playing basketball, their concepts of the team over the individual, their style of defense over gunning.

In sports, when a team meshes, jells, molds into something extra special, it is referred to in the locker rooms, and in the sporting press, as chemistry.

The Pistons were tinkering with their precious and delicate chemistry when they dumped Dantley and added Mark Aguirre.

Aguirre's attitude problems, his playing characteristics, had become infamous around the NBA.

The Pistons had missed winning the NBA finals the previous June by a few, quite significant, points. Now, in the 1988–89 season, their Bad Boys reputation had made them coverboys on slick magazines. But more than that, their combined skills had made them the strongest, most powerful, most respected club in the NBA. They went into L.A. on their February trip to the West Coast and back to the Forum, where they had lost Games 6 and 7 of the previous NBA finals. This time they drilled the Lakers, 111–103. It was the sixth straight victory for the Pistons.

Later that night, Jack McCloskey completed the trade he had been working on for a week or so. Chuck Daly went to Adrian Dantley's room to inform him he'd been traded. The coach and the player had been spatting, often, too often. Dantley was brokenhearted. It is known that he felt, deep inside that Isiah Thomas had caused him to be traded. Isiah wanted Mark Aguirre, his boyhood friend, on his team.

It would never be proven, but always suspected, that Isiah managed to convince Bill Davidson, whose Pistons had grown from league laughing stocks to near champions, that Mark Aguirre could provide the final element toward achieving the ultimate.

Isiah Thomas noted in his book, *Bad Boys*!, co-authored with Matt Dobek, in which they relived the 1988–89 season:

"... I chased down John Salley in the lobby, and he told me he had talked with A.D. He said, 'Zeke, we got your boy Aguirre, and you'd better be ready to handle it.' He meant, of course, that

it would be me who got the credit or blame for the trade, depending on how it worked out. Because it was such a blockbuster deal, involving big-name players, everyone seemed to have an opinion. My own first reaction was, 'Here we go again. Another controversy, and once again, I'm right in the middle of it.' Since Mark is such a good friend of mine, most people naturally assumed that I had plotted and manipulated behind the scenes to pull it off, and if it didn't work out, I was going to take a lot of heat.

"My second reaction was a selfish one. I was concerned about how the fans would treat me. I have really busted my butt for the Detroit Pistons ever since I came here, and I certainly wasn't going to be happy if everyone started booing . . .

"For the first time I can remember, there was complete silence on the team bus. By unspoken agreement, every player has his own seat, and Bill Laimbeer always sits behind me . . . He leaned over and said, 'Junior, no matter what happens, I'm in this with you.' I appreciated that."

Mark Aguirre took the first plane to join his new club in L.A. He was aboard the Pistons' plane, waiting at LAX, when the rest of the players arrived from practice the morning after the trade. The Pistons flew north to Sacramento, where the Kings were based already having posed as the Rochester Royals, Cincinnati Royals and Kansas City-Omaha Kings in previous NBA lives. That night Isiah asked Aguirre to join in a small dinner affair with some of the other Pistons.

The dinner, in the hotel dining room, was designed to go over the club's special ground rules with the newcomer. Everybody was aware of Aguirre's reputation. Everybody was aware of the danger of upsetting the championship chemistry on the ballclub. Isiah, Laimbeer, Rickey Mahorn and Vinnie Johnson sat around the table, the club elders, assumed control to initiate this outsider onto the Pistons. It was more than a speaking of the ground rules. It was delivering a riot act.

In Isiah's *Bad Boys!* book, he said:

"'Mark, welcome to the Pistons. Here's what's expected of you. First, you have to learn what it means to be a Piston. One thing it means is playing hard every minute of the game you're on the court. There are no nights off on this team. Second, your game won't be evaluated on the basis of how many points you score. On this team, every player has a role which best helps the team effort, and every player is expected to accept that role. That's how we win. You were a star in Dallas. Here in Detroit, our ninth man on the squad is as popular as you were in Dallas . . . "

One by one, as they ate dinner, the Pistons hit Aguirre with warnings and threats.

According to the book of Isiah, Laimbeer said: "The only reason I like you is you're a friend of Isiah's. If you weren't Isiah's friend, I wouldn't even talk to you. All the things I've heard and read about you have been bad. I don't care if they're true or not. Isiah said to give you a chance, so I'm giving you a chance."

Rickey Mahorn spoke next: ". . . Everybody knows you're a great offensive player, but I don't really care. Defense wins games, and we are an outstanding defensive team . . . if I get beat and you're not there to help me, that's it for you. I guarantee you I'll be hollering at Chuck to get you out of the game."

Vinnie Johnson finished up the lecturing: ". . . Backing you up is the best defensive player in the game, Dennis Rodman, and at the end of the game, Chuck goes with defense . . . In the fourth quarter, you may not miss a shot, but Chuck's going with Rodman in the last couple of minutes because defense is going to win that game. Just remember, it's nothing personal, it's just how we win."

Their points made, the diners permitted Aguirre to make the final statement: "I know you've heard a lot about me, but no matter what you've heard, I want you to know I'm here for one reason, and that's to win a championship. I promise you I will do anything to win. Isiah's known me since we were kids, and he knows what I'm all about. I'm glad you're giving me a chance because that's all I need."

Next day, Aguirre participated in his first practice with the Pistons at Sacramento. First, Aguirre tried to shoot and Rodman guarded him so tightly, he couldn't get a shot off. Aguirre tried to drive the lane. Mahorn moved in and knocked Aguirre into a heap on the floor. The Pistons bumped and clubbed Aguirre until he was battered and exhausted.

It was welcome to the club. The initiation to the Pistons.

Over the remainder of the 1988–89 season, the Pistons won thirty of their thirty-six games. Aguirre's scoring production dipped to 15.5 points per game, playing less than he ever had before. But his team finished first in the division. Aguirre was playing the role McCloskey had gotten him to play.

"All I've always wanted was to play on great teams and win basketball games," Aguirre told the *News'* Bryan Burwell early in the 1989 playoffs. "Now, I'm finally doing it. On all these teams I played for, there weren't a lot of players willing to respect my talent. I love to play the game and I really know how to play this game . . .

"In the situations I've been in, I was always expected to carry situations, and it was looked upon in the wrong way. It was looked upon where everybody figures you're it, you're totally it. And it causes friction among teammates.

"But scoring is what I do. I score. I put up numbers. That's what I know how to do best. If I was a great rebounder, I'd be putting up great rebounding numbers. But I'm a scorer. I study it. I know how to do it with the best. For some reason, wherever I went, that caused a problem. Here it's different. Teammates realize what I do and how it will help the team.

"There were times in Dallas when I wasn't in the game and we lost it and I was still the cause of it. My feeling was, 'If I'm the cause of the loss, please let me be in there to lose it.' We're a team. We're the Mavericks. I don't lose it. WE lose it. I got tired of dealing with it. I'm just so happy to be playing for this Pistons ballclub that really knows how basketball should be played. They play it here like a union . . .

"I'm just glad it was these guys and not some other team. A lot of them knew me, knew I wasn't anything like the guy they'd been reading about. All I asked was that they don't judge me by anything other than the way I behave here.

"I wasn't some jerk, and I wanted the chance to prove it."

The Pistons won their first championship in June, with the sweep of the Lakers. The Pistons might have won it without Mark Aguirre on their side. Nobody's certain. But the facts are simply this: after the trade in February, with Aguirre,

"All I've always wanted was to play on great teams and win basketball games."

the Pistons' record was 45–8, four rounds of 1990 playoffs included.

Mark Aguirre made additional headlines with the Pistons struggling in defense of their championship in 1989–90. He was injured in January and missed three games. Rodman started at small forward in his spot. When Aguirre was ready to return, he had a suggestion.

"I need time to get back in and get my rhythm," he told Terry Foster. "And you don't want to mess with the starting lineup. I think Dennis is playing well. It will take me time to get back where I need to be."

Mark Aguirre was volunteering to stay on the bench, come off it when Chuck Daly wanted to make a substitution. He was suggesting that he surrender his starting position.

Chuck Daly accepted the suggestion—for the welfare of the ballclub.

It wasn't total harmony. One night, when the reigning champions were playing the Miami Heat, Aguirre tried to score a three-pointer when he was off balance. Later in the same game, he

screwed up a three-on-one break when he flipped the ball behind him and the pass went right to a trailing Miami player.

After that gaffe, Daly rushed over to the press table and grabbed a phone and yelled: "Aguirre."

Mark thought he was being shown up. Daly confessed, indeed, that he had goofed, that he had shown up the ultrasensitive Mark Aguirre.

The second championship, in Portland in June 1990, was more difficult and more appreciated than the first. Perhaps, again, the Pistons might have won that championship without Mark Aguirre on their side. But the facts were that in a fraction of one season plus another entire season, the Pistons won 119 games and lost but 36 after Aguirre had been traded to them—two NBA championships included.

But even after helping the Pistons to two championships, Mark Aguirre has never managed to escape the reputation he brought upon himself in Dallas. Even the NBA's publicity department, which could be expected never to dwell on anything negative, went forward with a documentation of the truth in a press release about Aguirre. It said of his seasons in Dallas: ". . . the match was never perfect for Aguirre and the Mavs. He had his differences with coaches, teammates and the media, and on more than one occasion expressed a desire to be traded."

This was a rare kind of press release. Usually, they extol any virtues that might be uncovered at league headquarters about an athlete.

This release went on to say to America's sporting journalists: "Aguirre did his best to rid himself of the selfish image he acquired in Dallas." *Selfish Image?* The NBA propagandists went on to say in this most candid press release: "After injuring his back in January, he saw Dennis Rodman take his starting forward spot. Rodman helped the Pistons go on a 24–1 streak, and when Aguirre returned to health, he told Coach Chuck Daly to keep Rodman in the starting lineup, for the good of the team."

Of course, the moral of this press release, after all, was redemption and the values of teamwork. It went on to quote Isiah Thomas about his friend Mark: "That's just him wanting to be known as a winner. All through his career, people were saying, 'Aw, he's a loser . . . I know for a fact in my mind, and I think in all the players' minds, had he not been on this basketball team, there's no way we would have won back-to-back championships."

As the Pistons begin their quest of the unlikely Three-peat, something had fouled the chemistry. It isn't quite as pure. And the first flap of the 1991 playoffs on this team known to have its flaps involves Mark Aguirre on the night Daly yanks him from the game against Atlanta, then shoves him into garbage time.

The next day, with Aguirre's left arm in the hard cast after his middle-of-the-night hospital run, efforts are made to restore the peace on the ballclub.

Daly is contrite.

"I might have overreacted as a coach," he tells the mob of reporters, who have dredged up sins from Aguirre's Dallas past. "I don't remember what happened. I wanted a rotation, a defensive rotation. Hands up, box out, that's all."

And Aguirre accepts the coach's self-humbling explanation.

"He told me he might have gotten a little hyper about the situation," Aguirre said when he was surrounded by press. "Chuck admitted he might have been out of character about this thing. I don't know what he thought was wrong. I didn't do anything wrong. I followed his instructions, and he let me have it big time. I just felt I shouldn't have gotten it. It's water under the bridge right now.

"You're going to be pissed off for a second, but not to the point where you don't know what's happening on the floor. We are going to be men about this."

He denies that he defied Daly by refusing once to return to the game. But there are those who insists it is true.

He explains he wears the cast because his left wrist and thumb ache, but shoot, he'll play Game 3 of the series the next day in Atlanta.

And so he does, after the cast has been removed as quickly as it was placed on the arm in the middle of the night. Daly gives him fourteen minutes and Mark scores five points.

The issue is settled—until the next time. Daly has made his point emphatically and then soothed the player's sensitive spots with the caress of soft apology.

V—Buddha

James Edwards was a rookie with the L.A. Lakers in 1977. He was a third-round draft choice, which was more a slur on a guy's ability and potential than a comment of confidence that the guy some day will grow into a millionaire and wear the diamond rings sported by champions.

Edwards was tall, 7 feet 1, so the Lakers took a shot. They already had such an athlete of towering height on the team. The incumbent was regarded as a performer of some skill, with a sky-hook shot and a work ethic, and the desire to dominate underneath and win. The player's name was Kareem Abdul-Jabbar.

". . . nobody expected me to make the team," Edwards would recall a dozen years later for Mitch Albom of the *Detroit Free Press*. "I remember Kareem told me not to get discouraged. He invited me and a couple of other rookies to his house one time. We were like, 'Oh God! This is Kareem's house! Look at all this stuff!'

"Anyhow, I did make the team."

The third round of the draft was such, for so many years, that third-rounders hardly were ever qualified to make the clubs that drafted them. Mostly, they were picked to serve as practice fodder at training camp. Ultimately, the third round was regarded as such a waste of time the NBA would abolish it. It would cut off the draft after two rounds. That was enough, already!

So James Edwards beat the system when he made the Lakers as a third-rounder out of the University of Washington.

He beat the system through the years. And early in his rookie season, after Kareem beat the bejabbers out of Kent Benson, Edwards was in the Lakers' starting lineup. Kareem had busted up his hand. Edwards started while Kareem's hand healed. He displayed some roughness beneath the boards and an ability to block shots and do some scoring.

He was an NBA pro. But he was a transient. After twenty-five games with the Lakers, he was summoned by Jerry West, the coach.

West told Edwards the Lakers needed a pure shooter and had just gotten that player in a trade. The pure shooter was Adrian Dantley, from the Indiana Pacers. To get Dantley, the Lakers had to toss rookie James Edwards into the trade.

James rushed off to join his second team. His plane landed in Indy in a snowstorm. He played that night for the Pacers.

The Lakers might have been in a hurry to dispose of James Edwards. But he was welcomed with poetic praise in Indiana.

"Somebody upturned a gold watch," said Bobby Leonard, the Pacers' coach, another who had a way with words.

Out in L.A. Edwards had made some sort of impression on the Lakers' assistant coach, who filed a memory away for later use. Jack McCloskey.

Edwards played for the Pacers for three seasons, plus.

He made an impression in Indiana, too. Among those impressed was the man who came in as the aide to head coach Leonard in 1979. The name of the assistant head coach was the wayfaring Jack McCloskey.

In 1981, Edwards moved on to his third NBA club. He signed as a free agent with the Cleveland Cavaliers, a club with a circus image. The situation was such in Cleveland that during Edward's first season there the Cavs employed four head coaches. The third of these coaches survived 41 games, with a 9-and-32 record. He would recall later that his tenure extended for ninety-three days. "Ninety-three days in a Holiday Inn," he would say later in his second coaching life. Chuck Daly.

At Cleveland, James Edwards forced a second-year center into a backup role. The center in this puzzling version of This Is Your Team was named—Bill Laimbeer.

This was the early 1980s. This entire group of participants was doing plenty of traveling.

James Edwards played a season and a half for the Cavaliers and then he was traded to his fourth NBA club. He went to the Phoneix Suns for one flesh player, a bag of cash and, nicely, a third-round draft choice that would be somewhat worthless.

The next four and a half seasons would be spent in Phoenix. There would be some troubles, some problems, some heartache.

Then on February 24, 1988, at the NBA trading deadline, Edwards was traded once more, to team No. 5. Phoenix dealt him to the Detroit Pistons—and one of the weirdest reunions imaginable. The Pistons gave up Ron Moore and a second-round draft choice in 1991 for Edwards.

The general manager who manufactured the trade to Detroit's advantage was—Jack McCloskey.

The coach to whom Edwards reported on this team that was just placing itself among the NBA's elite clubs was—Chuck Daly.

The center Edwards would substitute for when Daly went to his backup players was—Bill Laimbeer.

A teammate on his fifth team was—Adrian Dantley.

A little more than three months after the trade, in the spring of 1988, they would all wind up where none of them ever had been before— in the NBA finals.

Edwards grew to his 7 feet 1 in Seattle, and his background differed from most of his teammates who had been collected by McCloskey. Buddha's father was an engineer. James himself, growing up in Washington state, had an affinity for the water and for boats. One of his life's enjoyments was sitting in solitude on his boat, in meditation.

Young James was not gifted with the basketball talents of an Isiah or a Magic or a Michael Jordan—or a Kareem. He was tall, but not a natural. He was hit with a severe setback as a ninth-grader, his freshman year in high school. Edwards went out for the team and was cut. His torso was so thin he didn't have the proper upper body strength for the physical elements of the game.

"I didn't like to bump and grind," Edwards told Terry Foster of the News. "I didn't like that contact. Everybody else was a lot bigger and stronger than I was."

He might have quit then. Some kids would. James Edwards went out and worked to improve himself. He took a ball and spent hours shooting. The jump shot. Fading away from the basket, jumping, shooting, hitting. The fade would become his shot. And years later, it would help him to be selected low in the NBA draft— and to make it, unlike the ninth grade in Seattle.

Eventually, he made the high school team at Seattle Roosevelt. He was 6 feet 8 at the time, and his team won the state championship. James Edwards went off to play college ball for the Washington Huskies—and he kept growing. As a man and in stature.

His college performances did not send him into the hot draft category of some of his contemporaries such as—Tree Rollins, Cedric "Cornbread" Maxwell, Otis Birdsong or Bernard King. But he was worth a third-round pick by the Lakers. It would be a longshot. The Lakers, after all, had Kareem and they had three first-round picks that year. In camp, Edwards would have to fight with the three first-rounders —Kenny Carr, Brad Davis, and Norm Nixon— for a spare spot on the eleven-player roster. James Edwards made it, for 25 games at least in Los Angeles, before he was sent off to start his grand tour of the NBA.

James Edwards was thirty-two years old and late in his eleventh season in the NBA when he joined the Pistons. He had grown a powerful Fu Manchu mustache and had a somber, sometimes baleful visage. The brooding face resembled the statuary of a Japanese diety. They called James Edwards by the nickname of Buddha. And he fit instantly into the precious bonding that the Pistons call their chemistry.

"It just gives us tremendous insurance," McCloskey said the day he completed the trade. "He can back up Billy, and if anybody goes down with an injury we've got a veteran center who can also play power forward."

". . . I had him in Cleveland, so I know his capabilities in the low post," Daly told writer Corky Meinecke. "I think it was a wise risk on our part."

The risk was that Edwards left Phoenix tagged with a drug rap, a bum rap.

James was one of three Suns players indicted in 1987 on charges of trafficking in cocaine and marijuana. As part of it, there were vicious rumors of point-shaving involving Edwards. None of the charges was ever proven. The case never went to court. The upshot was Buddha admitted to marijuana usage. The NBA put him on one of its one-year rehabilitation programs while he played on. After a year of counseling, the record of his admission was scrubbed.

The most serious result of the affair was the personal scars. Because it involved athletes, it attracted a huge amount of press coverage. The bite of the media is sharper against those who are known.

This case came to be known as the Phoenix Witch Hunt.

But a year later, with the playoffs looming and with a quality club, the Pistons took the risk on James Edwards despite the rap he carried.

"That's not a concern at all," said McCloskey.

But it would be a concern for James Edwards through the next several years. There was a stigma. A former teammate, Walter Davis, had testified against Edwards. It seemed, to Edwards, to be a set up.

"It still affects the way I think," Edwards told Mitch Albom in the spring of 1990, two years after he joined the Pistons. "I learned people will smile in your face, but be looking out only for themselves. I was an easygoing guy in Phoenix. I would have helped anybody. I learned my lesson."

Edwards continued to protest his innocence in Detroit. "I don't do things like that," he told Albom.

He became more reclusive. He spent less time at parties, more time alone on his boat.

"I have all the friends I need," he told Albom. "It takes me a long time now to trust anybody or to open up. That Phoenix thing really hurt me and my family. I'm still not over it."

It was with Edwards playing the backup role to Rick Mahorn and to Laimbeer that the Pistons ended the curse of the Celtics in the playoffs of 1988.

"We're riding the Buddha Train," was the way Spider Salley phrased the successes of the Pistons.

Whipping the Celtics in the playoffs, at last, was the breakthrough for the Pistons. It was a night of celebration. Thousands of the fans poured out of the stands at the Silverdome, where the Pistons were playing for the final season, and danced on the floor, clogging it with their jitterbugging. The date was June 3, 1988. It was a dividing point in history. All that had gone before through more than three decades of giggles and ineptitude could be packaged as something to be forgotten from the ancient past. The rest would be new and superior and efficient and for those who had discovered this team yearning to be discovered, it would be something wonderful.

And Buddha Edwards was a major reason. He had meshed in with the potpourri of vagabonds

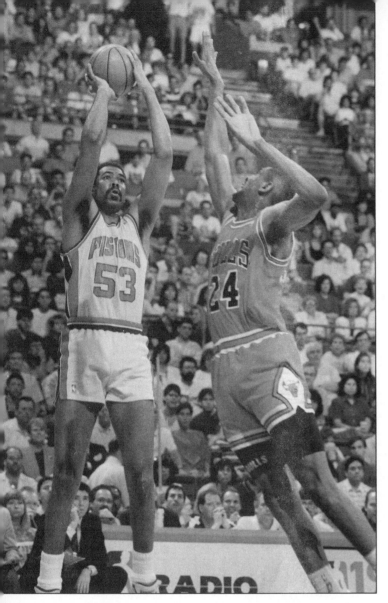

Edwards launches his deadly jumper.

collected by McCloskey. None had progressed as far as the NBA finals before.

Now after the Pistons lost the seventh game to the Lakers, James Edwards nearly abandoned his new club. The Suns had made him available to the Pistons at the trading deadline in February 1988, simply because they were going to lose Edwards anyway. While so much ado was made about Chuck Daly going through the NBA finals that year, supposedly without salary and neglected because he didn't have a new contract, James Edwards actually did not have a contract. He was a free agent and available to any club willing to sign him when the playoffs ended. And given James' proclivity to journey from club to club, Phoenix had decided to collect a body for him from Detroit.

At the end of the playoffs, it was the Pistons'

responsibility to sign Edwards or lose him to free agency. He was rapidly advancing toward his thirty-third birthday. It was his last chance for a killing.

Buddha's agent was Reggie Turner, who was such a tough infighter in his negotiations NBA general managers regarded him as their sworn enemy. According to the NBA grapevine, translated as the writers' gossip network, Jerry Colangelo, the Suns' GM, once told Turner to get the devil out of his office when they hit a snag in negotiations for Edwards. Colangelo didn't want any more of that stuff, another motive for dispensing of Edwards.

Now suddenly, in the summer of 1988, there was an auction going on in NBA inner sanctums for James Edwards. The Atlanta Hawks made an offer, supposedly $3.2 million for four years, and the New Jersey Nets bid $2.7 million for three years. Turner mentioned in interviews that the Lakers and the Philadelphia 76ers were also interested in signing the free agent James Edwards.

But Jack McCloskey is a tough infighter, too. He made an offer—and then went off on vacation. McCloskey felt pretty confident for one elementary reason—James Edwards, with eleven seasons in the NBA, had never played on an NBA championship team. He had money, a boat, security, memories of overcoming prophecies that he'd never make it in the NBA. But he lacked the ring that champions boast about.

So while Turner's auction for James Edwards' contract signature went on, McCloskey played tennis at Shanty Creek, a northern Michigan resort. One day McCloskey decided to make a long distance call to Turner just to see how the auction might be going.

They agreed to terms on the telephone—supposedly at $2.5 million for three years.

"Divine intervention," Turner told the *News'* Jim Spadafore when discussion was made about McCloskey's unscheduled phone call.

Turner said Edwards had been about to sign with the Hawks and had plane reservations to Atlanta for the formalities. The reservations could be cancelled.

"While I was talking to James about the offers made by Atlanta and New Jersey, Jack calls. We didn't know how to get a hold of him. I thought James was going to Atlanta. He was really close. James asked about the Pistons, but Jack was out of town. The Hawks improved their offer but wanted a decision right then."

That was the story told to the *Detroit News*.

The story Turner told the *Atlanta Constitution* was that the Hawks did not pursue Edwards very heavily because they were more interested in signing Moses Malone. The Hawks saw how the money was escalating, Turner said, and prefered to use it for Moses.

"I really didn't want to go with Atlanta or anyone else," Buddha told the *News*. "I feel Detroit has a better team and the fans have really accepted me. The Pistons have good chemistry. And next year, we'll be just as good or better."

So out of this scenario of typical NBA contract maneuvering and doublespeak:

Moses signed with the Hawks.

James signed with the Pistons. He would go on to win rings, back-to-back.

There are few givens in pro sports. Among those are athletes will age and ultimately lose some of their skills and after that some of their worth. But they will not be able to understand this normal process of the body wearing down. And no matter what, when a player signs a contract he will realize that salaries escalate and by the last year of the contract he will begin to think he's underpaid. Agents will use all the negotiating dodges at their command and try to make up new ones as they go along. But then, so will general managers.

The 1990–91 season was not exceptionally pleasant for James Edwards. He had the two rings and the large contract, and at age thirty-five was playing in a sport, which he had expected to reject him when he was a younger man.

He had been a pillar for the Pistons. When they won their first championship by beating the Lakers in 1989, Edwards counted the numbers. He was aware the Pistons could protect eight players in the expansion draft to stock the new Minnesota Timberwolves and Orlando Magic. He counted off eight names he guessed would be protected, without reaching his own. He figured he would be the player plucked by one of the new clubs.

Two days after winning the championship, during the celebration parade in Detroit and the massive victory rally at the Palace, McCloskey battled to make a deal to save the Pistons their first sacrificial expansion offering. McCloskey couldn't swing it. The players were together as a team when McCloskey summoned the player to be sacrificed to an expansion team. Not Edwards as expected, but Rick Mahorn.

The loss of Mahorn ripped at the player and all his teammates and the multitudes of fans. It ripped at Edwards because he and Mahorn were very close on The Bad Boys. But as Edwards explained to Mitch Albom: "The Pistons like me."

Early in the second championship season, Chuck Daly would elevate Buddha to the starting lineup in the spot left by Mahorn. Salley was given the first chance and played better coming off the bench. With Edwards starting along with Laimbeer up front, the Pistons won fifty-two of their last seventy games in 1989–90. They went on in that fashion to beat all their rivals in the playoffs, taking out the Portland Trail Blazers in five games in The NBA finals.

James Edwards was Daly's starter in the 1990–91 season. But it was much, much different. The club struggled through the season. And Buddha, popular as ever at The Palace, sulked. It was the final season of his contract. At age thirty-five, his value had diminished. His agent asked McCloskey for a new contract—three more years.

Otherwise, Edwards said: "Pay me or trade me."

Turner said five clubs were interested in obtaining Edwards.

McCloskey responded by saying, according to Terry Foster in the *News*: "You have my blessing to work out a trade. Good luck. Just make sure it's beneficial to the Pistons."

"The writing on the wall is getting clearer all the time," Turner told the *News*. "James is playing the best basketball of his career the last three years. When would he have more trade value than he does now?"

No trade was made. James Edwards continued playing a role for the Pistons into the 1991 playoffs. He continued serving as one of the club's elder statesmen. When the Hawks embarrassed and endangered the reigning champion Pistons by winning Game 1 on their own court in the best-of-five first-round playoff series, James Edwards casually told reporters: "It's a shame we have to go down there and win a game. We're going to win down there. Guaranteed!"

Just like Joe Namath in the Super Bowl. Guaranteed. It was another example of the enormous confidence the Pistons had in their own abilities to win. And they did win, one game in Atlanta as guaranteed, then they polished off the Hawks in Game 5 to win the series.

Edwards was asked by Mitch Albom one day whether it was better to have success early or late in an NBA career.

Buddha answered the question with Buddha-like wisdom: "Better late than never."

Still, the contract haggling continued into the summer of 1991. Turner said Edwards had a contract offer in Italy. Bent on refortifying the Pistons, McCloskey felt compelled to breakup the old champions. Trader Jack dealt Buddha to the Los Angeles Clippers.

FOURTH QUARTER

I—The Early Eighties

One of Jack McCloskey's notions in the summer of 1980, after the 16-and-66 debacle, was to hire Chuck Daly as the Pistons' head coach. But Jack first offered the job to Dr. Jack Ramsey, the erudite coach of the Portland Trail Blazers. McCloskey and Ramsey were longtime friends. Ramsey was locked into his contract at Portland and was required to reject the Detroit offer.

McCloskey then considered Daly, rooted in the Philadelphia style of grunt defense. Jack knew it would take years, perhaps a decade, to build the Pistons into a contending team from the ruins left by Dick Vitale. Out of Philly himself, McCloskey wanted a coach with expertise in defense.

He and Daly had somewhat similar backgrounds. Both were former coaches at Penn. Both had worked in coaching in the ACC, where the basketball is practical and stylish. Both were well into the passionate, middle-age part of life.

Daly was employed as an assistant coach with the Philadelphia 76ers, aide to Billy Cunningham on a team featuring Julius Erving. He had a deep resume in coaching and seemed overqualified to toil as an assistant. He was ready to coach his own NBA club as head man. But Chuck opted to remain in Philly at the time, according to the *News'* Bill Halls, due to family responsibilities.

With Daly and Ramsey unavailable, McCloskey had to conduct a manhunt for a coach to take over his team. He offered the job to at least one other guy and got at least one other turndown. Coaching the Pistons was not exactly valhalla for guys who'd fantasized about coaching in the NBA most of their professional lives. Then the job was offered to Scotty Robertson, a friendly, decent man. He was a heart-attack survivor, not the sort of life-threatening medical background that would enforce a guy seeking the position as head coach of the Detroit Pistons.

But, he grabbed the challenge. Scotty became the Pistons' sixteenth coach in their twenty-fourth season in Detroit at the start of the 1980–81 season.

Excerpts from a column by Jerry Green in the *Detroit News,* October 10, 1980:

There was Ray Scott, the brooding, bearded Othello, who carried the briefcase and was a winner.

He gave way to Herbie Brown, the New York slicker who arrived in town with only a pair of slacks and a sweater to his name. He wound up trying to jump through a hoop wearing a jumpsuit, sometimes uncertain which was right and which was left.

Brown gave way to sedate, suave, wine connoisseur Bob Kaufmann, who wore a three-piece suit like a lawyer would. He was hired to straighten things out because he had a background in the business. But the boss didn't always understand what he was talking about.

Kaufmann gave way to Dick Vitale, who arrived shot out of cannon, dancing the buggaloo, yapping about paradise and reVITALEization in a native New Jersey holler. He went into orbit one night when a whistle sounded and has not been seen since, though the echoes still reverberate to downtown.

Vitale gave way to Richie Adbuato, who pointed to himself when everybody said "Who?" He had prepared for the opportunity at a small college in Jersey and seemed like a very decent, innocent guy. Of course, he didn't hang around very long and when he was given his ticket from town everybody was still saying "Who?"

We have now reached current events and:

"I talk country . . . I'm from the South, but I've been around," said Scotty Robertson, who arrived in town after three other guys selected ahead of him turned the job down for one reason or another.

So Scotty Robertson is the Pistons' sixth coach in less than six seasons.

Another of those pro basketball seasons opens tonight. The Pistons have provided some comic relief to this town for 24 years now . . . Robertson will be a certified genius if the Pistons can improve on their 16-and-66 record.

But the new guy does more than talk country. He

talks a good deal of common sense. It sounds better than all this stuff about Pistons' paradise and lox-and-bagels diplomacy.

"We just want to make the right decisions," said Robertson, familiar with the Pistons' history.

"I think Jack McCloskey represents stability. Basketball people are making basketball decisions. I think that's important.

"All basketball decisions are made by Jack McCloskey, Scotty Robertson, Don Chaney and Will Robinson."

Important? It's critical for this franchise with dreamboat ownership of corporate whizzes and lawyers. Now, if it holds, the ideas will come out of a braintrust consisting of a general manager, a basketball coach, his assistant and an old coach and scout.

On all other NBA franchises, it takes the teams 24 seconds to shoot. It has taken the Pistons 24 years.

Basketball concepts by basketball men. How bright! Owners Bill Davidson and Ozzie Feldman finally thought of it. They've turned over the keys to the kingdom.

"They promised Jack McCloskey and me . . . they apparently had made some mistakes and if we felt they were mistakes we would not have to live with them," Robertson said.

"As a coach, I can't coach Kareem, Marques Johnson or Magic Johnson. They're on other teams. I'm not going to cry to you. I'm not going to cry to Jack. I'm not going to cry to the public. I'm going to coach the players we have.

"We have a helluva long way to go.

"We're not very good. Here's a different guy coaching. The obvious response from the public and from the media is here's more of the same, just with a different guy. We're on the right track.

"We've got to prove ourselves. If it was easy, I wouldn't be here. If the damn job was easy, I wouldn't be here. Anything easy is not worth it.

"Look at the Lions. Everybody's excited. So when we do the job two or three years from now, think how great it'll be.

"It's a hazardous job, but I love it. I was with the New Orleans Jazz and then I was out of basketball. I went into the real estate profession and I made a lot of money. I lived in a big house on a golf

The Pistons await the start of a playoff game in historic Boston Garden in 1987.

Scottie Pippen tries to cut off Vinnie Johnson as he heads to the hoop.
(*K. Dozier*)

James ''Buddah'' Edwards scores a forceful two points. (*K. Dozier*)

Dennis Rodman battles Boston's Robert Parish in the low post. (*K. Dozier*)

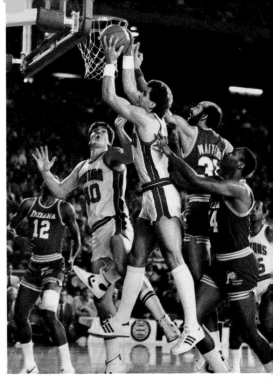

Kelly Tripucka, the Pistons second No. 1 draft choice in 1981, goes strong to the basket against the Indiana Pacers. Tripucka led Detroit in scoring during the 1982 and 1983 seasons. (*W. Anderson*)

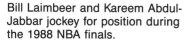

Bill Laimbeer and Kareem Abdul-Jabbar jockey for position during the 1988 NBA finals.

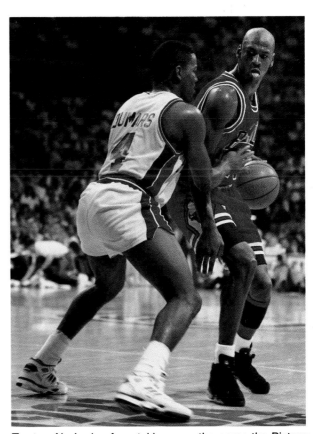

To stop Air Jordan from taking over the game the Pistons developed the so-called "Jordan Rules," which often meant Dumars was responsible for stopping Michael Jordan. (*K. Dozier*)

Laimbeer voices his displeasure to a foul call that went against him. (*K. Dozier*)

Portland's Terry Porter (30), Jerome Kersey (25), and Buck Williams converge on Isiah Thomas, leaving a man open under the hoop for Isiah to find. (*K. Dozier*)

No, it only looks like Joe Dumars is taking on the entire Lakers squad by himself. Dumars had plenty of help as Detroit defeated Los Angeles in four straight to claim its first World Championship.

Chuck Daly works the sidelines during the 1990 NBA finals. (*K. Dozier*)

Edwards jumps out to meet Michael Jordan during Game 4 of the 1991 Conference finals. (*K. Dozier*)

Adrian Dantley drives and dishes versus Chicago during Game 1 of the Chicago-Detroit series in 1988. The Pistons would go on to defeat the Bulls in three straight playoff series. (*M. Green*)

Isiah weaves through the Celtics defense for a reverse layup during the Pistons' 110–101 loss to Boston in Game 2 of the 1987 Conference finals.

John Salley maneuvers into position for a hook shot over Kevin McHale of the Celtics. (*K. Dozier*)

Rodman slams home two against the Bulls during the 1989 Conference finals.

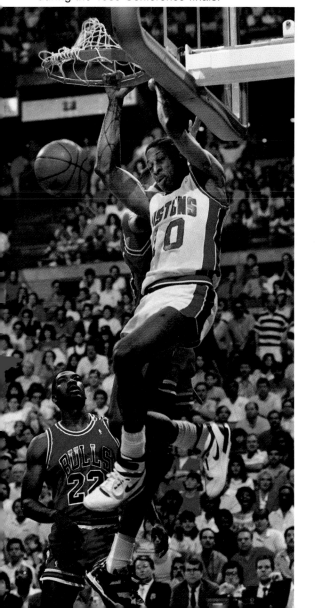

Mark Aguirre shoots the fallaway over San Antonio's Sean Elliott. (*K. Dozier*)

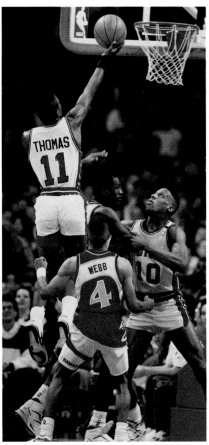

The leader of the Bad Boys, Rick Mahorn, beats Atlanta's Moses Malone to the rebound. (*K. Dozier*)

Spud Webb can only watch as Isiah glides in for a layup against the Hawks. (*K. Dozier*)

The Pistons celebrate their Back-to-Back NBA Championships. (*K. Dozier*)

course. But I went back to basketball in Buffalo as an assistant to Cotton Fitzsimmons for $20,000.

"I love it. It's brutal. It sometimes consumes me. It consumes my family."

That doesn't sound too much like country to me. It's honesty and it's emotion and it's belief. This is the guy with the toughest sports job in town and the hope is he can keep the bosses out of the office for the three years he has in the contract.

I doubt seriously, with the club Robertson inherits, if the Pistons can even equal 16 victories this season. His immediate goal is to put a competitive team on the floor, which is a miracle objective.

At least Robertson isn't trying to fool anybody with bombast and shooting cannons.

"I feel good about the direction the Pistons are going," Robertson said. "But we're not very bleeping good."

That said, the Pistons started off to who knew where!

There was deep concern by the NBA commissioner, that former Democratic politico Larry O'Brien, that the Pistons could make a go of it. He did not care for the Pistons idea of playing their games at the Pontiac Silverdome, far from the inner city. Basketball is known as a city game, and it required a thirty-mile haul to get to the Pistons' game. O'Brien suggested the Pistons had to move back downtown if they were ever going to succeed.

"I'm concerned about the franchises in Cleveland and Detroit," O'Brien said in comments to the *News*. "The way the economy is headed, people are going to think more and more about conserving gas, and the first place they cut back on is entertainment . . .

"Attendance figures usually reflect the success of the teams. . . . However, the situations in Cleveland and Detroit are based as much on economy as the performance of the teams."

O'Brien's insight might explain why the Democrats had a losing record longer than the Pistons. The Pistons had tried it downtown, at Olympia and Cobo, and it wasn't the economy that caused the public to ignore them. They didn't win. It was that logical.

And the Pistons lacked the basic necessities to turn into a winning ballclub as they started the 1980–81 season.

Kent Benson was a decent enough guy. He played hard, had a strong work ethic and was a fine human being. But he did not have the basketball ingredients of the departed Bob Lanier.

Terry Tyler and John Long, Pistons out of Dick Vitale's devotion to the University of Detroit, hustled, gave the traditional 100 percent every night. They had the talent to play in the NBA, but not as the dynamos of a ballclub. Phil Hubbard played as well as he could. Keith Herron was patched into the lineup. Larry Drew, the first-round draft choice McCloskey had managed to rescue in the Lanier deal, displayed significant promise. Greg Kelser was injured.

And then, the Pistons still had Bob McAdoo.

Scotty Robertson's declaration was totally accurate: The Pistons weren't very bleeping good.

The Pistons had lost the final fourteen games of the 1979–80 season. Now they proceeded to lose the first six of the new season, with the new regime. The twenty losses in succession meant the Pistons, in a broken-arrow sort of way, had tied the NBA record for historic futility. The 1972–73 Philly 76ers had managed to lose twenty straight in the same season, for the straight-arrow record.

Now in Game 7 of the 1980–81 campaign, the 0-and-6 Pistons trailed the 76ers by just a single point. They had the ball with sixteen seconds left. Scotty Robertson called a time out to set up the strategy for the last shot. They played the ball in close, to the low post, where it went into the hands of Kent Benson. Benson started to drive for the prospective winning hoop with ten seconds on the ticking clock. He dribbled and oops!

"I got the ball in time to go to the hoop, and I dribbled it off my foot," Benson would say later to the pack of journalists inquiring, hey, what happened.

Philly, with the incomparable Dr. J, snuggled over the ball to escape the groping fangs of this desperate basketball by running out the remainder of the clock. So the Pistons went to 0-and-7 for the season—and their losing streak, over two seasons, was extended to twenty-one games.

Billy Cunningham, the Philly coach, damned the Pistons with praise in response to a question from the *News'* Bill Halls:

"Detroit really played with intensity. They

were relentless going to the boards. They will just have to win games like this, the way we have."

Assistant coaches in the NBA are hardly ever interviewed. Cunningham's assistant was not asked for his thoughts on this particular night in November 1980. But obviously, he would have said: "Jeez, was I smart turning down that Detroit job." You could picture Chuck Daly looking into the mirror in the locker room as that thought tore swiftly through his head.

That all-star intangible, intensity, enabled the Pistons to end the losing streak one game later. With intensity, the Pistons managed to subdue the Houston Rockets, 112–109, to produce the first victory for Scotty Robertson in Detroit. And the second of his NBA coaching career. In two jobs in two towns, Scotty smilingly headed back to Detroit that night with an accumulative career coaching record of 2-and-22.

But coaching in the NBA was more gratifying that making a hundred grand a year peddling houses and vacant store space.

Bob McAdoo missed the fun at the beginning of the 1980–81 season. He had a foot injury.

"One of the doctors who examined it this summer said it was one of the biggest bone spurs he had ever seen," McAdoo said.

The Pistons had to play on without the guy who was supposed to score for them.

In December, McCloskey traded Kelser to the Seattle Supersonics for a 1983 first-round draft choice. Kelser got to Seattle. He was examined by the Sonics' doctors. The Sonics sent him back to Detroit and reclaimed their 1983 draft choice.

"He didn't pass the physical examination," said Dr. Ben Paolucci, the Pistons' physician. "It's like buying a used car. You look at it and you don't like it."

But the NBA is not like a used-car lot. Whoever heard of a used-car dealer taking back a vehicle with a bum wheel.

That's what Kelser had, a bad knee.

Jack McCloskey was informed about the broken deal during the fourth quarter of a game in which the Pistons were being thumped by the Knicks at the Silverdome. McCloskey had to take the phone call from Seattle at the edge of the baskeball floor, squatting down, in full view of that night's mob, counted officially at 4,083.

Kelser was welcomed back to Detroit.

Meanwhile, Bob McAdoo opted to be ready. He played 30 minutes against the Rockets and scored 15 points. The Pistons lost. That appearance snapped his missed-game streak, carried over from the previous season, at fifty-one games, due to the foot pains and a strained stomach muscle. McAdoo was off on another streak. He played in his second straight game the following night against the Chicago Bulls. This time he played 29 minutes and scored 15 points. The Pistons lost.

"He played hard . . . and he practiced hard," Robertson told Bill Halls.

Then the Pistons announced that McAdoo would be unable to accompany the team on its trip to Atlanta. He had redamaged the hurting foot the night he played in his second straight game.

The Pistons followed their merry route through the season.

McAdoo returned in January. He survived for four more games. On January 22, he played against the Bulls and in 10 minutes he missed all four of his shots and committed four turnovers. Robertson removed McAdoo from the game. Something hurt him. The Pistons lost.

A month later, the Pistons announced that Bob McAdoo had been benched for the remainder of the season. "Benched," indeed, was the word used in the announcement. Jack McCloskey said it would not be necessary for McAdoo to attend any more of the Pistons' practice sessions and he didn't have to bother showing up at games, either.

Bob had squeezed a grand total of six games into the season—for his reported paycheck of $525,000.

In early March, McAdoo complained that he was ready to play and the Pistons refused to let him. So, McAdoo said, he was going to file a grievance against the naughty Pistons. McCloskey placed McAdoo on waivers. And darn it if the New Jersey Nets did not claim McAdoo and stick him into their lineup. He played the last ten games of the season for them. And he would play five more seasons in the NBA, with the Lakers and 76ers, and pick up two NBA championship rings.

For Detroit, the Pistons had rid themselves of the curse of Dick Vitale, the man who had dispatched the rights to a fine player and two first-round draft picks to the Celtics because he was keen on Bob McAdoo.

One additional note of memorabilia came out of this 1980–81 season, as the Pistons struggled along in their own special fashion. Good, old Butch van Breda Kolff, once upon a time their coach for as long as he could stand it, had gotten another coaching position. He became newsworthy again when he refused to pay fines charged for a bunch of his technical fouls. Butch got himself suspended by the league for his indescretions, which included team dissension and recent poor team performance.

Oh, this league was not the NBA. Butch had become coach of the New Orleans Pride, of the Women's Professional Basketball League. With Butch suspended, his assistant was required to take over the coaching of the team. This suddenly elevated assistant coach was a dignified man with beard and the glowering look of Othello. His name was Ray Scott.

Back in the NBA, the Pistons finished up Scotty Robertson's first campaign as coach with a 21-and-61 record. As a drawing card, their average attendance was 5,569—or just about what it was the last season downtown when tiny crowds caused them to abandon Cobo Arena. Larry O'Brien's concern about Detroit as a pro basketball town had been justified. Bill Davidson's concern was closer to the pocket. The Pistons had lost more than a million dollars.

From a positive viewpoint the club did manage a five-game improvement—and it placed the Pistons nice and high in the draft rotation.

Indeed, the Pistons were back in their coinflip routine, this time tossing with the year-old expansion Dallas Mavericks for the top of the draft.

The flip was April 30,, just a few days before the 1981 NBA finals. The Pistons had the call. In Detroit, a radio station had conducted a poll of listeners as to whether Jack McCloskey should call heads or tails. Heads won.

McCloskey went to New York for the all-important coinflip in Larry O'Brien's office.

Jack looked outside the window before he called the flip.

"I looked at the cathedral across the street and felt a little bit of prayer might help us," McCloskey told Bill Halls.

O'Brien tossed the coin and it spun over and over and landed—tails. It was the twelfth time in thirteen years the coinflip had come out tails. Thanks to a Detroit radio audience Dallas won the toss and the chance to pick the best pro prospect available in college basketball.

"I guess the Southern Baptists won that one," McCloskey told the *News*.

"It would have been tremendously significant if Ralph Sampson had come out." But Sampson, 7 feet 4, had elected to stay in school at Virginia.

"We could still get a very good player," McCloskey said. "Other teams are vitally interested in our second pick and a trade is a distinct possibility.

"What we need more than anything else is an outstanding player; someone who can either score or make the play at a crucial time. Creativity is the important thing. We've got a nucleus of five or six good players, but there's not enough creativity on our ballclub.

"I'm very partial to good big people. But the fact there is such an outstanding player as Isiah Thomas available could make a difference.

"I like Thomas very much. But I don't think he'll necessarily go first in the draft."

Thomas had said aloud that his hopes were he could play for the Chicago Bulls. The other topnotch player available was another Chicago-produced athlete, Mark Aguirre, who played for DePaul. But it was written that Aguirre had a bad attitude.

"The jury's still out on that," McCloskey told Bill Halls in the *News*.

Dallas could win only fifteen games in its first expansion season after the NBA had gone through another of its periodic geographic alterations. The Mavs were needier than the Pistons.

"We need a big man most of all," Norm Sonju, the Mavericks' GM, told the *News*. "But we're not going to draft for position. We're going to listen to anyone who calls."

A couple of clubs were trying to maneuver themselves up in the draft rotation. The New Jersey Nets had three first-round picks, including the third choice in the order behind Dallas and Detroit. They were considering packaging all three in a shipment to the Mavericks and moving to the top of the draft. Then the Bulls were fourth in the order and figured Isiah Thomas would be a sensational hometown draw, fresh from leading Bob Knight's Indiana team to the NCAA championship. The Bulls were said to be interested in swapping their first-round position plus a veteran player to Dallas so they could go first and pick Thomas.

There was some sort of divine intervention this day in Larry O'Brien's office in New York for Jack McCloskey. The Pistons had a second first-round pick, their compensation from the Kansas City Kings, who had signed Leon Douglas. In a drawing, the Pistons won the right to draft ahead of the Utah Jazz later in the first round when they claimed their second No. 1 pick.

The Celtics poured through the championship series to beat the Houston Rockets in six games. The Celts had been rebuilt—with young Larry Bird. They also had added veterans Chris Ford and M.L. Carr in deals with the Detroit Pistons plus Robert Parish and Kevin McHale, cashed in for No. 1 draft choices obtained courtesy of Dick Vitale.

But at least, the Pistons no longer had Bob McAdoo.

The NBA's 1981 draft was scheduled for June 9. No team had been able to convince the Mavericks to trade away their choice location atop the draft. All the mock drafts, dreamed up beforehand by mock journalists, listed Dallas as taking the smiling nonpareil Isiah Thomas of Indiana. Detroit, going next, would draft Mark Aguirre, who did not often smile.

Jack McCloskey agreed with these pre-draft guessers. He had started negotiations with Aguirre's negotiators.

Then Isiah said he didn't want to play in Dallas.

Two days before the draft, the Mavericks announced they would use the top pick to select —the bugles should blast a fanfare here—Mark Aguirre.

There was absolute shock in the Pistons' inner sanctum. Joy, excitement, sheer happiness.

McCloskey had envisioned that the Pistons must have a creative player who can make things happen and also score.

"We'll absolutely take Isiah unless somebody makes us a fantastic trade offer we can't afford to turn down," McCloskey told Bill Halls.

Then McCloskey confessed: "We had an agreement with Aguirre."

Oh well, Jack determined, he would start afresh negotiating with Isiah Thomas.

Down in Dallas, the coach of the Mavericks spoke out about Mark Aguirre:

"He ranks with Bird, Magic Johnson and Bill Walton in being able to change the flow of a game. I was very impressed with him. I asked him hard questions, and I got very easy, efficient answers."

Somewhere in the future, Dick Motta would call Mark Aguirre a "coward" and a "jackass." But on this day, he beamed with pleasure when the Mavericks selected Aguirre first man off the board.

And the Detroit Pistons, after years of slapstick, beatings, and citizen apathy, would select Isiah Thomas and then Kelly Tripucka of Notre Dame in the first round. The draft would have a remarkable impact upon a franchise and the area where it played.

The 1981 scene at the Main Event in the Silverdome did not pack the theatrics of draft day two years earlier, when Dick Vitale, director of the show, Dick forked over $50,000 to induce the Milwaukee Bucks to permit the Pistons to draft ahead of them.

What Jack McCloskey lacked in showmanship at the draft, he made up for in quality selections.

"Isiah Thomas is obviously a player who has charisma, the magic touch and charm," McCloskey said to reporters. "And he is loaded, loaded with talent. It was our top priority to get a player of his caliber."

Scotty Robertson had all sorts of fantasies about a quick turnabout for the Pistons with his two rookies.

"Tripucka is the kind of guy who gets floor burns on his knees and elbows," Scotty told Bill Halls in his country twang. "He's a player who wants the ball in the last five seconds when the score is tied or you're one point behind."

"I'm not unhappy about coming to Detroit," Thomas said. "It has the capability of being a winning team. I'm not saying Dallas is a bad organization. But Detroit is closer to winning."

Confident words about a team that had lost sixty-six and sixty-one games the two previous seasons.

Draft day is always full of sweet talk. Then it ends and the general manager has to sign his new rookies. The acrimony starts.

NBA salaries were starting to soar at the beginning of the 1980s, subsidized by richer TV contracts. Pro basketball, at last, had become a challenger to pro football and baseball. And the athletes were benefitting from the new popularity, well overdue. Still, it was a common belief that only three clubs in the NBA could turn a profit—the Knicks, the Celtics and the Lakers. New York was rich in basketball heritage with the cigar chompers focused on the point spreads at the Garden. Boston had tradition and a winning team. L.A. had a winning team, and the Lakers, with Magic and Kareem, had become the cult team for the Hollywood glitterati.

But Detroit had not been able to operate on the star system and had been a money loser for its two brands of owners since Fred Zollner transplanted the franchise from Fort Wayne. You doubted if Bill Davidson and his cohorts would accept losing a million dollars plus for many more years.

Now Isiah Thomas would be able to fit this burgeoning NBA star system—once Jack McCloskey got him signed.

Thomas wanted to play in Chicago, but reluctantly accepted Detroit.

Smiling and wise, Isiah had been quipping, "In Detroit, I won't have anybody to pass the ball to."

Kelly Tripucka wanted to play for the Knicks or Nets, in New York or New Jersey, his home state. He popped a salvo at Detroit, the city, the people, the basketball team during the summer while engaged in rough contract negotiations.

"All I know about your city is that it's the talk of the NBA," Tripucka, the Notre Dame man, told the *News'* Jay Mariotti. "I hear it's the last place you want to go—not only for basketball, but as a city. The team won twenty-one games last year and lost sixty-one. I've never been on a losing team and don't know if I can play on a losing team.

"The only time I was in the area was when we played Michigan in the Silverdome two years ago. I remember it was cold, and I hate cold weather. I know a lot of people from Notre Dame who now live in Detroit, and everybody says the city's bad, the city's terrible. They tell me there are some beautiful suburbs . . . But I have to be a city person. I've got to be in the city . . .

"I'm in love with New York and everything about it. I'm fascinated by it all—the big press, the Broadway shows, the Yankees and the Knicks. To play here would be a dream."

McCloskey managed to get Thomas signed first. Isiah's agent was George Andrews, a Chicago attorney who also represented Earvin Johnson and Mark Aguirre. McCloskey had been in accord with Andrews when it appeared the Pistons would be drafting Aguirre.

During the summer, the GM and agent worked on a contract for Thomas. Isiah signed for four years for $1.6 million.

Tripucka's negotiator was the highly regarded and tough Bob Woolf, the Boston-based star agent whose stable of clients included Larry Bird. Woolf was known to conduct hard negotiations with general managers, then cutting a deal at the last possible moment. Kelly's reluctance to play in Detroit seemed a ploy to force the Pistons to deal him to the Knicks or the Nets in the East. There were plenty of reported rumors involving a deal with the Knicks, although McCloskey insisted he would not trade Tripucka.

McCloskey was as tough a dealer as Woolf. Tripucka finally signed his Pistons contract two days before training camp was scheduled to open in Ann Arbor in the first week of October. It was a three-year contract for $600,000.

Scotty Robertson's fantasies turned brighter. "Kelly is a player who will be aggressive and will give you all he has," Robertson told writer Jay Mariotti of the *News*. "Also, he is a player who can shoot better than most of the guys on this team."

Isiah Thomas would have a guy to pass to in Detroit, after all.

But Scotty was already hearing a bit of chirping about his abilities to take his talented new players and mold the Pistons into a team that could win.

Dave Bing, returned to Detroit following his retirement from active playing, addressed the Detroit Sports Broadcasters Association on the merits of the Pistons just before camp opened.

"I'm not necessarily sold on the coaching

situation," said Bing. "I will admit it's a tough situation for him."

Robertson would be hearing from other doubters soon enough.

The rookie Isiah Thomas was twenty years old when he made his impression on the NBA. He was a lovable kid with a taste for fried chicken and chocolate chip ice cream.

The club was touting him as the savior of the franchise. But that same word had been used when the Pistons drafted Bailey Howell, two decades and more earlier. It had been used to describe David Bing and Bob Lanier. They had arrived with fanfare in Detroit.

But with Howell, with Bing, with Lanier, the praise and the marketing pitch were never accompanied by ruffles and flourishes. They were basketball players, after all, and they had joined the Pistons in the 1950s, the 1960s or the 1970s. Those were different times—the Paleolithic Age in matters of huckstering pro basketball.

For the first time now, there was serious peddling of Pistons souvenirs.

The Pistons hiked the price of their local TV rights, which had been a terribly hard sell in other years. Now they latched onto a subscription TV outfit, using a pioneer cable concept, plus a station for a package of over-the-air telecasts.

With the lure of Isiah Thomas and Kelly Tripucka, the Pistons doubled the number of their season-tickets holders.

The Pistons decided they'd need to raise the noise level and develop additional entertainment attractions for their fans. They blasted more music, and with Gus the Vendor from Cobo no longer dancing his time-out Twist, they hired a group of young women to do their steps on the basketball floor. They did not wear very much clothing, and they were given the name of The Classy Chassis.

And in the spirit of this heightened exposure to pro basketball, the two Detroit daily newspapers, the *News* and the *Free Press*, decided to send beat journalists along on the travels of the Pistons.

Isiah was attuned to the moment.

"I understand the position this franchise is in," he told Jay Mariotti. "As far as feeling the pressure, I know people are expecting quite a bit from me, but I don't allow myself to feel any. I have expectations myself—to win, to win as many games as we possibly can. I'm pretty sure we're going to lose more games this season than I've lost in my whole career. But if we can win as many games as we possibly can win, I'll be happy.

"If we win 25 games, and that's as many as we possibly can win, I will have reached a goal . . ."

"He will make the right decisions under pressure," Robertson told the *News* during training camp at Ann Arbor. ". . . Everyone says you can't build a franchise around a guard, but I don't say that. He is just what we need on this club right now."

Isiah was signed quickly to two endorsement deals—for shoes and with an athletic equipment company. He and agent Andrews were being cautious.

"He's not a box of cereal," Andrews said.

"Some people are reluctant to do things because of the ballclub. It's going to take winning for Isiah to approach an Earvin Johnson in the way of endorsements."

"Things are looking up for us," Tom Wilson, the Pistons' executive director and the man in charge of their marketing, told Jay Mariotti. "Most of the interest has been created by Isiah. Our philosophy is that we bottomed out at the end of our 16-win season. Once you've been where we were, there's no way to go but up."

Although Scotty Robertson received more media knocks before the 1981–82 season even opened, the Pistons broke training camp with great expectations. There were suggestions in the papers that Scotty be replaced—immediately. He wasn't. McCloskey insured that Scotty was safe.

Isiah Thomas made his professional debut on October 30, 1981. The Pistons played the Milwaukee Bucks at the Silverdome. It can be looked back to as an historic evening. A franchise that had passed almost all of its previous seasons playing in the doldrums, that had been scoffed at and ignored, now was striving to alter its image theatrically with new athletes, with a new outlook.

But the drama and the history of the moment were, strangely, lost on the sports fans of Detroit. The Pistons had sold Isiah, they had huckstered in the city and the suburbs, they managed to attract true, hard-news publicity.

And, even with the increased number of season-ticket customers, the Pistons could lure only 9,182 spectators to the Silverdome for the 1981–82 opener and Isiah Thomas' debut. It was a curious slice of apathy, caused by the years of ineptitude and mismanagement.

Perhaps years later, 200,000 might claim they attended Isiah's pro debut. He wowed the tiny audience that night. With the perpetual smile, he broke into the pros by scoring 31 points—and carrying his team to a 118-113 victory over Milwaukee, the team that had been the best in the division one season earlier. The Pistons did not go ahead until the final four and a half minutes; unusual basketball drama there for Detroit.

Isiah hit four free throws in the final twenty seconds to save the game.

Afterwards, he told the *News'* Jay Mariotti: "I wasn't nervous at the line. I just wanted to go up there and get the game over with so I could get to the locker room."

Excerpts from a column by Jerry Green in the *Detroit News,* November 6, 1981:

An evening with the Pistons. . . .

The bandwagon rolled north on I-75.

It was another night with a choice.

Hockey game around the corner from the office—Red Wings doing OK.

Basketball game in the boondocks—Pistons going crazy, with Isiah Thomas.

Prefer hockey any time. Any time but last night.

The Frontrunners Association of America had its meeting at the Silverdome. Folks from the East, from the West—me, all the way from downtown Detroit—congregated to watch Isiah.

First Impression: Isiah has the classy chassis.

Second Impression: Scotty Robertson is all right.

He's a forthright guy, which is most important. He tells you the Pistons can be humbled fast. He tells you that his basketball team is a couple of years away, even with Isiah.

It's fine after all those Pistons coaches who kept tooting their horns until you were knee deep in their bull.

I prefer Scotty to all the coaches here who fed us with their propaganda, then failed to match their boasts . . .

Detroit is experiencing a miraculous rise to mediocrity. The town could have three .500 teams this season—Pistons, Red Wings, Lions. How easy to be satisfied!

His third pro game and Isiah already has been immortalized on T-shirts. They cost 8 bucks at the Pistons' concession stands. (Top ticket price is $9.)

The Pistons got new home uniforms. Gray? Silver because it is their silver anniversary in Detroit, and they play in the Silverdome? They look like they have been laundered in dirty water and have ring around the collar all over.

Change soap. Bring back the white uniforms . . .

More noise during the timeouts than during the game. The Pistons have sold the time during the timeouts for commercials to airlines, auto dealers, beer, assorted enterprises. Pro basketball keeps trying to hide itself in the bushes . . .

Now it's exciting. The Pistons score 13 straight points. Kelly Tripucka goes out of bounds and flattens the guest sitting next to Bill Davidson, who owns the team. Davidson almost gets bowled over himself. But he rises smiling.

At halftime, he is still smiling. After all these years he owns a team that can play basketball.

"They're getting better," he said—and for the first time he has a happy look.

More impressions: John Long works hard.

Isiah makes things happen. And he's always smiling.

Kelly Tripucka is a tough competitor . . .

Attendance reports: 12,114 at the Red Wings, but they don't count so well; 5,116 at the Pistons, who invented the phantom crowd count in their early days . . .

It's traditional pro basketball. It all boils down to the last three minutes.

The Pistons stave off the Nets 109-103. They stay unbeaten. Only 79 more games to go.

Final impression: The Pistons, with Isiah and Kelly, are one player away from being genuine championship contenders. The one player's name is Ralph Sampson.

Something funny happened. Next time the Pistons played at the Silverdome people showed up, real live people with fannies to put into the seats. They created a traffic jam on the roads outside the building, to be treasuered as an historic first for pro basketball in Detroit.

Maybe it was the magic of Isiah . . . maybe the town was turned on by the Pistons' 3-and-0 getaway in their dishwater gray uniforms at the start of the season . . . maybe it was the magic of the Boston Celtics, the ruling champions and their Larry Bird.

Whatever, 15,085 showed up for a pro basketball game. It was duly certified as the second largest crowd in the franchise's history. And it would serve as a trendsetter for seasons in the future:

Whenever the Pistons drew hordes of people into the arena to watch them they'd get the bejabbers beat out of them. The Celtics clubbed the Pistons 129–88, even with the advent of Isiah. It seems the Pistons never could do much against the Celtics.

In mid-November, with the club doing okay, Jack McCloskey jumped back into the trademarket. Greg Kelser, not appreciated by either McCloskey or Robertson, was unloaded again to the Seattle Supersonics. This time Kelser passed the Seattle physical and the trade held. This was the deal for a dynamo of shooting guard, who could warm up fast and hit from outside, who played the tough type of ball played on the asphalt playgrounds of Brooklyn—Vinnie Johnson. Vinnie had been unappreciated in Seattle.

But he seemed to fit in quite well into the Detroit backcourt with rookie Isiah Thomas and John Long.

It would be etched as the first of Jack McCloskey's astute deals aimed toward acquiring the parts that might be able to win a championship. Some day!

Isiah and the Pistons went into New York City, that basketball playground, for the first time on the first of December. Isiah was a hot property in this command center of the American communications industry. At 8:30 on the morning of the day before the game in the Garden, Isiah was picked up by a limousine and a chauffeur and taken to Rockefeller Center. There, Bryant Gumbel and the starry-eyed crew from NBC's "The Today Show" were waiting to ask questions of the wise twenty-year-old who had left college

in Indiana to display his skills in professional basketball.

"It's just another thing to do," Isiah responded when Jay Mariotti asked him if such exposure excited him. "This is no big deal."

"I'm sorry," Gumbel said, joshing at Isiah, "I'm sick and tired of making stars of twenty year olds."

Isiah grinned and when Gumbel asked seriously if he was surprised at the swath he was making in the NBA, Thomas said:

"I'm surprised our team has done as well as it has. That has been most pleasing."

Isiah's on-camera spontaneity would sharpen through the years.

And winning would have to be learned, too. The early success of the Pistons could be classified as moderate, no more. The Pistons were 8-and-5 around Thanksgiving and soon were 8-and-8. They were well polished off in the game in the Garden—112–100, their third consecutive defeat. This after not only the intensive TV exposure, but the typical overkill that the New York newspapers bestow upon visiting royalty.

"You can't go out and play the way we did and expect to win," Thomas said.

It was a lesson in reality.

The Pistons would remain stuck in their losing streak, stretching it to eight.

The transition from Bob Knight's ultra-successful college game to the pros caused some bewilderment for Isiah Thomas in the early season. There was a flap between the rookie and the coach, Scotty Robertson. Isiah said he was confused about his assignments, whether he was supposed to emphasize his passing game, or his shooting, or his defense. He figured Scotty didn't want him to shoot so much . . . and it was upsetting. From his side, Robertson figured Isiah was hogging the ball.

"I'm a player, not just a lead guard," Thomas complained to the writers.

Scotty told Isiah to cool it.

"Teams were beginning to play him for the drive," Scotty would explain. "I said we wanted him to learn the pro game, to give up the ball a little more.

"That was much more a media thing than an actual thing. There was never a confrontation between Isiah and myself. Isiah made the statement that he didn't know what his role was.

"That's not true. He knew what his role was. But I was talking to him about priorities. I wanted him to pass the ball first, play defense second and score third. I didn't tell him not to shoot. I told him to shoot when he had a good shot."

Kelly Tripucka was a revelation for the Detroit fans with his style of uncontrolled flying basketball. There were nights when the highlight was Tripucka diving through the first rows of customers in his efforts to save a ball about to go out of bounds. A couple of times during his rookie season, he was kayoed—once knocking heads on the floor with teammate Terry Tyler, who played with a powerful work ethic coming off the bench as a sixth man.

But despite his showmanship and on-the-court hustle, Tripucka continued to whiz and moan in interviews. With a sour puss, he told Jay Mariotti one day:

"Everybody said coming in here that I couldn't run, couldn't shoot, couldn't pass, couldn't play basketball. Well, I didn't say that, and I knew it wasn't true. I have a tremendous amount of self-confidence and I knew I could play in this league. I'll be honest and say I'm a little surprised I've done as well as I have."

In January, rookie Isiah Thomas was selected to the Eastern squad for the 1982 NBA All-Star Game to be a teammate of Larry Bird's and an opponent of Magic Johnson's. He was in with the elite. Kelly Tripucka sulked that he didn't make the All-Star squad and said so.

The next day, Tripucka was added to the team by Larry O'Brien when Danny Roundfield, from the Atlanta Hawks, withdrew because of an injury. Tripucka said it was like Santa Claus showing up late.

The Pistons were struggling in February 1982 when Jack McCloskey struck again at the witching hour—as the clock ticked close to midnight and the trade deadline.

Tossing in an additional draft choice and using Paul Mokeski's Polish heritage as bait, McCloskey slickered the Cleveland Cavaliers into yielding two players. McCloskey gave up first and second-round draft choices along with Phil Hubbard and Mokeski for the two.

It was reported in the press that the main addition to the Pistons was Kenny Carr, the

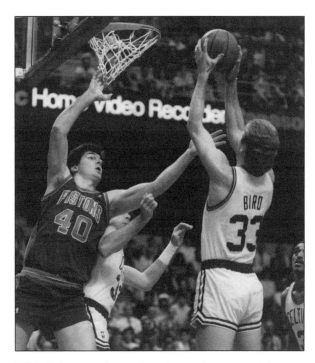

Bill Laimbeer was thought to be a minor part of the deal that brought him to Detroit from Cleveland.

highly touted power forward. Carr's reputation was as a strong rebounder who could score, according to the articles, with the best at his position in the entire NBA. It was reported, also, that he arrived with a sour disposition and a threat to team morale.

Carr's background—a racially mixed marriage —and his moods were dissected at length. And oh yeah, the second newcomer joining the Pistons was that moon-faced center who had been a benchwarmer over in Cleveland—the player just tossed into the trade to make it seem even, Bill Laimbeer.

With Carr, the Pistons now figured to have a strong, solid starting unit.

And Ted Steptien, the Cleveland owner, who dealt with McCloskey felt it was a good idea to get rid of Laimbeer, the backup center, because he had recently signed another center to an $800,000-a-year free-agent's contract. The free-agent center who made Laimbeer expendable in Cleveland was James Edwards.

On a night in March 1982, when the Pistons were losing again to the Celtics, the publicity people handed out ballots. Fans could vote for the Silver Anniversary Detroit Pistons team. It

159

was a simple function to write in the five best names of the old players—George Yardley, Dave DeBusschere, Bob Lanier, David Bing, and Gene Shue.

On the basis of one season, Isiah Thomas could not yet crack that distinguished lineup.

It was written by a columnist who would never forget, in the *News*: "This Pistons' Silver Anniversary All-Time All-Star team has one thing in common. The Pistons traded every one of the five of them away to other teams."

When the Pistons announced this official honor team, it included a sixth player—the deserving Bailey Howell. Never forget that they traded him away, too.

Late in the season, Tripucka was the target of a hard elbow tossed in a series by a rookie for the Washington Bullets. The league fined the culprit a grand for his bad-boy behavior. The rookie's name was Rick Mahorn.

The Pistons did manage to win more than twenty-five games in Isiah Thomas' rookie season. They won thirty-nine ballgames, against forty-three losses. That record, in itself, represented a huge improvement over the Detroit club of the previous two seasons. The Pistons were eighteen games better with Isiah and Tripucka than they had been the season before. They came in third in the Central Division. But they missed the playoffs, for the fifth successive season.

The impact of All-Stars Isiah and Kelly on Detroit and its sports fans, in the final tally, was not dramatic, despite the hoopla and the hard sell and the improvement in the quality of basketball. Attendance nearly doubled in the 1981–82 season to an average of 9,910. It was the best in the history of the franchise. But shoot, the Pistons had averaged almost that many customers the season they moved to the Silverdome, 1978–79, with Dick Vitale and his screamin' meamies.

The Pistons had started upward, on the floor and in the seats, but it would be a distant journey.

It was the turn of Pat Riley's Lakers to win the NBA finals again in the spring of 1982. With Magic playing the magnificent role, the Lakers licked the Philly 76ers for the championship in six games.

There was a postscript to this series. One of the Lakers earning a championship ring was—Bob McAdoo, the vagabond and erstwhile scoring champion.

McAdoo sent a message back to the Pistons via the *News'* Jay Mariotti:

"They won a few games last season, but they could have won more if they kept Bob Lanier and I. If they would have kept us, I think that team could be good enough now to challenge Philadelphia, Boston and Milwaukee. But they chose to do things their way. I understand people up there think they've improved a lot. I don't think they've improved that much."

So there!

Jack McCloskey got rid of Kenny Carr as quickly as he could after the 1981–82 season. Much of the reason had to do with controversy in the locker room. But also, McCloskey had deprived himself one first-round draft pick in the February deal for Carr and Laimbeer. An effective building process had only started. All the first-rounders McCloskey could stash away were essential to the growth of the Pistons.

So, McCloskey shipped Carr to the Portland Trail Blazers just before the 1982 draft, for a No. 1. Then Jack participated in the draft for the second time in two years armed with two first-round draft choices. But 1982 was not a vintage year for draftees. There wasn't a Magic or a Bird or an Isiah available in the draft.

James Worthy went first off the board—in defiance of the old wives' tale that the draft is designed to make all clubs equal to their rivals. The Lakers, the reigning champions, got Worthy.

When it came time for the abuilding Pistons to draft, McCloskey took Cliff Levingston on the ninth pick of the first round and then Ricky Pierce as the eighteenth selection.

They would prove to be adequate NBA pros, but they could not deliver the impact and instant excitement of Isiah and Tripucka as rookies.

Scotty Robertson went into his third training camp with the Pistons in the autumn of 1982 figuring he had enough quality on his club to reach the playoffs.

"I feel I've proven I can coach here," Scotty told Bill Halls. "I'm certainly not the best coach in the league, but I'm not the worst, either. I'm somewhere in between."

That self-appraisal covered his ballclub, too.

The Pistons had stopped being the worst team in the NBA. They were certainly not the best. They were somewhere in that huge basketball Bermuda Triangle—in between.

"We don't have to be ashamed of losing to Detroit," said Larry Bird one day in Boston in the fall of 1982. "They're a damn good team."

The Pistons weren't so damn good that the Celtics would fear losing to them. But with Thomas and Tripucka and Laimbeer and Vinnie Johnson, the Pistons could give most teams a go of it on most nights.

And interest stirred among the sportsgoers of the greater Detroit area. Pro basketball had become hung up on media-created catchy numbers, like triple doubles. Well, in Detroit, for the first time in the history of the franchise, the Pistons were hitting double digits in attendance on most nights—that is, 10,000 or more. Every now and then, they'd attract 15,000 or 20,000. It was a helluva improvement, considering.

". . . There's charisma here," Scotty Robertson told Bill Halls as the Pistons made their way through the early NBA schedule. "There's some interest among the fans."

Julius Erving came to town with the 76ers and he said:

"I don't know if they had a three, four or five-year plan in mind, but they appear to be in midphase. Scotty obviously had something on the drawing board and Kelly and Isiah have helped accelerate it."

"This franchise is no longer a laughingstock," Robertson said. "Now it's a valuable piece of real estate. That's because of the owner's willingness to turn the basketball operation over to Jack. This thing has been turned around. I've certainly had some part in it, and I'm proud of that."

It was a gratifying experience for Robertson.

He had been fired after fifteen games because he couldn't make a brand, new expansion team win in New Orleans. He had gone to work in real estate. He had given up a $100,000-per-year income out of his love for the game of basketball.

"In real estate, every time you make a deal, you go to the bank," Robertson told Bill Halls. "Financially, it was very rewarding. But I discovered I was motivated from an ego standpoint. I found it more important to write my name on the board in the real estate office when I made a sale than it was to collect my paycheck. I missed being in front of 10,000 people when I went to work.

"I had written to every team in the NBA and told them I would work for nothing to get a chance to get back in the league. But no one would give me an opportunity."

The New Orleans Jazz and the ziggy after fifteen games, fourteen of those defeats, continued to nag him in his thoughts.

"It was the first thing that had happened to me in my coaching career," he said. "I felt like the world was crumbling down all around me."

At last he was hired for an assistant's job, at twenty grand for the season. He suffered the heart attack, survived, came to an awareness that he was mortal, and now there was this gratification at age fifty-two because a basketball team in Detroit was making some progress.

"I always said if I ever back in this league," he said, "I was never going out again."

Scotty did not know everything that was going on around him as his club was creeping toward mediocrity, while Isiah Thomas was learning the pro game, while Bill Laimbeer was discovering that finesse was not required by every athlete in the NBA. Scotty did not know that there was some disenchantment with his coaching methods. From people in high places. You started to hear rumors around town.

The club played well enough through the early months of the season. The Pistons were second in the Central Division in January of 1983. They developed the ability to win games on the road.

Late in the month, against the Chicago Bulls, Kelly Tripucka went wild with the basketball in his hands. Shoot, shoot, shoot; score, score, score. For the night, Tripucka scored 56 points —more than Dave Bing ever scored in a game, more than George Yardley had ever scored in a game. Kelly was saluted for breaking Bing's twelve-year-old club record of 54 points in a game, just as David had once been heralded with breaking Yardley's club record of 52.

These were individual heroics, all connected in some manner with the tradition of the team— for after Tripucka's record performance, the team itself became connected with the Pistons' inglorious history. The Pistons of 1982–83 started to sink.

They dropped back to third place. There were failures, again. Quickly, the ancient quest for a .500 season became impossible. It ended in April. And although they had become a popular attraction for the rich and famous who lived in the suburbs north of the city—prominent folks such as Bob Seger, who rocked with the Pistons at almost every home game—the season record was 37-and-45. The Pistons had slipped into a retreat, despite all the promise and progress. They had drawn a club record in attendance— an average of 12,733 per game. But the final reckoning was another spring in which the Pistons failed to qualify for the playoffs. They had endured six seasons in which they finished with losing records and missed the playoffs.

Jack McCloskey was one of those in a high place who was disenchanted with the coaching.

Immediately after the season ended, McCloskey summoned Robertson. The message was that no matter what Robertson had said the previous December, he was going out again. His world would crumble around him again. Robertson got the ziggy, in the same manner as all of them in the long, long line of Pistons coaches who had worked and suffered and hoped before him.

It seemed to many of us who wrote about this basketball club through the years that this was a terribly unfair firing. The club had improved tremendously out of the ruins left by Dick Vitale. But sentiment never ruled in professional sports—and the harsh cruelty of that fact was never more apparent. Jack McCloskey had learned this reality himself a decade earlier when he, too, had been shafted at Portland and was so dismayed he sought refuge in a West Indies hideaway. At the time, he never wanted to see another basketball game.

McCloskey had to have reason. It was that the Pistons had not improved on defense during Robertson's three years as head coach. Robertson had taught Isiah Thomas some tricks of the game; he had taken Laimbeer and turned him into a forceful, useful basketball player; he had found spots for Vinnie Johnson and his flaming shooting streaks.

But the Pistons had remained losers, despite their progress and their allure. Another man would have to be chosen to finish the job.

McCloskey, his face taut and grim, said:

"Winning or losing or not making the playoffs was not instrumental in this decision. Fifty percent of the game is on the defensive end. The teams that make the playoffs and win championships are the teams that play defense. This is a matter of principle, a matter of coming along during the season. It is just not a matter of points allowed. It's a matter of percentage. Teams were making too high a percentage of shots against us.

"Scotty didn't teach the kind of defense you need in this league. You can have poor individual defenders and still play well defensively. You can still have good team defense. We didn't."

Robertson said he did not plan to become a recluse and vanish in the Islands. The night he was fired he attended the Pistons' team dinner and spoke to the players and the writers.

"I'm very disappointed, I'm shocked," he said in the *News*. "Even though there has been speculation for six weeks, I didn't think it would happen. In my mind, I've done a good job.

"I've gone through the hard times with this team. I wanted to be part of the good times."

"I knew it was a possibility, but it's a sad situation to see a coach fired," Bill Laimbeer told Bill Halls. "He did so much for me. He brought me here, put me in the starting lineup and had confidence in me. It was the greatest thing that ever happened to me."

As the playoffs began elsewhere, the new array of rumors started in Detroit. The *News* reported on April 22, 1983, that Jack McKinney, coach of the Indiana Pacers and former coach of the Lakers, had been contacted. The name of Phil Johnson, former coach of the Kansas City Kings and at that time an assistant with the Utah Jazz, was also prominently mentioned. Don Chaney, Robertson's assistant on the Pistons, was considered a candidate. So was Cotton Fitzsimmons, disenchanted with his job as head coach in Kansas City.

Another name was that of a Philadelphia broadcaster who had been an assistant with the 76ers and a head coach of the Cleveland Cavaliers, a one time head coach and schoolteacher at Punxsutawney High School in Pennsylvania: Chuck Daly.

It was well-documented in the papers that McKinney was the original choice. He was not interested in the Detroit job. It is understood that it was offered to other coaches, presumably Dr. Jack Ramsey, still in Portland and still unwilling to leave.

This time, however, Chuck Daly indeed was interested in pulling out of his Pennsylvania roots and going to Detroit to coach a basketball team with a tradition of pratfalls and defeat and coaches' insecurity.

On May 17, 1983, with the NBA finals just started, Jack McCloskey introduced Chuck Daly as the new head coach. There was nothing to indicate that anything would be different for Daly than it had been for the sixteen other men in this laughable lineage. Nothing at all!

The result of the NBA Finals of 1983 were different, though. With Chuck Daly just getting accustomed to reading the barbs in the Detroit newspapers, the Philly 76ers—his old team—completed a four-game sweep of the Lakers for the championship.

Chuck Daly—named head coach of the Pistons on May 17, 1984.

II—The Mid-Eighties

Chuck Daly arrived in Detroit much better prepared to work for the Pistons than Herbie Brown had been nine or so years earlier. Daly was ready. He had a wardrobe!

Pat Riley, in L.A., had made coaching in the NBA a matter of grooming and fashion. Riley greased WD-40 into his hair and slicked it backwards. His suits were spotless, knife-edged creases to the trousers, the jackets tailor-fitted. He stood immaculate in front of the bench in the Forum, where the crowd consisted of cinema-star dazzle, sporting dark shades and designer blue jeans. Jack Nicholson hero-worshipped Magic Johnson.

Detroit is a lunch bucket town, shot-and-beer, with an unrequired zest for sports. That is Detroit's culture, sports, games. Chuck Daly came into this blue-collar atmosphere, and it was suggested he possessed a clothes-envy of Pat Riley. He was in his fifties. But his head was combed in a wavy pompadour. His face was unlined. And his favorite suits were double-breasted, browns, blues, pearl grays, with white

shirts. Chuck prefered some wildly florid neckties, that would cause immediate violation of Ivy League eligibility regulations.

And whether he could coach in the NBA—particularly the defensive phase—was to be debated as the Pistons went through training camp as a prelude to the 1983–84 season.

Of course, the new mood had to be punctuated with a touch of controversy. Jack McCloskey was engaged in a battle with two agents—a pincers movement against him—in attempts to sign Antoine Carr, the No. 1 draft choice. Camp opened without Carr, as it had started the previous year without first-rounders Cliff Levingston and Ricky Pierce. They eventually signed. Their late arrivals upset the club's equilibrium and caused damage well into the season, to the point that it might have been a first straw leading toward Scotty Robertson's dismissal at the season's end.

Now McCloskey could not make headway in negotiations with Carr's two agents. Jack finally said the hell with it. Carr could go to Italy and play for lira and pasta. Chuck Daly would be forced to coach his first season without a first-round draft choice. His young veterans—Thomas, Tripucka, Laimbeer, Johnson—had been primed to reach the playoffs, this time for sure.

Maybe.

Daly told the *News'* Bill Halls that three weeks in camp was hardly sufficient time to establish different, improved offensive and defensive concepts.

"But we'll spend a great deal of time defensively because that's where you have to hang your hat."

The season started with the Pistons playing the Celtics. It was no longer a disgrace to lose to the Pistons, Larry Bird had said at another time. But on this late October night in the Silverdome he had something else to say. The NBA referees had taken their whistles and gone on strike against the league. The games would have to be played with irregular tooters, men willing to put on the stripe shirts for a few bucks and act as reserve NBA officials.

In the third quarter, as Bird guarded one of the Pistons near the edge of the court, he became upset with a decision by one of the strike refs. Bird barked at the guy through his thin, round, wimpish beak.

"Scab," said Bird, the one time garbage-truck worker in French Lick, Indiana, who became a Boston millionaire because he was tall and could shoot basketballs.

The sub official heard Bird. But he would not cross his hands in the form of the letter T to call a technical foul.

They weren't very good refs.

Starting quickly, Daly's Pistons moved toward the top of the Central Division. Their fourth game was versus the Milwaukee Bucks, with Bob Lanier at center.

Very late in the first half, there was a flurry beneath the basket. There was some jostling, some elbows tossed, typical NBA jungle stuff in the post. Suddenly, Bill Laimbeer was flat on the basketball court. Laimbeer was writhing with pain, obviously hurt, as Mike Abdenour, the trainer, rushed to administer first aid. What had happened had happened so fast, few of those in the stands saw it. Lainer, his fist clenched, had delivered a crushing punch in the nose to Laimbeer.

"He slugged him," said eyewitness Bill Davidson, the Pistons' owner. Davidson's seats were at the edge of the court, behind a basket. He told Bill Halls: "They'll never get away with it. It's on film."

But the two scab refs, still working with the zebra strike continuing, didn't see the punch. So, Lanier was not kicked out of the game. He could play on.

Laimbeer was groggy. It could have been a ten-count KO. But then he got up and he, too, played on—and outplayed and outrebound Lanier. When it ended, with the Pistons victorious, 106–93, and sharing first place in the division, Laimbeer told Bill Halls:

"I thought my nose was broken. It may be . . . I really don't know what happened. I heard a whistle and a foul call. The next thing I knew I was on the ground. It's unfortunate that he wants to play that way. He's a president of our players association and we're against violence. It was unprovoked as far as I'm concerned. I never even saw it coming.

"I can't afford to retaliate. He makes a lot more money than I do. I can't afford a $10,000 fine. It could have been a career-ending injury. I didn't expect it from him. I do now."

The occasionally brooding, often-mystical former Piston Lanier told Bill Halls: "I felt something inside and I don't feel good about it. The situation had nothing to do with what went on out on the court. It had nothing to do with Bill personally. I got this thing in my mind. I guess it manifested itself in that way. It's something I'm going through personally. I have some court things going on with my father."

Lanier had appeared in court in Michigan that morning regarding the death of his father, two years earlier. Robert Lanier, Sr., had been run down and killed in a traffic accident in Oakland County, not far from the Silverdome.

The Pistons sent the videotape of the punch to Laimbeer's nose to the league. Larry O'Brien, the commissioner, considered the complaint, watched replays of the one-punch knockdown, and fined Lanier $5,000. Lanier also wrote letters of apology to Davidson and Laimbeer.

Laimbeer was ticked because the fine wasn't larger.

But a reputation had been started. Bill Laimbeer was a very tough dude who played physical basketball and the centers around the NBA were not going to like him very much.

On the night of December 13, 1983, the Pistons played in the thin, rare Rocky Mountain air of Denver. They went out against the Nuggets and after four quarters, the score was knotted at 145 for each team. In the first overtime, each club scored 14 points. In the second overtime, the Pistons scored 12 points and the Nuggets matched the tally with their own dozen. It was 171–171 starting the third overtime period.

It was then that the Pistons managed to outscore the Nuggets with 15 points to 13. The final score was: Pistons 186, Nuggets 184. Isiah Thomas led the Pistons with 47 points; John Long scored 41; and Kelly Tripucka scored 35. Denver had its shooters, too—Kiki Vandeweghe with 51 and Alex English with 47.

So it was, the same franchise that had won the lowest-scoring game in the history of the NBA —the Fort Wayne Zollner Pistons in their 19–18 victory over the Minneapolis Lakers thirty-three years earlier—also won the highest-scoring game ever played in the league.

Each game totalled up as one in the win column of the standings.

On a frigid day in January 1984, as the world geared up its hysteria in advance of another Super Bowl, an event also was occurring in Detroit. I took congnizance of the fact by resurrecting the greatest moments in the twenty-seven-year history of the Detroit Pistons. There were two highlights in that time. No. 1, of course, in this outpouring of nostalgia was Wilt Chamberlain's hitch aboard the school bus to Toledo, as arranged for by the Pistons' travel agent.

Then . . .

Excerpts from a column in the *Detroit News*, January 13, 1984:

. . . The second of these highlights, crammed into slightly more than a quarter-century, is occurring right now.

The Detroit Pistons are sole occupants of first place in their NBA Central Division. If the Pistons have ever been in first place in mid-January before, the information is written on scriptures and hidden in a tomb somewhere.

The team that never has finished first is threatening to do exactly that. The bandwagon is careening down the highway. Frontrunners are emerging with yawns from behind their masks of apathy. The town is talking about the Pistons.

The Philadelphia 76ers are not in first place in their division. The Los Angeles Lakers are not in first place in their division. But the Pistons are tops, the leaders, in theirs. They could be a genuine miracle.

"The Pistons were not a good team when I got here," Kelly Tripucka said yesterday. "We had 21 wins that year.

"It's like we've come back from the dead."

It is a fair analogy.

Kelly Tripucka is the hot gun on this first-place ballclub. He has enormous assistance, of course, but Kelly is the top shooter.

. . . Tripucka said, "There were frustrations when I got here. I had to get used to losing . . . but I'd always been a winner before.

"So this was different. Being in first place . . . you know, teams that are consistently on top, it's harder for them to stay there than get there because teams are always gunning for you. They know you're the best and they go after you harder. It's like Nebraska in football."

The curiosity of the first-place Pistons in a league in which there are currently the second-place Lakers and the second-place 76ers is, naturally, a phenomenon of geography . . .

"They're still playing very good basketball," Kelly said. "Boston is in first place in Philadelphia's division. One of them is always in first place. Portland's playing well in the Lakers' division. In our division, Milwaukee's not playing well.

"Maybe that's the reason we're in first place. Basketball is a long season. They can still take us. But if we go down, it won't be without a fight."

That, in a nutshell, is the encouraging aspect of the Pistons. They are not yet a first-place ballclub. They are not yet in the championship arena with the Lakers, the 76ers, the Celtics. The pro basketball miracle in Detroit is that the Pistons have become qualified challengers for first; they have become genuine contenders for the playoffs.

For a traditional also-ran with a history of atrocious bungling, this can be regarded as progress. Years of 16-and-66, 21-and-61 have caused a smattering of skepticism . . . a dab of negativism. Such reactions have lingered since long before the Pistons' famous bus journey to Toledo more than 20 years ago . . .

"Detroit has not had much to cheer about," Tripucka said. "It's an improvement from what it used to be. They finally got some talent.

"The fans come out and we don't play well, and they boo. They cheer when we win. We're a fun team to watch. People come out and they get their money's worth. And that's what it's all about—people getting their money's worth.

In some regions of higher basketball interest, Kelly Tripucka is regarded as somewhat of a hot dog. That he is a showoff on the floor with theatrical mannerisms and flashy gestures. He was heavily criticized in L.A. last year for such behavior. It was said he was regarded the same way in that other basketball seat, New York City.

"If I'm a hot dog," rebutted Tripucka, "I want to know what everybody else is.

"I call it hard work. It's the way the game should be played, and if people and writers don't like it, they're in the wrong business."

No matter, there is a pro basketball bandwagon rolling in this town, for the first time. Kelly Tripucka, along with colleagues Isiah Thomas and Bill Laimbeer, is responsible for the unprecedented success. Wind up the 24-second clock, toot the whistles, cancel all the old observations about it all being jammed into the last three minutes . . . a longtime skeptic is softening.

"I haven't been in first place since I was in high school," Tripucka said. "It's different when you're in high school."

Yeah, you ride to games in a school bus.

That January night, the first-place Pistons drilled the Chicago Bulls in comeback fashion at the Silverdome. They'd rattled off a six-game winning streak; they'd won eleven of thirteen games.

The shootout at Denver, the 186–184 truple overtime game, was an aberration for this Detroit team. The Pistons were in first place, winning, because Chuck Daly, and assistant Dick Harter, had taken the gunners and taught them to play defense.

"I don't know when it happened, but I'm glad it did," Isiah told Bill Halls during the winning streak. "I think defense has saved us a lot. We go down and throw the ball away, or miss a shot, or make a mistake, and our defense at the other end saves us and gives us another opportunity."

But these Pistons were still young and tender, and the euphoria could not be everlasting. Not even for ten days. With the winning streak at six, the Pistons went into Chuck Daly's old hometown of Philadelphia to play the champion 76ers. The then second-place 76ers. It was a blast. Moses Malone, who might have been a Piston with any sense of smarts, pummeled them with 34 points and 16 rebounds. Dr. J scored 26 poinds. The winning streak ended with a cruel defeat, 128–117.

Reality returned.

The Pistons lost to the New Jersey Nets, who were never much, at home in the Silverdome.

"It looked like we were running in the mud," Daly told the reporters in his postgame commentary.

And the Pistons spent the remainder of the season running in and out of the mud.

April is baseball season in Detroit. It always has been. Opening Day is a holiday-like in the city. Kids actually do play hookey; so do bankers and lawyers and politicians. They all wind up, gray-flanneled, preening and posing at Tiger Stadium, in the box seats. Few of them had ever paid much heed to pro basketball.

And this April 1984, there were great expectations in Detroit for the Tigers. They had narrowly missed in the 1983 pennant race. They expected to win it in 1984. And when the Tigers started the baseball season by winning and winning again and winning some more enroute to an historic 35-and-5 start, the newly muscular Pistons were relegated to secondary status. As usual.

Except this time the Pistons had achieved their annual franchise goal of hitting the .500 standard. With Chuck Daly coaching and Isiah Thomas maturing, with Bill Laimbeer belting and Kelly Tripucka shooting, the Pistons finished at 49–33. It was their second best record of all the seasons in Detroit. The Pistons did not finish first in the Central, they were a game short of Milwaukee. But they had carried themselves close to the NBA aristocracy.

And for the first time in seven years, the Pistons qualified for the NBA playoffs.

The opponents in the first round were the New York Knickerbockers, coached by verbiage-ridden Hubie (not Herbie) Brown, in a best-of-five series. The Pistons, with the better season record, gained the homecourt advantage. At least, the Pistons had the *hometown* advantage.

Daly has a pet saying, a cliche: "What goes around, comes around."

And it would.

It was a hellacious series.

The Tigers might be running off from the rest of baseball, but at last, finally, Detroit proved it could split its civic personality to root for two teams at the same time.

With the crowd going nuts, the Pistons lost their first playoff game since the spring of 1977 to the Knicks by a tiny point, 94–93. Bernard King killed the Pistons with 36 points. Two nights later the Pistons squared the series with 113–105 victory, as the crowd in the Silverdome went even nuttier. Bernard King scored 46 points for the Knicks.

The next two games were in Madison Square Garden, New York. The Knicks won Game 3, 120–113, as Detroit watched on TV. Bernard King murdered the Pistons with 46 points, again.

Well, said the media, the Pistons gave it a good shot, they had a nice ride, chalk it as a year of progress—but . . . Then playing with enormous courage, the Pistons beat back the Knicks in Madison Square Garden, hostile territory, 119–112, on a Wednesday night. The Pistons commanded the TV ratings. Cheers. The series was tied for a second time. Bernard King scored 41 points, and his team still lost.

And now, the decisive fifth game was scheduled for Detroit.

That's when what went around decades earlier, came around again.

In olden days, the Pistons had been evicted from the Olympia Stadium and had to play playoff games at the University of Detroit Memorial Building. Once, this team of homeless waifs was forced to play an NBA playoff game at the high school gym in suburban Grosse Pointe.

Now, about to play one of the most critical games in the franchise's history—the decisive Game 5 of a 1984 playoff series—the Pistons were evicted from their home base again. The Silverdome was booked for motorcycle races. Bumped once more, the Pistons had to take their crucial playoff game to downtown Detroit, back to the riverfront, to play in Joe Louis Arena, the Red Wings' hockey rink.

They laid down the floor used by Detroit's moveable Continental Basketball Association entry, the Spirits. And the Pistons would take on the Knicks on a minor-league floor.

But even so, Detroit was gripped by the hysteria of pro basketball.

"The most difficult job I've had this year is getting them back to the level of intensity that we had in New York Wednesday night," Chuck Daly told Bill Halls. "When we get high and win, we sometimes have a letdown in the next game. We haven't handled that very well this year. When we win our thought process drops off. When we lose, we usually get more intense. If we think that way this time, we're in deep trouble.

"The final game in any playoff series is different than all the others . . .

"What we'll have is a big crowd on a neutral court. We've played in maybe thirty different arenas this year. We can't do anything about that. The game is on the schedule. Let's play it. I'm glad we'll have a big crowd. That's super. I'm happy. But we've got to come ready to play. That's the way the Knicks come out to play every night."

And Chuck had to figure out some way to stop —at least neutralize—Bernard King.

The winner of Game 5 would go off to play the next series—versus the Boston Celtics, who were winning.

Excerpts from a nostalgia piece in the *Detroit News*, May 15, 1990:

The tickets went on sale at 10 in the morning, and when they did, the line of people went around Joe Louis Arena and along the riverfront all the way to the Boblo Boat docks.

All for a basketball game in a town with wayward team that had been rendered homeless by a Supercross motorcyle event.

The date was April 27, 1984, and the attraction that suddenly drew out the people was Game 5 of the NBA playoffs—Pistons vs. Knicks.

. . . Chuck Daly was the rookie coach of the Pistons. Isiah Thomas, at age 22, was a third-year professional.

So we will take the time machine back . . . to then, when only a cockeyed optimist dared believe the Pistons would ever ascend to the NBA championship. The Pistons, in 1984, had not qualified for the playoffs in seven years. Four years earlier they had been 16–66, most pitiful in the NBA, in a season they began with Dick Vitale in a frenzied condition as their coach. They would improve, in another year, to 21–61.

And then on this April night in 1984, in a city frenzied over a baseball team, the people lined up in a rush for basketball tickets.

It was the night, after several abortive flirtations, that pro basketball finally became part of this city.

What aroused the fans was the game they had seen the Pistons play two nights earlier on television . . . They would be home for Game 5—well, not quite home.

"A foreign court," Daly told the press. The Pistons had played all season at the Silverdome. They knew how the ball bounced on the court there; they were familiar with the shadows, with the lighting. But they had been booted out by the zoom-zoom of the motorcycle competition. The Pistons were just tenants, and the Silverdome had previously contracted bookings.

So on this Friday night in downtown Detroit, the Knicks and the Pistons conducted the theater of basketball. In this same town, playing about a mile away, the Tigers went against the Cleveland Indians. The Tigers had begun the season with a 16–1 roll, on the way to their epic 35–5 start and the world championship.

The atmosphere was electric, the folks giddy that Friday night in downtown Detroit.

It was steaming hot inside Joe Louis for the players and for the 21,208 people who had managed to buy tickets. The Pistons were not yet a mature team. They were behind. The Knicks led by eight points with 1:57 left. The fans cheered the Pistons' gallant show, maybe next year.

Then Isiah got the ball. He got it again. And again. In 92 seconds, Isiah Thomas, possessed, scored 16 points. The Pistons tied it at 114 on Thomas' three-pointer with 23 seconds left. Neither team could score. It went into overtime.

At Tiger Stadium, 34,112 fans watched transfixed as the Tigers, so dominant, struggled against the Indians. They had packed into the outfield stands at 6 o'clock on this humid night. The Tigers had

become the biggest sports story in America. TV tripods were stacked around the infield.

The Tigers were tied 3–3. And oddly, there were cheers at times during the lulls in the baseball game. The baseball fans were listening to the dramatic twists of the basketball game down on the riverfront.

Overtime began at Joe Louis. The Pistons jumped ahead on a basket by Bill Laimbeer. They had a chance to increase the lead, but Trent Tucker stole the ball for the Knicks. They tied it.

Then Bernard King, matching Isiah with a prodigious scoring effort, converted an offensive rebound into a two-handed slam. The basket put the Knicks ahead with 3:29 left. The Pistons fell behind by six, then cut it to two with a minute left.

It was then that Thomas fouled Bill Cartwright and fouled out with 37 seconds left. Isiah had scored 35 points and had assisted on 12 baskets as he walked to the bench, Joe Louis rocking with the tribute of the fans.

The Pistons lost it, 127–123, as King scored 44 points to tack onto his string of 36, 46, 46 and 41 in the series.

Bill Laimbeer finished with 14 points and 17 rebounds. Vinnie Johnson chipped in with 16 points.

"It was like a 15-round heavyweight boxing match," Daly said to the press, "and they were the last team standing."

The sighs of the radio listeners at Tiger Stadium could be heard as the Pistons lost and the baseball game went on with its own drama. The Tigers, too, went into overtime, extra innings. And the baseball continued toward midnight and then into early Saturday morning, into the 19th inning. Then these champions-to-be committed three errors . . . Cleveland won 8–4 . . .

. . . Isiah Thomas does have a videotape of the 92-second segment during which he scored 16 points.

"They sent me a tape of it," he said. "Nope, I've never watched it."

April 27, 1984—This was the night the Pistons took over the town. And afterwards, the rival coaches swapped verbal exaggerations. As Chuck had in comparing this basketball game to a heavyweight title fight, Hubie Brown blathered off thinking he was Don King.

"I've been around a long time and I've never been in a game like that, where there were so many big plays," Hubie told the media, in his preparation mode for the day he would cause America to doze off as a TV analyst. "They went out swinging and Isiah Thomas' effort in the fourth quarter was a staggering punch to us."

Chuck Daly summed up for the press: "I've never enjoyed a team so much in in my life . . . Going into training camp I was pretty nervous. We weren't big and we didn't have a post-up player. In the playoffs, that's of primary importance . . . I think we've made strides and grown as a group. But that doesn't mean anything in terms of our roster. Our offseason will be as interesting as the regular season."

Jack McCloskey had some work to do. The contracts of Tripucka, Vinnie Johnson, and John Long had expired. It would be another lean year for draft choices and the Pistons' record had taken them deep, into the twentieth spot, in the first-round rotation. The No. 1 from the previous season, Antoine Carr, still hadn't been signed.

McCloskey had made a bunch of trades—to get cannon fodder types such as Tom Owens, Ray Tolbert, David Thirdkill and Earl Cureton. But it had been two years since McCloskey had made a major trade to produce a frontline player for the Pistons; not since Bill Laimbeer.

The Pistons had aspirations now of climbing anther step—to the level of the Lakers and the Celtics.

Even Bill Davidson was pleased with the progress.

"It was a very satisfying year," he said to Bill Halls. "A lot of positive things happened."

But there was the glaring negative. A major-league sports franchise should never have been kicked out of its own arena by motorcyclists and forced to play a decisive game in another building. Pro basketball was drawing people now in Detroit. Twice during the 1983–84 season the Pistons had drawn more than 35,000 spectators to games at the Silverdome, the two largest attendances in NBA history at the time. For the season, the Pistons' average crowd had jumped again by more than 3,000 per game, to 15,939.

The onetime little franchise that could do nothing right—could manage maybe 2,000 on Turkey Pop Gun Night—had led the league in attendance for the first time.

The syndicate of owners had just signed a rental agreement to play three more years at the Silverdome. But the guys were starting to think maybe it would be a pretty good idea to build their own basketball facility so they'd never be made homeless again during the playoffs.

The Celtics and the Lakers played a captivating series in the NBA finals—Bird versus Magic again. America watched, enchanted. Detroit watched, envious, fantasizing the way it might be some day, maybe not too far distant. The Celtics won the championship in the seventh game, deep into the month of June.

And less than a week later, Jack McCloskey made his move to deal the Pistons upward, maybe another half step toward the elite. He obtained Danny Roundfield, a forward, from the Atlanta Hawks for two of his previous first-round draft choices. Jack gave the Hawks Cliff Levingston, who had never quite crashed into the top group in Detroit, plus the signing rights to Antoine Carr, who had never joined the Pistons, plus two second-round draft choices to be cashed in.

It was a huge price to pay for one guy who was devoid of star credentials, in hopes of plugging a position.

A couple of days later, the Pistons drafted Tony Campbell out of Ohio State to serve as a body on the bench.

Then over the summer there would be all that stuff trying to sign the free agents, and that new restriction the pro basketball had put in to keep the athlete/millionaires from pickpocketing the owners to the poorhouse—the salary cap.

Isiah Thomas spent the summer of 1984 with his mind set on basketball. He built a gymnasium in his house. Each day he would dribble and shoot, shoot and dribble. He had been in the pro league for three years. In that time, he had established himself as one of few celebrity players immediately recognizable by mention of only his first name.

Kareem! America knew and it did not have to be told that he was Kareem Abdul-Jabber, a 7-foot-2 giant with a sweeping sky hook shot.

Magic! Dr. J! Larry!

And Isiah!

The television wizards understand celebrities, and Isiah had been brought in as a commentator for the NBA finals the previous spring, after the playoff drama against the Knicks.

He was standing courtside, looking over the parquet floor during the warmups—Magic, Larry, Kareem practicing their shots for Game 5.

Isiah, speaking softly, his smile intact, told Bill Halls, covering for the *News*:

"We'll be here next year."

The Detroit Pistons had vaulted in stature in the NBA.

Their stature was such that other clubs coveted their athletes.

Jack McCloskey's summertime task, now that he bolstered his lineup with the acquisition of Danny Roundfield, was to keep guys from escaping.

McCloskey had to try to stop three veterans from jumping to other ballclubs. That new devil free agency threatened to destroy the Pistons. August and September were months of difficult negotiations.

Vinnie Johnson's contract was up, and he was been pursued by his boyhood favorites, the Knicks.

The Cleveland Cavaliers wanted Kelly Tripucka.

Pro basketball's free agency stipulations differed from the way it was in baseball and football. The wooing team would submit an offer sheet to the desired player, sort of a promise of a dowry. The player could agree to the money figures, then his old team had the option of matching the offer in fifteen days to keep him.

In late August of 1984, as Detroit's sports interest focused on the Tigers' shambles-making of the American League pennant race, Vinnie Johnson received a firm offer from the Knicks. It would pay $1.5 million for three years. McCloskey entered preliminary talks with the possibility of striking up a trade with his GM counterpart on the Knicks—a graying gentleman who still harbored some feelings about the Pistons, Dave DeBusschere.

On the other edge of this cutting blade, McCloskey slashed the Pistons' offer to Tripucka, made during the previous season, by $200,000 a year to 450 grand. Jack criticized Tripucka's play on defense. Kelly had been the man assigned to

Bernard King in the playoffs. And King had sizzled him an average of 42.5 points per game in the five games.

Tripucka responded to the Pistons' blatant negotiations ploy by mouthing off. He told the *News*: "They almost made me feel unwanted. If I'm not wanted in Detroit, I'll go elsewhere." But Cleveland? The Cavs were reported about to ready an offer sheet to Tripucka.

"Kelly has directed me to get him out of Detroit," Bob Woolf informed the *News*. "I've told the Pistons of his wishes . . . He likes the people and the city, but he doesn't feel management has treated him fairly . . . Cleveland certainly is sincere."

Woolf said some other clubs were interested, too. Sincerely.

"If every player got offended that way it would be difficult for all of us," McCloskey said, returning fire. "Kelly is a big boy now. He ought to be able to take a little constructive criticism."

McCloskey had one additional signing problem. John Long, still vital in the Pistons' scheme, also was not signed and was very balky.

So it went into September with training camp near.

McCloskey's tactic then became clear. Under the free-agency matching arrangements he was allowing the offering clubs to do the actual dickering with Tripucka and with Johnson.

The Cavaliers, indeed, did give Tripucka an offer sheet. It was worth $6.3 million dollars and was designed to cover the next seven years, with a signing bonus and a complex arrangement of deferrred payments. The contract would last through the 1990–91 season.

McCloskey was ticked. He hinted trade.

But in the end, he matched Cleveland's offer to Tripucka. Kelly would remain with the Pistons, bound to them by the system for at least one more season before he could be traded away, should McCloskey wish to get rid of him then. McCloskey just wasn't going to allow Tripucka to abandon the Pistons without compensation.

"It's a load of bricks off my back," Tripucka said. "I feel like I won the lottery. I was fully prepared to play in Cleveland the next seven years."

Ugh!

The Pistons also matched the Knicks offer to Vinnie Johnson. Those negotiations had been less acrimonious. And Vinnie really didn't want to go anywhere else.

"Signing with New York was business," Vinnie told the *News*, using himself as the illustration of the manner in which business was now being conducted in the new, enriched NBA. "I knew Detroit wanted me and I wanted to play in Detroit. We signed with New York and sat back to see what happened."

Two guys didn't like what happened.

John Long read about the money Kelly and Vinnie would be making and increased his demands for a new contract.

Businessman Bill Davidson, who had to put his imprint on the payroll checks, denounced the entire system and the Cleveland Cavaliers, who had forced up Tripucka's salary in Detroit.

"Trampling on so-called partners," Davidson said. "It was reprehensible."

But then, the Pistons were happy campers during the annual training period. The Tigers were winning the World Series, and the Pistons had great expectations themselves.

"One thing is that we are going to have to understand that every time we go out to play we'll get everybody's best punch," Isiah told Bill Halls for the *News'* season preview. "We'll be a lot like Muhammad Ali when he was champ. Mentally, we have to understand that."

"We know we're going to have a very good ballclub, maybe one of the best in the league," said Bill Laimbeer in a rare moment. "Obviously we have to go out and prove it. We have to keep our basic playing group, and we have to stay injury free . . . we think we have a chance to go all the way."

Chuck Daly, starting his second season, feared the Chicago Bulls, who had suffered in the doldrums for years.

"We could be a better team, but it's possible we might not score as many points or win as many games as we did last year simply because of the strength in the Eastern Conference. Chicago is vastly improved. Dramatically, improved."

Chuckie was a hardened pessimist. He listed all the other rivals in the conference as being improved, too. But he kept coming back to the Bulls.

They had had a high pick in the draft rotation, and they used it for an exciting young athlete who had played for North Carolina and, during the summer, won a gold medal in the Olympics on Bob Knight's USA team. The rookie's name was Michael Jordan. Chuck Daly started getting creepy feelings at the image of what Michael might be able to do with the basketball.

With a national TV contract on CBS, with the athletes becoming free-agency millionaires, pro basketball had graduated to major league status, even in the view of hardened cynics. The NBA had had remained status quo geographically for half a decade, since the Dallas Mavericks were added to the league in expansion at the beginning of the decade. But now again, starting the 1984–85 season, the league returned to the moveable franchise bit. The San Diego Clippers, once upon a time the Buffalo Braves, rode a covered wagon up the coast to move into the Los Angeles territory and share the territory with the Lakers. But Jack Nicholson and the movie colony would refuse to split their loyalties. The L.A. Clippers were welcomed with yawns.

No yawns in Pontiac.

The Pistons did not start off well in the 1984–85 season. They were soon in third place. The Bulls were off ahead, and so were the Milwaukee Bucks, who had long been the dominant team in the Central Division.

By January 1985, the situation was clear. The Bucks were ahead in the division. The Pistons had taken another step—and the Bulls, with the tiny steps of rookie Michael Jordan, had slipped behind and out of consideration. Once again, as it was with the Pistons when Isiah joined them three years earlier, it was being proven that one-player teams cannot win in the NBA.

The Pistons went off and won a three-game road trip. They won despite Isiah playing with an injured ankle in New York. They won despite Kelly getting himself shaken up in an auto crackup in New Jersey. They won despite the freezing weather in New Orleans.

Travel is the toughest part of life in the NBA.

"Most road games I can't get to sleep until four o'clock in the morning," Chuck Daly said. "I play the game over and over. Then I wake up at six to catch the plane to the next game."

On this three-town road trip, Daly had the

option of taking the Pistons home to Detroit for a night after the visit to New York and Jersey. He chose to head straight for New Orleans. The Atlanta Hawks had scheduled a dozen of their home games in the Louisiana Superdome after the Jazz tooted off to Salt Lake City a few seasons earlier. The reason Daly had skipped going home was the favorable weather factor at New Orleans. He figured it'd be seasonably comfortable down there.

The Pistons' plane landed in a snow and ice storm. The temperature was six degrees—above. A sheet of ice covered the freeway in from the airport. The team bus had to detour because icy overpasses and bridges were closed. Southerners don't get much practice driving on ice and don't become very good at it.

"Figures," Daly muttered to Bill Halls. "It's amazing anyone can win on the road in this league."

The Pistons went on a tear in the first month of 1985—winning seven of eight.

But the Bucks were perfect for 1985. The two clubs charged into February, the Bucks in first place, the Pistons hanging about four games behind. Milwaukee had an eleven-game winning streak when the Pistons went there to play on February 4, 1985. Tripucka had a sprained ankle and Danny Roundfield was hobbled with a bum knee. Neither of the wounded could play.

No matter, the Pistons won the game 113–111 in overtime, with Bill Laimbeer shooting the game winner. The Bucks' streak was snapped. The Pistons had a run of eleven victories in twelve games. Laimbeer displayed the scoring facet of his multiple skills. He scored 32 points.

It was a game in which the Pistons kept making errant in-bounds passes and escaping anyway from danger. Laimbeer made one such foolish pass.

"It is uncharacteristic for me to make a dumb play like that," said Laimbeer. There were times when he could target himself.

The Pistons had proven—to themselves anyway—they could play the game and beat the better teams, in the home arenas of those teams. The summation word was—maturity.

They had advanced to that step.

One day Chuck Daly was conducting a clinic at a rec center run by Leon The Barber on the West Side of Detroit. Daly went through his routine, explaining some theories of coaching, some techniques of play.

"I need a volunteer," Daly said to the pack of students in the stands.

A guy stepped from the seats.

"I'll volunteer," said the guy.

He was a tall guy, who looked familiar and looked as if he might have some moves on the floor.

"It was Marvin Barnes," Daly would say later, laughing. "Bad News. He came out and did some moves."

Soon the Pistons took a silly step backwards. They had not yet killed off all their terrible habits from the old days. They continued to have that losing habit on the certain nights when they had exceptionally large crowds.

On February 16, 1985, the Pistons played the Philly 76ers at the Silverdome. The Pistons had been winning, they had been stirring, and they were stirring the town. It was becoming fashionable to go to the Pistons, duck beneath the temporary stands at halftime and purchase cotton candy from the food stands. Some of the town's swells would sit courtside in the third quarter, trying to get the sticky stuff off their patrician mugs.

The largest crowd to watch an NBA game, since Fred Zollner had a dream, journeyed out to the Pontiac boondocks to check out the Pistons on this night. They pulled in 43,816 to watch them in battle against the 76ers. The attendance figure, like the playing area, was jerry-rigged. The Pistons, despite their successes, needed to continue their policy of selling cut-rate tickets— or giving them away free in 2-for-1 promotions to people who bought a certain number of hamburgers in the latest grease-crammed fast-food marketing venture. Buy one basketball ticket, get one free. Maybe you'll be able to find someone willing to go with you. Gas stations used to give you free air and check your oil. Now you got a fill-up, and they gave you a dollar basketball ticket.

The difference now was, folks weren't tossing the freebies into the garbage bin any more. So nearly 44,000 showed up this promotion night, and it was a load for the history books.

The game was a battle. Moses Malone decked

Laimbeer and the officials must have been counting the house because they neglected to call a foul. One of the intellegensia in the cheap seats tossed a coin to the floor as a result, The coin hit referee Earl Strom in the left eye. The gravity force of the coin knocked down Strom. He got up and finished the game.

The Pistons lost it, as they were wont to do before any sizable mob of people, 125-114. Suddenly, they had lost five of six games.

The fadeout continued, and now the Pistons were hit with dissension and accusations. Kelly Tripucka remained sidelined with his sprained ankled. The club missed his scoring impetus. Nearly a month after he was injured, the Bucks came to the Silverdome—first place versus second. In their own building, the Pistons were nipped by the Bucks, 113-112, the sixth loss in eight games. It was the twelfth game Tripucka had missed and the Pistons had lost seven of them.

There were 20,542 spectators at this game. And when Tripucka walked out to courtside dressed in his street duds, they jeered and hooted at him. His rabbit ears could pick out some specific things yelled at him. They accused him of bailing out, dogging it, malingering—not nice words for an athlete who in other times would dive and skid on the floor to fight for the ball, who would fling his body into their seats to save the ball.

But when Bill Laimbeer made the same sort of accusation after the one-point loss to Milwaukee, it meant there was a serious rift in the team's harmony.

"It's the longest sprained ankle I've ever seen," Laimbeer told Bill Halls. "It's swollen whenever he plays on it. Every sprained ankle I've ever seen stays swollen until the end of the season. He may be out all season. What we're really waiting for is Rounds to come back [Roundfield had missed sixteen games following knee surgery]. He can really help us because he's a defensive player."

Laimbeer played every game, every night, once during this season with a 102-degree fever, another time with a bum shoulder and bum knee. He would play every game in a consecutive game streak until the league suspended him for fighting with an opponent.

Isiah Thomas was playing with a badly bruised thigh. He diplomatically did not criticize Tripucka's fortitude.

Tripucka did not respond to Laimbeer's barbs. But he had some comments for the fans, fed by the media, who criticized his mettle.

"I wish the the people who accuse me of not wanting to play would come over to my house and face me man-to-man," he challenged in an interview with the *News*. "The accusations are a low blow. The last thing anybody can accuse me of is not wanting to play. You have to put a gun to my head to say I can't play.

"I'm mad and disappointed. I don't think any of the fans who are on me or the newspapers are doctors. They don't know the whole story . . . I can't run and I can't jump. And if I can't do those things, I can't play."

The Pistons had Tripucka examined by a specialist, then announced he'd be out two more weeks.

He returned finally, still hobbled, after missing seventeen games. First place in the Central was a forgotten wish.

In the first week of March 1985, the frozen Michigan winds came raging across the state and ripped off the plastic roof of the Silverdome. This most functional of America's domed stadiums was immediately transformed into an open air arena.

True to tradition, the Pistons were orphans once more.

Back downtown they went to Joe Louis Arena on the riverfront. They were welcomed to share the building by the Red Wings' management. The Red Wings had been trying hard to lure the Pistons to their building as permanent tenants.

And then on the night of Match 11, 1985, the Pistons were orphaned again. Joe Louis Arena was booked for an ice show. The Pistons would always get last licks.

So with an outpouring of nostalgia, the Pistons had to move again, down the street along the Detroit River, to their old stomping grounds of Cobo Arena. They went back to memories of Gus the Dancing Vendor and to stories of the Cobo ticket sellers dozing off in their booths, because business was so lousy.

For this one-night stand, the Pistons played the Los Angeles Clippers, much-moved transplants themselves, on the old floor in the old Cobo atmosphere with the torn seats. This time the Pistons won, and this time they sold out the 10,000-seat house.

Upstairs in the balcony, Gus shook up the ghosts of nostalgia with his driving, bowing twist. Isiah, Kelly, Lam, and the current Pistons wondered just what the devil was going on.

Due to injuries, and perhaps their displacement to a temporary home, the Pistons ultimately finished thirteen games behind the Bucks in the Central Division. They won their last five games to boost the season record for the 82 games to 46-and-36. They had actually skidded by two games over the previous year.

For the first time since Fred Zollner had moved them out of Fort Wayne for the promised land of Detroit, the Pistons had two successive winning seasons. The old ambition to hit .500 was a matter to be chronicled in history. The Pistons fancied themselves as bonafide contenders.

And for the second time in two seasons, the Pistons led the NBA as a draw. They averaged 16,867 in attendance at their Silverdome home and their two downtown homes away from home.

They opened the playoffs against the New Jersey Nets in their rented digs at Joe Louis.

"It'll take a miracle to beat New Jersey," Daly, the playoffs pessimist, told the News' Bill Halls.

The Nets had mastered the Pistons five times in six games during the season.

"They handled us pretty easily," said doomsayer Daly. "They all but toyed with us."

Daly feared what the Nets might do to the less experienced Pistons in the best-of-five first-round series.

At playoff time, pro basketball's ownership got glinty eyes. They saw the opportunity to pay some of the salary of a Kelly Tripucka, Isiah or Laimbeer. Playoff time became pay-up time.

Bill Davidson and Tom Wilson, the Pistons' chief executive, must have believed the Pistons already had created a miracle. They wiped out the customary ticket policies for the playoffs and jacked up the face prices. They went up to $14 for the peanut gallery to $22 courtside.

Detroit was not quite yet prepared to accept such ticket prices; there remained those still dubious that the town was prepared to accept the sport of pro basketball.

It wasn't exactly like electricity was crackling all over town just because the eternally long basketball shootouts were starting. The first playoff game, in which the Pistons miraculously bombed the Nets 125–105, attracted exactly 10,465 customers at the inflated prices. That meant, the Pistons played in front of 11,000 unoccupied seats. Once 10,000 plus would have been an outstanding crowd for the Pistons. But not in 1985.

"Where were they?" said Kelly Tripucka, the well-experienced expert on fan behavior. "The Tigers playing? They're not in the playoffs yet. It's disappointing. I thought with all the support the Tigers get . . . everybody gets . . . the Red Wings . . . Tommy Hearns . . . we'd be in that category. It's PLAYOFF time . . .

"They're so anxious and screaming for us to come downtown here. Now we're down here in a playoff atmosphere with a chance to go very far in the playoffs, and you're playing to a half-empty arena. It's not too thrilling to go out there."

Excerpts from a column by Jerry Green, in the *Detroit News*, April 21, 1985:

. . . It is a vexing game, this pressurized sport played in an extension of winter.

. . . Daly grinned and frowned at the same time, a rare ability he has . . .

"I guess the most memorable playoff series I was in was with Philly against Boston," said Daly . . . "We were in Boston leading by six with a minute and a half to go. We were ahead 3-to-1 in the series. Only a minute and a half. We would have won the series.

"They come back to win the game. They come back to win the series.

"Then there was the year with the Lakers. Kareem gets hurt. They put Magic at center and they won the series."

It is an L.A. game. It is a New York City game. It is a Boston game. It is a Philly game.

It is not a Detroit game.

In other towns, only first names or nicknames are necessary for identification.

Whisper Magic, the city knows the subject is Earvin Johnson, tall, happy prodigy from Lansing, Michigan.

Julius Erving could sign his checks Dr. J or The Doctor and the bank would cash them. And put the checks in frames on the wall.

Kareem Abdul-Jabbar is renowned by his first name alone. It is enough to create the vision of a 7-foot-2 apparition wearing goggles.

The phenomenon, in its way, has touched Detroit to a degree. The odd Bloomfield Hills matron might snap at the mention of Isiah. Isiah Thomas cuts a figure in town.

But pro basketball is not a Detroit game. Not yet. Maybe never.

The other towns have had champions. They have played in these bitter, raw playoff series that prolong the winter.

As Kelly Tripucka so bitingly noted when he clamped the fans the other day, Detroit gives the Pistons no respect. The Pistons can't get a crowd for the playoff with the Nets. Detroit does not treat the Pistons with the reverence of the Tigers—or the Red Wings—or Thomas Hearns.

The jacked-up ticket prices for the playoffs are the main reason . . . Freebies and cut-rate tickets have created a false security. The Pistons led the NBA in attendance with papered houses.

Now they are being ignored by all but the wealthy in the first round of the playoffs . . .

It will take more than free samples to make pro basketball a Detroit game. It will take some years of championship quality performances . . .

The Pistons licked the nemesis Nets in Game 2 of the playoffs on a Sunday night before another paltry gathering at Joe Louis. But on this night, the Pistons established a trademark that would be mandatory if they were ever to rise to the level of champions. This trademark was their bench. These are the guys who sit there watching the other guys play and sweat while their own muscles feel like they've been grabbed by rigor mortis. They must concentrate on the game when they're not in it. And suddenly when the coach yells "hey, Benny," they must strip off their warmups in one motion and run into the game in another.

Detroit's players off the bench were Kent Benson and Terry Tyler. Together they carried the Pistons when the Nets led this game entering the fourth quarter. Off the bench, they mashed the Nets.

Benson, at one end of the court, muscled his man, outgrappled him and got the ball. He flipped it out and, seconds later, he was at the other end. Isiah passed the ball back, and Benson drove a wedge between two defenders and scored. He was fouled and made the free throw. A quarter that started with the Nets ahead turned in the Pistons' favor on Benson's rebound.

There was a bruise or two on Benson's face when we approached him in the locker room. There were some welts on his body. He was marked by the stray elbows that are regulation in the game.

Benson, pushed from the starting lineup years before, said how he had kept his faith. Between shoves and muggings on the floor, he read The Bible.

"You've got to rise to the challenge," he said, explaining his role. "The only thing that is difficult in that situation is sitting on the bench. You kind of cool off. Your muscles start to stiffen up a bit. It takes a little while to get things going . . .

"There have been some down times. But there have been more up periods than down periods—even adjusting to my so-called role play.

Benson revealed that he had been one of Bill Davidson's best customers. For four years, he had purchased 100 tickets for every Pistons game. He distributed them to underprivileged kids.

Kent was the guy who came to the Pistons five years earlier when Jack McCloskey offloaded Bob Lanier.

"I made the statement I wasn't coming here to fill Bob Lanier's shoes," Benson said after the second victory over New Jersey.

He laughed. Lanier took his size 20s, reported as 22s, to Milwaukee. Benson wore just size 15s.

Up 2-zip in the series, the Pistons headed east to the New Jersey Meadowlands. It wasn't exactly time yet for the populace to plan roasting a police car on the corner—a scene America's finest sports journalists had eyewitnessed the previous October when the Tigers won the World Series. But the Pistons were on the verge of winning a playoff series for the first time since 1976.

There was one mystery. There was a scowl on Isiah's face, and it looked out of place. He transported the warmest smile in sports. He could outsmile the Mona Lisa any day. Under normal circumstances, there was this smile when he dribbled. He smiled when he took a jump-shot. He smiled at the free-throw line. He smiled when Daly dragged him off the court and sentenced him to time on the bench. He smiled when the referee tooted his whistle and made another bum call against Isiah and Detroit.

But now there was this scowl on the face that usually smiled, this perpetual frown.

"I'm smiling on the inside," Isiah said. "The smile's still there."

A few nights earlier, after the Pistons had won Game 2 in Detroit, Laimbeer noticed the same glumness on Isiah's face.

"Is something the matter?" said Laimbeer. "You all right?"

"Yeah," said Isiah.

His own teammates seemed unable to keep up with Isiah in this New Jersey series. There had been moments Isiah had been so revved up he dragged his teammates behind him. And he was lugging along his memories, as added cargo. Memories of the year before and the series the Pistons lost in the fifth-game OT to the Knicks on Isiah's most brilliant night; memories of missing the playoffs entirely in his first two seasons in the NBA.

Winning in the playoffs had become a personal mission, a crusade.

"I felt like I was playing at one speed," Isiah told me, "and everybody else on my team was playing at another.

"I had to slow down."

The Pistons made it a sweep over the Nets in the Jersey Meadowlands. They won Game 3 with a gallant comeback. During the second quarter, the Pistons had been down by a dozen. There was chaos on the court. Then Mike Gminski, a slow, lumbering center, popped from outside. The ball went over Bill Laimbeer, who didn't raise his arms in defense.

"Where are you?" Daly yelled from the bench. Daly stomped his foot, paced—his typical courtside activities. He yelled again at Laimbeer, who was returning downcourt. Laimbeer waved at the bench—like, take a hike Daly.

Daly and Thomas plot strategy.

"Start playing, start playing," Daly yelled back.

The Pistons were headed toward panic. Daly called time out. The players, sweating, panting, sat on the bench. This is normally a time for strategy. But Daly ignored his clipboard. He turned psychologist, motivator, tyrant.

"Bill, you got to force it," Daly yelled.

"Leave me alone," Laimbeer yelled back.

The angry shouts were audible nearby in the press row at the Byrne Meadowlands Arena in the New Jersey swamplands.

"You got to see it," Daly yelled again.

"OK, OK," Laimbeer responded. Loudly. "Dammit, I'm going to get going."

Moments later Gminski drove the baseline right by Laimbeer.

And suddenly, Laimbeer, seething, was sweeping the basketball off the boards. He was belting players around underneath. Daly had switched on a flame thrower.

"You should have done that at the beginning," Daly yelled out on the floor. "You screwed up."

A little internal bickering was good for a needy club.

And in the fourth quarter, after they had trailed by five points with one minute thirty-nine seconds left and by one point with nineteen seconds left, the Pistons won the game. With the nineteen to go, John Long and Isiah trapped Micheal Ray Richardson and forced him to turn the ball over, back to Detroit. Daly called a time out to plot a play. And then the Pistons won it by one point, 116–115, on a shot two ticks before the final buzzer. They won it because they played with poise and had fortitude and were able to shoot and had become a good basketball team with the knowledge that it had some sort of destiny awaiting them.

Excerpts from a column in the *Detroit News* by Jerry Green, April 25, 1985:

He had carried the great agony with him for a year, even when he smiled. There had never been a pain like it.

So this April, when he had a chance for some redemption, he wore a mask of gloom. A scowl is totally out of character for Isiah Thomas.

Isiah Thomas is a basketball player for the ages. There are nights when his abilities abandon him for a quarter, a half. Sometimes they are missing for an entire game. There are rare games when his touch is absent for 47 minutes and 58 seconds. And then Isiah, in one flash of brilliance, is Isiah again.

The Pistons played a very rare basketball game last night. It was a basketball game for the ages. It was, undoubtedly, the most heroic game played by the Pistons since they bootlegged their franchise from Fort Wayne to Detroit. That was 28 years ago. That was five years before the birth of Isiah Lord Thomas III into a family of nine children in a west side Chicago ghetto.

Last night, the Pistons won a playoff series with a 116–115 victory over the Nets. It was a game the Pistons ought to have lost. In this game, Isiah Thomas missed layups. He lost the ball. In the final minute, he missed two free throws. In the final 19 seconds, he dribbled away 17 seconds, behind the key and into the corner.

Then he shot the basketball. The shot was dead, solid, perfect, swishing through the basket.

This is the kind of theatrical stuff that is the playoff right of Magic and Dr. J and Larry Bird.

One year ago, the Pistons were cruelly kayoed from the playoffs in five brutal games by the New York Knickerbockers.

The memory, the pain of that defeat, is what has haunted Isiah Thomas. He has suffered a 12-month hangover . . . He spoke of last year now:

"On the court during the games, I had one of the best feelings I ever had. Then it stops so suddenly, it was so dramatic. To go from a high to a low. So fast, so suddenly.

"It was so difficult to go to practice every day and be playing and then bang . . . suddenly, you have nothing to do.

Isiah Thomas sat in a lockerroom surrounded by boisterous, noisy, delerious athletes. The Pistons had not won a playoff series in nine years. It was the first time, the first taste for them . . . Isiah, Kelly Tripucka, for John Long and Terry Tyler, for Bill Laimbeer and Vinnie Johnson.

There is much basketball ahead. There are the Celtics. "They've beaten us like a drum," said Coach Chuck Daly, "and I've felt like I've been inside the drum . . .

"We're just a hot basketball team right now," said Isiah Lord Thomas III. "I'm glad we beat Jersey. But I feel bad for the guys on that team. There are so many plays in a game. Every one of those guys can look back at a play they didn't make.

"I've missed shots at the buzzer this year."

It was in this playoff series that the Pistons' continuous drive for recognition, respect, acceptance became painfully obvious. They did not draw fans for playoff basketball . . .

The Pistons felt they were rejects in their own town.

Last night in the New Jersey Meadowlands, the Pistons achieved their metamorphosis. They grabbed and groveled and spent most of a playoff game chasing the Nets. Their shooting was terrible. Their bench was the scene of hot tempers. Their star missed layups and vital free throws.

And they still won.

Isiah Thomas, a player for the ages, cast off the great agony he had carried with him for a year. He smiled—again. The Pistons, playoff winners, gained what they had been seeking most—recognition, respect, acceptance.

That night in New Jersey the victorious athletes spent the night in celebration. It was long after midnight when the coach dragged himself back to the hotel, his brow wrinkled with the torture of too little sleep.

"Having fun?" asked a guy at the bar.

"No," said the coach. "I feel like a deflated balloon."

And so the Pistons headed toward Boston and the parquet floor at the ancient Garden in the next series, best-of-seven. The Pistons hadn't played the Celtics in the playoffs since 1968. Back then the two foes had mashed each other through six games—and the Celtics—with Bill Russell, John Havlicek and Bailey Howell—of course, had won the series. And the Celtics had continued forward to win their ninth NBA championship in a period of ten years.

Now, seventeen years later, the Pistons and Celtics were matched again. The Celtics now with Bird and McHale and Parish.

Boston had the league's best record for the season, 63-and-19. And they had beaten the Pistons and Chuck Daly, in a phrase, like a drum.

The Celtics came in exhausted after winning their first series with Cleveland. They were battered.

So in the second-round opener, they broke the Pistons' eight-game winning streak. They introduced the Pistons to the true meaning of playoff basketball—not one of these preliminary series. The Celtics beat the Pistons, 133–99, in Game 1. A difference of 32 points. Robert Parish had a party night against Laimbeer. Parish scored 27 points and had 16 rebounds. Laimbeer scored 1 point. He took two shots and missed both. He had 3 rebounds. He played only 22 minutes.

"I played the worst game I ever played as a Detroit Piston," Laimbeer told the press in the cramped visitors locker room in the Garden. "I let my teammates down. But I'll be back."

"We were embarrassed by the final score," said Kelly Tripucka. "The non-basketball fan will read that and say we're a lousy ballclub."

There was a bit of physical stuff. Isiah got jabbed in the left eye by Larry Bird. "He seriously tried to tear my eye out," Isiah said to Bill Halls. "But that's all right."

"He was just frustrated," said Bird.

Between Games 1 and 2, on the offday in Boston, Laimbeer told Halls:

"Obviously, we've got to get more physical."

"Laimbeer isn't exactly a finesse player," said Bird.

The Pistons were more physical in Game 2. They were developing a reputation. Bird went toppling over and took a cut on his chin and got a bloody face when decked by one of Laimbeer's stray elbows.

"I'm glad to see him bleeding just to prove he's mortal," Daly would say.

Later, trying to stop Bird from shooting, Laimbeer drove toward him and clipped him again. Angered, Bird threw the ball from the middle of the court and into the seats.

But intimidating Larry Bird was impossible. He scored 42 points in this second game in Boston. The score was much closer this time, but Boston won again, 121–114. Laimbeer managed only 12 points.

"Of course I was upset," Bird told the press when asked about Laimbeer's tactics. "Bill was frustrated. I caught a couple of elbows. We can get physical, but I didn't want to get into a big fight because we had the lead.

"I'm sure if it keeps up, something might happen."

The Pistons were down two games to nil, with the next two games in Detroit, at their borrowed home, Joe Louis.

Something did happen in Game 3. In the third period, with the Pistons holding a four-point lead, Robert Parish crushed an elbow into Bill Laimbeer. Bill fell to the floor—maybe taking a theatrical flop to for the officials. He got up and approached Parish. The dour, never-smiling Par-

"Laimbeer isn't exactly a finesse player," said Bird.

ish slapped Laimbeer with an open hand. The officials stopped a fight. Maybe.

"I felt he took some cheap shots at me," Parish told the Boston press.

"I'm not going to run away from the guy," Laimbeer would tell Bill Halls. "But if I take a swing at him, I'm out of the game. It hurt them more than it hurt us because it was his fourth foul."

The Pistons again were unable to sell out Joe Louis. The game drew 14,209, which left 7,000 seats without fannies in them. But after this small donnybrook, the crowd was in the game.

So was Terry Tyler, off the bench with all his energy and all his fire. Terry scored 16 points in the fourth quarter. He hit on eight of nine shots in the period. He defended against Bird and held his man to two free throws for the quarter.

Fired up in his own style at last, Laimbeer scored 27 points in the game and seized 13 rebounds. The Pistons won it, 125–117. The Celtics were no longer invincible.

Cedric "Cornbread" Maxwell, who once had been offered to Dick Vitale for the Pistons before he demanded Bob McAdoo, took note of Laimbeer:

"He's taken more flops than the fat lady at the circus."

Larry Bird made a postgame peace statement to Bill Halls about Isiah: "I blocked his shot. I won the battle, he won the war. He's just awesome. I don't see how a little guy like that can go among the big men and score. It looks so easy. I have a lot of respect for him as a player and as a person."

The key word was RESPECT.

Between Games 3 and 4, the two sides exchanged a series of angry words

"They're cocky," said Laimbeer to the writers, somehow keeping a straight face.

"We're the world champions, you have to be cocky," said Cornbread Maxwell.

"I guarantee something will break out if they let it go Sunday like they did Thursday night," Parish told the press. "Elbows were flying and everytime we play something happens. That's the way Laimbeer plays.

"They can treat us any way they want to as long as we win the ballgame," Laimbeer responded. "The talk doesn't bother me one bit."

It was natural talk for a game to be played in a hockey rink. But with all the buildup about blood and stuff, the Pistons drew all of 141 more customers than they had for the third game.

The talk was just talk.

Instead the 14,350—plus a national TV audience—got to see vintage Vinnie Johnson.

Vinnie came rolling off the bench when the Pistons needed him most. With the Pistons trailing by 11 points in the fourth quarter, they rallied to win, 102–99. Vinnie scored 22 points in the twelve minutes. He hit on 10 of 11 of his shots. With Boston still ahead by four with four minutes to play, Vinnie rattled off 8 straight points. He scored 34 for the game.

In those last minutes, Isiah kept yelling advice at Vinnie.

"I said, 'hey Zeke, should I pass the ball?'" Johnson told the News' Mike O'Hara. "He just told me to keep it going."

Very neatly, the Pistons, with their two victories at Joe Louis, had squared the series.

"I don't think it's overly complicated why we lost two games," the always quotable Cornbread Maxwell told the media. "It was just a case of two guys—Tyler and Johnson—having career games."

And nearby, the Celtics' Danny Ainge took note of Vinnie Johnson and observed: "If that guy in Chicago, William Perry is The Refrigerator, Vinnie Johnson is The Microwave. He heated up in a hurry."

But the Pistons were required to take their game back to Boston Garden. They hadn't won there for three years. And still going!

Before Game 5, a thief broke into the visitors' locker room and stole Pistons road blue jersey No. 11. Isiah's number. Jerry Dziedzic, the equipment man, had to give Isiah a spare with No. 42 etched on it.

"It was too baggy," said Isiah.

A ready-to-wear alibi, maybe.

"My head really wasn't in it the first part of the game," Isiah told the media. "My uniform wasn't with me and it threw me off a little bit. I just din't feel right."

This time, the fourth quarter belonged to Larry Bird. He scored 17 points in the period and 43 for the game. The Celtics won it 130–123 —and the Pistons were one defeat from elimination."

"Catch me after we beat them," Bird told the press. "I've got some awesome quotes for these guys after we get done with them."

And now it was back to Detroit for Game 6—and this time the people filled all the seats at Joe Louis Arena and those who could not obtain seats purchased tickets entitling them to stand in the aisleways and clog the corridors.

It was such a gala affair, Chuck Daly said: "I think I'll wear a tuxedo."

When he walked onto the floor wearing a nifty brown suit, somebody yelled: "Where's the tux?"

"No courage," said Chuck.

The crowd of 21,193 followed the game in despair. The Pistons were barely in it, despite a bravura performance by Isiah Thomas. He scored 37 points.

"A lot of times I was getting hit and grabbed," said Thomas, back in his No. 11 in the home whites. "But that's part of the game."

So are turnovers. And the Pistons, usually so sure, so certain, coughed up the ball nineteen times to the Celtics in a suicide ritual. Two turnovers buried the Pistons in the fourth quarter.

In the bitter end, the score was 123–113, and the Celtics, still reigning champions, advanced into the next round.

The Pistons reflected on 1984–85 as a season of enormous progress—and built ambitions for future years.

"I thought all along we had a solid club and we accomplished what we were capable of doing," said Chuck Daly, in summary.

It had been a mean, physical, angry series between two clubs of players who didn't particularly care for each other. The Detroit basketball image was just beginning. But when it ended, the Pistons flooded the floor to shake hands and hug the Celtics with an outpouring of congratulations.

In the postmortem, Larry Bird's promised awesome quotes weren't that powerful, but did include the ultimate slam: "I can't say they're better than Cleveland."

Bird continued: "It was a good series, but not one of the toughest. Our last series against Cleveland took a lot out of us. They've got a short way to go to be one of the leading teams in the league, though. I give them a lot of credit. A lot of words were said. In the end, we have a lot of respect for each other."

And the Curse of the Celtics continued!

Funny, the Celtics had an easier time with the 76ers in the next series than they'd had with Detroit. They wiped out Philly in five games and continued on to the NBA finals. It was Bird against Magic again. It was Magic's turn to win. The Lakers beat the Celtics for the 1985 championship in six games.

A week after the finals ended, Trader Jack McCloskey struck again. It had been painfully obvious in the playoffs that the Pistons needed a mighty strong forward if they were to step further along in their ambitions. Danny Roundfield had not given the Pistons what they'd expected in his one season in Detroit.

His knee bothered him and he missed a number of games due to surgery. Other times, he didn't seem to care. One night, at the Silverdome, he left the bench in uniform, went to the locker room and returned in his street clothes. Then, saying his knee bothered him, he begged out of the sixth playoff game with Boston when he might have helped.

McCloskey moved him along to the Washington Bullets for two players. One was Mike Gibson, who would last half the 1985–86 season. The other player was a glowering individual who would sometimes deliver a leering, sinister smile. He had the reputation of playing with a roughhouse style. His name was Rick Mahorn, and McCloskey theorized that maybe he would mesh in a terrorizing manner with Bill Laimbeer.

The 1985 draft was the day after the trade. The Pistons, ascending in the league, had placed themselves eighteenth in the draft rotation. It was at this draft that the league inaugurated its draft lottery system, concocted out of the brain of David Stern, the new NBA commissioner.

The old coinflip, that had been a bugaboo of the Pistons once upon a time, and the worst-record-goes-first methods had been scrapped by decree. Now, the seven dregs teams, not in the playoffs, were shuffled up into a raffle.

Rather coincidentally, the team plucked first out of the lottery the first year was the team the new NBA marketeers were convinced had to be successful and latch onto the most marketable player. So it was that New York won No. 1 in the lottery. And so it was that the Knicks took Patrick Ewing, the giant franchise player from Georgetown.

The Pistons, in their No. 18 position, drafted that unsung athlete from McNeese State who had been recommended to McCloskey and whom he had personally scouted—Joe Dumars.

Trade . . . Draft . . . Coach!

Jack McCloskey completed his sticky business within a few days in June 1985. He had the power forward to mesh muscles with Laimbeer. Mahorn would be able to do that. He had the young shooting guard to mesh with Isiah. Dumars should be able to do that.

And he had Chuck Daly, handcuffed, returning to the Pistons after the passionate wooing from his homeboy Philadelphia 76ers. So what if the Pistons management came out as the villain in the Daly derby. So what if after establishing one price tag for the 76ers to kidnap their coach they set a second, exorbitant price. The negative press, the furor, would fade over the summer.

It did. And Daly took a philosophical attitude about being held captive in a job he had preferred to leave. He dwelled on the Pistons' progress.

"At the beginning of last season," Daly told the *News'* Bill Halls. "I would have said it would be tough to get to this position.

"But when you get there, you want more."

Still, the coaching situation would have to be resolved. Prevented from jumping to Philly, Daly accepted an extended contract from the Pistons. McCloskey thought they had an agreement on a deal. Daly changed his mind. So, Chuck went into the training camp in September without any assurances about his future. One year remained on his original Detroit contract. His quasi-lame duck situation would work as a subplot to the Pistons' efforts toward progress throughout the season.

The coach and the GM locked in battle, a matter of obvious discord.

The addictive impact of reaching the playoff level of playing the Celtics well gave the Pistons dreamy ambitions for the season of 1985–86. They had proven themselves to the forecasters, those self-style wizards who knew the league so well that they can pick the standings for the following season before the training camps open in September. For the first time the Pistons were regarded with such esteem, a number of these wizards nominated the club in a variety of magazines to finish in first place in the Central Division. If true, it would be the end of an era. The Milwaukee Bucks had been first-place finishers for six consecutive years.

Once again, the NBA altered its map, westward. Once again, it was the same ancient franchise yanking out its roots and pulling out the covered wagon and heading off for new territory.

The Kings participated in this Moveable Feast IV into Sacramento. Thus, this club completed the original Rochester Royals' migration across the American continent, with brief layovers in Cincinnati still named the Royals, then in Kansas City-Omaha as the share-your-home-team Kings, then in Kansas City alone as the Kings, and at last to Sacramento, preserving the name Kings.

But no matter how far they traveled, they hadn't figured out the way to win a championship since they had been uprooted from the quintessential minor-league town of Rochester.

Then, neither had the erstwhile Fort Wayne Zollner Pistons.

The Pistons opened the 1985–86 schedule with a spurt. Mahorn had bolstered the club with his toughness. Dumars adapted well, better than most of the first-round draft choices who'd been tooled at schools more prominent that McNeese State.

They nipped Milwaukee—the team they had to unseat to claim first place—at the buzzer in the season opener at the Silverdome.

Kelly Tripucka was acting up again. He got into it with an official in early November. Kelly was griping and griping and finally Joe Crawford, the ref, slapped a T on him—a technical foul. Tripucka couldn't hit from the floor, compounding his troubles. The fans were on him again. That's when Kelly responded to one guy several rows behind the Pistons bench, using a number of bleep words not normally uttered at your common garden party in Grosse Pointe. The mob of women and children within earshot was reported as horrified.

Well, maybe not. But some guardians of the press were. So an issue was made of the matter and then the issue died without further damage, except to destroy the myth that athletes are all goodie goodies. Some do have hot tempers that get out of control, just as real human begings do.

"Nope, it's not important," Chuck Daly told the writers when asked if Kelly might be fined for his indescretion. "It's happened before."

After a month or so, the Pistons had an 11–5 record. They had developed the knack of rescuing ball games with late histrionics—proving, again, the last-three-minutes theory of pro basketball.

But then, the Pistons fell into a malaise. It seemed, to close observers, that their interest waned.

They were in a horrible slump at New Year's 1986. They had plummeted to below .500. They lost six games in succession. Through the first week of January, they had lost thirteen of their previous games.

It was more serious than a slump. Something seemed drastically wrong with the Pistons.

Critics started the knee-jerk search for the reasons. Some foolishly speculated that the reasons began with Chuck Daly; that he was sulking because he'd been denied the opportunity to go to Philadelphia; that he'd lost interest, that he tended to care more about the 76ers than the Pistons.

Such rot caused Daly to bristle.

"What you're seeing is a very unusual change going on," Daly was quoted as saying in the *News*. "We didn't see this before the season started, but we aren't at all the same team we were a couple of years ago. It's very strange and hard to get a handle on."

Something had happened to the Pistons' offense. It no longer raged up the court, with Isiah the spearhead. It had become slow, sluggish. And the blame was dropped on Rickey Mahorn, the newcomer. Mahorn wasn't fast enough to keep up, the snipers said. He was out of shape, overweight.

And McCloskey had to admit that part of it was true—that Mahorn did not fit in because of his bulk.

Earl Cureton and Kent Benson were used by Daly at the power forward spot that had been etched in for Mahorn.

"For two years we pushed up the floor very, very well," Daly told Dave Dye. ". . . We'd run through a lot of our mistakes. But now we can't do that. Zeke is so much quicker than everybody else that the fastbreak is out of sync."

"We have different personnel now than the last two years," said Isiah Thomas, already in his fifth season. "We don't have as quick of athletes as we used to. We aren't a fastbreak team any more.

". . . Whatever is best for our team. This is a challenge to see if I can put my talent into that style and still be productive."

Other snipers pointed to the loss of Terry Tyler. Terry, with the huge work ethic, had signed as a free agent with the new Sacramento Kings. He was proving to be irreplaceable.

There were printed suggestions that Jack McCloskey would have to make radical changes in the Pistons at the end of the season. McCloskey read such suggestions with proper cynicism.

"I like our nucleus and the fact that it's still young," he told the hawkish media. "We just need to play harder on defense."

"We weren't known to play much defense the last couple of years," said Daly. "But you'd be surprised how much more we played than we are now."

The slide continued through the month of January.

The Detroit doomsayers got busy with their poison pens . . .

Excerpts from a column by Jerry Green in the *Sunday News*, January 19, 1986:

Chuck Daly is a big boy now. He knows that when everything cracks around him he cannot:

Spank Isiah Thomas.

Make Kelly Tripucka go stand in the corner.

Have Bill Laimbeer write "We won't flub up again" 100 times on the blackboard.

Chuck Daly used to coach in Cleveland. He understands the whims of franchise owners in moments of distress. He realizes there's a bull's-eye etched on the chest of every coach/manager . . .

He is aware that when a team goes through a long pratfall, such as that experienced currently by the Pistons, only one man is vulnerable.

He is.

He's the coach.

It goes with the territory.

"It isn't like I'm a rookie in this business," Chuck Daly said yesterday. "I know what can happen."

It hardly matters that Daly is the best man alive right now for the job of coaching the Pistons. It means nothing that the Pistons have had some of the most successful years since they went into business in Detroit during his regime. It would be foolishly sentimental to believe his bosses are not considering making him the scapegoat for their own failures. This, even though they squeezed him to stay in their employ last spring and tortured him when he had the opportunity for better security and wages with the 76ers.

The Detroit club has won but five of its last 20 games. It is a stinking disappointment. It will play the Lakers today, then embark on a five-game trip to the hinterlands.

The hard question is, will Chuck Daly still be coaching the Pistons when they return home 10 days from now? The history of this franchise, its lengthy roster of former coaches quickly fired, says no. The history of sports says no.

"As a coach, I realize the ramifications," Daly said. "But I haven't seen any kind of panic."

Chuck Daly hasn't panicked. That is the best thing. Predecessors have. Dick Vitale once was dragged shrieking from courtside.

The other night the Pistons managed to win one.

"A relief," said Laimbeer.

"Fizz-fizz," said Daly the morning after. "There's a certain amount of relief."

Reprieve is a more accurate word.

"I don't think anybody thought we'd go into this kind of tailspin," Daly said. "I thought we could lose four, win two—that kind of thing.

"I don't think anybody thought the egg was that fragile.

"Guys get disjointed. It's a selfish game by nature. But we've got to play as a team."

It, naturally, is the coach's responsibilty to force the team to play as a team. Examine what is different between this year's team and the teams of the last two years . . . there was some maturing, a bit of progress, a touch of promise.

Some say the departure of Danny Roundfield damaged the Pistons. But the clearest memories of Roundfield in his year in Detroit are of him limping to the bench to sit there in his snazzy street clothes.

More, it says here, that the club's refusal to retain Terry Tyler was most damaging.

"He might have made a difference," Daly said. "Who knows?"

Terry Tyler seldom started ball games . . . His job was simple. When the Pistons fell into a lull, he jumped off the bench and juiced up the ballclub on the floor. His presence was electric. He didn't start ballgames. He merely won them . . .

". . . The Philly thing is a closed door," Daly said. "Doors open. Doors close.

"That door's closed. I keep trying to keep this one open."

The best man for the job has his bull's-eye showing.

It might be in rereading that column and reanalyzing the situation on that Sunday morning in January 1986, that the words were premature, that Daly had not yet reached the point of danger. The Detroit Pistons were team with a history of impatience and hysterical gut reactions. Bill Davidson was a very secretive man. But in the twelve years he had been principal owner of the ballclub, he had fashioned the quick ziggy. Ray Scott, Herbie Brown, Bob Kauffman, Dick Vitale, and Scotty Robertson had coached the Pistons during Davidson's proprietorship and caught the blade.

It was logical for any historian of this franchise to figure the coach could be in peril when his team, picked to finish first, had just lost fifteen of twenty games. There was the additional matter of the continued contractual stalemate between McCloskey and Daly. It still had not been resolved, it remained a bothersome issue.

Chuck Daly's hands were still smudged from reading the Sunday paper when the Pistons went onto the Silverdome court to play another game. It was to be the feature on CBS-TV. And because it was TV, it was scheduled to start at the bizarre hour of noon in Detroit. It was not actually the Pistons, who were the feature attraction on this slice of TV entertainment. The Lakers were in town, and the Pistons were there to serve as the opponent, the foil to what some of the journalists/speculators were referring to as the best pro basketball team of all time.

Such claims, usually, result from ideas that flash through the heads of dreamy editors, with little sense about the day before yesterday. So it was in this case. The Celtics had won eight NBA championships in succession, and ten in eleven years. But that all had been lost in a time capsule. The reigning champion Lakers came into town with a 31-and-6 record for the 1985–86 season—to see headlines: Best Team Ever?

The game had all the magic to make it the perfect show for TV. Earvin Johnson. Kareem. Isiah. The fans nibbling at their pink cotton candy, a mob of 28,548 . . . and a ballgame with a wild, crazy, unexpected finish.

What happened was James Worthy put in two free throws to tie the game at 115-115 for the Lakers with a few seconds left. Then with Laimbeer passing the ball for Tripucka with the clock cut down to less than five seconds, Worthy snapped at it, ticked it and, for a flash, seemed to have a steal and a clear run to the basket and victory. But Tripucka snapped the ball away and heaved a shot toward the basket from twenty-six feet. It went through, from three-point range, with two seconds to play. The Pistons won 118-115—and the Lakers went back to the Coast. Beaten, by a team in a terrible slump, with a coach whose tomorrows had been the subject of conjecture.

The Pistons were still below .500, at 19-and-21, and they were in third place in the division, eight games out.

But whatever pressure there might have been on Chuck Daly . . . it was relieved.

And by March, Daly had managed to regroup his ballclub. The Pistons won twenty of their next twenty-six ballgames and with a 111-101 victory over the Indiana Pacers at the Silverdome assured themselves of a spot in the playoffs for the third straight season. And as the Pistons finished it up, McCloskey delivered the ultimatum to Daly as the Pistons barnstormed through California: Sign this last contract offer in five days, or forget it.

Daly signed for two more seasons. He was not thrilled. And the long negotiations between McCloskey and Daly, much of it reported in the public press, had to have an unsettling impact on the hired players, and their season.

It was a season of odd swings, odd mood shifts . . . a fast start, a fast finish, a slow in-between, a change in style . . . a season, in the final reckoning, that had been considered a disappointment, since there had been so much optimism at the beginning. Attendance remained about the same, an average of 16,957—and this time the roof remained attached to the Silverdome for the entire season.

The Pistons finished with a 46-and-36 record, the same as it had been the previous season. They placed third. Milwaukee won a seventh successive division title. And the Pistons also finished behind the Atlanta Hawks.

And they drew the Hawks in the best-of-five first round of the playoffs.

The playoffs were cruel, swift, decisive—unlike the season before, when the games were loaded with drama and the finish had provided such optimism.

The Pistons were blasted out in four games. The Hawks won the first two games in Atlanta, without a sweat.

Tripucka had been hired to produce ghost-written columns for the *News*, and he pointed out how the Pistons had lost the first two games in Boston in 1985. Always hope, and it prevailed when the Pistons won Game 3 in the Silverdome.

But then in what sometimes can be the marvelous theatre of basketball the Hawks won Game 4 in the Silverdome. They edged the Pistons in double overtime by one point, 114-113.

The defeat deprived the Pistons of a chance for a playoff rematch with the Celtics, who had toyed with young Michael Jordan and the Chicago Bulls in their first round. But more, it turned around the Pistons' schemes for the next several seasons.

Jack McCloskey had the nucleus; he assembled a team that could get to the playoffs and sometimes win an early series. But it was obvious that the Pistons, as they were then, needed changes—and McCloskey set about to supply some new bodies before camp in the fall of 1986. At least, he had Chuck Daly captured for the next two seasons.

While McCloskey reevaluated and plotted, the Celtics and Houston Rockets played each other in the NBA finals. Houston Rockets? They knocked off the team headlined five months earlier as the possible Best Team Ever in five games in the Western Conference finals. With the Lakers out, Bird and the Celtics rolled over the Akeem Olajuwon and Ralph Sampson in six games, some quite nasty, to win Boston's NBA championship No. 16.

The Pistons were positioned in the eleventh spot in the first round on draft day in 1986. Cleveland had the first lottery pick and drafted Brad Daugherty, from North Carolina. The Celtics had traded to obtain the second pick. They claimed Len Bias, from Maryland. In a few days, Bias would be dead in Maryland, killed by drug abuse.

But on draft day, the Celtics celebrated their good fortune in being able to claim such an outstanding young athlete to fit into their championship team. And down in Maryland, Len Bias celebrated his good fortune in being drafted by the great Boston Celtics. His tragedy would shake sports—and the entire nation.

There was a glamor name left when the Pistons' turn came around. McCloskey grabbed him—7 feet, maybe just 6 feet 11, John Salley, out of Georgia Tech.

They went into the second-round, which is a wild grabbag of guys regarded as candidates for the burgeoning pro leagues in Spain and Italy and Greece, or fodder for the Continental Basketball Association. The NBA clubs gamble they might hit a target in the second round, once in a while. In fact, Cleveland once passed a second-round draft choice to Philadelphia in exchange for a guy who wasn't even a player. Chuck Daly.

It was then, early in the second round in 1986, that Jack McCloskey announced that the Detroit Pistons selected: Dennis Rodman, from Southeastern Oklahoma State. He was twenty-five, somewhat aged for a rookie—and nobody had ever heard of him, except for the Detroit scouts who flushed him out, Stan Novak and Will Robinson, plus Jack McCloskey, and a white family named Rich in Bokchito, Oklahoma.

A deal is not done in a day, unless there is the pressure of the trading deadline in February. Then, there is the hourglass torture, with all the grains of sand pouring away exactly at midnight.

But now Jack had the luxury of time in his talks with the Utah Jazz. He used up much of the summer in these conversations. The deal was completed August 21, 1986. The Pistons would get Adrian Dantley, age thirty, twice NBA scoring champion, who would be moving to his fifth team. In his travels, he had acquired a reputation. He liked to shoot. He played with an individualist's style. He did not always merge into the team concept. He had occasionally feuded with his coaches; among them was Utah's round and jolly Frank Layden, who wanted eagerly to get rid of Adrian.

McCloskey also nudged two semi-worthless second-round draft choices out of the Jazz.

In exchange, the Pistons parted with two of their longtime standbys. Kent Benson, whom they had received for Bob Lanier; and Kelly Tripucka, who had come bracketed with Isiah Thomas in the 1981 draft.

Actually, the Pistons had been on the brink of trading Tripucka for Dantley six months earlier, under the pressure of the NBA deadline in Feburary 1986. It fell through—and later the inclusion of Benson and the draft choices made it possible.

"So we finally pulled the trigger," the grandiloquent Layden told the media of Salt Lake City.

Layden would have liked to have pulled the trigger on Dantley long before.

"We didn't get along," Layden told the press. "I didn't want him back. He didn't want to come back. Put it this way: if we were married it would have ended up in divorce—or murder."

As is the custom in trades, the new club always welcomes the new guy with smooches and love. There never has been a general manager who admits at the press conference that he goofed on the trade he just made. The GM is still thinking about, boy, how smart I am.

"I knew Adrian Dantley very well," McCloskey told the Detroit press. "I had him in Los Angeles and he was a team player there. There was no problem. Sometimes you have a problem with a coach, but unless Frank Layden comes along there won't be any problem here.

"We're getting a guy who averages a third more points than Kelly. Adrian is a great scorer, maybe one of the greatest scorers in the league's history. He's a post-up player, and that's what the coaches have been wanting. He may post-up as well as anybody in the league. He gives our team a new dimension."

Dantley was elated to be able to flee from Salt Lake and move to a team in contention. His problems with Layden stemmed from a contractual flap. They flared again when Dantley came to the defense of young Karl Malone, who was being victimized in a tonguelashing by Layden at the bench.

"Some people say it'll be good for me because I won't have all the problems off the court to think about," Dantley said when the *News'* Dave Dye contacted him. "But as far as being mentally tough, I don't think I ever let the coach affect my play."

It was a deal that pleased everybody—except, of course, Kelly Tripucka. The Pistons had been trying to dump him for months. He had become a crybaby whose complaints irritated McCloskey and Daly as much as his lackidaisical efforts on defense. They needed a scapegoat for the disappointing season they'd had in 1985–86 and for the tailkicking they'd received in the playoffs.

Kelly would be that scapegoat. And he would burn when he learned about the trade and the manner in which he heard about it.

He was playing golf back in New Jersey when the Jazz prematurely slipped out the announcement of the trade. The Pistons had been trying to hold off the release. McCloskey made a couple of phone calls to New Jersey in trying to locate Kelly to notify him that he'd been traded away.

Instead, Kelly learned about it in the locker room after he'd finished his round of golf.

He refused to talk to the Detroit media when they called him for reaction. The Pistons' scapegoat made the journalists his scapegoat. But after a few days of ducking, Tripucka came out of solitary confinement to give an interview to the *Newark Star-Ledger*. And so his words drifted back to Detroit.

"I think that they've stayed the same for so long that they're just making changes for the sake of changing," Tripucka said to the Newark paper in his denunciation of the Pistons.

"When they drafted me, that team was in oblivion, down in the dumps. Look now, I've helped build it.

"Our fans got better and better each year. I felt I was part of that . . . I've talked with people in Detroit and a lot of fans are upset about the trade . . . Here's a guy three years older than me. The big question mark about him is his attitude . . . he's been with five teams, there's always rumors as far as him getting along with his teammates . . .

"I found out in a very demeaning way. I was playing in a golf tournament. We had just played in the rain, and I was in the locker room getting dressed when some kid comes running in. He obviously didn't know I was there. He yelled out, 'hey, Kelly Tripucka just got traded to the Jazz for Adrian Dantley.'

"I was shocked."

And there were those who questioned the wisdom of the deal. These naysayers cited Dantley's desire to have the ball in an offense designed for the ball to be controlled by Isiah Thomas.

The Pistons had been and would still be Isiah's team. The other four guys were satellites, playing around him.

McCloskey had entered his make-a-trade mode and he was not done. Next day, with the stories about Dantley and Tripucka clogging the sports sections, Jack dealt again. He wanted a strong bench forward and obtained Sidney Green from the Chicago Bulls. To get Green, McCloskey shipped off relaible Earl Cureton, who'd been with the Pistons in a reservist/morale booster role for three years. The Pistons also donated one of their excess second-round draft choices.

The shakeup was completed during training camp at the University of Windsor, in Canada. McCloskey dealt away John Long to Seattle for a pair of those always useful future second-round draft choices.

There was sadness when Long left camp. He was the final linkage between the Pistons' past and the present—Vitale and Daly. Three days later, Long, who had been rooted in his hometown of Detroit for eight NBA seasons, was traded a second time. Seattle relayed him to the Indiana Pacers.

The Pistons had been redone between seasons. Starting out the 1986–87 season, they were a young club, anchored around three veterans—Isiah, Laimbeer, and Dantley. The other two starters were Mahorn and Joe Dumars, the kid in the outfit. The Pistons, due to McCloskey's maneuverings, had a fortified bench—a vital positive in the drive to take another step toward the NBA finals and the ultimate championship.

Sixth man off the bench was Vinnie Johnson, now heralded as the Microwave. And beyond V.J., there were the rookies Salley and Rodman.

It was a mighty impressive array—on paper, at least.

The attendances had been escalating through the years. More and more of the suburban swells were discovering the sport. Perched into the front-row seats, courtside at the Silverdome, a student of modern cultist behavior could see individuals dressed in black leather, short skirts, tailored bluejeans, sequined tops over gold lame pants, Armani sportsjackets, warmup suits, studded windbreakers, three-piece gray flannel suits favored by conservatives in buttondown collars.

Bill Davidson, who attended games in open-necked sportshirts, and his fellow investors had decided to abandon the Silverdome as soon as they could. They could draw mobs to their games, 40,000 or more, but it was not a basketball arena. It was the corner of a covered—sometimes—football stadium, also used for Springsteen concerns, motocross events, and tractor pulls. There was always the danger that the Pistons could be dispossessed for a critical playoff game.

So Davidson and his colleagues purchased a tract of land in Auburn Hills. They would build and operate their own basketball arena. And the team that thirty years earlier had moved into Detroit because it was a major-league town would be moving even farther from downtown and the city.

Through the decades that they had been relegated to the inside pages of the newspapers, reduced to one sentence containing the score on the TV sports news on Channels 2, 4, and 7 at 11:17, clumped in the radio ratings by the hockey game, the Pistons had struggled to develop a media personality. The baseball team had its Ernie Harwell, whose godly voice was immediately identifiable with the Tigers. The pro teams in the other sports had their broadcasters who could be associated, by the public, with the Lions or with the Red Wings.

But there never had been such an individual who would turn the public on and have the people say: he's the voice of the Pistons. Indeed, the Pistons had about as many play-by-play men on a variety of coathanger stations as they had coaches and GMs. This was the club that once had taken its broadcaster and made him the general manager—and the promotion of Don Wattrick in desperation, years before, tickled sports writers with long memories.

Now the Pistons developed their own devoted radio following on a major station that fed a network of other outlets throughout Michigan. George Blaha, voice of the Pistons, became as integral a part of the basketball persona as Bill Laimbeer.

And Blaha developed a style that was distinct in a way that enhanced the joys of pro basketball in Detroit.

For example, Joe Dumars dribbled across the midcourt line and in his mind's eye the listener could imagine the scene as the player dribbled the ball from side to side and then launched an arching shot. "Street music on the rainbow," yelled Blaha into the mike, and the listener, becoming basketball wise, knew exactly how the shot looked as it traveled toward the basket.

Bill Laimbeer hitting from behind the circle. Blaha on the radio: "Laimbeer from downtown."

Dumars, again, scoring a three-point basket. Blaha: "The triple got nothing but net."

The Pistons moving downcourt, trying to hold a lead late in the third quarter. Blaha: "2 and 52 left here in the third."

These were word pictures—and there was an eager audience.

The Pistons' locker room in the Silverdome was a well-lighted place. It was a large room, with trainer Mike Abdenour's area secluded, out-of-bounds to nosy sports writers. The players could slip in this sanctuary before or after games and not be bothered answering questions.

But facing the corridor was a huge window, and the Pistons had not thought of using one-way glass. Peeping Toms could see everything going on inside, if they were so inclined. And any reporter with a mind became adept at using his eyes as well has his ballpoint pen and notebook, or nowadays, his microcassette tape recorder.

Inside Abdenour's room with its rubbing tables and benches an observer might see Bill Laimbeer immersed in the hot tub, reading a newspaper. You could see Adrian Dantley getting his ankles taped by Abdenour. Then Adrian rotating his head, trying to loosen his neck muscles.

Outside, Isiah might be at his locker in the corner, sitting on a stool, stringing shoelaces through the eyes of new sneakers.

"Isiah. New shoes?" The reporter started off with small talk, a device to warm the mood.

"Jump higher, shoot better, that's basketball," Isiah responded, continuing with the shoelaces.

"Are you going to pass Adrian the basketball?"

"Pass him the ball? Nah! Shoot it myself."

You wandered around on the blue-carpeted floor of the locker room. The reporters clustered near Salley, the rookie. The reporters exchanged gossip, rumors.

By NBA rules, you had to leave the locker room forty-five minutes before gametime.

You walked out and took a final peek through the window into the trainer's room.

Isiah was now in the tub, a Walkman stuffed to his ears.

Despite all of Jack McCloskey's digging, the Pistons did not roar to success when the bell rang for the 1986–87 season. The Atlanta Hawks were the club in the division that the Pistons feared now, not the Milwaukee Bucks. The Hawks had wiped them out the previous spring in the playoffs. But on this opening night in the Silverdome, the Bucks were the opponent. And the Bucks drilled the Pistons.

The reporters clustered outside the locker room after the game until the security guard let them in. The NBA has a ten-minute cooling off period. Then any media person with a credential was supposed to be allowed to enter. The mob advanced about ten steps into the corridor. That's where Chuck Daly was waiting to conduct his interviews.

"Not a good night," he might say. "We're not there yet. We're not in the class with Atlanta yet. Not yet with Philly or Boston."

Four or five guys with video cams fought for vantage points. The TV reporters tethered to the cams stuffed their microphones into Daly's mouth. The writers for the papers tried to squeeze closer to grab Daly's words for posterity.

And a few of us slipped away and into the players room, to Isiah.

"They're still good," said Isiah. "We're a better team. I have no doubts in my mind we'll be a very good basketball team. If we'd won, everybody would be saying how great we are."

The new man, Adrian Dantley, was down the way. He was asked how he was fitting into the Pistons' schemes.

"Need confidence," Dantley told the roving writers. "I got to get used to players I played against for six years. You got to keep at an even level because you can't get too high when you win or low when you lose . . . because there are so many games."

Bill Laimbeer was across the way.

"Tonight you saw a lack of cohesiveness as a twelve-man team," Laimbeer told the writers.

Back across the carpet to Isiah, where a new group of media people had gathered.

"You can't judge a team on one night's performance," Isiah said. "And like last year, you can't say we're a great team on one night's performance, when we won."

Routine stuff. It was opening night, but the postmortems would be pretty much the same after every game during the season.

Considered the most talented team the Pistons had ever assembled, they nonetheless got off to an old-fashioned 3-and-6 start. Early on, the Hawks were running ahead in the division. In the early season, they handled the Pistons before the home mob at the Silverdome. And they were invincible on their homecourt in the Omni in Atlanta.

By mid-December, the Hawks had moved ahead of the Pistons by six games in the division race.

The week before Christmas the Pistons went into Atlanta for another match with the Hawks at the Omni.

It was a nasty game. Late in the first half, Vinnie Johnson, the normally mild-mannered Microwave, was bumped by the Hawks' Tree Rollins. Tree was so named because he was 7 feet 1 in height and had the torso of an oak. Vinnie never took any stuff when he played the game on the asphalt playgrounds of Brooklyn. He wasn't going to take any, either, on the wooden floor of Atlanta. He charged after Tree. He did not think of the key statistic in the tale of the tape—that he was giving away eleven inches to Tree.

What followed was the typical NBA fight. There were a couple of punches, lots of milling, whistles, ejections, angry postgame comments, followed by fines.

"I didn't throw the first punch," Vinnie told Dave Dye. "I went after him, but I shoved first. I didn't punch. He punched first. I think I had just cause to go after him. I had to let him know I'm not going to take that crap. He elbowed me right on the shoulder."

The Pistons were gathering a reputation around the league as a very aggressive, malevolent basketball team.

That night, the Pistons beat the Hawks by eleven points. The Hawks were no longer invincible on their home court.

Funny, but the Pistons went off on a winning roll.

Jack McCloskey made another trade in midstream at the end of January. He reasoned that the Pistons needed another high body for the bench. He traded for Kurt Nimphius, 6 feet 11, from the Los Angeles Clippers. It would be for immediate help only. Nimphius would be a free agent at the end of the season. The price was extravagant—the Pistons' first-round draft choice for 1987 plus one pick out of their stock of second-round selections. The trade was a calculated risk, and Nimphius would be gone after twenty-eight games.

Jack couldn't score every time.

The deal did not damage the Pistons' mix, though. By mid-Feburary, they had passed over the Milwaukee team, and they had caught the Hawks for leadership of the division.

Excerpts from a column in the *Detroit News* by Jerry Green, February 22, 1987 . . .

Saturday night pro basketball live—and Bill Laimbeer's eyes narrowed into slits. He was ready to sizzle, to fry.

The Pistons have been in town for 30 years. It has never been like this before . . .

Bill Laimbeer stood out there on the glistening hard floor of the Silverdome as they introduced the athletes. He did not blink. His torso heaved with tension. He flashed his laser eyes at his Detroit teammates. He turned and glared at the bench of the Atlanta Hawks and reduced them with his evil eye.

Laimbeer was possessed, and so was his team. And so was the crowd—44,970—all legitimate . . .

This was high-intensity stuff, and the Pistons won it, 102–97. They led from the first shot to the final SCARE. First place beating second place. It is a rollicking, crazy February in this town.

"It puts them down three in the loss column," said Laimbeer. "It puts us up on them in two of the tiebreakers."

He had lugged a six-pack into the sauna with him. When he returned, he had one silver can left in his hand.

His talk of stats, advantages and playoff edges was the talk of the Celtics or Lakers. It was rare talk. Never before.

"That's the way first-place teams talk," said Bill Laimbeer.

"We are a first-place team.

"I keep track of those figures. It was an important game. It was a home game. This was a game we had to go out and win and we did win. We had to go out and take care of business."

This was a blood game. Pro basketball can be that way. There is all the finesse, all the whirling, all the ballet steps by gracefully tuned, elongated athletes. But so much of it is blood and brutality.

That is the style in which Laimbeer plays the game. He plays with the finesse of a scorched bull. His rivals were Kevin Willis and Jon Koncak. He matched them, sharp elbow thrust for sharp elbow, forearm shiv for forearm shiv.

"Yes, I was intense before," Laimbeer said of his slitted eyes. "I wanted to be a major key . . ."

Moments after the game began, Willis flattened Laimbeer beneath the Detroit basket. Laimbeer bounced on the floor and bounced up. His run is an urgent plod. So he urgently plodded . . . the other way. He and Willis greeted each other with an exchange of elbows underneath the Atlanta basket. And Laimbeer took the rebound away— the precious defensive rebound. He heaved the ball the length of the floor, a perfect pass to Adrian Dantley, alone, who scored a simple layup.

It is a sweet blend. The blood mixes with the sweetness and the swiftness. The Pistons play at a .667 clip, the pace of champions.

The franchise has been at it 30 years—and it never happened before. Not with a DeBusschere or a Bing or a Yardley or a Howell or a Bellamy or a Scott.

"War at the Silverdome," Chuck Daly had called the Saturday night game.

Daly has been a realist through his years of gradual improvement in Detroit. His repeated statements have been that the Pistons are not there yet—not there with the Celtics, not with the Lakers, not with the 76ers, not with the Hawks. The truth was proven when his team was toppled in the playoffs.

But now it is first place and playing like first place.

There yet?

"Questionable," said Daly, live on this Saturday night . . .

"Questionable.

"I'm uncertain about the size factor. This is the most talent I've had, the most talent.

"The Celtics, the Lakers, they've been there. Have we passed the 76ers? I don't think so.

"There's a couple of clubs above," and Daly raised his hand high, "and the rest.

"I think we're in the rest. Somewhere . . ."

Isiah Thomas offered the dissenting opinion to his coach's presumed realism.

"I agree that we're one of the elite teams," Isiah said in that February of the 1986–87 season.

Isiah was on the bike in the locker room. He pushed the pedals slowly round and round. The wheel turned and the spokes floated into a blur. Isiah's face flashed with the usual mirth. The bike was riveted to hits spot, stationary.

Like the bike, the Pistons had been locked on a stationary fixture.

He continued to pedal. The wheel turned. Softly.

"See. I'm not excited," Isiah said. "I'm not overwhelmed because this is what I expect.

"It is the first time we've been elite, and it's time, and that's why they brought me here. It's more gratifying than any season because everybody said we couldn't win and put up with the elite teams. Everybody asked me, 'don't you want to play with Boston, L.A.? The best!'

"And I said, 'if you work hard enough, you'll be good enough, and we'll be up there. Critics of mine, they say I was doing too much before and not enough now. They say you got to be seven feet to win in this league. How can a guy 6-1 make a team win?"

Chuck Daly did have it pegged with accuracy. There was a night the Portland Trail Blazers visited the Pistons in the Silverdome. On this night, as the season moved toward the final stage, the flaws remaining in the team of Isiah, the team of Laimbeer, showed up. The Pistons still lacked a certain something.

They had learned to win as a first-place team could, it was written. They could dominate. They could intimidate. They could burn up with the emotion and intensity of the critical games. They imitated the Celtics and the Lakers in that winning function.

But it was the theory here that the Pistons had not yet learned to lose in the manner that a first-place team loses. That savvy slip of knowledge might be the final item, I wrote. There was a special, dignified type of defeat when champions must lose—defeat with honor.

On this night, the Trail Blazer's had crunched

Thomas and Dantley are all smiles during the final minutes of a 43-point playoff victory over Washington.

them 123–111, right in Isiah's house. The Pistons lost with dishonor. They had been on a five-game winning streak and were talking first-place boast talk, and they were blown out.

Blowout is an ugly, cruel word. It describes mismatch or capitulation or disparity in the quality of talent. The elite clubs of the NBA never got blown out.

But on this night, the Pistons had been because they'd thumbed layups off the glass, missing a dozen chip shots. On this night, loyalists in the cultist crowd of 26,833 started walking out in a cascading rush early in the fourth quarter. On this night, the Pistons had trapped themselves with a loss of poise.

It was written in summary: The Pistons cannot shove into the NBA's elite until they discover the savvy tricks of *losing* in the style of a first-place team. No blowouts. No capitulation. No honor.

So it was that the Pistons were mere temporary occupants of first place during the 1986–87 season. They were too erratic still, too flawed. They failed to finish in first place for the thirtieth successive season.

The Hawks recaptured first place in the Central from the Pistons, along with the critical perk for finishing with the superior record—home-court advantage in the playoffs. The Pistons had climbed above the half-century standard for the second time, finishing at 52-and-30. But it was second place, a whopping five games behind the Hawks.

Nevertheless, the city had become daft about the Pistons. The Pistons led the NBA in attendance again. They averaged 22,152, an improvement of more than 5,000 for each of the forty-one home dates.

The Pistons had become a profitable enterprise.

But they still had never finished first. They had never won more than one playoff series in any single season. They had never, truthfully, been one of the elite clubs in the NBA.

And now they had played themselves into the obstacle of playing most of the playoffs with the road-court disadvantage—if they succeeded in scraping through the first round.

These best-of-five first-round series had been a bugaboo for the Pistons, since they had started qualifying for the playoffs with regularity. Twice in the previous three years they had been bumped off in best-of-five opening rounds.

This time they played the Washington Bullets. The Pistons won it in a sweep, the three-game minimum. They had only one perilous game, Game 3, on the road in the Capital Centre, Landover, Maryland. That was a one-point game, but the Pistons won it, 97–96. They could advance on, into danger. Their second round foe was the Hawks, in a best-of-seven series, with four of the games scheduled for the Omni in Atlanta.

The Pistons snatched the homecourt edge from the Hawks in Game 1, with another one-point victory. It was Pistons 112, Hawks 111. Atlanta won Game 2 at home. Games 3 and 4 were in the Silverdome, Isiah's house. The Pistons took a 2–1 edge with a victory in the third game, 108–99. Game 4 was on a Sunday afternoon, a showpiece, on national TV—Isiah Thomas pitted against Dominique Wilkins, according to the marquee billing.

Excerpts from a column by Jerry Green in the *Detroit News*, May 11, 1987.

The ball went in and now he was hugging it in his stomach and doing his war dance beneath the basket. Isiah Thomas was tromping on the glistening wood of the court. He was doing all this until Rickey Mahorn hoisted him in the air toward the roof of the Silverdome.

The moment was laden with . . . history. Isiah was aware of it. He dwelled on it. It flooded his head during the time-outs in which the strategies were established for victory and defeat.

"In the huddle I was thinking about how they beat us last year in the same kind of game," Isiah said,

"and how they celebrated on the floor and partied and danced and high-fived, and I said I can't lose that way again.

"I said if I get this basketball I'm making it. No way am I going to miss it."

He swept around and made it. Dribbling, driving, shooting underhanded, scoring, dancing.

The Detroit Pistons have never advanced so far, so smartly, so brightly with such success, never since they moved to this community 30 years ago. They have a 3–1 stranglehold now in the playoffs over the Atlanta Hawks, one of their perennial tormentors. One more victory, one more—and the Pistons move onward in these playoffs. One more and they move to the NBA semifinals, the pro game's Final Four.

"This was the biggest game in this franchise's history," said Isiah. "It was the most important in the history of the Detroit Pistons."

He kept saying it. The Pistons won, 89–88 . . . and he made the winning basket with one second on the clock.

This was absolute drama, this was the crisp ballet of pro basketball at the pressure point.

Isiah takes the pass-in with five seconds left. There have been double time-outs, the Hawks ahead by one. He takes it from Adrian Dantley and he sweeps around John Battle and he swoops it under Antoine Carr and he dances.

"Moments like these are moments you dream about when you're asleep at night," Isiah said. "Or what you dream about when you're a kid. Or what you dream about right now . . .

"If you miss that shot, you got to be prepared to make it next time.

"A lot of players when they miss they can't make that shot again. They can't do anything for three weeks.

"I said if I got the basketball I was making that shot.

"I had to."

Isiah . . . is in pro basketball's celebrity bracket with Magic and Dr. J and Bird and Kareem . . . But all those others have played on championship teams. Their individual heroics have created concrete results.

But the Detroit Pistons have never survived the second round of the playoffs. Never. Visions of the

Hawks celebrating on the Pistons' floor just last year.

"I feel we're a very good basketball team," Isiah said . . . "We're as good as anybody playing. We need the bounces.

"We're good enough to match up against anyone now . . ."

It was graduation day. For the Pistons. For Isiah. He won, he was awarded his college degree in absentia.

His mother, Mary, collected his degree in his place down at Indiana. He talked to her on the phone immediately after the game.

"She was crying," said Isiah. "She said, 'I'm so happy you got the degree.'

"She told me she didn't know I was going back to school. She said, 'you little devil.'"

Joe Dumars drives for a layup with Dominique Wilkins of the Hawks in hot pursuit.

He was back at his locker and the lights were on him. This was his moment, a rare, special moment. He was asked what he told his mother about his shot.

"I didn't tell her," he said. "She didn't ask. She was so happy I got my degree. It was a happy Mother's Day."

And you, Isiah, what means more to you—the degree or the shot?

"Definitely, the shot," he said. His smile was dazzling.

The afternoon of Game 5 in Atlanta, Chuck Daly took time out as his players napped at the the Marriott Hotel in Atlanta. He lounged, in a preciously rare moment of pregame relaxation, at the swimming pool.

"Isiah's on the cover of *Sports Illustrated*," I told him.

"That's the kiss of death," said Daly. "Like two black cats."

That night, the Hawks battled ahead, the Pistons drove back. The Hawks retaliated. Bill Laimbeer got into a shoving battle with Dominique Wilkins. Wilkins wanted to kill him. The Hawks were ahead at the half.

Halftime shows in pro basketball do not consist of blaring marching bands and wiggling drum majorettes. More, it is the theatre of the absurd—guys who can balance two stilts one atop the other, or kids who do speed dribbling. In this case at the Omni, a wooden dummy of Laimbeer with No. 40 painted onto it figured prominently in the entertainment.

A guy with a chain saw cut Laimbeer's effigy into two portions. The Omni crowd loved it. Laimbeer was hated in Atlanta, too. But the chain saw murderer missed Laimbeer's heart.

The Hawks buttressed their lead in the third quarter and into the fourth. Atlanta went up by a dozen with fewer than nine minutes to play.

I had an early deadline and started pounding the keys of my computer to make the morning edition of the *News* back home. I was nearly finished with a piece that said the Pistons would have to go home to play Game 6.

Then the Pistons overcame the huge deficit. They charged back. Vinnie Johnson, the Microwave, turned on. Vinnie scored 15 points in a flash. Daly dug into his bench. He had Isiah and Rickey Mahorn out there with Vinnie and the rookies, Spider Salley and the Worm, Rodman. Rodman got into Dominique's face on defense. Vinnie stole the ball from Dominique on the trap. Then Isiah stole it from Dominique. The Pistons streaked ahead. I erased everything I had written. I started with a fresh column, about the Pistons' gallant comeback. They won. They beat the Hawks, 104–96. They advanced to the next round, the Eastern finals, further than they had ever been before.

They would have to meet the Boston Celtics, again.

In the locker room, Chuck Daly held a can of Budweiser in his hand and suggested the reporter look at him, at his straight teeth, his grin, his face ruddy and fresh, unlined.

"I thought we were a pretty good club," he said. But not in the class of Boston or L.A.—until this night in Atlanta.

"The guys knew how good they are before I did," Daly said.

Bill Laimbeer sat grinning along a wall. His beefy face was aflame with happiness. Isiah had saved a special smile just for this night.

"Zeke kept coming to me in the third quarter and saying, 'we're gonna win it, we're gonna win it, we're gonna win it,'" Daly said. "We were ten down and my starters were struggling, and he's saying we're gonna win it.

"It's unbelievable . . . This is the culmination."

And then a story developed in this jubilant locker room in Atlanta.

It was more than a year old, a well-kept secret. Back then, in late March 1986, when Daly was given the ultimatum to sign in five days or else—the Pistons were trying to push him out. They planned to dump Daly, who once had begged the Pistons to release him so he could go to Philly and was refused. Now they wanted him gone. But smart heads prevailed.

Isiah and Laimbeer invaded the inner sanctum and convinced management that Chuck Daly was needed by the Pistons.

"Chuck's one of the rare coaches in the league who will let Isiah have freedom," Thomas said.

It was not a culmination at all. The Pistons were halfway there. Now they had another series . . . against Boston, and the Curse. The Celtics owned the precious homecourt advantage. The Pistons had lost fifteen successive games on the parquet floor at the Boston Garden, atop the

Dantley looks to the hoop during the 1987 Conference finals. He would be knocked out of Game 7 with a head injury.

grimy North Station. The Celtics had the Garden and the championship experience. They knew the angles and how to handle the ball when the whole building vibrated as the nine o'clock train chugged from the station on the Boston & Maine tracks for Portland, Maine.

The Pistons had six days off to sooth their hangovers, heal their injuries, prepare for the Celtics. They headed into Boston for the first game of the Eastern Conference finals, which is a much catchier name than the NBA semifinals. Same thing. David Stern had turned the NBA into a marketing product. And pro basketball was selling, deep into what tradition once insisted would be the exclusive time period for baseball season.

On May 19, 1987, the Boston papers were filled with the articles about the basketball rudeness of the Pistons—of Laimbeer, of Mahorn, of Rodman, the large-eared rookie. And that night the Detroit Pistons were beaten in the first game they had ever played in a conference finals series.

The Celtics handled them, 104–91. Sixteen losses in a row on the parquet floor.

Two nights later, that streak of frustration was streched to seventeen. The Celtics beat the Pistons again, 110–101. At times, it seemed, the rivals were trying to score on the off-tackle play.

The Pistons were down 2–0 of the best-of-seven when they returned home to the Silverdome for Games 3 and 4. They had been in this same sort of jam two years earlier—the playoff year when Larry Bird said, in what he considered an awesome quote, that the Pistons weren't as formidable as Cleveland.

The television network rules . . . so the Pistons and Celtics were required to play on successive weekend days for CBS's select national audience. The Pistons blitzed the Celtics twice in the Silverdome, 122–104 and then 145–119. There was pushing, grabbing, shirt pulling. Bill Laimbeer had become very unpopular with Parish and Bird.

The rivals trooped back to Boston for Game 5. With two victories over the Celtics, the Pistons had confidence now. They were the emerging team. The Celtics were the old champs. It was quite that simple; the Pistons had developed a mindset, that they could beat the Celtics. What the hell if Game 5 was in Boston!

Larry Bird gets a hand on John Salley's shot. (*K. Dozier*)

So they did it. They went out and matched the Boston Celtics. They went out and Isiah drove them into a lead, a most fragile lead, in the final moments. Then the Celtics booted the ball out of bounds with five seconds remaining. Dennis Rodman went dancing up the court, with his arm waving high, in the faces of the Boston fans. The Pistons had a victory in the Garden. The Curse, it was finally broken. All the Pistons had to do was pass the ball in and let the five seconds fade way.

That's all!

Why the Pistons neglected to call a time out at this moment in time to allow the heat of their emotions to cool, to calm themselves from their peak of excitement, to organize themselves for a proper inbounds pass—it was a question they would live with forever, without a logical answer.

Isiah bounced the ball at the edge of the court, on the side corner, near the Celtics' basket. Only Laimbeer was around. The other guys were busy celebrating. Isiah flipped it in the direction of Laimbeer. Bird stepped in the path of the ball. He intercepted it. He relayed it to Dennis Johnson. Johnson popped the ball in the basket.

The Curse continued. Boston 108, Detroit 107!

It was the most painful defeat in the history of the Pistons, since the day Fred Zollner, in a fit of enlightenment, established a basketball team to represent his factory in Fort Wayne, Indiana, before World War II.

The Pistons dragged home for Game 6, heartbroken, on the brink of elimination. But it was a measure of what the Pistons had become that they did not lose Game 6. Any lesser team would have. The pain and bitterness stuck with them. But they beat the Celtics, 113–105, at the Silverdome. And the prize for winning was one more visit to Boston and the Garden for Game 7.

The date was May 30, 1987. Again, as they had four nights earlier in Boston, they controlled the tempo and the angers flashed between the teams. Parish had punched Laimbeer. Bird had thrown the basketball at Laimbeer in a fury. The Pistons again matched the Celtics. On this afternoon, Vinnie Johnson and Adrian Dantley drove for the ball and met head on. Their skulls collided. Dantley was knocked cuckoo and had to be carted off the floor and taken to the hospital.

Mahorn shoots over Robert Parish.

The Pistons still had their chances to win. But they didn't.

Larry Bird scored 37 points. In the end, the reigning champion Celtics won. The final score was 117–114, Boston. The Celtics would return to the NBA finals.

And in the small, tight locker room in the Boston Garden, above the North Stadium, the irrational angers and emotions poured out of the mouths of Pistons for the benefit of America's media. Dennis Rodman spoke about Larry Bird's whiteness and the words flared into a racial controversy. The controversy would upstage the NBA finals and another championship series between the Celtics and Lakers.

Dennis Rodman would vanish to the house where he had lived with a white family in Oklahoma. But his remarks and the furor would not go away.

"I think over the next couple of years, this will be a very much improved team," Jack McCloskey told Bill Halls in postmortem. "Hey, this is a team you have to enjoy. They are good people. I really enjoy watching them play, and I like the approach the coaches have taken."

McCloskey would have to do just a bit more

tinkering before the Pistons could take another step, the critical step to the edge and over. The Pistons did not have a No. 1 draft choice in 1987. It had been surrendered for Kurt Nimphius, wasted actually. But Jack had some ideas, and the players he had assembled had not yet gotten to their individual peaks.

Magic and Bird went off in another one of their duels that aroused the TV network into spasms of ecstasy. And Magic won again. The Lakers dethroned the Celtics in six games of the NBA finals . . . as Isiah Thomas and Bill Laimbeer and Joe Dumars watched, suffering at their thoughts of what could have been.

III—The Late Eighties

They had migrated to Detroit thirty years earlier as strangers, and for the bulk of the three decades the Pistons had remained outlanders in their adopted hometown. Through most of these thirty years they had attracted some curiosity seekers, had provided their new city with moments of slapstick comedy and had employed seventeen head coaches and nine general managers. They had traded away Yardley and Shue and Howell and DeBusschere and Bing and Lanier, without equitable return. They used seven scattered arenas as their supposed homecourt, including Toledo.

During the first thirteen years, they never had a record touching .500, establishing a league standard for futility. They had but seven winning seasons. They never finished first in a division. Nor had they ever reached the stratopheric region of the league's championship series.

Examining the entire package, three decades of toil and trying to peddle a sports product and collect a respectable fan clientele, the Pistons were abject failures.

But entering the 1987–88 training camp, four of those rare winning records had occurred in the four previous seasons. The same coach had served four complete seasons—despite some storms about quitting or being fired. And that in itself was a longevity standard for Pistons coaches. The previous May, the Pistons had advanced for the first time as far in the playoffs as the NBA semifinals. Only then had they lost in seven angry games. They had built a team and the people came. The audience contained more than curiosity seekers now. They had built a cult of supporters. They had led the league in attendance in each of the past four years.

The thirtieth anniversary of the Pistons setting foot in Detroit, with Charley Eckman in charge and Walter Dukes in tow, went unmarked by ceremony. In fact, it passed by unnoticed.

The 1987–88 Pistons were engaged in training camp for another season, the beginning of the fourth decade in Detroit. Their own new arena with luxury suites and similar perks in Auburn Hills, north of Detroit, beyond Pontiac, was more than a hole in the ground. The construction gang would be finished in time for the following season.

By then, the Pistons dreamed, they could be NBA champions.

This franchise, with its cleansed and purified image, was that close now. But Chuck Daly, starting his fifth season as the team's coach, would not confirm that.

"Everybody automatically looks at last year and figures we'll move right into the finals," Daly told the *News'* Corky Meinecke on the eve of the season opener. "Well, we were fortunate to get where we were. The expectations are high, which is fine, but I don't think we can sit back and allow other people's expectations to direct us and take away from our work habits and mental approach to the game."

It was amazing that good ole Chuck hadn't developed worry marks.

"The Clippers lost four guys last year. If we would have lost four guys last year, we would have been terrbile, too. We would have been in the draft lottery, too."

Again, Daly expressed fear of the Chicago Bulls, within the Central Division.

". . . it's easily as strong as any division in the league from top to bottom," he told the *News* . . . "Chicago is probably the most improved club, and Indiana and Cleveland have all that youth and talent . . . This is a bigger challenge than any year since I've been here. We climbed the mountain a little ways last year. One time.

"That ain't like doing it year in and year out, and winning it once in a while. Like the Lakers and Celtics have."

The Pistons' ownership syndicate could have revised the blueprints for the Auburn Hills arena to put in a violins section.

As was his custom, Jack McCloskey tinkered some with the manpower, this time to hone a club considered capable of dethroning the Celtics—at last—in the Eastern Conference.

The Pistons had burned up their first-round selection in the 1987 draft for Nimphius. Now he had opted to leave for the San Antonio Spurs as a free agent.

So at draft time, McCloskey traded for William Bedford, who had been a problem player with the Phoenix Suns. McCloskey knew he was gambling on Bedford. William had been connected with a drug situation on the Suns, in which he exchanged court testimony for immunity from prosecution. He was accused of lacking any sort of work ethic, the sort of which infected the Pistons. Al Bianchi, then an assistant coach with the Suns, said of Bedford: "He's the laziest kid in America."

The price was steep—the Pistons' first-round draft selection for 1988. That meant, the Pistons would be minus a No. 1 in two successive drafts. But William was 7 feet 1. And general managers and coaches always feel self-assured they can alter the bad habits of athletes with their own distinctive methods. In Bedford's case, he was so tall, with so much promise, the Pistons believed they could let him fill in immediately while cultivating him for the future.

Late in training camp, McCloskey, in frustration, had to give up on Sidney Green, who had spelled Rickey Mahorn at power forward. Green was sent to the New York Knicks. The Pistons received Ron Moore for the bench—plus another of those second-round draft picks.

The Pistons opened their final season at the Silverdome with a victory over the New York Knicks. The storyline for New York was the debut of Rick Pitino, making his NBA stop of his teams-he-has-coached tour. He must have been horrified. The game was a mess. It had 65 turnovers in it. And the Pistons whacked the Knicks with a late rally. The opener drew 28,676 customers, and they loved it.

So did Daly. His worst fear had been averted.

"Well, we got a win," he told the media when they charged through the double doors into the corridor in the locker room. "At least we won't go 0-and-82."

Inside, where the players dressed, Daly had posted a huge blown up photograph of an NBA championship ring. The Pistons had advanced a far distance from the time when the goal was to cross over .500.

Right after the game, the Pistons went to the airport. The first roadgame of the new season was the following night, in Milwaukee. Bill Davidson had splurged for a jet plane to carry the Pistons from town-to-town. Roundball One was outfitted with twenty-four reclining seats with stereo headsets, a sofa, and a bunch of TV sets and VCRs. It was there after each game, waiting for the players and coaches, then it would fly off into the night to the next destination.

No more prancing through airports, dodging gawkers and autograph seekers, flying Northwest Airlines with the great unwashed, squeezed into seats with about as much room as, er, a school bus. No more would Chuck Daly have to pace his suite at the Guest Quarters in Philly or Wyndham in San Antonio till four in the morning, replaying the game, then rush to the airport for the 7:35 morning flight to Denver.

He could pace the aisle in Roundball One, or watch the tape of the game on the VCR.

The Pistons were the only NBA team with their own wings. It could be an edge for a team in contention.

In late November, Jack McCloskey offloaded one of his stock of second-round draft choices to obtain Darryl Dawkins from the Utah Jazz. Dawkins was legend around the NBA. He had been the first player to fragment a glass backboard into a million shards with the very force of a slam dunk. Chocolate Thunder was the nickname. From the planet Lovetron. He had played for Philly, Jersey, the Jazz—and he'd never won a championship ring. He was thirty and had a reputation and showed up flabby. McCloskey felt he could spell Laimbeer in the middle.

But Jack did not know if Dawkins could still play at his age with the huge body beaten by years of skirmishes in the middle. He was acquired as a role player on a club so very close to championship caliber. He was with the Pistons, to mix with a quality club fitted with individual stars who had somehow blended with marvelous chemisty. It was written that Dawkins could endanger the delicate balance of this winning formula.

"I don't got one yet," Dawkins said, looking at Daly's photo of the championship ring. "I'm planning on getting one here."

"He won't upset the chemistry here," Isiah vowed. "We're too strong."

True. Dawkins played a few minutes that night against the Spurs during garbage time of the Pistons' 141–111 victory. He got a Standing O when Daly sent him into the game. He scored four points and blocked a shot by San Antonio's Greg Anderson. Accomplishing that role play, Dawkins turned toward Anderson. And winked.

The four points would be all Darryl Dawkins would score for the Pistons in the entire season. He got into one more game. Then, because of his condition, he was dropped from the active roster.

But he was a delicious part of pro basketball history.

The first week in December, with the Pistons riding in first place in the division, the Celtics arrived in Pontiac in their first confrontation since the previous May. The Detroit media played this regular-season game up as Game 8.

Adrian Dantley was asked his memories of Game 7, when he was kayoed in the collision of heads with Vinnie Johnson.

"I don't remember anything from the point of contact," said Dantley.

"There is no Game 8," said Laimbeer, scoffing at the media hype notion.

"Not Game 8," said Isiah. "It was a seven-game series. Those are the rules . . . Think about it? Yeah. I thought about it. Yeah. I lived it over.

"The thing I really thought about was Vinnie and Adrian. It just wasn't our time. Too many freaky things happened.

"Give Boston credit. They were hurt. Tired. They have every excuse. And they didn't die?

"Carry-over? Nah!"

Nah! But Bird did not offer to shake Laimbeer's hand before the tipoff.

Carry-over?

Bird played versus Rodman. Attacker versus defender. Rodman scored over Bird and raised a fist toward the roof to the roars of 35,523 rooting for the home guys. Bird twirled, spun and scored on the underhand shot and evoked a pained silence. Rodman jumped over Bird and put it in. Rodman stole the ball out of Bird's hand. Rodman stole the ball a second time from Bird. The noise of appreciation shook the place. Bird scored over Rodman. The expression on Bird's face read total disdain.

The entire night they played each other in silence.

"He didn't say anything," Rodman would say later. "I wanted to say, 'Hi. Any hard feelings? I'm sorry.' But I just kept my mouth closed."

"That's history," said Isiah. "Yesterday and today is tomorrow's history."

The Pistons won this game—but all it was was a game between two hellish rivals on a December night during the regular season. The score was Detroit 128, Boston 105. A blowout. No blood, no strange stuff, just bygones being bygones. Tomorrow's history had not yet happened in this season.

During the Boston game, the Pistons announced the selected name for their new 21,000-seat basketball arena in Auburn Hills. They had held a contest to name the place and had received 75,000 entries. A committee of Metro Detroit business people picked the winning suggestion.

It was as announced in dramatically hushed tones to the 35,000 plus at the Silverdome as: "The Palace of Auburn Hills."

Living up to their rich tradition, the fans greeted the momentous announcement with thunderous boos.

The Pistons waltzed into the new year with one of the spiffiest records in the entire league. They had had a ten-game winning streak. Adrian Dantley scored 25 points or more in seven of them. The Pistons were dominant, they were mighty. On most nights.

But the weird things happened to them, too.

In their first game in January 1988, they went to Colorado to visit the Denver Nuggets, the strongest team in the Midwest Division. The Nuggets beat the Pistons, not a surprise on the road. But the score was Denver 151, Detroit 142.

The Pistons trooped aboard Roundball One for the luxury flight to Atlanta. There, a couple of nights after the Denver debacle, the Pistons lost to the Hawks. This time the score was Atlanta 81, Detroit 71. Half as many points for the Pistons in Georgia as they had scored in Colorado. With a dire result in the standings. The Pistons fell below the Hawks in the standings, back into second place.

The Pistons were nagged by that most dreaded malady—inconsistency.

Chuck Daly felt the winning streak might have had one negative reaction among the Pistons.

"It's hard because you get into such a comfort zone," Daly told Corky Meinecke. "You almost get a feeling of invincibility because you're playing so well. Then you have to go out into the real world and learn how to survive again."

And with the Pistons' ascent toward the NBA's elite, there was the shoot-'em-down factor faced by all good clubs.

"You've got these vipers out there every night," Rickey Mahorn told Meinecke. ". . . there won't be a game where we can really relax. It's going to be intense every night. It's like we're Boston or L.A. Every night somebody's coming out there to kill us."

So it was that the Indiana Pacers could rev themselves up to beat the Pistons one night; the Washington Bullets another night.

And on another night, the Lakers edged the Pistons by two before 40,278 in the Silverdome. The Pistons had the ball for the last shot with the score tied at 104. The scheme was to get it to Isiah, so he could create, as Daly and assistants Dick Versace and Ron Rothstein plotted it out. But two Lakers in their regal purple trapped Isiah, covered him, and he was forced to flip the ball to Laimbeer for the final shot. Laimbeer had to shoot from too far away. The ball rammed against the back of the rim, where the support was located. It rebounded off the iron, high. And dropped to the floor. There was a scramble for the loose ball. It was picked off by the champions in purple. The Pistons fouled. With two seconds, the Lakers broke the tie. Final, Lakers 106, Pistons 104. Defeated again, at the bitter end.

It was written: The class that separates champions from contenders is this ability to win, on a road court, in a hostile town, against a good team that is not quite good enough.

"The team of today versus the team of tomorrow," Laimbeer was told in the pain of the locker room.

Laimbeer looked up with that face that is fierce with intensity and yet, sometimes, angelic.

"We're the team of today," Billy said with an athlete's impatience. "We're just not playing like it."

"Detroit is right there," said Pat Riley, the coach of the Lakers, to the media marvels. "This is a team that feels it can win it all."

In the room, Isiah admitted to Corky Meinecke that he remained haunted by the weak pass he had made that cost the Pistons Game 5 in the playoffs the previous spring—and in the end, killed their opportunity to reach the NBA finals.

"You get only so many chances as a pro," Isiah was quoted as saying. "Think of all the guys who've played pro ball, then look at those who have a chance to compete for a championship. There's only a select few that get that opportunity. If you get that chance, you better take advantage of it."

The prophecy from Isiah!

In mid-January, the Pistons played the Chicago Bulls. Michael Jordan came driving for the basket. Rickey Mahorn came charging for Michael. The Chicago players came charging off their bench toward Mahorn. So the teams fought, the Pistons and Bulls, with clenched fists and hard shoves.

The whistle tooter called Mahorn for a flagrant foul.

Then in New York, Rod Thorn, the executive vice president of the NBA, studied the ref's report and tapes of the brawl. Thorn fined Mahorn $5,000 and suspended him for one game.

Rick Mahorn was building a reputation similar to that of his accomplice, Bill Laimbeer. Somewhere, a poet of the press romantically referred to the Pistons as bad boys. A monicker in the making.

Rod Thorn, the NBA's enforcer, would become a thorn for the Pistons. He obviously was a man lacking in sentiment. This was the same Rod Thorn, who nearly a quarter of a century earlier had been tossed into Charley Wolf's memorable fiasco of a deal that would be included in the Pistons' all-time bummers. Thorn judged his old team as harshly as any of the others. The current Pistons, not fulling versed in their club's history, theorized that another of Thorn's old jobs colored his beliefs. He was a former general manager of the Bulls, back when Michael Jordan was a rook.

But Thorn's ruling didn't bother the Pistons as much as the comments they read in the Chicago papers the next day, as they pushed off for another town. Jordan was quoted as saying the Pistons were the dirtiest team in the NBA and that they intentionally tried to hurt players on the other clubs.

Michael joined another diety of the NBA in taking his turn to condemn the Pistons for what could appear to be an overexuberant style of play. Red Auerbach, still with Celtics after all these years, had told the Boston writers that the Pistons played dirty basketball.

When the media guys asked Chuck Daly for a reaction, he riposted: "Well, Red doesn't have to worry about it any more. We've sent Billy and Rickey to charm school."

On the last weekend of January 1988, America and the world had been smothered by the weeklong hype advancing Super Bowl XXII in San Diego. The drums thumped, America's media magicians cranked out piles of copy and tons of video tape for the edification of the masses between parties—all before a football game was played.

The Friday night before Super Bowl, the Pistons played another basketball game with the Celtics in a corner of the football stadium in Pontiac. The people that night flooded out of the seats of the jerry-built basketball arena and into the two tiers of football sideline seats far away from Isiah and Bird on the court.

There was a ticket giveaway promotion that Friday night, January 29, 1988. But when the people watching the game were counted, they totalled to 61,983, almost as large as the count that would watch the Super Bowl two days later. It was the largest crowd ever to watch a pro basketball game—in fact, any sort of basketball game. And it would likely remain an NBA attendance record forever, with the Pistons evacuating the Silverdome for their own chummy Palace.

The out-of-town papers had picked up on the trashing of the Bad Boy Pistons for a perceived lack of basketball etiquette.

Out in L.A., in the *Herald-Examiner,* it was written:

"The Pistons? They lack the killer instinct."

Same town, same paper: "Dirtiest team in the NBA."

So it was amusing that Al Davis, impressario of the dark and sometimes ugly Los Angeles Raiders of football treachery, had seen something he liked in the Pistons. Davis called the Pistons the Raiders of basketball. He sent them a batch of black Raiders T-shirts, caps, and jerseys.

These new Bad Boys of basketball, they returned the respectful treatment. Their Bad Boys emblem would be the skull and crossbones— an insignia of the Raiders.

And again, Chuck Daly was on the edge. He was working the final year of his contract in 1987–88, with the negotiations dragging as they had before. McCloskey and Daly were stalemated.

Speculation flared again. One night in February, as the Pistons played in Philly against the now-in-turmoil 76ers with Dr. J retired, a banner was unfurled in the Spectrum: "BRING BACK CHUCK DALY."

The banner was yanked down. But it was known that Harold Katz, the 76ers' owner, was wild about Daly and would go after him. Katz had just fired Matt Guokas, the coach he had appointed three years earlier when the Pistons had made it impossible for Daly to skip town.

The speculation turned up, and Daly turned coy.

The Pistons were close, he had helped build the team. He had become a recognized figure in Detroit. He was begged to appear in TV commercials. The job of coaching the Detroit Pistons, once upon a time, had evoked sympathy for the unfortunate individual. Now it became a position of prominence.

Daly, dressed nattily, was now featured in TV commercials with his pal Sparky Anderson.

"I'm very happy here," Daly would say. "I haven't thought anything about it."

Sure!

The Pistons regained first place in the Central. They put on another winning streak after the All-Star break in February. They were too good for Atlanta. They could bash the Chicago Bulls at home, with 40,000 spectators behind them in the Silverdome. They could bash the Bulls on the road, in Chicago Stadium. The Bulls were a one-man attack force, Michael Jordan. But he lacked a team to play with him on his side.

At the trade deadline, Trader Jack McCloskey scored another hit. Seeking size, seeking experience, he made the deal to obtain James Edwards, the old pro and onetime third-round draft choice who had moved around the league from the Lakers, to Indiana to Cleveland to Phoenix. McCloskey gave the Suns Ron Moore, the rookie acquired just before the season from New York for Sidney Green. To make the trade sweet enough for Phoenix, McCloskey tossed in an always available second-round draft choice, this one for use in 1991—three years in the future. The Pistons had Buddah for the bench now, for the playoffs.

In mid-March, the Pistons licked the Sacramento Kings in the Silverdome. It was the sixteenth successive victory on their home court. The objective now was to win more than 50 games for the season, gain the homecourt advantage in as many playoff rounds as possible, try to gain the edge over the Celtics at playoff time.

The Boston Garden continued to spook the Pistons. They had learned to manhandle the Celtics at home. They could almost handle the Celtics in Boston Garden. But not quite, not yet. They had lost twice more during this season in Boston.

"The home court is such a factor if you get to the finals," Daly said on this night in the middle of March, with a month left in the schedule. "Right now we're one game down to Boston in the loss column—and they're better and deeper than last year."

Daly, on this night, had hit the arena in a black Fedora, brimmed tipped over the eyes, and a black coat, the collar upturned around the neck. Very dapper. Very sinister. The style of a hit man from Las Vegas.

The odds on the Pistons bumping off the Celtics, bumping off the Lakers, becoming the NBA champs?

"No, no," protested Daly, "I'm not an oddsmaker."

But then . . .

"I think it's feasible," Daly said. The prince of pessimism, he apparently had been drugged with truth serum. "I think this club this year is a little bit better than the club last year. Particularly on defense, and the bench.

"But in reality the bench and depth are not so important in the playoffs, because you go to the iron more. In other words, you play your regulars more."

The serum had worn off fast.

"But," said Daly, "this year there are more minefields. The sixth, seventh, eighth teams are more dangerous. A la Cleveland, Philadelphia, Washington, New York, Indiana, that's your first-round opponent . . .

"The ultimate problem is . . . You have to go through Boston and Los Angeles, which have been there, champions, seven of the last eight years.

"We've reached a peak or a challenging position. I was surprised last year that we reached the position to go to the finals—a little earlier than expected."

The Pistons were geared. They were aiming, rolling, a team on a mission, happy now and proud, unshakable in their belief.

And then, in the last days of March, they were shaken.

Excerpts from a column by Jerry Green in the *Detroit News,* March 31, 1988:

William Bedford was suspended late in the 1988 season.

Len Bias, dead. Drugs.

Chris Washburn, rehabilitation. Drugs.

Roy Tarpley, rehabilitation. Drugs.

William Bedford, rehabilitation. Drugs.

It's plain scary.

These men were the cream of the NBA college draft two years ago. They were four of the first seven athletes picked off the board.

One by one they fell. They collapsed in front of the availability and lure of drugs. Abusers. They did it to themselves.

Bias went to his death a day or two after the Celtics drafted him out of Maryland. He had been a college legend. A hero. And he died too young, a terrible tragedy.

Then, it was believed, Bias' death would not be totally in vain, not the complete waste of a human life. He would be remembered as an example to his fellow basketball athletes. They would remember that he died doing drugs and they would resist the temptations.

"Imagine you love chocolate," Chuck Daly said Wednesday when the shock of Bedford's problem struck the Pistons. "You have to give up chocolate forever."

It's tough. Chocolate is not cocaine; an overdose of chocolate does not kill. But Daly's analogy illustrates the point: the human being is weak. He succumbs to his desires. He ignores the consequences.

Chris Washburn, then Roy Tarpley, now William Bedford in the trail of Bias.

It's scary.

It's so scary because these are young men, just beginning to live their lives, play their careers. It's scary mostly because this drug situation for basketball does not start in the NBA for most of them. These were college players two years ago . . . It starts in the high school gyms and on the playgrounds.

In the NBA, it is magnified. One after another they go—Micheal Ray Richardson, Orlando Woolridge, the cream of '86. Now William Bedford of Detroit . . .

"I saw it coming," Dennis Rodman said Wednesday noontime of William Bedford's case.

Rodman is Bedford's closest friend on the Pistons.

"I saw it coming, but I didn't want to realize that," Rodman said. "We kind of ran together.

"I told him if he had any kind of problem, he's got to come forth with it.

"He has some childish ways. He wanted to do this, do that. Buy this, buy that.

"He's like a kid who'd never grown up. He'd like to buy things. Like Walkmans, radio. Other things."

And drugs.

How does it happen? William Bedford just turned 24, with a wife and a baby. Why?

"It's tough because you got a lot of money," Rodman said. "You got to discipline yourself. The biggest challenge for me was to realize I got all this money, coming off the street."

The Pistons were jocular in their Wednesday shootaround. Bill Laimbeer laughed. John Salley grinned and flipped a ball over his head and threw his arms out. "Relax man," he joked to teammates.

Isiah Thomas could evoke no feeling of pity or sorrow for Bedford, although he said Bedford should be retained in the team family. The job is to win games, Thomas said, a championship for Detroit.

"We needed a focal point anyway," said Daly . . . "We just dropped two games. We need a focal point."

Len Bias is dead from doing drugs. He died nearly two years ago.

Still, nobody can believe the message.

With a focal point, the Pistons played on. Fighting for first place, the Pistons went into Atlanta in early April. Rickey Mahorn got into it again with the Hawks. He elbowed Randy Wittman. The Bad Boy. Then Mahorn shoved Tree Rollins and got into a fight with Cliff Levingston. The brawl unsettled the Hawks and the Pistons thrived. They won the game, fended off the Hawks in the contest for first, and carried on.

The final week of the regular seasons they defeated the Washington Bullets on the road, with Adrian Dantley scoring 31 points. It was the fifty-third victory of the season for the Pistons—breaking the standard for total victories for the franchise. They would win one more game, finish with a 54-and 28 season record.

And for the first time ever, this Detroit franchise won a division title, finished in first place. The Pistons celebrated their finish with a champagne bash. Splashing it on each other, kids reverting to the sandbox.

They won the Central Division by four games over Atlanta and Chicago. Their attendance soared again in their final season at the Silverdome, averaging 26,012 attendees over the season. For the first time in the forty-odd years since some rich visionaries had established a pro basketball league, a team drew more than one million fans over a season. The finally first-place Pistons . . . in the town that the NBA once wished it could abandon.

But first place now was merely a stepping stone to the higher aspirations of this ballclub. The people of Detroit, after all, had this longtime playoff mentality. But now reaching the playoffs was no longer suitable. The NBA finals had become the objective. It translated into crushing the Curse—the Boston Celtics and the mastery they had retained through the ages over the Pistons. It meant the Pistons must win a basketball game in the Boston Garden, where they had been haunted. With their playoff misdeeds, the weak pass-in and the cracking of heads, included, the Pistons had been beaten in twenty-one consecutive games in the musty old Garden.

The Pistons had failed in their season-long quest for the precious homecourt advantage in the serious portion of the playoffs. Though the Pistons had finished first—and that certainly merited a banner hanging from the rafters to proclaim the deed—the Celtics and Lakers also had finished first in their divisions. And the Celtics and Lakers had won more games than the Pistons, the decisive factor in earning the homecourt advantage.

But before Boston, the Pistons had the certain preliminaries to take care of—two playoff series with other, lesser, clubs.

The Pistons drew Washington in the first round, the best-of-five elimination. The prior April the Pistons had blown out the Bullets in a three-game sweep. Hah!

Bill Laimbeer reached into his locker to get dressed after practice on the day before the playoffs started.

"I wore my Raiders sweater," Laimbeer said. With pride.

The comparision between the teams, the Raiders and Pistons, had taken hold on America's mass media. The Pistons' image on national TV and in the slick magazines was characterized as being the same as the Raiders'. The assassins. The thugs. The clubbers.

"It was fun at the time," Laimbeer said. "A joke. But there was so much adverse publicity because the media were getting carried away.

"In Milwaukee, the paper had a headline about me: Pistons' Prince of Darkness" . . .

"Of the court, I'm a completely different person, I like to think. I don't think I'm an intimidator. I think I'm a professional basketball player who goes about his job. I don't get into fights. If you see me in an altercation, it's because the other guy is swinging at me."

The stereo blared through the locker room, rapping out the words and music. It should have been a trio of fiddles, because there stood that famous pacifist, Bill Laimbeer.

The Pistons played rusty and rotten in their first game of the playoffs. They were up against a team that had finished with a 38-and-44 record during the regular season. All that distinguished the Bullets from any other loser was that they possessed the tallest and shortest benchwarmers in the league—Manute Bol, 7-feet-6, who had prepped on the searing desert of Africa's The Sudan, and Tyrone Bogues, 5-feet-4 out of the heart of Baltimore.

They finally won it, at home, the Pistons did, after playing three quarters of flat basketball. They lacked drive, fire, intensity. They were drab, dull, plumb awful. Times were the Pistons clunked five shots in succession.

The difference was the Pistons had Isiah in the clutch. He got himself 14 points in the fourth-quarter rally, 34 for the game. The Pistons won it, 96–87.

"That's what superstars are all about," said Daly.

In Game 2, the Pistons were flat-out lethargic again. For the second time, at home, they played on the edge, touched it—and escaped. This time, the Pistons got away with a one-point victory, 102–101. The Bullets, the team with the sub-.500 record, led these would-be champs by a point with sixteen seconds to play. The Pistons were rescued by a bank shot off the glass by—of course, Isiah, to win it. Win it, only after Washington's Jeff Malone missed his final shot.

"Getting one more win against them, it could be murder," Daly said. "World War III!"

Daly was prone to exaggerations. You could not be sure if he meant it. But he was right.

The Pistons did not win Game 3. The series had switched to the Bullets' homecourt in the Capital Centre in Landover. Again the Pistons played without passion. The score was tied with nineteen seconds, the Pistons had the ball. But this time they were unable to work it to Isiah for another game-winning shot. Joe Dumars had it. He wanted to get rid of it. He couldn't. The Bullets ganged up on Isiah. They wanted Du-

mars to take the shot. Joe had been missing in Games 1 and 2 back home. In Game 2, he had connected on only two of eleven. Dumars was forced to take the final shot with two seconds left, from behind the free throw line. The ball struck iron and bounded away. Joe was two for twelve. The Bullets won it in overtime, on Jeff Malone's deadeye shooting, 114–106.

Between Games 3 and 4, Chuck Daly was busy. He was still hogtied in his contract negotiations. His contract was expiring, at the end of May, in less than a month. If the Pistons did manage to play into June, against the Celtics, then advance to the finals, Chuck would technically be coaching without a contract, though his paychecks would continue. And while the Pistons were bivouacked in Maryland, struggling against the Bullets, Daly lost his leverage.

Unable to wait, the 76ers hired a coach. They signed Jim Lynam, who had been the interim coach after Guokas got the Philly version of the ziggy, for three seasons.

Chuck Daly would have to work out something with the Pistons, if he wanted to remain in coaching. The strain of the playoffs, at age fifty-eight, gave him some fleeting thoughts about becoming a general manager on some club, somewhere.

The Pistons did not win Game 4, either, on the Washington court.

The year before, when the Pistons had eliminated the Bullets in a three-game sweep in the first round of the playoffs, Moses Malone had castigated his teammates for quitting. Moses had migrated from club to club through his NBA career, after the Pistons had skipped him over in the dispersal draft of the folding American Basketball Association more than a decade earlier.

He was now thirty-three years old, in the thirteenth year of a marvelous pro career that had begun when he was nineteen and fresh out of high school. He had won the NBA's MVP award three times and had been on a championship club in Philly.

Now, it was felt, he was staging a last hurrah in these playoffs for the Washington Bullets. And in this Game 4, he called it all back—and because of him the Pistons were dispatched into a trauma, full fright.

In the final sixty-five seconds, Moses twice shot his jumpshot, the ball propelled toward the basket low and flat, without an arch to it. And twice he connected. That was the difference as the Bullets handed it to the Pistons again, 106–103. This time the Pistons squandered a four-point lead in the last two and a half minutes. Laimbeer lost a ball. Isiah traveled. Rodman misfired a pass. Mahorn committed a foul.

The Pistons had entered the playoffs with too much swagger. Daly had seen it. It was noticeable in their carriage, their manner. They had a divisional first-place banner among their souvenirs. How many teams have ever celebrated with a champagne-spraying bash after winning just a division? The Pistons hadn't been thinking about the Bullets. They were thinking about the Celtics. The Lakers. The Bullets had come in with their pride. Nothing more.

And the Pistons had been taken to the limit, to Game 5, by a team with a fourth-place record of six more losses than victories.

Game 5 was on a Sunday afternoon, starting time 3:30, as selected by CBS. It could have been doomsday for the Pistons.

Before the game, Daly went to Laimbeer. Their conversation was brief. Coach and player. Through the years they had had heated conversations, shouted at each other in the midst of playoff games. Angry, cursing, emotional.

This time Daly said, softly: "Bill, why aren't we as passionate as we should be. I don't see the passion of last year."

Laimbeer gave Daly his perplexed schoolboy look.

"I don't know," he said.

Laimbeer related the conversation after Game 5.

The Pistons won it. They clubbed the Bullets, 99–78. Rodman burned up the Bullets in the fourth quarter, waving his arm in triumph, scoring 12 points.

"It's emotion," Laimbeer said, hardly audible below the blaring music of the amplifiers in he locker room. "This was how we played last year. We brought our intensity level to what it should be. It wasn't there the first four games . . .

"Before the game, Chuck had a meeting and said, 'get the ball to Bill early.' Hype the emotion."

Laimbeer came out pop-eyed and crazy. He was jumping, his face blazed with emotion. He paced, as though caged, during the long TV-caused delay before the game. When the game at last began, Laimbeer popped.

He went pop and scored from the outside. He went pop again and scored his second basket from outside. The Pistons were off. Laimbeer held off Moses Malone. Dumars, on defense, took away Jeff Malone's shooting eye—and rediscovered his own.

"What a relief to have this series over," Laimbeer said. "The media painted it as an easy series for us."

You wondered in retrospect how a quality team, a team of pride and passion, a team with championship pretentions, could tumble into such a predicament. How could it deliver dull, uninspired performances in the playoffs? Right here, you found what separated the Pistons from the Celtics. The Pistons from the Lakers. The teams the Pistons boasted they're good enough to challenge. Those teams always excel. Those teams could bring fire out of the Pistons. But it stayed a mystery why the Pistons struggled with the Bullets in a lollipop series. Daly was unable to explain it. Laimbeer couldn't. So it would remain a concern.

"A lot of good things came out of this series," said Laimbeer. "This series taught us every game is tough."

Escape-artist Chuck Daly already knew that.

"Long live Laimbeer," said Daly.

No doomsday for the Pistons. They survived, to go onward in the playoffs—against Michael Jordan and his Chicago Bulls.

The Pistons and Bulls had not played each other in the playoffs since Dave Bing's misfired inbounds pass in the seventh game in 1974. Now the Pistons were a quality team with a chance to reach the NBA finals. And the Bulls were a team with one quality player and a group of young accomplices. Michael Jordan had become the newest marvel with a one-name identification.

Michael was there with Kareem and Magic and Bird, and, yes, Isiah. He was finishing his fourth season. And for two seasons now, he was the NBA's scoring champion. In 1987–88, he had averaged 35 points per game, his tongue sticking out in an affectation, driving the line, the baseline, halting, jumping, switching shooting hands in midflight. He was truly miraculous. But he played with a young surrounding cast, players not yet ready to take on the championship team

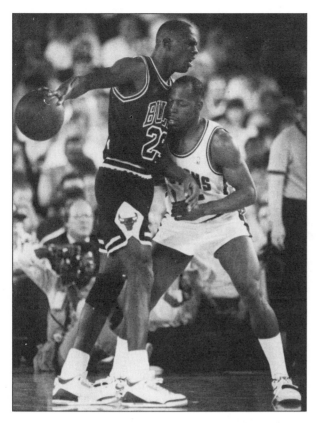

V.J. plays tight D on M.J.

challenge. Two of the guys were rookies, Scottie Pippen and Horace Grant. John Paxson was a light scoring guard.

As a team, the Bulls had won fifty games. But they had not been tournament tested.

There was one subplot. Isiah and Michael did not care for each other. Three years earlier, according to *Sports Illustrated*, Isiah had concocted a plan to keep the ball out of Michael's hands at the NBA All-Star Game. The idea was to show up Jordan, then a rookie. Magic Johnson, Isiah's friend, was on the other team, but he sanctioned the plan, *SI* reported.

Michael never cared much for Isiah after the incident.

The Bulls just were not prepared to handle the Pistons under playoff conditions in the best-of-seven series. The Pistons drilled the Bulls in five games. They split the first two games in Detroit, the Pistons winning Game 1 by a 93–82 score, then the Bulls won Game 2 in the Silverdome 105–95. With the series switched to Chicago Stadium in Isiah's boyhood neighborhood, the Pistons won Games 3 and 4 by blow-out tallies

of 101–79 and 96–77. Back home the Pistons finished off the Bulls, 102–95, in Game 5.

The Pistons' passion was back.

They had reached the Eastern Conference finals. Boston again, if the Celtics could miraculously overhaul the Atlanta Hawks.

The Celtics then went into their typical plucky playoff mode. They won games in their own fashion, winning after they seemed to be beaten. Twice they were on the brink of elimination in their series with the Hawks. They had been down three victories to two. Then they beat the Hawks by two points on the road, in Atlanta, in Game 6. And then back in the Boston Garden, they survived again against the Hawks by two points again while the Pistons, already conquerors of the Bulls, were waiting for them.

And now the Pistons headed toward the series they had spent a year preparing for.

They had failed in their season-long objective to win more games than the Celtics and, thus, obtain the odd-game for the Silverdome—the precious homecourt advantage.

If, if, the Pistons were to kill the Curse of the Celtics at last they would be forced to win a game in the Boston Garden, with the building vibrating from the rattle of the departing trains. The Pistons had lost every of the twenty-one games they'd played there, since 1982.

Larry Bird delivered his customary speech about the Pistons the day before the series opened. Headlines!

"I sort of like the way they play," Bird told reporters, "but it's the stuff the league lets happen—the fouls after the whistle and the way they try to get in their little cheap shots. If they can take someone out, they take you out. The league likes that stuff because it's good press and creates an image for a team . . . But I can't blame them. If you can get away with it, do it.

"I don't expect them to be any different this time. But if things get out of control, we'll just have Parish blindside them and that'll end that . . . we can handle it ourselves."

And there was a message for Laimbeer as he arrived to play in the city of his birth.

"Personally, I don't like him," Bird told the reporters.

On the night of May 25, 1988, the Pistons beat the Celtics on the parquet woodwork of the Boston Garden. The score was 104–96. Isiah Thomas scored 35 points for the winners, including two three-point plays during crunch time of the fourth quarter. Bill Laimbeer, who had played in 646 regular-season games, injured his shoulder and was forced from the game, thus becoming listed as doubtful for future games. In victory, the Pistons took a one to nil lead in the NBA Eastern Conference finals and claimed the luxury of the homecourt advantage in the seven-game series. It was the first time that the Pistons had won in the Garden since 1982.

Those were the plain facts.

Emotionally, the victory was an exuberant experience for the Pistons. Haunted for years by the Celtics, particularly after the horrors of the playoffs one year earlier, the Pistons had put a visible crack in the Curse of the Celtics.

Chuck Daly sought to temper the mood with reality.

"Boston really looked tired," he told the writers. "It looked like Atlanta took a lot out of them.

"Let's not forget that it's a seven-game series."

Game 2 went one night later, no rest for the wicked, er, the Celtics.

The doubtful Bill Laimbeer did play, because of the miracles of modern medicine—or guts.

"You know me," Laimbeer told the *News'* Cocky Meinecke. "And winning stops a lot of pain."

The Pistons lost Game 2, almost in the old, haunting deja vu manner. The Celtics won it, 119–115, in double overtime. They won it with a break on a call from the officials. But the Pistons allowed it to escape.

"We were awesomely lucky," K.C. Jones, the Celtics' coach, admitted to the press.

For the first time, there was open disenchantment among the Pistons with Adrian Dantley. And Dantley himself had become disenchanted with the Pistons, complaining of a shortage of playing minutes in the playoffs.

But in this Game 2, the one-time NBA scoring champ, missed a free throw with eleven seconds left. Thus, regulation ended with the score tied, at 102. In the second OT session, Adrian would miss two more free throws when the score was tied at 113.

What cost the Pistons, though, was the three-pointer that Kevin McHale scored with his black sneaker implanted on the three-point line. The shot came with seven seconds remaining in the first overtime. Seconds earlier, Isiah had shot a legitimate three-pointer to put the Pistons up by three, 109–106.

The three officials gathered in caucus to discuss the validity of McHale's desperation launch. They decided they did not see his foot on the line and gave Boston the three points. Thus, the game was tied again after the first OT and permitted to continue into the second OT.

So the Pistons returned home, losers of Game 2, for Games 3 and 4 at the Silverdome. They had the edge in the series, and they had also established a mini-curse over the Celtics in their own building. The Pistons had licked the Celtics eight straight at the Silverdome.

But even with this edge, the Pistons continued to squawk about the ruling in Boston.

Ron Rothstein, the assistant coach, was the bag man. He showed up in Daly's office lugging a black satchel. He unzipped the bag and dug out two video tapes.

"Wait till you see TBS," Rothstein said to Daly and Dick Versace, who stood by, a full-of-ears listener.

Daly sat back to watch. Rothstein plugged the tape into the machine. He flipped the switch. The machine whirred, the tape went through it, a series of pictures emerged.

McHale had the basketball. He stepped backward with it. Then he shot it—a flat, ugly prayer of a shot with his team three points behind. The ball went swish. McHale raised both arms upward in the three-pointer signal.

In the next scene, three confounded officials were in heated discussion.

"Geez," said Versace.

The Pistons had been robbed in Game 2. The pictures showed, graphically, that the toe of McHale's black sneaker was on the line. The basket for which he was credited with three points was worth only two.

"Can't do a thing about it," said Daly. "There are no TV replays in this league. It's spilled milk."

In Game 3, the Pistons were ahead by fourteen points in the third quarter. The Celtics then made their move—and the lead was sliced to twelve, to ten, to eight. Larry Bird twirled a shot with a tremendously high arc. The lead was now six.

There was fear on the Detroit bench. You could see it gripping them. Just those flashes of strain, of worry—the sweat, that sense of history.

The Celtics were charging. How they could charge! Sixteen world championships, a million comebacks, a thousand miracles. Cousy and Havlicek and Russell and Bird. They choked the enemy with heroic tradition.

Time for panic? No, no—time for the journeyman to the rescue.

James Edwards shoved back history on this Saturday afternoon in late May 1988 in the Silverdome. He thwarted tradition. Edwards, chomping his gum, anger in eyes, his Fu Manchu bristling with ferocity, hoisted the Pistons and rescued them in this moment of fear and peril. He scored four baskets in the last four minutes of the period. He delivered the Pistons back to safety. Back to their comfort zone.

It was precisely his role, the reason Jack McCloskey had traded for him three months earlier.

The Pistons won Game 3 by a 98–94 score and again went in front in these finals. They had now twice defeated this rival that strikes them with horror and envy. And afterward, James Edwards, the one-time third-round draft choice, the one-time backup to Kareem, the guy with four other clubs in his touring book, said in a storybook statement:

"This is my once-in-a-lifetime chance. I've been in the league eleven years, and it's winding down for me. This is my chance to get my championship ring."

There was a crowd of reporters around Edwards, and he was asked how he learned that he'd been traded from Phoenix, a rinky-dink ballclub with a nasty past and a vague future.

Edwards was at home, he said.

"I was playing Nintendo," Edwards said. "A video game."

The phone rang.

"You've been traded," the voice told him. A pause. "To Detroit."

Edwards packed and rushed to the airport. He was familiar with the routine.

In the other room, Larry Bird told the media: "The difference between this year and last? They got James Edwards. He can make instant offense for them."

Baseball had been Detroit's tradition-rich sport since the first years of the century, since Ty Cobb. The Tigers had won their pennants, played in their World Series, and in the spring of 1988, they were defenders of the American League East title.

So a funny thing happened at the Detroit ballpark on the nights the Pistons were involved in their playoff games with the Celtics. The Detroit ballplayers, during their baseball games, would slip out of the dugout. They would slink up the runway to the clubhouse. They would go up there on a pretense, for a cup of coffee or on a trip to the . . . But the real reason was that the Pistons were on TV.

Their own team was out on the ballfield playing and here were these bench players cheering around the clubhouse set.

And after the baseball games, the ballplayers would stand in the middle of the clubhouse, alternately cheering and groaning as the baskets were scored in the Pistons versus the Celtics. They'd be wrapped in towels or standing stark naked. And there was Sparky Anderson, the great baseball manager, looking up and second-guessing his colleague, Chuck Daly: "He should have . . ."

The cult sport of pro basketball had captured all segments of Detroit society.

But the mentality of the Detroit fan sometimes dipped to the obscene or the obnoxious or the uncouth. A guy behind the basket at the Silverdome unfurled a bedsheet banner in Larry Bird's face: "I hate Boston."

The guy in the front row dangled a Leprechaun tied at the throat to a noose. It was a cute toy, if it was meant to be a toy.

The crude. The rude. The lewd. The basketball playoffs were bringing out the worst of Detroit, I wrote in the *News*. The games were intense, bloody, hectic. They were bits of theater, of individuals performing with heroism. The rivalry between the Pistons and Celtics had turned into competition unmatched in any sports. It was tight and emotional . . . a war between teams, sometimes with knuckles, elbows, knees, rhetoric.

But it had seeped off the edges of the basketball court. It had slipped beyond sportsmanship and into the area of bitter hatred. It had brought out public vulgarity.

The Boston Celtics were a team in decline. But they were a team with a rich, wonderful heritage. The Celtics were hooked eternally into the history of all sports. And I felt Detroit was starting to ridicule the Celtics. There was a lack of proper respect, proper admiration.

The Pistons themselves showed this respect. Chuck Daly showed it. He presented an analogy—of death and the plight of the Celtics. How death came, and you saw the victim die, and you saw the victim buried—and after the funeral you wondered how the victim would return to get you.

That was respect and admiration.

Chuck had another analogy. "The Celtics are like a snake," he said. "You kill it in the morning. But it's still twitching at sundown. You got to chop its head off."

But then Chuck Daly, once upon a time, lived in Boston when he coached Boston College. He was able to appreciate the wonderful cultural and historical offerings of that city. The pro basketball team, included.

The Pistons played Game 4 in a funk. They could muster only ten points in the first quarter. Again their motivation had vanished. In one sequence over more than ten minutes of the first half, the Pistons missed twenty shots in succession. They were the team that couldn't shoot straight. And in the end, it would beat the Pistons.

They were behind by ten at halftime, and then rallied. They went into the fourth quarter with an eight-point lead. It seemed they had played themselves out of their funk. Then they took another pratfall. They reverted to their first-quarter inaccuracies, and again they were held to ten points for the period. They didn't shoot straight again, on the last shot, that might have won it. Joe Dumars shot and as the ball ap-

Dennis Rodman and Fred Roberts get tangled up in Game 4 of the 1988 Conference finals.

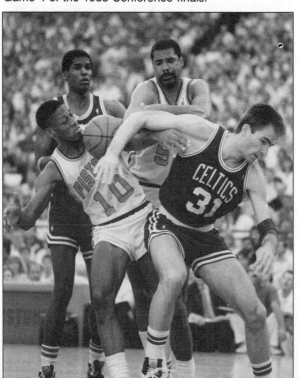

proached the hoop, Robert Parish jumped with his hand extended in the air. There were several versions of what happened.

But the verdict was the Pistons lost 79–78 in Game 4. The series was square at two victories for each club—and the Celtics had recaptured that invaluable homecourt advantage with the series returning to Boston Garden and all its mystique for Game 5.

Daly's snake was twitching.

Afterwards, the Pistons were loud and cranky. They used the TV replays from all angles to show that something rotten was happening to the Pistons. Game 4 went in dispute and controversy, just as Game 2 did. The Pistons claimed goaltending. And the replays showed the play over the final eight seconds—Isiah passing to Laimbeer passing to Dumars; Joe shooting, the ball touching metal, and Parish's fingers poking the netting of the basket. Vintage goaltending, perhaps. But those dastardly referees ruled no, not goaltending, and explained that Dumar's shot had no chance of going in. Thus, no goaltending.

"To beat the Celtics," Isiah said in his corner of the quiet locker room, "you have to beat more than a basketball team. You have to beat a mindset. The Celtics aren't supposed to lose. And everybody thinks that.

"Anybody *human* thinks that."

Daly's contractual stalemate continued, and his contract actually expired between Games 4 and 5. Some of those in the media picked up on it and wept that Daly was a coach without a contract with the playoffs on—and shame on the Pistons, shame on Jack McCloskey for being so cruel. Negotiations had even been halted.

It made a good story, sympathetic to Daly. But nobody bothered to check . . . but if they had, Daly could have told them it was his idea to suspend the contract negotiations until after the season so as not to distract him from his job of coaching his team.

It all made sense.

The Pistons' funk continued into Game 5. They were flat, dead, disinterested. The Celtics dominated the first half. They lead by fourteen at the break. Early in the third quarter, Parish scored and put the Celtics ahead, 56–40. Sixteen points, in the horror chamber of the Boston Garden.

Chuck Daly gave up stomping the floor in front of the bench. He sat down and crossed his arms. To wait and watch the fadeout of a dream that lasted a year, then when it seemed to be coming true had . . .

Then Dantley started scoring. Isiah started hitting. The Pistons were slicing into the huge Boston bulge. By the end of the third quarter, they had cut it to a five-point deficit, 70-65. Then at the start of the fourth quarter, they scored ten points while the Celtics went blank. The Pistons had taken the lead, 75-70. The Celtics rallied again. And at the end of four quarters, they were even. deadlocked, 92-92.

The Pistons blew the Celtics out in overtime. Dantley put the Pistons ahead to stay on a three-pointer. Thomas added to the lead with four points, his last scoring on a 35-point night. The Pistons won it, 102-96. They had won a second playoff game in the Boston Garden. They had put themselves to the edge of the NBA finals for the first time, one victory away.

And they would play Game 6 back at the Silverdome, home.

"I took off my coaching hat and became a cheerleader tonight," Daly told his postgame media klatch. "I turned the clipboard over and said, 'I'm nothing but a cheerleader.' And that's the way it's going to be from here on out . . .

"We have one game to win, which is absolutely the biggest game in the history of the franchise."

Roundball One was buzzing with the Pistons aboard, on the trip from Boston back to Detroit in the dark of night after Game 5. The Pistons had won and were flying home with the joy of being so close to accomplishment.

"It was a white-knuckler," Ron Rothstein would recall later. "The plane was bouncing. There was lightning."

Then he said: "They never let you win easy, do they?"

Bill Laimbeer arrived in the Pistons' locker room on the evening of Game 6 lugging an article smuggled in his bag. He showed it to some of his teammates and the early press pests. They laughed at Laimbeer's searing symbolism. Laimbeer went off to Mike Abdenour's training retreat with fiercely smug expression on his face.

In the room, by his locker, Isiah assessed the impact of the game.

"I've never played in a game as big as this one," he told the *News'* Corky Meinecke. "And I don't know how I'm going to respond. Every step is a new step for me.

"We haven't cleared the hurdle, but we've made the jump. And we're high enough in the air to know we can get over it."

"If we can't win it now, we don't deserve to," Daly, never brimmed over with optimism, told the press.

The date was June 4, 1988. A Friday night. The Pistons were on the edge of where they'd never reached before. A mob of 38,912 —including true fan Bob Seger, the rocker—came out to cheer them along.

Boston, carried by its pride, went off strongly. The Celtics had played through the series with mystifying loss of their shooting accuracy. They had a bunch of injuries; Bird was playing hurt, he had trouble with his shooting eye, too. Parish had a bum knee along with his inborn scowl. Only Kevin McHale had been hitting for the Celts. And he proudly carried his team.

But McHale could not do it alone.

And the Pistons blew open the game in the third quarter, as the crowd started its craziness.

Dumars tries to fight through a Robert Parish pick. (*K. Dozier*)

Adrian Dantley exhorts the crowd after scoring two against the Celtics.

The Pistons went up by seventeen. Then that old pride stirred the Celtics into a rally. They had been champions; they had been to the NBA finals for the past four years; they had the richest tradition in pro basketball, the eminence. They refused to fold before this upstart team from Detroit, with the reputation of playing basketball while lacking basketball etiquette.

The Celtics slashed the Pistons' lead by ten points, to seven in a gasp in the fourth quarter. But by then only a last minute remained. And the Celtics still fought. But it was too late.

The Pistons won it, and before it was officially ended, the fans clambered from the grandstands and flooded the court and danced and cheered and jumped. The Pistons were headed for the NBA finals, finally, after thirty-one seasons in town . . . after decades of ineptitude.

The guards had to battle the fans off the court so the game could be played to its end. Then Adrian Dantley flipped in a free throw with three seconds left. The final score was Detroit 95, Boston 90.

The Curse of the Celtics was done. The head had been sliced off the wiggling snake. The hurdle had been jumped. All the metaphors that go with victory had been conquered.

The fans stormed the court again to resume their joyous dancing. They climbed the backboards and rolled over the basket stanchions.

Out of this chaotic scene, there were certain scenes visible to the deadline-pressed journalists who were smashing away at keyboards near midnight.

Kevin McHale came running down the court to the bench, where the Pistons themselves celebrated. He grasped Isiah Thomas' hand in congratulations, and then whispered, as revealed in Isiah's own book:

"Zeke, don't be happy just getting to the finals, go out there and win it."

A different scene had occurred in the last minute. A bunch of the Celtics evacuated the bench and headed for the locker room, early, so they could avoid congratulating the Pistons and witnessing the celebration.

"That's when I knew we had it, when they were leaving the court," Isiah said of the Celtics' flight.

"I don't like the Detroit Pistons, that's all," Danny Ainge told the *News'* Bill Halls when asked his rooting interests in the finals . . . I cannot root for them."

And Larry Bird told the writers of the projected finals: "If the Pistons are allowed to hold, grab and push James Worthy like they did me, it will be to their advantage. If the Lakers go out and run, I can't see it being much of a series."

But as the Pistons tried to remain composed amid the jubilation of the mobs who somehow crashed their locker room, they were not certain which team they'd play in the NBA finals. The Lakers and Dallas Mavericks still had not finished the business of the Western Conference final series. They had a meeting the following afternoon to determine an opponent for the Pistons.

In the locker room, strangers taunted the media people.

"Well, what do you think of the Pistons now?" a leering guy with some age on him in a Pistons' T-shirt snapped at me, a reformed critic.

"Wonderful," I said. "Only took them thirty-one years."

And I shoved as close as I could to Laimbeer's locker to wait for him to speak and display what he had brought with him hidden in his bag.

Excerpts from a column in the *Detroit News*, by Jerry Green, June 4, 1988:

Bill Laimbeer arrived lugging a sickle in his equipment bag.

"Where's that snake?" he said. He waved the crescent shaped piece of sharp metal. His eyes were ablaze.

In one swish, Laimbeer sliced up the tension that had been gripping the Pistons on this night of nights.

The snake is dead. The Boston Celtics are dead. Killed Friday night, not by the sickle—but the hammer.

It was Chuck Daly's graphic imagination that produced the snake, the locker room joke . . . "You got to chop it's head off."

Well, the Pistons bludgeoned the head off the snaky Celtics, 95-90. And even then, right down to the very end, the Celtics snapped and twisted . . .

"I was worried we'd be like Milwaukee," Laimbeer said. "Bang on the door, bang on the door, lose to Boston. Like Milwaukee lost to Boston all those years when I first got here, and then the one year they beat Boston, they lost to Philly. I was afraid of that."

. . . it has happened so often, the downtrodden team, the struggler, the team that has banged on the door for eternity is just happy to be there. Delighted to reach the championship round. The mission over, then these newcomers fizzle.—their grins intact.

"That's not us," said Laimbeer. "Not us. We're mentally tough. We know how to play basketball. And beyond that, we're professional. Like Vinnie Johnson."

. . . Friday night was the clincher but the Pistons were psyched by the Celtics until that Game 5 in Boston.

"Yes and no," said Bill Laimbeer.

"Yes, the Boston Celtics had us talking to ourselves.

"No, we knew we could do it. We had that mental toughness. We knew we could beat them. We just had to do it."

Laimbeer got up from his locker, sickle still in his bag. He walked across the locker room, through the crowd. He walked to where Isiah sits in the corner.

Spider Salley does the "We Beat Boston Boogie" after the Pistons beat the Celtics in the Conference finals in 1988.

"What'd I tell you two months ago?" Laimbeer said, his voice loud.

Isiah responded softly. "Destiny," he said.

The morning after, Isiah awakened. For a moment he wondered. Then he bolted from his bed. He bolted for the front door. He stopped. He smiled.

"I woke up and ran to the mailbox," he said. "I had to check the papers to see if we won. I wanted to make sure I wasn't dreaming."

One dream had come true, confirmed by the papers and their World War II headlines. The Pistons were certified as the new conquerors.

"FINALLY," the *News* said on the front page, and it was true.

"You can talk about the greatest players," Isiah said. "But the winners are those who advanced their team to the championship. The key is getting to this championship.

"You can talk about Wilt Chamberlain and Bill Russell, and you say Bill Russell is the best because he won the most championships. Wilt had the best statistics."

"Like Michael Jordan?" I said to Isiah.

"The very best player," said Isiah. The dart had landed. Michael Jordan and the Bulls had been defeated in five playoff games by the new conquerors.

"We beat the Celtics," Isiah went on. "Nobody beat Larry Bird, Kevin McHale, Robert Parish, Danny Ainge, Dennis Johnson. We beat their tradition and the hardest thing we had to beat was the mindset of the Celtics."

Then he mentioned his contract. Daly wasn't the only figure with contract talks suspended as the Pistons went to the finals. Isiah was aiming to join Bird and Magic in the $2 million to $3 million dollar category. His longterm contract had become obsolete at $750,000 per season.

"The Pistons have decided to do something about it," Isiah said. "Since I am a bit underpaid."

That afternoon the Lakers, the reigning champions, won their Game 7 of the Western Conference finals over the Mavericks, 117–102. L.A. would be seeking NBA championships, back-to-back, against the Pistons. Magic versus Isiah!

They were the closest of friends, Magic Johnson and Isiah Thomas. Magic had named a room in his mansion in Bel Air "The Isiah Thomas Suite." Whenever Isiah went to California for reasons other than basketball, he stayed at Magic's house. In his own bedroom. Isiah left a California wardrobe in his closet to wear when he was there.

And often when Magic returned to his roots in Michigan, he would stay at Isiah's place. Magic was always agreeable to participation in Isiah's charity games.

"It's been a fantasy of ours for years, playing each other for all the marbles," Magic told the late Shelby Strother of the *News*. "Now, it's reality. Head to head. The marbles, the chips. The money."

And then Isiah told Strother: "I've seen every championship series since I've been in the league. I wanted to learn what it took to be a champion. I observed."

The previous six years since he'd entered the NBA, Isiah had a spectator watching Magic and the Lakers play the finals five times.

"Earvin is my friend, one of the best people in the world," Isiah told Shelby Strother. "And we have been there for each other a lot. But he's not

John Salley plays cameraman in order to videotape the Pistons first trip to the NBA finals.

going to tell me the secret of how to be a champion. It's a secret he and Larry Bird have shared. And neither one of them ain't going to tell me how it's done."

With the Lakers holding the homecourt advantage, Game 1 of the NBA finals was played at the Forum in Inglewood, California, on June 7, 1988. Jack Nicholson sat in the front row between the team benches. Jack was so close, in his black glasses, he could high-five the Lakers and occasionally did. Or goose the visiting coach, which Dick Motta once accused him of doing, according to stories in the press. Spangles and silicone were visible all over courtside, in locations that were underpriced at more than 400 bucks per seat. Quiche gobblers made up much of the nearby crowd. But they were all basketball savvy; the Lakers, in L.A., had been one of the early NBA success tales.

Then the players were introduced and walked onto the floor to play the game.

Magic and Isiah greeted each other. They embraced and kissed each other on the cheeks.

Preliminaries concluded, the Pistons proceeded to play Game 1 as if they'd been competing in the NBA finals ever since the franchise was formed. There had been the usual unflattering stories about how the team in the finals for the first time comes out with a batch of jitters and queasy stomachs.

The Pistons disproved the theories by rattling off the first eight points. By halftime, the Pistons had the Lakers seventeen down. Adrian Dantley, who had played for the Lakers and was attuned to atmosphere, was hitting like magic. He scored 34 points for himself in what Isiah would write in his *Bad Boys!* was the best game of his career. The Pistons won the first NBA finals game in their thirty-one seasons of representing Detroit by a score of 105–93.

Jack Nicholson did not do much high-fiving. And Isiah had shown that he did not need Magic Johnson to show him how winning a game in the NBA finals was done.

The homecourt advantage, considered so vital by the media analysts, had been claimed by the Pistons.

Life at the finals was not all basketball for the Pistons. There were some distractions; part of the atmosphere of the NBA finals. The Pistons went into a ga-ga tourist's mode in La-La Land. Between Games 1 and 2, the Pistons were invited to the Playboy Mansion.

"I'd never been in a mansion like that before," Vinnie Johnson would say later. "I'd never been in any mansion before.

"There's so much excitement in L.A., you can get caught up in all that. The movie stars, the cars, the clubs. It wasn't so much distracting as it was new to us . . .

"All the media attention, it hits you, like, wow, this is the biggest, man . . ."

The Lakers were recharged for Game 2 at the Forum. They were strong early. The Pistons stormed back to tie in the fourth quarter. But this time, with Magic playing his vintage game and James Worthy conncecting with his shots, the Lakers won, 108–96.

The basketball finalists now went cross-country with the entourages to play the next three games at the Silverdome, thirty miles north of Detroit. The format for the finals was different, because of the travel distances, than in the other seven-game playoffs. It was 2–3–2, which could give a lesser team the edge if it managed an upset in either Game 1 or 2 on the road. The Pistons had.

Detroit, and environs, went electric with expectation over the city's first NBA finals game. The World Series had been played in the city. There had been a Super Bowl in the Silverdome six years earlier, but with two teams from other towns. Otherwise, it had been more than three decades since a Detroit team had played in town in an NFL championship game (pre-Super Bowl era) or the NHL's Stanley Cup finals. So the media went gushy about the event in town, in outpouring of public cheerleading that embarrassed any journalist with professional pride in his profession and interest in unemotional objectivity.

Game 3 was played on June 12, 1988, before 39,188—no freebies—at the Silverdome. The jitters finally did catch the Pistons. Or perhaps it was their occasional fit of lethargy. The Detroit players didn't shoot well. It was tight for a half. At the start of the second Worthy scored all eight points of a Lakers run. Despite Isiah's bravura performance with 28 points, the Pistons lost again, 99–86. On their homecourt, in the first game of the finals ever played there.

The defeat had a rather sobering effect on the citizens. They had been on a high ever since the Pistons did away with the Celtics.

But the series was building toward a dramatic conclusion. The Pistons had been in front in the series, now the Lakers were in front, and then . . . the Pistons started off Game 4 with a refortified confidence. Isiah and Magic had bussed cheeks, as had become their custom, to the voyeuristic thrill of CBS and its TV people. This was Adrian Dantley's game. He kept putting in those little layups of his on his twisting drives to the basket. The Pistons led at halftime by seven and by eighteen after the third quarter. They'd win the game 111–86 with Adrian scoring 26, to tie the series at two victories per team. But this was a bare part of the story.

According to Isiah in his autobiography, Magic had told him before the finals that there'd be mayhem if the two kissers met in the lane. Magic would slam him if Isiah tried to drive the lane. Isiah drove down the lane in the fourth quarter. Magic slammed him. Isiah responded with a shove. Hey, the kissing friends were fighting. They laughed about it after the game, two basketball players playing their game. As

Dantley heads to the hoop and then dishes to the trailer.

Chuck Daly liked to say: "It's a three-game series now. First team to win two wins."

Isiah had damaged his back, but kept on playing despite missing some practice sessions. He admittedly was taking painkillers. It was the sort of injury that could have driven a normal athlete out of the game. But Isiah had been waiting an entire career to play in the NBA finals. He was not a normal athlete. He played on motivation and guts, over the agonizing pain.

The Pistons were back in their funk as Game 5 started. The Lakers jumped ahead 12–0. They upped that to thirteen points, before Daly took Isiah to the bench and sent out Vinnie Johnson, the Microwave. Vinnie rallied the Pistons. They went ahead by nine. This would be the Pistons' last hurrah at the Silverdome, with The Palace more than a glint on a blueprint for the next season, and the 41,732 cultists in attendance, largest NBA playoff crowd ever, chomped at their cotton candy and roared at the excitement. Isiah wrote that he'd never played before a more energized crowd . . . all but visiting fireman Jack Nicholson. Despite some sky-hook heroics by Kareem, the Pistons withheld the Lakers through the second half. The Pistons won it, 104–94—and had themselves a 3–2 series lead going back to L.A. and the Forum for Game 6—and if need be, Game 7.

It would be a superior script to anything they could write down the boulevard at Paramount.

The Pistons went out to win the championship in Game 6. They had reversed the flow of the

Salley is all over this Mychal Thompson shot during Game 4.

series again; they had the proof that they could match the Lakers; they had the confidence; they had the edge.

And they broke in front in the sixth game, with a spurt. The Pistons went up by six in the first quarter. The Lakers counterattacked in the second quarter and took a seven-point lead.

Now it became a raw match, Earvin Johnson versus Isiah Thomas. Isiah started hitting from faraway and the Pistons came back. He scored 14 points at the beginning of the third. The Pistons picked off the ball and Isiah led the break down the court, toward the basket. He passed off to Dumars, a typical quick-trigger flip to the man driving in. And just as he got the ball of, Isiah went into Michael Cooper. Isiah's right sneaker landed on Cooper's. Isiah went careening to the court. He would say, as he writhed on the floor, the pain shooting through his right ankle, that he thought he had broken his leg.

They carted Isiah to the Pistons' bench. Mike Abdenour went to work on the ankle. It wasn't broken. It was torn up inside, sprained. But on the floor the Pistons were playing the Lakers with the NBA championship within their grasp.

"Tell, Chuck I'm ready to go back in," Isiah said to Abdenour, as recorded in his own book.

Isiah returned. He kept on popping; his ankle kept on throbbing its messages of pain. He scored 11 points in a four-minute span of the third quarter—25 points plus one severe injury for the period. The Pistons went into the fourth with a two-point lead. Another quarter, and they could be champions.

The Pistons nursed their lead through the fourth quarter, into the last minute. They had a three-point lead, 102–99.

Just one minute away, sixty seconds.

Byron Scott scored for the Lakers to cut the lead back to one. The Pistons were unable to score. The Lakers got the ball again. It went into Kareem Abdul-Jabbar. Kareem was forty-one years old, still one of the mightiest forces in the NBA. He went to hook the ball. There were fourteen seconds left in the game. Then the whistle tooted. Foul on Laimbeer. Billy made a horrible face, protesting his innocence.

Kareem hit the two free throws. The Lakers had slipped ahead, 103–102. The Pistons had fourteen seconds to score the winning basket. They called time out.

Thomas and Mahorn are able to relax late in Game 4 with the Pistons up big. Detroit won the game 111–86.

Daly plotted a play, for Isiah, of course. They completed the inbounds pass this time. Instead, misfortune had a different form. Isiah and Adrian cracked into each other. The Pistons didn't score. The Lakers held 103–102, and their fans streamed onto the court. The series was tied, and there would be a Game 7—Lakers versus Pistons. Magic versus Isiah. Maybe. Isiah had scored 43 points in trying to win the championship himself in Game 6, but he had this terribly damaged ankle that would naturally enlarge with heavy swelling in the two days between games.

Every Detroit sportscast, every article dwelled on the state of Isiah's ankle, what the X-rays looked like, how it was being treated, how it seemed impossible that he would be able to play in Game 7. Dr. Ben Paloucci and Mike Abdenour became featured subjects on the newscasts beamed back from L.A. to Detroit.

The columnists wrote that there was no chance Isiah could play. He was too badly injured, the ankle had ballooned, he couldn't walk on it so how could he run on it and take all the jarring and shaking required to make the stops and starts of a basketball game?

All these media people in L.A. did not know Isiah Thomas. They dwelled on the ankle while neglecting to look into the heart and the guts and the brain. The mindset, as Isiah had said before the finals.

In his *Bad Boys!*, Isiah says that once Norm Nixon missed a game for the Lakers due to a

separated shoulder. Isiah was watching the game with Mark Aguirre. Isiah told Aguirre, as repeated in his book: "I'd have to be dead for them to keep me out of the lineup."

He himself doubted he could play. The L.A. Raiders of pro football infamy were the Pistons' alter egos out of another sport. And Al Davis offered the Pistons use of the Raiders' training and medical facilities for treatment of Isiah's ankle.

He was not dead, so when Game 7 of the 1988 NBA finals started on June 21, Isiah Thomas was in the Pistons' lineup.

Again the Pistons went into the early lead. They were ahead by five at the half. And again the flow changed. The Lakers were ahead by ten at the end of three.

The Pistons challenged again. They cut the Lakers' lead to one point. The Lakers reopened it to three, 103–100. Dennis Rodman went up and blocked a shot by Kareem. Vinnie Johnson grabbed the loose ball and fired back to Rodman. The Pistons came back down with the ball. Rodman halted and shot from fifteen feet with thirty-nine seconds left. The shot missed. The Lakers held on. They won the seventh game, 108–105. They were NBA champions, Back-to-Back.

"I don't know what was going through my mind," Rodman told Bill Halls in the locker room. "I'm not a jumpshooter. But I just leaped and took it. It was long and hit the back of the rim. I had a clear path to the basket for a layup. I just took a dumb shot. I should have taken it in."

Another postmortem on another night of despair in another locker room at the end of another playoff series.

As the fans mobbed the Lakers on the floor,

Isiah, sporting his Raiders T-shirt, answers questions about his injured ankle.

John "Spider" Salley managed to reach Kareem Abdul-Jabbar.

"Thanks," said Salley, "I learned a lot from you."

All the Pistons had learned, even Laimbeer. Billy told reporters: "Now I understand why Boston and L.A. protect the finals so hard. It's fun to be here. I'm glad I was here to see how to act when we win it."

The Detroit Pistons . . . they had been within sixty seconds of winning the championship in Game 6, they had a multitude of chances to win in Game 7. They had taken one more step, in reaching the finals. They still had one more step to go.

The defeated Pistons were welcomed home with a civic rally at Hart Plaza in downtown Detroit, cheered by a crowd that appreciated their efforts.

"THANKS," said the *Detroit News* in a headline on the front paper of the newspaper, in a typesize normally used to honor victory in war.

Jack McCloskey's workload increased immediately after the finals. Those few weeks in late June are always the busiest for the GM. He has the draft coming up before the month ends. The trades that had been discussed long ago in January are either completed—or fall through. And there is the matter of contracts. The negotiations with Chuck Daly and Isiah had to start up again, right away.

And in 1988, there was the added situation of another change in the NBA's geography. The history of the NBA continued to be a moveable feast, especially now that pro basketball had hit a lode of gold through the machinations of marketing-brilliant David Stern and the escalating TV contracts he was negotiating.

The league would be adding four new territories in the new two seasons, two in 1988, two more in 1989.

The new expansion would bring the Charlotte Hornets, to grab at the basketball-insane trade of the Carolinas, and the Miami Heat into the league the first season. The following year expansion teams in Orlando and Minnesota would enter the NBA.

It meant the established clubs would have to stock the newcomers with live athletes. Each club would have to cough up one veteran each season, after protecting a chosen top eight.

McCloskey drew up his list for the expansion draft for Charlotte and Miami two days after the finals ended in June. There were nine players he wanted to protect, but one of them would have to be listed as available. So, after considerable soul searching, McCloskey included the name of Vinnie Johnson on the Pistons' expansion list along with Ralph Lewis, Chuck Nevitt and Walker Russell, all benchmen.

The Pistons lucked out. The Hornets chose Lewis, who had spent the entire near-championship season with the Pistons and got into fifty games.

Vinnie Johnson was saved—to play again for the Pistons.

For the second straight year, the Pistons went into the annual NBA draft without a selection in the first-round. Efforts to trade for one did not pan out. Unless, McCloskey made a deal before the start of the next season, the Pistons would resume their drive for the championship with the same basic cast.

The news on draft day was that Chuck Daly was there and participated, not the unemployed coach at all. He was slaving loyally for the team, though he technically no longer worked for the Pistons.

"I anticipate I'll be back," Daly said. "I like to use the word anticipate."

Daly was not the vagabond nor misformer Larry Brown was. Brown had just skedaddled from collegiate coaching again to coach San Antonio in a five-year deal for $700,000 per year. Larry—that natty dressing Herbie Brown's brother—had vowed his allegiance to Kansas before his skip out back to the pros. But Larry Brown's deal had to aid Daly's cause.

"Larry Brown's a unique situation," Daly said. "I don't have the marquee name he has."

A few days later, the Pistons announced that Daly had signed a new three-year contract, through the 1991–92 season. It was a few weeks before Daly's fifty-eighth birthday. A clause in his contract permitted him to escape during a fifteen-day period, if he so chose, but would be forbidden to go to another team as coach. And throughout the NBA, GMs worked for considerably less than the $675,000 base salary, plus incentives, Daly would receive from the Pistons each year.

Isiah Thomas' negotiations lagged.

His right ankle had been placed in a cast and Isiah had to maneuver on crutches. One summer day he was in the Pistons' offices. Mike Abdenour worked on the puffiness.

Isiah told me about life on crutches.

"The other day when it was 104, I was out driving and passed a Dairy Mart. I had to stop. I ordered the biggest strawberry shake I could get. I picked it up and took a drink. Then I said, 'it's too hot.' I wanted to go to my car to finish it.

"I got on my crutches and . . ."

He held out his hands, in helpless fashion. He couldn't work the crutches and carry the shake at the same time.

The NBA marketers, with a notion for peddling their game, realized quickly they had a new commodity in the Detroit Pistons. The Pistons were a fresh entity for the American purchasing public. That's everybody with ownership of a TV machine. The trait of the Pistons was . . . well, mayhem.

So the entertainment branch of the league that had admonished and punished the Pistons so often for being Bad Boys now capitalized on their charm-school virtues as a selling tool. NBA Entertainment, Inc., produced a video soon after the conclusion of the finals.

It went something like this, with a guitar riffing in the background:

Isiah: "Yeah, we're the Bad Boys." He emitted a giggle.

A flick of music.

Rodman: "Everybody wants to see us fight." Music.

Vinnie: "Just win, baby, whatever it takes." Music.

Mahorn: "When you got a Detroit Pistons uniform on . . . you just got to have that little edge in your system."

More music, a tune called "Bad to the Bone," was played according to *Rolling Stone,* by George Thorogood. And next, a series that displayed the Pistons in basketball action: Mahorn dumping Charles Barkley with a hit from behind; Mahorn bumping Larry Bird with his ample hip; Mahorn whacking and staring down Charles Oakley of the Knicks; Isiah dumping Danny Ainge, an old friend.

Isiah: "If we're gonna be the Bad Boys, we've gotta act like the Bad Boys."

Fade out.

The league put this video on sale for consumer dollars. More than 20,000 of the videos were peddled at $19.95 a pop . . . so to speak.

It was noted that there was an absentee from in the Pistons' NBA-sponsored video. Bill Laimbeer said he does not participate in such commercial ventures, except for charity. How noble!

The team that once chugged to basketball games in school busses and played a playoff game in a suburban high school gym went into business in its own palacial arena on November 5, 1988. Opening night, blazing spotlights circled beams into the heavens. And rather than a school bus in the parking lot, there were rows of limousines that had transported the basketball cultists to The Palace of Auburn Hills to cheer on the near-champions. The athletes showed up in their own vehicles—Porches and BMWs.

Inside The Palace, Bill Davidson and associates had sold out 180 luxury suites. They had sold out the courtside seating at more than $100 a pop per game—for locations comparable to those that had cost, whenever somebody might want one, $7 at Cobo. The plush building, with its seating for 21,454 customers and guaranteed sellouts for years, had cost $70 million. The owners were eager to make it back as fast as they could.

The people yelled their heads off as the Pistons rolled up banners to The Palace's rafters to commemorate the Central Divison and Eastern Conference titles from the 1987–88 season. Now the Pistons' singular goal was an NBA championship banner.

Bill Laimbeer had summarized the mood as the Pistons went into training camp at Windsor a month earlier:

"I'm getting tired saying wait till next year. We said wait till next year after the Boston series in 1987. And then we had to say it again. It gets a bit tiring. At some point, we're going to have to do it.

"We don't need respect now. We need the ring."

Isiah and Jack McCloskey came to accord on the renegotiated contract the night before camp opened. It's doubtful if there ever were serious trade talks involving Isiah. With the Utah Jazz . . . or any other team. Ploys and threats and dares and wounded egos are all fair in contract negotiations.

The Palace of Auburn Hills

His ego soothed, now in a pay class with Magic and Bird and Jordan, Isiah had total purpose. Magic had played for a championship team. Bird had. Dr J had.

Isiah was absent from the list.

There had been a smattering of changes.

Chuck Daly had a defector, who left with the Pistons' blessing. Ron Rothstein now had his own team. He was appointed the first head coach of the Miami Heat, a stress job without any hope of survival long enough for the team to become a winner. Brendan Malone, an assistant on the Knickerbockers, replaced Rothstein on the staff that included assistant Dick Versace.

Daly had become a head pro coach himself so very late in his career. But now he was becoming a coaching guru. Dick Harter, a former assistant, was the new head coach of the second expansion franchise, the Charlotte Hornets.

The Pistons had two rookies in camp, both out of the stock of second-round draft choices. They were Fenno Denbo and Michael Williams. The best they could expect was a collection of bench splinters in their warmup suits. If they stuck.

And William Bedford was back with another chance. He had been in rehab, near L.A., as the Pistons played in the NBA finals. Not all his teammates greeted Bedford on his return.

Isiah wrote in *Bad Boy!*: "Unless and until William Bedford decides that he wants to be a changed person and lead a clean life, I think he's always going to have the same problems he had leading to training camp."

There was one other semi-newcomer. Darryl Dawkins, the mammoth man from the planet Lovetron, was back for another shot, off the suspended list.

The Pistons were already 1-and-0 when they opened at The Palace. They had started off the 1988–89 schedule in Chicago against Michael Jordan and the Bulls. They were the same old Bulls. One man without a cast. The Pistons double-teamed Michael Jordan and won the opener, 107–94. Of course, there had to be a near fistfight. Isiah and Bill Cartwright were the antagonists.

Two nights later, amid the glitter, they played their game in their new home building. The visitors were the debutante Charlotte Hornets, with their expansion culls. Included on the side of the Hornets was the premier player obtained in the expansion draft, Kelly Tripucka. Kelly had finally gotten his wish to be moved out of Utah, though the prospect of playing for a new team of pickups had to be harrowing.

The Pistons were hardly awesome contenders in this first game with their brand new banners hanging overhead. They managed to beat the

Hornets, 92–85. But the killer instinct that champions require was missing.

It was the first time in six years the Pistons had started a season with victories in the first two games, back-to-back.

And quickly, the Pistons extended their winning streak in a serious way. They beat Philadelphia on road to go 3-and-0, then played the refurbished Atlanta Hawks at The Palace. The Hawks had added Moses Malone and Reggie Theus between seasons. The Pistons figured the Hawks, with Dominique, would be their most formidable opponents within the division. But the Pistons struggled in this first meeting of the new season, overcame a twelve-point deficit and won the game in overtime. The Pistons remained undefeated through four games.

It was not a picnic at the beginning. Following the victory over the Hawks, the Pistons were required to hop to Boston and meet the Celtics in the Garden. The curse/snake was dead. But the Garden remained an edifice haunted by witches and their craft. Of course, it was fight night again. A rematch between Laimbeer and Parish. Nobody landed a punch, except the refs. They tossed both out of the game. The Pistons again rallied in the fourth quarter to win it to stretch their record to 5-and-0.

The Dallas Mavericks, who had carried the Lakers to seven games in the Western finals the prior spring, were the Pistons' sixth opponent. It mean that Isiah would be playing against his old boyhood friend, Mark Aguirre. In the first quarter, Mark headed for the basket for the Mavs. The Pistons' defender, Adrian Dantley, moved in on Aguirre. Aguirre's elbow connected with Dantley's jaw and broke the upper jawbone. It meant Dennis Rodman would be promoted to the starting five. The bench was vital in this game—Darryl Dawkins came in, roaring as he had in his younger days. The Pistons' were still unbeaten, 6-and-0.

The Pistons flew off to San Antonio and beat the Spurs to make it seven straight—and then continued on to Phoenix. With Joe Dumars and Isiah pinpointing from the backcourt, the Pistons whipped the Suns.

They were 8-and-0—and six of their victories had been on the road.

There was much ado in the national press about the Pistons' getaway. Historians dug into the records to discover Great Starts in Pistons History. They didn't have to go very deep. Once before the Pistons had actually started 9-and-0. It was back in when Butch van Breda Kolff was the coach—and Dave Bing was the star and Bob Lanier was a rookie.

Chuck Daly told Isiah and the guys he'd like his Pistons to match and break that record. The western trip continued, into Houston, for their fourth road game in five nights. This time the Pistons had the lead entering the fourth quarter. Then they lost it to the Rockets, 109–98.

They were 8-and-1. There went history, the Pistons couldn't match Bing and Lanier in their 9-and-0 start. But a footnote in the history book would have added that the Pistons at the end of that season so long ago missed the playoffs.

The Pistons were careening along, but they were unable to shake the Cleveland Cavaliers, an unexpected challenger in in he division.

On the Sunday of Thanksgiving weekend, the Lakers came to The Palace for the first time. The game got a tremendous buildup—national exposure on CBS and all. Kareem, now 41, had announced that he would be playing his final season in the NBA. He was making his farewill tour and in each arena the home club made a special affair of it and presented him with a memento for his retirement, such as an easy chair or a portrait. Though it was early in the season, the Lakers wouldn't be back to Detroit with Kareem, unless they and the Pistons both made the finals again. So this was the Detroit stop on Kareem's farewell tour—and the crowd in The Palace rendered this august and revered longtime rival a mighty Standing O.

CBS had taped both Isiah and Magic for the pregame hype. Then both of them went out and played another classic. The Pistons dismissed any nagging doubts that might have lingered over the summer on this November night. The Pistons managed to hold off a late charge by the Lakers and Magic. They won, 102–99.

"We just wanted to beat these guys whether it was the finals or not," Rodman told the *News.*

The Pistons were in first place going into December. But they had been catching injuries. Adrian missed a few games with his busted jaw; James Edwards went out with an ankle sprain.

In the middle of the month, the Pistons had difficult divisional games on successive nights. The Milwaukee Bucks beat the Pistons, 119–110, the first time they had lost in The Palace.

"Hey, Milwaukee played great," Dantley told the *News*. "Everybody thinks we're a machine.

If so, the machine had a broken gear. Next night, in Cleveland the Pistons fell to the Cavaliers, 119–98. The Pistons forfeited their claim to first place for the first time in the season. The Cavs moved in.

The struggle continued into the New Year, 1989. Right after New Year's the Pistons' lost their innovative assistant, Dick Versace, with the patted down, curly white hairdo. Versace became the third head coach in the NBA trained at the benchside of Chuck Daly in Detroit. He was appointed coach of the Indiana Pacers. Three nights later Versace showed how much he had learned from his mentor. His Pacers upended the Pistons in Indianapolis, 113–99. Then the Pistons lost their next game when the Knicks beat them in The Palace. The Pistons had been beaten in three of the first four games of 1989.

But they lost more than a game against the Knickerbockers. Joe Dumars broke his hand. The medical staff—Ben Paloucci and Mike Abdenour projected that Dumars would be lost to the club for five or six weeks. And Isiah, writing in his *Bad Boys!* said: "In many ways, Joe may be our most valuable player." In addition, Rickey Mahorn was incapacitated by more spasms in his back, a chronic problem.

The oomph had gone out of the Pistons' scoring machine. Dantley had been Versace's project, they were close. And with Versace gone, Dantley's scoring prowess fell off.

The Pistons rallied to beat the Celtics at The Palace, but a week later they were back to their old ways. The lost in the Boston Garden. It was their sixth loss in succession on the road, where they had played with such skill and success in the early weeks of the season.

A few nights later, the first-place Cavaliers went into The Palace for a game that the Pistons considered critical. The Cavs outplayed the Pistons badly before the homefolks, the the static mob of 21,454 Palace swells in their tailor-made jeans and glittering furs with team T-shirts swelling underneath. In the third quarter, the Cavs had the Pistons by sixteen. It was then that all hell broke lose.

Bill Laimbeer and Brad Daugherty swapped elbows undernath a basket. Then they started tossing punches at each other's high-up chin. Most basketball fights turning into a flurry of gangly arms and legs. This one was nasty. Laimbeer always boasted that he never threw a punch—and never would unless he was punched first. This time he clenched his hands and used his fists. He popped Daugherty a good one. Isiah, nearby, would write that he saw Daugherty's eyes glass over. Both pugilists were tossed out.

Perhaps fired by the fight, the Pistons rallied from seventeen points down to tie the game with some awesome defense. Then in the final seconds, a point down, Isiah missed the set-up shot that might have won. The Cavaliers prevailed, 80–79. The Pistons had fallen five games out, in a race they were expected to dominate.

After all, who was Cleveland?

A discarded Cleveland coach from long ago was plainly worried about the slide of the Pistons. Chuck Daly.

He told the *News*: "We went to the mountaintop last season and had a very good training camp. But somewhere along the line we lost something, and we're not playing as well as last season. The game is simple, but the people are complex. We have some conflicts going."

Asked to amplify on the conflicts, Daly told the media: Basic selfish problems."

It was an unhappy ballclub—and even Isiah's brimming confidence had waned. "A lot of teams in this league have gotten better," he said in an interview. "Up to this point, we haven't. Whether we're good enough to win it all, I don't know."

Rod Thorn, the onetime Piston working as the justice of peace in the league office, administered the punishment. There would be heavy fines—plus each player would be suspended for one game. Bill Laimbeer would never forget and never forgive. The one game on suspension was the first he missed since he joined the Pistons seven years earlier. He was mighty proud of his consecutive-game streak, 685 in succession, the fourth longest streak in the history of the NBA. He had targeted No. 1, the 906 consecutive-games record of Randy Smith over eleven years with an array of franchises.

"We all knew deep down that the first time I defended myself, Rod Thorn would make an example of me," Laimbeer groused to the *News*.

The rumors started then. Daly had said the Pistons had some conflicts going. Whatever they were, the Pistons players read, or heard, that the club would soon be making a major trade—Adrian Dantley to Dallas for Mark Aguirre.

As the gossipy speculation got hotter about a trade, then withered away because nothing happened, the Pistons regrouped. They started climbing toward Chuck Daly's mountaintop. They rattled off seven successive victories. And this winning streak revealed the many virtues of the Pistons—elements other clubs lacked.

The streak started with a twenty-five-point victory over the Sacramento Kings at Auburn Hills. Dennis Rodman led the scorers with 24 points. Then, the Pistons whipped the Bulls in

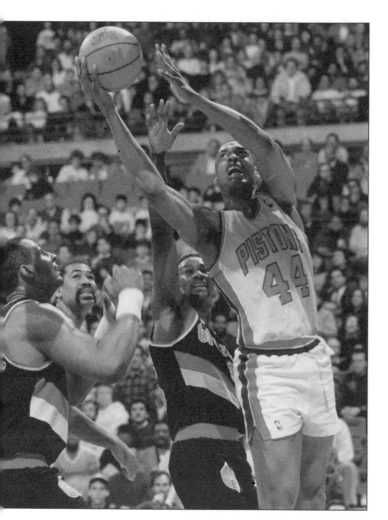

Mahorn displays pure power against Portland. (*K. Dozier*)

Chicago again by six in overtime. Isiah was high scorer with 34 points. Detroit was a team with balance and a bench. The Bulls tried to match the Pistons with a single player, certainly the most talented in the game, Michael Jordan. Five and a bench beats one every time.

Then the Pistons went into Philly. They beat the 76ers by eighteen. This time, the high scorer was Dantley, not unnerved at all by the trade rumors, in his best game with the Pistons.

"I want to make this straight," Dantley told the *News,* "I want to stay in Detroit. I have a good feeling. But you never know."

The game after the trip to Philly, the Pistons beat Jordan and the Bulls again at The Palace by eleven. This time Vinnie Johnson was the high man with 27.

Next game the Pistons whipped the Bucks by eleven at The Palace. This time the leading scorer was Laimbeer with 22 points.

That's five games, five victories, five different leading scorers.

No other team in the NBA played with matching manpower.

The streak continued into L.A., where the Pistons beat the Lakers by eight at the Forum. It was their first trip back since the galling defeats the prior June in Games 6 and 7 of the finals. Joe Dumars, returned from his fractured hand, joined the leading scorers' list, No. 6 on it, with 23 points.

Then the Pistons finished off their winning streak by beating the Kings in Sacramento by eleven. Johnson, Dumars and Laimbeer each scored 20. The streak was finally snapped two nights later by the Golden State Warriors, by two points in OT, at Oakland.

By then, the trade was done—and Mark Aguirre had joined the Pistons full of joy.

It happened on the fifteenth of February, in the wee hours after the Pistons had beaten the Lakers in L.A. Adrian Dantley departed the Pistons with a broken heart.

"No matter what anybody says, this ain't got nothing to do with basketball," Adrian said to the late Shelby Strother of the *News*. "I'll have something to say about it, but not now. I wanted a ring in Detroit. I still want a ring. Tell the people I had a great time with them. Those two and a half years were some of the best years of my career."

That night in Sacramento, Isiah, Laimbeer, Vinnie and Rickey Mahorn took Aguirre to dinner with them. Each one, in turn, told Aguirre what it meant to be a member of the Pistons—and that he'd better shape up, or else.

Reaction to the trade was intense back in Detroit. Dantley had blended into this chemistry the Pistons boasted about, overcoming an individualistic, selfish basketball style. He had become popular with the customers. McCloskey was blasted on radio, TV, in the papers for upsetting something that had been working so well.

It was well known that Isiah and Aguirre had been chums since boyhood. And there was considerable conversation that Isiah had orchestrated the trade to bring in his friend.

It became a hotter talk topic when writer Corky Meinecke interviewed Adrian's mother, Virginia, and she came down on Isiah, whom she had welcomed into her home for meals when the Pistons visited Washington. Detroit fans snickered at Virginia Dantley's choice of words when she called Isiah a con man and said that his royal highness gets whatever he wants. And there were some Detroit fans, as much as they praised Isiah, who agreed that it could be the truth.

Despite the winning streak, the Pistons remained stuck far behind the Cavaliers. They had another ministreak of three victories. Aguirre shotmaking was an immediate boon. In New Jersey, he scored 31 in a twenty-six-minute explosion in leading the Pistons to an eighteen-point victory over the Nets.

There was another injury. Spider Salley broke an ankle and the progosis was he'd be out for three weeks. Darryl Dawkins, who had given the Pistons some bulk, was dropped on waivers. McCloskey was looking for a shooting guard to bolster the Pistons. He scrounged around and found John Long, who had been dropped by Indiana. Long gleefully rejoined his hometown team, in a support role.

The Pistons went across the lake to play Cleveland on the last night of February, in the Richfield Coliseum in the Ohio outback. The pro basketball epidemic had taken over Cleveland, a town deprived of culture and bereft of champions. Now the Cavs were in first place, ahead of these supposedly championship-contending Pistons, and Cleveland was agog. And it was even better when the Cavaliers whipped the Pistons' butts by sixteen points. It was the third straight head-to-head meeting in which the Cavs beat the Pistons. As a sidelight, Rickey Mahorn was hooted by the Cleveland fans for pitching an elbow at Mark Price, the quick guard who geared the Cavs' offense. The refs didn't even bother to whistle a foul on Mahorn . . . but.

The month of March started with the Pistons six games behind Cleveland in the Central Division. By the Ides of March, the Pistons had reclaimed first place.

They won nine games in succession. They lost one. They won another eight in a row. They lost one. The won another five in succession. They lost one. The won another five in a row, to finish the regular season.

On March 1, after the night before in Cleveland, the Pistons had been 36-and-16. The would finish the schedule with a 63-and-19 record. They would win twenty-seven of their last thirty ballgames.

It was a mighty effort for a team under fire from its coach for locker room conflicts and loss of intensity, playing hardly as well as the season before.

In the NBA, Rick Mahorn came off as—he took up the cadence—"the meanest bleeper-bleeper who ever walked on the face of the Earth." He said it with a grin. But it was not the sinister, evil grin he displayed on the basketball court when he had just busted an opponent. The assignment was to portray the other side of Mahorn.

Without publicity he collected a stack of gift certificates he won from a sporting goods sponsor as Pistons player of the game. He took them to the store and used them to buy twenty-five Pistons jackets. They were solid, winter-lined, authentic pieces of gear in a variety of sizes. He took them, still wrapped in their cellophane, and stuffed them into Salvation Army clothing-collection boxes. He drove off with the grin, satisfied that some Detroit kids would receive warm Pistons jackets from an anonymous doner.

"My charities?" he said to the writer. "I don't talk about it."

Then he did.

"I grew up less fortunate than people, and people gave us a hand. Now I'm more fortunate. I keep the tradition growing.

"It's something you do for yourself. For inner peace. From my heart and not just because I have to."

Mahorn's routine was to drop in to visit a kid in a hospital bed . . . to show up at Special Olympics. He would do it without notice, without noteriety.

The previous spring, through the playoffs and into the losing finals, Mahorn played with agonizing back pains. He was operated on to cure the chronic problem. Soon this 6-foot-10 figure in a hospital robe began appearing in the children's wards at Beaumont Hospital.

"I went down to see a kid with cancer," Mahorn said. "He gave me a T-shirt. Just to get down there, to see him smile. Laughter, it makes you feel good. There's something about kids. They get you away from reality. Kids are the best thing you can have.

"Laimbeer, Edwards and myself, we have a free-throw competition through the season. It ends with us making donations to our favorite charities.

The headline image of Mahorn around the league was of the ruffian, the bully with the clenched fist.

"The rough guy," said Mahorn. "I take my job seriously. When I'm on the court, it's forty-eight minutes.

"Then off the court . . . a lot of people don't know the other side of me."

How could Rick Mahorn be a Bad Boy!

The Pistons' rally to first place had started when the Microwave lit it up on the first of March against the Utah Jazz. Vinnie scored 19 points in a row in the second quarter. From then on, to the end of the season and into the playoffs, the Pistons were ablaze. VJ scored 34 points in that game against the Jazz. The Pistons won 96–85. Two nights later they cracked whatever mastery the Cavaliers had on them. With Laimbeer scoring 24, they did in Cleveland, 96–90. The Pistons were fired to beat the Cavaliers because Rod Thorn had again delivered his punishment to The Bad Boys. Mahorn collected

a $5,000 fine for busting Mark Price with an elbow. Thorn called it a flagrant elbow after viewing the video of the play, even though not foul had been called. All the Pistons were ticked by Thorn's justice.

"It's the Detroit Pistons against the world," Laimbeer told the *News'* Terry Foster.

In the next two weeks, the Pistons rolled over Miami, Denver, Seattle, Philly, Washington, Indiana and Boston in succession. Different guys took their turns leading the scorers—Dumars with 25, Isiah with 27 and 34, Laimbeer with 24, Dumars again with 30 and Vinnie with 30.

During the streak, on March 14, the Pistons recaptured first place at Indiana with a 129–117 victory over Dick Versace and his Pacers. The Pistons' reputation was being flavored with each game—and naturally, on the night they moved back into first, there was another fight. This time it was James Edwards fighting with Stuart Gray.

The winning streak was broken by the Milwaukee Bucks. The one loss shoved the Pistons back down to second place. Only temporary. Then the Pistons took off again, beating Atlanta, San Antonio, New Jersey. With the victory over the Nets, ignited by Joe Dumars' 35 points, the Pistons went back into first place. Then they protected their lead by beating Charlotte and Dallas.

The Dallas game featured the first return of Adrian Dantley to The Palace in the green road uniform of the Mavericks.

There was touching reunion between Isiah and Adrian on the floor. The fans cheered the departed Dantley. Isiah greeted Adrian with a grin and put his arms around his former teammate. But there weren't any cheek-smooches. Adrian glowered back at Isiah and whispered some secret words into his ear. The Pistons won the game, 90–77 . . . their fifth victory in that winning streak . . . and the Mavericks' tenth straight defeat.

The Pistons' winning streak continued on a western road swing, Utah in double OT, Seattle and the L.A. Clippers. Throughout this victory streak, eight straight, the scoring again was distributed—Isiah with 26 and 30 in two games, Laimbeer with 21, Dumars with 35, then Thomas with 25 and Joe again with 27 and 23.

The Trail Blazers took it to the Pistons at

Portland the first week of April. From then on, the Pistons would win all but one of their last eleven games. They beat the Bulls back-to-back on successive nights, at the Palace and then by 114–112 in OT when Vinnie scored 30—and there was another fistfight.

The Pistons and Bulls had not been friendly—their rivalry heated by Michael Jordan's and Isiah Thomas' supposed feud. Certainly, they were not kissing friends. Surely, Jordan did not care for the Pistons' rough basketball tactics. And it seemed, at least, that there were pangs of envy in Chicago because of the Pistons' team successes. On this night, the combatants were Isiah, at 6 feet 1 and Bill Cartwright, with a one-foot advantage. Despite the size disparity, Isiah was aggressor. He had picked the ball away from Cartwright. Isiah, in his book, wrote that he saw Cartwright take a roundhouse swing at him and then punch him a second time in the head. Thomas had been cut, he said, a couple of earlier times by Cartwright during the season. This time Isiah swing back. He duked it pretty good against Cartwright. A bunch of other fights broke out. And Laimbeer and Mahorn rushed to save Isiah against Cartwright.

Lucky they did. Isiah emerged from the fight with a broken left hand. Rod Thorn again dealt severely with the Pistons' reputation. Isiah got a $5,000 fine and a two-game suspension. Cartwright got away with a $2,500 fine and a suspension for one game.

The doctors looked at Isiah's broken hand, placed it in a cast—and said he'd be incapacitated for six to eight week, deep into the playoffs.

Isiah missed two games. The two suspension games. The Pistons won both of them without him, over Milwaukee and Washington.

Then they played Cleveland, which still had wild hopes in the race to finish first in the Central. Lenny Wilkens, the Cavs' coach, started moaning that Isiah's suspension should have carried over to two games in which he was physically able to play. That protest failed.

Dumars and Vinnie started in the backcourt. Isiah came off the bench and played some with his hand protected by a cast. It was Vinnie, who carried the Pistons. He scored 31 points in the twelve-point victory at The Palace.

Six nights later, the Pistons did it again down on Cleveland's homecourt, winning by sixteen. Dumars blistered with his shotmaking, with 42 points against the Cavs for his career best. That night the Pistons clinched first place in the Central Division. Again.

The only loss in these final eleven games was by four in Madison Square Garden to the Knicks.

When it was all packaged, the Pistons had gone above the sixty-victory standard, an awesome achievement for a franchise that had struggled nine years earlier to win sixteen for an entire season. They sold out every one of their 21,454 seats at Palace for every one of their forty-one games. And their finishing record for the 1988–89 schedule was 63-and-19. It was by far the best record in the NBA.

With an unsurpassed record—the Lakers were closest with fifty-seven victories—the Pistons had a mighty claim on the homecourt advantage through the entire playoffs. If, or course, they did not foul up and get themselves eliminated before the finals.

Isiah flashed back into history as the Pistons prepared to start their attack in the playoffs.

"We didn't have any tradition, we were just the Pistons," he said in an interview with Shelby Strother. "Just another team in the league. That was eight years ago. Now we have tradition, I think. The Celtics have had it for forty years. The Lakers have had it almost as long. You think about those two teams, and you know what they do, how they do it. That's tradition.

"Our basketball team has it now, too."

Remove the fangs from the snake and it becomes an innocent, unintimidating creature. Thus it was with the Celtics. Larry Bird had been damaged, out for the season. The Celtics, without him, were fortunate to reach the playoffs. The mighty had dropped so far, so quickly, and now the Pistons, the team on the ascent, drew the Celtics for the first round of the playoffs—the preliminary best-of-five go-around.

There was no need for fear of a curse this playoff spring. Bill Laimbeer left his sickle hanging with the garden rakes in the garage. Long tormented by the Celtics, the Pistons had turned tormentors.

They swept through the first round with 101–91 and 102–95 victories at The Palace, then put the Celtics out of their misery in the ancient haunted house of Boston Garden, with the trains rattling below, 100–85. It all ended with a mini-brawl—Mahorn vs. Kevin McHale and Joe Kleine.

"We're the best team in the league and we wanted to get it out of the way quickly," Laimbeer told the *News'* Terry Foster.

Rolling Stone discovered the Pistons around playoff time. Laimbeer, Mahorn, Isiah wound up romanticized in the pages normally devoted to Madonna and Sinead O'Connor. The Pistons were *Rolling Stone*'s kind of guys. The freelance writer who did the piece, Jeff Coplon, aptly described his subjects thusly: "In the cultish NBA, if the Celtics were White America's team and the Lakers were Club Hollywood, the Pistons belonged to Qadaffi."

Smiling Rickey Mahorn told the *Rolling Stone* man: "I love contact. Intimidation is how I make my money. You get yourself so motivated and geeked up. But I never try to hurt anybody. In basketball, you could take anybody out any night. But we're all human; we're all human."

Laimbeer and Mahorn were the stars of the article, eulogized by Isiah. He was quoted as saying: "They used to punch us in the stomach, score a basket and call us sissies. We just had to sit and take it. But all that ends with Horn around."

The piece ran with a picture of Lam and Horn. Rickey had on shades, a Bad Boys cap, black gloves without fingertips and his teeth biting the nets off a basketball hoop. Laimbeer had on his *Rolling Stone* sneer, the black glasses, and he had punctured a basketball with his fingertertips.

The rock hardcore of, er, Mainstream America, had been introduced to the Detroit Pistons.

The picture was such a hit to Laimbeer and Mahorn, it would be reprinted as a poster for sale to the masses. Laimbeer, firm in his conviction not to capitalize on his reputation, turned his proceeds over to charity.

The Milwaukee Bucks were designated to be the Pistons' victims in the second round, best of seven. They had finished fourth in the Central, in which the top five clubs—Pistons, Cavs, Hawks, Bucks and Bulls all finished above .500.

The Bad Boys swept the Bucks, too, in the four-victory minimum. They won Game 1 by an 85–80 score at The Palace—and the closeness of the result scared the stuffings out of Chuck Daly.

"We dodged the bullet big-time," Daly said in his postmortem. "And it's going to be that kind of series."

Detroit won Game 2 at home, 112–92, them broomed the Bucks out on their homecourt in Milwakuee, where a newspaper headline once had described Laimbeer as The Prince of Darkness. The scores were 110–90 and 96–94. In Game 4, the Pistons rallied from a ten-point deficit at the half to win by the two points.

"I told them they had two choices," Daly told the *News'* Terry Foster. "They could play hard for the next twenty-four minutes or they would have to play Milwaukee on Wednesday for forty-eight minutes. They're smart men."

Through two rounds, the Pistons were undefeated in the playoffs—with a dozen victories in a row, continuing the streak started during the season.

The Chicago Bulls had succeeded the Celtics as the Pistons' hate-rivals. They had had their fights—Isiah versus Cartwright, Mahorn and Laimbeer against all Chicago comers. During one of them, Mahorn had slamdunked the Bulls' coach, Doug Collins, onto the press table.

The Bulls, clearly, were not as impressed as NBA Entertainment, Inc.'s marketing profiteers with the endearing charms of the Pistons. There were the wails and whines from Michael Jordan about the Pistons' style of play, dirty, in his descriptions. Michael had become the best player in pro basketball, the most productive. His tongue hanging out, he would drive for the basket and make shots with acrobatic twists that no other human being could mimic. He was making millions in endorsements.

But he was a superstar on a fifth-place ballclub. They had finished sixteen games behind the Pistons in the division. The Pistons had won every one of the six games between the two teams during the season.

There were two powerful impressions about Jordan and the Bulls. 1. Added to his supreme, individual brilliance was Michael's mighty motivation; he played with the highest level of motivation in the league. He burned to beat the Pistons. He was driven to lead his team upward, step after step, in the very way the Pistons had done it. 2. The Bulls, despite their outcries about foul tactics beating them, were jealous of the Pistons' successes.

With his motivation, and skills, Michael had driven the Bulls through two playoff series over clubs with superior records. They eliminated the Cavaliers in the decisive fifth game of the first round, by a single point, on the enemy's court in Richfield. Then they wiped out the New York Knicks, who had finished in first place in the Atlantic Division, in six playoff games.

They were doing the Cinderella bit. Upset victors in two rounds of the playoffs, they were charged up for the Pistons, the team they despised, feared—and envied. Less than forty-eight hours after eliminating the Knicks, the Bulls polished off the Pistons in the first game of the Eastern finals at The Palace. The Pistons had their winning streak going in double digits. If not invincible at home, they were practically so.

But the Bulls whipped them in Game 1, by the tune of 94–88, behind Michael's 32.

Michael had said beforehand that if the Bulls won Game 1, they'd win the entire series. Pishposh, Isiah responded, as expressed in his autobiog: "I laughed to myself because I knew he had left one crucial thing out his calculations: experience versus nonexperience. This was the Bulls' first experience in a conference finals matchup, and there's no way he could have known how tough a seven-game series would be."

Isiah was talking about mental toughness, a trait that can be acquired only by some and only through the years, in competition. The way the Pistons themselves had, playing the Celtics.

Poise and pride was the motto of Al Davis' Raiders. And it could be the guiding principle, also, to the NBA's version of those rogues and renegades. The Pistons won Game 2 over the Bulls, 100–91—and were mad as hell in victory.

"We have been able to play and execute regardless of the opponent we play," Isiah said in his postgame remarks. "We are not moving the ball well. I don't like the way we're playing basketball."

The deadlocked series switched to Chicago Stadium, with the Bulls now possessing the home-court advantage.

Aguirre can't believe the call during Game 1 against the Bulls.

In Game 3, the Pistons had fourteen-point lead with less than seven minutes to play. It was uncharacteristic of this club to blow a such a lead late in any game. This night they did. It was 97–97 when Daly called time out with twenty-eight-seconds left. The Pistons had the ball. Daly wanted to set up the winning play. There was another one of those disputes at the bench. Laimbeer was yelling at Daly, to set up a play for Isiah. "Isiah's the one who got us here," Laimbeer shouted, as documented in Isiah's book, "he'll be the one to win it for us."

The Pistons melted eighteen seconds off the clock and Isiah moved to take the shot for a winner. But before he did, the whistle tooted. And Laimbeer, trying to set a screen, was grabbed for committing an offensive foul. An inopportune call that most likely would never have been called on any other player, except Bill Laimbeer. The Bulls got the ball and Jordan got the gamewinner with three seconds left. The final was 99–97—Michael scored 46—and the Bulls were up in the series, two victories to one.

226

In any sport, the division line between champions and pretenders runs between those who display mettle in adversity and those who scoot away and quit. Isiah—many of the Pistons—could not sleep during the night after the loss in Game 3. They were mulling over this issue. According to Isiah, they wrestled with the question—Do we stop or do we go on? The easy thing would be to quit! Jordan was killing them by himself. He was getting little help—none of any value from the other Bulls—Scottie Pippen, John Paxson, Cartwright.

At breakfast, following the night of tossing in the sack, Isiah met with Dumars, Mahorn and Aguirre for breakfast. They discussed defense on Jordan. The Detroit club had been single-teaming Jordan, mostly with Dumars, sometimes even with Laimbeer . . . and he was destroying the Pistons. The players, over their bacon, thought it might be a good idea to go back to the double-team trap that had worked well enough on Jordan during the regular season.

Isiah and Dumars made the suggestion to Daly at practice. Daly listened and nodded. He was this kind of coach—not a despot, not a dictator . . . he allowed the hired athletes to have suggestions. So it was that the Pistons switched defensive concepts versus Michael—a concept that would be referred to romantically, by the gimmick-minded media, as The Jordan Rules.

Faced with the possibility of a 3-1 deficit in the series, the Pistons went to Game 4 at Chicago Stadium with the new idea. Daly jokingly told Isiah not to blame him if the altered defense alignment against Jordan turned out to be beatable. Isiah, joshingly responded, that he guaranteed that the Bulls would not top the 80-point total. The Pistons displayed their mettle. The won it, and Isiah had it pegged correctly; the score was 86-80. Michael was limited to 23 points. Isiah scored 27 himself. Salley and Rodman controlled the rebounding. The series was squared again, two apiece, and the Pistons had taken back the homecourt edge.

And the Pistons won Game 5, too, in the same fashion back at The Palace. Holding Jordan to a subpar 18 points, the Pistons were 94-85 victors.

Game 6 was back in Chicago, with Game 7 scheduled for The Palace, as it is always written in the agate in the papers, if necessary.

It was not necessary. The Pistons did not stop Michael this time. His shotmaking and motivation were so much that he scored 32 points. The rest of the Bulls vanished. Pippen caught a stray elbow in the eye—Laimbeer's elbow, natch; accidental, natch; no foul called. Knocked cuckoo, Pippin played one minute and did not score.

Isiah's shotmaking and motivation were so much that he scored 33 points. He played on a team. That showed. The Pistons won the Game 6, in Chicago, 103-94. They would return to the NBA finals.

On the court, when it ended, there was a tender scene. Michael Jordan embraced Joe Dumars. Michael whispered, according to what Dumars told the *News'* Bryan Burwell: "Bring the championship back to the East. Bring it to the East."

Bill Laimbeer chortled to the media in the tiny, dank locker room, where fifteen years earlier David Bing had shed tears of playoff defeat, in the bowels of Chicago Stadium.

"It'll be the bad guys against the good guys," Laimbeer said through that semi-angelic, semi-malicious grin. "Hopefully, the bad guys will win."

Pippin's prediction was not registered.

In the marvelous traditions of sport, it is chic to root for the underdogs, the downtrodden, the oppressed. And against the dynastic champions. It is America's sense for sympathetic creatures, the nation's love of the Cinderella fairy tale. Now along came the Pistons, the longtime comic franchise that had never won anything. And they had acquired an image—of their own making—of Public Enemy No. 1. Their preening villainy had a charm to it. But these downtrodden were unloved in the cities across America with NBA ballclubs—except for their own.

What was it like to be in command of the despised—to lead this team known as The Bad Boys?

"Strong men with strong personalities," Chuck Daly told the Shelby Strother. "When I became a coach, I looked at the talent in the league and said 'I can't harness it all.' It scared the hell out of me. I knew I had to have control, but I knew it also had to be delicate."

And Isiah told the writer about his coach: "It's easy to be a dictator. But fear is not a great motivator. Chuck allows a certain freedom to exist. He allows Rick Mahorn to know who he is and be Rick Mahorn. He allows Dennis Rodman to be Dennis Rodman. Players come here, maybe searching for themselves. And Chuck has created this environment where someone can make the turnaround himself."

Isiah Thomas does not forget. Now as the Pistons prepared for the NBA finals of 1989, with the best record in the league, Isiah's mind drifted back to the previous June. June of 1988, the night of Game 7, after the Pistons had lost by one point in Game 6 and three in Game 7, when they had been at the very point of winning the championship—and then had lost.

"The thing I recall most vividly is walking into the shower after the seventh game and seeing Bill Laimbeer sitting in the middle of the shower room floor, water over his body, slumped down, crying," Isiah wrote in *Bad Boys!* ". . . I walked in, touched him, and he looked up. 'Next year is our year,' he said. We promised each other right there that we wouldn't be sitting on a shower room floor crying in June 1989."

To reach the finals for the fourth successive June, the eighth time in nine years, the ninth time in eleven years, the Lakers had swept through three rounds of the 1989 playoffs. They had won eleven playoff games and lost zip.

An era was ending. Kareem Abdul-Jabbar would be retiring after twenty seasons in the NBA. He had gone from the young Lew Alcindor, with the Afro cut on the Milwaukee Bucks, to the forty-two-year-old renamed Kareem, with the goggles and shaved skull and reputation as one of the game's beloved legends.

And there were the other subplots—Isiah and his kissing crony, Magic; the haberdashery wars between Chuck Daly, in his double-breasted sharkskins, his head pompadoured, and Pat Riley, in sharp suits and jackets, his head combed straight back and stuck in place by chicken drippings. Chuck Daly had coached his team through the development years, step-by-step in progress until the Pistons had achieved a level never reached before by the franchise. Riley had a team that had maintained such a level through all nine seasons that he had been the Lakers' coach. They had finished first in their Pacific Division each of the nine seasons. They had won four NBA championships.

The Lakers were reigning back-to-back NBA champions—and now they were aiming for what the media were terming THREE-PEAT—that ugly bastardization of words that Riley himself had created.

Isiah and Magic meet in the NBA finals for the second straight year.

Two Detroit fans show their support for John Salley and the Pistons.

points in the fourth quarter, as the Detroit fans shieked for blood. It was a 108–105 victory for the Pistons. They were up two victories to none to the two-time reigning champions.

"We don't feel sorry for the Lakers," Laimbeer told Terry Foster.

"I'm just so upset," Magic told the press. "I kept asking why. Not now! Why after all the hard work."

The reigning champions went off to defend their realm at The Forum for Games 3 and 4, and Game 5, if necessary. They were damaged,

Salley starts to celebrate the Pistons 109–97 victory over the Lakers in Game 1 of the 1989 NBA finals.

The preludes would be better than the series.

The 1989 NBA finals started on Tuesday night, June 6, at The Palace of Auburn Hills. The Lakers were below full strength. They would have to play without Byron Scott, who had been No. 3 on their scoring list through the season, behind Magic and James Worthy. Scott was out for the duration with a pulled hamstring.

Game 1 opened with the now routine cheekbussing between Isiah and Magic. In their weakened condition, the Lakers were not a match for the Pistons. Isiah outscored Magic, 24 points to 17. Dumars had 22, Vinnie added 19—the Pistons killed them with three guards and won the first game, 109–97.

The Lakers were more competitive in Game 2, back at The Palace. For three quarters, they had the Pistons whipped. The fourth quarter started with the Pistons eight points in the rear. But they were driving. The Lakers lost Earvin Johnson partway through the third quarter. He tore up his left hamstring and hobbled from the court. The Lakers had been deprived of both players in their starting backcourt—opposite the heart of the Pistons.

With Magic off the floor, the Lakers were dead. Joe D was the scoring catalyst again. He drove the Pistons and finished with 33 points. The Pistons outscored the Lakers by eleven

wounded, shellshocked. Magic planned, gamely, to play in Game 3. He lasted five minutes. He couldn't run, he failed to score, he could barely pass. Even without him, inspired perhaps by the courtside presence of the ever-loveable Jack Nicholson, the Lakers fought a pitched battle with the Pistons through the third quarter. They connected on nine of ten shots in a flurry—and Joe Dumars matched them shot for shot. Joe scored 21 points in the third; in one stretch he scored all 17 points notched by the Pistons. Still, the Lakers went into the fourth quarter with a two-point lead. Dumars and Isiah rallied the Pistons, again. Detroit won it, 114–110—with 31 from Dumars, 26 from Isiah and 17 from the third guard, Vinnie.

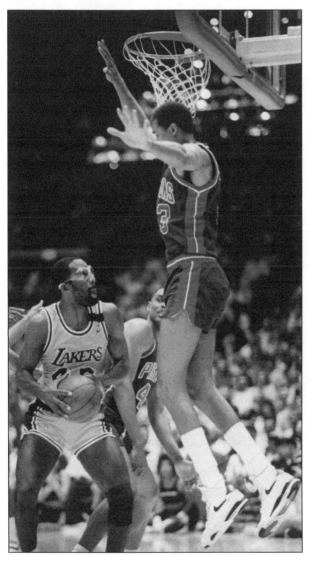

James Worthy's heroics weren't enough for the Lakers.

Detroit was in total command of the NBA finals. The Pistons had the 3–0 lead in games. The Lakers were without Magic now. Without Scott. Jabbar, who scored 26 in Game 3, was playing with the age of his forty-two years. They were resolute, gallant champions—and they were on the verge of being swept, losing their championship on their own court before their glitzy movie-star audience.

"Until I see it happen, then I will believe it," Chuck Daly told the media.

But even Chuck, this prince of pessimism, knew the ultimate was there for his basketball team.

The champagne was already delivered, icing inside The Forum, and the souvenir caps that seemed to pop up instantaneously upon the clinching of a championship—proclaiming Pistons 1989 NBA champions—had already been manufactured and stashed in hiding, for usage at the proper moment. That was the way it was on the night of June 13, 1989, in Inglewood, California.

The Pistons went out to play this proud, maimed opponent—and it required a helluva effort. The Lakers, with James Worthy firing away as a one-man attack gang, took a twelve-point lead in the first quarter. The Pistons cut it to a half dozen by the intermission. They cut it down another four points in the third quarter.

Entering the fourth quarter, the Pistons trailed by two points, a single bucket. And only then did the Pistons, with their full complement of athletes, cruise by the Lakers. Worthy scored 40 points, many too few to rescue his team. The Pistons won it, 104–97. A sweep!

They were champions of the NBA—this franchise founded to promote the products of a factory in Fort Wayne, Indiana, and moved thirty-two years before to Detroit . . . champions, this franchise that gave away the best of its players, that pulled the radio broadcaster from his microphone and put him in charge, that fired coach after coach after coach, that had moved from site to site to site, this team afflicted by the curse of the Celtics, this franchise of The Z and Reggie Harding and Gus the dancing vendor and Herbie Brown and Butch van Breda Kolff and Marvin Barnes and Dick Vitale . . . this franchise, the Detroit Pistons, had become champi-

1989 NBA CHAMPS

ons of the universe in the money-making sport of professional basketball.

And a city that had ignored and laughed at this franchise for so many years, that city erupted in celebration. Mobs roamed the Detroit streets, trashed the town and each other; they honked car horns and turned cars over.

Out in California, Joe Dumars, the unemotional, quiet assassin of the Pistons, told the media: "This is great. When there is something in front of you and you chase it for so long and it is so hard to get, that brings all thye emotions out of you."

Dumars had scored 22, 33, 31 and 23 points in the sweep of the Lakers. He was picked as the series MVP, by a unanimous vote.

The partying started in the Pistons' locker room and continued through the night. The retreat to the sandbox mentality that grabs all brand new champions.

Champagne is the drink of champions. But this champagne was used for squirting and dousing and mixing with the shaving cream that had been mushed through the heads of the champion athletes as shampoo. Bill Davidson hugged the huge golden NBA championship trophy—The Larry O'Brien Trophy—for the obligatory "how d'ya feel" TV interview. He got sprayed by champagne, all over his gray head and gray Glenplaid jacket.

Very little of the champagne was used for drinking. Isiah and Billy Laimbeer grabbed one jug of the stuff and lugged it into the same Forum shower room where the year before they had cried and vowed they'd win the championship in 1989. Now they popped the cork and toasted each other.

"I'm in Heaven; I'm floating, floating, floating," Isiah told the *News'* Shelby Strother. "God—I'm free. I'm cured. My obsession has been realized."

The Pistons jumped aboard the team bus, still in their blue road uniforms, stinking of sweat and champagne. They rode that way to their hotel in Marina del Rey, for the party. Some stayed in their basketball uniforms. The music blared and the purple and blue and green light beams flickered around the ballroom—and they drank and they danced. Jack McCloskey—age sixtysomething—climbed aboard a chair and

high kicked his legs in a funky version of a never-named dance.

He had said, years before, they would advance step by step by step, and he built them, and they had. Now he was high stepping.

Dennis Rodman was still wearing his blue No. 10 Pistons' jersey the following afternoon when Roundball One, lugging the champs, landed amid the mobs of cheering fans at Willow Run Airport, west of Detroit. Dennis jumped off the plane, ran down the ramp and started high-fiving the fans.

Detroit is not a city of sophistication—in the way that New York is, or L.A., or San Francisco, or even Chicago is. It is a hard, working man's town—a lunchbucket town, a shot-and-a-beer town. But the people are rugged and devout about their sports and loyal to the city's teams. Sports—other than whatever TV sitcom you might see before it is cancelled for the next season—is the outlet for the people. They are good people, for the most part, with deep roots and feelings for their varied heritages—and when one of the city's teams wins a championship, the passions tumble over, and they are united.

Sometimes, too, the celebrations become too wild, too violent, people are wounded, some die—and across America, the media scrutinize Detroit from afar. And the city's image worsens.

The Bad Boys, for certain, were the perfect hardscrabble team for Detroit. They were not as mean nor terrible as they were made out to be. There was some love there and some romance and tons of heart.

Right then, two days after the Pistons completed their sweep of the Lakers and ascended the final step to the NBA championship, Detroit didn't give a damn what the rest of America wanted to believe about it—or its basketball franchise.

It was June 15, 1989—and in Detroit there was a parade and the cheers of victory—and at the end of the day, a stunner of disappointment that stuffed a damper onto the whole bit.

The people lined the streets of Woodward Avenue—once the main artery of the central city —from Grand Circus Park to Kennedy Square . . . not far from Cobo Arena, where pro basketball games had been played in a different era. The cops estimated the mob at 125,000. The champions jumped from the parade floats and stood before the adoring throngs and spoke endearing banalities into the public address microphone.

Rickey Mahorn was greeted by thunderous cheers. He played to the crowd. He exhorted the people into their sheeplike chant of "Baaaad Boys, Baaaad Boys, Baaaad Boys . . ." Rickey cupped his right ear, and the people chanted louder.

The Pistons were loaded into a bus and transported the forty miles or so, back to Auburn Hills. There, the second stage of the celebration was scheduled before another mob of 12,000 inside The Palace. Each Piston spoke again.

Jack McCloskey led off: "When I first came here, everybody said the Pistons were losers. The players were losers. The coaches were losers. The front office people were losers. Sometimes winners are losers who just won't quit."

Dennis Rodman cried as he spoke: "I want to thank my mother for coming and Byrne Rich. I want to thank the people who rock this roof. I want to thank God. And I think you all know how hard I fought through a lot of things to get where I am today." Dennis broke, and Isiah consoled him.

Rickey Mahorn said, grasping Jack McCloskey's hand: "Thanks for helping me with my weight problem."

He again led the crowd in the BAAAD BOYS chant and went to each of his teammates, nuzzling each on the cheek.

Then the party ended, and the euphoria had to be crushed by weight of reality.

The NBA was going through the second stage of its latest, planned geographical alteration. The Minnesota Timberwolves and Orlando Magic were to join the NBA for the 1989–90 season, a year after Charlotte and Miami.

For procedural purposes, with the college draft scheduled for late June, the allocation of expansion veterans was planned for the second day following the conclusion of the finals.

It meant Jack McCloskey had to draw up another list to protect eight players before he could lead cheers for the great unwashed.

During the parade and other gala events of the day, McCloskey was on a cellular phone, trying to concoct a trade and protect one additional player. Jack could not make the trade.

While the Pistons yelled and cheered and cried for the people at The Palace, the NBA conducted its expansion draft via conference call.

One of the players on the stage—one of the champions—would be gone, culled by a team that still did not own a basketball nor a jockstrap.

When the rally at The Palace ended, the champion players gathered in a private room. It was off limits to all, particularly the media. The players inside, now sagging after days of joy and celebration, supposedly looked around at each other. As Isiah said later, they all knew one of them would be gone. Some of them kept glancing at Vinnie Johnson and at James Edwards.

Then McCloskey opened the door and asked to talk to Rickey Mahorn.

And the Pistons knew—the prototype Bad Boy had been chosen for sacrifice, taken away from them.

"We went from one of our happiest days to one of our saddest," Chuck Daly told the cluster of writers out in the hallway.

Mahorn had been taken second in the expansion draft, by the Minnesota Timberwolves.

Another group surrounded McCloskey. Jack was trying to explain his reasoning, why.

Mahorn walked past, trying to get out of The Palace. He had not stopped even to clean his gear from his locker.

"I have nothing to say, I don't feel like talking, man," he said.

A crowd of the people had gathered outside The Palace gates, where the players park. Mahorn came out. The people cheered him and went into the Baaaad Boys chant. They were unaware—then—that Rickey Mahorn belonged to another team.

Mahorn got into his car. A TV reporter jammed a microphone through the driver's-side window. "It's a business deal," Mahorn mumbled, painfully, making a huge effort not to flood over with tears. Then, he drove off to nurse his grief in private.

"You go out and win, and it all seems like a fantasyland," Joe Dumars told the *News'* Bill Halls. "Then you come back to reality. This takes the punch right out of the celebration."

"We almost had a three-way deal with two teams so that we wouldn't lose one of our key players," McCloskey told the press.

". . . This was really a tough decision and a sad, sad day for everyone. We feel like we've been penalized for having too much depth. We went over and over this."

The deciding factor was Mahorn's chronic back problems. So he went rather than Edwards or Johnson, both of them older.

For sure it was a tough call. But the Pistons gave up some heart and soul here, and toughness. And a beautifully cynical humor, and the sinister smirk that went with it.

Horn, with his noteriety, had signed, during the playoffs, his first contract to endorse basketball shoes for New Balance.

"I think I'll call them Air Horns," Mahorn had joked to the writers.

Then, there are the perks that are reserved, traditionally, for the champions.

Wheaties announced that the Pistons would be pictured on their orange and blue cereal boxes, for distribution at stores in Michigan—and, natch, Toledo.

And George Bush invited the Pistons to make the honored championship pilgrimage to the White House. They flew to Washington on Roundball One, reunited as a team for this one day the week after winning the championship. Rickey Mahorn had planned to fly commercially, on his own, to Washington. But then he switched and flew with the Pistons, because he had been part of all of it.

The Pistons presented President Bush with an autographed basketball, a game jersey and Bad Boys and world championship T-shirts.

"On the court they are the Bad Boys of basketball," said Bush. "But off the court, people see the kinder and gentler side of the Detroit Pistons."

The president also recalled that Bill Laimbeer, that elbow-equipped Republican, had predicted during the presidential campaign the autumn before during an electioneering stop in Michigan that they'd see each other at the White House.

"He said he'd meet me at the White House in June," Bush said. "Actually, he was sure he would be here. I wasn't so sure about me."

Then Isiah Thomas spoke and said the Pistons would no longer refer to themselves as the Bad Boys.

"We have been called the Bad Boys of basketball," Isiah told George Bush. "Actually, we are nice guys. Really. We are a team in the true sense of the word. One of our members is leaving, and there can be only one Bad Boys basketball team. This was it.

"You said hello to the Bad Boys here today. Now you have to say good-bye. That's it."

For the first time in three years, the Pistons possessed a first-round draft choice. But as the best team in the league, they were at the end of the line. They drafted twenty-seventh. Their pick was Kenny Battle. It was then trade time. McCloskey swapped Micheal Williams, who had played so infrequently for the champions, and the draft rights to Battle to the Phoenix Suns, his old trade partner. In exchange the Pistons received the rights to Anthony Cook, who had been the Suns' first-round draft choice. McCloskey envisioned Cook eventually fitting into the void vacated by Mahorn. But Cook would reject the Pistons and sign to play basketball in Greece. McCloskey did not fret over the decision.

He felt for the Pistons to repeat as champions they would have to add to their veteran bench strength. Jon Koncak became McCloskey's objective as a free agent. Koncak had been the backup center for the Atlanta Hawks, a seven-footer with some skills and a promising future.

McCloskey made an offer for $2.5 million for one year for Koncak. The figures created earthquake tremors around the NBA. Koncak was not even a starter. He had a scoring average below five points per game. He was a decent rebounder, but hardly extraordinary. The Hawks, under league rules, had fifteen days to match the offer—or the Detroit offer sheet Koncak had signed would become valid and Atlanta would lose him. The Hawks were irate. McCloskey's GM peers around the league were astounded and angered. Jack had flipped the NBA's salary structure out of kilter.

The Pistons did not get Koncak. The Atlanta club, forced by the Pistons, made him an acceptable offer of $13.2 million for six years.

And around the league, the Pistons were

regarded as heavies not only on the basketball floor, but in the front office, too.

The Pistons spent the summer of 1989 basking in the glow of their championship; warding off the overkill from their admirers; and trying to beef up the squad.

One Saturday in August, Chuck Daly went to Detroit Metro Aiport to meet a friend's plane. Once he would have been unrecognized. Now he was mobbed by travelers. He stood there shaking hands, grinning, bobbing his head, signing his name to the scraps of paper they thrust at him. People gathered around him, ignoring their suitcases as the luggage rode round and round on the baggage carousels.

"This has been something, I've never seen anything like it, all summer," Daly told a traveling writer who happened to be returning home from a baseball assignment.

He kept shaking hands. Southpaw.

"It really hurts," he had told the *News*' Bob Wojonowski, who inquired about Daly's sore right elbow. "The doctors say its tendinitis, and the only thing they can figure is I signed too many autographs and shook too many hands . . . I shake with my left hand and try to explain."

Dennis Rodman happened to attend an MTV concert at The Palace—old MTV star Chuck Daly wasn't performing, incidentally. The concertgoers discovered the Worm among them. They surrounded him and started tearing at his clothes. They tore off his shirt. Rodman fled for backstage.

"They're nice people and they mean well," Rodman told Wojonowski. "But if they hadn't stopped, I'd have been left with nothing on . . ."

Matt Dobek, the team's PR man and Isiah's co-author, was besieged with requests for personal appearances by the athletes.

"Do you realize I get people wanting to have a player come to their son's bar mitzvah," Dobek told the *News*.

The summer was busy for Joe Dumars, the quiet Piston. He signed a new contract—$8 million for six years. Down in Natchitoches, he got married to Debbie. And he went off to Disney World, as the MVP of the NBA finals.

Bill Laimbeer played golf, went fishing—and reflected on the injustices of life. He considered retiring, because his colleague in cruelty, Rick Mahorn, had been taken away.

"We had lost a physical player and all the physical responsibilities would fall on me," Laimbeer would tell the press. "I knew it would be a very long season for me."

He also told Isiah of his intentions. Isiah convinced Laimbeer that he was just going through a phase. Isiah mentioned money—Laimbeer, rich from birth, still could find uses for a million and a half bucks; camaraderie—Laimbeer had been bonded with the group; another championship—Laimbeer lusted for it.

Before the Pistons reassembled for the 1989 training camp in Windsor, McCloskey beefed up the roster with two free agent veterans; neither as expensive as Jon Koncak.

He signed Scott Hastings, whose abilities as a standup comic matched his talent on the basketball floor. Hastings was 6 feet 11 and had played for the Knicks, Hawks, and Heat through the years. He wouldn't play much, but he'd provide laughs and he would be a good guy for the Pistons to have on their side whenever a benchclearing brawl happened to break out.

Then McCloskey signed David Greenwood, who had been in the league for ten seasons with the Bulls, Spurs, and Nuggets. Far back, Greenwood had been drafted by the Bulls as the second-player taken in the first round. The year was 1979. The Lakers had the first pick off the board that year. His name was Earvin Johnson, a.k.a. Magic.

In addition, William Bedford, who had not been active at all during the championship season while continuing his rehab program, returned to the roster.

Thus fortified, the Pistons were confident of being strong enough to repeat.

They still had to prove themselves, they felt. The doubters, the cynics, the skeptics argued that the Pistons were cheese champions. After all, the critics wrote and said, they'd beaten a broken team. The Pistons, these doubters claimed, had won the championship only because the Lakers didn't have Magic and Byron Scott.

There had been rumors all summer that the Minnesota Timberwolves would have to trade Rickey Mahorn. He didn't want to play for the expansion T-Wolves. Mahorn threatened to go to Italy and play the season with the Glaxo Verona club. One rumormonger printed that Mahorn would be traded to the Bulls. The Pistons certainly didn't want that, Mahorn riding shotgun for Michael Jordan in their own Central Division. Pat Riley said publicly that the Lakers had tried for three weeks to trade for Mahorn. Rickey riding shotgun for Magic was not appealing, either.

For certain, the Pistons tried to talk trade with Minnesota to get Mahorn back. But the T-Wolves obviously wanted too much, more than the Pistons could offer.

A week before the season opened, Mahorn was traded. He went to the Philadelphia 76ers— for three draft choices, a 1990 first-round selection and two No. 2s. He'd be teaming with Charles Barkley in a City of Brotherly Love version of the Bad Boys.

A week before the season, the Pistons played the 76ers in the SkyDome in Toronto. That wonderful Canadian town was treated to a hockey game on the basketball floor. The fight broke out between James Edwards and Mike Gminski. Isiah jumped into the fight to help Buddha. Fortunately, Barkley and Mahorn were not playing that night for the Sixers.

No penalty box in basketball, the fight participants were all ejected and fined.

"A lot of teams are coming after us because we don't have Rick," Edwards told the *News'* Terry Foster. "They think we won't stand up. If we allow them to crack us, they will crack us for the entire game. We have to stand up for ourselves."

The Bad Boys—no matter what Isiah had told President Bush, the name still grabbed at the Pistons—were ready to start defending their championship.

Opening Night was November 3, 1989, with the Knickerbockers the opposition, at The Palace.

In the *News* that day, the late Shelby Strother quoted Chuck Daly about the ingredients needed for a repeat:

"The atmosphere for winning must be there. It's all about discipline, which leads to commitment, which leads to execution. It's a selling job. We convinced people that the rewards are greater teamwise. Nobody made the first, second, or third All-NBA team from Detroit. Yet we won

Dumars scored 26 points and played stellar defense in the 1989–90 season opener against the Knicks.
(*K. Dozier*)

the championship. We have four potential 30-point scorers on this team. But we would not have won the championship that way. We realized this, and I hope we still realize it."

Shelby then quoted Laimbeer:

"It's human nature that this year is going to be a lot harder than last year was. You're just never as hungry as when you're starving, like last year. It's going to be hard to get back to that mindset. We're not the same team personnel-wise and that will take some adjustment. But we do have a tremendous nucleus of pride. And we were able to see what was possible when everyone gave his best effort. We have proof that style works."

Then Daly was quoted again:

"I won't use the word repeat, although that naturally is our goal. I'm calling our mission the Daly Double."

David Stern traveled from New York to present the Pistons their diamond-encrusted championship rings as the 21,454 fans made the rafters shake. The championship banner was unveiled, high above—just as the Celtics have sixteen such banners dangling above the floor in the Boston Garden.

As a marketing gimmick, the Pistons handed out 20,000 replicas of the championship ring on key chains to their fans.

The idea of that ticked off Bill Laimbeer, who was not shy about saying so.

"I've worked nine years for this, and it kind of cheapens it," Laimbeer groused to Terry Foster.

"If they are going to give something out like that, do it on another night. And advertising that it is a special commemorative ring makes it sound like they're giving away an actual championship ring, which does not sound right."

Each of the champions, remaining champions, walked up individually to receive the ring from Stern. The ring was priced at $4,000, 14 karat gold with eight diamonds on it, shaped like the bulky NBA championship trophy. The ring had an inscription etched inside: "Bad Boys, Detroit 4, Los Angeles 0."

The ring key chains given to the fans—didn't Laimbeer once beg them for their support?—cost a buck sixty. And they were paid for by Campbell Soup, sponsor of the promotion.

And that night, the Pistons had a new theme song blaring from The Palace's high-volume amplifiers: M.C. Hammer's "U Can't Touch This." It lifted the crowd to their dancing feet.

It will be recorded that the Pistons won their opener 106–103 over the Knicks, with Joe Dumars scoring 26. Spider Salley won the starting job at power forward, in Mahorn's place. With the same array, the Pistons won their second game, at Washington, beating the Bullets, 95–93.

But these champions would not start off their defense with a lengthy winning streak, as they had in November the season before. They received a message in the third game. Michael Jordan and the Bulls licked them, 117–114. They held Michael to 40 points.

And the message became more profound when they lost, on the road, to lightweight Indiana, coached by Dick Versace, and Ron Rothstein's second-year Miami Heat.

Indeed, the Pistons were no longer a starving basketball team.

They went briefly into first place in the division in the middle of November, the night of their first meeting with the Celtics. The rivalry had cooled with the decline of the Celtics. The Pistons won it, 103–86. Dumars was the top scorer with 27; he was the top scorer in most every game.

When the Pistons fell into second place, Daly decided Salley would be more valuable off the bench than starting. (*K. Dozier*)

The Pistons were playing under pressure—the pressure they had never felt before, the pressure they never knew existed. It was the pressure of playing as reigning champions.

"Every game, every team gets up for you because we're the champions," Laimbeer would say over and over to the writers.

The Pistons fell into second place. They were playing with an inconsistency that troubled Daly. He had a ring, he had security; but they didn't mean he'd ever stop worrying.

One night he had a long skull session with Isiah. Then Daly decided that Spider Salley was more valuable coming off the bench and providing an instant lift. So, he demoted Salley, back to the pines—and made Buddah Edwards a starter.

The Pistons left on their first trip to the West Coast at the end of November. It was a five-gamer, first port of call, Portland. The Trail Blazers made mincemeat of the champions,

102–82. It was the twentieth successive loss for the Pistons' franchise in Portland.

There was one uplifting game in which the Pistons restored some juice to their suffering egos. They returned to The Forum for their single scheduled appearance on the road against the Lakers. The lovable Lakers fans were among those who regarded the Pistons as cheese champions.

A banner greeted the Pistons: "How do the Pistons spell NBA championship—HAMSTRINGS."

This night the Lakers did have Magic Johnson and Byron Scott. And there was some beautiful theater. Magic scored 28 points against the Pistons, and he enabled the Lakers to force the game into an overtime period. The score was 97–97 entering the OT. Then the Pistons, with their defense playing to kill, shut out the Lakers over the five extra minutes. The Pistons scored 11 points themselves during the OT and won the game, 108–97. Dumars, natch, led the Detroit marksmen with 26.

Hamstrings, indeed! It was Hammertime.

But the Pistons could not rise above second place. A week later they went to Philly, to visit Rickey Mahorn for the first time. Rickey and Barkley had been aptly named Bump and Thump by the Philly romantics.

It was speculated that war might break out; it is an old media habit to guess about dire possibilities in the routine hyping of events.

"It won't feel strange hitting each other," Laimbeer, accommodating as ever, told the press people before the game. "It'll be just like practice used to be. But when he tags us coming down the lane, Rickey will smile and just keep on playing."

There was one confrontation, relatively minor. Laimbeer wasn't involved. It was Isiah taking on Mahorn. Nothing severe.

The 76ers won it, 107–101. Mahorn was the Philly force. He scored 22 points and had 14 rebounds.

That night, the Pistons dropped into third place. The week after that, in the middle of December, the Pistons lost to the Clippers in L.A., the Jazz in Utah, and the Warriors at Golden State in Oakland. The reigning champions of the NBA were in fourth place in their own division, with a 13–10 record.

They would spend Christmas 1989 and New Years 1990 lolligagging between fourth and third.

America's media started wondering what's wrong with the Pistons. Outside of Detroit, they were writing that, pretty much, with glee. This was not the most popular of ballclubs.

"Every town we've been in, they keep writing that we're not playing like the defending champions," Daly told writers on the road. "What does that mean? This is a new year, not last year . . . It's always like a dream, winning a championship. You see somebody else do it, and you keep wishing that somebody was you. Then you win it, and find that there are new problems . . . But they're all worth it."

Deep inside his head, Daly knew that the main problem was complacency, that reduction in the hunger level. He knew the Pistons had the talent to repeat; and that it was very early in the season; and that the best way to knock off the lethargy was through hard knocks.

His theory was correct. The Pistons won their final game of 1989 over New Jersey—and then would win the first five of 1990. The sixth victory of the streak was over the Bulls at The Palace, by ten points. Dumars scored 28 and his defense held Michael to 16 points. Off the bench, Spider Salley stuffed one shot back into Michael's face and chortled later, to the writers:

"We're in a groove right now."

It was January 9—and that night, the Pistons edged past the Bulls into first place.

The mood of the locker room, again . . .

Bill Laimbeer was sitting on a hardwood bench in the cramped locker room of the archaic Boston Garden. His eyes were narrowed and focused on the tiny apparatus in his hand. He punched at some buttons. He was engrossed in his miniature Nintendo game before the Pistons had to play the Celtics.

"Did you win?" I asked him when a game ended.

"No," Laimbeer muttered and started another game.

"You're eyes look like your out there on the floor playing the Celtics," I said.

"That's because you're competing against the game," said Laimbeer.

Competition is competition is competition.

William Bedford sat against a far wall, talking to a writer from the *Boston Globe*.

Isiah came into the locker room.

"One million, I'll take it," said Isiah in reference to a story making the rounds about Frank Sinatra. Isiah started weaving, holding a make-believe microphone, singing. "Start spreading the news . . . . New York, New York." Isiah stopped singing. "OK, pay me," he said.

"Hey, I won a game," Laimbeer yelled across the room.

The winning streak ended at Boston, where the Witch of Salem crossed her hexing fingers at Laimbeer. When Billy picked up his sixth foul, he walked off the parquet floor. As he did, he raised both arms toward the Celtics' championship banners attached to the roof and then and bowed to the basketball fans who populate the city of his birth. Their boos from the balcony increased two more notches in volume.

"They were waiting for it, they wanted it," Laimbeer said later, the ham emerging in the tiny locker room where the Pistons have despaired and spoke in harsh criticism and exuded in joy in the Boston Garden.

"But in Atlanta, they're probably a little more nasty. Atlanta is a little more innovative."

Michael Jordan was ticked at Isiah, again.

Some promoters suggested a Michael versus Magic one-on-one competition, a TV gimmick for $1 million. TV had been begging to show-piece Magic and Michael against each other.

Isiah said such a TV contest would be phony and ridiculous. He was head of the NBA Players Association and spoke out against it in that capacity. The NBA refused to sanction the scheme, also.

"I wonder what Isiah's position would be if he were playing Magic," groused Michael on ESPN. "Of course, if he were playing Magic, nobody would want to see it."

Isiah responded to the sour grapes in a statement to the *News*: "As long as my team keeps winning, that's all that matters."

In mid-January, the Pistons lost by four in Philly to Mahorn and Barkley, who scored 30. Two games later the Pistons, the Lakers showed up for their seasonal visit to The Palace. It was another rocking session. The Pistons had won their seven previous meetings with the Lakers, including the sweep in the 1989 NBA finals. But the Pistons were still being accused of winning their championship only because Magic and Scott had been injured.

Aguirre's benching seemed to strain Isiah's relationship with Daly. (*K. Dozier*)

240

Perhaps so. The Pistons blew a decent, early lead. Then their frustrations hit them. Laimbeer shoved Magic, and the players from both clubs got involved in the melee. In the fourth quarter, after the Lakers had evaporated the deficit and started to dominate the Pistons, Isiah got into it with Mychal Thompson. Isiah landed some punches to Mychal's head and got himself kicked out. The Lakers had gone to the Pistons' own roughhouse tactics—pushing, shoving, aggressive basketball—and it worked. The Lakers wiped out the Pistons, 107–97.

The loss dropped the Pistons down into second place, by a half game, behind the Bulls.

Chuck Daly felt the Pistons had lost some of their spark. They were playing drab basketball. He decided to pump something new into the chemistry. Amid controversy, Daly changed his starting unit about this time. Mark Aguirre was removed from the starting unit at small forward. Dennis Rodman was promoted to starter. Perhaps Aguirre would contribute more to the team effort coming off the bench. Rodman, with his emotion, cheerleading, pointing his finger toward the roof when he grabbed an offensive rebound and scored, with his total verve, might reignite the Pistons.

They were a team, but they were individuals. Isiah was Aguirre's chum. It was here the Pistons were touched by controversy. The benching of Aguirre seemed to strain the mood between Isiah and his coach. Isiah refused to discuss the situation with reporters.

The Pistons were in second place for two days after losing to the Lakers. Then they went into Chicago Stadium to face the Bulls again in one of their blood battles. The Pistons hammered the Bulls in front of their own fans, again, 107–95. Michael scored 31; Isiah got 26 and the team he had around him won it.

The Pistons had reclaimed first place. Three nights later, on January 26, at The Palace, the Pistons licked the Phoenix Suns, 107–103. Laimbeer had a mighty game, with 31 points and 23 rebounds.

But those were plain statistics. Not the kind of stats that mattered. As Isiah had wanted, the Pistons would keep winning. They would keep winning through the All-Star break in February until they won thirteen consecutive games. It was

a record winning streak for this franchise that had started off in Detroit with thirteen consecutive losing seasons.

Then after a single loss to the Atlanta Hawks, the Pistons would rattle off twelve more victories in succession. Over a period of eight weeks, from late January to late March, they would post a 25-and-1 victory record. Daly's decision to start Rodman in Aguirre's place had had an impact. The coach knows basketball. By the time the Pistons were stopped from streaking, their bulge over the Bulls was eight games within the division.

David Bing was selected for induction to the Basketball Hall of Fame in Springfield, Massachusetts, in February 1990. It was a high honor for the old Piston from the disadvantaged days. Bing had moved back to Detroit after finishing his career in exile. He had become prosperous in the steel industry and his stature as a citizen expanded. He employed hundreds of minority people at Bing Steel. And there was talk that some day Dave Bing would enter the court of politics and run for mayor of Detroit.

His anger about the way the Pistons had treated him, leading to his trade from Detroit, had cooled years before. He was a frequent spectator when the Pistons played at The Palace.

Terry Foster interviewed Isiah Thomas about Bing. Isiah recalled the times when he and Mark Aguirre would sneak into Chicago Stadium:

"The Pistons-Bulls rivalry was so intense, but Dave was a guy you never rooted against. His jumper was so sweet. Every time he took it you thought it was going in."

Isiah was so taken with Bing's class and style that he copied some of the moves out of his repertoire.

As the Pistons roared along, stretching their lead in their 25-and-1 Hammertime, there were daily reports about Chuck Daly's future. It was written, as though it had been etched in stone, that he'd give up coaching after the playoffs and sign on with NBC as a talking head.

Chuck's own occasional moods supported the media guesses about his heading. There was the night he sent Ben Paloucci to the courtside seats to fetch some theatre tickets for him in mid-game against Miami. What more evidence did a reporter need to pump out more wild speculation?

There were, of course, other nights when Daly danced and jigged up the sidelines, along the edge of the court, in his usual animated fashion. One night Daly ventured out there in his double-breasted blues, his floral necktie neatly in place. He arms flourished and he was in mid yell when—oooooh, he hit a wet spot with his spiffy, shiny black shoes and they went up and he went down. Right onto the flap vent of his jacket. He was quickly helped to his feet and resumed his duties, dignity only scratched. If it didn't make Chuck think about what the hell he still needed this kind of stuff for, it made the courtside eyewitness reporters think exactly that.

NBC was taking over the NBA telecasts—in a $600 million deal for four years, starting in 1990-91—and Daly might be the ticket as a courtside analyst. Pat Riley was also on the rumormonger's list. There would be room for both of them.

Chuck wouldn't talk much about it.

The new TV contract was one example of pro basketball's rampaging popularity after decades of apathy in most of the nation's population centers. David Stern was given a new contract as NBA commissioner. He had marketed the game into a bonanza.

And the owners rewarded him for it. They gave him a five-year deal that, according to the *New York Times,* included a $10 million bonus and an annual salary of $3.5 million. Adding and multiplying on a calculator indicated that the commissioner had a $27.5 million package.

Pro basketball became the only sport in which the commissioner was in the same salary bracket as the athletes.

Despite the twin winning streaks that added to 25-and-1, Isiah harked back to the loss of Mahorn and felt it would have an impact on the Pistons' place in history.

"People look back on last year's team and realize that it was one of the greatest teams in the history of sports," Isiah told writer Roland Lazenby for a feature piece in *The Sporting News.* ". . . The things we did to win, people don't necessarily understand yet. But I think that two, three, four years from now, people will look back and start patterning their teams after us.

"Expansion hurt us, but it's also hurt just about every other team. Now, there are no more dominant teams in the league. Had we been able to keep our team together there still would have been a dominant team. We could have won three out of the next four years.

"We're capable of winning it this year. But you look at next year and the year after. Those are question marks because the team's getting a little older. The older guys are playing more minutes. Therefore, you don't have the luxury of having them for four years. You burn them out in two . . .

"The Lakers had tradition. The Celtics had tradition. They could be themselves. We, as the Detroit Pistons, needed a gimmick to get people to respect us. People never respected the Detroit Pistons. Even the officials didn't respect us. Having won the championship, we don't need hooks now. We don't need gimmicks."

Isiah, in February 1990, had it down pretty much the way it was—and the way it would be.

It was March 2 when the 76ers and Rickey Mahorn made their first appearance of the season at The Palace. The Pistons made it an occasion; in a special ceremony, they awarded Mahorn his championship ring. He got a raucus standing ovation, a tribute in a town that does not always salute the enemy, even when he used to be a friend.

But the ring and the cheers were all that Mahorn got that night. He delivered a forearm or two to Laimbeer and Dumars, all in the game. And Rickey threw the basketball at James Edwards, his best friend who just happened to be his host the night before.

Mahorn's Sixers blew a four-point lead in the final 10.8 seconds. Isiah banked in a three-pointer. Then after the strategy sessions, he stole Philly's inbounds pass—something he might have learned from Larry Bird. He fed the ball to Dumars, who drove in with the layup. All that, and Barkley tied the score on a free throw and the game went into OT. The Pistons then won it, 115-112. It was their fourth straight victory and seventeenth in eighteen games.

"We're enemies during the game, but afterwards we'll go out an get a beer," Edwards would tell the *News'* Jim Spadafore. "But [this time] he was too ticked off to get a beer because we beat them."

On March 20, the Pistons won the twelfth game of their second winning streak, 117–96, over the Bucks at Milwaukee. They had a 51-and-15 record with their eight-game lead. That night Buddha Edwards was the high scorer with 21 points. Daly had moved Edwards into the low post. The new tactic worked with a series of high-scoring games for Edwards—21 in the victory over New Jersey, 21 again when the Pistons beat Charlotte, 16 when they beat Dallas.

Two nights later the streak was broken at Houston. Hakeem Olajuwon scored 26 for the Rockets in a 115–110 victory.

That was the start of another rocky period for the Pistons. They lost three in a row, with San Antonio and Dallas beating them down in Texas after the loss at Houston.

The trip was disastrous. Joe Dumars' broke his hand, the left one again. Just as last year, the medics said Joe D would be out for at least a month—until the playoffs, at least.

The Pistons played in an erratic manner through the rest of the schedule, in late April. They would go 8-and-8 over the final 16 games, their edge lost, wondering again about their powers and destiny. Twice their lead was withered to two games.

Usually, still, it was Edwards leading them in scoring—25 in a loss to Milwaukee, 29 in a loss to Atlanta, 22 in a narrow victory over Orlando.

Three games before the end of the season, the 76ers returned to The Palace.

It had been true, as Isiah had prophesized. The Pistons were not really The Bad Boys any more. That part was a legend in history. They had some fights, but not many main events. During the season, they had seldom heard from Rod Thorn and been spanked by his peculiar sort of justice.

But in April, the nice guys were switching to their playoffs mode. Against Orlando, Laimbeer was whistled down for nicely nudging the Magics' Jerry Reynolds in the head. Seconds later, Laimbeer took a potshot backhander from Reynolds, presumably invoking the eye-for-an-eye rule. The refs missed it. Laimbeer and Reynolds started yelling at each other, obviously in disagreement about their favorite rides at Disney World.

Rod Thorn fined both the combatants, slapping the higher fine on Reynolds for tossing the punch at Laimbeer. Reynolds was assessed $3,500, Laimbeer $750. Thorn must have thought The Bad Boys had become the, er . . . Nice Guys!

Now, on April 19, Barkley and Mahorn and Laimbeer and Isiah appeared on the same court at The Palace. Rather combustible ingredients after a season of simmering. During the season, Barkley had appeared on the "Arsenio Hall Show." He had vowed to Arsenio, and the audience of insomniacs, and himself, that he would punch out Laimbeer.

The game proper did not have enormous meaning for the Pistons. Three nights earlier, as they sat in their homes, they had clinched first place in the Central for the third straight year. They backed in on the night off. Dick Versace's Indiana Pacers knocked off the Bulls, making it impossible for Michael Jordan and his companions to catch Detroit. Most important, it meant a homecourt advantage if the Pistons and Bulls would happen to get together again in the Eastern Conference finals.

However, the game with Detroit was critical

A broken hand sidelined Dumars for the last month of the season. (*K. Dozier*)

for the 76ers. They were battling with the Celtics for the title in the Atlantic Division.

As the opponents sat in their respective locker rooms on opposite corners of The Palace, Sir Charles Barkley wrote out a message and had a ball-boy courier deliver it to Laimbeer. The message, with its choice expletives displaying a fine command of the English language, did not exactly commend Laimbeer for a noble style of playing basketball and for his aristocratic upbringing.

The game that ensued was punctuated, somewhat, by curses at each other and forearm shivs of intensity somewhat stronger than love taps.

Barkley's trash talk was audible to the media, at the side of the court, and to the patrons in the expensive seats down front. The first prelim occurred in the second quarter. Joe Dumars, who had again beaten the medics' prognostications on his recovery, tried to test his brittle hands by taking a pop at Mahorn. Joe shot better than he punched. He swung and missed. Mahorn grinned.

In the third quarter there was some bumping between Mahorn and Laimbeer. Rickey was somewhat ticked that he had not heard anything from Laimbeer all season long. Must have affected poster sales. Their bumping, shoving match resulted in technical fouls for both.

Later in the third, Isiah took umbrage at Mahorn and clenched his also brittle hands. Isiah, giving away nine inches and an estimated half-ton of avoirdupois, brushed Mahorn with one of several punches. The refs, led by veteran Jake O'Donnell, booted Isiah from the game. Mahorn grinned.

Meanwhile, Barkley was playing a helluva game amid his outbursts of taunts. The 76ers had a decent lead as the game wound through its final minute. Charles had scored 36 points. Fourteen point eight seconds before the finish, Mahorn drove toward the basket for a layup. Worm Rodman whammed Mahorn for a foul. They made little gestures at each other.

Laimbeer retrieved the loose ball. Billy stuffed the ball into the face of poster-pal Mahorn. After that, things tended to happen.

Barkley, fulfilling the vow he had made on Arsenio, delivered a left hook to Laimbeer's face. Sir Charles landed heavily.

Laimbeer—attacked, and thus free to fistfight by his own credo—punched back at Barkley. Laimbeer landed heavily.

Next, a mob of players was tangled on the floor, punching. And the most noticeable punches were being scored onto the shaven head and grimacing face of Sir Charles Barkley by Scott Hastings, who had departed his usual dozing location at the distant end of the Pistons' bench.

Off to the side, buddies Edwards and Mahorn were seen dancing a hot gavotte. Mahorn had a handful of Edwards' jersey in his grasp. It did not look like they planned to go drink beer together later.

Once Jake O'Donnell and his two striped-shirt partners along with Palace security men halted the donnybrook, Barkley, Laimbeer and Hastings were excused for the rest of the night. The ejected Laimbeer and Hastings were required to take a route past the visiting bench occupied by the 76ers.

Hostilities were about resume, but this time they were limited to badinage. All the athletes stretched the limits of their vocabularies.

As Barkley was being escorted from the arena, one of the Detroit intelligensia seated near an aisleway seat attempted to take one more punch at Sir Charles. Barkley tried to leap the railing toward his assailant and found the distance too great to punch back. So Barkley responded by spitting at the fan's face, a method of player-fan association that would become a habit for Charles.

For the record, the 76ers won the game, 107–97, their third of the season's four meetings with the Pistons.

Postfight Quotes . . .

Laimbeer displayed an ugly, reddish bump on the side of his face in the locker room.

"Nobody really cares about him," Billy said to Bill Halls. "He's a loser. Barkley threw the first punch. He hit me first. What he said was insignificant. He said nothing intelligent. That's basically how he talks."

"He had a shot at the title," Barkley, who fancied himself as the NBA's heavyweight champion, told the press. "He lost. I got in three or four good punches. Then Hastings sucker punched me. Jake O'Donnell told me that. I know exactly who did it, and I'm gonna get his butt. Yeah, I'm gonna get that bleeper."

Barkley's trophies included two bruises and a red gash that trickled blood as he delivered his macho prattle into the recorders of the journalists. He swigged champagne as he spoke. The blood mixed with the champagne that had been poured over his skin head. The victory had clinched the title in the title in the Atlantic for the 76ers—and generated the possibility of a Detroit-Philly rematch in the Eastern Conference finals.

"I guess he's going to have to chase a loose ball and dive on the bench," Hastings said when told Barkley had vowed to get his butt in revenge.

About his after fight engagement with the over-brave fan, Barkley told the reporters: "He swung at me for no reason. I tried to get at him, but I couldn't. So I spit in his face . . ."

"I clearly saw Hastings sucker punch Barkley," said O'Donnell, the ref. "Every player on both benches will be fined."

"I don't care if I get fined," Barkley told the writers. "I make $3 million (truthfully, $2.6 million). What's a couple of thousand dollars? . . . But I don't give a damn about the brawl. I'm going to party."

Rod Thorn viewed the tapes. And his justice prevailed. He became the world's champion of fine slappers. When everything was accounted for, the fines totalled $162,500. It was a record for fighting in professional sports, ice hockey included.

What's a couple of thousand dollars?

Charles Barkley and Bill Laimbeer, as the main-eventers, got $20,000 each. Hastings, as the sucker off the bench, got $10,000. Isiah got $7,500 for his earlier setto with Mahorn. Each of the ten players—five from each club—who dashed off their benches to get into it was fined $500. The Detroit and Philly franchises were fined $50,000 each for failure to control their employes.

In addition, Thorn whacked Laimbeer, Barkley and Hastings with one-game suspensions.

And some folks view wrestlemania and an art form!

The Pistons beat the Bulls, 111–106, in the season finale. They finished the season with a 59–23 record, four games below the level of the previous season, second best in club history. The Pistons' attendance record was perfect again, forty-one successive sellouts at The Palace.

Now they had to shoot for the toughest accomplishment in all sports—repeating as champions. The Pistons were targets for all comers. They had earned themselves the homecourt advantage throughout the Eastern finals. But not all the way, this time. If they and the Lakers managed to survive to the NBA finals for the third straight year, the Pistons would not have the homecourt edge. The Lakers did not disintegrate with the retirement of Kareem. They had played through the season with a 63-and-19 record, the NBA's best. The smart guys, who gauged such things in advance, figured the Lakers could take the Pistons, if they met in the finals. But the championship round was more than a month away. It would be silly to look so far ahead.

The Pistons' first-round opponent would be the Indiana Pacers, Dick Versace's team that squeezed into the last spot in the playoffs, with a 42–40 record.

Daly, of course, was worried. The Pistons had been stumbling for a month.

"It's a new season—the first team to fifteen wins," Daly told the press. "We've got to get back to our work ethic. We've been casual with the ball and you can't afford to do that in the playoffs or you're not going to be around very long . . .

"I talked to John Madden about when he coached the Raiders and wanted him to tell me about the mentality of being a defending champion, and he gave me great advice. He said he wanted to defend their title in training camp, in the first game and all through the regular season. But with that attitude, he said, they didn't have anybody with any energy left when the playoffs came around.

"I don't want that to happen to us."

Vinnie Johnson also spoke about being the target all year for every other club in basketball. Vinnie had not had a vintage season. The Microwave had dimmed. His scoring average had dropped drastically, below double figures, to 9.8 points per game. It was his worst season since he joined Detroit.

"We know everybody wants to knock us off," Vinnie told Clifton Brown of the *New York*

Times. "We've never gone into the playoffs as the champs, and that will mean more pressure. But we feed off that.

"We've always been like the bad guys, anyway. Other teams don't like us. Fans don't like us. But we look at it as a challenge. If we win Back-to-Back championships, people still might not like us. But they'll have to respect us."

"It'll be an all-out war," Daly told the writers before best-of-five series with the Pacers.

The writers donned their steel helmets.

The war was over in three routs. The Pistons swept the Pacers, 104–92, 100–87, and 108–96. Spider Salley turned it up now that the Pistons were in the playoffs, slamming back a bunch of Indiana shots. There was only one near fight, in the first minute of Game One. Rodman and Detlef Schrempf did a bit of shoving, and each was hit with a techninal.

CBS pulled John Salley across the court during practice to perform a rap song for the Game 2 pregame intro. The lyrics had something to do about how the Pistons were going to repeat and slam all those guys on the other teams and stuff. Isiah spotted Spider at the mike with the CBS crew and ran his finger slantwise across his throat. Spider removed the mike and for the first time in his life rejected the chance to perform in TV.

"We got enough people shooting at us," Isiah told the reporters. "We don't need to pour no gasoline on the fire."

The highlight of the series occured in this first game at The Palace. Daly split the seem of his trousers in mid-tirade at the refs. He continued yelling, and coaching.

"Sure, I knew it was ripped," Daly told the writers. "But I've got a great pair of shorts underneath."

The Pistons had to wait six days for the next round while the Celtics and Knicks clubbed each other around in the East.

While this was going on, Rodman finally received his recognition as the NBA's Defensive Player of the Year, when he broke down in tears.

The Pistons spent their practice time preparing to play the Celtics for the fourth straight spring in the playoffs. The Celtics were up two victories to zero over the Knicks when the Pistons eliminated Indiana. Then, funny, the Knicks beat the Celtics twice in Madison Square Garden. It was even. Back in Boston Garden, the Knicks completed their comeback from the 0–2 deficit and beat the Celtics by seven points.

It was the Knicks' turn to play the Pistons. The Pistons did a quick brush up on the Knicks scouting report and dropped into the second round. The Pistons could just have well spent the week of intensive practice touring Tibet. They slaughtered the Knicks, 112–77, in a schoolyard-basketball Game 1 at The Palace.

The Knicks were pooped from beating the Celtics. Garbage time came early—with the Pistons ahead by forty-two midway through the fourth quarter. Chuck Daly cleared his bench, tossing onto the floor Hastings, David Greenwood, William Bedford and veteran Gerald Henderson, who had been signed during the season for experienced bench aid at guard.

"I'm a lot like Red Auerbach's cigar," Hastings told the press after the laugher. "When I got in the game, it means it's over."

Two nights later, the Knicks provided more competition for the Pistons. But Detroit won it, 104–97, with Edwards and Laimbeer outmuscling the Knicks' giant, Patrick Ewing. Edwards scored 32 points. Laimbeer, for the fifth successive game in the playoffs, led his club in rebounds.

The Pistons had a 2–0 edge in games as the series switched to New York. Daly had his stylized, built-in warning. The Knicks had been down two games to the Celtics, too, and won the series.

But there was validity to Daly's thoughts. The Knicks won Game 3 at the Garden, before a celebrity crowd, 111–103. Ewing was unstoppable. He hit for 45 points, including a long-distance jumper worth three points. Hitting the shot, Ewing exchanged high fives—or was it low fives?—with Spike Lee, the erudite filmmaker out of Brooklyn who appears with Michael Jordan in Nike commercials.

While in New York, the citadel of American communications as well as the home of Nathan's hot dogs, the issue of Chuck Daly's tomorrows flaired anew. Gossip grabs. NBC was located in New York. The rumors became thicker and thicker that Chuck would utilize the escape allowance in his contract and flee to the network when it started doing NBA in 1990–91. The New

York tabloids fell all over the story, along with ESPN and the media-fawning *USA Today*. Even the august *New York Times* mentioned the rumors, in passing. It was not only New York, though. Some of the Detroit media believed that Daly would probably be leaving the Pistons after the end of the playoffs.

Daly was playing it straight up the middle, being noncommittal. He hinted that some day he would have to start taking it easier, yet he insisted that he was addicted to coaching. In essence, though, Daly had slipped his intentions out rather clearly a few weeks earlier in a piece in the *News* by Bryan Burwell:

"I'm a lifer as a coach. When you have time to sit down and think about something like this, 'Wow, I haven't done anything else in my life.' Where would I be without it? Could I exist without it? The practices, the travel, the crisis management. You know, when the summer comes, as tired as I am, when I'm sitting down and I see a plane fly overhead, I say, 'Hey, maybe I should be on it' because that's my way of life. I had never thought about being anything else for the rest of my life. All of a sudden, you have to start thinking about it. I just say to myself, 'I like what's going on. Do I want to do anything else?'

"As I go along in life . . . I realize where you have to make your money is in your area of expertise, doing what you do best. You go in

James Edwards (32 points) got the better of Patrick Ewing in Game 2 of the 1990 playoffs. (*K. Dozier*)

Dennis Rodman looks to score two with a little flair. (*K. Dozier*)

these other areas, you're out in left field, as an interloper so to speak. But I know the league. I know basketball. I know the players. It's an area I feel comfortable with. Maybe I like the challenge of being part of building something from scratch."

The message was there. The media do not always pay attention!

The Knicks were handicapped immediately in Game 4, when Patrick Ewing got trapped in foul trouble. He didn't score a point in the first half, then got thirty in the second half. There couldn't be any squawking about the officiating by the Pistons this time. The refs helped them to a 102–90 victory in the Knicks' building.

The series returned to The Palace for Game 5, with the Pistons in command three victories to one. Again, the Pistons lacked killer motivation. At the first time out, Spider Salley was spotted again peaking at Comedy Clips on the multicolored Palace scoreboard. His teammates on the floor were sluggish. And with a hellish rain outside, the roof of The Palace had sprung a leak. The mopping crews had to take over for a bit. When the game resumed, Dumars popped and it was an airball.

So it was that Chuck Daly reminded his athletes that they'd be forced to make another trip to New York if they didn't start shagging it. Chuck, this man of wisdom, decided to permit Mark Aguirre a night out of his doghouse. He put Aguirre into the game late in the first quarter. Aguirre was allowed to play his individual game, which was shoot-shoot-shoot.

He started by popping in a three-pointer. Just before halftime, he grabbed an offensive rebound and rammed in the basket. All in all, he had 17 points in the second quarter and had reversed the tempo of the game.

Spike Lee sat at courtside, in his Brooklyn Dodgers cap, jumping up every time his beloved Knicks did something. The Knicks led it during the third quarter. Then Vinnie Johnson warmed up and scored a basket. blue-collar style, and Salley rose from the floor and blocked a shot by Ewing. The Pistons won it, 95–84, and moved onward to the Eastern Conference finals for the fourth time in four years. Against an opponent to be determined. Aguirre had led the way with 25 points off the bench.

The locker room was jammed with well-wishers. Spike Lee, the consummate jocksniffer, had apparently reversed loyalties and was snapping pictures in the Pistons' locker room. Across the way, Laimbeer was beeming in triumph.

"Relentless, relentless, wave after wave," said Laimbeer. "That's our game. Ewing got tired. It's a series, not a game. We can sustain. We get better as it goes along.

"We do a good job of wearing people down. If we get tired, the other team is really tired. See, we play eighty-two playoff games a year. All our games at playoff games.

"Rings and money, that's what it's about. MONNNNN-NEEEE!"

Charles Barkley had promised he'd see the Pistons again in the Eastern finals. The Pistons did not particularly relish such a matchup. Barkley and Mahorn and the 76ers had beaten the Pistons three of four during the regular season. Charles spoke junk. To get to the Pistons, the Sixers had to travel via Chicago. The Bulls wiped out Philly in five games.

Instead, the Pistons would get Michael Jordan again. That other gifted speechmaker.

Michael had that blood feud with Isiah. It had been intensified during the season when Michael's one-on-one million-dollar matchup with Magic had been aborted. Jordan had publicly belittled Isiah.

Now Jordan was praising the Lakers as the best team in the NBA—reviving the cheese-champion opinions.

"They're the best," Michael said of the Lakers, as quoted by Mike Downey in the L.A. Times. "They're the best until somebody proves different. All Detroit really proved is they could beat the Lakers without Magic and Scott. We'll see this year if they can do it again. But first they've got to get by us."

The year before, after the Pistons had eliminated them in six games in the Eastern finals, the Bulls had given Doug Collins the ziggy as their coach. It was a cruel act. Collins had helped build and train the Bulls. But in the NBA any coach, no matter how talented, can get himself brushed aside for a new man. It happened how many times in Detroit?

The new coach was Phil Jackson. In the 1960s, he was a child of the times. A tall hippie.

He was a hippie when he played for the Knicks and was with them when they won the NBA championship in 1973. His roommate was Bill Bradley, the future United States senator from New Jersey, and never a hippie.

Jackson had changed his lifestyle and become a coach with a talent for innovation. He'd come up from coaching the Albany team in the Continental Basketball Association; and it was his coaching mind, as much as anything, that had enabled the Bulls to beat the 76ers.

Now he would match up with Chuck Daly . . . with certain similarities in their careers.

"There's definitely a hate factor when they play us," Spider Salley said to the press about the Bulls during the idle time of waiting for a proper CBS Sunday start to the series.

"We're their Boston. It was always something big when we played the Celtics. We're what Chicago shoots for."

The analogy was perfect. The Pistons had knocked the Bulls out of the playoffs two years running. The Bulls trembled with the Curse of the Pistons.

And Daly played along again with the mysterious Jordan Rules that the Pistons used to trap and haunt and taunt Michael.

After a gap of four days—they could have started the series sooner except for CBS—the Pistons went back at it against the Bulls at noon on May 20, 1990.

"I thought it was a rugby game more than a basketball game," Phil Jackson would say at his postgame press session.

It was ugly. Michael was hitting early. Then he got hit. He and Rodman, rotating into double coverage, collided late in the first half. Michael went down on his rump and damaged his left hip. Even so, he scored 26 points in the first half. The Bulls had the Pistons by four at the half. Then, at halftime, Daly switched to another segment of his secret Jordan Rules. Michael would get only six more points, handicapped by his injury.

And Joe Dumars, in addition to serving as the main defender against Michael, turned deadeye. In the third quarter, when the Pistons took over the game, Dumars scored 18 points. He outscored the entire Bulls team by himself.

The Pistons won Game 1, 86–77. Dumars had 27 points on a day when Isiah was missing and the Pistons were rusty.

"That's the way it is on this team," Dumars told the *News'* Bill Halls in the last cubicle in the Pistons' locker room. "You get hot, you don't have to call for the ball. They'll get it to you. We'll ride a person until he drops."

"We were crappy," Rodman, sitting next door, told Terry Foster of the *News*. "I screwed up a lot."

"This was the best chance they had to steal one out of our building," said Buddah Edwards, across the room. "I shot bad. Isiah shot bad. We didn't play well."

The Pistons had played lucky and had the one hot hand, Dumars.

Joe D had the hot hand again in Game 2 at The Palace. The Pistons went up by seventeen points in the second quarter, led by fifteen at the half. Michael Jordan walked sullenly to the Bulls' locker room. What went inside during the intermission was a state-of-the-art temper tantrum. Those in the hallway could hear yelling— in Michael's voice. They could hear a folding metal chair being booted over.

The words probably had some impact. Anyway, when the third quarter started, the Pistons relaxed and admired the Bulls' comeback. Before the teams were very deep into the third, the Pistons' entire lead had wasted away. The Bulls led. And then Dumars again rescued the Pistons. They won it, 102–93, and had a 2–0 lead in the series. Dumars scored 31. And Michael, hobbled, was limited to 20 on a sad shooting night. He was in a very foul mood.

Before the ink-stained wretches and the electronic media marvels with their elbowing crews were allowed entrance into the Bulls' inner sanctum, Michael came charging out. He pushed through the media mob.

"I ain't got no time," Jordan said when a TV guy stuck a mike in his mug.

Then Jordan escaped into the Bulls' team bus that was parked on a ramp inside The Palace. He sat there and stewed.

Horace Grant leaked Michael's thoughts to the invading media.

"He said the guys are playing like bleep," Grant said, as quoted by Bill Halls. "He didn't want to name any names, but he was right. The guys know who they are. We were embarrassed.

"Mike feels some guys aren't giving their all, and I don't blame him. He's giving his all and gets upset when other guys don't do the same. We played terribly. I've never seen Michael that upset.

They were naming names in the Chicago papers. In the *Chicago Tribune,* Bernie Lincicome wrote that Bulls should notify the missing persons bureau about a lost forward—Scottie Pippen.

The *Trib*'s Skip Myslenski asked Bill Laimbeer if the Bulls were in a similar position as the Pistons were in 1988 when they finally managed to beat the Celtics in a playoff series. Laimbeer, as always, spoke the truth. "They're not that good yet," he told the reporter.

CBS had arranged another four-day hiatus between games, for weekend audiences. Time enabled Michael to do some healing—and his teammates to do some soulsearching. Games 3 and 4 were to be played in Chicago Stadium.

There was time between games for Rod Thorn to view some more video and collect more fine revenue. James Edwards had slapped the Bulls' Ed Nealy during Game 2 and tossed a punch. Buddah got kicked out. Now Thorn hit him with a $3,500 fine.

The Bulls were upset because Edwards was not suspended.

Michael had remained mum to reporters ever since he fled from them in The Palace. Now on Saturday afternoon, May 25, in Chicago Stadium, the Bulls spotted the Pistons a fourteen-point lead in Game 3. Michael, resolute, rallied the Bulls. He got help from Pippen. The Bulls, defeat in their faces, rallied back. They took over the lead in the third quarter. From outside, Jordan hit a three-pointer.

He turned and the TV camera focused in on his face. His tongue was out, and he said: "Yes, yes, yes." His face was twisted with emotion. This was Michael Jordan full of fire, passion—and you noted, he's the rare athlete who makes all those millions from playing the game and from endorsements of his Nike Air Jordans and his soft drink and his cereals and everything else, and he raises his motivation level.

He was the artist on the basketball floor. And he had to be, because these were the Pistons and they fought him. The Bulls did not win until Aguirre missed a thirty-foot three-point shot that could have tied with seconds left, but went astray. The Bulls won it, 107–102. Michael scored 47. Pippen had 29. Isiah fought the strong battle. He scored 36. Not enough. And Laimbeer, mysteriously, had 0.

"First doughnut of my career, I think," Laimbeer told the late Shelby Strother.

Two days later, on Memorial Day afternoon, they played Game 4 back in Chicago Stadium. The Bulls' came out with a smothering, trapping defense that had been the Pistons' own weapon to stop them in Detroit. Phil Jackson's defense forced the Pistons into a series of lost balls, errant passes, turnover mistakes so uncharacteristic of the reigning champions. Michael remained ablaze. This time the Bulls took the lead early and they held it and held it until the forty-eight minutes were up. They did not rattle and collapse when the Pistons cut a nineteen-point Chicago lead to three in the third quarter. The Bulls won, 108–101. Michael scored 42. His teammates scored enough to offset 26 by Isiah, 24 by Dumars and 20 by Rodman. Laimbeer again had problems. He scored 4 points. He'd missed on twelve of thirteen shots in the two games. The Bulls even dared to shove him around a bit. Pippen did—and got himself a technical foul.

Bill Laimbeer was wrong. The Bulls had become that good. They had squared the series at two victories each. The home team had been the winner in each of the games.

The odds had lenthened on the Daly Double!

"I'm fed up with the way our intensity had been," Daly told the media in postmortem. "You can't just expect to waltz in and repeat as NBA champions. We've had it easy all year. This is the first time in the playoffs that our backs are against the wall, and if we don't respond right now offensively and defensively we can forget about repeating . . .

"Every team wants what we have. We own the title. It's up to us how badly we want to keep it."

No matter what their travail, the Pistons refused to surrender their flair. It was ingrained, part of the character that made them special—beloved in Detroit, detested in Chicago and in every other town in the NBA. A team of heroes at home, villains everywhere else.

Throughout the playoffs, the athletes had

been wearing T-shirts around the locker room, in their cars, at home, with a message that revealed their always mellow mood. Scott Hastings had them made up:

"Have You Hugged Bill Laimbeer Today?"

Now Laimbeer showed up with his own message when he arrived at The Palace the night of Game 5. He wore a button: "Heaven doesn't want me. Hell is afraid I'll take over."

Billy got his shot back. Buddah rediscovered his shot. Chuck Daly rediscovered Mark Aguirre. In that manner, the Pistons controlled the game. Laimber scored 16, Edwards 13—and when unleashed from Daly's doghouse, Aguirre burned with emotion and scored 19. Mark was the key. Daly said so. And, of course, so was Joe Dumars, who had to defend Jordan pretty much alone. Rodman had hurt his ankle and played just six minutes. The rest of the time he spent near the bench, jumping up and down on a small trampoline, trying to work movement into the ankle.

The Pistons won it, 97–83, for a three games to two advantage in the series.

"With Jordan, there's nothing you can do but work, hope and pray, and Joe did all three," Daly told the writers about Dumars' defense.

Michael managed only 22 points.

And again, there was an angry scene with angry words.

Pippen roughly took down Laimbeer late in the game. He was called for the T, again. When Laimbeer arose, he strolled over to Jordan and said something. Laimbeer wanted to take over hell.

"He said if Scottie can get away with that kind of hard foul, then he's going to break my neck," Michael told the Chicago writers, who passed it on to the Detroit press.

Did Laimbeer really threaten to break Michael's neck?

In the Pistons locker room, sitting on a towel at his locker, Laimbeer put on the innocent look out of his repertoire of multiple faces.

He first addressed the knockdown by Pippen.

"The league office will take care of it accordingly," Laimbeer said. "If that was me, the league office would hang my ass."

Somebody asked: "Did you tell Jordan 'we could break your neck any time we want?'"

"Have You Hugged Bill Laimbeer Today?"

"I did not say 'we could break your neck any time we want,'" Laimbeer said.

"What did you say?"

Silence!

"Huh?"

"No comment," said Laimbeer.

So off they went, back to Chicago, for Game 6, the blood boiling. It was Friday night, June 1, prime time on CBS.

Before the game, Rod Thorn administered justice again. This time he fined Scottie Pippen $2,000 for misbehavior against the body of Bill Laimbeer. Thorn was being fair, being an alumnus of both enemies.

The loudmouth who does the PA blabbing at Chicago Stadium proclaimed that his audience was the noisiest basketball crowd in America. Not the brightest, just the noisiest.

And the boos and jeers and hoots were the loudest when the guy introduced Bill Laimbeer to the mob. They had read the reported remarks about breaking Michael's neck. Laimbeer loved the recognition.

On the floor, where basketball rivals often shake or touch hands, sometimes even smooch, Michael reached out his hand. He was offering to tap hands with Laimbeer. Laimbeer looked at Jordan, sneered and ignored this little expression of understanding, if not friendship.

Then the Bulls beat the bejabbers out of the Pistons again. By the third quarter, the Pistons were down by sixteen. Michael popped a three-pointer and turned away with a half-grin.

In the end, the Bulls won, 109–91, a blowout. And again the series was tied at three victories and going to Game 7.

"Guess what," Chuck Daly said to the media folk, "it's a one-game season."

Nonsense, but at the moment of utterance Daly could not look ahead to at least four more games in another series if the Pistons did survive in Game 7.

More, it showed the true value of the regular season that often becomes boring and dull for the traveling athletes, their series of plane hops and late arrivals and storms and one-night hotel stopovers.

"This is why we play those cold January and February nights, when nobody's paying attention," Dumars said to the media.

"We played all season for this one game to be at home," said Laimbeer to assembled media. ". . . That's why we put ourselves through a season of abuse . . . We torture ourselves for eighty-two games for situations just like this . . ."

"That is why The Palace was built," Isiah told Charlie Vincent of the *Free Press*. "For situations like this."

Through the years, after the Pistons had become competitive, during duress in Boston or Atlanta in the playoffs, Isiah had said often: "Now we're going to Isiah's house."

Now Game 7, winner to advance to the NBA finals, would be played in Isiah's house, The Palace of Auburn Hills. The reward for winning more games than the other team during the eighty-two-game schedule was the homecourt advantage in the playoffs. And the Detroit Pistons had gained that edge over the Bulls on the icy, blustery nights of February and March.

There was an intangible. Historians discovered in their research that the Pistons had played three previous Game 7s. They had lost all three—on the road.

"Seventh games are tossups," Phil Jackson said to the Chicago writers.

Magic Johnson stood in the hallway near the locker rooms at The Palace. A visiting fireman. Game 7 between the Pistons and Bulls would be starting shortly on Sunday afternoon, June 3.

He was asked about the cheese-champions stigma that the Pistons still had to lug with them almost a year after winning their first NBA finals.

"I think they've already proved themselves," Magic said. "Even though we were hurt last year. They beat everybody they had to."

"But like you and the Lakers in 1980," I said, "you won the championship with you playing center with Kareem hurt?"

"I see what you're saying," Magic said about the Pistons still being required to offer proof of their quality.

"If they have to prove themselves, they'll do that today, then," he said.

The ballgame started before a crowd that was pumped, pumped, pumped. It started with James Edwards shooting and unloosing an airball. It followed with Joe Dumar firing and unloosing another airball. It started with both clubs tentative, like the first round between two mighty heavyweights. And the analogy was valid because among the fans seated courtside was Muhammad Ali, who lived in his retirement on a farm in Michigan.

The Bulls—those upstarts with no championship tradition—took the lead in the first quarter. Isiah could not hit a basket until the last half minute of the first quarter. Missing as they did, the Pistons were mighty lucky to trail by only two at the quarter.

Now Chuck Daly displayed his own mettle. He displayed the experience that made him a championsip coach. He displayed the sort of gambling daring that would make most other NBA coaches wretch thinking about.

Daly put William Bedford onto the floor to start the second quarter. Bedford had barely played any minutes during the playoffs. Usually, he went into the game only when it was garbage time.

Not only that. Daly sent Vinnie Johnson, John Salley and Mark Aguirre onto the court with Bedford. And with Isiah, the only starter on the floor.

And with this bench-augmented unit, the Pistons blew open the ballgame. Isiah was possessed. He drove, he fed Salley through a tangle of arms for a basket. Vinnie popped from outside. Isiah drove, and scooped the ball through more arms for another basket. Salley went up for a huge slam. Aguirre drove through the middle to score with a scoop. Isiah scored off a triple pump through the middle. Aguirre grabbed an offensive rebound underneath and scored again.

In a flash, the Pistons had gone ahead by a dozen points.

Now Rodman was on the floor leading the crowd in cheers. And the crowd was responding. And the Pistons were ripping downcourt in a crosscross passing pattern to Rodman for another score, at the halftime buzzer.

The Pistons had the lead by fifteen at the half. It went to twenty-two points in the third quarter. The Bulls then made a charge. It was much too little and far too late.

It ended with the crowd chanting: "REEE-PEAT, REEEPEAT . . ." And it ended with Spider Salley scoring on a backward jam off Isiah's pass.

The Pistons won Game 7, by a 93–74 margin. They were going to the NBA finals for the third year in a row. Isiah had taken over in the game he had to take over. He had 21 points, 11 assists, 8 rebounds and a couple of blocked shots.

"He did what Isiah's supposed to do," Laimbeer would tell a group of writers, "go out there and lead us to a championship. That's his job. That's why he gets paid the big bucks."

For the Bulls, there was the agony of being bumped from the playoffs by the Pistons for the third year in a row. Michael had glorified himself in defeat with 31 points.

Isiah and Michael, longtime antagonists, met briefly, peacefully, on the floor.

"I told him the same thing I told him a year ago," Isiah would tell the media. "I told him not to give up, to keep trying. I know exactly what he's going through, and it's hard, extremely hard. His day will come."

Michael had been brilliant through seven blooded games. But his team didn't show with him for Game 7. Scottie Pippen scored only two points, hitting on one shot of ten, in forty-two minutes. Pippen complained that he had a migraine, that the pounding in his head destroyed his effectiveness. His performance in this critical game, his migraine alibi, would haunt Pippen throughout the next year. And in the Pistons locker room there were snickers that Scottie had his migraine because he'd spent the night before out gallivanting.

Spider Salley, as always, was the first to emerge from the sanctuary of the shower room and into the main locker room filled with the swarming press. He had blocked four shots and scored 14 points in lifting the Pistons when they needed it.

It was part of John's great plan to be first out of the shower room. The first guy out of hiding got his name in the papers, his comments on the TV news, ESPN, CNN, everywhere. The other guys didn't give a hoot. The mass interview was a pain to all the rest, but a steppingstone to something strong in his future to John. He could try out his laugh lines on the fawning media, rushed on deadlines, begging for somebody to quote.

"The Palace is our home," said Salley, towering over his semicircle of shoving listeners. "You don't want somebody coming into your home stealing. It was like they wanted to steal our dream."

Salley was asked if he felt sorry for Michael, defeated again.

"He's from Mars," Spider told his group. "Let him go back to Mars. We got things to do."

The Pistons had to prepare to play the Portland Trail Blazers in the NBA finals. Huh?

While the Pistons were struggling, struggling, struggling—in Daly's words—through the East, the bizarre had been occurring out West. The Lakers, with all their players available, were ridden out of the playoffs in the second round. The Phoenix Suns shockingly eliminated them in five games. Portland, meanwhile, had to rally mightily to defeat the San Antonio Spurs in seven games.

Then the Trail Blazers knocked off Phoenix in six games—and had to wait four days before the Pistons managed to join them in the finals.

Excerpts from an article in the *Detroit News* by Jerry Green, June 4, 1990:

From Magic, with love.

There will be no smooches this time in The NBA Finals, no little kisses on the cheek between Earvin Johnson and Isiah Thomas.

"I'm on vacation, OK?" said Magic, a Sunday visitor to the Pistons' locker room.

"The Finals? It's going to be intense. But I still pick Detroit. They got experience. It goes a long way.

"A lot of time that's more important than talent. And to have talent and experience! Oh, my."

Magic Johnson does not customarily schedule his vacations for early June. In eight of the last 10 years, he was busily occupied . . .

But now in his rare role of the vacationer, he became the best man available to size up this June's NBA Finals pitting the Pistons and the Portland Trail Blazers. He has that important experience in The Finals. His team plays in the same division as the Blazers.

"Portland's different from Chicago," Magic said . . .

"They're going to cause more problem in the open court. And they got more talent than Chicago."

. . . Johnson, the NBA's most valuable player, said that the Blazers match up better with the Pistons than the Bulls did. The Bulls were Michael Jordan and four other guys on the floor. The Blazers have the better balance—with Clyde Drexler, Terry Porter, Jerome Kersey . . .

Earvin Johnson, who has been part of so many championship celebrations, stood there as a spectator as the Pistons were barely festive in the clinching of this Eastern Conference title. He stood there with a Michigan State basketball '90 sweatshirt and a wistful smile.

The scene might have been surprising for its lack of player revelry. But the Pistons are like the Lakers now. They've become accustomed to going to The NBA Finals in early June. They know there are more games to be played, to be won if they can, before they can go on their own vacations.

"You're not excited," someone said to Bill Laimbeer, dressed only in a black NBA Finals cap, and a white towel. "How come?"

"Our whole team isn't excited," Laimbeer said. "We knew what was needed to win—A, B, C, D. That simple."

It was a stunning contrast from the mass jubilation, the fans dancing on the court, when the Pistons finally disposed of the Boston Celtics two years ago and won their first conference title.

"That was the first time, that was different," said Laimbeer. "But we've won only one championship . . ."

There was one day to hype the finals.
Portland, Maine, or Portland, Oregon?
Portland, where is it?
Portland, Washington?
Oregon? One of those squarish states out west? Like Montana or the Dakotas?
The Portland jokes started immediately after the Pistons had removed Chicago from the playoffs. Sophisticates versus bumpkins. Ho, ho. The Detroit media raged with their humor. For the edification of their citizens, they displayed maps. Portland, Maine—arrow pointing, not here. Portland, Oregon—arrow, here. Portland —didn't know there were two.
Portland—a Little League town.
Media checked into in Detroit from across America to cover the finals. They arrived from Italy and Mexico and Britain.
They got to Detroit, looked at the TV, checked the Portland jokes, digested the geography lessons aimed at the local citizenry—and they wondered who were the bumpkins, anyway?
The Pistons and Trail Blazers were barely acquainted with each other. They played each other twice during the season, no more. They split. The Blazers won by twenty early in the season on their home court in Oregon. The Pistons won the rematch at The Palace in January.
Now the Pistons, with their superior record for the season, owned the homecourt advantage, which had been so precious for them against the Bulls.
Bill Laimbeer was familiar enough for Kevin Duckworth to remember him. Duckworth was the Trail Blazers' center; he went 6 feet 11 and 270 pounds.
"He goes for the ball and will hit you in the face at the same time," Duckworth said at the NBA's day-off press session.

Duckworth said Laimbeer once whacked him on the jaw going for a rebound off a missed free throw.

"But he apologized," said Duckworth. "It's nothing personal with me."

Duckworth wasn't that familiar with Laimbeer, after all.

Game 1 of the 1990 NBA finals was played Tuesday night, June 5, at The Palace. Chuck Daly had one day to prepare a plan for Portland. The Pistons were so pooped after the Chicago series they didn't even stage a normal practice before Game 1.

Daly obviously had rebuilt his wardrobe believing there'd be another clotheshorse matchup with Pat Riley at the finals. Chuck showed up for Game 1 in a double-breasted brown sharkskin suit and the explosive necktie. Pat Riley didn't show up. A guy named Rick Adelman did . . . Mr. Generic, in plain, piperack threads . . . to coach the Portland team. Adelman had once been a backup guard in Portland and with a popourri of other NBA clubs. His coaching roots went back to Chemeketa Community College in Salem, Oregon. This was the matchup—the guy who started at Punxsutawney versus the guy out of Chemeketa.

Whatever it was Daly did to prepare the Pistons for the NBA finals, it took a while to set in. The basketball cultists in the grandstands at The Palace were electric; the basketball team blew a fuse.

Defense of their NBA championship started with the Pistons missing their first seven shots. Within a few minutes, the Trail Blazers, this team that lacked the feeling of playing under the pressure of the finals, had a 20–9 lead. Only Isiah could keep the Pistons relatively close. He hit four shots in the first quarter, going into his personal overdrive early.

But the rest of his team had come up flat again in a critical game. Underneath the basket, Joe Dumars missed three shots.

Perhaps the Pistons' highlight of the first half occurred after Spider Salley rejected a shot by Drazen Petrovic, the Blazers' Yugoslav import.

Scott Hastings jumped off the Pistons' bench and hollered:

"Take that, Commie."

The Pistons managed to tie the score twice, but they could not get ahead of Portland. The Blazers were back in front by eight late in the third quarter. They bumped it to ten points five minutes into the fourth quarter. With six minutes, fifty-eight seconds left in the game, Daly called a time out. He reached into a bag and pulled out an ammonia capsule and gave it to Isiah. Isiah snapped it under his nose. Wake up!

When the game resumed, Thomas scored and then scored again, Dumars scored, Aguirre scored. In a flash—in less than two minutes—the Pistons had whittled Portland's lead to three. Adelman signaled for a time out. Then he called

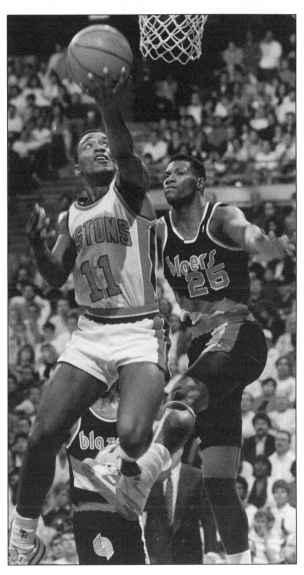

Isiah was almost unstoppable in Game 1 of the 1990 NBA finals. (*K. Dozier*)

another. When the game resumed, Thomas, in one swirling minute, stole the ball, scored two free throws, then grabbed a rebound, popped in a three-pointer to tie the score at 94 with 3:40 on the clock. He followed with a jumpshot as Detroit went ahead for the first time in the entire game with 2:24 left. Then Isiah popped in a three-pointer.

In a swift, crushing assault of slightly longer than five minutes, the Pistons had taken a ten-point deficit and created a five-point lead. The Pistons won Game 1 by a 105–99 score. As the game wound through its final seconds, during a time out, Laimbeer leaned toward Isiah at the Detroit bench.

"You've always been my idol," said Laimbeer, a huge grin.

Isiah scored 33 in a bravura performance that would rank with any single-handed display by Michael Jordan or Magic Johnson or Larry Bird. Sixteen of Isiah's points were scored in the rally that won it. He had a run of ten straight.

"It's will, not skill," said Isiah when the media clustered around him at his locker.

"We were dead in the water, belly up," Daly told the press.

Somebody asked Isiah about the extra juice after he'd whiffed the ammonia.

"I've studied the Boston guys," Isiah said to his group. "I remember them struggling and seeing Bird pop a tablet. I always learned from them. It's like . . . ever been hit in the nose and it makes your eyes water.

Isiah had entered one of those zones again in those last seven minutes. He explained later: "Everything comes into focus . . . Everything on the court seems to get slower . . . Gets clearer . . . Everything slows down . . . Everything you do goes right . . . be it rebounds or shots or passes . . ."

There had been other times in other playoff games when Isiah had become immersed in this zone. Against the Knicks in 1984, when he scored 16 points in ninety-four seconds. Against the Lakers in 1988, when he scored the 25 points in the third quarter of Game 6 of the finals, when he tore up his ankle.

On the off day, between Games 1 and 2, they asked Isiah what his best game in the zone had been.

"The Lakers game was a pretty darn good performance," he told the media of the nation and the world. "What happened in the game against the Knicks will never happen again.

"But I would have to put this one last night No. 1 because we won the game, and lost the other two."

If the NBA ever did a video anthology about the classic basketball games, Game 2 of the 1990 finals would belong at the beginning.

This game started as though the Pistons would dominate the Trail Blazers, having won the first game in such a stunning fashion. The Pistons were up by eight points early. Soon they were down by twelve.

But hasn't it been the contention all along that any thing that occurs in a pro basketball game doesn't matter until the last three minutes?

It had been that way in Game 1. It would be again in Game 2.

Laimbeer was a deadeye shot on this night. James Edwards kept the Pistons viable with 24 points by himself in the third quarter.

But still, Portland led by six entering the fourth.

"How many miracles can you expect?" Daly yelled to his players at the bench.

How many, indeed?

With three minutes and change on the clock, Laimbeer unloosed a shot from three-point range and hit. He'd tied the score with that shot, at 86–86. Next time down, Laimbeer shot and hit another three-pointer. The Pistons were up, 89–86, and the mob in The Palace was going daft.

Then Clyde Drexler fired back for the Blazers, three points, and it was tied once again, 89–89.

Thomas drove to put the Pistons up again, this time by two. It continued into the final minute, to the final seconds. Salley made it a three-point lead with a free throw. Drexler cut it to two, missing one free throw, hitting the other, with 44.3 seconds left.

The Pistons missed in their turn, and the coaches jockeyed; each called a strategy time out with 21.1 seconds left. Then with 10.2 seconds left, Terry Porter hit two free throws to tie it again, 94–94. Isiah missed a last shot bid.

The game continued into overtime. In the same manner.

When Laimbeer hit a three-pointer, the Pistons led by four, 102-98, with a minute and a half left in OT. Drexler responded with two free throws and Porter with a jumpshot to tie the game at 102-102 with 27.0 seconds left.

They battled on, and Portland got the ball again. With 9.6 to go, Buck Williams sank two free throws to put the Blazers up, 104-102.

The Pistons came down again—a routine basket could tie it again, send it into a second OT. That was the commonsense play, but these were the Pistons. Laimbeer got the ball and popped from three-point range again.

He hit from there—his sixth three-point basket of the game. The Pistons had the lead, 105-104, with 4.1 seconds left. Adelman, composed, quickly called a Portland time out to devise a plan. Aguirre jumped off the Detroit bench and hugged Laimbeer. Laimbeer waved his arms in caution. He would say later:

"They came running to me, and I told them the game was not over. I looked at the clock. There were four seconds left, which in the NBA is an eternity."

From here to eternity!

On the pass-in, Dennis Rodman put a handcheck on Drexler. The whistle blew. "When the whistle blows, it's always a foul," Laimbeer would tell the press. It was a chintzy, often overlooked foul. But a foul.

Drexler connected on two free throws with 2.1 seconds left. Portland was ahead, 106-105. Daly called a time out. Then the Pistons tried their luck once more with 1.5 seconds left. As the buzzer went off, Edwards desperation shot was soaring above the backboard.

The Trail Blazers had won Game 2 at The Palace by the one-point difference. They were going home to Portland, their own arena in Oregon, with the NBA finals square at one victory apiece.

They'd gained the home court advantage—and tons of respect—while visiting in Michigan.

Rick Adelman took his shots at the Portland bashers in the jubilation of the Blazers' locker room at The Palace. Hell, he'd earned it. The juvenile delinquency of the Detroit media against Portland had continued. The Portland media were getting involved in the nonsense with retaliatory shots.

"Detroit, a French word meaning 'Let's move to Houston' . . . explained an editorial in The Oregonian, the Portland daily.

Now Adelman was hot about the disrespect shown for his basketball team.

"It seems nobody realizes how good we are," said Adelman, as quoted by the News' Bob Wojnowksi in the wake of Game 2. "We lose Tuesday night and the BRILLIANT Dick Vitale says the series will be a blowout. He obviously hasn't seen us play all year, because anybody who says that is just plain dumb.

"I'm just getting tired of it. You'd think by the time a team got to the finals people would have done their homework and tried to find out who we are. How can people not know us? Just ask somebody. Ask me. Ask my mother. Ask my father."

Ask Chuck Daly.

Or Laimbeer!

"We can't expect to put ourselves in a hole and crawl back, crawl back every time," Laimbeer said.

He had scored 26 points—18 on his accuracy with the three-point distant shots—and he had captured 11 rebounds. Edwards also had 26 and Isiah had 23. Only Drexler had scored more than any of the Pistons' trio, with 33. But the Pistons had lost to a team that had played with poise and smarts and passion.

"At times tonight we played stupidly, and at times we played unemotionally," Laimbeer said into the microphones in his face.

There was a simple formula now. Games 3, 4 and 5 would be played in Portland. The Pistons would have to win one of the games there to repeat as NBA champions.

Isiah had never played in a winning game in Portland. Laimbeer had not played in a winning game in Portland since he had joined the Pistons. Chuck Daly had not coached in a winning game there since . . . since he coached the Cleveland Cavaliers once upon a time for ninety-three days and had already been told he'd be fired as soon as that Western roadtrip was over.

There was much ado about the Pistons' inability to win in Portland. They had lost twenty successive games there, *in Oregon*! As with the Salem witch who crossed fingers to cast her spell on Bill Laimbeer in Boston, the Portland hex was more nonsense fodder for media consumption, than reality for the athletes.

Last time the Pistons had beaten the Trail Blazers in Portland was 1974. Bob Lainer and Dave Bing played for the Pistons then. Rick Adelman was a guard for Portland. Jack McCloskey had just gotten the ziggy as coach of the Trail Blazers. Since then, the Pistons had employed six coaches, Herbie Brown and Dick Vitale included, and had gone through three generations of players.

All that mattered to Daly and Laimbeer and Isiah was that the Pistons had to win one game, somehow, in Portland—or they'd lose their championship without there ever being a Game 6 or Game 7 back in The Palace of Auburn Hills.

"It's a big deal if you can't win in another building," Daly told the *News'* Terry Foster. "But we've faced that over the years in Boston and L.A., so we're used to it, and it's all part of the game. We're a proud team and we've faced adversity before."

The city of Portland was a revelation for the media tourists, even those who had been taking giggles at it. There was fresh air—and rain—and the mighty Columbia River Gorge and snow-capped Mount Hood to the east—and rain—the gigantic evergreens toward the craggy, jutting Pacific coast to the west—and rain. It was soggy, but stunning. It was no wonder that former pro basketball players, consigned to what they thought was an NBA outpost in the West had stayed to live their post-athletic lives in Oregon.

One of these was Terry Dischinger, who hailed originally out of Indiana. Dischinger had reminiscences of enduring the worst of both clubs at play in the 1990 NBA finals. He had performed for the Detroit Pistons during the most-comical franchise years of the 1960s. Liberated from the Pistons, he had migrated to the Trail Blazers, the NBA's newest losers.

I went to visit Dischinger to obtain the views of the NBA championsip round from the guy who had played for both teams when they were the pits. Excerpts:

LAKE OSWEGO, Oregon—Back when he played for the Pistons, Terry Dischinger would practice taking his shots over an upraised broom held in the hands of a helper. The idea was to simulate game conditions—scoring over the towering peaks, Wilt Chamberlain and Bill Russell.

"I did it to arc the ball, get it up in the air," Dischinger said. "To develop concentration. I did it in the pros. I remember doing it in the Boston Garden. The next night we'd be trying to shoot over Russell. Hah!"

Terry Dischinger, 6 feet 7, always was a thinker as well as an athlete. Now, at 49, Dr. Terry G. Dischinger is a rare spectator as Detroit and Portland play in The NBA Finals. He played for the Pistons and the Trail Blazers during the times when these two clubs were suffering growing pains.

"When I was in Detroit, the team was always in a state of flux," Dischinger said. "We were either changing coaches or changing players.

"When I came here to Portland, they'd just hired a new coach. Jack McCloskey. He'd never coached the pros. I felt it was difficult for a college coach to get used to an 82-game schedule. We started out pretty well. There were quite a few personnel changes."

But Portland was the place he decided to live with his wife, Mary, and their three children. He left basketball after one season with the Blazers. He went off to the University of Tennessee to continue his dental studies and earned his second degree. His first was in engineering at Purdue, where he was an All America.

He returned to Oregon and began his practice in orthodontics in this princely suburb of Portland . . . Displayed on the main wall of his waiting room are Dischinger's USA uniform and Gold medal won at the 1960 Olympics in Rome.

"Oscar Robertson, Jerry West, Jerry Lucas were on that team," Dischinger said. He was hesitant about showing his trophies as a matter of modesty. But then he decided his clients would like to look at them. The walls inside the clinic itself are festooned with souvenirs, newspapers and artifacts celebrating the Portland Trail Blazers.

"This is the Palace of Lake Oswego," he said.

The doormat, briefly, happened to be a Pistons T-shirt, purchased for the occasion of a Detroit visitor's arrival.

Dischinger's loyalties are evident. He lives here. His kids were educated here. One son was an Oregon All-State basketball player. Dischinger is a Blazers season ticketholder . . .

Now . . . Dischinger talked about the old days, those tough seasons in Detroit. Crowds sometimes hit 2,000 at Cobo Arena. The Pistons sometimes won and sometimes lost. Sometimes, but not often, people cared.

"I was never in a situation where the team was together for a while," Dischinger said. "One year in Detroit, when we were in the same division as Milwaukee, Phoenix and Chicago, we started out 12-and-0. The next year half the team was gone. Talk about chemistry. Then it was all gone.

"What do I remember about playing at Cobo? I remember you could hear individual people—because there weren't that many."

This terrible chaos . . . In six seasons, he played for seven coaches. One of the seven was himself. He was tapped, named acting coach, when Butch van Breda Kolff couldn't take it any more and left NBA coaching ten games into the 1971–72 season. Dischinger was listed, officially, as the Pistons' coach for two games.

"I'm the only coach in history never to win a game," Dischinger said.

"A lot of great talent came through there . . . Guys like Dave DeBusschere, Happy Hairston, Tom Van Arsdale, Ray Scott, Eddie Miles. We just never put it all together."

Those seemed to be hopeless days for the Pistons. There were times when the NBA sought to move the franchise out of Detroit. Fred Zollner . . . fought the league to prevent the move.

"I don't think I ever felt hopeless," Dischinger said. "More frustration that we couldn't move more into the upper eschelons. We could compete.

"What's difficult at that level is to keep believing mentally that you have the ability to win. You're really in trouble when you stop believing you can win.

"Personally, the thing I did best was I could score. I was not a great rebounder. I was adequate on defense. I didn't feel I got the ball enough to do what I did best. That was kind of a personal frustration for me."

Just about the time the Pistons were starting a climb in the 1970s—Dave Bing was on the club then, Bob Lanier was a rookie—Dischinger went to another team suffering the growing pains. The Pistons traded him to Portland in a three-club deal. Detroit got Fred Foster in return.

The Trail Blazers were an expansion club, a dismal one, in their third season.

"We had a lot of young guys," Dischinger said. "Sidney Wicks was in his second year. Larry Steele was in his second year. Lloyd Neal was a rookie. Ollie Johnson was a rookie. It wasn't so much frustration because I could see the end of my career. I was just trying to help the younger guys.

"I asked to be traded by the Pistons. I told Ed Coil that this team was not winning with me. I was halfway through dental school, and I was looking for a place to make home.

"I wanted to go to Phoenix. Detroit couldn't make a deal. I didn't want to come here. I'm glad I did.

He can play golf year-round and carries a .5 stroke handicap, almost scratch. And he can watch the Trail Blazers.

"I didn't believe I'd be a fan," said this ex-Piston/ex-Blazer. "I thought I could be a professional. Observe it.

"This year, I became a fan."

Such is Blazermania.

And the glass-encircled Memorial Coliseum near the banks of the Willamette River rocked with Blazermania on Sunday afternoon, June 10, 1990. The Pistons were villains everywhere; Bill Laimbeer was detested. And now the Pistons were at a disadvantage in a rabidly hostile environment against a basketball team that had been belittled in a town that had been ridiculed.

Beyond those elements of emotion, the Pistons had been playing in the finals with mechanical problems. The Pistons, basically, were at their strongest when they could attack with a three-guard philosophy. With Vinnie Johnson, doing the Microwave bit, hopping off the bench and lighting up the arena with baskets.

In Games 1 and 2 against Portland, Vinnie had missed 9 of his 10 shots. Including the Chicago series, he was in a 3-for-24 slump. With the superheated coverage of the finals, Vinnie's friends were reading all about his misses back in Brooklyn.

"I got nothing to say," Vinnie said when the reporters asked him to talk about his lost shooting eye. "Not a word.

Chuck Daly had one lineup change for Game 3. Mark Aguirre would be starting at small forward. Dennis Rodman had been the starter since the middle of the regular season and all through the playoffs. Now Rodman's sprained ankle was so bothersome, Daly had to make the switch.

Before the game Matt Dobek was summoned to the telephone. Debbie Dumars was calling from Detroit. Joe Dumars II had died in Natchitoches. Debbie was keeping her pact with her husband. Don't tell Joe. Dobek told Chuck Daly and Jack McCloskey and Bill Davidson. Isiah was told. None of them would tell Dumars until after the game that his father had died.

Again, Game 3 started with the Trail Blazers moving ahead, then the Pistons making one of their charges led by Isiah. Detroit had a four-point lead after one quarter.

It is in these championship games that the coaches earn their feed. Experience matters. So does coaching touch, the feel for positioning personnel, and the unexpected use of the mid-game hunch. Chuck Daly started the second quarter with another strange array on the floor. He left Isiah in the game. He put Salley in. Nothing unusual in that. But then Daly went to the extreme end of his bench, to Scott Hastings and David Greenwood—the two guys who customarily sat there, joked with the fans, joked with each other, led cheers. And as the fifth guy on the floor—rejecting Isiah's notion—Daly went to the misfiring and uncharactistically silent Vinnie Johnson.

Daly had a hunch. It turned into a brilliant stroke.

Vinnie, who had been one-for-ten, connected on his first shot. The subs held the lead, then added to it. Vinnie hit a three-pointer. Then he scored another jumper. He scored again, and then again.

It the time it takes for a microwave to take your beefsteak and make it done like dinner, Vinnie Johnson had 13 points. And the Pistons had an eleven-point lead.

It'd be twelve in the third quarter, then reduced to seven before the nastiness started. Drexler slammed the ball at Laimbeer, who had fouled him. The Portland crowd booed.

Vinnie returned in the fourth quarter. He hit a jumper, to open the lead to ten. Later he hit another jumper, to open the lead to fifteen. By the time, Buck Williams delivered a chop across Laimbeer's neck and jaw, the issue had been decided. Laimbeer fouled out a minute later. The Portland crowd emitted a derisive cheer. It was the sort of moment that Laimbeer loves. His team was far, far ahead, on the road, and he went through his routine. He bent in a deep, mocking bow and waved to the home fans, the dirty villain.

The Pistons won it, 121–106, the franchise's first victory in Portland since 1974, after twenty successive defeats. There had been no voodoo involved, no hex, no problem in winning the game that had to be won in Portland. The Pistons had reclaimed the homecourt advantage; they had a two games to one lead in the series. It was Vinnie Johnson's turn to be the key figure. He scored 21 points.

In the subdued locker room of the victors, Joe Dumars was sympathetically led to a telephone to speak to his wife back in Detroit.

There was the relief of this needed victory mixed with the sorrow for Joe Dumars, who had never been involved in any controversies on this team and had only friends among all his teammates.

Chuck Daly and Isiah went to the NBA's interview room; Vinnie talked in the locker room of his agonies, of the street game he had learned as a lad in Brooklyn and honed to sweetness in the NBA, of not being forced to read about his slump any more. Bill Laimbeer put on the black Fedora and regaled the writers.

"Joe made one shot, running down the lane, a high shot," Isiah told the sporting press of the world, as only Isiah could, "and it went in. After that, we looked at each other and smiled, and I said to myself, 'your father put that one in. You sure didn't have anything to do with it.'"

"We broke a seventeen-year streak," Daly said at the press conference. "This was the time and place to do it. Obviously, we were in a precarious position. Now we can take it home. The last thirty-three, thirty-four months, we've played 330 games, you get the feel. You can tell the mood on the plane, the mood in practice. You get to deal with the egos.

"We were very emotional. I sensed that yesterday at practice. Vinnie? I've coached here seven years. I know Vinnie."

In the locker room, Laimbeer explained the internal communication among the champions. He had given Vinnie Johnson a verbal hug in the pregame locker room.

"It was a mental thing with Vinnie," Laimbeer said. "I talked to him. I explained to him we were behind him even if he shot 1-for-500."

"Bill definitely gave me a big lift," said Johnson. "He said, 'you're two men.' He almost called me at three o'clock in the morning."

Among all the Pistons' victories over the previous few seasons, as they became contenders and then champions, Laimbeer ranked this one near the top.

"The third-best win for this club," he said, squinting beneath the Bruise Brothers Fedora. "The others were Boston two years ago, when we finally beat them, and got over the hump. And the first game with L.A. two years ago in the finals, when we won."

"Bigger than last year when you guys won the championship?" I asked him.

"Last year was too easy," Laimbeer said. He relished the war.

With this relish, the Pistons went out to play Game 4 two nights later. Joe Dumars, conferring with his family in Louisiana and his wife in Detroit, decided to remain with his team. It was the way his father would have wanted it, the family said.

And on the offday between Games 3 and 4, there was renewed speculation about Daly's future and unknowing media guesses that he was committed to NBC-TV for the next season. The guesswork had been triggered on this day-in between by Pat Riley. Riley had upstaged the finals by announcing his resignation as coach of the Lakers after so many seasons of victory. It was common knowledge he would join the network as a slicked talking head. NBC wanted two such former coaches as it took over the NBA telecasts from CBS—and had offered Daly the other assignment.

Chuck kept grinning and thrusting, while reminding all the preening guessers that coaching was in his blood. Sometimes you have to hit guys in the head with a bludgeon before they can figure things out.

The pattern continued in Game 4. The Trail Blazers streaked off ahead. The Pistons played, typically it seemed, without adrenelin. By the end of the first quarter, the Blazers had a ten-point lead. And Vinnie Johnson was on the floor for Detroit. He warmed up by hitting his first shot.

Then, in the second quarter, he connected on a couple more jumpers as the Pistons caught up and tied the score. The Blazers retook the lead. It was then that Joe Dumars, possessed, drove the lane, ordered Salley out of the way, and scored. In quick succession, Dumars scored three field goals and then another just before half. The Pistons had a five-point lead at the half. They did all this with Isiah scoring only two points.

They built the lead to sixteen in the third quarter. They did all this with Isiah scoring four three-point baskets. He scored 22 points in the twelve minutes.

But starting the fourth quarter, the Pistons' lead had been cut to ten. The Pistons were struck by turnovers and lethargy. And with six minutes left, all but one point of the immense lead had vanished.

Within a minute, Terry Porter hit a jumper from along the baseline. The house shook with cheers. Three times now the Pistons recapatured the lead. And twice the Trail Blazers took it back. Now it was Dumars twice hitting two free throws and then a jumper. The Pistons took a two-point lead, 106–104, into the last minute. Buck Williams made a free throw, but missed a second with 35.6 seconds left. Laimbeer was called for fouling Drexler in the scramble for the rebound. He'd fouled out. It was a weak call, after the stuff Laimbeer oftimes gets away with, and he left with a spurt of billingsgate. At the bench, he slammed a water bottle to the floor. Then Drexler made two free throws. The Blazers had slipped in front once again, 107–106, with 31.8 seconds left.

Here Chuck Daly called the Pistons' final time out. He set up a play for Isiah. The ball went to Isiah in the corner. He faked a step backwards and shot. With 25.7 seconds remaining, the Pistons were ahead again, 108–107.

The Trail Blazers worked back up toward their basket. Terry Porter drove toward the basket. He had the ball and then he didn't. Dumars bumped the ball away from Porter, and the refs didn't call a foul. Isiah grabbed the free ball and was fouled. He put in the two free throws with 8.4 seconds to play. It was Detroit 110–107, but there was to be more in the precious few seconds left. Adelman called the time out to set up a play for Portland. The Pistons quickly fouled Porter to forstall a shot at a three-point basket. Porter made the two free throws with 6.5 left. It was 110–109 favor the Pistons, and they had the ball.

The previous December the Pistons had signed Gerald Henderson as a backup guard because of his experience in the NBA. He had played ten seasons, mostly for the Celtics, and had been on two championship teams. Daly had Henderson in the game at this juncture because of this experience. Henderson was fed the ball on the inbounds by Edwards. Henderson had a free route to the basket and with 1.3 seconds left he scored the uncontested layup for a 112–109 Detroit lead.

Daly stomped on the floor with great anger. Another basket was exactly what he did not want. The tactic was to work the ball, dribble it, waste time away. Henderson had given the Blazers time to score a three-pointer and tie it. Especially if the timekeeper was a tad sluggish.

And for a bit, as the Portland crowd danced and cheered, it seemed as if that was what happened. Danny Young shot and the ball zoomed half the distance of the floor, thirty-five feet, and went in with the buzzer still echoing. The officials gathered at the timer's table and consulted each other. They talked and considered. Players from both sides smothered them with their special viewpoints. It was good, the Portlands yelled. No good, said the Detroits.

Then, the refs waved their arms. No good. Too late. They ruled the shot had been launched after the buzzer.

Now the Pistons danced, and they danced off the court, 112–109 victors, with a three games to one lead in the finals. They had won two games in three days in Portland. And they were one victory from repeating as NBA champions.

In the interview room, Daly was still shaking. He had this terrible sense of deja vu after Henderson scored the basket that had almost damaged the Pistons.

"All I could think about was Isiah's pass in Boston," said Daly. He did not have to recount history for the media.

"I didn't really yell at him," Daly added. He meant Gerald Henderson, just as he did not yell at Isiah that terrible night when Larry Bird intercepted the pass-in so many playoff games ago.

"Did we win or what?" said Henderson, so close to being a goat.

There were heroes in this game. The Pistons won it, basically, because of their triumvrate of guards. Daly had gone back to a bizarre alignment—the three-guards system. He teamed Isiah with Dumars and Johnson with a couple of twin peaks. They provided a scat attack that confused the Blazers. Isiah scored 32 points—30 in the second half. Dumars, who had stayed to play in tragedy, scored 26. Vinnie scored 20.

The Trail Blazers lacked the manpower to match them.

In the locker room, John Salley talked about many things—including his view of the last shot by Danny Young that didn't count.

"That last shot took four seconds to get off," said Spider. "I was going strictly Brooklyn on that, Brooklyn one, Brooklyn two . . . four seconds. I could see the headline: 'Salley Beats Up Ref.' They must pay that man who runs the clock a lot of money."

Somebody said to Salley that he was one game from winning a lot of money, Or was it the championship ring that mattered most? Salley looked at Aguirre nearby.

"Mark, what's bigger the ring or the money?" yelled Spider.

Aguirre, who had been able to adapt his one-man scoring binges into the conservative offensive framework of the Pistons, looked back at Salley. He responded:

"You ask me, and I left 36 points a game!"

Game 5 would be broadcast to more than seventy-five countries, according to the NBA's tub-thumpers and bean counters. The listening audience included NBA fans in Qatar and Zimbabwe.

"Did'ja ever think you could win two games out here?" a man had asked Isiah during the off day in Portland.

"I thought they would be long odds," said Isiah. "But if any team is capable of that, it's us."

Asked the same question, Chuck Daly responded simply: "No."

But now, as the Pistons went out to play the Trail Blazers in Game 5 on June 14, 1990, four cases of Cooks American champagne were already chilling, just in case. And the manadatory caps bearing the legend: PISTONS—BACK-TO-BACK 89–90 WORLD CHAMPIONS—had been stashed away in a secret hiding place, along with the customary T-shirts with the identical message. Again. Just in case.

The Blazers took their customary early lead. But this time Isiah altered his pattern. He had been winning the games with his scoring in the

Edwards shoots over Kevin Duckworth in Game 5. (*K. Dozier*)

second half. This time he had his eye earlier. At the end of the first quarter, he turned and banked a spinning shot off the glass for a four-point lead. Early in the second quarter, he popped one of his three-pointers to boost the lead to six points. He kept shooting, but the Trail Blazers refused to be chopped liver themselves, even in such a negative situation. They kept the Pistons close enough, to a four-point advantage, at the half.

And at the start of the third quarter, the Trail Blazers made a run. The lead fluctuated between the teams for a while. But then Portland got control. The Blazers led by as much as eight in the early fourth quarter.

It was then that Chuck Daly went to the Microwave. The score was 76–69 Portland, with nine minutes left. Vinnie Johnson hit a jumper and then another jumper and then a turnaround jumper, in a fifty-six-second spree. Then he popped in two free throws within the next minute. He has scored eight successive points on the floor—and the Pistons regained the lead at 77–76.

It was a briefly held lead and then the teams would slug it out until it was 81 for each. There was less than five minutes to go when the Trail Blazers made another run. Drexler, Porter, Kevin Duckworth, Buck Williams—they fired and rattled off seven points while holding the Pistons without a point for three and a half minutes.

For all those who put stock in the ancient belief that NBA games mean terribly little until the last three minutes, this Game 5 was for you.

The Trail Blazers had a seven-point lead, 90–83, with two minutes, two seconds left. They needed only to hold on—and they would go back to Michigan, to The Palace, for a Game 6 on Sunday.

With this 2:02 left, Daly called time out.

"You want to go back to play in Detroit?" Daly told his players, Dennis Rodman would say later. "We can win it here."

The Pistons put the ball in play and got it into Vinnie Johnson's hands. He scored with 1:50 left on his jumper. On the play Drexler fouled him and fouled out. Vinnie hit the free throw. It was 90–86, favor of Portland.

The Blazers used up as much time as they

could, shot, missed and Laimbeer seized the rebound. Down came the Pistons and got it to Vinnie. He shot his jumper and scored. It was 90–88, favor of Portland with 1:21 to go. With 43.1 seconds left, the Pistons forced a jumpball. They won the jump. This time they got the ball to Isiah. He hit the shot with 36.5 seconds left. The Pistons had tied the score, at 90–90.

The Memorial Coliseum—the people in it, anyway—had turned hysterical. They must have been going beserk, too, in Zimbabwe.

Portland again worked the ball up court. They got the ball to Terry Porter and he . . . he threw it away. Detroit ball, 20.1 seconds left. Daly called a time out to set up a last shot for Isiah.

Rodman made the inbounds pass—this time. He passed it to Isiah. Isiah dribbled, he waited, letting time go; he was off balance. He saw Vinnie. He passed it to Vinnie. Four seconds to go. Vinnie dribbled and shuffled to his left. He shot from seventeen feet, arching the ball high above Jerome Kersey, and the ball went into the orange, iron hoop and fell and rode the force of gravity through the netting.

The game clock on the wall of the arena flickered 00.7. It was Detroit 92, Portland 90. And a fraction of a second later, the Detroit Pistons—once the laughing stock of pro basketball—had completed the Daly Double, had become the third franchise in the history of the NBA to win championships BACK-TO-BACK!

The locker room was a mad, mad scene—once you could battle through the swarm of well-wishers, Detroit fans who had found their way to Portland, Oregon, despite the media maps that could have sent them to Maine. The Pistons were back in the sandbox. Champagne squirted off the ceiling and heads and down necks. Bill Laimbeer put on the black Fedora and his face lit up like one of those little HAV-A-NICE-DAY smile buttons.

"At halftime, I told Vinnie, 'you're going to make the winning shot,'" Laimbeer said.

"Why him?" I asked Laimbeer.

"Because he's Vinnie Johnson," Laimbeer said, rolling on, mobbed by writers, pressed by TV cameras.

"Last year the championship was for everybody else. The organization. The city. The fans. Everybody else. This year it was for us.

Buddah enjoys championship number two. (*K. Dozier*)

"We talked about it all year. It was for us, the twelve players in this room.

". . . everybody wanted a piece of the Detroit Pistons, but we survived. . . . we thought we didn't get all the respect we should have after last season . . . now I think they know now how special and good we are . . ."

They were champions, back-to-back, and there wasn't any modesty in this locker room.

"We were real close to winning three in a row," Isiah said, harking back to the first time the Pistons were in the finals and could have won. He had scored 29 points in this Game 5 and was selected as the MVP of the finals. No contest.

"We came out here with the idea that we had to win Sunday," Isiah said. "I thought we'd win one here. Then we won Sunday. Then we won Tuesday, then Thursday. Three games out here. We had adversity all year . . .

". . . for four or five years, we felt we were one of the best teams in basketball history.

"We may not always be pretty, but this team knows how to win. We just know how to win.

"We are champions—and everybody gave us their best shot."

This time all America—and much of Europe, Africa and Asia, too—knew that the Pistons had proven themselves as champions.

The Pistons partied for hours in the Mayfair Ballroom at the Benson Hotel in downtown Portland. Invited guests could have champagne poured for them by Bill Laimbeer or discuss how tough things were with Chuck Daly or speak words of sympathetic admiration to Joe Dumars for his grit. It was a noisy party—and when Bill Laimbeer left, he no longer had the black Fedora that had become his NBA finals talisman.

And back in Detroit, people ran out into the streets to celebrate a team winning a championship. They do this now in all cities.

By the time the police regained control of the streets of Detroit and its suburbs, eight people had died. Four of them died—children and youths—when a man raced his car into them on a city street. A man died after he toppled off a roof. Another, mixing with a group of celebrants, was shot to death. Police reported that 23 others were wounded by gunshots, that 3 persons were stabbed and that there had been 104 assaults.

WDIV-TV, Channel 4, sent reporter Anne Thompson into the streets to report on the victory celebration. A celebrant swinging a baseball bat smashed the windows of the WDIV car and the reporter's forehead was gashed.

Countless store windows were smashed by looters. Celebrants threw bottles at police vehicles and cursed the cops.

A nurse at a suburban hospital reported fights among celebrants in the emergency room. They had been taken there to repair injuries.

A city, its people, its media cheered because a team of basketball millionaires had won a championship. And there were only eight deaths. Only the families of the dead wept.

Mayor Coleman Young and other civic leaders blamed the media for overkilling the story.

The Pistons flew Roundball One to Detroit the following day. They were greeted by throngs at Willow Run Airport, then dispersed to head home. Some would go to Louisiana for the funeral services of Joe Dumars' father the next afternoon.

Isiah Thomas arrived home to find his wife, Lynn, in tears. WJBK-TV, Channel 2, had gone on the evening news spectacularly with a report that Isiah had been linked with a federal gambling probe. A friend of Isiah's, a former neighbor, was under investigation. Isiah had given the man his paycheck to cash on occasion, so he could avoid causing a stir if he went into a bank without a disguise. And you might understand what a stir Isiah might cause if he went into a bank wearing a disguise.

The FBI said Isiah Thomas was not being investigated.

Isiah blamed certain media outlets for bollixing the story. Since the FBI said Isiah was in the clear, he had a right to gripe.

The week after the Pistons won their repeat championship, they went through a repeat rendering of the honors.

Detroit repeated its parade for its team, followed again by a rally at The Palace. A mob estimated at 200,000 lined the streets in Detroit. Dennis Rodman again erupted with tears when the 21,000 inside The Palace gave him a two-minute standing ovation.

That night, John Salley tossed a party for anybody who wanted to attend at Joey's. Among those who showed up was M.C. Hammer, the rap singer who had written the Pistons' theme song, "U Can't Touch This."

The next day Isiah flew to New York to receive his trophy as MVP in the NBA finals. He had a story to tell about his boyhood days when he hung around Chicago Stadium and approached his favorite player, Walt "Clyde" Frazier of the Knicks, for an autograph.

"I never told this story," said Isiah, as reported by UPI. "I used to ask for gym shoes and autographs. I was standing outside the Stadium, it was wintertime, and Clyde had his big white fur coat. I asked him for his autograph and he said no."

But Isiah said he and his sister weren't perturbed by the snub.

"No, cause I got gym shoes," Isiah told his New York audience. "I was standing there with about five pairs of gym shoes from the Knicks and Bulls. I think he had to catch a bus or something."

Isiah talked about the Celtics of the 1960s.

"Their whole atmosphere, team atmosphere. They played perfect basketball. What we've done in the NBA is bring the old 1960s style back . . . The early part of the 1970s we had the one-on-one style. I'm just glad the Detroit Pistons brought back the team style."

The day after the Pistons returned to Washington to the White House for the now customary visit to President George Bush. It was a sweltering day in the Rose Garden. Isiah was holding the blue Pistons road jersey to present to the president. He handed it around and several Pistons used the jersey to mob the sweat from their faces. A photographer snapped both Isiah and Laimbeer in midwipe.

"I think they are going to have to give us a wing here at the White House," Isiah told George Bush in front of the notetaking reporters. "They have the West Wing and the East wing. Maybe they need A Pistons Wing."

"Deja vu all over again as Yogi Berra would say," Bush said.

With the festivities done for another year, Jack McCloskey started planning for ways to induce Chuck Daly to stay on as coach. The Pistons were talking Three-Peat. And Isiah carried that goal along with him as he went west to California to make his appearance on "The Arsenio Hall Show."

IV—The Nineties

Surprise, surprise! Chuck Daly, the master of leverage, opted not to go to NBC and become a wise old talking head. He opted not to go to TNT or to the Denver Nuggets or anywhere else, as had been rumored for months, through the playoffs as the Pistons were winning their second NBA championship—and in the weeks following Portland and conquest and a permanent spot in jock history.

Read his lips! The man had been a coach since his twenties at Punxsutawny, Pennsylvania. Coaching had been his life, his obsession, through all those decades. And now that he was turning sixty, he was not giving up his profession. The zest remained. The lust to win had not diminished.

Walking the corridors outside The Palace offices, meditating, weighing dollar-sign sums,

considering his family, consulting his ego—judging it all—Daly's sole conclusion was he had to continue in coaching.

There was so much money, any direction he went. Family was not an issue. His wife, Terry, had journeyed with him from job to job through the years.

But . . . ego was an enormous consideration.

This was the man who carried a comb in his warmup suit to perfect his pomadeur on the practice floor. This was the man who dressed as dandy as he could on the bench, with his collection of suits and jackets and splashy neckties. This was the man who once told this writer to study his face to prove that it was unmarked, unlined.

"I would always look back and say I didn't try to get that third championship and it would always haunt me," Daly said at the press conference on July 10, 1990, when his decision was announced to the world.

He was the coach of back-to-back NBA champions. Only two other franchises, through all the years, had won championships in successive seasons. The Lakers did it three times—in 1949 and 1950, then in 1952 and 1953 when they played in Minneapolis, then 1987 and 1988 when they played in Los Angeles. And of course, there was the ultimate dynasty of the Celtics, their eight successive championships from 1959 through 1966 followed by two more championships in 1968 and 1969.

Three in a row would be a realistic goal for Daly. It had happened only twice. The motivation was real; if he continued to coach, Chuck Daly would be striving to join an exclusive circle. With Red Auerbach, the immortal among all NBA coaches. In all the years of the old BAA and the NBA, only two men had coached teams that had managed the Three-peat trick—Red, and John Kundla, in the fifties in Minneapolis.

There was an additional consideration. With Pat Riley gone off to TV's fantasyland, Chuck Daly would be the senior coach in tenure in the NBA.

Ego was a factor.

But Chuck had this golden opportunity, using this period of seeming indecision to bolster his income, to pad his security. He had the leverage, he had the Pistons in his grasp, he had Jack McCloskey in his grip—and he could squeeze.

So it was on this July afternoon, less than a month after the Pistons won their second championship, that it was McCloskey who broke the news. "A new contract . . . no terms . . . but if you want to check the new *Forbes* list."

The new deal provided Daly with guaranteed employment through the 1991–92 season, a one-year extension of the contract that had been negotiated, with leverage, after the near miss of the 1988 Finals. The new salary approached $700,000 a year. And as he had customarily worked into his contracts, Daly insisted an escape clause after the 1991 playoffs, if there happened to be an offer that he preferred.

One of those Daly contacted before his decision was made public was Isiah Thomas. Isiah had developed powerful spheres of influence. Back years earlier, when the Pistons were struggling and Daly himself thought he would get the ziggy, Isiah supposedly interceded with Bill Davidson. The players backed Daly then. And they did through the championship seasons. But there was not total harmony. There was much publicity about a rift between Daly and Thomas during the 1989–90 season.

"We've had our ups and downs, lover's spats," Daly told writer Corky Meinecke in the *Free Press.* "I'm sure he's not always happy with me and I'm not always happy with him. But we're still family.

"I'm aware of what he is and what he can do."

One of the things Thomas could do was soften any stirrings in the locker room. And that was Daly's reason for consulting Isiah as the coaching contract was being renegotiated.

"There had to be more cooperation between the coaches and players and among the players," Daly explained to Meinecke.

"It's part of my job . . . to find ways to keep us winning," Daly told the late Shelby Strother of the *News* during the summer. "I understand this can flip over so easily on us. But the challenge is an incredible rush—going for three in a row . . . There will be that carrot out there in front of us all season . . . We're older, yes. But I don't think that experience factor can be overstated. We know what it's like, that long haul it takes to get to the championship. We've been through something no other team has for a couple of years. The value of that is incredible . . ."

Chuck had one more thing to say, about the reputation the Pistons had to lug with them into another season.

". . . Really, we're a bunch of pussycats once you get to know us."

The pussycat notion was not universally accepted. For one, Frank Layden, the windbag who once coached the Utah Jazz until he discovered he had a voice for doing NBA radio, had a different choice words to describe Daly's position. As quoted in the October 1990 edition of *Inside Sport* magazine, Layden said:

"Frankly, I would rather lose than coach a team such as Detroit. I'm not a whore. I couldn't stand to look at them for two years. Once you get the championship ring, is it really worth it to put up with those jerks?"

It was a question Layden himself was unable to answer. He had never gotten a championship ring.

"Hey!" Bill Laimbeer had resurfaced with a huge grin after a summer of privacy. He was walking across the basketball floor of the St. Denis Centre in Windsor, Ontario, Canada, where the Pistons had opened training camp for the 1990–91 season. Here this menacing figure was being as friendly as a poodle, glad to see the reporters he would start to cuss any day now.

He stuck out his hand for a handshake. My hand disappeared amid the callouses.

Laimbeer might not confess to his reading matter, but somehow he sees everything printed about himself and his ballclub. All the preseason magazines were on the stands, specualting on whether the Pistons could with a third successive NBA championship. Or whether Michael Jordan and the Bulls had caught up with the Pistons. Laimbeer had just seen the preseason issue of *HOOP*, the publication certified by the NBA itself, in essence David Stern's house organ.

"*HOOP* magazine is picking us fourth," Laimbeer said, and he was back with his mid-season sneer.

"The NBA doesn't want us to finish first."

One of the other annual magazines devoted to pro basketball caught a prognostication by Pat Williams, the circus-master who operated the Orlando Magic franchise down by DisneyWorld.

"They're due to get hit," Williams said of the Pistons. "They will have a major tumble. It's a cyclical thing. It's someone else's turn now."

It was true that the Pistons, after back-to-back championship seasons, still had a complex about their unpopularity within the league. They would continue to play the game with a chip on their shoulders.

Laimbeer's glowering visage had appeared in a basketball shoe commercial during the summer for Converse. FLOOR LAIMBEERS? Nah.

"If nice guys finish last, where's that leave us?" Laimbeer said in the commercial.

Chuck Daly had the Pistons billeted in a hotel on the Canadian side of the riverfront of the Detroit River. The athletes could see Detroit and the United States from their rooms. There was an international tunnel under the Detroit River and an international bridge over it. It was a mile across, the flow across the border was free, but going through the immigration and customs formalities could be a drag at times. The whole trip might take ten minutes.

But the United States of America was out of bounds for the Detroit Pistons during training camp.

"Detroit is off limits," said Laimbeer, discussing the rigors of training camp. "We've got to stay on this side of the river."

After the Lakers had won their back-to-back champions in 1987 and 1988, Pat Riley had come up with the word THREE-PEAT. It was an ugly bastardization of the language, but it made a word of enchantment for headline writers with puerile mentalities.

Laimbeer was asked about the motivation of seeking a third championship. He had spent a lot of time between putts during the summer thinking about it.

"Mooooo-neee," he said, in a way he had used the word before. "More bonuses."

Then he surprised when he compared the second championship season with the first.

"Easier mentallly, harder physically," he said. "I expect this year to be the same."

Chuck Daly had his players scrimmage for the crowd that packed the gym. The Pistons went through all the motions. Right off, Isiah stole the ball from young Lance Blanks, the only rookie expected to make the team.

The previous June, amid the aftermath of the second championship and the negotiations to bring back Daly, Jack McCloskey had drafted Blanks. Blanks was a guard from Texas. He was a first-rounder, but at the tail end of the rotation. The Pistons figured he could make the club as a bench player and be cultivated as a starter for the time when some of the team elders left the club.

He was the only rookie with a chance to make the squad. The Pistons would be pretty much static in their quest for a third championship. David Greenwood, upset because he had spent so much time in limbo on the bench, had jumped to San Antonio as a free agent. In his place, McCloskey signed 7-foot-1 Tree Rollins, who had spent a dozen years in the league.

When a team wins two successive championships, the general manager is actually in a precarious spot. He could keep all the key men who helped win those championships—or he could deal away one or two of them, while the players still retained some value, for younger, less experience players. Either way could be risky.

The Pistons would be going into the new season with five guys older than thirty—Edwards, Johnson, Laimbeer, Aguirre and Rollins. And before the 1991 playoffs would end the following spring, Isiah and Rodman would turn thirty.

"Injuries scare me," Daly said in the *News*. "Birthdays don't . . . They say they want another ring. I say fine with me . . ."

This was no more a team of eager kids. Or of hungry veterans.

"You could never match the hunger of the first championship," Isiah said at the training camp.

He also, in his own mind, proven his membership in the established elite of pro basketball by being selected as the MVP of the playoffs.

"A little guy had never done it before," he said. "A big guy had always done it. So there was pressure."

It was a temporary memory lapse—or Joe Dumars, the 1989 MVP, could be classified as a big guy, standing two inches higher than Isiah.

Isiah would be entering his tenth season in the league. And he would be entering it in anger.

The guilt-by-association innuendos had faded away over the summer months after the mishandling of the gambling probe story. But Isiah, quite obviously, carried a grudge against Channel 2, WJBK-TV. And now his reaction to an attempt to interview him by the station's Virg Jacques had become the hot topic of training camp.

Jacques claimed, on the air, that Isiah had grabbed him around the neck and had pushed him. The TV man said he would file suit. The words choke and strangle were used.

Isiah attracted a mob at Windsor. He said he felt his reputation had been smirched.

"There's not doubt in people's minds what I am and what I'm about," Isiah said. "Some people are trying to discredit that. When you get to the top, somebody's always trying to knock you down. It's no different with Joe Montana. The question is not whether it's right or wrong, or fair. That's how it is."

Moments later, Isiah and Jacques went into a room at the gymnasium and made their peace.

The basketball season could start on schedule.

It started with another presentation of the diamond championship rings at The Palace on November 2. The lights were doused and the champions ran out, individually announced by George Blaha, spotlighted to the mighty cheers of the basketball cult. Buddha Edwards ran out with three fingers raised. Jack McCloskey got loud cheers—where else would a GM be awarded hero's status?—and said "We got the Daly Double, now we go for the Trifecta."

Laimbeer had his game face. Actually, he had more than his game face. His cheekbone had been fractured during the exhibitions. He would be wearing a transparent plastic mask.

They would look like a team from Mars. Isiah would be wearing goggles to protect a ruptured tear duct in his eye.

Beyond those two with injuries, there was concern about about Dennis Rodman's still-agonizing ankle. The Pistons were prepared to place Rodman on the inactive list when he insisted he could play over the pain. But Daly decided to return Mark Aguirre to the starting lineup in Rodman's place in the early part of the season.

So it started. And as the Pistons got ready to go onto the floor the noise system blared with Hammertime.

M.C. himself came on the video screen above center court to say:

"It's time Detroit let them know they can't

Edwards and Laimbeer let the refs know that the correct call is a jump ball. (K. Dozier)

touch these . . ." And he pointed to the twin NBA championship trophies.

And then the Pistons started their drive for a third championship against the Milwaukee Bucks. They beat the Bucks, 115–104.

The long, long grind to the playoffs was underway.

The Pistons started it wonderfully well. Through November, they were 13–2. One of their two losses, in the first week of the season, was back at Portland. The motivation was different than it had been five months earlier, in the finals. The Trail Blazers busted the Pistons, 113–101. Then the Pistons finished November with a ten-game winning streak.

In the midst of the streak the Pistons were in

Miami to play the Heat. They became the first basketball team to appear on "Monday Night Football." Their alter egos, the L.A. Raiders, were engaged in a football match with the Miami Dolphins. And the camera panned the sidelines. All America saw the world champion Pistons adorned in Raiders' black T-shirts and caps. Laimbeer, of course; Isiah, grinning, of course, Dumars, Johnson.

The next night when the Pistons played the Heat, a Miami heckler yelled at Salley: "Hey, Salley baby, you got a girl's name." Spider, according to George Vecsey of the *New York Times,* responded: "Yeah, but I have two championship rings . . . [stage pause] Would you like me to show them to you?" Salley then showed the fan two fingers. Neither was a ring finger.

Chuck Daly was continually perplexed by Salley. One night Salley would be marvelous, scoring, blocking shots. Other nights his attention would focus on the comedy clips on the scoreboard.

"John is enigma wrapped in a riddle," Daly told the media. "I never know what I'm going to get from him. You know what to expect from others, but with John you never know who's going to show up."

Near the end of November, the Pistons were in a struggle at Atlanta. Laimbeer got into it with Dominique Wilkins, an old adversary. Some shoves, not much more. The Pistons went off on a tear and won the game. Laimbeer scored 25 points.

"That's our game," he told the writers. "That's when we're at our best. We're at our best when we go to war. Maybe we should be part of Operation Desert Shield."

America, with troops in Saudi Arabia, was girding up for war with Iraq.

Rod Thorn did not care for Laimbeer as the warrior. He dumped the heavier fine on Laimbeer as the troublemaker.

Rickey Mahorn was featured in *Sport* magazine, talking about a bunch of stuff.

WORST MOMENT?—"Being let go to the Minnesota Timberwolves after winning the NBA championship. You feel like the victory's embedded in stone. But it wasn't worth everything I thought it would be. I felt betrayed . . ."

MAHORN ON LAIMBEER—"At times everybody in the world thinks he's a bleep. A while back, I called him and said, 'Hey man, why haven't you called me?' And he says, 'Because your the enemy now.' But the best thing about Bill . . . we had two opposites that attracted. We could talk about everything—religion, racial barriers, politics—we'd disagree sometimes but we'd learn about each other. And I knew that this person had the attribute to win. We developed our own identities, we were The Bad Boys. I relished that. After the games, the reporters would come in. I'd say, 'Hey Bill, are we talking tonight?' 'Nah.' Then we'd yell, 'Get outta here,' and kick 'em out. It was fun with him."

GUY I RESPECT MOST—Adrian Dantley. "Ever since playing with him in Detroit, he's been an inspiration. A mature NBA player who puts everything into perspective. He works hard, takes care of his career, takes care of his life."

November ended as the best first month in the history of the franchise. The Pistons, in first in the division, were out ahead of the Bulls, in third, by four games.

Phil Jackson, starting his second season as coach of the Bulls, was already dismayed.

"I thought they'd get off to a slower start than they have," Jackson told Bob Verdi in the *Chicago Tribune.* "It's been their history. Then when they get their tenth defeat, they kick it in another notch . . . It's almost as if they want to be mentioned in the same breath with the great teams. Boston, the way they moved the ball. The Lakers, and their fast break. The Pistons. Gritty. If you ask me to give you a word to describe them, it would be GRITTY. That's their personality."

"I don't think we're as good as the Pistons at coming into a building, shutting down a team to the point where it deteriorates, then getting out of town with a victory," Michael Jordan said in the same column. "Hopefully, what we're building toward is a point where we can outnumber a team like the Pistons in a long series . . . If we fall too far behind Detroit, then I have to do whatever I can to change it. When do we reach that point? Never, I hope."

The Pistons started December with another streak. They lost four in a row, their longest losing streak in three seasons. They would lose seven of eight.

They made their first visit to the Lakers early in the month. Late in the game Laimbeer came down hard on James Worthy, who was headed for the basket. Worthy went after Laimbeer, but it was broken up before it became a fight.

"Typical Laimbeer," said Mike Dunleavy, who had replaced Riley as coach of the Lakers. "He has a chance to take a foul, he's going to accentuate it."

The Lakers blasted the Pistons, 114–90.

"We didn't see a good team," Daly told the *L.A. Times,* "we saw a great team. They are possibly better than ever before."

The Pistons were out of first place before the middle of December. The Bucks went past them. The Bulls were even with them, The Pistons went into Boston and lost at the Garden, 108–100.

"I'm like President Bush," Daly told the writers. "I'm just not ready to admit we're in a recession."

Laimbeer was given his customary welcome to Boston. The Herald ran a picture of Robert Parish with a fistful of Laimbeer's jersey, pulling on it.

Bill responded by telling the media: "That's the way it is everywhere we go. I've become more than a basketball player. I'm a basketball personality."

Bill Bonds of Detroit's Channel 7 did a bit on Laimbeer. Laimbeer told him: "I have to look at opponents as the enemy. You almost have to hate them."

The NBA schedulemaker, with little sense of theatre, did not match up the Pistons and the Bulls until the third week of December—after more than a quarter of the games had been played. This had become the NBA's most bitter rivalry.

Now with the Pistons reeling, losers of seven of their previous eight games, the Bulls went into The Palace sniffing blood. They were on the rise. But the Pistons were the back-to-back champs, and they had gotten there both times by handling the Bulls. Particularly at The Palace. The Bulls still could only aspire to what the Pistons had already accomplished.

So it was that the Pistons emerged from their slump and beat the Bulls, 105–84, in typical fashion. Michael scored 33. Isiah and Dumars each scored 19.

Next game the Pistons won again, beating the Hawks, 113–87, at The Palace—after Daly and Isiah were kicked out. Daly got the boot for debating one of the refs in a manner that lacked dignified decorum. Isiah got it for clenching his fist and using at against the body of the Hawks' Rumeal Robinson.

The Pistons continued their erratic journey through December.

The NBA schedulemaker, with TV on his brain, had the Pistons meeting the Bulls in a rematch in Chicago Stadium on Christmas afternoon on NBC, the new network. The Pistons were not pleased having to leave home and family on Christmas Eve. So Isiah and Laimbeer defied the club, skipped the Roundball One flight to Chi the day before Christmas, played Santa Claus to their young families, and then took off for Chicago at their own expense. Quite expensive. They chartered their own plane to catch up with the team.

This time Jack McCloskey—not Rod Thorn—would fine them.

But in immortal words of Charles Barkey, Isiah and Laimbeer didn't give a damn. A heavy fine is a pittance to sporting millionaires.

"I've always preached that family was more important than basketball," Laimbeer told interviewers, "and it was time to put up or shut up. I kind of put my money where my mouth was."

"Seeing my little boy open up presents, you just can't buy that," Isiah told the press. "We played didn't we? It isn't like we missed the game, or anything."

They played, they lost, they were full of lethargy. The Bulls beat them, 98–86, and afterwards Isiah detected something mysteriously the matter with the Pistons.

"From the coaching staff on down to the players, we're not going to get it done with this attitude," Isiah said in the aftermath to the media. "We may have to look in a new direction. New people, new enthusiasm . . . We slowed to a crawl. We didn't have the same emotional energy and enthusiasm in the second half. That seems to be out pattern this year . . . This is a totally different attitude than he had last December."

The Pistons had dropped to third place . . . two and one-half games behind Milwaukee— and two behind the Bulls.

NBC, which could toss and turn a rumor with the media veterans, figured there was dissension on the reigning champions. The network proclaimed that the other players were ticked off at

Isiah and Laimbeer because they had skipped the team flight to Chicago on Christmas Eve.

"They're just trying to throw stuff out and hope it sticks," Laimbeer responded when reporters approached him with NBC's allegation. "Well, it ain't going to stick here. It might stick some place else."

Erratic? Inconsistent? This was what Chuck Daly was getting paid huge bucks to figure out! The Pistons finished off the 1990 portion of the season with three victories. They started the 1991 part with eight more victories. The club that had been reeling with defeat and rumored dissension three weeks earlier would rattle off an eleven-game winning streak.

In the first game of the new year, the Pistons beat the Denver Nuggets at The Palace, 118–107. Dennis Rodman, starting again, scored 34 points, his career best, had 23 rebounds and 2 steals.

Daly gushed afterwards: "He's the best there is. He's a joy to coach. In all my years—high school, college and pro—he's the only player who goes all out every game. He never gets involved in the agenda, the head stuff."

With the club rising again, the Pistons got involved in another fistfight. This time it was intramural, at practice, between Aguirre and, of course, Laimbeer. Laimbeer was caught on video tape by WXYZ-TV, Channel 7, tossing a looping right. Daly broke it up.

The next night the Trail Blazers made their only season appearance in The Palace. The game received an exaggerated media buildup as a rematch of the finals. It was a contest. It went into overtime and the Pistons won it, 100–98, on Laimbeer's basket with 0.03 seconds left. A TV man rushed to Laimbeer with a microphone, figuring the victory had some profound impact: "What'd it mean?"

"That we won eight in a row," said Laimbeer, always the realist against media overkill.

Ever since its foundation, the NBA had clogged its veins with collections of minutia. Against the Trail Blazers—before he won the game—Laimbeer sucked in a rebound that some would consider historic. It was his 8,064th in the uniform of the Pistons. That number made him the club's all-time rebound leader, replacing Bob Lanier—if you can feature such a total. Not bad

for a guy about whom old coach/cum TV prattler Hubie Brown once said: "He can't jump over a piece of paper."

It might have been history to the NBA's stat counters. It was trivia to Laimbeer.

". . . means I've been here for a long time, and if you're not a pretty good player for an organization, you're not with it for a long time," Laimbeer told the *Free Press'* Charlie Vincent. "I guess it's a big deal."

While the Pistons were streaking, the Bulls also were hot. The two rivals vaulted past the Bucks. With their eleven victories in a row, the Pistons could not reclaim first place. They were a half game behind the Bulls. It looked as though it would be a hellacious race through the rest of January, February, March and April for the division title—and a homecourt edge in May.

But then Isiah' wrist went on him. His right wrist, his dominant wrist for shooting and dribbling. The medics said he had strained ligaments. Isiah missed two games. Then he tried to play against the Celtics in late January. He managed 3 points in 22 minutes.

Two days later, on January 25, 1991, the Pistons announced that Isiah Thomas would undergo surgery to fuse three bones in his right wrist. Doctors estimated that Isiah would be incapacitated for at least twelve weeks, most likely longer. The NBA playoffs would start in exactly—twelve weeks.

The Pistons, thus, would be without Isiah for the remainder of the regular season and probably into the playoffs . . . or so the doctors said.

"He has a very, very high pain threshold," Jack McCloskey said in his announcement to reporters. "He just couldn't go on. This is a very serious injury for him to stop playing."

Even with Isiah gone, the Pistons managed a five-game winning streak, turning into February. They surged back into first in the Central Division. Joe Dumars had moved to Isiah's position. Vinnie went into Joe's. Daly now figured he must use Lance Blanks, the rookie, sooner than he'd desired. McCloskey scrounged around for a guard and signed John Long. John had been out of the league, and McCloskey found him playing pickup games on the courts at Southfield, a suburb outside Detroit. It was John's third tour with the Pistons.

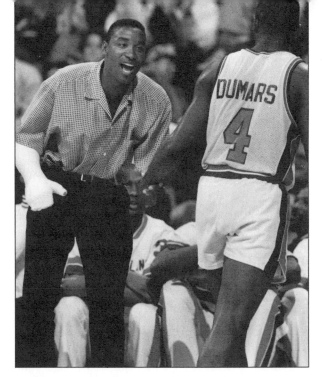

Isiah was forced into the cheerleader role for 5½ weeks in 1991 because of a wrist injury. (*K. Dozier*)

On February 7, the Bulls were scheduled into The Palace. Now there were reports of all sorts of dissension on the Bulls. They had the same problems they'd had the previous spring, when Michael lashed out at his teammates and stormed out of the locker room during the playoffs and took refuge on the bus. The players had been criticizing Phil Jackson; they had been criticizing Jerry Krause, the general manager; they had been grousing about each other. Scottie Pippen, quoted by writer Ted Green in *The National,* accused Krause of being a liar in regard to a contractual matter.

Vocal as usual, Michael had blasted Krause in public for not bolstering the Bulls by trading for Walter Davis, who went to Portland instead. Then Michael said if he were the GM rather than Krause, the Bulls would be a better ballclub.

Now, Michael envisioned the Pistons-Bulls game at The Palace as the pivotal game of the schedule.

He told the Chicago press: "We have to prove that we can win there if we're to have any legitimate chance of winning the championship . . . If we can't beat them without Isiah, then we have to question ourselves as to whether we're really that good of a team."

The Pistons had beaten the Bulls nine times in a row at The Palace.

The Bulls won it, 95–93, with Michael scoring 30. Michael, tongue out, hotly motivated, scored the last 10 points for the Bulls. Singlehandedly, he wiped out a four-point Detroit lead in the last four minutes. The Pistons missed their last four shots.

"Everyone says we can't win here," Michael told the media. "We proved them wrong . . . With Isiah out, it makes a difference . . . It's a great confidence builder from the mental aspect to know we can beat this team other than on our court."

"We got a monkey off our backs," was the way Phil Jackson described it.

The Bulls had achieved something. They had achieved what once, years earlier, the Pistons had achieved by winning a game in the Boston Garden.

And the Bulls were learning. They were displaying some Bad Boys habits of their own. Bill Cartwright got kicked out for delivering an elbow to the face of one of the Pistons. Bill Laimbeer's face, at least his Phantom of the Opera mask.

The Pistons hung two percentage points behind the Bulls at the All-Star Game on Feburary 10. Dennis Rodman was omitted from the team, and Jack McCloskey was outraged at the oversight. Hersey Hawkins, who played for the 76ers, was added to the squad because Larry Bird was hurt.

McCloskey delivered a public statement to the media:

"Today is a dark day in the NBA for effort, enthusiasm, talent and hard work. The league has elected a guard for injured forward Larry Bird . . . therefore bypassing possibly the greatest defensive player ever to play the game—Dennis Rodman. This is a gross injustice and cannot be explained rationally."

Gross injustice that it was, the complaint seemed to be overstated.

At least Sir Charles Barkley, Hawkins' Philly teammate, seemed to believe so.

"The reason it's so dark is because Jack lives in Detroit," Barkley told the inquisitive writers at the All-State site in Charlotte. "If it's so dark, tell Jack to turn the lights on."

Rodman? He wasn't nearly as upset as McCloskey. Dennis spent his All-Star break holiday where it's always dark—in Las Vegas in a casino.

After the break, the Pistons went into a spin.

They lost to Indiana at The Palace. Dumars scored 30 in defeat. Blanks, the rookie, was stripped of the ball on three successive possessions by Micheal Williams. Two years earlier, the Pistons had given up on Williams. They then lost to the Knicks in New York by twenty-eight points, embarrassingly watched by the nation on NBC-TV. Rodman blasted his teammates for giving up.

"I'm not sorry for what I said," Rodman, not hiding, told the media. "I don't care if they hate me . . . I told them that we're all men. They might not like my opinion, but they're still going to have to listen to it. We needed to play hard, like the Pistons have done for the last three seasons."

Joe Dumars was doing his gutty best, but he was playing with a terribly wounded big toe on his left foot. He barely could walk. The Pistons missed Isiah. And there was criticism that Isiah had not even showed up at the games, to sit on the bench in civvies, to cheer his team on.

"Face it," Daly said, facing the writers, "we have to learn we're basically a pretty average basketball team . . . Everybody thinks they're playing hard, but they're going to have to play harder . . .

"When you lose someone like Isiah, all you can do is circle the wagons. It's like L.A. losing Magic, or Boston losing Bird."

"The automatic pilot is broken now," Laimbeer told the press."

Chuck Daly was a journeyman in basketall until he was well into his fifties. Glory, for him, showed up late. But when it showed, it showed with splendor, and Chuck was able to work it to the hilt with his skill in matters of leverage. Hell, whatever he got, he'd earned.

And in mid-February 1991, with the Pistons in trouble, he received the most glorious honor of all. The Olympic committee appointed him head coach of the United States team at the 1992 summer Olympics in Barcelona. For the first time, the USA would be permitted to put NBA pros on the team. The college kids had gotten knocked around at the 1988 Olympics in Seoul. Basketball was our old peachbasket invention, but it had gained popularity worldwide. And there were times when tall Soviets and tall Yugoslavs were good enough to beat the Americans at our own game. When America lost, as it did at Seoul, our journalists always moaned: This never would have happened if we could have used our NBA players.

Well, in 1992, they would be eligible—and Chuck Daly was appointed to coach them because he had become, simply, the most prominent coach in the NBA. Michael Jordan, Magic Johnson, Karl Malone, Patrick Ewing, Charles Barkley, Larry Bird, John Stockton, Chris Mullin, David Robinson, and Scottie Pippen all on the same team; it was enough to make a coach drool. And to change a hardened pessimist into a gold-expectant optimist.

"It's the ultimate challenge in that you're assembling a team of the greatest basketball talent ever," Daly told the press in response to his honor. "I expect to come back from Barcelona with the gold medal."

February was a time for chants of USA, USA, USA anyway. The nation was at war in the Persian Gulf against Iraq. And as a sign of patriotism and troop support the Pistons, and all the other NBA teams, had American flags sewn onto their warmup jackets.

The Pistons had lost three of four and four of six when they played the Seattle Supersonics on February 18. Isiah had been criticized for not attending the games, for abandoning his team when he might have been able to provide an emotional boost. Rodman had tried to do his part with a resounding outburst—a la Michael Jordan—in the locker room in Detroit.

And the Pistons' loyalists—some of them—were starting to jump ship. Though they announced their 128th successive sellout of 21,454 at The Palace, there were large patches of empty red seats visible to all who cared to look. There were maybe 1,000 no-shows, an early warning that perhaps the passionate interest had peaked in the Pistons.

But Isiah was not a no-show on this night. He was the captain. It was his duty to close the locker room and talk to the athletes.

Then he held a press conference.

"The thing that really concerns me is that all of a sudden our goals are short-sighted," Isiah said. "We're looking to the short range. We have to look to long-range goals. We're a team that is going to be playing till June. We shouldn't be judging our team from February to April . . .

"This is not a pressure situation. The guys are putting too much pressure on themselves. Actually, it would be easier without me. The guys don't have to play up to my level . . . I don't think I ever bullshitted you people about our basketball team; right now I think our basketball team is as good as it ever has been . . . We are capable of winning the championship with what we have."

Through all his brave words, one refrain kept coming back—Bill Laimbeer's words after the Pistons won their second championship in Portland.

"This is Isiah's team," Laimbeer had said then. And it was true.

The Pistons, without Isiah, were dead meat.

And already, there were reports that he'd be back with the team long before the surgeons figured he would be.

On this night, he walked out to sit on the bench in his civvies. The crowd cheered. His right arm was encased in a huge cast, almost to the elbow. He was there as a one-armed cheerleader. He jumped off the bench and flipped his left arm in the air when the Pistons rallied. And it was noticed that he was providing a coaching input on the bench, talking to assistant Brendan Malone.

His presence had an impact. The Pistons won, 85–83, with Dumars circling left and driving through a forest of Seattle defenders with a hooking right-handed layup with two seconds left.

Jack McCloskey was working feverishly on making a trade for a guard. It was happy time for the rumor mongers. The Pistons needed a somebody to fill in for Isiah. And according to reports in Detroit and in basketball gossip columns throughout the NBA, the Pistons were offering Spider Salley as the bait. There were active rumors about Salley going to at least seven different NBA clubs. For seven different players.

"It's flattering because somebody wants to get me, but it's not so flattering that the team you're giving your blood and sweat for . . ." Salley told the *News'* Terry Foster.

McCloskey's wizardry at the trade deadline was semi-legendary. But no deal this time. The trade deadline went by with no action.

"There was a lot of talk, but no shooters," McCloskey told Foster.

Three days after the deadline, McCloskey signed Gerald Henderson again. Henderson had been in retirement in Philadelphia, president of a transportation company. He had playing intramural ball to keep in shape.

The Pistons had Long, thirty-four, and Henderson, thirty-five, two retired guys who'd been playing intramural ball, and they were chasing the Bulls and Michael Jordan.

At the end of February, the Pistons played the Lakers and Magic at The Palace in a Sunday afternoon feature on NBC-TV. The presence of the Lakers always intensified the Pistons' motivation. They played their finest game since Isiah's surgery. They led at the half by seven. NBC broke off at halftime to go to Saudi Arabia for a news update on the Persian Gulf War. It had been that way with the war on—the networks judged that America could take a dose of news.

The basketball game was tied at the end of regulation. In the OT, Aguirre gunned a shot that missed, an unwise choice, Edwards dribbled the ball off his leg, Rodman got his sixth foul, Vinnie missed a shot he used to be dead on and then missed a layup. Magic controlled the game. The Lakers won it, 102–96. And the Pistons left with grim faces.

Most of their losses now were like this one. They were close, then they lost in the last three minutes, the last seconds. It was the sort of games Isiah Thomas, when healthy, used to win for them.

Indeed, they were Isiah's team. The Pistons were reduced to .500 mediocrity while his wrist healed inside the plaster cast. They lost to the Charlotte Hornets. They lost to the Miami Heat, Expansion dregs. They lost to the New Jersey Nets. They had a five-game losing streak, their longest in five years.

After an eleven-point loss to Milwaukee at The Palace, Daly said: "This was the most disappointing loss in my eight years as coach here. We got a Jekyll-Hyde team on our hands here. They don't understand what they've got to do here."

Against Charlotte at home, the Pistons missed seventeen of their first twenty shots. There was bickering on the bench. You could hear it courtside, coming from the bench: "Shut up, shut up." Aguirre had a temper tantrum on a foul call. He pounded the press table with his fist. There were empty seats all over The Palace. In the final eleven minutes, they spurted—they hadn't bothered to play hard before that—and rescued the game. After all, this was Charlotte and this was the Pistons' homecourt.

"We miss his personality more than anything physical," Dumars told Bill Halls about trying to win without Isiah. "His competitiveness. We miss that a lot more than his 16 points a night."

"It's like we'd lost our commander in chief," Rodman told *Sports Illustrated* in a piece about the decline of the Pistons.

Leadership was a problem, though Isiah had said it wouldn't matter.

"When you leave it's like a McDonald's," Isiah had said one night. "Anybody can run a McDonald's. That's the way it his here. Anybody can lead this team."

It was plain now—a team loses a star in basketball, it's tougher than in any other sport. There are only five players on the floor. The Pistons realized this now. It was like when the Lakers lost Magic Johnson in the 1989 finals.

"It's like watching a patient die," Daly said on March afternoon in a post-practice press session. "You wonder if there's anything you can do . . ."

The Pistons kept falling further behind the Bulls—four games, five games, eight and a half. By the end of March, the Pistons were nine games behind Chicago. They were in a battle—with Milwaukee for second place in the division, anything they could get as a homecourt advantage in the Eastern bracket of the playoffs.

The games they managed to win they won ugly . . . scraping along, with their nagging defense.

"Hey, if you want pretty, go to the art gallery," Joe Dumars said to some writers.

Chuck Daly had been having some premonitions as his team struggled.

"This is a good team, a proud team," Daly told Bud Shaw in *The National*. "But how many teams—the Reds, the Celtics, the Lakers—have been able to get to the top and stay there? Something always happens to them.

"So I keep asking them, 'How do you want it to end? You have a chance to write an ending. How do you want it to end?'"

On April 5, the Pistons received a gift. Isiah Thomas flew off to Hartford, for an examination of his wrist by his surgeon. The wrist had healed. It was weak, sore, but Isiah had been working out, by himself, dribbling, trying to shoot with the wrist for several weeks.

He'd beaten the doctors' most optimistic prognosis by three weeks. Now he would be back after missing thirty-two games. In his absence the Pistons had won eighteen and lost fourteen; they had rallied and managed to win their previous four. They had gone from first place to nine games behind the Bulls.

After his exam, Isiah flew back to Detroit. He played that night against the Minnesota Timberwolves.

"I was so nervous I couldn't keep my hands dry driving to The Palace," Isiah told George Blaha on the pregame telecast on Channel 50. "I went into the locker room and looked at Lam, at Joe, and I forgot my routine."

He might not have remembered his ritual in the locker room. The rest was instinct. Isiah penetrated through the defenders for his first bucket. He played thirty-five minutes on his first night back. He scored 15 points. The Pistons won, 101–92.

"Isiah looked like he never missed a beat," Daly said in his postgame commentary.

The Pistons were still Isiah's team.

Isiah quickly regained his touch. But even so, the Pistons did not respond. Edwards, Salley and Aguirre all had bothersome backs. The Pistons had been saddled with injuries all season. Now with Isiah back they lost to the Knicks and the Bucks. The best the Pistons could do now do was finish second in the division, third in the East. They were ten games behind the Bulls. There were some shaky moods, plenty of bickering, on the club.

". . . do they want to die to win it?" Isiah said in an interview with Terry Foster. "And we got to die to win it. And I'm willing to. If there are some guys not willing to do that, they won't be around long. By the time the playoffs start, it's my job to make sure there are no stowaways."

They lost a third straight game, to Cleveland, on their own court.

Isiah delivered his second blast. The Pistons had become addicted to losing, he said.

"Nobody gives a damn around here any more and that includes the coaches," Isiah told the writers. "We've become comfortable with losing. It doesn't bother anyone any more. Nobody cares . . .

"It doesn't even hurt any more when you lose."

Two nights later, the Bulls came to The Palace for their final visit of the 1990–91 regular season. It was mid-April. On this night, all the Pistons could do was send a message to Michael Jordan and the Bulls. Stick some memories into the Bulls' fragile psyches. Preserve their home turf.

They clubs were tied entering the fourth quarter. The Pistons reached back a year and put on one of their rallies. They won it, 95–91. Michael scored 40 points. Isiah had 26 plus 16 assists. There were no stowaways. Laimbeer had 22 and Dumars 20—and the Bulls had to be wondering which variety of the Pistons would show up in the playoffs.

The Pistons remained a puzzlement through the final week of the regular season. They lost to the Pacers. They beat the Celtics, they beat the Hawks. They lost to the Bulls in Chicago.

They wound up with a 50-and-32 record, eleven games behind the Bulls, who finished 61-and-21. The Pistons' record was No. 3 in the Eastern Conference. It assured them of the homecourt advantage in the first round of the playoffs, versus the Atlanta Hawks. But after that, they could be in peril if they were required to play the Celtics and Bulls in the playoffs—or any of six clubs from the West, if they could survive to the NBA finals.

"To win fifty games with the injuries we had was phenomenal," Daly told the media.

Daly, too, was wondering which variety of Pistons would show up in the playoffs. That and the thoughts he had been lugging inside his brain for more than a month—how would it end for the Pistons, the team he had coached to NBA championships, back-to-back?

"We've been ready for this since the pre-season," Buddha Edwards said to the *News'* Terry Foster the day before the playoffs opened.

It was as though the eighty-two-game season

had meant nothing, that the Pistons had learned little.

"The season's boring," Laimbeer told the media.

How different it was this year! No more statements about the value of the homecourt; or this was why they played all those games on frigid nights in January and February, to gain the edge in a pivotal seventh game.

Dennis Rodman went off to visit his barber to get a new message carved into the back of his skull. In the past he had had ALEXIS etched there, in honor of his daughter; and he'd had WILD THANG cut into the hair, presumably in honor of himself.

Now for the playoffs he had TRILOGY—91—III branded into his head. Better than THREE-PEAT, the Trilogy became the Pistons'

Bad Boys At It—Laimbeer, Rodman, and Salley tangle with Bill Cartwright and Horace Grant of the Bulls during the final matchup between the teams in The Palace during the 1991 regular season. (*K. Dozier*)

obsession. At least, Chuck Daly hoped it would be an obsession.

"It's definitely more of a challenge this year," Isiah said on WJR radio. "It's all stacked against you. The odds are against it, we've won for two years."

Strange as it was, with the playoffs here, the Pistons were at their fittest. The backaches had gone away. Edwards, Salley and Aguirre were in top shape. Isiah's wrist, always worrisome, had endured a month of the rigors of the game.

In one move, Daly decided to start William Bedford against the Hawks. William had started the final four games of the regular season to rest Edwards. Now Daly planned to use Edwards off the bench.

Terry Foster surveyed the Pistons, asking which team they feared most in the Eastern playoffs. Most guys said Chicago.

"The Pistons," said Laimbeer. But which opponent. "The Pistons," said Laimbeer.

As always, he was very astute.

There was a whole new blast of electricity when the Pistons romped onto the court at The Palace for Game 1 of the best-of-five against Atlanta. The people believed the Pistons could do it again. Certainly, there was no alarm with the Pistons playing the Hawks in the opening round. The Pistons—no matter what sort of slump they were in—had won all five games with Atlanta during the season.

By the second quarter, it was obvious that the Pistons were involved in something more intense than a boring regular-season game. Spud Webb, 5 feet 7 and once a rejected Pistons draft choice, popped in two three-pointers for the Hawks.

In the third quarter, the Hawks were up on the Pistons by eleven, at 78–67. Webb had scored 12 points. Isiah had scored 1.

In the fourth quarter, Laimbeer got into it with Sidney Moncrief. Moses Malone rushed to Moncrief's aid. Laimbeer got ejected. About then the Pistons became aware these were the playoffs. Isiah rallied them, mostly with his floor play. They cut the Atlanta lead to two points, then tied the score at 93–93 with 2:27 left. This was the sort of game the Pistons had become accustomed to winning in the playoffs.

They lost. In the final minutes, the Hawks beat them at their specialty. Of course, in the last half minute, Isiah missed two free throws; Du-

mars missed a three-point shot; Salley lifted up an airball. The final score was Atlanta 103, Detroit 98. The Hawks were up by one victory— and this was one of those abbreviated series, first team to win three advances onward.

The faces in the Pistons' locker room afterward were faces of doom.

Daly realized it.

"In a five-game series, you lose that first game and you shoot yourself in the foot," he said. "We got to win a game there. We got our backs to the ball."

"The next game is crucial," said Laimbeer.

In the media hospitality freeload room before Game 2, the sports writers were telling graveyard jokes. "You coming back from Atlanta Wednesday?" asked one, to laughter. Game 3 would be in Atlanta Tuesday night, and the wisdom was that the Pistons would be getting swept.

The Pistons started sluggishly again. Isiah was

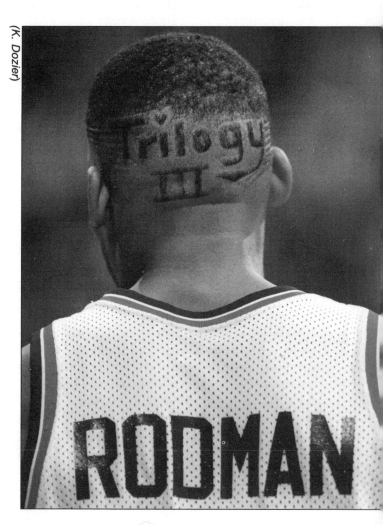

(K. Dozier)

278

missing, even a layup. Vinnie missed two shots. Then Isiah tossed the ball away.

The guards had been the Pistons' strength in their championships. And now they were not getting it from the guards. Yet, the Pistons were still dominating this game. They had an eleven-point lead at the half. Isiah found the target in the third quarter, and the Pistons started to romp.

But it was oddly quiet in The Palace. With the Pistons ahead by fifteen in the fourth quarter, it was so silent that Rodman, the cheerleader, raised his arms in supplication. And the rich, affluent audience of surbanites started screaming behind their team.

Some of the action was at the bench. Daly was catching angry stares from Mark Aguirre.

The Pistons won it, 101–88, to square the series. Now they would have to win one of the two games in Atlanta.

"That's not going to be easy," Daly said in his postmortem. "We got to win in their building or it's over."

And there was trouble in the locker room. That old, ugly team disunity had resurfaced.

Aguirre put on a tantrum because Daly had ignored him in the second half, then stuck him in for forty-four seconds of garbage time. The coach was showing he was boss. And Aguirre showed his pique by storming from the locker room, past the pack of journalists.

Laimbeer started grumbling about the press.

Then Laimbeer spoke to a few of the chosen. He said:

"We're the best at winning a series. We adjust. They adjust. We adjust. We've been the best at that for three years."

NBC-TV was rigging the schedule—a given for TV now. And it was running its promos of events to come. The network was pumping Magic versus Michael on the air.

I wondered just who the hell were the reigning champs, anyway!

Daly needed to avoid disharmony during the playoffs. It was difficult enough for him. He had to nip the business with Aguirre, who showed up at practice with his arm in a splint and bandages. Dick Motta was never able to handle Aguirre and his moods and outbursts.

But Daly was master of more than leverage in contract negotiations. He was the master han-

dler of his men. He cooled a nasty situation, by stating he overreacted, again massaging Aguirre's ego. It was an uncharacteristic display of humility by Chuck. But he had to do it.

Chuck could be the master at the Knute Rockne stuff, too, when it had to be.

It had to be at Game 3 in the Omni in Atlanta on April 30, 1991. In the sportswriting trade, they are called must games. There are a million wretched cliches to describe the Pistons' sitation. In a series in which the first team to three victories remains in business, on an enemy court in a hostile town, the Pistons had to break through the Hawks to win the third game. They could not dally and go into the fourth game down two victories to one, on the edge of elimination.

All this was very clear to the Pistons.

So here they were, behind by fifteen points at the end of the first quarter. Here they were behind by seventeen in the second quarter, and down by a dozen at halftime, 56–44. Only one of Vinnie Johnson's shooting sprees had kept the Pistons that close.

In the same locker room where the Pistons had once celebrated a monumental playoffs triumph early in their ascent—where Daly had boasted about his wrinkle-free face—the athletes sat down bedraggled—and vulnerable. They were on the edge—of being defrocked as champions.

Daly acted again, his back straight, his face sober. He grabbed a piece of chalk and went to the blackboard. He etched for all in the room to see: POISE . . . FRANTIC . . .

"Because," Daly would tell the media later, "we needed to stay poised . . . because we were too frantic."

Daly made one change for the third quarter. He ended the experiment with William Bedford on his starting unit. James Edwards was back with his group.

Pyschological ploys usually do not work with the pros. They're too suave, too sophisticated, too experienced. Too many cynics age thirty. But Daly's blackboard etchings worked.

The Pistons fired out in the third quarter. Dumars was marvelous. He hit a three-pointer about eight minutes into the half and the Pistons had caught up and passed the Hawks. Isiah was the usual Isiah on his thirtieth birthday. And the Pistons, down twelve when the third began, were up by five when the period ended. They carried on, won Game 3, by a 103–91 margin, the must game, and took a two victories to one lead in the series. Dumars scored 30 points, 24 of those after Daly's scribblings on the blackboard. Isiah had 19. Vinnie 17. The guards were back.

The Pistons had some space now. The worst that could happen would be a Game 5 on their homecourt.

Only Mark Aguirre remained without joy. He snapped back at his critics, the gentle people of the media, who had dredged up ancient questions about his team spirit.

"I don't see how that can be discussed considering the things I've given up to make this team better," Aguirre told the *News*. ". . . I've given up a contract. I gave up money. I've given up my starting position and I gave up minutes. I don't think any player in the NBA would. If they would, I haven't seen it."

Relapse. Another one. With the chance to eliminate the Hawks, give themselves a respite to repair wounds such as Isiah's aching hamstring, the Pistons self-destructed in Game 4. The game at the Omni was close for most of three quarters. It had been rough, in the Bad Boys image. Dennis Rodman was elbowed by Kevin Willis. Rodman got up and butted Willis, his head barging into the Atlanta player's chest. The reaction was worth a techincal foul. But this was a rare display of emotion by the Pistons in Game 4.

The Hawks won it, 123–111. The series was deadlocked again, two victories apiece. It was Sidney Moncrief, whose origins in the NBA dated back to Dick Vitale's expensive and extraneous draft shenanigans, who did the dirty work for Atlanta. Moncrief, rarely used, age thirty-four, came off the bench to play twenty-two minutes and score 23 points. His 12 points in the fourth quarter were critical. Bob Weiss, the Hawks' coach, had switched to Moncrief as a third-guard in his offense. Other coaches were stealing Daly's stuff.

Daly had mused in the public prints about how his athletes wanted it to end. And now they had a possible ending in their faces. They would be home for Game 5 versus Atlanta on May 5. Would this be doomsday?

"We can't give up the throne now," Rodman told Terry Foster. "We have to act like it's our last day here. If we don't come out fighting, it will be our last day."

As a prelude to Game 5, Bill Laimbeer had reexamined his relationship with the fans. They, the customers who were paying up to $150 a ticket, could be the good guys again—if they'd only yell louder.

"Our fans haven't found out they are going to have to work for this championship just like the players are," Laimbeer said to Terry Foster. "This is not going to be as easy as the last two . . ."

Laimbeer, presumably, had changed his mind and it would be OK if the fans could have a souvenir copies of the championship ring; that is if they yelled loud enough to drive the Pistons to victory.

Also now, on the Sunday morning before Game 5, the media took an extremely cautionary approach to one critical matter involving the Pistons' chances of victory. It was noted that the Pistons had gone 0-for-the-season in games telecast nationally by NBC. The reigning champions had turned up six conseuctive stinkers on the NBA's new Peacock Network. The modern media can never overlook a single salient fact when scrutinizing the psyche of ballclub.

Then maybe it was just Marv Albert's voice that bored the Pistons to sleep on NBC.

Well, the cursed Pistons smashed the NBC voodoo doll behind the vociferous urgings of their fans in the fifth game of the first round of the 1991 NBA playoffs. Also, Bill Laimbeer smashed Dominique Wilkins with an elbow— Dominique responded with a slap—and the Pistons smashed the Atlanta Hawks. The score was 113–81. Before America turned drowsy on this first Sunday afternoon in May, the Pistons had connected on their first five shots. Before the first quarter ended, the Pistons were up by fourteen. At halftime, they were up by seventeen. Isiah scored 16 in the first half, but no stats were kept on on the number of clicks made by TV sets turning off. By the time it ended, the fans earned their bread by chanting "THREE-PEAT, THREE-PEAT, THREE-PEAT!" Isiah finished with 26, Dumars with 20—and Rodman had soared with his emotions and grabbed 20 rebounds.

"We obviously played like champions," Daly said at his postgame media klatch. "Defensively, up and down the lineup, we were exquisite."

These strange Pistons had sent off another message to Michael.

But before they and Bulls could settle their differences, the Pistons had to go through Boston once again. Back to Boston Garden, above the train station, where the Pistons had experienced so many horrors but also rare moments of joy.

"It reminds me of the CYO and the PSL," Vinnie Johnson told Terry Foster in the *News*. "No question I love the Garden. It's old, just like my game."

The Celtics had come back in 1990–91 with the old cast, some new kids and a new coach. They won 56 games. It meant that the Celtics held the homecourt advantage on the same historic parquet floor.

"Someone told me Parish, McHale and Bird retired," Daly said to the writers. "But I see they are still playing."

The Celtics had been on the edge of elimination themselves in the playoffs. They beat Indiana in their decisive game with a second half rally, 124–121. Larry Bird was leader of the rally after he'd dove for a loose ball and landed flat on his face on the parquet floor. He'd been groggy in the trainer's room for forty-five minutes, then returned while the game went on. He drew a rousing ovation as he ran up the corridor into the arena. Then he won the game.

"He's Superman," said Derek Smith, one of the youthful Celtics, in the postgame media madcap scene.

So the Celtics were riding on emotion mixed with the new leadership of their rookie coach.

The new coach was Chris Ford. He was the same Chris Ford, who had been banished into exile from the Pistons by one Dick Vitale back in 1978. Vitale, after viewing him in three games, had decided Ford could not shoot a basketball straight. Ford was traded to the Celtics with a second-round draft choice for Earl Tatum. It was the first of Vitale's successful efforts to RE-VITALEIZE the Celtics.

"Dick Vitale, he helped build the Celtics," a man said to Ford during the 1991 playoffs.

"He helped a lot of people," responded Ford.

In Boston, Ford played on one championship team before heading off into broadcasting and then into coaching. He spent seven seasons as an assistant coach, before he backed into the head coaching job. Much the way Chuck Daly did in Detroit, not the top choice. Duke's Mike Krzyze-wski rejected the Celtics' job before Ford got it as the successor to the fired Jimmy Rodgers.

Backaches were epidemic, it seemed, in the NBA. In Boston, Superman had played the entire season with a bum back. The Celtics and Pistons had split their four games during the season. Bird had missed three of them due to his back troubles.

Now as the Pistons went off to Boston for Game 1, there were all sorts of memories rekindled about playoffs past. The fights—Laimbeer and Parish; Bird flinging the ball at Laimbeer; Isiah's errant pass that Daly kept recalling as the reason the Pistons had not played in the finals four years in succession; the Pistons breaking the curse at last on an joyous and historic June night in 1988; and the words once spoken by Dennis Rodman about Larry Bird, the words that triggered a regrettable racial controversy.

Oddly too, Larry Bird had just done a lengthy taped interview on ESPN. In this interview, he made an astonishing statement:

"A lot of people tell me I'm black on the inside and white on the outside."

It's a Superman, no it's a Bird . . .

Mortal after all, Larry Bird's back aches were so severe he had to miss Game 1. As a consequence, the Pistons were able to control the game from the first quarter on. They were ahead by eight in the fourth when Dee Brown, driving for the basket, stepped on the top of Isiah's right foot. Isiah went down. His right shoe was knocked off by the ferocity of the collision. Isiah hobbled up, off the floor, and left the arena. Game 1 ended, with the Pistons 86–75 victors, while Isiah was in the rear of an ambulance enroute a hosptial. The X-rays were negative. Dr. Ben Paolucci, the team physician, diagnosed Isiah's injury as strained ligaments.

"His foot looked ugly," Spider Salley told the media after the victory. "But you know Isiah. He has another foot."

The story was Bird would be able to play in Game 2, while Isiah was considered very doubtful.

"So what if Larry Bird plays!" said Laimbeer.

It was playoff time, and Boston remained a dangerous town for the Pistons. Through the years they had been besieged by cranks at their hotel. Phone calls to disturb the players in the middle of the night; weirdos making obscene calls or death threats. So the Pistons were checked into their rooms with phony names to afford them some peace and rest. They displayed plenty of ingenuity.

In a feature in the *News,* Terry Foster listed some of the pseudonyms the Pistons used on this trip to Boston. Traveling with them this trip were Jim Morrison, Kim Basinger, Mickey Mantle, Roger Maris—and Hannibal "The Cannibal" Lechter. The Cannibal was the name used by Buddah Edwards, taken from the character of the mass-murderer played by actor Anthony Hopkins in the film, *Silence of the Lambs.*

His cover blown, Buddah would have to adopt another name on the Pistons' next trip. Perhaps Jack Nicholson would work.

Isiah and Bird dressed in their respective uniforms for Game 2, back in the Garden. The day off between games had helped Bird's back just enough. But it wasn't enough time for Isiah. Bird

Reggie Lewis (35) seems to have Dumars' shot measured during Game 2 of the Boston playoff series.

played. Isiah watched and led cheers. Gerald Henderson started in his place for the Pistons.

The Pistons and Celtics had been shunted to a 1 p.m. starting time on an ordinary Thursday. The Boston Bruins had first dibs on the Garden for their Stanley Cup playoffs hockey game on Thursday night.

It was not the best of times for the Pistons. They were listless without Isiah. The Celtics controlled the first half. Only Aguirre's shooting—17 points in the first half—enabled the Pistons to stick close. In the third quarter, the Pistons slipped off to a five-point lead. During the quarter, the game had to be stopped when a pigeon waddled across the floor. The refs and Kevin McHale pursued it. Chuck Daly gave a tight, cynical smile. The pigeon screwed up any momentum the Pistons had. But it was more Larry Bird than the pigeon bird. Larry scored only 16 points, but his presence was a tonic for the Celtics. The won it, 109–103, to level the series.

"My first thought was of Dave Winfield and the seagull," Larry Bird, always thinking kind thoughts, told the *News'* Bill Halls. "I thought somebody might grab it and rip its neck off."

The Pistons had snatched the homecourt advantage, but they had their deep concerns about Isiah. They had won the game in which Bird didn't play. The Celtics had won the game in which Isiah didn't play. Now Isiah had two additional days to rest his foot.

Games 3 and 4 would be at The Palace. The Celtics had never won there in the three years since the Pistons' facility had been in business; they had played The Palace nine times and lost nine games.

It was Saturday afternoon, the eleventh of May, NBC-TV, both Isiah and Bird in the starting lineups.

The Pistons played as though they'd never been in The Palace before. They came out missing free throws. The Celtics were out in front immediately and in control when Rodman and Bird tangled in the first quarter. Bird had a grasp on both the ball and Rodman's head with the ears into which he used to stick 25-cent pieces. Rodman reacted by shoving Bird over the bank of squatting photographers at courtside. Bird landed on his tail. He got up and continued

Laimbeer finds himself on the receiving end of an elbow from Robert Parish in Game 3.

playing with his sore back. The Pistons continued missing free throws. By halftime, the margin was thirteen points, favor of the Celtics.

"You got to play harder to win at home than on the road in the playoffs," Daly said at halftime when an NBC microphone was stuck into his unlined face.

Isiah was struggling on the floor. He had very little movement. He had endured agony throughout this season, first with his eye injury, then his hamstring, then his wrist and now this foot that he virtually had to drag along as he dribbled. And the Pistons kept missing, layups now along with the misfired free throws.

On the bench, Daly might have been wondering again how it would end for the Pistons.

On this Saturday, it was piteous to watch a championship disintegrate.

Marv Albert, at the NBC mike, seemed to delight in rubbing it in.

The Pistons dropped twenty-three points behind.

"An embarrassing performance by the defending NBA champions," Albert told America in the voice that was as New York as cheesecake.

The Pistons dropped thirty points behind.

"This has now turned to sheer humiliation," Albert intoned.

It was profound journalism for once by television, but the guy at the mike seemed to relish the disaster.

Garbage time came early. The scrubs went into to flap around until the clock wound out. When it ended, Isiah was grinning on the bench —or was it grimacing? And next to him, Laimbeer was glowering. The final score was 115-83. And the Celtics had captured a 2-1 lead in the series. The Pistons had made 17 of 36 free throws. It was that bad. They made 33 of 99 field goal attempts. Worse.

And Larry Bird hardly had been a factor with 10 points. Isiah was less of a factor, seven points in his 26 minutes.

"I should have sat out," Isiah confessed to the media mob at his corner locker. "My mind kept telling me I could do it. One play my hamstring pulled up and I said, 'Forget it.' On another it was my foot, and I said, 'forget it.' I just didn't have enough to get over the hump."

And across the way, Laimbeer told the press: "Today was a total, complete mental disaster."

How does a championship team recover from a thirty-two-point defeat?

No matter what, the Pistons made great satire. They continued to capture the imaginations of showbiz.

"Saturday Night Live": produced a skit on the sporting favorite of the American people and entitled it: Silence of the Laimbeers. It was worth a fast chuckle.

"I could care less," said Laimbeer. Then . . . "Hey, I'm a public person. You can poke fun at me all you want. I'm well compensated."

The night of the thirty-two-point defeat by the Celtics, "Entertainment Tonight" featured the Pistons games—well, everything but basketball.

That slice of TV brain candy delved into a typical night in The Palace. It put a mike on club CEO Tom Wilson and showed Comedy Clips (Spider Salley's favorite); Nestles Crunch Time Moment of the Game (film clips of heroic shots); Ball Racing (huge cheers as three differently colored dots do five laps around the Palacevision message board, no wagering please); the Century 21 Shoot For Gold halfcourt, three-point shot (the chosen fan never can reach the hoop from midcourt); Dunham's Fast Break Contest (two three-footers in oversized Pistons shirts race each other up and down the court dribbling basketballs and try to be the first toddler to sink a basket); Celebrity Free Throw Shooting (a local hack politician has twenty-four seconds to make a fool of himself in public); the Noisemeter (shriek your heads off, you guys in the 150-buck seats, and watch the needle go over the top).

All this during, with the Frisbee-catching dog the star attraction at halftime.

"More than just the Pistons, it's an entertainment oddysey," giggled "Entertainment Tonight."

The TV program made it seem as if Bill Laimbeer were earning his $1.9 million doing a walk-on part in a dog-and-pony show.

Isiah Thomas walked along the dark passageway in the bowels of The Palace some ninety minutes before Game 4. He was dressed in his street clothes, color purple. He had a starboard list, limping badly on his injured foot. He displayed that grin that had become his trademark.

Mike Abdenour, the trainer, examined the injured foot. It still hurt. Abdenour had more time in service with the Pistons than any of the ballplayers. He had been the head trainer for 15 years and had been assistant trainer, at fifteen bucks per game, before that. He had seen club-owners, general managers and coaches go and come.

He had a variety of functions beyond that of taping ankles and making certain the water in the whirlpool would not scald the watchamacallits off the millionaire athletes. He was in charge of hotel reservations on the road and making certain the team busses were on the tarmac when Roundball One pulled into a town at 4 in the morning after a game in Sacramento.

He was also a valued pointman on the bench, when not placing an ice bag on a paining shoulder. During time outs. he was the observer who kept track of the other team's bench activity and substitutions while Daly was busy delivering instructions and plotting plays.

The Pistons defense collapses on Reggie Lewis in the lane.

And most important he was watchguard of the 24-second clock. When the Pistons had the ball, working for a shot and the clock wound down to five seconds left, Abdenour's voice boomed out over the arena:

"GO TO IT; GO TO IT." If it was Vinnie or Joe or Isiah with the ball, they had to get a shot launched in a hurry, before the twenty-four seconds expired. Time and again, Abdenour's alarm enabled the Pistons to score a basket a flicker before the deep belch of the buzzer.

He did not have the a glamor job in the NBA. But he had two championship rings and he was the first guy to hug Chuck Daly when Vinnie Johnson hit his championship winning shot with :00.7 on the clock the year before in Portland.

He called himself "The cut man for the Bad Boys."

And now with the Pistons again in jeopardy,

Abdenour looked at Isiah and said, so very simply:

"He can't play."

Isiah could play with a bum eye, a bum wrist, a bum hamstring, even as he did at L.A. three years before in the finals, with a bum ankle if it was taped by Abdenour. But a bum foot doesn't work on a basketball court.

Daly juggled his guards again in the emergency. Dumars took Isiah's spot at point guard, running the offense, and Vinnie Johnson became a starter at the shooting guard. Gerald Henderson was back on the bench.

The day, May 13, was Dennis Rodman's thirtieth birthday. In ceremonies before Game 4 started, he was presented with the NBA's Defensive Player of the Year Award for the second time. It helped to arouse the crowd.

How does a championship team recover from a thirty-two-point defeat?

The Pistons did it by charging out with the stuff that had been missing two days earlier—intensity, emotion—and this time, shooting accuracy. Buddah Edwards hit the first four shots and then added two free throws and the Pistons survived the first quarter with a three-point lead and were safe enough at halftime with the score tied.

In the second quarter, Bird and Rodman were close together on the floor. There was no shoving this time.

"I hate to say this," Bird said to Rodman, "but congratulations. You deserved the award."

"Thanks, Larry," said Rodman.

Rodman didn't have any time for further conversation. He was busy guarding Bird, then switching to McHale, then to Kevin Gamble, then to Reggie Lewis, then to Brian Shaw.

His assignment was defense and rebounding.

Mark Aguirre's assignment was shooting.

In the third quarter, Aguirre connected on two three-point baskets. Then he scored on an off-balance shot, banked off the glass, and added a free throw. His nine-point spree opened the game. The Pistons led by six at the end of the third. They held their lead through a safe fourth quarter.

When it ended, the Pistons had redeemed themselves, regained their pride, and had beaten the Celtics, 104–97. They had squared the series at two a piece.

And Joe Dumars and Dennis Rodman had played themselves into a fit of exhaustion. Dumars played every second of the forty-eight minutes. Rodman had played all but the final 9.8 seconds of the game. Aguirre had scored 34 points, the most since he'd been with the Dallas Mavericks on a team with a different philosophy. Dumars had 24 points.

And Dennis Rodman—the birthday celebrant—he had five points. But then he had taken only one shot the entire night. He did his job just as Daly planned. Dennis defended against all five positions during the game. And he had dominated the backboards with 18 rebounds.

Rodman had packages of ice on both knees and his right shoulder, and the pain of fatigue on his face after the game.

"This is a lot harder than it was three years ago," he said at his locker. "We were on a mission then to beat Boston, beat Boston. Now we're expected to beat Boston."

And Rodman had even been spoken to by Larry Bird! You could sense the irony in that.

Spider Salley slams home two points over the Celtics' Ed Pinckney.

"Do you think Bird really meant it," I asked him in the locker room long after the game, "seeing as you had once remarked about an award he won?"

Rodman grinned. He was very weary.

"I think he meant it," Rodman said. "He's not that bad a guy. He had a smile on his face. It was the second time he talked to me. I wish he'd speak to me more. I think he respects me. He doesn't want to admit it. He's not a bad guy."

While the Pistons struggled with the Celtics, the Bulls zoomed in the opposite bracket. They reached the Eastern Conference finals for the third successive year by polishing off the 76ers in five games. They'd have to wait for an opponent. The Pistons and Celtics had possibly three more games, if a seventh was necessary, before one would qualify to face Michael and his teammates for honors in the East.

The Bulls had a vested rooting interest. Scottie Pippen, the migraine man, spoke openly on TV about his choice. He said into the microphone he hoped the Bulls could play the Celtics.

Not Michael.

Michael told print reporters in Chicago: "Until we beat the teacher, we're still in the learning stages."

The Pistons had taught the Bulls about how to win in the playoffs three years in succession. Michael wanted revenge.

Isiah went out on the parquet to take his warmups before Game 5 in the Boston Garden. Another two days of tender, loving care had enabled him to maneuver a bit on his right foot. It was decided he would not start; but he would play.

"If you go back in a seven-game series, the team that wins Game 5 usually wins the series," Isiah told the media before the game. His reasoning hardly had a scientific or historic basis —to wit, the Pistons beat the Lakers Game 5 of the 1988 finals. But it sounded good on TV.

Isiah got into the game midway through the first quarter after Vinnie was charged with two fouls. The Pistons were down by seven. With Isiah's playmaking the Pistons were ahead by the end of the quarter. In the second period, Isiah replaced Joe Dumars. It was Joe's first rest in three games. By halftime the Pistons had forged a ten-point lead. It went to eighteen in the third as Vinnie turned Microwave again.

Then the Celtics, with Bird burning, rallied back in the fourth. They cut it to nine, then to four, then to two. Larry Bird, overcoming the agonies in his back, was in one of those zones. He shot again, scored, and tied the score at 100–100 with 3:38 to play. Twice Laimbeer broke tie scores with shots from the outside. The Celtics brought it back to 106–106 in the final minute.

With four seconds left on the 24-second clock and Mike Abdenour's cries of "GO TO IT" echoing through the Garden, Laimbeer stepped backwards two steps and fired a daring, outside shot over Bird's reaching arm. That broke the tie with 38.4 seconds to play. It was 108–106, Detroit. The Celtics brought the ball back. Reggie Lewis had it. Dumars stuck his body in Lewis' path, froze and was knocked over by the collision. Charge or block, offensive foul or defensive foul? This was Boston. The refs ruled offensive foul, in favor of Dumars. Now it was 110–106, Detroit, and the Celtics came back again with less than twenty seconds left. Dee Brown had the ball and went up and came down heavily on— Joe Dumars. Offensive foul, again. Twice Dumars had sacrificed his body, already weary and bruised. Down the stretch, in the last 12.4 seconds, Joe made six free throws.

The Pistons won it, again in Boston Garden, 116–111. It was three victories to two in the series. One more victory for the Pistons and Michael Jordan would have his wish to try again against the teacher.

"We bent, but we didn't break," Joe Dumars told the reporters in the tiny locker room in the Boston Garden, where so much of the Pistons' history had occurred. He had scored 32 points. Laimbeer had 24 and Vinnie also had 24.

"If they're going to play smaller guys on me in the playoffs, we've got to make them pay," Laimbeer said postgame on the TNT cable network, which did the game for a national audience. A slap at Bird!

"I love to win in this building. Our instincts and natural tendencies come out and when instincts take over, we have great players. We can win when we don't have to think."

Isiah had gone 0 for Game 5 in Boston. He had hobbled through fifteen minutes, contributed six assists plus the inspiration. His own teammates debated his value as a leadership force.

"You know, they said we couldn't win without Isiah," Rodman had said, "we couldn't create things. We proved we could.

True! They did.

"This is Isiah's team." Bill Laimbeer kept repeating the statement.

True too!

Now again, the Pistons would start Game 6 with Isiah on the bench in a supplementary role. Vinnie would be starting with Dumars in the backcourt. It was Friday night May 17, 1991, and they were back at The Palace. The Bulls were getting impatient in Chicago, waiting for an opponent. The Pistons were aware they would be playing again on Sunday afternoon, in less than 48 hours—either Game 7 in Boston Garden, or Game 1 of the conference finals against the Bulls.

In a similar situation three years earlier, on a Friday night of a Game 6 playoff match with the Celtics, Laimbeer had flipped a sickle into his equipment bag. The weapon to chop the head off the symbolic writhing snake that the Celtics had been.

The Pistons now were the snake to the Bulls.

Laimbeer left his sickle at home.

The Pistons made a fast getaway without Isiah. They were up by eleven points inside seven minutes. They led by six after a quarter. Dumars had a classic period for himself with 16 points —on three-pointers, knifing drives and one magnificent hookshot from the low post.

They maintained their advantage to the halftime, with Isiah playing a bit in the second quarter. Dumars had 25 points at the half.

The Pistons went ahead by seventeen during the third quarter. The fans damn near broke the noisemeter. The Celtics were a team broken into bits. Parish was hurting so much that he didn't even put on his uniform. He sat on the bench in a brown suit. Bird was spending much of the time lying on the floor at the bench to reduce the pain in his aching back.

But there was something ingrained in the character of the Boston Celtics. They smashed back and cut the Pistons' seventeen-point lead to seven entering the fourth quarter. The THREE-PEAT chant went up from the Detroit crowd.

The Celtics cut the Pistons' lead to three points.

It was bitterly contested basketball between two longtime rivals, dotted with magificent performances.

Isiah, back in, connected on a three-pointer. Kevin McHale hit his own three-pointer. Bird, back in, scored on a fallaway jumpshot. They went past the magic three-minutes-left barrier. With 2:13 left, Bird scored two free throws—and the Celtics were ahead, so unexpectedly, 100–99. The exchanged the lead a couple of times. With 1:20 left, Dumars tied it at 103–103 with a jumper. The Celtics had a basket by McHale wiped out by a very debatable offensive goaltending call. With Detroit ahead, 105–103, with 21.4 seconds left, Dumars, the 89 percent foul shot shooter, missed two free throws. Reggie Lewis tied it for the Celtics, 105–105, with 7.8 seconds on the clock.

Game 6 went into overtime.

Snap, the Celtics quickly went up by four in the OT. The THREE-PEAT chants had faded away, to total silence. There was a ripple of applause when Edwards popped in a jumper. The Pistons were now behind by two. They got the ball again.

"GO TO IT, GO TO IT!" Mike Abdenour's shriek went along the court at the speed of sound.

Isiah tossed the ball up a flash before the 24-second buzzer went off. The ball went in for three points. The Pistons led, 110–109. Reggie Lewis scored. The Celtics led, 111–110. It was Isiah's turn again. He popped in a jumper. The Pistons led, 112–111. It said 1:41 on the clock. Salley rebounded a missed shot by Boston. Laimbeer popped in a jumper for a 114–111 lead. Dee Brown barged into Rodman and was called for traveling. Isiah popped in a jumper for a 116–111 lead. Now just twenty-five seconds were left and the noisemakers were noisy again. The Pistons had it. They won, 117–113; they had eliminated the Celtics again. They were going to the Eastern finals for the fifth time in five years.

It was another rescue mission by Isiah. In the final two minutes, twenty-three seconds of the overtime period, as his team reached the edge of defeat at home, Isiah, crippled by a painful foot, had scored 8 points. He finished the game with 17 points. Dumars had 32 in another bravura performance. They could go engage Michael Jordan again.

"We're not the favorites, we're the underdogs," Isiah said in the subdued locker room. "That's the way it is." There wasn't any champagne this night. He was in a monologue mode. "Everybody was kinda waiting for me to do something and I didn't know what I was going to do. Situations kind of presented themselves. Every play was such a big play. Every shot. Every rebound. A big play.

"Some of the best basketball ever played in the NBA has been the Pistons-Celtics. The Celtics-Lakers. The Pistons-Lakers."

Isiah was sending one more message to Michael.

"Pippen said on national TV he wanted to play Boston," said Laimbeer, with his gloating grin. "We were all watching it on TV in our hotel rooms. We called each other up, 'See this?' Beep, beep, beep. 'You see that?'

"It's fun to play Chicago because they're so competitive now. It ain't about who's better. You go home like this . . . (he held his head in his hands). Next day, 'that was fun.' We enjoy the mental competition. That's the best part of it."

When Game 6 ended, Isiah had ran down the court to embrace Kevin McHale. McHale had once, three years earlier, gone to Isiah with congratulations and words of encouragement. This was on the night that the Pistons finally had beaten the Celtics in the playoffs and reached the NBA finals. McHale went to Isiah as the other Celtics vanished, refusing to congratulate the team that had beaten them. Now, in another victory, Isiah had deliberately sought out Kevin McHale for an embrace and a handshake and some private words.

Isiah was alone at his locker when asked why he made the special effort to seek out McHale.

"I just wanted to let those guys know what an honor it is to play against those guys," Isiah said. "They were some of the great players. I wanted Bird to know it was a great honor to play against him. I told Kevin to tell Larry."

What the Celtics had been to the Pistons for years . . . until the Pistons had snapped the head off the Celtics at last in 1988 . . . the Pistons were now to the Bulls.

And through it all, through the anguish, bitter moods had gnawed at Michael Jordan. He had chastised his teammates in defeat. He had hidden in the team bus, refusing to talk, a recluse. He was the greatest basketball player in the world—the most magnificent individual force in the NBA. Nobody could dispute that. But he was unfulfilled as a professional athlete. He had not won a championship in the NBA. And he had been deprived because he, and his team, had been beaten down by the Pistons.

"They're our nemesis," Jordan told the *News'* Vartan Kupelian as the Bulls prepared to play the Pistons again. "They've knocked us out of the playoffs the last three seasons. We know to get a world championship, we have to get past them."

"All year long they've been saying they want to play us," said Isiah Thomas. "Well, here we are."

"We asked for it and now we've got it," Horace Grant told the writers.

"This is for everybody—for the fans, for television, for the writers, for everybody," Jordan said to the press people.

For everybody—except Scottie Pippen. And Scottie had become a player.

They darkened the decrepit Chicago Stadium and turned on a spotlight to introduce the Chicago Bulls to "the greatest basketball fans in the world." These greatest fans in the world had just finished booing and cursing the reigning back-to-back world champions. Isiah, who grew up in the neighborhood. Laimbeer, the masked man, who was a visitor on his thirty-fourth birthday. Now they roared as each of the Bulls ran out with the torch burning on him as though he were Arnold Schwarzenegger at some premiere of a made-in-Hollywood fantasy.

Game 1 of the NBA's Eastern Conference finals was about to begin.

And seconds after it began, Joe Dumars was trying to cover Michael Jordan on an inbounds pass. Smash. Michael's arms whipped out and hit Dumars on the chops.

Not long after that, Michael's elbow unexpectedly catupulted out and dug into the body of Dennis Rodman. Soon after that, Michael was shouting something that was not overly complimentary at Mark Aguirre. And before the first

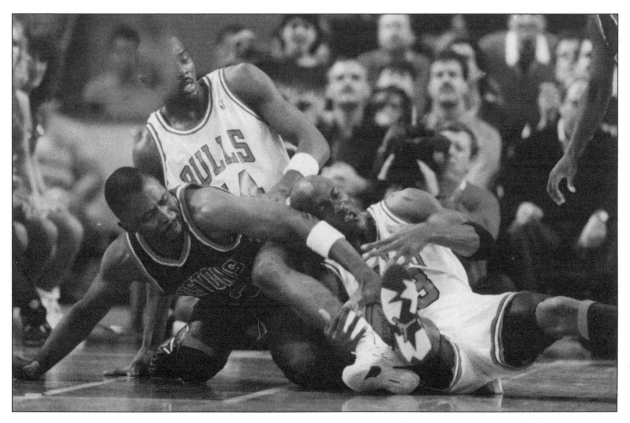

Aguirre and Michael Jordan scramble for a loose ball during Game 1 of the Eastern Conference finals.

half was over, Michael was back at Rodman, shouting and screeching.

Rodman would later tell the media, "He said, 'You're the best defensive player in the league and you can't stop me.'

"I said, 'You're a great player.'

"He looked at me and said, 'You can't stop me.'

"I said, 'OK, you're right, I can't stop you. If I was Michael Jordan could you stop me?'"

The Bulls were out with their defense pawing and clawing and trapping the Pistons. They were out blocking shots and stealing the ball. They were out with different guys hitting the basket. They were out with guys coming off the bench and outdueling the Pistons. They were out with the elbows and the shoves.

The Bulls had studied the teacher for three years in the playoffs. They had learned. Phil Jackson had urged them onward. They were outplaying the Pistons—and beating them with the Pistons' own game.

Michael was not shooting with his usual brilliance. But the rest of the guys were.

The Bulls dominated the first quarter and led by eleven. They led by eight at the half. In the third quarter, the champs made a run. The Pistons went ahead by a point with five minutes left in the third. Jordan was cold, and then he was on the bench.

And the Chicago subs blew the Pistons away. Guys with unfamiliar names. Will Perdue, Craig Hodges, Cliff Levingston, once a Piston. B.J. Armstrong. The bench, winning it in Pistons fashion.

The Bulls beat the Pistons, 94–83, in Game 1. And Michael, with 22 points, was more talk than show.

In relating Michael's harangue early in the game, Rodman added to the reporters: "He said they had a great team. OK, whatever he says. He wants to talk, he can talk.

"But until you see some championship banners in this building, all he can do is say they're a great team . . . He's always been confident. But you can have all the confidence in the world, and if you don't win, it don't mean anything at all."

"It was time to learn from the past," Jordan told the writers. "We can't let them intimidate us with that little cheap stuff. If they were going to give us their little cheap stuff, we weren't going to take any of their junk."

If Chicago had a hero, it was Scottie Pippen. He scored 18 points and stole the ball six times.

On the day off between games in Chicago, the NBA announced its most valuable player for the season. Even Dennis Rodman couldn't argue about the overwhelming choice. Michael Jordan won it, virtually doubling the vote total of Magic Johnson. It was the second time Michael was MVP.

"I'm envious of the Detroit Pistons, the Los Angeles Lakers, the Boston Celtics—the teams that have won championships," Jordan told the media at the MVP press conference. "That's something I badly want to taste. It's the driving force for me right now. Winning the MVP is great . . . But I'd much rather be standing here in June, waiting to receive a championship ring . . ."

He also tried to explain what was going on with all his vocal jousting on the court. "The game is supposed to be a game of sportsmanship. That part of the sport they have taken away. Some teams go out and play that way now because they've had success with it. I don't know where it got started. Laimbeer probably . . . If they start talking trash, I talk trash back. Let's see how they react when they get some of the same treatment they've been handing out."

The pupil-teacher hate relationship went on.

Game 2 began with the usual Second City dramatics, the darkened court, the dramatic entrances. Then it turned to more ferocious basketball. Early on, there was a contretemps between Rodman and Pippen, who had vowed not to take any more stuff. Pippen shoved Rodman. The refs gave Pippen the T.

Again the Pistons couldn't keep up. Despite 16 points by Dumars in the first quarter, the Bulls opened a five-point lead. The Pistons kept flipping the ball away again on errant passes, rushed and bewildered by Phil Jackson's version of the trap defense. His defense was designed with a single purpose. "To make their offense frenetic," Jackson explained. Isiah wasn't scoring. And Laimbeer couldn't hit. The Bulls commanded

The Detroit-Chicago series was highlighted by tough, physical play and plenty of banging.

the game all the way. They went up by seventeen points.

There had been two earlier flagrant fouls called by the overreacting refs against Dumars and Salley, stinking calls. But in the fourth, Isiah nailed Jordan for the third flagrant foul against Detroit. Laimbeer got into it, too. The old champs had lost their poise.

It was 105–97 for the Bulls, the Chicago crowd serenaded the Pistons with a version of "Hey, Hey, Goodbye."

"They are very hungry," Chuck Daly said, addressing the press postgame, with the Bulls up two games to nothing in the series. "They are better athletes, but they are a lot like we were at that point."

Daly's giants were AWOL. Laimbeer managed two points after scoring four in Game 1. Edwards scored one point, Salley two. Isiah had 10. Only Vinnie, with 29 off the bench, and Dumars, with 24, enabled the Pistons to finish with a respectable score.

"We can smell it," Pippen told the writers. He'd scored 21. Michael had scored 35.

There was one other stat of note. In the two games, the Bulls were awarded seventy-six free

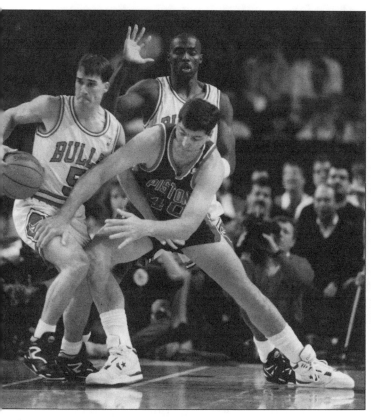

John Paxson turns to head up court after making the steal from Laimbeer.

with a decent TV audience, Bill Laimbeer rested an aching knee. And, he reflected about his newest offering to American culture. A video game firm based in California announced its newest Nintendo product: "Bill Laimbeer's Combat Basketball."

The promotional hype explained: "In the year 2030, after permanently injuring a dozen opponents and shortening the careers of hundreds of others, Bill Laimbeer is forced to retire from professional basketball. Unable to play, he is elected commissioner of the NBA. Shortly after, he fires all the referees . . . and eliminates rules against fouls. The sport develops a new meaning as players wear protective armor and the action really heats up. 'Finally, basketball is a combat sport,' impassions Laimbeer. 'This is the way basketball was mean to be! No wimps, no sissies. Just brutal, hard-core action.'"

With knees, elbows, fists—and the electronic fans throwing bombs and missiles at the electronic players.

"The league is gonna have a fit," Laimbeer told Charlie Vincent of the *Free Press*.

Once Laimbeer said he would not exploit from his reputation for profit. He had turned the proceeds of his Bad Boys poster with Rick Mahorn over to charity.

"I'm gonna keep this money," Laimbeer said.

A contradiction?

"It's not a bad thing, it's a fun game," Laimbeer said.

A contradiction?

"Right. I'm gonna keep this one."

Combat basketball? During the interlude, there were stories on Chicago TV about Aguirre challenging Pippen to meet him in the parking lot after a game at Chicago Stadium. Pippen said OK.

Aguirre said: "I didn't say that. He was saying bleep, bleep, bleep.

Saturday afternoon at The Palace, and before Game 3, Ken Calvert, the Pistons' courtside announcer, did his cheerleading best to incite the home crowd. "In ten seconds we will be joined by the NBC network. Let's show them we have the best basketball fans in the world." A programmed mob of lemmings opened its vocal cords to greet the Detroit Pistons. And then the mob opened again to greet Michael Jordan with a massive boo.

throws and the Pistons forty. It was a ratio of nearly two to one. In Detroit, the disk jockeys wept more about the officiating than did Chuck Daly.

Salley did comment about the way the refs were calling fouls against the Pistons: "We're not only the Bad Boys, we're the terrible boys."

The Pistons were going home for Games 3 and 4. The Bulls had handled the Pistons with such ease that a sweep seemed as if it would be a merciful end to the run of the back-to-back champions.

"We're going to have to respond big time in our own building . . . and our crowd is going to have to be a factor as their crowd was in Chicago," Daly told interviewers.

He was turning it over to the guys in the $150 seats, the swells in their suits and neckties who lose it and get up dancing when "The Heat Is On" blasts through the speakers at The Palace.

While the teams took three days off while waiting for NBC to allow them to play Game 3

The Pistons see Game 2 slipping away.

The crowd was into it, just as Chuck Daly had requested. This was suppose to be the homecourt advantage that the Pistons needed if they were to rescue their championship honor.

But the Pistons missed the message.

The Bulls went on a tear to a 6–0 lead. Embarrassed twice in Chicago, how could the Pistons come out without any fire, without any intensity? Daly paced back and forth at the Detroit bench, his flower-patterned necktie flapping. His champions committed two offensive fouls and one turnover in the early going. The Bulls led by sixteen points ten minutes into the first quarter.

The Pistons were shrieking at the bench during time outs, as they had years before.

"Our offense sucks," Laimbeer yelled, loud enough to be heard by the writers at the press table nearby. "All we do is stand around and shoot twenty footers."

The Pistons managed to cut the Bulls' lead to eight by the end of the first quarter. They went in front by two briefly in the second quarter on a slamdunk by Salley. The Bulls rallied right back and led by eight again at the half. Horace Grant stole the ball twice to ignite the rally.

Scottie Pippen had bailed out, complaining of migraine the last time he'd been in a playoff game at The Palace. Now, in the third quarter, he

scored eight points in quick succession. Jordan scored. Cartwright scored. The Bulls were up by sixteen.

Nothing could save the Pistons.

During the third quarter, George Maskin, the Pistons' PR man from the horrible years when they faked attendance counts and were a floating franchise in their own town, plopped into the seat next to me.

"I came here from a Bar Mitzvah at Shir Shalom," Maskin said. "The rabbi said, 'Say a prayer for the Pistons.' Then he ripped the refs in a prayer."

It couldn't help the Pistons.

The best the Pistons could do was cut their deficit to five points in the fourth quarter. The Bulls held them off and won the game, 113–107. They had a three victories to none lead over the back-to-back champions.

"We're gonna sweep them," Pippen yelled as the Bulls ran up the runway to the locker room where only a year before Michael had ranted at them and questioned their fortitude.

Michael was one victory away from killing the enemy that had tormented him for three years; one more from completing his mission.

The writers from across America stood in the Pistons' locker room. There was utter silence. A single huge, white Converse basketball shoe, size 18, was stuffed into the trash barrel in the corner. Its owner was, presumably, Bill Laimbeer. He was a Converse man.

The press people waited forty-five minutes and some started to drift away. There had been so many victories celebrated in this locker room. Finally, Isiah showed up. The media remnants, those with patience or safe deadlines. gathered around his locker.

Isiah spoke in his soft voice. He had played as brilliantly as he could, with all his flair and magic. He had scored 29 points. But Jordan had 33 and Pippen had 26, and the Bulls were too much. The Pistons had been equal to the Bulls through the last three quarters. But the Pistons were unable to overcome their self-destructive first quarter.

"I'm not an optimist," Isiah said. "I'm a realist. If I didn't think we could come out and make a series of it, I'd tell you we can't win. But I think we can make a series of it . . .

"The next game they win is going to have to be the hardest game they ever had to win in their lives . . .

"Coming into the playoffs, I knew we were at a disadvantage because everybody else played a season. We were set back when I had my injury. We were nowhere where we would have been if I had not had an injury. I wouldn't say intensity is our problem. The other team is beating us."

He was asked about the impact of the first seven minutes of the game . . . the Pistons could not recover from that dreary spell.

"I wasn't surprised," Isiah said, "because it was that way in the first two games . . .

In the Bulls' locker room, Horace Grant said to the writers around him: "The dragon isn't dead yet. We have to cut off his head Monday."

It was a vaguely familiar statement!

On the Sunday day off between Games 3 and 4, it all spilled out of Michael Jordan after the Bulls' practice session. The greatest basketball player in the world told the cream of America's sports journalism his exact opinion of the Detroit Pistons—and their championship era.

"The people I know are going to be happy they're not the reigning champions any more," Michael said, as quoted by Bill Halls in the *News*. "We'll get back to the image of a clean game. People want this kind of basketball out . . .

Isiah greets fans outside The Palace before Game 4.

"When Boston was the champion, they played true basketball. Detroit won. You can't take that away from them. But it wasn't clean basketball. It wasn't the kind of basketball you'd want to endorse.

"We're not trying to lower ourselves to their kind of play. I may talk some trash. But we're playing hard, clean basketball. They've tried to provoke us, and we've kept our poise . . .

"I don't feel we're overconfident, but we want to kill this team. I know Thomas feels there's still some hope. He's got to believe that. He's the leader. But I'd rather be in our position than his. We've worked hard to get here. It wasn't given to us.

"Maybe the odds are against us winning in a sweep. But I think we can sweep this team.

"And if we can get by this team, we can win it all."

Michael went on, gloating: "The Pistons have a great defense and they'be beaten us with it in the past. But we're doing to them what they used to do to us. We're disrupting their offense. We're making them panic. We're making them crumble . . ."

Chuck Daly had been wondering for weeks how it would end for the Pistons. Now, he said:

"We've won two championships on the road, and I'd hate to see it die here, in our own building."

It was time for desperation changes and choice words from the cliche collection—back-to-back champions with backs against that old historic wall.

Chuck's desperation change was to elevate Mark Aguirre into the starting lineup again in place of Dennis Rodman. Aguirre would give the Pistons a shooter's chance.

Game 4 was played in the afternoon of the Memorial Day holiday, a Monday, May 27, 1991.

For the first nine minutes, the two rivals belted each other with pure and beautiful basketball. The Pistons played with their highest intensity of the series. Laimbeer and Edwards emerged from their doldrums. They were able to score. Aguirre put in a couple. Isiah ran the attack on the floor and was popping. These were more like the Pistons who had won back-to-back championships.

But it was strange. They were unable to pull away from the Bulls. A four-point lead was the best the Pistons could manage. Pippen was hot and scored 10 points. It turned nasty. Laimbeer and John Paxson shoved and almost punched each other. The Pistons' bench turned hot. Assistant Coach Brendan Suhr was called for a technical foul. That set Daly off. Chuck got a T, too. The score was 24-all at the time. Paxson sank both free throws off the technicals. The Bulls slipped ahead. They would stay ahead. In a flash they led by eight points.

Soon it was ten points in the second quarter. Laimbeer, wearing his Phantom of the Opera mask, hacked Pippen and drew a flagrant foul. As Pippen reeled, Rodman shoved him from behind. Pippen was driven down to the floor, hard, face first, into the bank of photographers and beyond them toward the front-row seats.

The champions had lost their cool. This was the dethroning of a champion, and it was not pretty. By the end of the third quarter, the Bulls led by seventeen. In the fourth, the lead went to twenty. Droves of fans, once so passionate and adoring, started leaving the building, hoping to beat the traffic jams outside The Palace, on the road named Two Championship Drive. The Pistons were being deserted.

Laimbeer was on the bench. With 7:37 left, Isiah left the game. As he reached the bench, Laimbeer reached out and they slapped hands. Isiah sat next to Laimbeer. Laimbeer said something to Isiah and laughed. Isiah nodded.

Daly sent Isiah back in. Edwards and Salley were seated at the far end of the bench. Their faces showed masks of defeat. Buddha's arms were folded across his body as he watched the game. The Bulls were toying with the Pistons.

With 4:38 left, and the Bulls ahead by twenty-three, Daly took out Isiah, Dumars, Rodman, Aguirre and Bedford, who had played much of the last quarter. Laimbeer went onto the floor and embraced Isiah and embraced Dumars. They congratulated each other for their two championships, for the time when they had been the best team in the NBA. Aguirre walked toward the bench and Isiah ran to embrace him. Then he hugged Rodman.

The fans who were left stood and gave the defeated champions a lengthy ovation.

It ended in garbage time . . . in an arena abandoned by half the fans that had adored this team for five years . . . for the years when it suffered against the Celtics, then broke the curse, for the years of losing to and then beating the Lakers in the finals, for the year when it went to Portland and won the championship there, for the years when it was powerful and young enough to frustrate the Bulls in the playoffs.

It ended with the Pistons playing Scott Hastings, Tree Rollins, Gerald Henderson, John Salley and Vinnie Johnson on the floor. Then Bedford came back to replace Vinnie. Vinnie trundled off to join the good company of almost ex-champions on the bench. It ended with the scattershooting. throw it up, shoot and shoot some more garbage time, like a night in January in Sacramento.

It ended with the Detroit crowd chanting. "GO L.A., GO L.A., GO L.A." The Lakers and Magic Johnson had not yet qualified for the Bulls' opponent in the finals. But Michael Jordan had griped himself out of their favor.

And as these final moments flicked away, you could see Isiah seated on a barrier at the end of the court. He was smiling. Laimbeer was with him. He was laughing.

They were plotting. The getaway.

We don't congratualate the Bulls, Laimbeer was saying. No shaking hands.

Isiah agreed.

He was smiling and you could see Laimbeer laughing.

We walk out of here before it's over. They agreed.

Daly disagreed. He suggested they go out by

congratulating the Bulls. They elected to reject his advice.

Laimbeer suggested they ignore the media in the locker room. The hell with them. Dumars demurred.

With fifteen seconds to play, the Pistons left their bench and started toward the locker room.

The Celtics—Bird, Parish, all but Kevin McHale—had once snubbed the Pistons in this manner on that historic night at the Silverdome in 1988. The Celtics had walked out as the Pistons were making it into the NBA finals for the first time.

Now it was time again for the ritual of passage. And to get to the locker room, the Pistons were required to parade past the Bulls' bench, where Jordan and Pippen, victors, were in celebration.

With 7.8 seconds left in garbage time, the whistle blew and everything stopped on the floor. The fleeing Pistons kept going. They went by in single file—Laimbeer, Isiah, Rodman, Aguirre, others. They did not glance at the Bulls as they kept walking, off the floor, out of the arena. They went out defiant, angry, proud. Only Dumars stopped and was seen shaking the gifted hand of Michael Jordan, his rival and also his friend.

The game ended the few seconds later. The Bulls had won it in a sweep, 115–94 in the fourth game. Chuck Daly walked up to Phil Jackson and they shook hands.

The music was shockingly loud in the locker room.

This was the Pistons' locker room—not Michael Jordan's. He was headed for the NBA finals and all the pressures that go with being the champions. The music in the Pistons' locker room, down the passageway beneath The Palace, was not a dirge. It was blasting, it was raucous. The Pistons were going "Whew! It's over." They had lost and snubbed their conquerors. They had behaved much like the Celtics. They had etched a spot in the history of pro basketball.

"I'm going to relax my body, relax my mind," Isiah Thomas said. "Sit in the sunshine. And you don't know that pressure . . . because you're not under it. I don't think anybody realizes what we've been through all these years, It's a cruel form of torture. There's nothing to compare what we've gone through, what we had to endure physically and mentally.

"You look back on what we accomplished . . . you hate to see our run end . . . If with this team we didn't cash in and win the championship, we would have been bitter, it would have been a tragic story. But we maxed out. When you max out, you max out. We had great years together. It's a happy time. Like for once in the last six, seven years we can relax.

"When history judges this team, people will look back and and say, we were one of the greatest teams. We were able to grind it out.

"This was not a sad story. The things we accomplished, we made history."

"I was more emotional about this loss than the two games that won the championships for us," Chuck Daly told the media. "To tell the truth, it was hard to say some things in the locker room. But there were no sad songs for us.

"I couldn't be happier with this group and what they accomplished. They've been to three finals, won two rings and gave it their best shot this year . . .

"Try winning two championships in a row and for a third successive one, and see the toll it takes."

Daly, on his own TV show on WDIV with Bernie Smilovitz, would say in a final assessment: "I've said all along the team with the most toys wins. And toys are post-up people."

Bill Laimbeer emerged from his hiding place in the shower room. A mob of media surrounded him.

"They won," he said. The questions were tossed in flurries at him. "They won," he said. Another question. "They won," he said. Channel 4 stuck a mike in Laimbeer's unmasked face. "They won," he said.

"Your emotions?" he was asked by a reporter.

"I'm gonna kill myself; they won."

"They won. They won. They won."

The first wave of media people gave up. Another group surrounded Laimbeer.

"They won," he said.

Behind him, Laimbeer spotted this reporter taking notes.

"Are you counting them?" he asked me.

"Yep, thirty-four 'they wons.'"

He grinned. This was his newest game, Combat Journalism.

Finally, he unburdened himself of a thought

or two for a couple of Detroit media men. "We congratulated each other when we came off. We just appreciated the torture we went through. Our families went through. You don't understand. The fans don't understand. We just congratulated ourselves."

Laimbeer got up to leave the locker room.

"Did you deliberately walk out without congratulating the Bulls?" somebody asked him.

Laimbeer walked out without answering the question.

Dennis Rodman remained in the seclusion of Mike Abdenour's trainer's room for a long time. When he came out, he stood in a corridor and explained his actions and his feelings. He felt no regrets that he had shoved Scottie Pippen hard to the floor; no regrets about the trash spoken between the two hostile teams.

"The world don't end because you lost one series," Rodman said. "If the Celtics can do it, the Lakers can do it, we can, too.

"Chicago? If they're such a great team, go prove it. They're not a great team at all. To be a great team, you got to be the Celtics, the Lakers, and go through it for a long time.

"They're not a great team. All they did was bitch, complain, bitch, complain. They don't give us no credit. Michael, he got all the money. He ought to buy the team and change it. Nothing was given to us."

Rodman leaned against the cement block wall, wearing a T-shirt with a message that said, "I'm So Bad." He was asked if he had any regrets.

"Should we?" he said. "Oh, they did a great job. No way. They can go now and boast—the Pistons have lost, the world is safe again. Life without the Pistons, the world is safe . . .

"If you live by the sword, you die by the sword."

It was a while later when Isiah Thomas walked out of the locker room. His teammates had gone. He was lugging his equipment bag, going out to meet his wife, Lynn, who was waiting.

Got one more question! About your leaving the court without congratulating the Bulls . . .

"Was it choreographed?" Isiah said. "Of course it was. They didn't show us any respect. Why should we show them any?"

While the Detroit media ignored the implications of the Pistons' choreographed march off the court, the deliberate snubbing of Jordan and the Bulls, the national press turned it into a cause celebre. In the aftermath, as the Bulls waited for the Lakers to eliminate the Trail Blazers in the West, the Pistons caught media flak from all over.

Ira Berkow, the erudite sports columnist of the *New York Times* wrote about the Pistons' premature departure: ". . . It was a miserable display of sportsmanship, but it was consistent with their play during the game. It was one of the ugliest displays of basketball in memory . . . And when the Pistons, in their puerile behavior left the court, their coach should have blocked their path: 'Game's not over yet. Get back there and sit down.'

"Daly didn't. His team disgraced not only itself, but the N.B.A. Next year he will be coaching a team wearing jerseys with "U.S.A." on them. It's a sobering thought."

Bernie Lincicome, columnist for the *Chicago Tribune,* wrote: "May the Pistons rest in pieces . . . The NBA should consider Detroit so dangerous to the good health of basketball, not to mention the general decency, that they break it up and send its various parts to places so distant that it can never be reassembled.

"Dennis Rodman, the smirking vermin, should be sent first and farthest away, some place without a ZIP code, running water or a decent mattress.

"Bill Laimbeer, the sucker-punching oaf, needs a long rest in a tight suit, one of those with arms that tie in the back.

"Isiah Thomas, the sneaky little puppeteer of this mob, ought never again be given anything sharp to play with, unless he turns it on himself.

"The whole, thuggish bunch of them, including our nascent Olympic coach, Chuck Daly, should be frisked before being allowed to enter public places . . .

"One of the side benefits of the Bulls whipping the Pistons is that many local lives and flammable cars will now be saved from the usual victory celebrations . . ."

Two days after the Pistons lost the Eastern Conference finals to the Bulls, Dennis Rodman signed a perfectly typewritten letter to Scottie Pippen. Dennis had—suddenly—turned contrite. He had also been fined $5,000 by Rod Thorn, NBA minister of justice. In the letter, Rodman apologized to Pippen and said: ". . . I am not the type of player of which I have been accused. The situation was one of those things which should not have happened . . ."

"I'm not convinced he wrote the letter," Pippen told the press in Chicago. "If he did, it's a confession, but I don't believe it's going to make up for the scars on my chin."

Bill Laimbeer finally spoke out about the manner in which the Pistons left the arena.

". . . It would have been good sportsmanship for them to keep their mouths shut," Laimbeer told Frank Beckmann on WJR radio. "Quit whining and crying the whole time. Basically, before the playoffs even started, they were whining and bitching about the Pistons being too tough for them. Hey, it's a man's game. You come, play like a man, and you go home like a man.

"Every year that we won we didn't get adulation from other people, nor did we expect it. So why should people expect it from us? We don't understand how they can put themselves on a high moral ground.

"Who are they? They're nobody. Just for Michael Jordan to think that he is better because he looks better in the air doing his job. I mean, who is he? Big deal. It's only a game . . .

"I could care less what Chicago says. We're our own people. The only people we have to believe in and answer to are the twelve guys in the locker room."

Chuck Daly, a few weeks earlier, had wondered how it would end and suggested that the Pistons would write their own ending. Bill Laimbeer—the Bad Boy forever—just wrote it!

Bibliography

Basketball Weekly.

Chicago Tribune.

Detroit Free Press.

Detroit News Archives.

Detroit Pistons 1990–91 Media Guide.

Frank, Stanley. "Coaching the Pros Is a Cinch, He (Eckman) Says." *Saturday Evening Post,* 19 February 1955.

Hollander, Zander, ed. *The Modern Encyclopedia of Basketball.* New York: Dolphin Books, 1979.

Inside Sports.

Lazenby, Roland. *The Official Detroit Pistons Yearbook, 1990–91.* Dallas: Taylor Publishing, 1990.

The National.

NBA Guide, Sporting News.

NBA Register, Sporting News.

Salzberg, Charles. *From Set Shot to Slam Dunk—The Glory Days of Basketball in the Words of Those Who Played It*. New York: Dell Publishing, 1987.

Sport Magazine.

Sports Illustrated.

Thomas, Isiah, and Matt Dobek. *Bad Boys!* Grand Rapids: Masters Press, 1989.

USA Today.

"The Year of The Bad Boys, 1988–89." *Detroit News,* 1989.

Other Books by Jerry Green

Year of the Tiger, Coward-McCann, 1969

Detroit Lions—Great Teams, Great Years, NFL Properties/Macmillan, 1973.